AMERICAN
SIGN LANGUAGE
DICTIONARY

AMERICAN SIGN LANGUAGE DICTIONARY

Revised Edition

Martin L.A. Sternberg, ED.D.

ILLUSTRATIONS BY HERBERT ROGOFF AND EDUSELF

Abridged edition of *American Sign Language*

HarperPerennial
A Division of HarperCollins*Publishers*

To the memory of
Fannie and Irving Sternberg

HarperCollins books may be purchased for educational, business, or sales promotional use. For information, please write to: Special Markets Department, HarperCollins Publishers, Inc., 10 East 53rd Street, New York, NY 10022.

FIRST EDITION

Library of Congress Cataloging-in-Publication Data
Sternberg, Martin L. A.
    The American sign language dictionary / Martin L. A. Sternberg ; illustrations by Herbert Rogoff and EduSelf. — Rev. ed., 1st ed.
        p.   cm.
    Rev. ed. of: American sign language dictionary. 1st Perennial Library ed. 1990.
    "Abridged edition of American sign language."
    ISBN 0-06-273275-7
    1. American sign language—Dictionaries. I. Sternberg, Martin L. A. American sign language dictionary. II. Title.
HV2475.S78   1994
419—dc20   94-37905

95 96 97 98 99 ❖/CW 10 9 8 7 6 5 4 3

Contents

Acknowledgments

The original work from which this revised edition is derived, *American Sign Language: A Comprehensive Dictionary,* is the culmination of a period of endeavor that goes back to 1962. Two abridgments have since appeared: *American Sign Language Dictionary* (1987), and *American Sign Language Concise Dictionary* (1990). The current work is a revised and enlarged edition of the *American Sign Language Dictionary.*

In order to maintain continuity in the evolution of this project, members of the original General Editorial Committee are listed on pages ix and x.

My many friends who use sign language have been a constant source of information (and inspiration) in the identification and inclusion of new signs in this book. To them, my sustained appreciation and applause.

Bringing this project into the Computer Age from its index card and hand-illustrated status has been a major challenge, sometimes a source of trepidation and frustration, but ultimately a unique achievement. This could never have been accomplished without the sustained help and guidance of Kenneth S. Rothschild, my teacher, friend, and major supporter, who not only set up the format for the computer but came to my side countless times to help me out when I was in trouble. Lorri Kirzner gave willingly of her knowledge and expertise to resolve transient difficulties I encountered with the database. Her smile and patience make her a very special person.

The illustrations have been produced using the latest current technology, which leaves me breathless when I contemplate the work to produce the original Unabridged Edition, a project of nineteen years! The new procedure involved making videotapes of the signs using different models and then freeze-framing appropriate poses. These poses in turn produced computer-generated drawings—rapidly and accurately. Randi F. Kleiman coordinated this multi-faceted operation. She is another unique contributor who deserves unfailing appreciation.

Likewise, certain people need special recognition. The two illustrators, Meravi Geffen and Case Ellerbrock, did an outstanding job within the constraints of time and deadline pressures. They were ably assisted by Rachel Ackerman, Eva Cohen, David Fogel, and Jimmy Mizrachi, all under the executive direction of Nissim Halfon. Jack Berberian produced the videotape, which used the talents and modeling skills of Alan R. Barwiolek, Patrice Joyner, and Marie Taccogna.

Herbert Rogoff, the talented artist who did the original freehand drawings appearing in editions past—many of which remain among these pages—is thanked yet again.

Marilee Foglesong, Children's Librarian, New York Public Library, offered valuable suggestions for drawing up an appropriate list of signs for children.

With this project, my publisher, HarperCollins, demonstrates a major commitment to the dynamic new world of multimedia publishing. Nancy Dickenson, Director of New Media, has had the vision and drive to design a multifaceted CD-ROM edition of this work. She has been ably assisted by Paul Shustak, a very experienced programmer and software designer.

In spite of her multiple duties as Vice President and Publisher of HarperCollins Interactive for the Adult Trade Group, Carol P. Cohen, who has been involved with this project from its inception, has kept up a lively and close interest in the development of this new edition.

Robert Wilson, my editor, is the latest and very much the best of a long line of editors under whom I have worked. Thirty-two years is a long time to be affiliated with a single publisher, and Rob's commitment to me and this always-expanding project demonstrates the wisdom of my choice of HarperCollins as my publisher.

Elaine Verriest, supervisor, HarperReference production, and freelance copyeditor Linda H. Hwang improved this edition through their care, diligence, and attention to detail.

Finally, Theodora Zavin, my literary adviser, has been a reassuring presence throughout the development of the new edition and the production of the CD-ROM versions.

Martin L.A. Sternberg , Ed. D.
New York, 1994

General Editorial Committee

(Unabridged Edition)

Editorial Staff

Edna S. Levine, Ph.D., Litt.D., *Project Director.* Late Professor Emeritus, New York University, New York, NY.

Martin L.A. Sternberg, Ed.D. *Principal Research Scientist and Editor-in-Chief.* Adjunct Professor, Adelphi University, Garden City, NY; Adjunct Associate Professor, Hofstra University, Hempstead, NY.

Herbert Rogoff, *Illustrator.* Former Associate Research Scientist, New York University, New York, NY.

William F. Marquardt, Ph.D., *Linguist.* Late Professor of English Education, New York University, New York, NY.

Joseph V. Firsching, *Project Secretary.*

Consulting Committee

Elizabeth E. Benson, Litt.D., *Chief Consultant.* Late Dean of Women and Professor of Speech, Gallaudet University, Washington, DC.

Leon Auerbach, L.H.D., *Senior Consultant.* Late Professor of Mathematics, Gallaudet University, Washington, DC.

Special Consultants

Charles L. Brooks, *Vocational Signs*
Nancy Frishberg, Ph.D., *Editorial*
Emil Ladner, *Catholic Signs*

Abbreviations

adj.	Adjective
adv.	Adverb, adverbial
adv. phrase	Adverbial phrase
alt. phrase	Alteration
arch.	Archaic
Brit.	British
colloq.	Colloquial, colloquialism. Informal or familiar term or expression in sign
condition. suffix	Conditional suffix
eccles.	Ecclesiastical. Of or pertaining to religious signs. These signs are among the earliest and best developed, inasmuch as the first teachers of deaf people were frequently religious workers and instruction was often of a religious nature.
e.g.	*Exempli gratia.* L., for example
esp. interrog.	Especially interrogative
i.e.	*Id est.* L., that is
interj.	Interjection
L.	Latin
loc.	Localism. A sign peculiar to a local or limited area. This may frequently be the case in a given school for deaf children, a college or postsecondary program catering to their needs, or a geographical area around such school or facility where deaf persons may live or work.
obs.	Obscure, obsolete
pl.	Plural
poss.	Possessive
prep.	Preposition
prep. phrase	Prepositional phrase
pron.	Pronoun
q.v.	*Quod vide.* L., which see

sl.	Slang
v.	Verb
v.i.	Verb intransitive
viz.	*Videlicet*. L., namely
voc.	Vocational. These signs usually pertain to specialized vocabularies used in workshops, trade and vocational classes and schools.
v.t.	Verb transitive
vulg.	Vulgarism. A vulgar term or expression, usually used only in a colloquial sense.

Pronunciation Guide

The primary stress mark (′) is placed after the syllable bearing the heavier stress or accent; the secondary stress mark (′) follows a syllable having a somewhat lighter stress, as in **interrogate** (ĭn tĕr′ ə gāt′).

Symbol	Example	Symbol	Example
ă	add, map	o͝o	took, full
ā	ace, rate	p	pit, stop
â(r)	care, air	r	run, poor
ä	palm, father	s	see, pass
b	bat, rub	sh	sure, rush
ch	check, catch	t	talk, sit
d	dog, rod	th	thin, both
ĕ	end, pet	th̸	this, bathe
ē	even, tree	ŭ	up, done
f	fit, half	ū	unite, vacuum
g	go, log	û(r)	urn, term
h	hope, hate	yo͞o	use, few
ĭ	it, give	v	vain, eve
ī	ice, write	w	win, away
j	joy, ledge	y	yet, yearn
k	cool, take	z	zest, muse
l	look, rule	zh	vision, pleasure
m	move, seem	ə	the schwa, an un-stressed vowel representing the sound spelled
n	nice, tin		*a* in *above*
ng	ring, song		*e* in *sicken*
ŏ	odd, hot		*i* in *clarity*
ō	open, so		*o* in *melon*
ô	order, jaw		*u* in *focus*
oi	oil, boy		
ou	out, now		
o͞o	pool, food		

Explanatory Notes

Sign Rationale

This term, admittedly imprecise semantically, refers to the explanatory material in parentheses which follows the part of speech. This material is an attempt to offer a mnemonic cue to the sign as described verbally. It is a device to aid the user of the dictionary to remember how a sign is formed.

Verbal Description

The sign and its formation are described verbally. Such terms as "S" hand, "D" position, "both 'B' hands," refer to the positions of the hand or hands as they are depicted in the American Manual Alphabet on page xvii.

Terms such as "counterclockwise," "clockwise," refer to movement from the signer's orientation. Care should be taken not to become confused by illustrations which appear at first glance to contradict a verbal description. In all cases the verbal description should be the one of choice, with the illustration reinforcing it. The reader should place himself or herself mentally in the position of the signer, *i.e.,* the illustration, in order to assume the correct orientation for signing an English gloss word.

Sign Synonyms

Sign synonyms are other glosses for which the same sign is used. They are found at the end of the verbal description, following the italicized *Cf.* and are given in SMALL CAPITAL LETTERS.

It is important to remember that the words listed after the *Cf.* do not carry an equivalent sense in and of themselves. Because meaning for the signer springs from the sign, apparently unrelated glosses can be expressed by similar movements.

Illustrations

A) Illustrations appearing in sequence should not be regarded as separate depictions of parts of a sign. They are fluid and continuous, and should be used in conjunction with the verbal description of a sign, for they illustrate the main features of the sign as one movement flows into the next.

B) Arrows, broken or solid, indicate direction of movement. Again, they are designed to reinforce the verbal description and, where confusion may arise, the reader is cautioned to review the verbal description, always keeping himself or herself mentally in the position of the illustration (the signer).

C) As a general rule, a hand drawn with dotted or broken lines indicates the sign's initial movement or position of the hand. This is especially true if a similar drawing appears next to it using solid lines. This indicates terminal position in the continuum.

D) Groups of illustrations have been arranged as far as possible in visually logical order. They are read from left to right, or from top to bottom. Where confusion is possible, they have been captioned with letter A, B, C, etc.

E) Small lines outlining parts of the hand, especially when they are repeated, indicate small, repeated, or wavy or jerky motions, as described in the verbal section of an entry. ANTICIPATE is an example.

F) Arrows drawn side by side but pointing in opposite directions indicate repeated movement, as described in the verbal section of an entry. APPLAUD is an example.

G) Illustrations giving side or three-quarter views have been so placed to afford maximum visibility and to avoid foreshortening problems. The user of the dictionary should not assume a similar orientation when making the sign. As a general rule, the signer faces the person he or she is signing to.

H) Inclusion of the head in the figures permits proper orientation in the formation of certain signs. The head is omitted where there is not question of ambiguity.

American
Manual
Alphabet

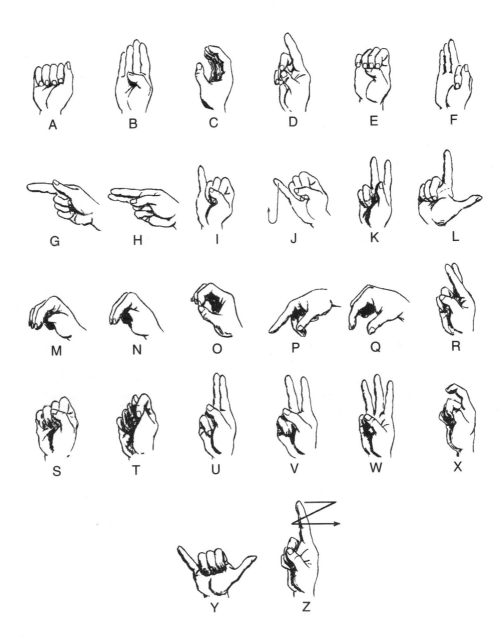

AMERICAN
SIGN LANGUAGE
DICTIONARY

ABANDON (ə băn′ dən), *v.*, -DONED, -DONING. (To throw something aside.) Both "S" hands are held with palms facing at chest level and then thrown down and to the left, opening into the "5" position. *Cf.* CAST OFF, DISCARD, FORSAKE 1, LEAVE 2, LET ALONE, NEGLECT.

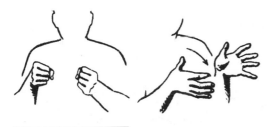

ABBREVIATE (ə brē′ vǐ āt′), *v.*, -ATED, -ATING. (To squeeze or condense into a small space.) The "C" hands face each other, with the right hand nearer to the body than the left. Both hands draw together and close deliberately, squeezing an imaginary object. *Cf.* BRIEF 2, CONDENSE, MAKE BRIEF, SUMMARIZE 1, SUMMARY 1.

ABBREVIATION (-shən), *n.* See ABBREVIATE.

ABHOR (ab hôr′), *v.* (To push away and recoil from; avoid.) The two open hands, palms facing left, are pushed deliberately to the left, as if pushing something away. An expression of disdain or disgust is worn. *Cf.* AVOID 2, DESPISE, DETEST, HATE, LOATHE.

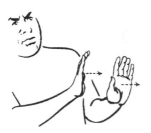

ABILITY (ə bĭl′ ə tĭ), *n.* (An affirmative movement of the hands, likened to a nodding of the head, to indicate ability or power to accomplish something.) Both "A" hands, held palms down, move down in unison a short distance before the chest. *Cf.* ABLE, CAN, CAPABLE, COMPETENT, COULD, MAY 2, POSSIBLE.

ABLE (ā′ bəl), *adj.* See ABILITY.

ABOLISH (ə bŏl′ ĭsh), *v.*, -ISHED, -ISHING. (Removing.) The right "A" hand, resting in the palm of the left "5" hand, moves slightly up and away, describing a small arc. It is then cast downward, opening into the "5" position, palm down, as if removing something from the left hand and casting it down. *Cf.* DEDUCT, DELETE 1, ELIMINATE, REMOVE, SUBTRACT, SUBTRACTION, TAKE AWAY FROM.

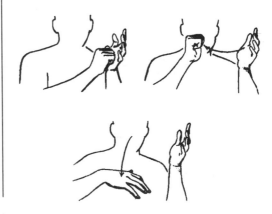

ABORTION 1 (ə bôr′ shən), *n.* (The baby is removed from its mother's womb.) The right hand grasps the stomach and then is thrown down and open.

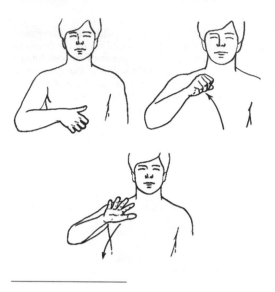

ABORTION 2 *n.* (A variation of ABORTION 1; taking from.) The right fingers scratch against the left palm as if removing something. The right hand is then thrown down and open.

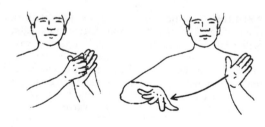

ABOUT 1 (ə bout′), *prep.* (Revolving about.) The left hand is held at chest height, all fingers extended and touching the thumb, and all pointing to the right. The right index finger circles about the left fingers several times.

ABOUT 2, *adj.* Same as ABOUT 1 above, but both hands are held in the "H" position. *Cf.* ALMOST.

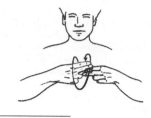

ABOUT 3, *adv.* (In the general area.) The downturned open "5" hand moves in a counterclockwise direction in front of the body. *Cf.* THEREABOUTS.

ABOVE (ə bŭv′), *adv.* (One hand moves above the other.) Both hands, palms flat and facing down, are held before the chest. The right hand circles horizontally above the left in a counterclockwise direction.

ABSENCE (ăb′ səns), *n.* (A disappearance.) The right open hand, palm facing the body, is held by the left hand and is drawn down and out, ending in a position with fingers drawn together. The left hand, meanwhile, may close into a position with fingers also drawn together. *Cf.* ABSENT, DISAPPEAR, GONE 1, VANISH.

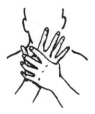

ABSENT (-sənt), *adj.* See ABSENCE.

ABSENT-MINDED (mīn′ dĭd), *adj.* (The mind is gone.) The index finger of the right hand, palm back, touches the forehead (the modified sign for THINK, *q.v.*). The right open hand, palm facing the body, is held by the left hand and is drawn down and out, ending in a position with fingers drawn together. The left hand, meanwhile, has closed into a position with fingers also drawn together.

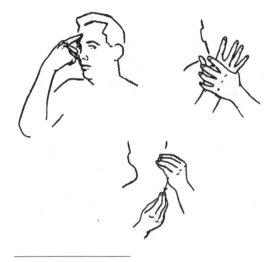

ABSOLUTE (ăb′ sə lōōt′), *adj.* (Coming forth directly from the lips; true.) The index finger of the right "D" hand, palm facing left, is placed against the lips. It moves up an inch or two and then describes a small arc forward and away from the lips. *Cf.* ABSOLUTELY, ACTUAL, ACTUALLY, AUTHENTIC, CERTAIN, CERTAINLY, FIDELITY, FRANKLY, GENUINE, INDEED, POSITIVE 1, POSITIVELY, REAL, REALLY, SINCERE 2, SURE, SURELY, TRUE, TRULY, TRUTH, VALID, VERILY.

ABSOLUTELY (ăb′ sə lōōt′ lĭ), *adv.* See ABSOLUTE.

ABSTAIN (ab stăn′), *v.* (Withdrawing or getting off.) The curved right index and middle fingers, sitting in the hole formed by the left "C" or "O" hands, are pulled up and out.

ABUNDANCE (ə bŭn′ dəns), n. (A full cup.) The left hand, in the "S" position, is held palm facing right. The right "5" hand, palm down, is brushed outward several times over the top of the left, indicating a wiping off of the top of a cup. *Cf.* ABUNDANT, ADEQUATE, AMPLE, ENOUGH, PLENTY, SUBSTANTIAL, SUFFICIENT.

ABUNDANT (ə bŭn′ dənt), *adj.* See ABUNDANCE.

ACCEPT (ăk sĕpt′), *v.,* -CEPTED, -CEPTING. (A taking of something unto oneself.) Both open hands, palms down, are held in front of the chest. They move in unison toward the chest, where they come to rest, all fingers closed. *Cf.* WILLING 1.

ACCESS (ak′ ses), *n., v.* (Going into.) The down-turned right fingers move under their left counter-parts.

ACCOMPANY 1 (ə kŭm′ pə ni), *v., -NIED, -NYING.* (To go along with.) Both "A" hands, knuckles together and thumbs up, are moved forward in unison, away from the chest.

ACCOMPANY 2, *v.* (Going forward together.) Both "A" hands, knuckles and thumbs touching, move forward in unison. *Cf.* GO WITH.

ACCOMPLISH (ə kŏm′ plĭsh), *v., -PLISHED, -PLISHING.* (Penetrating the heights.) The "D" hands, palms back, are held at each side of the head, near the temples. With a pivoting motion of the wrists, the hands swing up and around, simultaneously, to a position

above the head, with palms facing out. *Cf.* ACHIEVE, PROSPER, SUCCEED, SUCCESS, SUCCESSFUL, TRIUMPH 2.

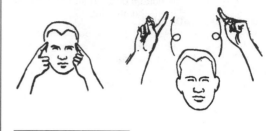

ACCORDING (TO) (ə kôr′ dĭng), *adv.* (A likeness; a sameness.) Both index fingers, held together at one side of the body near waist level, point forward. As they travel to the other side of the body they separate an inch or two and come together again. *Cf.* ALSO, AS, SAME AS, TOO.

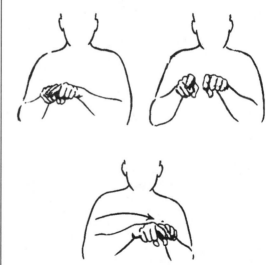

ACCUMULATE (ə kū′ myə lāt′), *v., -LATED, -LATING.* (Gathering in.) The right "5" hand, its little finger edge touching the upturned left palm, is drawn in an arc toward the body, closing into the "S" position as it sweeps over the base of the left hand. *Cf.* COLLECT, EARN, SALARY 1, WAGE(S).

ACCURATE (ăk′ yə rĭt), *adj.* The right index finger, held above the left index finger, comes down rather forcefully so that the bottom of the right hand comes to rest on top of the left thumb joint. *Cf.* CORRECT 1, DECENT, EXACT 2, PROPER, RIGHT 3, SUITABLE.

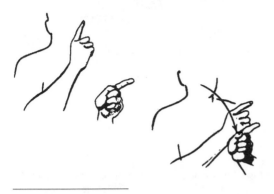

ACCUSE (ə kuz′), *v.,* -CUSED, -CUSING. (The blame is firmly placed.) The right "A" hand, thumb pointing up, is brought down firmly against the back of the left hand, held palm down; the right thumb is then directed toward the person or object to blame. When personal blame is acknowledged, the thumb is brought in to the chest. *Cf.* BLAME, FAULT, GUILTY 1.

ACCUSTOM (ə kŭs′ təm), *v.,* -TOMED, -TOMING. (Bound down to custom or habit.) Both "S" hands, palms down, are crossed and brought down in unison before the chest. *Cf.* BOUND, CUSTOM, HABIT, LOCKED, PRACTICE 3.

ACHE (āk), *n., v.,* ACHED, ACHING.(A stabbing pain.) The "D" hands, index fingers pointing to each other, are rotated in elliptical fashion before the chest–simultaneously but in opposite directions. *Cf.* HARM 1, HURT 1, INJURE 1, INJURY, PAIN, SIN, WOUND.

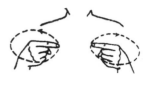

ACHIEVE (ə chēv′), *v.,* -CHIEVED, -CHIEVING. (Penetrating the heights.) The "D" hands, palms back, are held at each side of the head, near the temples. With a pivoting motion of the wrists, the hands swing up and around, simultaneously, to a position above the head, with palms facing out. *Cf.* SUCCEED, SUCCESS, SUCCESSFUL, TRIUMPH.

ACQUIRE (ə kwīr′), *v.,* -QUIRED, -QUIRING. (A grasping and bringing forward to oneself.) Both hands, in the "5" position, fingers curved, are crossed at the wrists, with the left palm facing right and the right palm facing left. They are brought in toward the chest, while closing into a grasping "S" position. *Cf.* GET, OBTAIN, PROCURE, RECEIVE.

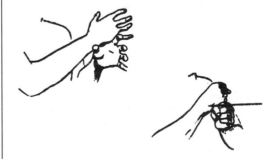

ACROBAT (ak′ rə bat), *n.* (The body movement.) The right index and middle fingers rest in the upturned left palm. The right hand leaves the left, assuming a palm-up position. The index and middle fingers swing in the air in a clockwise circle, and then the two fingers "land" again in the left palm. *Cf.* GYMNASTICS.

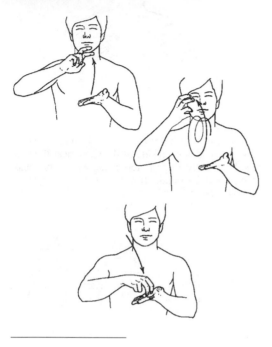

ACROSS (ə krôs′, ə krŏs′), *prep., adv.* (A crossing over.) The left hand is held before the chest, palm down and fingers together. The right hand, fingers together, glides over the left, with the right little finger touching the top of the left hand. *Cf.* CROSS, OVER.

ACT 1 (ăkt), *v.,* ACTED, ACTING, *n.* (Motion or movement, modified by the letter "A" for "act.") Both "A" hands, palms out, are held at shoulder height and rotate alternately toward the head. *Cf.* ACTOR,

ACTRESS, DRAMA, PERFORM 2, PERFORMANCE 2, PLAY 2, SHOW 2.

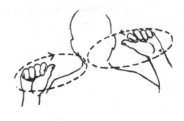

ACT 2, *v.* (An activity.) Both open hands, palms down, are swung right and left before the chest. *Cf.* ACTION, ACTIVE, ACTIVITY, CONDUCT 1, DEED, DO, PERFORM 1, PERFORMANCE 1.

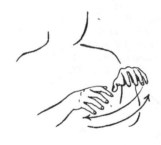

ACTION (ăk′ shən), *n.* (An activity.) See ACT 2.

ACTIVE (ăk′ tĭv), *adj.* (Activity.) See ACT 2.

ACTIVITY (ăk tĭv′ ə ti), n. See ACT 2.

ACTOR (ăk′ tər), *n.* (Male acting individual.) The right hand moves to the forehead and grasps an imaginary cap brim (MALE root sign). The sign for ACT 1 is then given. This is followed by the sign for INDIVIDUAL: both hands, fingers together, are placed at either side of the chest and are moved down to waist level. *Note:* The MALE root sign is optional.

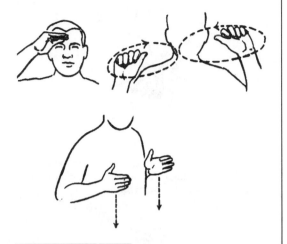

ACTRESS (ăk′ trĭs), *n.* (Female acting individual.) The thumb of the right "A" hand moves down along the line of the right jaw from ear to chin (FEMALE root sign). The sign for ACT 1 is then given. This is followed by the sign for INDIVIDUAL: both hands, fingers together, are placed at either side of the chest and are moved down to waist level. *Note:* The FEMALE root sign is optional.

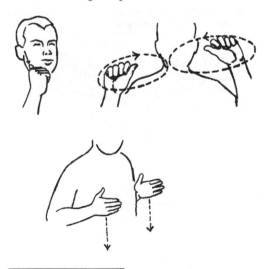

ACTUAL (ăk′ chōō əl), *adj.* (Coming forth directly from the lips; true.) The index finger of the right "D" hand, palm facing left, is placed against the lips. It moves up an inch or two and then describes a small

arc forward and away from the lips. *Cf.* ABSOLUTE, ABSOLUTELY, ACTUALLY, AUTHENTIC, CERTAIN, CERTAINLY, FIDELITY, FRANKLY, GENUINE, INDEED, POSITIVE 1, POSITIVELY, REAL, REALLY, SINCERE 2, SURE, SURELY, TRUE, TRULY, TRUTH, VALID, VERILY.

ACTUALLY (ăk′ chōō ə lĭ), *adv.* (Truly.) See ACTUAL.

ADD 1 (ăd), *v.,* ADDED, ADDING. (To bring up all together.) The two open hands, palms and fingers facing each other, with the left hand above the right, are brought together, with all fingers closing simultaneously. This sign is used mainly in the sense of adding up figures or items. *Cf.* ADDITION, AMOUNT 1, SUM, SUMMARIZE 2, SUMMARY 2, SUM UP, TOTAL.

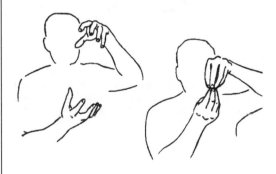

ADD 2, *v.* (A mathematical symbol.) The two index fingers are crossed in the sign for PLUS. *Cf.* ADDITION, PLUS, POSITIVE 2.

ADD 3, *v.* (Adding on.) The index and middle fingers of the right "H" hand, palm up, are swung up and over until they come to rest on the index and middle fingers of the left "H" hand, held palm down. *Cf.* ADDITION, GAIN 1, INCREASE, ON TO, RAISE 2.

ADDITION (ə dĭsh′ ən), *n.* See ADD 1, 2, OR 3.

ADDRESS (ăd′ rĕs), *n., v,* -DRESSED, -DRESSING. (Same rationale as for LIFE 1, with the initials "L.") The upturned thumbs of the "A" hands move in unison up the chest. *Cf.* ALIVE, LIFE 1, LIVE 1, LIVING, RESIDE.

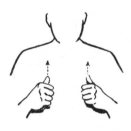

ADEPT (ə dĕpt′), *adj.* (A sharp-edged hand.) The right hand grasps the little finger edge of the left firmly. As it leaves this position, moving down and out, it assumes the "A" position, palm facing left. *Cf.* EXPERIENCE 1, EXPERT, SHARP, SKILL, SKILLFUL.

ADEQUATE (ăd′ a kwĭt), *adj.* (A full cup.) The left hand, in the "S" position, is held palm facing right. The right "5" hand, palm down, is brushed outward several times over the top of the left, indicating a wiping off of the top of a cup. *Cf.* ABUNDANCE, ABUNDANT, AMPLE, ENOUGH, PLENTY, SUBSTANTIAL, SUFFICIENT.

ADMINISTRATION 1 (ad min is trā′ shən), *n.* (Handling the reins.) The signer manipulates a pair of imaginary reins back and forth.

ADMINISTRATION 2, *n.* (A fingerspelled loan sign.) The letters "A-D-M" are spelled out.

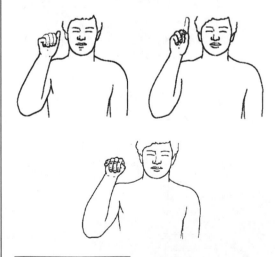

ADMISSION (ăd mĭsh′ ən), *n.* (Getting something off the chest.) Both hands are held with fingers touching the chest and pointing down. They are then swung up and out, ending with both palms facing up before the body. *Cf.* ADMIT, CONFESS, CONFESSION 1.

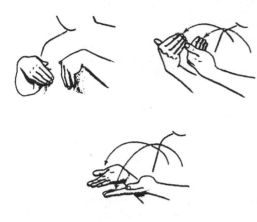

ADMIT (ăd mĭt´), *v.*, -mitted, -mitting. See ADMISSION.

ADMONISH (ăd mŏn´ ĭsh), *v.*, -ISHED, -ISHING. (Tapping one to draw attention to danger.) The right hand taps the back of the left several times. *Cf.* CAUTION, FOREWARN, WARN.

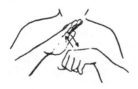

ADOPT (ə dŏpt´), *v.* (Take and keep.) The right hand grasps onto an imaginary object to the right, and then the two hands assume the "K" position, palms facing each other, with the right resting on the left.

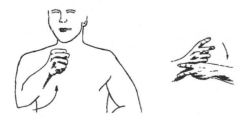

ADULT (ə dult´), *n., adj.* (The letter "A"; the FEMALE and MALE root signs.) The thumbtip of the right "A" hand is placed first on the right jawline, and then moves up to touch the right temple.

ADULTERY 1 (ə dul´ tər ĕ), *n.* (Turning the corner, out of sight of the spouse.) The right cupped hand makes a U-turn around the left "D" hand. The movement is repeated.

ADULTERY 2, *n.* (Jumping from a spouse to another person.) The left hand is held in the "V" position, palm facing the signer. The right hand, in the "A" position, moves in a small arc from the left index to the left middle finger.

ADVANCE (ăd văns´, -väns´), *n., v.,* -VANCED, -VANC-ING. (Moving forward, step by step.) Both hands, in the right angle position, palms facing, are held before the chest, a few inches apart, with the right hand slightly behind the left. The right hand is brought up, over and forward, so that it is now ahead of the left. The left hand then follows suit, so that it is now ahead of the right. *Cf.* PROGRESS.

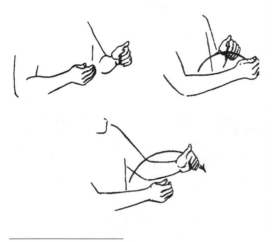

ADVANCED (ăd vănst´), *adj.* (Something high up.) Both hands, in the right angle position, are held before the face, about a foot apart, palms facing. They are raised abruptly about a foot, in a slight out-ward curving movement. *Cf.* HIGH 1, PROMOTE, PRO-MOTION.

ADVICE (ăd vīs´), *n.* (Take something, *advice,* and disseminate it.) The left hand, held limp in front of the body, has its fingers pointing down. The fingers of the right hand, held all together, are placed on the top of the left hand, and then move forward, off the left hand, assuming a "5" position, palm down. *Cf.* ADVISE, COUNSEL, COUNSELOR, INFLUENCE 3.

ADVISE (ăd vīz´), *v.,* -VISED, -VISING. See ADVICE.

ADVOCATE (ad´ və kāt´), *v.,* -CATED, -CATING. (One hand upholds the other.) Both hands, in the "S" posi-tion, are held palms facing the body, the right under the left. The right hand pushes up the left in a gesture of support. *Cf.* ENDORSE 2, SUPPORT 2.

AFFILIATE (ə fĭl´ ĭ āt´), *v.,* -ATED, -ATING. (Joining together.) Both hands, held in the modified "5" posi-tion, palms out, move toward each other. The thumbs and index fingers of both hands then connect. *Cf.* ANNEX, ATTACH, BELONG, CONNECT, ENLIST, ENROLL, JOIN, PARTICIPATE, UNITE.

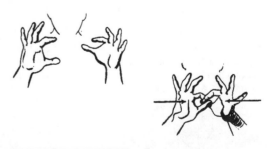

AFRAID (ə frād´), *adj.* (The heart is suddenly cov-ered with fear.) Both hands, fingers together, are placed side by side, palms facing the chest. They quickly open and come together over the heart, one on top of the other. *Cf.* FEAR 1, FRIGHT, FRIGHTEN, SCARE(D), TERROR 1.

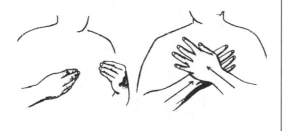

AFRICA 1 (af′ ri kə), *n.* The "A" hand, thumb pointing to the face, makes a counterclockwise circle around the face. This is considered a racist sign and should generally be avoided.

AFRICA 2, *n.* (The shape of the continent.) The hand, in the "A" position, opens, and the index and thumb trace the shape of the African continent in the air. This is generally considered the most acceptable and racially neutral sign for Africa.

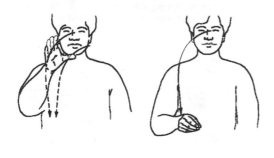

AFTER (af′ tər, äf-), *prep.* (Something occurring *after* a fixed place in time, represented by the hand

nearest the body.) The right hand, held flat, palm facing the body, fingertips pointing left, represents the fixed place in time. The left hand is placed against the back of the right, and moves straight out from the body. The relative positions of the two hands may be reversed, with the left remaining stationary near the body and the right moving out.

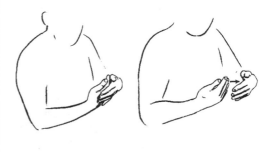

AFTER A WHILE (hwīl), *adv. phrase.* (A moving on of the minute hand of the clock.) The right "L" hand, its thumb thrust into the palm of the left and acting as a pivot, moves forward a short distance. *Cf.* AFTERWARD, LATER 1, SUBSEQUENT, SUBSEQUENTLY.

AFTERNOON (af′ tər nōōn′, äf-), *n., adj.* (The sun is midway between zenith and sunset.) The right arm, fingers together and pointing forward, rests on the back of the left hand, its fingers also together and pointing somewhat to the right. The right arm remains in a position about 45° from the vertical.

AFTERWARD (ăf´ tər wərd, äf-), *adv.* See AFTER A WHILE.

AGAIN (ə gĕn´), *adv.* The left hand, open in the "5" position, palm up, is held before the chest. The right hand, in the right-angle position, fingers pointing up, arches over and into the left palm. *Cf.* REPEAT.

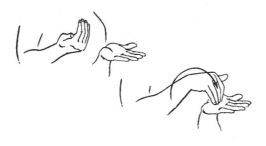

AGAINST (ə gĕnst´, -gānst´), *prep.* (Opposed to; restraint.) The tips of the right fingers, held together, are thrust purposefully into the open left palm, whose fingers are also together and pointing forward. *Cf.* OPPOSE.

AGE (āj), *n.* (Age, in the sense of chronological age; the beard of an old man.) The right hand grasps an imaginary beard at the chin and pulls it downward. *Cf.* OLD.

AGGRAVATE 1 (ag´ rə vāt), *v.,* -VATED, -VATING. (The stomach turns.) The right claw hand makes a series of counterclockwise circles on the stomach. A look of distress or annoyance is assumed.

AGGRAVATE 2, *v.* (The emotions well up and explode.) Both downturned hands are placed at the stomach, right fingers pointing left and left fingers pointing right. Both hands move up slowly and then come apart explosively, with palms now facing each other. An expression of distress or annoyance is assumed.

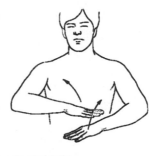

AGO (ə gō´), *adj., adv.* (Something past, behind.) The upraised right hand, in the "5" position with palm facing the body, is held just above the right shoulder and is thrown back over it. *Cf.* FORMERLY, ONCE UPON A TIME, PAST, PREVIOUS, PREVIOUSLY, WAS, WERE.

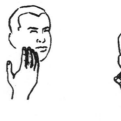

AGREE (ə grē´), *v.,* -GREED, -GREEING. (Of the same mind; thinking the same way.) The index finger of the right "D" hand, palm back, touches the forehead (the modified sign for THINK, *q.v.*, and then the two index fingers, both in the "D" position, palms down, are brought together so they are side by side, pointing away from the body (the sign for SAME). *Cf.* AGREEMENT, CONSENT.

AGREEMENT (-mənt), *n.* See AGREE.

AHEAD (ə hĕd'), *adv.* (One hand moves *ahead* of the other.) The two "A" hands are placed side by side in front of the chest with thumbs and knuckles touching, and the thumbs pointing outward from the body. The right "A" hand moves ahead until its heel rests on the left knuckles.

AID (ād), *n., v.,* AIDED, AIDING. (Helping up; supporting.) The left "S" hand, thumb side up, rests in the open right palm. In this position the left hand is pushed up a short distance by the right. *Cf.* ASSIST, ASSISTANCE, GIVE ASSISTANCE, HELP.

AIM (ām), *v.,* AIMED, AIMING. *n.* (A thought directed upward, toward a goal.) The index finger of the right "D" hand moves up to the index finger of the left "D" hand, which is held above eye level. The two index fingers stop just short of touching. *Cf.* AMBITION, GOAL, OBJECTIVE, PERSEVERE 4, PURPOSE 2.

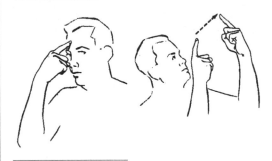

AIR (âr), *n.* (Creating a breeze with the hands.) Both hands, in the "5" position, palms facing, are held at face height. Pivoting at the wrists, they wave back and forth, fanning the face.

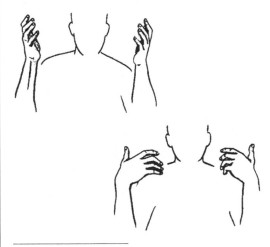

AIRPLANE (âr' plān'), *n.* (The wings of the airplane.) The "Y" hand, palm down and drawn up near the shoulder, moves forward, up and away from the body. Either hand may be used. *Cf.* FLY 1, PLANE 1.

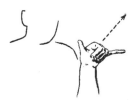

ALARM (ə lärm′), *n.* (The striker hits the bell.) The right index finger, pointing down or out, strikes the opposite palm repeatedly.

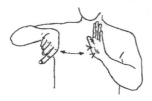

ALASKA (ə las′ kə), *n.* (The letter "A"; the fur-lined hood.) The right "A" hand moves from the left side of the face to the right, describing an arc over the head.

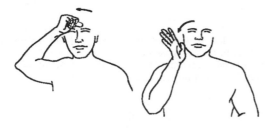

ALCOHOL (al′ kə hôl), *n.* (The size of the jigger.) The right hand, with index and little fingers extended and remaining fingers held against the palm by the thumb, strikes the back of the downturned "S" hand. *Cf.* LIQUOR 1, WHISKEY.

ALIKE (ə līk′), *adv.* (Matching fingers are brought together.) The outstretched index fingers are brought together, either once or several times. *Cf.* IDENTICAL, LIKE 2, SAME 1, SIMILAR, SUCH.

ALIVE (ə līv′), *adj.* (The fountain [of LIFE] wells up from within the body.) The upturned thumbs of the "A" hands move in unison up the chest. *Cf.* ADDRESS, LIFE 1, LIVE 1, LIVING, RESIDE.

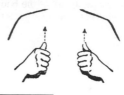

ALL (ôl), *adj., n., pron.* (Encompassing; a gathering together.) Both hands are held in the right angle position, palms facing the body, and the right hand in front of the left. The right hand makes a sweeping outward movement around the left, and comes to rest with the back of the right hand resting in the left palm. *Cf.* ENTIRE, UNIVERSAL, WHOLE.

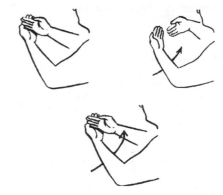

ALL AFTERNOON (af′ tər nōōn′, äf-), *adv. phrase.* (The sun, at its zenith, travels across the sky to sunset position, at the horizon.) The left arm is held before the chest, with the hand extended, fingers together, and palm facing down. The right elbow rests on the left hand, with the right hand extended, palm facing out. The right arm, using its elbow as a pivot, moves slowly down until it reaches the horizontal. *Cf.* AFTERNOON.

ALL ALONG (ə lông′, əlŏng′), *adv. phrase.* (From a point up and over.) In the "D" position, palms down, both index fingers touch the right shoulder and then are brought up and over, ending in a palm-up position, pointing straight ahead of the body. *Cf.* ALL THE TIME, EVER SINCE, SINCE 1, SO FAR, THUS FAR.

ALL DAY (dā), *phrase.* (From sunrise to sunset.) The left arm is held before the chest, palm down, fingers together. The right elbow rests on the back of the left hand. The right hand, palm up, pivoted by its elbow, describes an arc, from as far to the right as it can be held to a point where it comes to rest on the left arm, indicating the course of the sun from sunrise to sunset.

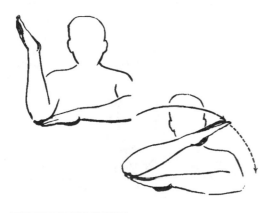

ALLEGIANCE (ə lē′ jəns), *n.* (Support.) The knuckles of the right "S" hand push up the left "S" hand.

ALLIGATOR (al′ ə gā tər′), *n.* (The mouth.) Both "5" hands are held against each other, fingertips pointing forward. With the heels of the hands connected, the hands come apart in a wide arc, imitating the opening of a large mouth.

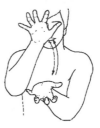

ALL MORNING (môr′ nĭng), *adv. phrase.* (The sun, at sunrise position, rises until it reaches its zenith.) The right arm is held horizontally before the body, palm up and fingers together. The left hand, palm facing the body, is placed in the crook of the right elbow, and the right arm rises slowly until it reaches the vertical.

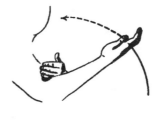

ALL NIGHT (nīt), *adv. phrase.* (The sun, having set over the horizon, continues around the other side of the earth, until it reaches the opposite horizon.) The left arm is held before the chest, hand extended, fingers together, palm down. The right arm rests on the back of the left hand, with palm down, fingers extended and together. The right hand, pivoted at its wrist, describes a sweeping downward arc until it comes to a stop near the left elbow.

ALLOW (ə lou′), *v.,* -LOWED, -LOWING. (A permissive upswinging of the hands, as if giving in.) Both hands, palms facing and fingers pointing away from the body, are held at chest level, almost a foot apart. With an upward movement, using their wrists as pivots, the hands sweep up until the fingers point almost straight up. *Cf.* GRANT 1, LET, LET'S, LET US, MAY 3, PERMISSION 1, PERMIT 1, TOLERATE 1.

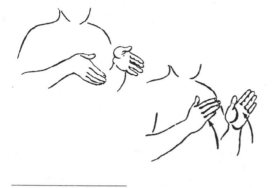

ALL RIGHT (rīt), *phrase.* (A straightening out.) The right hand, fingers together and palm facing left, is placed in the upturned left palm, whose fingers point away from the body. The right hand slides straight out along the left palm, over the left fingers, and stops with its heel resting on the left fingertips. *Cf.* O.K. 1, PRIVILEGE, RIGHT 1, RIGHTEOUS, YOU'RE WELCOME 2.

ALL THE TIME (tīm), *adv. phrase.* See ALL ALONG.

ALL YEAR; ALL YEAR 'ROUND (yĭr; round), *(colloq.), adv., v. phrase.* (Encircling the planet.) The left hand, in the "S" position, knuckles facing right, is encircled by the right index finger, which travels in a clockwise direction. It makes one revolution and comes to rest atop the left hand. *Cf.* AROUND THE WORLD, ORBIT.

ALMOST (ôl′ mōst, ôl mōst′), *adv.* The left hand is held at chest level in the right angle position, with fingers pointing up and the back of the hand facing right. The right fingers are swept up along the back of the left hand. *Cf.* ABOUT 2, NEARLY.

ALONE (ə lōn′), *adj.* (One, wandering around in a circle.) The index finger, pointing straight up, palm facing the body (the number *one*), is rotated before the face in a counterclockwise direction. *Cf.* LONE, ONLY, SOLE.

ALPHABET 1 (ăl′ fə bĕt′), *n.* (The movement of the fingers in fingerspelling.) The right hand, palm out, is moved from left to right, with the fingers wriggling up and down. *Cf.* DACTYLOLOGY, FINGERSPELLING, MANUAL ALPHABET, SPELL, SPELLING.

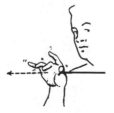

ALPHABET 2, *n.* (The A-B-C.) The signer finger-spells "A-B-C," and then the hand, with fingers wriggling, moves from left to right. See previous entry.

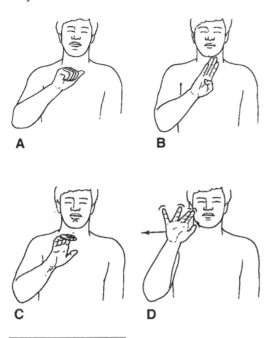

A   B

C   D

ALSO (ôl′ sō), *adv.* (A likeness; a sameness.) Both index fingers, held together at one side of the body near waist level, point forward. As they travel to the other side of the body they separate an inch or two and come together again. *Cf.* ACCORDING (TO), AS, SAME AS, TOO.

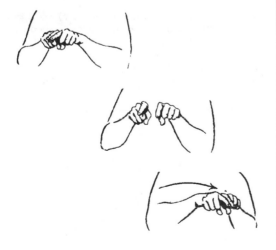

ALTAR (ôl′ tər), *n.* (The construction or shape of the altar.) Both "A" hands, palms down and thumbs touching, separate and move down.

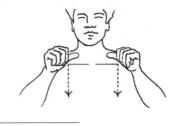

ALTRUISM (al′ trōō iz əm), *n.* (The heart is open.) The right hand is held against the heart. It moves out and forward with a flourish, ending with the palm facing left.

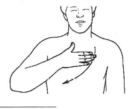

ALWAYS (ôl′ wāz, -wĭz), *adv.* (Around the clock.) The index finger of the right "D" hand points outward, away from the body, with palm facing left. The arm is rotated clockwise.

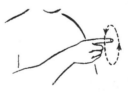

AM 1 (ăm; *unstressed* əm), *v.* (Part of the verb to BE.) The tip of the right index finger, held in the "D" position, palm facing left, is held at the lips, and the hand moves straight out and away from the lips. *Cf.* ARE 1, BE 1.

AM 2, *v.* (The "A" hand.) The tip of the right thumb, in the "A" position, palm facing left, is held at the lips. Then the hand moves straight out and away from the lips.

AMAZE (ə māz´), *v.*, -MAZED, -MAZING. (The eyes pop open in amazement.) Both hands are held in modified "O" positions with thumb and index fingers of each hand near the eyes. These fingers suddenly flick open, and the eyes simultaneously pop open wide. *Cf.* AMAZEMENT, ASTONISH, ASTONISHED, ASTONISHMENT, ASTOUND, SURPRISE 1.

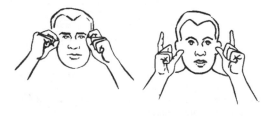

AMAZEMENT (-mənt), *n.* See AMAZE.

AMBITION (ăm bĭsh´ ən), *n.* (A thought directed upward, toward a goal.) The index finger of the right "D" hand touches the forehead, and then moves up to the index finger of the left "D" hand, which is held above eye level. The two index fingers stop just short of touching. *Cf.* AIM, GOAL, OBJECTIVE, PERSEVERE 4, PURPOSE 2.

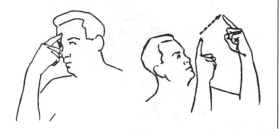

AMBITIOUS (ăm bĭsh´ əs), *adj.* (Rubbing the hands together in zeal or ambition.) The open hands are rubbed vigorously back and forth against each other. *Cf.* ANXIOUS, DILIGENCE, DILIGENT, EAGER, EAGERNESS, ENTHUSIASM, ENTHUSIASTIC, INDUSTRIOUS, METHODIST, ZEAL, ZEALOUS.

AMBULANCE (am´ byə ləns), *n.* (The flashing light.) The right hand, fingers extended, is positioned above the head. It rotates in imitation of a flashing emergency light.

AMEND (ə mend´), *v.* (Add something on.) The open left hand is held either with palm facing the body or facing right. The right hand, palm down and a space maintained between the thumb and the other fingers, swivels up and grasps the little finger edge of the left hand, as if inserting a clip on a stack of papers.

AMERICA (ə mĕr′ ə kə), *n.* (The fences built by the early settlers as protection against the Indians.) The extended fingers of both hands are interlocked, and are swept in an arc from left to right as if encompassing an imaginary house or stockade.

AMIABLE (ā′ mĭ ə bəl), *adj.* (A crinkling-up of the face.) Both hands, in the "5" position, palms facing back, are placed on either side of the face. The fingers wiggle back and forth, while a pleasant, happy expression is worn. *Cf.* CHEERFUL, CORDIAL, FRIENDLY, JOLLY, PLEASANT.

AMID (ə′ mĭd′), *prep.* (Wandering in and out.) The right index finger weaves its way in and out between the outstretched fingers of the left hand. *Cf.* AMIDST, AMONG.

AMIDST (ə′ mĭdst′), *prep.* See AMID.

AMONG (ə mŭng′), *prep.* See AMID.

AMOUNT 1 (ə mount′), *n.* (To bring up all together.) The two open hands, palms and fingers facing each other, with the left hand above the right, are brought together, with all fingers closing simultaneously. This sign is used mainly in the sense of adding up figures or items. *Cf.* ADD 1, ADDITION, SUM, SUMMARIZE 2, SUMMARY 2, SUM UP, TOTAL.

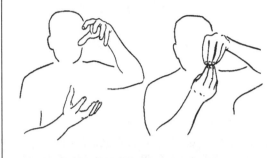

AMOUNT 2, *n.* (Throwing up a number of things before the eyes; a display of fingers to indicate a question of how many or how much.) The right hand, palm up, is held before the chest, all fingers touching the thumb. The hand is tossed straight up, while the fingers open to the "5" position. *Cf.* HOW MANY?, HOW MUCH?

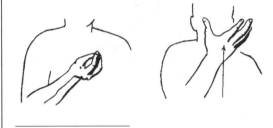

AMPLE (ăm′ pəl), *adj.* (A full cup.) The left hand, in the "S" position, is held palm facing right. The right "5" hand, palm down, is brushed outward several times over the top of the left, indicating a wiping off of the top of a cup. *Cf.* ABUNDANCE, ABUNDANT, ADEQUATE, ENOUGH, PLENTY, SUBSTANTIAL, SUFFICIENT.

ANALYZE (an' ə līz), *v.* (Pulling apart.) Both down-turned curved index and middle fingers pull apart repeatedly.

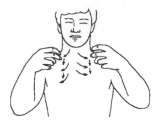

ANCESTORS (ăn' sĕs tĕrz), *n. pl.* (A series of parents, in the past.) The upright open hands are held facing each other before the right shoulder, right palm facing left, left palm facing right. In this position the hands move back over the shoulder, alternately executing a series of up-down, circular motions.

ANCHOR (ang' kər), *n., v.* (Dropping the hook.) The right "3" hand is held palm facing left. This represents the vessel floating on the surface of the water. The downturned curved left index finger is "thrown" overboard and goes down, and the signer leans back against an imaginary rope or line to set the anchor in place on the bottom.

AND (ănd; *unstressed* ənd; ən), *conj.* The right "5" hand, palm facing the body, fingers facing left, moves from left to right, meanwhile closing until all its fingers touch around its thumb.

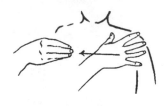

ANGEL (ān' jəl), *n.* (A winged creature.) The fingertips of both hands rest on the shoulders, and then the hands go through the motions of flapping wings, pivoting up and down from the wrists, and held at shoulder level. The eyes are sometimes rolled upward, indicating something celestial.

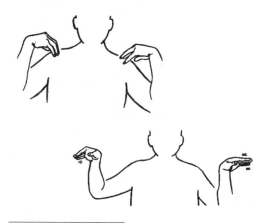

ANGER (ăn' gər), *n.* (A violent welling-up of the emotions.) The curved fingers of the right hand are placed in the center of the chest, and fly up suddenly and violently. An expression of anger is worn. *Cf.* ANGRY 2, ENRAGE, FURY, INDIGNANT, INDIGNATION, IRE, MAD, RAGE.

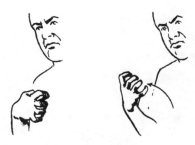

ANGLE (ang′ gəl), *n.* (Outlining an angle.) The left hand is held in the "L" position, palm facing forward. The right index finger moves down the left index and along the thumb, tracing a right angle as it does.

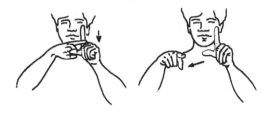

ANNEX (ə nĕks′), *v.,* -NEXED, -NEXING. (Joining together.) Both hands, held in the modified "5" position, palms out, move toward each other. The thumbs and index fingers of both hands then connect. *Cf.* AFFILIATE, ATTACH, BELONG, CONNECT, ENLIST, ENROLL, JOIN, PARTICIPATE, UNITE.

ANGRY 1 (ăn′ grĭ), *adj.* (Wrinkling the brow.) The "5" hand is held palm toward the face. The fingers open and close partially, several times, while an angry expression is worn on the face. *Cf.* CROSS 1, CROSSNESS, FIERCE, ILL TEMPER, IRRITABLE.

ANGRY 2, *adj.* See ANGER.

ANNOUNCE (ə nouns′), *v.,* -NOUNCED, -NOUNCING. (An issuance from the mouth.) Both index fingers are placed at the lips, with palms facing the body. They are rotated once and swung out in arcs, until the left index finger points somewhat to the left and the right index somewhat to the right. Sometimes the rotation of the fingers is omitted in favor of a simple swinging out from the lips. *Cf.* ANNOUNCEMENT, DECLARE.

ANIMAL (ăn′ ə məl), *n.* With the curved fingertips of both hands resting on either side of the chest, and acting as anchors, the arms are moved alternately toward and away from each other.

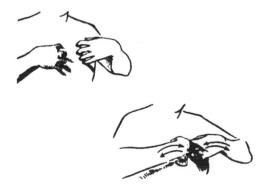

ANNOUNCEMENT (-mənt), *n.* See ANNOUNCE.

ANNOY (ə noi′), *v.*, -NOYED, -NOYING. (Obstruct, block.) The left hand, fingers together and palm flat, is held before the body, facing somewhat down. The little finger side of the right hand, held with palm flat, makes one or several up-down chopping motions against the left hand, between its thumb and index finger. *Cf.* ANNOYANCE, BOTHER, DISRUPT, DISTURB, HINDER, HINDRANCE, IMPEDE, INTERCEPT, INTERFERE, INTERFERENCE, INTERFERE WITH, INTERRUPT, MEDDLE 1, OBSTACLE, OBSTRUCT, PREVENT, PREVENTION.

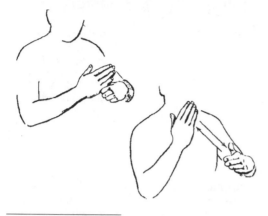

ANNOYANCE (ə noi′ əns), *n.* See ANNOY.

ANNUAL (ăn′ yōō əl), *adj.* (Several years brought forward.) This sign is actually a modification of the sign for YEAR, *q.v.* The ball of the right "S" hand, moving straight out from the body, palm facing left, glances over the thumb side of the "S" hand, which is held palm facing right. As this contact is made, the right index finger is flung straight out, and the right hand, in this new position, continues forward. This is repeated several times, to indicate several years. *Cf.* EVERY YEAR, YEARLY.

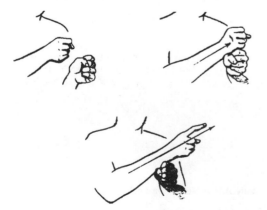

ANOINT (ə noint′), *v.* (Pouring holy water on the head.) The "a" hand, holding an imaginary pitcher by the handle, tips it over above the head to pour water on the head.

ANOTHER (ə nŭth′ ər), *adj.* (Moving over to *another* position.) The right "A" hand, thumb up, is pivoted from the wrist and swung over to the right, so that the thumb now points to the right. *Cf.* ELSE, OTHER.

ANSWER (ăn′ sər; än′-), *n.*, *v.*, -SWERED, -SWERING. (Directing a reply from the mouth to someone.) The tip of the right index finger, held in the "D" position, palm facing the body, is placed on the lips, while the left "D" hand, palm also facing the body, is held about a foot in front of the right hand. The right index finger, swinging around, moves toward and stops in a pointing position a few inches from the left index fingertip. *Cf.* MAKE RESPONSE, REPLY 1, RESPOND, RESPONSE 1.

ANTICIPATE (ăn tĭs′ ə pāt′), *v.*, -PATED, -PATING. (A thought awaited.) The tip of the right index finger, held in the "D" position, palm facing the body, is placed on the forehead (modified THINK, *q.v.*). Both hands then assume right angle positions, fingers facing, with the left hand held above left shoulder level and the right before the right breast. Both hands, held thus, wave to each other several times. *Cf.* ANTICIPATION, EXPECT, HOPE.

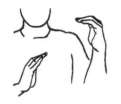 

ANTICIPATION (-pā′ shən), *n.* See ANTICIPATE.

ANTLERS (ănt′ lərs), *n. pl.* (The branching of the antlers from the head.) Both hands, in the "5" position, palms up, are placed at the head, thumbs resting on the head above the temples. *Cf.* DEER, ELK, MOOSE.

ANXIOUS (ăngk′ shəs, ăng′ shəs), *adj.* (Rubbing the hands together in zeal or ambition.) The open hands are rubbed vigorously back and forth against each other. *Cf.* AMBITIOUS, DILIGENCE, DILIGENT, EAGER, EAGERNESS, ENTHUSIASM, ENTHUSIASTIC, INDUSTRIOUS, METHODIST, ZEAL, ZEALOUS.

ANY (ĕn′ ĭ), *adj., pron.* The "A" hand, palm down and thumb pointing left, pivots around on the wrist, so the thumb now points down.

ANYHOW (ĕn′ ĭ hou′), *adv.* Both hands, in the "5" position, are held before the chest, fingertips facing each other. With an alternate back-forth movement, the fingertips are made to strike each other. *Cf.* ANYWAY, DESPITE, DOESN'T MATTER, HOWEVER 2, INDIFFERENCE, INDIFFERENT, IN SPITE OF, MAKE NO DIFFERENCE, NEVERTHELESS, NO MATTER, WHEREVER.

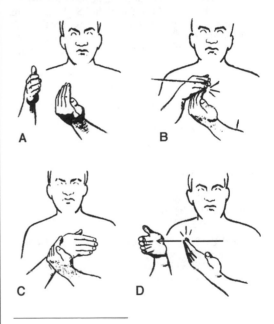

A   B

C   D

ANYONE (ĕn′ ĭ wŭn′), *pron.* (Any and one.) After forming either of the two signs for ANY, the "A" hand, moving up a bit, assumes the "1" position ("D"), palm out.

ANYWAY (ĕn′ ĭ wā′), *adv.* See ANYHOW.

APART (ə pärt′), *adv.* (The hands are moved *apart*.) Both hands, in the "A" position, thumbs up, are held together, with knuckles touching. With a deliberate movement they come apart. *Cf.* DIVORCE 1, PART 3, SEPARATE 1.

APOLOGIZE 1 (ə pŏl′ ə jīz′), *v.*, -GIZED, -GIZING. (The heart is circled, to indicate feeling, modified by the letter "S," for SORRY.) The right "S" hand, palm facing the body, is rotated several times over the area of the heart. *Cf.* APOLOGY 1, CONTRITION, PENITENT, REGRET, REGRETFUL, REPENT, REPENTANT, RUE, SORROW, SORROWFUL 2, SORRY.

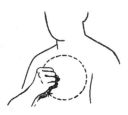

APOLOGIZE 2, *v.* (A wiped-off and cleaned slate.) The right hand wipes off the left palm several times. *Cf.* APOLOGY 2, EXCUSE, FORGIVE, PARDON, PAROLE.

APOLOGY 1 (ə pŏl ə jĭ), *n.* See APOLOGIZE 1.

APOLOGY 2, *n.* See APOLOGIZE 2.

APOSTLE (ə pos′əl), *n.* (A follower.) Both "A" hands, one behind the other, move forward in unison. The sign for INDIVIDUAL is then made: both open hands, palms facing each other, move down the sides of the body, tracing its outline to the hips.

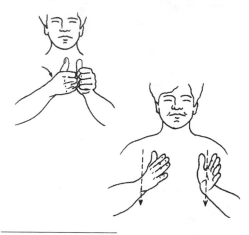

APPARENT (ə păr′ ənt, ə pâr′-), *adj.* (Something presented before the eyes.) The open right hand, palm flat and facing out, with fingers together and pointing up, is positioned at shoulder level. Pivoting from the wrist, the hand is swung around so that the palm now faces the eyes. Sometimes the eyes glance at the newly presented palm. *Cf.* APPARENTLY, APPEAR 1, LOOK 2, SEEM.

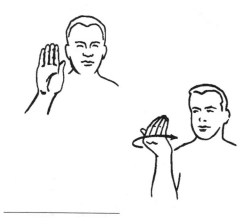

APPARENTLY (ə păr′ ənt lē, ə pâr′-), *adv.* See APPARENT.

APPEAR 1 (ə pîr′), *v.*, -PEARED, -PEARING. See APPARENT.

APPEAR 2, *v.* (Popping up before the eyes.) The right index finger, pointing up, pops up between the index and middle fingers of the left hand, whose palm faces down. *Cf.* POP UP, RISE 2.

APPETITE (ăp' ə tīt'), *n.* (The upper alimentary tract is outlined.) The right "C" hand, palm facing the body, is placed with fingertips touching midchest. In this position it moves down a bit. *Cf.* CRAVE, DESIRE 2, STARVATION, STARVE, STARVED, WISH 2.

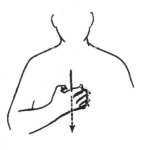

APPLAUD (ə plôd'), *v.,* -PLAUDED, -PLAUDING. (Good words coming from the mouth; clapping hands.) The fingertips of the right hand, palm flat and facing the body, are brought up to the lips, so that they touch (part of the sign for GOOD, *q.v.* The hands are then clapped together several times. *Cf.* APPLAUSE, COMMEND, CONGRATULATE 1, CONGRATULATIONS 1, PRAISE.

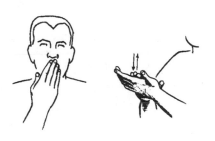

APPLAUSE (ə plôz'), *n.* See APPLAUD.

APPLE (ap'əl), *n.* (A chewing of the letter "A," for *apple*. The right "A" hand is held at the right cheek, with the thumb tip touching the cheek and palm facing out. In this position the hand is swung over and back from the wrist several times, using the thumb as a pivot.

APPLESAUCE (ap' əl sôs), *n.* (Eating an apple with a spoon.) The sign for APPLE is made. An imaginary spoon is then brought up to the mouth.

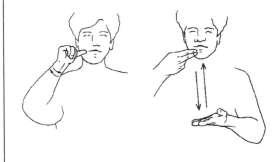

APPOINT (ə point'), *v.,* -POINTED, -POINTING. (Taking unto oneself.) The right hand, palm out, is extended before the chest, index finger and thumb in an open position, the other fingers separated and pointing up. The hand is drawn in toward the chest, and the index and thumb close at the same time, indicating something taken to oneself. *Cf.* CHOOSE, SELECT 2, TAKE.

APPOINTMENT (ə point'mənt), *n.* (A binding of the hands together; a commitment.) The right "S" hand, palm down, is positioned above the left "S" hand, also palm down. The right hand circles above the left in a clockwise manner and is brought down on the back of the left hand. At the same instant both hands move down in unison a short distance.

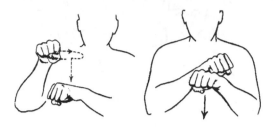

APPRECIATE (ə prē' shǐ āt'), *v.,* -ATED, -ATING. (A pleasurable feeling on the heart.) The open right hand is circled on the chest, over the heart. *Cf.* ENJOY, ENJOYMENT, GRATIFY 1, LIKE 3, PLEASE, PLEASURE, WILLING 2.

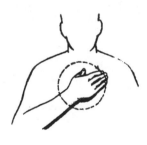

APPROACH (ə prōch'), *v.,* -PROACHED, -PROACHING. (Coming close to.) Both hands are held in the right angle position, fingers facing each other, with the right hand held between the left hand and the chest. The right hand slowly moves toward the left. *Cf.* NEAR 2, TOWARD 2.

APRON (ā' prən), *n.* (Tying the apron.) The signer mimes tying apron strings behind the back.

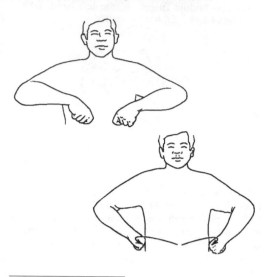

ARCHITECTURE (är' kə tek chər), *n.* (The letter "A"; the roof and walls of a building.) Both "A" hands, palms facing forward and thumbtips touching, move apart and then straight down. Also ARCHITECT.

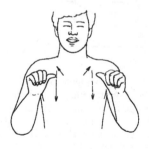

ARE 1 (är), *v.* (Part of the verb to BE.) The tip of the right index finger, held in the "D" position, palm facing left, is held at the lips, and the hand moves straight out and away from the lips. *Cf.* AM 1, BE 1.

ARE 2, *v.* This is the same sign as for ARE 1, except that the "R" hand is used. It is an initialized version of ARE 1.

AREA (âr′ ĭ ə), *n.* (The letter "A"; the limitations or borders of the area.) The "A" hands, palms facing down, are positioned with thumbtips touching. They separate, move in toward the body, and then come together again at the thumbtips. The movement describes a square or a circle.

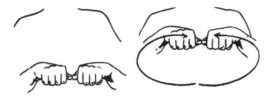

ARGENTINA 1 (är′ jen te′ na), *n.* (Playing a guitar.) The signer goes through the natural motions of playing a guitar.

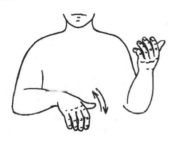

ARGENTINA 2, *n.* The thumbtip of the "A" hand touches both sides of the forehead.

ARGUE (är′ gū), *v.,* -GUED, -GUING. (An expounding back and forth.) The index fingers here represent the two sides of the argument. First the left index finger is slapped into the open right palm, and then the right makes the same movement into the left palm. This is repeated back and forth several times. *Cf.* ARGUMENT, CONTROVERSY, DEBATE, DISPUTE.

ARGUMENT (-mənt), *n.* See ARGUE.

ARISE 1 (ə rīz′), *v.,* -ROSE, -RISEN, -RISING. (Rising up.) Both upturned hands, held at chest level, rise in unison, to about shoulder height. *Cf.* RISE 3.

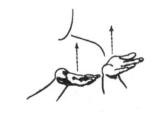

ARISE 2, *v.* (Getting onto one's feet.) The upturned index and middle fingers of the right hand, representing the legs, are swung up and over in an arc, coming to rest in the upturned left palm. *Cf.* GET UP, RAISE 1, RISE 1, STAND 2, STAND UP.

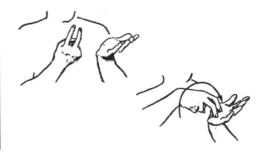

ARITHMETIC (ə rĭth′ mə tĭk), *n.* (A multiplying.) The "V" hands, palms facing the body, alternately cross and separate, several times. *Cf.* FIGURE 1, MULTIPLY 1.

wrists so that the palms now face the body (a class or category, all together as one unit).

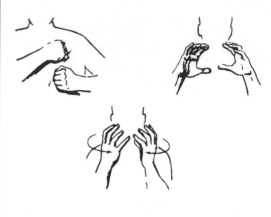

ARIZONA (ar′ ə zō′ nə), *n.* (The letter "A"; the dryness.) The thumbtip of the right "A" hand moves across the lips from left to right, as if drying the mouth.

ARMS (ärmz), *n. pl.* (Bearing arms.) Both "A" hands, palms facing the body, are placed at the left breast, with the right hand above the left, as if holding a rifle against the body. *Cf.* SOLDIER.

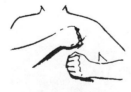

ARMY (är′ mĭ), *n.* (A group of arms-bearers or soldiers.) The sign for ARMS is made. The "C" hands, palms facing each other, then pivot around on their

AROUND 1 (ə round′), *adv.* (Circling *around.*) The left hand, all fingers pointed up and touching, is encircled by the right index finger, pointing down and moving clockwise.

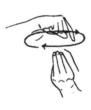

AROUND 2, *prep.* (Turning a corner.) The left open hand is held palm down. The right index finger moves around the left fingertips, from the index to the little finger.

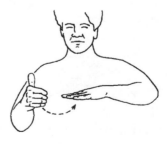

AROUND 3, *adv, adj.* (Moving *around* an area.) The downturned "5" hand moves in a counterclockwise fashion.

AROUND THE WORLD (wûrld), *adv. phrase.* (Encircling the planet.) The left hand, in the "S" position, knuckles facing right, is encircled by the right index finger, which travels in a clockwise direction. It makes one revolution and comes to rest atop the left hand. *Cf.* ALL YEAR, ALL YEAR 'ROUND, ORBIT.

ARRANGE (ə rānj'), *v.,* -RANGED, -RANGING. (Placing things in order.) The hands, palms facing, fingers together and pointing away from the body, are positioned at the left side and held about a foot apart. With a slight up-down motion, as if describing waves, the hands travel in unison from left to right. *Cf.* ARRANGEMENT, ORDER 3, PLAN 1, PREPARE 1, PROGRAM 1, PROVIDE 1, PUT IN ORDER, READY 1.

ARRANGEMENT (ə rānj' mənt), *n.* See ARRANGE.

ARREARS (ə rirz') *n.* (Pointing to the palm, where the money should be placed.) The index finger of one hand is thrust into the upturned palm of the other several times. *Cf.* DEBIT, DEBT, DUE, OBLIGATION 2, OWE.

ARREST (ə rěst'), *v.,* -RESTED, -RESTING. (Seizing someone by the clothing.) The right hand quickly grasps the clothing at the left shoulder.

ARRIVAL (ə rī' vəl), *n.* (Arrival at a designated place.) The right hand, palm facing the body and fingers pointing up, is brought forward from a position near the right shoulder and placed in the upturned palm of the left hand (the designated place.) *Cf.* ARRIVE.

ARRIVE (ə rīv´), v., -RIVED, -RIVING. See ARRIVAL.

ART (ärt), n. (Drawing on the hand.) The little finger of the right hand, representing a pencil, traces a curved line in the upturned left palm. Cf. DRAW.

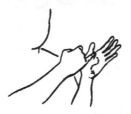

ARTICULATE (är tik´ yə lit), adj. (Speaking with skill.) The right index finger, pointing left, describes a continuous small circle in front of the mouth. This is a sign for SPEAK. It is followed by the sign for SKILL: the right hand grasps the little finger edge of the left firmly. As it leaves this position, moving down and out, it assumes the "A" position, palm facing left.

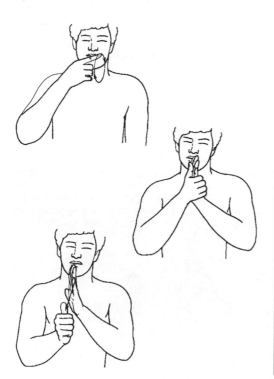

ARTIFICIAL (är tə fish´ əl), adj. (Words deflected from their path, straight out from the lips.) The index finger of the right "D" hand, pointing to the left, moves in front of the lips, from right to left.

ARTIST (är´ tĭst), n. (An individual who draws.) The sign for ART is made, followed by the sign for INDIVIDUAL: both hands, fingers together, are placed at either side of the chest and are moved down to waist level.

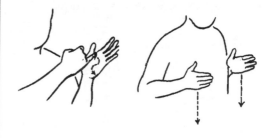

AS (ăz; unstressed əz), adv. (A likeness; a sameness.) Both index fingers, held together at one side of the body near waist level, point forward. As they travel to the other side of the body they separate an inch or two and come together again. Cf. ACCORDING (TO), ALSO, SAME AS, TOO.

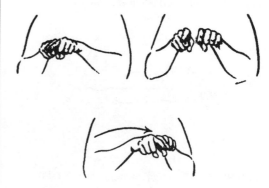

AS A MATTER OF FACT *phrase.* (Straightforward, from the lips.) The right index finger is placed up against the lips. It moves up and forward, in a small arc.

ASHAMED (ə shāmd′), *adj.* (The color rises in the cheek; an attempt is made to hide the head.) The backs of the fingers of the right hand, held in the right angle position, are placed against the right cheek. The hand moves up along the cheek, pivoting at the wrist, so that the fingers finally point to the rear. *Cf.* BASHFUL, SHAME 1, SHAMEFUL, SHAME ON YOU, SHY 1.

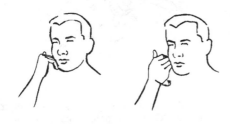

ASK 1 (ăsk, äsk), *v.,* ASKED, ASKING. (Pray tell.) Both hands, held upright about a foot in front of the chest, with palms facing and fingers pointing straight up, are positioned about a foot apart. Moving toward the chest, they come together until they touch, as if in prayer. *Cf.* INQUIRE 1, REQUEST 1.

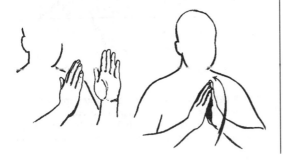

ASK 2 *(colloq.), v.* (Fire a question.) The right hand, held in a modified "S" position with palm facing out, assumes a position with the thumb resting on the fingernail of the index finger. The index finger is flicked out and forward, usually directed at the person being asked a question. Reversing the direction so that the index finger flicks out toward the speaker indicates the passive voice of the verb, *i.e.,* to be ASKED. *Cf.* INQUIRE 2, INTERROGATE 2, INTERROGATION 2, QUERY 2, QUESTION 2, QUIZ 2.

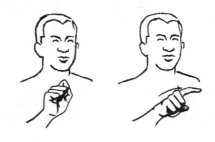

ASK 3, *v.* (Firing questions.) The index fingers of both "D" hands repeatedly curve and straighten out as the hands are alternately flung forward and back, as if firing questions. *Cf.* EXAMINATION 2, INQUIRE 3, INTERROGATE 1, INTERROGATION 1, QUERY 1, QUESTION 3, QUIZ 3.

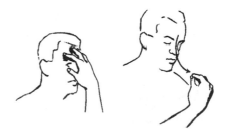

ASLEEP (ə slēp′), *adv.* (The eyes are closed.) The fingers of the right open hand, facing the forehead, are placed on the forehead. The hand moves down and away from the head, with the fingers closing so that they all touch. The eyes meanwhile close, and the head bows slightly, as in sleep. *Cf.* NAP 1, SLEEP 1.

ASSEMBLE 1 (ə sĕm´ bəl), *v.*, -BLED, -BLING. (Assemble all together.) Both "5" hands, palms facing, are held with fingers pointing out from the body. With a sweeping motion they are brought in toward the chest, and all fingertips come together. This is repeated. *Cf.* ASSEMBLY, CONFERENCE, CONVENE, CONVENTION, GATHER 2, GATHERING, MEETING 1.

ASSEMBLE 2 *v.* (Many people coming together in one place.) The downturned "5" hands, fingers wriggling, come toward each other until the fingertips almost touch.

ASSEMBLY (ə sĕm´ blĭ), *n.* See ASSEMBLE 1.

ASSET (as´ et), *n.* (Putting a plus into the pocket.) The index fingers form a plus (+) sign, and then the right "F" hand moves down an inch or two against the right side of the body, as if placing a coin into a pocket.

ASSIST (ə sĭst´), *n.*, *v.*, -SISTED, -SISTING. (Helping up; supporting.) The left "S" hand, thumb side up, rests in the open right palm. In this position the left hand

is pushed up a short distance by the right. *Cf.* AID, ASSISTANCE, GIVE ASSISTANCE, HELP.

ASSISTANCE (ə sĭs´ təns), *n.* See ASSIST.

ASSOCIATE (ə sō´ shĭ āt´), *v.*, -ATED, -ATING. (Mingling with.) Both hands are held in modified "A" positions, thumbs out. The left hand is positioned with its thumb pointing straight up, and the right hand, with its thumb pointing down, revolves above the left thumb in a clockwise direction. *Cf.* EACH OTHER, FELLOWSHIP, MINGLE 2, MUTUAL, ONE ANOTHER.

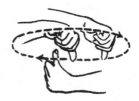

ASSOCIATION (ə sō´ sĭ ā´ shən), *n.* (A grouping together.) Both "C" hands, palms facing, are held a few inches apart at chest height. They are swung around in unison, so that the palms now face the body. *Cf.* CIRCLE 2, CLASS, CLASSED, CLUB, COMPANY 1, GANG, GROUP 1, ORGANIZATION 1.

ASSORTED (ə sôr´ tĭd), *adj.* (Separated many times; different.) The "D" hands, palms down, are crossed at the index fingers or are held side by side. They separate and return to their initial position a number of times. *Cf.* DIFFERENCE, DIFFERENT, DIVERSE 1, DIVERSITY 1, UNLIKE, VARIED.

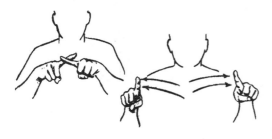

ASSUME (ə sōōm'), *v.*, -SUMED, -SUMING. (To take up.) Both hands, held palms down in the "5" position, are at chest level. With a grasping upward movement, both close into "S" positions before the face. *Cf.* PICK UP 1, TAKE UP.

ASTONISH (ə stŏn' ĭsh), *v.*, -ISHED, -ISHING. (The eyes pop open in amazement.) Both hands are held in modified "O" positions with thumb and index fingers of each hand near the eyes. These fingers suddenly flick open, and the eyes simultaneously pop open wide. *Cf.* AMAZE, AMAZEMENT, ASTONISHED, ASTONISHMENT, ASTOUND, SURPRISE 1.

ASTONISHED *adj.* See ASTONISH.

ASTONISHMENT (-mənt), *n.* See ASTONISH.

ASTOUND (ə stound'), *v.*, -TOUNDED, -TOUNDING. See ASTONISH.

ASTRONAUT (as' trə nŏt), *n.* (The "R" for "rocket"; the liftoff.) The base of the right "R" hand rests on the back of the downturned left hand. The "R" hand shoots up. The sign for INDIVIDUAL 1 then follows.

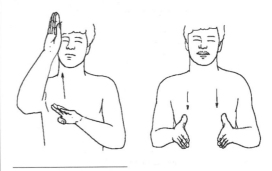

AT (ăt; *unstressed* ət; ĭt), *prep.* The left hand is held at eye level, palm facing out and fingers together. The right hand, palm down, fingers also together, moves over to the left, so that the right fingertips come to touch the back of the left hand. This sign is seldom used; most signers prefer to spell out "AT" on the fingers.

AT A LOSS (lôs, lŏs), *phrase.* (The mind is frozen; the thought is frozen.) The index finger of the right "D" hand, palm facing the body, touches the forehead (modified THINK sign, *q.v.*. Both hands, in the "5" position, palms down, are then suddenly and deliberately dropped down in front of the body. A look of surprise is assumed at this point, and the head jerks back slightly. *Cf.* DUMBFOUNDED 1, SHOCKED 1.

ATHLETE (ath' lĕt), *n*. (One who does exercises.) Both "A" hands, palms facing the chest, move in alternate forward circles. The sign for INDIVIDUAL 1 then follows.

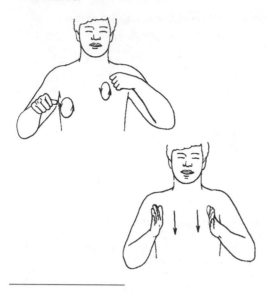

ATOM (at' əm), *n*. (The letter "A"; around the world.) The right "A" hand makes a circle around the upright left fist.

ATTACH (ə tăch'), *v*., -TACHED, -TACHING. (Joining together.) Both hands, held in the modified "5" position, palms out, move toward each other. The thumbs and index fingers of both hands then connect. *Cf*. AFFILIATE, ANNEX, BELONG, CONNECT, ENLIST, ENROLL, JOIN, PARTICIPATE, UNITE.

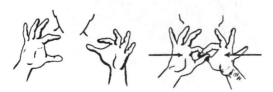

ATTACK (ə tăk'), *n*., *v*., -TACKED, -TACKING. (Striking against.) The clenched right hand strikes against the open left palm.

ATTEMPT 1 (ə tĕmpt'), *n*., *v*., -TEMPTED, -TEMPTING. (Trying to push through.) The "A" hands, palms facing before the body, are swung around and a bit down, so that the palms now face out. The movement indicates an attempt to push through a barrier. *Cf*. EFFORT 1, ENDEAVOR, PERSEVERE 1, PERSIST 1, TRY 1.

ATTEMPT 2, *n*., *v*. (Trying to push through, using the "T" hands, for "try.") This is the same sign as ATTEMPT 1, except that the "T" hands are employed. *Cf*. EFFORT 2, PERSEVERE 2, TRY 2.

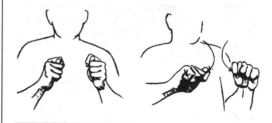

ATTEND (TO) (ə tĕnd'), *v*., -TENDED, -TENDING. (Directing one's attention forward; applying oneself; concentrating.) Both hands, fingers pointing up and together, are held at the sides of the face. They move straight out from the face. *Cf*. ATTENTION, CONCENTRATE, CONCENTRATION, FOCUS, GIVE ATTENTION (TO), MIND 2, PAY ATTENTION (TO).

ATTENTION (ə tĕn' shən), *n*. See ATTEND (TO).

ATTITUDE (ăt´ ə tūd', -tōōd'), *n*. (The letter "A"; the inclination of the heart.) The right "A" hand describes a counterclockwise circle around the heart, and comes to rest against the heart.

ATTORNEY (ə tûr' nĭ), *n*. (A law individual.) The upright right "L" hand (for LAW), resting palm against palm on the upright left "5" hand, moves down in an arc, a short distance, coming to rest on the base of the left palm. The sign for INDIVIDUAL is then added: both hands, fingers together, are placed at either side of the chest and are moved down to waist level. *Cf*. LAW, LAWYER, LEGAL.

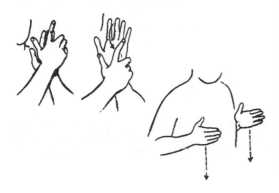

ATTRACT (ə trăkt'), *v*., -TRACTED, -TRACTING. (Bringing everything together, to one point.) The open "5" hands, palms down and held at chest level, draw together until all the fingertips touch. *Cf*. ATTRACTION, ATTRACTIVE.

ATTRACTION (ə trăk' shən), *n*. See ATTRACT.

ATTRACTIVE (ə trăk' tĭv), *adj*. See ATTRACT.

AUDIOLOGY (ô´ dē ol' ə jĕ), *n*. (The "A"; at the ear.) The right "A" hand, held at the ear, pivots slightly back and forth. Both "A" hands may also be used, at both ears.

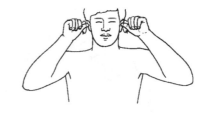

AUNT (ănt, änt), *n*. (A female, defined by the letter "A.") The "A" hand, thumb near the right jawline (see sign for FEMALE), quivers back and forth several times.

AUSTRALIA 1 (ô strāl' yə), *n*. (The turned back brim of an Australian hat.) The fingertips of the right "B" hand are placed against the forehead with palm toward the face. The hand is then drawn away from the face and turned so that the palm faces outward. The open hand then strikes back against the right side of the head.

AUSTRALIA 2, *n.* Both hands are held in the "8" position, palms down. The signer flicks out the middle fingers of both hands twice. This is a native Australian sign.

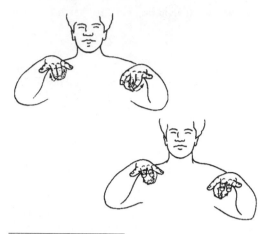

AUTHENTIC (ô thĕn′ tĭk), *adj.* (Coming forth directly from the lips; true.) The index finger of the right "D" hand, palm facing left, is placed against the lips. It moves up an inch or two and then describes a small arc forward and away from the lips. *Cf.* ABSOLUTE, ABSOLUTELY, ACTUAL, ACTUALLY, CERTAIN, CERTAINLY, FIDELITY, FRANKLY, GENUINE, INDEED, POSITIVE 1, POSITIVELY, REAL, REALLY, SINCERE 2, SURE, SURELY, TRUE, TRULY, TRUTH, VALID, VERILY.

AUTHORITY (ə thôr′ ə tē), *n.* (The letter "A"; the muscle.) The right "A" hand describes an arc on the left arm muscle as it moves from shoulder to the crook of the elbow.

AUTISM (ô′ tiz əm), *n.* (Cut off from the world.) Both "C" hands, palms facing, are positioned at the temples. They move around so that they now cover the eyes.

AUTOMATIC (ô tə mat′ ik), *n., adj.* (The shift lever attached to the car's steering column.) The left index finger, slightly curved, is held up. The right index finger, also slightly curved, palm up, slides up and down the left index finger.

AUTOMOBILE (ô′ tə mə bēl′, ô′ tə mō′ bēl, -mə bēl′), *n.* (The steering wheel.) The hands grasp an imaginary steering wheel and manipulate it. *Cf.* CAR, DRIVE.

AUTUMN (ô′ təm), *n.* (A chopping down during harvest time.) The right hand, fingers together and palm facing down, makes several chopping motions against the left elbow, to indicate the felling of growing things in autumn.

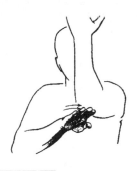

AVAILABLE (ə vā′ lə bəl), *adj.* (A spot or place is empty, therefore available.) The middle finger of the right downturned "5" hand makes a small counterclockwise circle against the back of the downturned left hand.

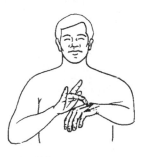

AVERAGE (ăv′ ər ĭj, ăv′ rĭj), *n., adj., v.,* -AGED, -AGING. (Halfway between top and bottom.) The right open hand, held upright, palm facing left, rests its little finger edge across the index finger edge of the downturned, open left hand. In this position the right hand moves back and forth several times, rubbing the base of the little finger along the edge of the left hand.

AVIATOR (ā′ vĭ ā′ tər, ăv′ ĭ-), *n.* (An individual who flies a plane.) The sign for either AIRPLANE 1 or AIRPLANE 2 is made, and this is followed by the sign for INDIVIDUAL 1: both hands, fingers together, are placed at either side of the chest and are

moved down to waist level. *Cf.* FLIER, PILOT.

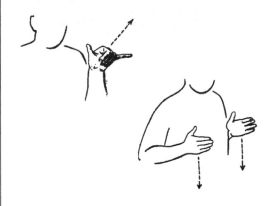

AVOID 1 (ə void′), *v.,* -VOIDED, -VOIDING. (Ducking back and forth, away from something.) Both "A" hands, thumbs pointing straight up, are held some distance before the chest, with the left hand in front of the right. The right hand, swinging back and forth, moves away from the left and toward the chest. *Cf.* EVADE, EVASION, SHIRK, SHUN.

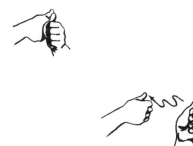

AVOID 2, *v.* (To push away and recoil from; avoid.) The two open hands, palms facing left, are pushed deliberately to the left, as if pushing something away. An expression of disdain or disgust is worn. *Cf.* ABHOR, DESPISE, DETEST, HATE, LOATHE.

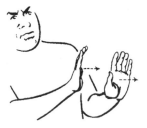

AWAKE (ə wāk'), v., adj., -WOKE or -WAKED, -WAK-ING. (Opening the eyes.) Both hands are closed, with thumb and index finger of each hand held together, extended, and placed at the corners of the closed eyes. Slowly they separate, and the eyes open. *Cf.* AWAKEN, WAKE UP.

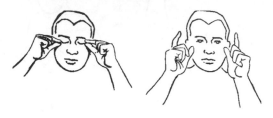

AWAKEN (ə wā' kən), v., -ENED, -ENING. See AWAKE.

AWARD (ə wôrd'), n., v., -WARDED, -WARDING. (A giving of something.) Both "A" hands, with index fingers somewhat draped over the tips of the thumbs, are held palms facing in front of the chest. They are pivoted forward and down, in unison, from the wrists. *Cf.* CONTRIBUTE, GIFT, PRESENT 2.

AWFUL (ô' fəl), adj. (Throwing out the hands.) Both hands, their fingertips touching their respective thumbs, are held, palms facing each other, near the temples. They are thrown out before the face,

assuming "5" positions, palms still facing. *Cf.* DREADFUL, TERRIBLE, TRAGEDY 1, TRAGIC.

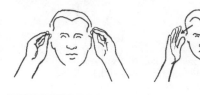

AWKWARD (ôk' wərd), adj. (Clumsy in gait; all thumbs.) The "3" hands, palms down, move alternately up and down before the body. *Cf.* AWKWARD-NESS, CLUMSINESS, CLUMSY.

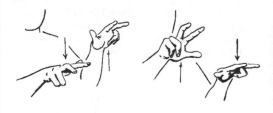

AWKWARDNESS n. See AWKWARD.

AXE (aks), n. (The chopping.) The left arm is held straight up from the bent elbow. The little finger edge of the upturned right hand then makes a series of chopping movements against the left elbow. *Cf.* HATCHET.

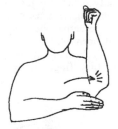

B

BABY (bā′ bǐ), *n., adj., v.,* -BIED, -BYING. (The rocking of the baby.) The arms are held with one resting on the other, as if cradling a baby. They rock from side to side. *Cf.* INFANT.

BABYSITTER (ba′ bǐ sıt er), *n.* (The baby is kept or cared for.) The sign for BABY is made: the upturned right arm is placed atop the upturned left arm, and both arms rock back and forth. The right "K" hand is then placed on its left counterpart to "keep" the baby in place.

BACHELOR (băch′ ə lər, băch′ lər), *n.* (The letter "B.") The right "B" hand, held with palm facing left and fingers pointing up, touches the left side of the mouth and then moves back across the lips to touch the right side of the mouth.

BACK (băk), *n.* (The natural sign.) The right hand moves over the right shoulder to tap the back. *Cf.* REAR 1.

BACKGROUND 1 (băk′ ground′), *n.* (The area below.) Both hands, in the "5" position, palms down, are held before the chest, the right under the left. The right hand moves under the left in a counterclockwise fashion. *Cf.* BASIS, BELOW 1, BOTTOM, FOUNDATION.

BACKGROUND 2, *n.* (The letters "B" and "G"; underneath.) The right hand, in the "B" position, is held under the downturned left hand. The "B" changes to a "G."

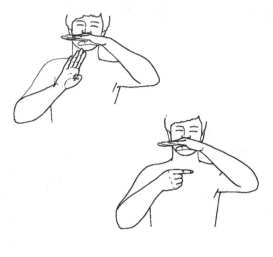

BACKPACKING (bak′ pak ing), *n.* (Slapping the backpack.) Both hands reach over the shoulders to pat a backpack.

BACON (bā′ kən), *n.* (The curled up slice after frying.) Both hands, in the "H" position, are held with middle and index fingers touching. The hands move apart and the index and middle fingers execute wavy movements as they separate.

BAD (băd), *adj.* (Tasting something, finding it unacceptable, and turning it down.) The tips of the right "B" hand are placed at the lips, and then the hand is thrown down.

BAGGAGE (băg′ ĭj), *n.* (The natural sign.) The downturned right "S" hand grasps an imaginary piece of luggage and shakes it up and down slightly, as if testing its weight. *Cf.* LUGGAGE, SUITCASE, VALISE.

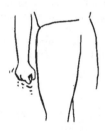

BAH! (bä), *interj.* The outstretched right hand, palm facing forward, is thrown forward and down in a forceful manner. The signer assumes an expression of annoyance or disapproval. An even more effective nonmanual accompaniment to this sign would be an explosive release of breath. *Cf.* PHOOEY!

BAKE (bāk), *v.,* BAKED, BAKING, *n.* (Placing the bread in the oven.) The upturned right "B" hand, representing the bread, is thrust slowly forward under the downturned left hand, representing the oven. *Cf.* OVEN.

BALANCE 1 (băl′ əns), *n., v.,* -ANCED, -ANCING. (The natural sign.) The extended right index and middle fingers are placed across the extended index and middle fingers of the left hand, which is held with thumb edge up and fingers pointing forward. In this position the right hand rocks back and forth, as if balancing.

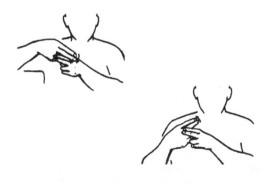

BALANCE 2, *v., n.* (Maintain equilibrium.) Both downturned open hands move alternately up and down, as if balancing on a tightrope.

BALD 1 (bôld), *adj.* (A bald patch.) The middle finger of the open right hand makes several circles on the back of the left "S" hand, which is held with palm facing down.

BALD 2, *adj.* (Devoid of hair.) The right middle finger makes a continuous clockwise circle on top of the head.

BALL (bôl), *n.* (The shape.) The curved open hands are held with fingertips touching, as if holding a ball. *Cf.* ROUND.

BALLET (bal′ ā), *n.* (The toes held "en pointe.") Both hands, fingers together, point straight down. They move up and down in successive order.

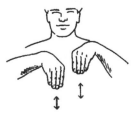

BALLOON (bə lōōn′), *n.* (Blowing up.) The signer mimes blowing up a balloon. The cupped "C" hands expand and the cheeks are puffed out.

BALONEY (bə lō′ nǐ), *(sl.)*, *n.* The right "S" hand is held with its thumb edge over the tip of the nose, palm facing left; in this position the right hand is then twisted forcefully to the left, until the palm faces down.

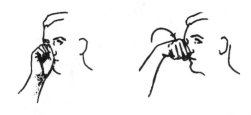

BAN (băn), *v.*, BANNED, BANNING, *n.* (A modification of LAW, *q.v.;* "against the law.") The downturned right "D" or "L" hand is thrust forcefully into the left palm. *Cf.* FORBID 1, FORBIDDEN 1, PROHIBIT.

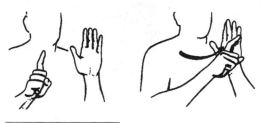

BANANA (bə nan′ ə), *n.* (The natural sign.) Go through the motions of peeling a banana, the left index representing the banana and the right fingertips pulling off the skin.

BANDAGE 1 (băn′ dĭj), *n.*, *v.*, -AGED, -AGING. (Applying a Band-Aid.) The index and middle fingers of the right hand are drawn across the back of the downturned, left "S" hand, as if smoothing a Band-Aid. *Cf.* BAND-AID.

BANDAGE 2, *v.*, *n.* (Bandaging the hand.) The right "H" hand makes a series of clockwise circles around the left fist.

BAND-AID (bănd′ ād), *n.* See BANDAGE 1.

BANDIT (băn′ dĭt), *n.* (A mustachioed thief.) The fingertips of both "H" hands, palms facing the body, are placed above the lips and are drawn slowly apart, describing a mustache. Sometimes one hand only is used. This is followed by the sign for INDIVIDUAL: both open hands, palms facing each other, move down the sides of the body, tracing its outline to the hips. *Cf.* BURGLAR, BURGLARY, CROOK, ROB 3, ROBBER, ROBBERY 1, THEFT 3, THIEF 2.

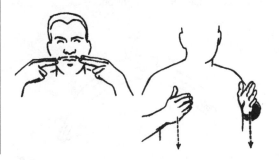

BANK 1 (bangk), *n.* (The "B" letters; a house or building.) Both downturned "B" hands describe the shape of a building's roof and walls.

BANK 2, *n.* (Stuffing money into a piggy bank.) The signer mimes stuffing money into a small toy bank.

BANKRUPT (băngk' rŭpt, -rəpt), *n., adj.* (The head is chopped off.) The tips of the right fingers are thrust forcefully into the right side of the neck. *Cf.* BROKE.

BANQUET (băng' kwĭt), *n., v.,* -QUETED, -QUETING. (Stuffing food into the mouth.) Both closed hands come to the mouth in alternate continuous circles. *Cf.* FEAST.

BAPTISM (băp' tĭz əm), *(eccles.), n.* (The sprinkling of water on the head.) The right hand sprinkles imaginary water on the head. *Cf.* SHOWER.

BAPTIST (băp' tĭst), *(eccles.), n.* (The immersion.) Both "A" hands, palms facing and thumbs pointing up, swing over simultaneously to the left, with the thumbs describing a downward arc. *Cf.* BAPTIZE.

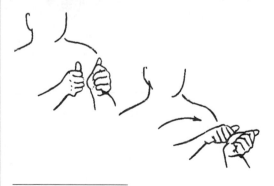

BAPTIZE (băp tĭz´, băp' tĭz), *v.,* -TIZED, -TIZING. See BAPTIST.

BAR (bär), *n.* (Raising the beer stein or mug.) The thumb of the right "A" or "Y" hand is brought up to the mouth. *Cf.* SALOON.

BARBECUE 1 (bär′ bə kyōō), *n., v.* (Turning the spit.) Both horizontal index fingers, pointing toward each other, execute simultaneous clockwise turns.

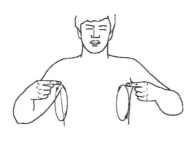

BARBECUE 2, (A fingerspelled loan sign.) The letters "B-B-Q" are fingerspelled.

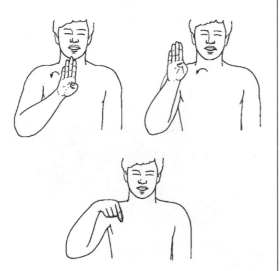

BARBER (bär′ bər), *n.* (The scissors at both sides of the head.) The two "V" hands, palms facing the sides of the head, open and close repeatedly as the hands move alternately back and forth. *Cf.* HAIRCUT .

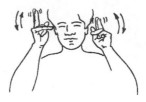

BARE (bär), *adj.* (Devoid of everything on the surface.) The middle finger of the downturned right "5" hand sweeps over the back of the downturned left "A" or "S" hand, from wrist to knuckles, and continues beyond a bit. *Cf.* EMPTY, NAKED, NUDE, OMISSION, VACANCY, VACANT, VOID.

BARK (bärk), *v., n.* (The opening and closing of the barking dog's mouth.) The hands are positioned palm against palm before the body, with the fingertips pointing forward. With the bases of the hands always touching and serving as a hinge, the hands open and close repeatedly, with the stress on the opening movement, which is sudden and abrupt. *Cf.* SCOLD 3.

BAROMETER (bə rom′ ə tər), *n.* (The letter "B"; rising and falling.) The downturned right "B" hand moves up and down along the upright left index finger.

BASE (bās), *n., adj.* (Motion downward.) The right-angle hands are held up before the head, fingertips pointing toward each other. From this position, the hands move down in an arc. *Cf.* DEMOTE, LOW, LOWER.

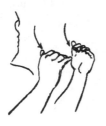

BASEBALL (bās′ bôl), *n.* (Hitting the ball with the bat.) The signer mimes hitting a ball with a baseball bat. *Cf.* HIT 2.

BASHFUL (băsh′ fəl), *adj.* (The color rises in the cheek; an attempt is made to hide the head.) The backs of the fingers of the right hand, held in the right angle position, are placed against the right cheek. The hand moves up along the cheek, pivoting

at the wrist, so that the fingers finally point to the rear. *Cf.* ASHAMED, SHAME 1, SHAMEFUL, SHAME ON YOU, SHY 1.

BASIS (ba′ sĭs), *n.* (The area below.) Both hands, in the "5" position, palms down, are held before the chest, the right under the left. The right hand moves under the left in a counterclockwise fashion. *Cf.* BACKGROUND 1, BELOW 1, BOTTOM, FOUNDATION.

BASKETBALL (băs′ kĭt bôl′), *n.* (Shooting a basket.) Both open hands are held with fingers pointing down and somewhat curved, as if grasping a basketball. From this position the hands move around and upward, as if to shoot a basket.

BASTARD (băs′ tərd), *n., adj.* (The letter "B.") The right "B" hand, held with palm facing left, fingers pointing up, strikes the middle of the forehead.

BAT (bat), *n*. (The hooked wings of the creature.) The index fingertips of the "X" hands, palms facing the body, are crossed and hooked on the shoulders, depicting a bat with folded wings.

BATH (băth, bäth), *n*. (The natural sign.) The closed hands move up and down against the chest as if scrubbing it. *Cf.* BATHE, WASH 3.

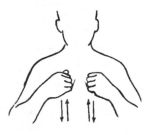

BATHE (bāth), *v.*, BATHED, BATHING. See BATH.

BATHROBE (băth′ rōb), *n*. (Bathing and slipping on a robe.) The signer rubs the body with the closed hands, and then mimes slipping on a bathrobe.

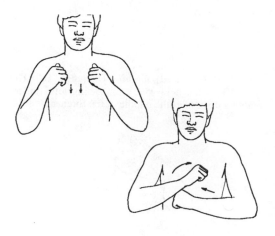

BATHROOM (băth′ rōōm′, -rŏŏm′, bäth′-), *n*. (The natural signs.) The sign for BATH is made, and then the sign for ROOM: the open hands, palms facing and fingers pointing out, are dropped an inch or two simultaneously. They then shift their relative positions so that both palms face the body, with one hand in front of the other. In this new position they again drop an inch or two simultaneously.

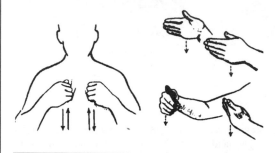

BATHTUB (băth′ tub), *n*. (Bathing and the shape of the tub.) The signer rubs the body with the closed hands, and then mimes shaping the bottom and sides of a bathtub.

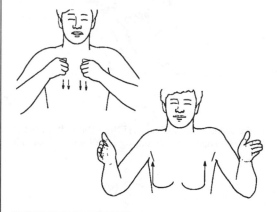

BATTER (bat′ ər), *n*. (The mixing motion.) The downturned right finger, placed in a cup formed by the left "C" hand, makes a series of rapid clockwise movements, as if mixing up a batter.

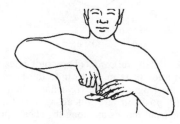

BATTERY (bat′ ə rē), *n.* (The "B"; making contact.) The left "B" hand is held palm out. The knuckle of the right index finger touches the left index finger repeatedly.

BAWL 1 (bôl), *v.*, BAWLED, BAWLING. (Tears streaming down the cheeks.) Both index fingers, in the "D" position, move down the cheeks, either once or several times. Sometimes one finger only is used. *Cf.* CRY, TEAR 2, TEARDROP, WEEP.

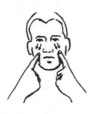

BAWL 2, *v.* (Tears gushing from the eyes.) Both "B" hands are held before the face, palms facing forward, with the backs of the index fingertips touching the face just below the eyes. From this position both hands move forward and over in an arc, to indicate a flow of tears.

BAWL 3, *v. sl.* (A flood from the eyes) Both down-turned claw hands move forward and down from the eyes.

BAWL OUT *v. phrase.* (Words coming out forcefully.) The "S" hands are held one atop the other, the right palm facing left and the left palm facing right. Both hands suddenly shoot straight out, opening to the "5" position. The sign is repeated once or twice.

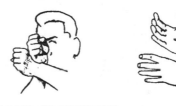

BE 1 (bē, *unstressed* bĭ), *v.*, BEEN, BEING. (Part of the verb to BE.) The tip of the right index finger, held in the "D" position, palm facing left, is held at the lips, and the hand moves straight out and away from the lips. *Cf.* AM 1, ARE 1.

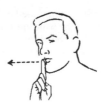

BE 2, *v.* (The "B" hand.) This is the same sign as for BE 1 except that the "B" hand is used.

BEAN(S) (bēn), *n.* (The beans in a pod.) The tips of the four right fingers move up and down simultaneously as they move along the left index finger from knuckle to tip. This sign is used generally for different grains.

BEANPOLE (bēn′ pōl′), *(sl.), n.* (A thin, tapering object is described with the little fingers, the thinnest of all.) The tips of the little fingers, touching, one above the other, are drawn apart. The cheeks may also be drawn in for emphasis. *Cf.* SKINNY, THIN 2.

BEAR (bâr). *n.* (Scratching; the bear hug.) Cross the arms, placing the right hand on the left upper arm and the left hand on the right upper arm; pull the hands across the arms toward the center, with a clawing movement.

BEARD 1 (bĭrd), *n.* (The natural sign.) The thumb and fingers of the right hand move down either side of the lower face, tracing the outline of a beard and coming together just below the chin.

BEARD 2, *n.* (In need of a shave.) The fingers of both open hands move up and down along either cheek.

BEAT 1 (bēt), *v.,* BEAT, BEATEN, BEATING. (The natural sign.) The left hand is held in a fist before the face, as if grasping something or someone. The right hand, at the same time, is held as if grasping a stick or whip; it strikes repeatedly at the imaginary object or person dangling from the left hand. *Cf.* WHIP.

BEAT 2, *v.* (Forcing the head into a bowed position.) The right "S" hand, placed across the left "S" hand, moves over and down a bit. *Cf.* CONQUER, DEFEAT, OVERCOME, SUBDUE.

BEAT 3, *n*. (A blow is struck.) The right fist strikes the left palm. *Cf.* BLOW 2.

BEAT 4, *v*. (Throwing someone over.) The right hand is held in a loose fist, with the thumb touching the middle and index fingers. The hand is thrust forward suddenly, with the index and middle fingers suddenly shooting out.

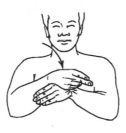

BEATEN (bĕ′ tən), *adj*. (The head is forced into a bowed position.) The right "S" hand, palm up, is placed under and across the left "S" hand, whose palm faces down. The right "S" hand moves up and over, toward the body. This sign is used as the passive voice of the verb BEAT. *Cf.* CONQUERED.

BEAU (bō), *(colloq.)*, *n*. (Heads nodding toward each other.) The "A" hands are placed together before the body with thumbs up. The thumbs wiggle up and down. *Cf.* LOVER, MAKE LOVE 1, SWEETHEART 1.

BEAUTIFUL (bū′ tə fəl), *adj*. (Literally, a good face.) The right hand, fingers closed over the thumb, is placed at or just below the lips (indicating a tasting of something GOOD, *q.v.*). It then describes a counterclockwise circle around the face, opening into the "5" position, to indicate the whole face. At the completion of the circling movement the hand comes to rest in its initial position, at or just below the lips. *Cf.* BEAUTY, PRETTY.

BEAUTY (bū′ tĭ), *n*. See BEAUTIFUL.

BEAVER (bĕ′ vər), *n*. (The action of the tail.) Both downturned hands are held at chest level, the right under the left. The right hand moves up sharply, its back slapping against the left palm. The action is repeated.

BE CAREFUL (kâr′ fəl), *v. phrase.* (The "K" for *keep* in the sense of *keeping carefully.* Both "K" hands are crossed, the right atop the left. The right hand moves up and down a very short distance, several times, each time coming to rest on top of the left. *Cf.* CAREFUL 3, TAKE CARE OF 1.

BECAUSE (bĭ kôz′, -kŏz′), *conj.* (A thought or knowledge uppermost in the mind.) The fingers of the right hand or the index finger, are placed on the center of the forehead, and then the hand is brought strongly up above the head, assuming the "A" position, with thumb pointing up. *Cf.* FOR 2.

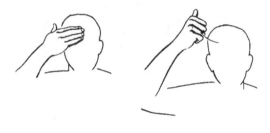

BECKON (bĕk′ ən), *v.,* BECKONED, BECKONING. The right index finger makes a natural beckoning movement. *Cf.* COME 2.

BECOME (bĭ kŭm′), *v.,* -CAME, -COME, -COMING. (To change from one position to another.) The palms of both hands, fingers closed and slightly curved, face each other a few inches apart, with the right above the left. They are pivoted around simultaneously, in a

clockwise manner, so that their relative positions are reversed.

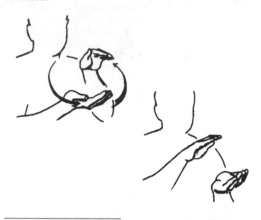

BECOME SUCCESSFUL *phrase.* (Soaring up into the stars.) The downturned right "B" hand is placed against the palm of the left hand. The "B" hand shoots upward smartly.

BECOMING (bĭ kŭm′ ĭng), *adj.* (Something that agrees with.) Both hands, in the "D" position, index fingers pointing straight out, are held before the body, palms facing and several inches apart. They are swung down in unison until the palms face down--bringing the two index fingers almost together and side by side, in "agreement" with each other.

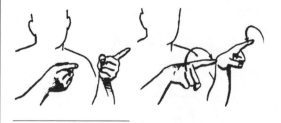

BED (bĕd), *n.* (A sleeping place with four legs.) The

head is tilted to one side, with the cheek resting in the palm, to represent the head on a pillow. Both index fingers, pointing down, move straight down a short distance, in unison (the two front legs of the bed), and then are brought up slightly, and move down again a bit closer to the body (the rear legs).

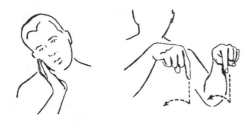

BEDROOM (-rōōm; -rŏŏm), *n*. The sign for BED is made, followed by the sign for ROOM. The open palms facing and fingers pointing out are dropped an inch or two simultaneously. They then shift their relative positions so that both palms face the body, with one hand in front of the other. In this new position they again drop an inch or two simultaneously. This indicates the four sides of a room. The "R" hands are often substituted for the open palms.

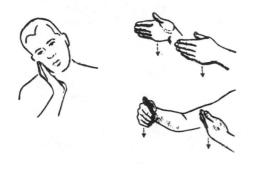

BEE (bē), *n*. (The bee's stinger is brushed away.) The index finger is placed on the cheek, and then the same hand makes a quick brushing motion off the cheek.

BEEF (bēf), *n*. (The fleshy part of the hand.) The right index finger and thumb squeeze the fleshy part of the open left hand, between thumb and index finger. *Cf.* FLESH, MEAT.

BEER (bĭr), *n*. (Raising a beer stein to the lips.) The right "Y" hand is raised to the lips, as the head tilts back a bit. *Cf.* DRUNK, DRUNKARD, DRUNKENNESS, INTOXICATE, INTOXICATION, LIQUOR **2.**

BEFORE 1 (bĭ fōr'), *adv*. (One hand precedes the other.) The left hand is held before the body, fingers together and pointing to the right. The right hand, fingers also together, and pointing to the left, is placed so that its back rests in the left palm. The right hand moves rather quickly toward the body. The sign is used as an indication of time or of precedence: *He arrived before me.*

BEFORE 2, *adv.* (One hand precedes the other.) The left hand, palm out and fingers together, is held before the body. The right, fingers also together, is placed back to back against the left, and moves rather quickly toward the body. The sign is used alternatively, but less commonly, than BEFORE 1.

BEFORE 3, *adv.* (Face to face.) The left hand, fingers together, palm flat and facing the eyes, is held a bit above eye level. The right hand, fingers also together, is held in front of the mouth, with palm facing the left hand. With a sweeping upward movement the right hand moves toward the left, which moves straight up an inch or two at the same time. *Cf.* CONFRONT, FACE, FACE TO FACE, PRESENCE.

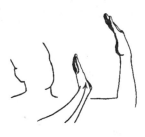

BEG 1 (bĕg), *v.,* BEGGED, BEGGING. (Holding out the hand and begging.) The right open hand, palm up and fingers slightly cupped, is moved up and down by the left hand, positioned under it.

BEG 2, *v.* (An act of supplication.) With the right hand clasped over the left, both hands are shaken gently before the body. The eyes often are directed upward. *Cf.* ENTREAT, IMPLORE, PLEA, PLEAD, SUPPLICATION.

BEGIN (bĭ gĭn'), *v.,* -GAN, -GUN, -GINNING. (Turning a key to open up a new venture.) The right index finger, resting between the left index and middle fingers, executes a half turn, once or twice. *Cf.* COMMENCE, ORIGIN, START.

BEHIND (bĭ hīnd'), *prep.* (One hand is after or behind the other.) Both hands, in the "A" position, are held knuckles to knuckles. The right hand moves back, describing a small arc, and comes to rest against the left wrist.

BELCH (belch), *n., v.* (Releasing a belch.) The right "S" hand is placed at the chest. The right index finger suddenly pops up, and the signer mimes releasing a belch.

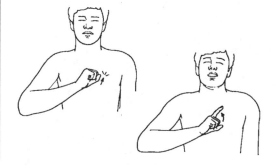

BELIEF (bĭ lēf′), *n.* (A thought clasped onto.) The index finger touches the middle of the forehead (where the thought lies), and then both hands are clasped together. *Cf.* BELIEVE, CONVICTION.

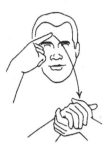

BELIEVE (bĭ lēv′), *v.,* -LIEVED, -LIEVING. See BELIEF.

BELL 1 (bĕl), *n.* (The bell's reverberations.) The right fist strikes the front of the left hand, and then opens and moves away from the left in an undulating manner, to indicate the sound waves.

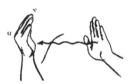

BELL 2, *n.* (Ringing a small bell to summon someone.) An imaginary small bell is held in the hand and daintily shaken back and forth.

BELL 3, *n.* (Pressing the button of the bell.) The right thumb is thrust into the open left palm several times, indicating the pressing of a bell button.

BELONG (bĭ lông′, -lŏng′), *v.,* -LONGED, -LONGING. (Joining together.) Both hands, held in the modified "5" position, palms out, move toward each other. The thumbs and index fingers of both hands then connect. *Cf.* AFFILIATE, ANNEX, ATTACH, CONNECT, ENLIST, ENROLL, JOIN, PARTICIPATE, UNITE.

BELOVED (bĭ lŭv′ ĭd), *adj.* (Clasping the heart.) The "5" hands are held one atop the other over the heart. Sometimes the "S" hands are used, in which case they are crossed at the wrists. *Cf.* DEVOTION, LOVE, REVERE.

BELOW 1 (bĭ lō′), *adv.* (The area below.) Both hands, in the "5" position, palms down, are held before the chest, the right under the left. The right hand moves under the left in a counterclockwise fashion. *Cf.* BACKGROUND 1, BASIS, BOTTOM, FOUNDATION.

BELOW 2, *adv.* (Underneath something.) The right hand, in the "A" position, thumb pointing straight up, moves down under the left hand, held outstretched, fingers together, palm down. *Cf.* UNDER 1, UNDERNEATH.

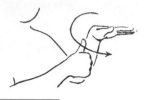

BELOW 3, *adv.* (The area below.) The right "A" hand, thumb pointing up, moves in a counterclockwise fashion under the downturned left hand. *Cf.* UNDER 2.

BENCH (bench), *n.* (The stretched out seat.) Both hands are held with curved index and middle fingers pointing down, depicting the sitting position. The palms may face either inward or outward. The hands separate, moving in opposite directions.

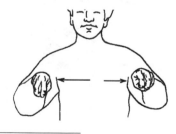

BE QUIET 1 (kwī′ ət), *v. phrase.* (The natural sign.) The index finger is brought up against the pursed lips. *Cf.* QUIET 1, SILENCE 1, SILENT, STILL 2.

BE QUIET 2 (Quiet and peace.) The open hands are crossed before the mouth, the right palm facing left, left facing right. Then both hands, held palms down, move down from the mouth, curving outward to either side of the body. *Cf.* BE STILL, CALM, QUIET 2, SILENCE 2.

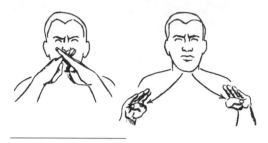

BERRY (ber′ ē), *n.* (A small item being picked off a branch.) The right fingertips grasp the tip of the left little finger and twist, as if plucking a berry. This sign is used for any berry, often with classifiers. *Cf.* CHERRY, VIRGIN 3.

BE SEATED *v. phrase.* (The act of sitting.) The extended right index and middle fingers are draped across the back of the same two fingers of the downturned left hand. The hands then move straight downward a short distance. *Cf.* CHAIR, SEAT, SIT.

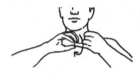

BEST (bĕst), *adj.* (The most good.) The fingertips of one hand are placed at the lips, as if tasting something (*Cf.* GOOD), and then the hand is brought high up above the head into the "A" position, thumb up, indicating the superlative degree.

BE STILL *v. phrase.* See BE QUIET 2.

BET (bĕt) *n., v.,* BET, BETTED, BETTING. (The placing or slamming down of bets by two parties.) Both open hands, palms up, are suddenly swung over in unison, to the palms-down position. Sometimes they are swung over one at a time.

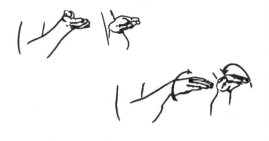

BETTER (bĕt´ ər), *adj.* (More good.) The fingertips of one hand are placed at the lips, as if tasting something (*Cf.* GOOD). Then the hand is moved up to a position just above the head, where it assumes the "A" position, thumb up. This latter position, less high up than the one indicated in BEST, denotes the comparative degree. *Cf.* PREFER.

BETWEEN (bĭ twēn´), *prep.* (Between the fingers.) The left hand, in the "C" position, is placed before the chest, all fingers facing up. The right hand, in the "B" position, is placed between the left fingers and moves back and forth several times. This sign may also be made by pointing the left fingers to the right, with the left thumb pointing up, and the right hand making the same back and forth motion as before, with the right little finger resting on the left index finger.

BEYOND (bĭ yŏnd´), *prep.* (One hand moves on to a place *beyond* the other.) Both hands, fingers together, and slightly cupped, are held before the chest, with the left hand in front of the right. The right hand moves up and over the left, and then straight out.

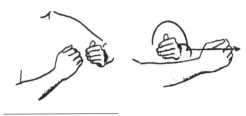

BIB (bib), *n.* (The bib is indicated.) The signer mimes placing a bib on the chest and fastening its strings behind the neck.

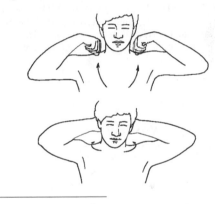

BIBLE 1 (bī´ bəl), *n.* (Literally, Jesus book.) The sign for JESUS is made: the left middle finger touches the right palm, and then the right middle finger touches the left palm (the crucifixion marks). The sign for BOOK is then made: the open hands are held together, fingers pointing away from the body. They open with little fingers remaining in contact, as in the opening of a book. This BIBLE sign signifies the Christian Bible.

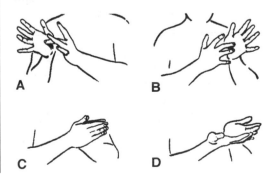

A   B

C   D

BIBLE 2, *n.* (Literally, holy book.) The right "H" hand makes a clockwise circular movement, and is then opened and wiped across the open left palm (something nice or clean with an "H," *i.e.,* HOLY). The sign for BOOK, as in BIBLE 1, is then made. This sign may be used by all religious faiths.

BIBLE 3, *n.* (The book from above.) The sign for BOOK is made: the hands, held together palm to palm, open and part, as if opening a book. They then close again as both hands, palms touching, are raised to a level above the head.

BIBLIOGRAPHY (bib´ lē og´ rə fē), *n.* (A book with lists.) The sign for BOOK is made: the hands, held together palm to palm, open and part, as if opening a book. The little finger edge of the right hand then moves down along the upturned left palm in a series of small jumps, from fingertips to the heel of the left hand, as if listing items one after the other.

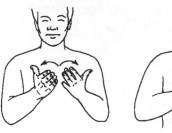

BICYCLE (bī´ sə kəl), *n., v.,* -CLED, -CLING. (The motion of the feet on the pedals.) Both hands, in the "S" position, rotate alternately before the chest.

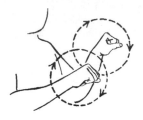

BIG 1 (bĭg), *adj.* (A delineation of something big, modified by the letter "L," which stands for LARGE.) Both "L" hands, palms facing out, are placed before the face, and separate rather widely. *Cf.* GREAT 1, LARGE.

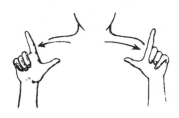

BIG 2, *adj.* (The height is indicated.) The right right-angle hand, palm facing the left, is held at the height the signer wishes to indicate. *Cf.* HEIGHT 2, HIGH 3, TALL 2.

BIG-HEADED (hĕd´ ĭd), *(colloq.), adj.* (The natural sign.) Both downturned "L" hands are positioned with index fingers at the temples. They move away from the head rather slowly, indicating the size or growth of the head. The head is often moved slightly back and forth as the hands move away. An expression of superiority is assumed. *Cf.* BIG SHOT, CONCEITED, SWELL-HEADED.

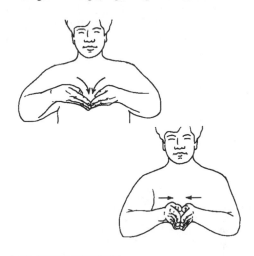

BIG SHOT (shŏt), *(sl.).* See BIG-HEADED.

BIG WORDS (wûrdz), *(sl.).* (Large expanses of written material as they appear on the page.) The right "Y" hand, palm down, is placed on the left "G" hand, above the wrist. The right hand, in this position, arcs up and over, coming to rest on the left index finger. In this sign the two fingers of the right hand represent the widest possible space that can be indicated, and the left "G" hand represents a single line on the page.

BILLFOLD 1 (bil´ fōld), *n.* (Placing the bills inside.) The little finger edge of the open right hand, palm facing the body, is slipped into the space created by the thumb and other fingers of the left hand. The signer then mimes placing the billfold into a back pocket. *Cf.* WALLET 2.

BILLFOLD 2, *n.* (Placing the bills in and folding the billfold.) Same as BILLFOLD 1, but after placing the bills in the billfold, the two hands, fingertips touching, are brought together palm to palm.

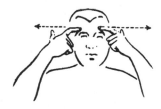

BILLIARDS (bil´ yərdz), *n.* (The game of billiards.) The signer, hunched over an imaginary cue stick, mimes striking the ball. *Cf.* POOL.

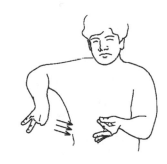

BILLION (bĭl´ yən), *adj., n.* (A thousand thousand thousands.) The sign for THOUSAND is made three times: the tips of the right "M" hand are thrust into the upturned left palm three times, each time a little closer to the left fingertips.

BIND (bīnd), *v.*, BOUND, BINDING. (The act of tying.) Both hands, in the "A" position, go through the natural hand-over-hand motions of tying and drawing out a knot. *Cf.* KNOT, TIE 1.

BINOCULARS (bə nŏk′ yə lərz, bī-), *n. pl.* (The natural sign.) The "C" hands are held in front of the eyes.

BIOLOGY (bī ol′ ə jē), *n.* (The "B"s; pouring from a test tube.) Both "B" hands, palms out, execute continuous alternating circles: the right moving counterclockwise and the left clockwise.

BIRD (bûrd), *n.* (The shape and movement of a beak.) The right thumb and index finger are placed against the mouth, pointing straight out. They open and close.

BIRTH 1 (bûrth), *n.* (Presenting the baby from womb to hand; a coming out from the womb to the waiting hand.) The upturned right hand is brought

forward from the stomach to the upturned left palm. *Cf.* BORN 1, NEE.

BIRTH 2, *n.* (The baby is presented.) Both open hands are held against the breast, one on top of the other, as if holding something to oneself. From this position the hands move out from the body and to either side, ending palms up. *Cf.* BORN 2.

BIRTH 3, *n.* (The baby is brought forth from the womb.) Both cupped hands, palms facing the body, are placed at the stomach or lower chest, one on top of the other. Both hands are moved out and away from the body in unison, describing a small arc. *Cf.* BORN 3.

BIRTH CONTROL *n. phrase.* (Preventing a baby from being conceived.) The sign for BABY is made: the upturned right arm rests on its upturned left counterpart, and both arms rock back and forth. Next the sign for PREVENT is made: the left hand, fingers together and palm flat, is held facing somewhat down. The little finger edge of the right hand, striking the thumb side of the left, pushes the left hand slightly forward.

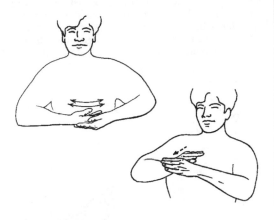

BIRTHDAY (bûrth′ dā′), *n.* The sign for BIRTH 1 or BIRTH 2 is made, followed by the sign for DAY: the left arm, held horizontally, palm down, represents the horizon. The right elbow rests on the back of the left hand, with the right arm in a perpendicular position. The right "D" hand, palm facing left, moves in an arc to the left until it is just above the left elbow.

BISEXUAL (bī sek′ shōo əl), *n., adj.* (Swinging from one sexual orientation to another.) The right curved downturned index and middle fingers, swiveling at the wrist, move to the left and right.

BISHOP 1 (bĭsh′ əp), *(eccles.), n.* (Kissing the ring.) The extended index and middle fingers make the sign of the cross before the face. Then the ring finger of the right "S" hand is kissed. This is the sign for a Catholic bishop.

BISHOP 2, *n.* (The shape.) The downturned open hands, fingers together, move up from either side of the head, and the fingertips come together, forming an arch over the head, to describe the bishop's miter.

BITCH (bĭch), *(sl.), n.* (The letter "B"; the "female" portion of the head.) The right "B" hand is brought up to the chin.

BITE (bīt), *n., v.,* BIT, BITTEN, BITING. (The natural sign.) The index finger of the downturned hand is bitten.

BITTER (bĭt′ ər), *adj.* (Something sour or bitter.) The right index finger is brought sharply up against the lips, while the mouth is puckered up as if tasting something sour. *Cf.* DISAPPOINTED, DISAPPOINTMENT, SOUR.

BLACK (blak), *adj.* (The darkest part of the face, *i.e.,* the brow, is indicated.) The tip of the index finger moves along the eyebrow.

BLACKBOARD (blak′ bôrd), *n.* (The signs for black and write.) The right index finger moves over the right eyebrow, from left to right. This is the sign for BLACK. The right hand then mimes writing something on the upturned left palm.

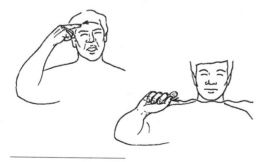

BLACK EYE *n.* (Swollen eye.) The right claw hand, palm facing the body, is placed over the right eye.

BLAME (blām), *v.,* BLAME, BLAMING, *n.* (The blame is firmly placed.) The right "A" hand, thumb pointing up, is brought down firmly against the back of the left hand, held palm down; the right thumb is then directed toward the person or object to blame. When personal blame is acknowledged, the thumb is brought in to the chest. *Cf.* ACCUSE, FAULT, GUILTY 1.

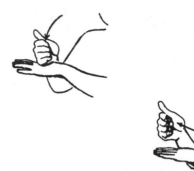

BLANKET (blang′ kit), *n.* (Pulling up the cover.) The downturned hands grasp an imaginary blanket edge and pull it up over the chest.

BLANK MIND *n. phrase.* (Wiping off the mind.) The right middle finger moves across the forehead from left to right, indicating an emptiness within. This sign is derived from BARE or EMPTY.

BLEED (blēd), *v.*, BLED, BLEEDING, *adj.* (Blood trickles down from the hand.) The left "5" hand is held palm facing the body and fingertips pointing right. The right "5" hand touches the back of the left and moves down, with the right fingers wiggling. *Cf.* BLOOD.

BLESS (blĕs), *v.*, BLESSED or BLEST, BLESSING. (Blessed; forgiveness.) The "A" hands are held near the lips, thumbs up and almost touching. Both hands move down and out simultaneously, ending in the "5" position, palms down. The right hand, palm flat, facing down, is then brushed over the left hand, held palm flat and facing up. This latter action may be repeated twice.

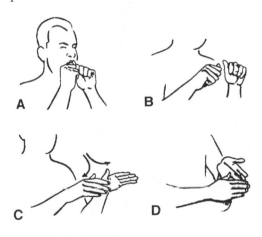

BLIND (blīnd), *adj.* (The eyes are blocked.) The tips of the "V" fingers are thrust toward the closed eyes. *Cf.* BLINDNESS.

BLINDFOLD (blīnd' fōld), *n., v.* (The natural sign.) The signer mimes tying a blindfold over the eyes and fastening it behind the head.

BLINDNESS (blīnd' nĭs), *n.* See BLIND.

BLOND (blond), *adj., n.* (Yellow hair.) As it moves up over the right side of the head, the right "Y" hand makes the sign for YELLOW: it twists back and forth repeatedly, swiveling at the right wrist.

BLOOD (blŭd), *n.* See BLEED.

BLOOM (bloom), *n.* (Flowers or plants emerge from the ground.) The right fingers, pointing up, emerge from the closed left hand, and they spread open as they do. *Cf.* DEVELOP 1, GROW, GROWN, MATURE 1, PLANT 1, RAISE 3, REAR 2, SPRING.

BLOOMINGDALE'S *n. loc.* The right index finger, held pointing into the throat, twists back and forth repeatedly, swiveling at the wrist. This local sign does not seem to have any coherent explanation, although it is widely used wherever this department store can be found.

BLOW 1 (blō), *v.,* BLEW, BLOWN, BLOWING, *n.* (The blowing back and forth of the wind.) The "5" hands, palms facing and held up before the body, sway gracefully back and forth, in unison. The cheeks meanwhile are puffed up and the breath is being expelled. The nature of the swaying movement—graceful and slow, fast and violent, etc.—determines the type of wind. The strength of exhalation is also a classifier. *Cf.* BREEZE, STORM, WIND.

BLOW 2, *n.* (A blow is struck.) The right fist strikes the left palm. *Cf.* BEAT 3.

BLOW YOUR STACK *sl. phrase.* (The lid blows off the pot.) The downturned right hand rests on the left hand, in the "C" or "O" position. The right hand suddenly goes up, its wrist swiveling back and forth as it does.

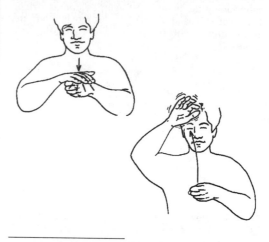

BLUE (bloo), *n., adj.* (The letter "B.") The right "B" hand shakes slightly, pivoted at the wrist.

BLUFF (blŭf), *n.* (A double face, *i.e.,* a mask covers the face.) The right hand is placed over the back of the left hand and pushes it down and a bit in toward the body. *Cf.* FAKE, HUMBUG, HYPOCRITE, IMPOSTOR.

BLUNT (blunt), *adj.* (The letter "B"; straight forward.) The right "B" hand is placed on the forehead, palm facing left. It moves straight out forcefully.

BLURRY (blûr' ĭ), *adj*. (One hand obscures the other.) The "5" hands are held up palm against palm in front of the body. The right hand moves in a slow, continuous clockwise circle over the left palm, as the signer tries to see between the fingers. *Cf.* UNCLEAR, VAGUE.

BLUSH (blŭsh), *v.*, BLUSHED, BLUSHING. (The red rises in the cheeks.) The sign for RED is made: the tip of the right index finger of the "D" hand moves down over the lips, which are red. Both hands are then placed palms facing the cheeks, and move up along the face, to indicate the rise of color. *Cf.* EMBARRASS, EMBARRASSED, FLUSH, MORTIFICATION.

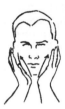

BOARD OF DIRECTORS *n*. (The letters "B-D"; the Roman toga.) The right "B" hand, starting at either shoulder, sweeps across the chest, ending in a "D" at the opposite shoulder.

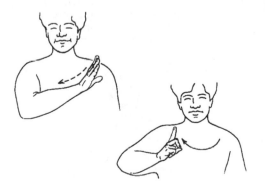

BOARD OF TRUSTEES *n*. (The letters "B-T"; the Roman toga.) The right "B" hand, starting at either shoulder, sweeps across the chest, ending in a "T" at the opposite shoulder.

BOAT (bōt), *n*. (The shape; the bobbing on the waves.) Both hands are cupped together to form the hull of a boat. They move forward in a bobbing motion.

BODY (bŏd' ĭ), *n*. (The body is indicated.) One or both hands are placed against the chest and then are removed and replaced at a point a bit below the first. *Cf.* PHYSICAL 1.

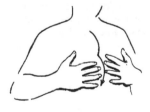

BOOK (boŏk), *n*. (Opening a book.) The open hands are held together, fingers pointing away from the body. They open with little fingers remaining in contact, as in the opening of a book.

BOOKLET (bŏŏk' lĭt), *n.* (A book with a narrow spine.) The left hand, fingers together, is held upright, palm facing right. The right hand wraps around the lower edge of the left and travels up to the little finger. This denotes a narrow object. The sign for BOOK is then made: the hands are placed together, palm to palm, and then opened, as if opening a book. Sometimes this latter sign is omitted. *Cf.* MAGAZINE, MANUAL, PAMPHLET.

BOOKSHELF (bŏŏk' shelf), *n.* (Books side by side along the shelf.) The sign for BOOKS is made: the hands open repeatedly. The right hand, palm facing left, then moves to the right, slowly and deliberately.

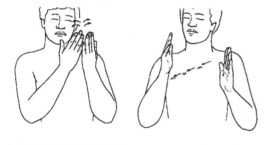

BOOT (bŏŏt), *n.* (The height of the boot.) The little finger edge of the right hand is drawn across the wrist of the downturned left hand.

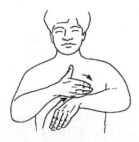

BORDER/BORDERLINE (bôr' dər), *n., v.* (The line.) The fingertips of the downturned right hand are drawn along the index finger edge of the left hand, held palm facing the body. The tip of the right little

finger alone may be substituted for the right fingertips.

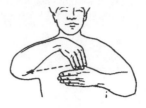

BORE (bōr), *v.,* BORED, BORING, *n.* (A dryness, indicated by a wiping of the lips.) The "X" finger is drawn across the lips, from left to right, as if wiping them. *Cf.* DRY, DULL 2.

BORING 1 (bôr' ĭng), *adj.* (The nose is pressed, as if to a grindstone wheel.) The right index finger touches the tip of the nose, as a bored expression is assumed. The right hand is sometimes pivoted back and forth slightly, as the fingertip remains against the nose. *Cf.* MONOTONOUS, TEDIOUS.

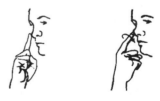

BORING 2, *adj.* (The movement of the grindstone.) The left hand is held with palm facing right. The thumb edge of the right "S" hand is placed on the left palm and does a series of clockwise circles. This sign may be preceded by the index finger briefly touching the nose.

BORN 1 (bôrn), *adj*. (Presenting the baby from womb to hand; a coming out from the womb to the waiting hand.) The upturned right hand is brought forward from the stomach to the upturned left palm. *Cf.* BIRTH 1, NEE.

BORN 2, *adj*. (The baby is presented.) Both open hands are held against the breast, one on top of the other, as if holding something to oneself. From this position the hands move out from the body and to either side, ending palms up. *Cf.* BIRTH 2.

BORN 3, *adj*. (The baby is brought forth from the womb.) Both cupped hands, palms facing the body, are placed at the stomach or lower chest, one on top of the other. Both hands are moved out and away from the body in unison, describing a small arc. *Cf.* BIRTH 3.

BORROW (bŏr′ ō, bôr′ ō), *v.*, -ROWED, -ROWING. (Bring to oneself.) The "K" hands are crossed and moved in toward the body.

 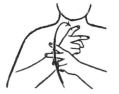

BOTH (bōth), *adj., pron.* (Two fingers are drawn together.) The right "2" hand, palm facing the body, is drawn down through the left "C" hand. As it does, the right index and middle fingers come together.

BOTHER (bŏth′ ər), *v.*, -ERED, -ERING. (Obstruct, block.) The left hand, fingers together and palm flat, is held before the body, facing somewhat down. The little finger side of the right hand, held with palm flat, makes one or several up–down chopping motions against the left hand, between its thumb and index finger. *Cf.* ANNOY, ANNOYANCE, DISRUPT, DISTURB, HINDER, HINDRANCE, IMPEDE, INTERCEPT, INTERFERE, INTERFERENCE, INTERFERE WITH, INTERRUPT, MEDDLE 1, OBSTACLE, OBSTRUCT, PREVENT, PREVENTION.

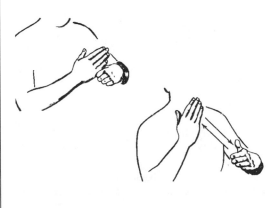

BOTH OF US *phrase*. (Two people interacting.) The right "V" hand, palm up and fingers pointing left, is swung in and out to and from the chest. *Cf.* US TWO, WE TWO.

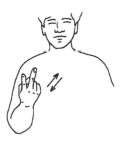

BOTTOM (bŏt′ əm), *n.* (The area below.) Both hands, in the "5" position, palms down, are held before the chest, the right under the left. The right hand moves under the left in a counterclockwise fashion. *Cf.* BACKGROUND 1, BASIS, BELOW 1, FOUNDATION.

BOUND (bound), *adj.* (Bound down to custom or habit.) Both "S" hands, palms down, are crossed and brought down in unison before the chest. *Cf.* ACCUSTOM, CUSTOM, HABIT, LOCKED, PRACTICE 3.

BOX 1 (bŏks), *n.* (The dimensions are indicated.) The open hands, palms facing and fingers pointing out, are dropped an inch or two simultaneously. They then shift their relative positions so that both palms face the body, with one hand in front of the other. In this new position they again drop an inch or two simultaneously. *Cf.* PACKAGE, ROOM 1, SQUARE, TRUNK.

BOX 2, *v.,* BOXED, BOXING. (The natural sign.) Both clenched fists go through the circular motions of boxing. *Cf.* FIGHT 2.

BOY 1 (boi), *n.* (A young male.) The MALE root sign is made: the thumb and extended fingers of the right hand are brought up to grasp an imaginary cap brim, representing the tipping of caps by men in olden days. The downturned right hand then indicates the short height of a small boy.

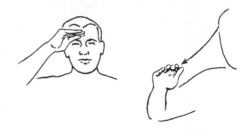

BOY 2, *n.* (A modification of the MALE root sign; the familiar sign for BOY 1.) The right hand, palm down, is held at the forehead. The fingers open and close once or twice.

BOY SCOUT (skout), *n.* (The salute.) The Boy Scout salute is given.

BRACELET (brās′ lit), *n.* (The natural sign.) The curved thumb and index finger of the open right hand are wrapped around the left wrist.

BRAG (brăg), *v.*, BRAGGED, BRAGGING. (Indicating the self, repeatedly.) The thumbs of both "A" hands are alternately thrust into the chest a number of times. *Cf.* SHOW OFF.

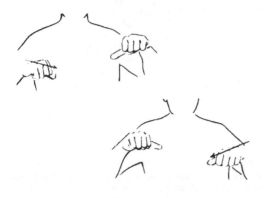

BRAKE (brāk), *n., v.* (Pressing the brake pedal.) The signer uses the right hand to mime pressing the brake pedal of a car.

BRANCH (branch), *n.* (The offshoot of the tree.) Both open hands, facing out, are held with index finger edges touching. The right hand moves up along the edge of the left, curving right as it reaches the left fingertips.

BRAVE (brāv), *adj., n., v.*, BRAVED, BRAVING. (Strength emanating from the body.) Both "5" hands are placed palms against the chest. They move out and away, forcefully, closing and assuming the "S" position. *Cf.* BRAVERY, COURAGE, COURAGEOUS, FORTITUDE, HALE, HEALTH, HEALTHY, MIGHTY 2, STRENGTH, STRONG 2, WELL 2.

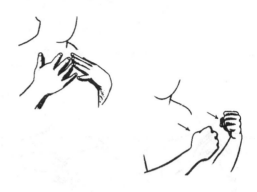

BRAVERY (brā′ və rǐ), *n.* See BRAVE.

BRAZIL (brə zil′), *n.* (Possibly having to do with the feathered headdress of a native.) The fingers are placed on the forehead and the hand moves in a slight counterclockwise direction. A native sign.

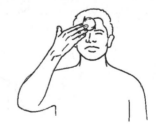

BREAD (brĕd), *n.* (Act of cutting a loaf of bread.) The left arm is held against the chest, representing a loaf of bread. The little finger edge of the right hand is drawn down over the back of the left hand several times, to indicate the cutting of slices.

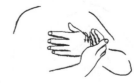

BREAK (brāk), *n.*, *v.*, BROKE, BROKEN, BREAKING. (The natural sign.) The hands grasp an imaginary object and break it in two. *Cf.* FRACTURE.

BREAKDOWN (-doun), *n.* (A collapsing.) Both "5" hands, fingertips joined before the chest, swing down so that the fingertips face down. *Cf.* CAVE IN, COL-LAPSE.

BREAKFAST (brĕk′ fəst), *n.* (Morning food.) The sign for FOOD is given: the closed right hand goes through the natural motion of placing food in the mouth. This movement is repeated, followed by the sign for MORNING: the little finger edge of the left hand rests in the crook of the right elbow. The left arm, held horizontally, represents the horizon. The open right hand, fingers together and pointing up, with palm facing the body, rises slowly to an almost upright angle. The signs may also be reversed, as MORNING, FOOD.

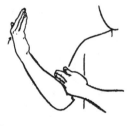

BREASTS 1 (brestz), *n.* (The location.) The right fingertips touch the left breast and then the right.

BREASTS 2, *n.* (The shape.) Both cupped hands are held over the breasts, to indicate the shape.

BREASTS 3, *n.* (The breasts hang.) Both upturned cupped hands are positioned under the breasts and move up and down an inch or so.

BREATH (brĕth), *n.* (The rise and fall of the chest in respiration.) The hands, folded over the chest, move forward and back to the chest, to indicate the breathing. *Cf.* BREATHE, RESPIRATION.

BREATHE (brĕth), *v.*, BREATHED, BREATHING. See BREATH.

BREEZE (brēz), *n.* (The blowing back and forth of the wind.) The "5" hands, palms facing and held up before the body, sway gracefully back and forth, in unison. The cheeks meanwhile are puffed up and the breath is being expelled. The nature of the swaying movement—graceful and slow, fast and violent, etc.—determines the type of wind. The strength of exhalation is also a classifier. *Cf.* BLOW 1, STORM, WIND.

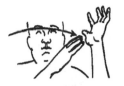

BRIBE (brīb), *n., v.,* BRIBED, BRIBING. (Underhanded payment of money.) The right hand, grasping an imaginary dollar bill, moves under the downturned left hand.

BRICK (brik), *n.* (The color red and the shape.) The sign for RED is made: the index finger moves down across the lips. The thumbs and index fingers then outline the shape of a brick, moving apart to indicate the length, and then closing to show the height.

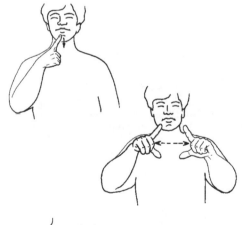

BRIEF 1 (brēf), *adj.* (To make short; to measure off a short space.) The index and middle fingers of the right "H" hand are placed across the top of the index and middle fingers of the left "H" hand, and move a short distance back and forth, along the length of the left index finger. *Cf.* SHORT 1, SHORTEN.

BRIEF 2, *adj.* (To squeeze or condense into a small space.) Both "C" hands face each other, with the right hand nearer to the body than the left. Both hands draw together and close deliberately, squeezing an imaginary object. *Cf.* ABBREVIATE, CONDENSE, MAKE BRIEF, SUMMARIZE 1, SUMMARY 1.

BRIGHT 1 (brīt), *adj.* (Rays of light clearing the way.) Both hands are held at chest height, palms out, all fingertips together. They open into the "5" position in unison, the right hand moving toward the right and the left toward the left. The palms of both hands remain facing out. *Cf.* BRILLIANCE 1, BRILLIANT 2, CLEAR, EXPLICIT 2, OBVIOUS, PLAIN 1.

BRIGHT 2, *adj.* (Reflected glistening of light rays.) The left hand, held supinely before the chest, palm down, represents the object from which the rays glisten. The right hand, in the "5" position, touches the back of the left lightly and moves up toward the right, pivoting slightly at the wrist, with fingers wiggling. *Cf.* GLISTEN, SHINE, SHINING.

BRIGHT 3, *adj.* (The mind is bright.) The middle finger is placed at the forehead, and then the hand, with an outward flick, turns around so that the palm faces outward. This indicates a brightness flowing from the mind. *Cf.* BRILLIANT 1, CLEVER, INTELLIGENT, SMART.

BRIGHT 4, *adj.* (Light rays glistening upward.) Both "5" hands, palms facing out, are held before the chest. They move up and out, all fingers wiggling to convey the glistening of light rays upward. This sign is an alternate for BRIGHT 2 and GLISTEN. *Cf.* BRILLIANCE 2.

BRILLIANCE 1 (bril′ yəns), *n.* See BRIGHT 1.

BRILLIANCE 2, *n.* See BRIGHT 4.

BRILLIANT 1 (bril′ yənt), *adj.* See BRIGHT 3.

BRILLIANT 2, *adj.* See BRIGHT 1.

BRING (bring), *v.,* BROUGHT, BRINGING. (Carrying something over.) Both open hands, palms up, move in an arc from left to right, as if carrying something from one point to another. *Cf.* CARRY 2, DELIVER.

BRITAIN (brit′ ən), *n.* (The English are supposed to be handshakers.) The right hand grasps and shakes the left. *Cf.* BRITISH, ENGLAND, ENGLISH, GREAT BRITAIN.

BRITISH (brit′ ish), *adj.* See BRITAIN.

BROAD (brôd), *adj.* (The width is indicated.) The open hands, fingers pointing out and palms facing each other, separate from their initial position an inch or two apart. *Cf.* WIDE, WIDTH.

BROAD-MINDED (brôd´ mīn´ dĭd), *adj.* (The mind is open, or wide.) The index finger touches the forehead to indicate the MIND. Then the sign for BROAD is made: the open hands, fingers pointing out and palms facing each other, separate from their initial position an inch or two apart.

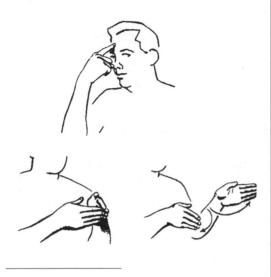

BROTHER (brŭth´ ər), *n.* (A male who is the same, *i.e.,* from the same family.) The root sign for MALE is made: the thumb and extended fingers of the right hand are brought up to grasp an imaginary cap brim, representing the tipping of caps by men in olden days. Then the sign for SAME 1 is made: the outstretched index fingers are brought together, either once or several times.

BROTHER-IN-LAW (brŭth´ ər in lô´), *n.* The sign for BROTHER 1 is made, followed by the sign for IN: the fingers of the right hand are thrust into the left. The sign for LAW is then made: the upright right "L" hand, resting palm against palm on the upright left "5" hand, moves down in an arc, a short distance, coming to rest on the base of the left palm.

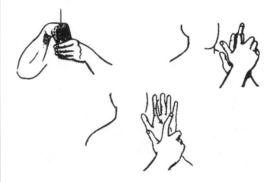

BROKE (brōk), *(sl.), adj.* (The head is chopped off.) The tips of the right fingers are thrust forcefully into the right side of the neck. *Cf.* BANKRUPT.

BROOM (broom, broom), *n.* (The natural sign.) The hands grasp and manipulate an imaginary broom. *Cf.* SWEEP 1.

BROWN (broun), *adj.* The "B" hand is placed against the face, with the index finger touching the upper cheek. The hand is then drawn straight down the cheek.

BUCKET (buk' it), *n.* (Hanging from the arm.) The arm is held outstretched, palm down. The index finger of the other hand makes a downward arch from wrist to elbow. *Cf.* PAIL.

BUCKLE (buk' əl), *n., v.* (Locking the buckle's catch.) Both hands are held palms facing the waist, with curved thumbs, index and middle fingers. These fingers slide together, knuckles interlocking, as if fastening the catch of a buckle.

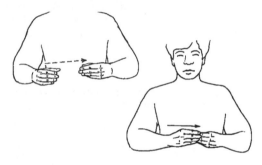

BUFFALO (buf´ ə lō), *n.* (The horns.) Both outstretched "S" hands are positioned palms out at the temples. They move away and twist so that the palms now face the signer. The "C" hands may be used initially at the temples, changing to "S" as they move away.

BUILD (bĭld), *v.,* BUILT, BUILDING. (Piling bricks one on top of another.) The downturned hands are placed repeatedly atop each other. Each time this is done the arms rise a bit, to indicate the raising of a building. *Cf.* CONSTRUCT 1, CONSTRUCTION.

BULB (bulb), *n.* (Twisting the bulb into its socket.) The sign for ELECTRIC may be made: the knuckles of the bent index fingers touch each other twice. The signer then mimes twisting a light bulb into its socket.

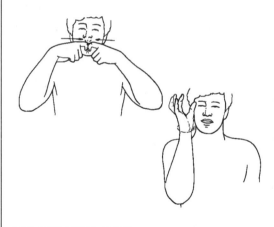

BULLSHIT 1 (bŏŏl' shit), *n., expletive.* (A fingerspelled loan sign.) The signer makes the letters "B" and "S." The hand is flung out while making the "S."

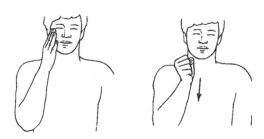

BULLSHIT 2, *n., expletive.* (The horns of a bull; the animal defecating.) The left downturned "Y" hand is held near the right shoulder. The closed left hand, positioned under the left elbow, opens suddenly into the "5" position. The movement may be repeated.

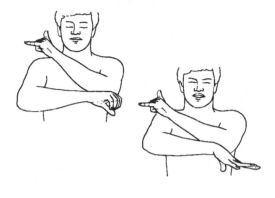

BUNDLE (bun′ dəl), *n.* (The shape.) Both "C" hands held about a foot apart, with palms facing, move up and come together as if squeezing the top of a bag.

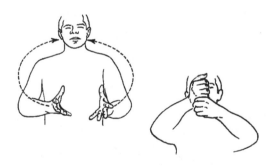

BUNK (bungk), *n.* (A two-tiered bed.) Both down-turned "U" hands are positioned one atop the other, about an inch apart.

BURGLAR (bûr′ glər), *n.* (A mustachioed thief.) The fingertips of both "H" hands, palms facing the body, are placed above the lips and are drawn slowly apart, describing a mustache. Sometimes one hand only is used. This is followed by the sign for INDIVIDUAL: both open hands, palms facing each other, move down the sides of the body, tracing its outline to the hips. *Cf.* BANDIT, BURGLARY, CROOK, ROB 3, ROBBER, ROBBERY 1, THEFT 3, THIEF 2.

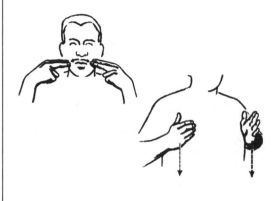

BURGLARY (bûr′ glə ri), *n.* See BURGLAR. The sign for INDIVIDUAL is omitted.

BURN (bûrn), *n., v.,* BURNED or BURNT, BURNING. (The leaping of flames.) The "5" hands are held with palms facing the body. They move up and down alternately, while the fingers wiggle. *Cf.* FIRE 1, FLAME, HELL 2.

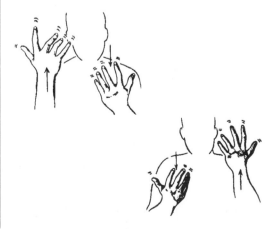

BURY (ber′ ē), *v.*, BURIED, BURYING. (The coffin is lowered.) The downturned right "U" hand slides down the outstretched left palm, whose fingertips face forward.

BUSY (bĭz′ ĭ), *adj.* (An activity of the hands.) The right "S" hand, palm out, glances back and forth against the left "S" hand, whose palm faces down.

BUSYBODY (biz′ ē bod ē), *n.* (One whose nose is into others' business.) The nose is touched with the index finger, which is then curved and thrust into a hole formed by the other hand.

BUT (bŭt; *unstressed* bət), *conj.* (A divergence or a difference; the opposite of same.) The index fingers of both "D" hands, palms facing down, are crossed

near their tips. The hands are drawn apart. *Cf.* HOW-EVER 1, ON THE CONTRARY 1.

BUTCHER (bŏŏch′ ər), *n., v.* (Stabbing a creature in the neck.) The right thumb "stabs" the right side of the neck. For the noun, the sign for INDIVIDUAL 1 then follows.

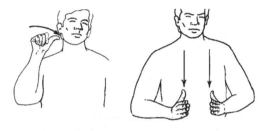

BUTTER (bŭt′ ər), *n., v.*, -TERED, -TERING. (The spreading of butter.) The tips of the fingers of the downturned right "U" hand are brushed repeatedly over the upturned left palm.

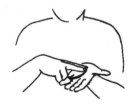

BUTTERFLY (bŭt′ ər flī′), *n.* (The natural sign.) The "5" hands, palms facing the body, are crossed and intertwined at the thumbs. The hands, hooked in this manner, move to and fro in vague figure-eights, while the individual hands flap back and forth.

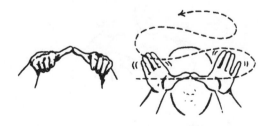

BUTTON UP *v. phrase.* (The buttons along the garment.) The right "F" hand describes the shape of the buttons as they are lined up on the chest, from waist to throat.

BUY (bī), *n., v.,* BOUGHT, BUYING. (Giving out money.) The sign for MONEY is made: the upturned right hand, grasping some imaginary bills, is brought down into the upturned left palm, and then the right hand moves forward and up in a small arc, opening up as it does. *Cf.* PURCHASE.

C

CABINET 1 (kab' ə nit), *n.* (Opening the doors.) The outstretched "B" hands are held side by side near the left shoulder at eye level, facing out. They turn in repeatedly, as if doors are swinging in. At each successive opening, the hands move slightly to the right.

CABINET 2, *n.* (Grasping the handles.) The signer mimes opening a pair of cabinet doors by grasping the handles. *Cf.* CUPBOARD.

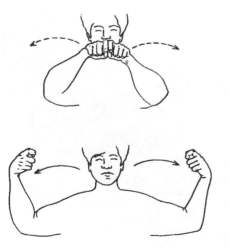

CAESAREAN SECTION (si zâr' ē ən sek' shən), *n.* (Cutting out the baby.) The sign for PREGNANT 1 is made: one or both open hands are placed on the stomach and move forward an inch or two, to indicate the swollen belly. The right thumb is then drawn across the stomach as if making an incision.

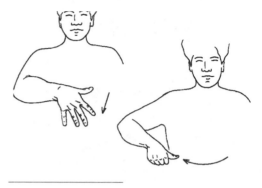

CAFETERIA 1 (kaf' ə tir' ē ə), *n.* (The letter "C"; a restaurant.) The right "C" hand is placed at the left corner of the mouth and moves over to the right corner.

CAFETERIA 2, *n.* (Eating and pushing the tray.) The signer lifts food to the mouth twice and guides a tray from left to right.

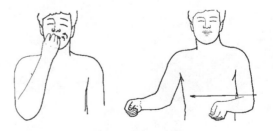

CAGE (kāj), *n., v.* (The bars.) Both "4" hands are held up, right facing left and left facing right. They switch positions and may move down slightly.

CAKE 1 (kāk), *n.* (The rising of the cake.) The fingertips of the right "5" hand are placed in the upturned left palm. The right rises slowly an inch or two above the left.

CAKE 2, *n.* (The letter "C"; cutting a slice.) The little finger edge of the right "C" hand, resting on the upturned left hand, cuts an imaginary slice of cake.

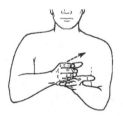 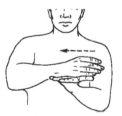

CALCULATOR (kal′ kyə lā′ tər), *n.* (The function and shape.) The left open hand, palm up, represents the keyboard. The index or middle finger of the right hand taps in numbers at random. The right thumb and index are then drawn down the left palm, outlining the shape of the calculator.

CALENDAR 1 (kal′ ən dər), *n.* (Turning the pages.) The right "C" hand, palm facing left, moves up the left palm, over the fingertips, and down the back of the hand.

CALENDAR 2, *n.* (A monthly schedule.) The sign for MONTH is made: the right index finger moves down along the inside edge of the left finger, which is pointing up. This is followed by SCHEDULE: the right "4" hand, palm against the left palm and fingers pointing up, moves down from the index finger edge to the little finger edge. The right palm next flips over so that it faces the body, and moves from the base of the left palm to the left fingertips.

CALF (kaf), *n.* (A small cow.) The sign for COW: one or both "Y" hands, palms facing forward, are positioned with thumbs touching the temples. Thecupped hands, palms facing, are then brought together to indicate something small.

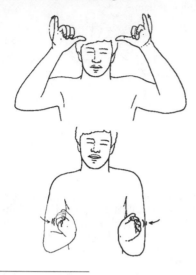

CALIFORNIA (kăl' ə fôr' nyə, -fôr' nĭ ə), *n.* (Yellow earrings, *i.e.,* gold, which was discovered in California.) The earlobe is pinched, and then the sign for YELLOW is made: the "Y" hand, pivoted at the wrist, is shaken back and forth repeatedly. *Cf.* GOLD.

CALL 1 (kôl), *v.,* CALLED, CALLING. (To tap someone for attention.) The right hand is placed upon the back of the left, held palm down. The right hand then moves up and in toward the body, assuming the "A" position. As an optional addition, the right hand may then assume a beckoning movement. *Cf.* SUMMON.

CALL 2, *n., v.* (The natural sign.) The cupped right hand is held against the right cheek. The mouth is slightly open.

CALLED *adj.* (NAME, indicating who is named.) The sign for NAME is made: the right "H" hand, palm facing left, is brought down on the left "H" hand, palm facing right. The hands, in this position, move forward a few inches. *Cf.* NAMED.

CALM (käm), *adj., v.,* CALMED, CALMING. (Quiet and peace.) The open hands are crossed before the mouth, the right palm facing left, left facing right. Then both hands, held palms down, move down from the mouth, curving outward to either side of the body. *Cf.* BE QUIET 2, BE STILL, QUIET 2, SILENCE 2.

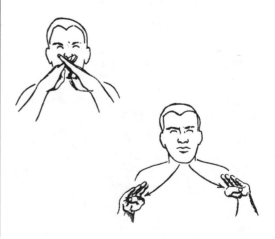

CAMEL 1 (kăm′ əl), *n.* (The shape of the neck.) The two "C" hands are placed at the neck. The right hand, palm facing up, moves up and forward in a long undulating curve, as if tracing the camel's long neck.

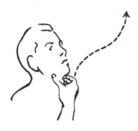

CAMEL 2, *n.* (The two humps.) The downturned right hand describes the two humps on the camel's back.

CAMERA 1 (kăm′ ər ə, kăm′ rə), *n.* (The natural sign.) The eye peers through the viewfinder of an imaginary camera, and the index finger clicks the shutter. This sign is used for a camera of the 35-mm type.

CAMERA 2, *n.* (The natural sign.) The signer peers down into the viewfinder of an imaginary camera held at the waist, and the thumb clicks the shutter. This sign is used for a camera of the box type.

CAMPFIRE *n.* (kamp′ fīr) (CAMP and FIRE.) Both "V" hands, fingertips touching, move down and out, describing a pyramid. This is the shape of a tent, associated with camp. The upturned wriggling fingers then move up and down alternately, describing the leaping of flames.

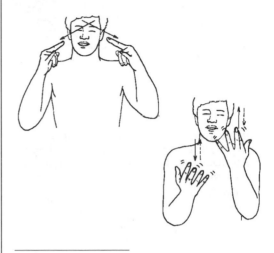

CAN (kan, kən), *v.* (An affirmative movement of the hands, likened to a nodding of the head, to indicate ability or power to accomplish something.) Both "A" hands, held palms down, move down in unison a short distance before the chest. *Cf.* ABILITY, ABLE, CAPABLE, COMPETENT, COULD, MAY 2, POSSIBLE.

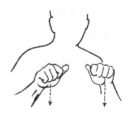

CANADA (kan′ ə də), *n.* (Shaking the snow from the lapel of an overcoat.) The hand grasps and shakes the right lapel.

CANCEL (kăn´ səl), *n., v.,* -CELED, -CELING. (A canceling out.) The right index finger makes a cross onthe open left palm. *Cf.* CORRECT 2, CRITICISM, CRITICIZE, FIND FAULT.

CANCER (kan´ sər), *n.* (Eating away the tissues of the body.) The right claw hand is placed on the thumb edge of the left hand and "eats" against the hand repeatedly.

CANDIDATE (kăn´ də dāt´, -dĭt), *n.* (Bringing oneself forward.) The right index finger and thumb grasp the clothing near the right shoulder (often the lapel of a suit or the collar of a dress) and tug it up and down gently several times. Sometimes one tug only is used. *Cf.* VOLUNTEER.

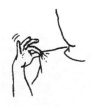

CANDLE (kăn´ dəl), *n., v.,* -DLED, -DLING. (Blowing the flame of the candle; the flickering flames.) The tip of the index finger of the right hand is placed at the lips and then it is placed at the base of the outstretched left hand, whose palm is facing out and

whose fingers are wiggling to denote the flickering of flames.

CANDY 1 (kăn´ dĭ), *n.* (Titillating to the taste.) The fingertips of the right "U" hand, palm facing the body, brush against the chin a number of times beginning at the lips. *Cf.* CUTE 1, SUGAR, SWEET.

CANDY 2, *n.* (Wiping the lips; licking the finger.) The right index finger, pointing left, is drawn across the lips from left to right.

CANE (kān), *n.* (A walking stick.) The signer mimes swinging a cane in the act of walking.

CANNING (kan′ ing), *n.* (Tightening the cover.) The signer mimes tightening the cover of a jar or can.

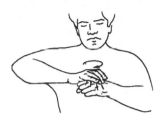

CANNON (kăn′ ən), *n.* (The recoil.) The right index finger points out and slightly upward. The right arm is jerked quickly forward and back, like the recoil of a cannon.

CANNOT 1 (kăn′ ŏt), *v.* (One finger encounters an unyielding quality in striking another.) The right index finger strikes the left and continues moving down. The left index finger remains in place. *Cf.* CAN'T, UNABLE.

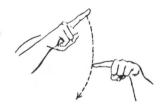

CANNOT 2, *v.* (Not able.) The sign for CAN is formed, followed by the sign for NOT: both hands, fingers together and palms facing down, are held before the body with the right slightly above the left. They separate with a deliberate movement, the right hand moving to the right and the left moving to the left. *Cf.* CAN'T.

CANOEING (kə nōō′ ĭng), *n.* (The natural sign.) The hands, grasping an imaginary paddle, go through the motions of paddling a canoe.

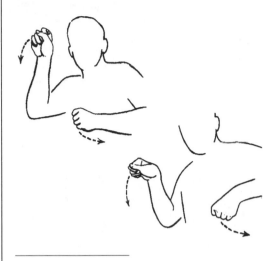

CAN'T (kănt, känt), *v.* See CANNOT 1, 2.

CAP (kăp), *n., v.,* CAPPED, CAPPING. (The natural sign.) The hand grasps the brim of an imaginary cap and pulls it down slightly.

CAPABLE (kā′ pə bəl), *adj.* (An affirmative movement of the hands, likened to a nodding of the head, to indicate ability or power to accomplish something.) Both "A" hands, held palm down, move down in unison a short distance before the chest. *Cf.* ABILITY, ABLE, CAN, COMPETENT, COULD, MAY 2, POSSIBLE.

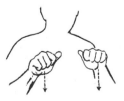

CAPACITY (kə păs´ ə tĭ), *n.* (The upper and lower limits are defined.) The right-angle hands, palms facing, are held before the body, the right above the left. They swing out 45 degrees simultaneously, pivoted from their wrists. *Cf.* LIMIT, RESTRICT.

CAPITAL (kăp´ ə təl), *n.* (The head indicates the head or seat of government.) The right index finger, pointing toward the right temple, describes a small clockwise circle and comes to rest on the right temple. *Cf.* GOVERNMENT.

CAPITAL LETTER (lĕt´ ər), *n.* (The size.) The right index and thumb, forming a "C," are held far apart. This sign is usually made only in context; here we are discussing printing.

CAPTAIN (kăp´ tən, -tĭn), *n.* (The epaulets.) The fingertips of the downturned right "5" hand strike the right shoulder twice. *Cf.* OFFICER.

CAPTION 1 (kăp´ shən), *n.* (The quotation marks are indicated.) The curved index and middle fingers of both hands, held palms out, move slightly to either side of the body, as if drawing quotation marks in the air. *Cf.* QUOTATION, QUOTE, SO-CALLED, SUBJECT, THEME, TITLE, TOPIC.

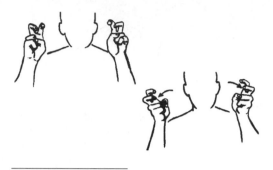

CAPTION 2, *n., v.* (Language or sentences spread out on the bottom of a filmed image.) Both "F" hands, palms out, are held together. As they separate they wriggle, pivoted by the wrists.

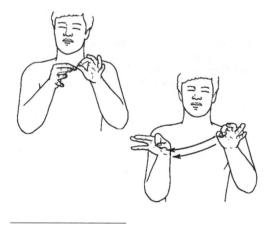

CAPTURE (kăp´ chər), *n., v.,* -TURED, -TURING. (Grasping something and holding it down.) Both hands, palms down, quickly close into the "S" position, the right on top of the left. *Cf.* CATCH 2, GRAB, GRASP, SEIZE.

CAR (kär), *n.* (The steering wheel.) The hands grasp an imaginary steering wheel and manipulate it. *Cf.* AUTOMOBILE, DRIVE.

CARD (kärd), *n.* (The natural sign.) The sides of the card are outlined with the thumb and index finger of each hand. *Cf.* TICKET 1.

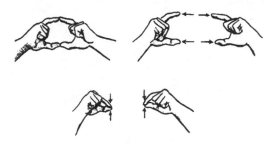

CARDINAL (kär´ də nəl), *(eccles.)*, *n.* (A red bishop.) The sign for RED is made: the tip of the right index finger moves down across the lips. The "R" hand may also be used. This is followed by the sign for BISHOP 1: the ring finger of the right "S" hand is kissed. This is the sign for a Catholic bishop. The red refers to the cardinal's red hat or biretta.

CARD PLAYING (plā´ ĭng). (The action of dealing out cards.) The signer goes through the motions of dealing out imaginary playing cards. *Cf.* CARDS, PLAYING CARDS.

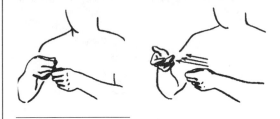

CARDS (kärdz), *n. pl.* See CARD PLAYING.

CARE 1 (kâr), *n., v.,* CARED, CARING. (Slow, careful movement.) The "K" hands are crossed, the right above the left, little finger edges down. In this position they describe a small clockwise circle in front of the chest. *Cf.* CARE FOR, CAREFUL 1, TAKE CARE OF 3.

CARE 2, *n., v.* (A variant of CARE 1.) With the hands in the same position as in CARE 1, they are moved up and down a short distance. *Cf.* CAREFUL 2, KEEP, MAINTAIN 1, MIND 3, PRESERVE, RESERVE 2, TAKE CARE OF 2.

CARE FOR (fôr), *v. phrase.* See CARE 1.

CAREFUL 1 (kâr´ fəl), *adj.* See CARE 1.

CAREFUL 2, *adj.* See CARE 2.

CAREFUL 3, *adj.* (The "K" for *keep* in the sense of *keeping carefully.*) Both "K" hands are crossed, the right atop the left. The right hand moves up and down a very short distance, several times, each time coming to rest on top of the left. *Cf.* BE CAREFUL, TAKE CARE OF 1.

CARELESS (kâr´ lĭs), *adj.* (The vision is sidetracked, causing one to lose sight of the object in view.) The right "V" hand, representing the vision, is held in front of the face, palm facing left. The hand, pivoted at the wrist, moves back and forth a number of times. *Cf.* RECKLESS.

CARPENTER (kär´ pən tər), *n.* (Manipulating a carpenter's plane.) The hands grasp and manipulate an imaginary carpenter's plane. This is followed by the sign for INDIVIDUAL: both open hands, palms facing each other, move down the sides of the body, tracing its outline to the hips.

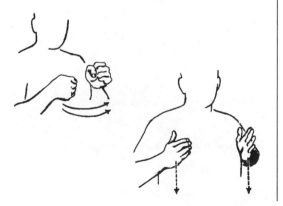

CARPET (kär´ pit), *n.* (The letter "C"; spread out over a surface.) The right "C" hand, facing left, slides over the downturned left arm, from forearm to wrist.

CARRIAGE (kar´ ij), *n.* (Rocking back and forth.) The signer mimes grasping a pram's handle and rocking it back and forth. *Cf.* PRAM.

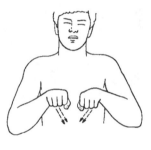

CARROT 1 (kar´ ət), *n.* (Biting a carrot.) The signer bites off a piece of imaginary carrot.

CARROT 2, *n.* (Shredding.) The right thumb vigorously "shaves" the outstretched index of the left "D" hand.

CARRY 1 (kär′ ĭ) v., -RIED, -RYING. (Act of conveying an object from one point to another.) The open hands are held palms up before the chest on the right side of the body. Describing an arc, they move up and forward in unison.

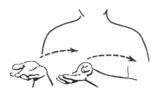

CARRY 2, v. (Carrying something over.) Both open hands, palms up, move in an arch from left to right, as if carrying something from one point to another. *Cf.* BRING, DELIVER.

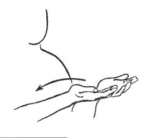

CARTOON(S) (kär tōōn′), n. (Funny drawings.) The sign for FUNNY is made: the index and middle fingertips brush repeatedly over the tip of the nose. The sign for DRAW then follows: the tip of the right little finger is repeatedly drawn down over the upturned left palm.

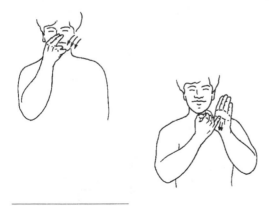

CARVE (kärv), v., CARVED, CARVING. (Chipping or cutting out.) The right thumb tip repeatedly gouges

out imaginary pieces of material from the palm of the left hand, held facing right.

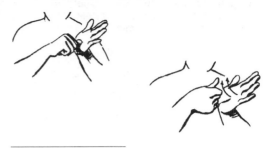

CASTLE 1 (kăs′ əl), n. (The buttresses and bulwarks.) Both hands, held in fists, are placed one on top of the other, arms held horizontally. The right arm then rises into the vertical position and its elbow is brought smartly down about an inch. The left arm then follows suit.

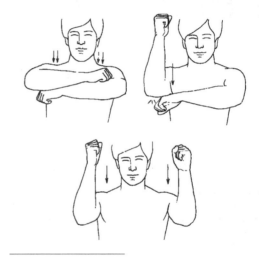

CASTLE 2, n. (The ramparts and towers.) Both "C" hands, held aloft and palms facing, are brought down and apart, in a series of successive movements.

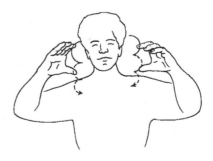

CAST OFF (kăst ôf), *v. phrase,* CAST, CASTING. (To throw something aside.) Both "S" hands are held with palms facing at chest level and then thrown down and to the left, opening into the "5" position. *Cf.* ABANDON, DISCARD, FORSAKE 2, LEAVE 2, LET ALONE, NEGLECT.

CAT (kăt), *n.* (The whiskers.) The thumbs and index fingers of both hands stroke an imaginary pair of whiskers at either side of the face. The right hand then strokes the back of the left, as if stroking the fur. This latter sign is seldom used today, however. Also one hand may be used in place of two for the stroking of the whiskers.

CATCH 1 (kăch), *n., v.,* CAUGHT, CATCHING. (The act of catching.) Both hands quickly come together, as if catching a ball.

CATCH 2, *v.* (Grasping something and holding it down.) Both hands, palms down, quickly close into the "S" position, the right on top of the left. *Cf.* CAPTURE, GRAB, GRASP, SEIZE.

CATCH 3, *v.* (Catching a ball.) Both hands go through the motions of catching a ball.

CATCHER (kăch´ ər), *n.* (One who catches a ball.) The sign for CATCH 3 is made, followed by the sign for INDIVIDUAL: both open hands, palms facing each other, move down the sides of the body, tracing its outline to the hips.

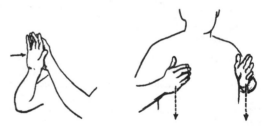

CATERPILLAR (kat´ ər pil ər), *n.* (The insect's crawling motion.) The right index finger makes a series of undulating forward motions as it "crawls" up the downturned left arm.

CATHOLIC (kăth´ ə lĭk, kăth´ lĭk), *adj.* (The cross.) The extended index and middle fingers make the sign of the cross before the face, moving down from the forehead and then across the face from left to right.

CAUGHT IN THE ACT 1 (kŏt ĭn *th*ĭ ăkt), *v. phrase.* (A pinning down.) The left "D" finger represents the one who is caught. The curved index and middle fingers of the right hand, palm facing down, are thrust against the left "D" finger, impaling it. *Cf.* CONTACT 2, CORNER 2.

CAUGHT IN THE ACT 2, *v. phrase.* (Impaled on a stick, as a snake's head.) The "V" fingers are thrust into the throat. *Cf.* STRANDED, STUCK 2, TRAP 1.

CAUSE (kŏz), *n., v.,* CAUSED, CAUSING. (Rays of influence emanating from a given source.) All the right fingertips, including the thumb, are positioned on the tip of the upturned thumb of the left "A" hand. The right hand, opening into the downturned "5" position, moves forward from its initial position. Instead of its initial position on the left thumb, the right hand is frequently placed on the back of the

downturned left "S" hand, moving forward as described above. *Cf.* INFLUENCE 2.

CAUTION (kŏ´ shən), *n.* (Tapping one to draw attention to danger.) The right hand taps the back of the left several times. *Cf.* ADMONISH, FOREWARN, WARN.

CAVE (kāv), *n.* ((Walking in and under a low ceiling.) With the left "C" hand downturned, the right index and middle fingers, bent over, "creep" under the left hand.

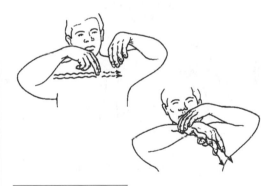

CAVE IN (kāv ĭn´), *v. phrase,* CAVED, CAVING. (A collapsing.) Both "5" hands, fingertips joined before the chest, swing down so that the fingertips face down. *Cf.* BREAKDOWN, COLLAPSE.

CAVITY (kăv′ ə tĭ), *n*. (The hole in a tooth.) The right index finger "drills" into a tooth. The mouth is of course held wide open.

CEILING (sē′ ling), *n*. (An overhead covering.) Both hands are held palms down above the head, index fingers side by side. The arms are separated while the signer looks up.

CELEBRATE (sĕl′ ə brāt′), *v*., -BRATED, -BRATING. (Waving of flags.) Both upright hands, grasping imaginary flags, wave them in small circles. *Cf*. CELEBRATION, CHEER, REJOICE, VICTORY 1, WIN 1.

CELEBRATION (sĕl′ ə brā′ shən), *n*. See CELEBRATE.

CELERY (sel′ ər ē), *n*. (The "C"; the stalk.) The thumbtip of the right "C" hand is placed on the tip of the left upturned index finger.

CELSIUS (sel′ sē əs), *n*. (The letter "C"; temperature.) The thumb of the right "C" hand moves up and down the upturned left index finger.

CEMETERY (sĕm′ ə tĕr′ ĭ), *n*. (The mound of a grave.) The downturned open hands, slightly cupped, are held side by side. They describe an arc as they are drawn in toward the body. *Cf*. BURY 1, GRAVE 1.

CENSUS (sen′ səs), *n*. (Counting people.) The fingertips of the right "F" hand move straight up the palm of the left, from heel to tips of fingers, as if adding up a column of figures. The sign for PEOPLE is then made: both "P" hands, palms down, swing in toward the body in alternate and repeated counterclockwise circles.

CENT (sĕnt), *n.* (The Lincoln head.) The right index finger touches the right temple and moves up and away quickly. This is "one cent." For two cents, the "2" hand is used, etc. *Cf.* CENTS, PENNY.

CENTER (sĕnt´ ər), *n., v.,* -TERED, -TERING. (The natural sign.) The downturned right fingers describe a small clockwise circle and come to rest in the center of the upturned left palm. *Cf.* CENTRAL, MIDDLE.

CENTIMETER (sen´ tə mē tər), *n.* (The "C" hands; the distance between.) Both "C" hands, palms out, are held with thumbtips touching. The hands move straight apart.

CENTRAL (sĕn´ trəl), *adj.* See CENTER.

CENTS *n. pl.* See CENT.

CERTAIN (sûr´ tən), *adj.* (Coming forth directly from the lips; true.) The index finger of the right "D" hand, palm facing left, is placed against the lips. It moves up an inch or two and then describes a small arc forward and away from the lips. *Cf.* ABSOLUTE, ABSOLUTELY, ACTUAL, ACTUALLY, AUTHENTIC, CERTAINLY, FIDELITY, FRANKLY, GENUINE, INDEED, POSITIVE 1, POSITIVELY, REAL, REALLY, SINCERE 2, SURE, SURELY, TRUE, TRULY, TRUTH, VALID, VERILY.

CERTAINLY (sûr´ tən lǐ), *adv.* See CERTAIN.

CHAIN (chān), *n.* (The links.) The thumbs and index fingers of both hands interlock, separate, reverse their relative positions, and interlock again.

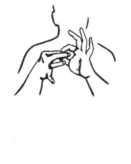

CHAIR (châr), *n.* (The act of sitting.) The extended right index and middle fingers are draped across the back of the same two fingers of the downturned left hand. The hands then move straight downward a short distance. *Cf.* BE SEATED, SEAT, SIT.

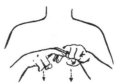

CHALLENGE (chăl´ ĭnj), *n., v.,* -LENGED, -LENGING. (Two individuals pitted against each other.) The hands are held in the "A" position, thumbs pointing straight up, palms facing the body. They come together forcefully, moving down a bit as they do, and the knuckles of one hand strike those of the other. *Cf.* GAME, OPPORTUNITY 2, VERSUS.

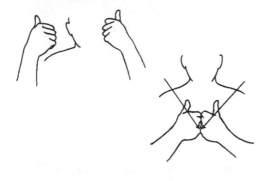

CHAMPAGNE (sham pān´), *n.* (Popping the cork.) The thumb flicks up from its position hidden in the closed hand.

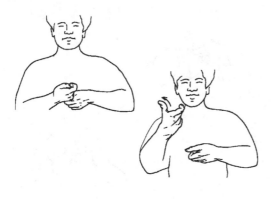

CHAMPION (chăm´ pĭ ən), *(sports), n.* (The head is crowned.) The upturned left index finger represents the victorious individual. The downturned "5" hand, fingers curved, is brought down on the left index finger as if draping it with a crown.

CHANCE 1 (chans), *n.* (Grabbing an opportunity.) The right cupped hand grabs an imaginary object from the upturned open left hand.

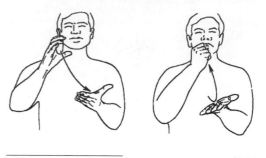

CHANCE 2, *n.* (Trying to push through, to an opportunity.) Both "C" hands, palms facing each other, move forward simultaneously, palms coming around to face forward.

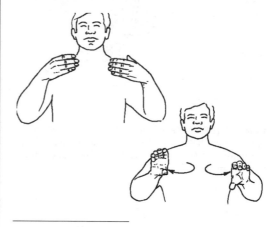

CHANGE 1 (chānj), *n., v.,* CHANGED, CHANGING. (The position of the hands is altered.) Both "A" hands, thumbs up, are held before the chest, several inches apart. The left hand is pivoted over so that its thumb points to the right. Simultaneously, the right hand is moved up and over the left, describing a small arc, with its thumb pointing to the left. *Cf.* CONVERT, MODIFY.

CHANGE 2, *n.*, *v.* (Dividing up or sharing.) The little finger edge of the open right "5" hand, held perpendicular to the index finger edge of the left, sweeps back and forth. This sign is used to mean changing money. Some signers use the right index finger over the left index finger, with the same orientation and motion as described before.

CHANGEABLE (chăn´ jə bəl), *adj.* (Changing again and again.) The "5" hands, fingers curved and palms facing, swing in unison, in alternate clockwise and counterclockwise directions, with the left and right hands alternating in front of each other.

CHAPTER (chăp´ tər), *n.* (A section of a page.) The palm of the left "C" hand faces right, representing a page. The fingertips of the right "C" hand, representing a section of the page, move straight down against the left palm.

CHARACTER 1 (kăr´ ĭk tər), *n.* (The heart is defined by the letter "C.") The right "C" hand, palm facing left, describes a circle against the heart.

CHARACTER 2, *n.* (The letter "C"; the face or appearance of something.) The right "C" hand, held palm facing left, executes a single counterclockwise circle, coming to rest against the left palm, which is facing forward.

CHARGE (chärj), *n.*, *v.*, CHARGED, CHARGING. (Nicking into one.) The knuckle of the right "X" finger is nicked against the palm of the left hand, held in the "5" position, palm facing right. *Cf.* COST, EXPENSE, FEE, FINE 2, PENALTY, PRICE 2, TAX 1, TAXATION 1, TOLL.

CHASE (chās), *v.*, CHASED, CHASING. (The natural sign.) The "A" hands are held in front of the body, with the thumbs facing forward, the right palm facing left and the left palm facing right. The left hand is held slightly ahead of the right; it then moves forward in a straight line while the right hand follows after, executing a circular motion or swerving back and forth, as if in pursuit. *Cf.* PURSUE.

CHAT 1 (chăt), *n., v.,* CHATTED, CHATTING. (Words tossed back and forth.) The open hands are held side by side with palms up, fingers pointing forward and slightly curved. In this position the hands swing back and forth from side to side before the chest. *Cf.* CONVERSATION 2.

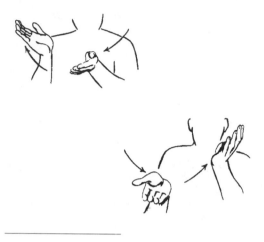

CHAT 2, *n., v.* (Moving the hands as in using sign language.) Both "C" hands, palms facing out, move alternately up and down.

CHAT 3, *n., v.* (A modified version of CHAT 2.) Both hands are held in the "C" position, palms facing out, but only the right hand moves up and down.

CHEAP (chēp), *(colloq.), adj.* (Something easily moved, therefore of no consequence.) The right fingertips slap the little finger edge of the upturned left hand.

CHEAT 1 (chēt), *v.,* CHEATED, CHEATING. (Underhanded-ness.) The right hand, palm down, is held with index and little fingers pointing out. The left hand, in a similar position, is held above the right. The right hand moves forward repeatedly, each time emerging briefly from under the left hand. The positions may be reversed, with the left hand doing the movement, or both hands can move simultaneously. *Cf.* DECEIT, DECEIVE, DECEPTION, DEFRAUD, FRAUD, FRAUDULENT.

CHEAT 2, *v., n. sl.* (Riding a pony.) The downturned right "V" hand straddles the index finger edge of the left hand, whose palm faces right. An up-down riding movement is used. This somewhat archaic sign refers to the "pony"—small, old, softcover study books designed to prepare one quickly for a school examination, usually high school or college undergraduate. These books seldom helped and often confused or hurt.

CHECK (chĕk), *n.* (A bank check.) The sign for CARD is made: the sides of the card are outlined with the thumb and index finger of each hand. This is followed by the sign for MONEY: the back of the right hand, palm up and fingers touching the thumb, is placed in the upturned left hand.

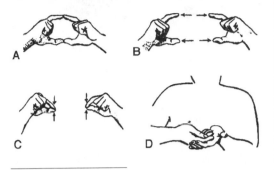

CHEER (chĭr), *n.* (Waving of flags.) Both upright hands, grasping imaginary flags, wave them in small circles. *Cf.* CELEBRATE, CELEBRATION, REJOICE, VICTORY 1, WIN 1.

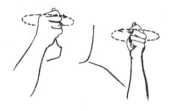

CHEERFUL (chĭr´ fəl), *adj.* (A crinkling-up of the face.) Both hands, in the "5" position, palms facing back, are placed on either side of the face. The fingers wiggle back and forth, while a pleasant, happy expression is worn. *Cf.* AMIABLE, CORDIAL, FRIENDLY, JOLLY, PLEASANT.

CHEESE (chēz), *n.* (The pressing of cheese.) The base of the downturned right hand is pressed against the base of the upturned left hand, and the two rotate back and forth against each other.

CHEMISTRY 1 (kĕm´ ĭs trĭ), *n.* (Pouring alternately from test tubes.) The upright thumbs of both "A" hands swing over alternately, in elliptical fashion, as if pouring out the contents of a pair of test tubes. *Cf.* SCIENCE 1.

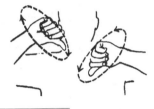

CHEMISTRY 2, *n.* (The letter "C;" pouring from test tubes.) Both "C" hands mime alternately pouring out the contents of laboratory test tubes.

CHERRY (cher´ ē), *n.* (Loosening a cherry from a branch.) The fingertips of the right hand grasp the end of the left little finger and twist back and forth as if loosening a cherry from a branch. *Cf.* BERRY, VIRGIN 3.

CHEWING GUM (chōō′ ing gum), *n.* (The chewing motion.) The thumb of the right "A" hand, held against the right cheek, swivels forward and back several times. Alternatively, the tips of the right "V" hand are placed at the right cheek and bend in and out. *Cf.* GUM.

CHICAGO (shǐ kô′ gō, -kä′-), *n.* (The letter "C.") The right "C" hand, palm facing out, describes an inverted "S" curve, moving down as it does.

CHICK (chǐk), *n.* (A small chicken.) The sign for CHICKEN is made: the right index and thumb, pointing forward, open and close at the lips. The cupped hands are then brought together, as if holding a small object.

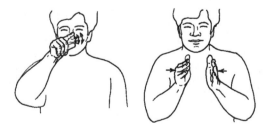

CHICKEN (chǐk′ ən, -ǐn), *n.* (The bill and the scratching.) The right index finger and thumb open and close as they are held pointing out from the mouth. (This is the root sign for any kind of bird.) The right "X" finger then scratches against the upturned left palm, as if scratching for food. The scratching is sometimes omitted.

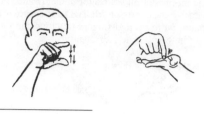

CHILD (chīld), *n.* (The child's height.) The downturned right palm is extended before the body, as if resting on a child's head.

CHILDREN (chǐl′ drən), *n.* (Indicating different heights of children; patting the children on their heads.) The downturned right palm, held before the body, executes a series of movements from left to right, as if patting a number of children on their heads.

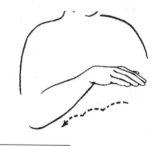

CHILE (chil′ ē), *n.* The right middle finger flicks an imaginary speck of dust from the left shoulder. A native sign.

CHILL (chĭl), *n.* (Chattering teeth.) Both "V" hands, fingers curved and the right hand held above the left, move very rapidly back and forth, in opposite directions each time, imitating the chattering of teeth. *Cf.* SHIVER 2.

CHILLY (chĭl′ ĭ), *adj.* (The trembling from cold.) Both "S" hands, palms facing, are placed at the sides of the body. In this position the arms and hands shiver. *Cf.* COLD 1, SHIVER 1, WINTER 1.

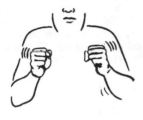

CHIMNEY (chim′ nĕ), *n.* (The shape.) The open hands, palms facing each other, are held a few inches apart. They move up together a short distance, come together an inch or two, and then continue their upward movement. *Cf.* SMOKESTACK.

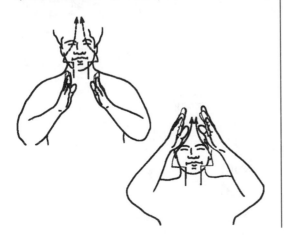

CHIN (chĭn), *n.* The chin is touched with the extended index finger.

CHINA 1 (chī′ nə), *n.* (Slanting eyes.) The index fingers draw back the corners of the eyes, causing them to slant. One hand is often used. In either case, this sign, formerly very popular and widely used, is today considered offensive and derogatory. *Cf.* CHINESE.

CHINA 2, *n.* (Same as above, but initialed with "C.") The thumb of the "C" hand is placed at the corner of the eye. Also derogatory and offensive.

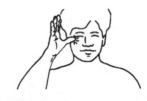

CHINA 3, *n.* (Tracing the buttons on the Mao uniform.) The right "G" hand, palm facing the upper chest, moves across from left to right, then down to the right side of the chest. This sign is used by native Chinese. It is slowly replacing other signs for CHINA.

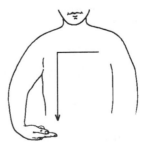

CHINA 4, *n.* (The finger touches a brittle substance.) The index finger is brought up to touch the exposed front teeth. *Cf.* DISH, GLASS 1, PLATE 1, PORCELAIN.

CHINESE (chĭ nēz´, -nēs´), *n., adj.* See CHINA 1.

CHOCOLATE (chôk´ ə lĭt, chŏk´-, chôk´ lĭt, chŏk´-), *n., adj.* The thumb of the right "C" hand, resting against the back of the downturned left "S" hand, makes a series of small counterclockwise circles.

CHOICE (chois), *n.* (Making a choice.) The left "V" hand faces the body. The right thumb and index finger close first over the left index fingertip and then over the left middle fingertip. *Cf.* EITHER 2.

CHOKE (chŏk), *v.* CHOKED, CHOKING. (Catching one by the throat.) The right hand makes a natural movement of grabbing the throat. *Cf.* STUCK 1.

CHOOSE (chōōz), *v.,* CHOSE, CHOSEN, CHOOSING. (Taking unto oneself.) The right hand, palm out, is extended before the chest, index finger and thumb in an open position, the other fingers separated and pointing up. The hand is drawn in toward the chest, and the index and thumb close at the same time, indicating something taken to oneself. *Cf.* SELECT 2, TAKE.

CHOREOGRAPHER (kôr ē og´ rə fer), *n.* (DANCE and TEACHER.) The sign for DANCE: the index and middle fingers of the right hand execute a rhythmic back-and-forth movement against the upturned left hand. Next, the sign for TEACH: the fingertips of each hand are placed at the temples. They then swing out and open into the "5" position. The sign for INDIVIDUAL 1 then follows.

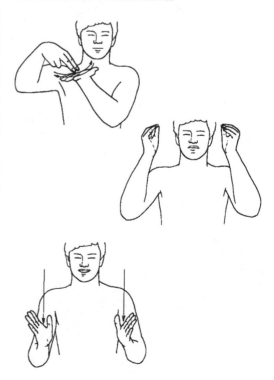

CHRIST (krīst), *(eccles.)*, *n.* The right "C" hand is placed against the left shoulder and slides down across the chest to the right hip. The movement from shoulder to hip outlines the band worn across the chest by royalty.

CHRISTIAN (krĭs´ chən), *n., adj.* (An individual who follows Jesus.) The sign for JESUS is made: both "5" hands are used. The left middle finger touches the right palm, and then the right middle finger touches the left palm. This is followed by the sign for INDIVIDUAL: both open hands, palms facing each other, move down the sides of the body, tracing its outline to the hips. Other ways to make this sign involve the signs for JESUS, and BELIEVER, FOLLOWER, or FRIEND. Another way is to make the signs for CHRIST and INDIVIDUAL.

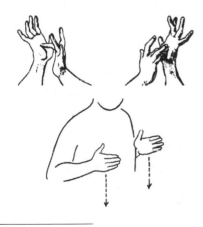

CHRISTMAS (krĭs´ məs), *n.* (The shape of the wreath.) The right "C" hand, palm facing out, describes an arc from left to right. *Cf.* XMAS.

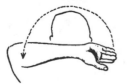

CHURCH (chûrch), *n.* (The letter "C," set up on a firm foundation, as a building.) The base of the thumb of the right "C" hand is brought down to rest on the back of the downturned open left hand. The action may be repeated twice.

CIGAR (sĭ gär´), *n.* (The shape.) The right hand, in a grasping position and palm facing left, moves forward from the slightly open mouth, closing into the "S" position.

CIGARETTE (sĭg´ ə rĕt´, sĭg´ ə rĕt´), *n.* (The dimensions of the cigarette.) The index and little fingers of the right hand, palm facing down, are placed upon the left index finger, so that the right index finger rests on the knuckle of the left index finger and the right little finger rests on the tip of the left index finger.

CIRCLE 1 (sûr´ kəl), *n., v.,* -CLED, -CLING. (The circle is described.) The index finger, pointing down or out, describes a circle.

CIRCLE 2, *n., v.* (A grouping together.) Both "C" hands, palms facing, are held a few inches apart at chest height. They are swung around in unison, so that the palms now face the body. *Cf.* ASSOCIATION, CLASS, CLASSED, CLUB, COMPANY 1, GANG, GROUP 1, ORGANIZATION 1.

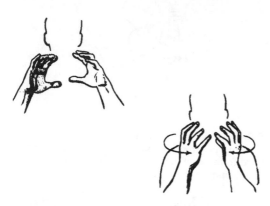

CIRCUMCISION 1 (sûr′ kəm sizh en), *n.* (Cutting the foreskin.) The tip of the right thumb makes a clockwise circular movement around the tip of the left thumb.

CIRCUMCISION 2, *n.* (A variant of CIRCUMSION 1.) The fingertips of the right hand grasp the tip of the left index and pivot in a clockwise manner.

CITY (sĭt′ ĭ), *n.* (A collection of rooftops.) The fingertips of both hands are joined, the hands and arms forming a pyramid. The fingertips separate and rejoin a number of times. Both arms may move a bit from left to right each time the fingertips separate and rejoin. *Cf.* COMMUNITY, TOWN.

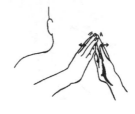

CIVILIZATION (siv ə lə zā′ shən), *n.* (Around the world with the letter "C.") The right "C" hand makes a circle around the left fist.

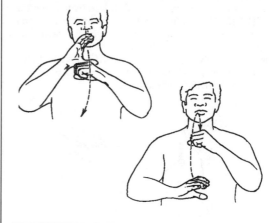

CLAP (klap), *n., sl.* (A slang term for GONOR-RHEA: the penis is infected, *i.e.,* covered with the disease.) The right claw hand is brought down on the tip of the left index. Although gender-specific here, this sign may also be used for female gonorrhea. *Cf.* GONORRHEA.

CLASS (klăs, kläs), *n.* (A grouping together.) Both "C" hands, palms facing, are held a few inches apart at chest height. They are swung around in unison, so that the palms now face the body. *Cf.* ASSOCIATION, CIRCLE 2, CLASSED, CLUB, COMPANY 1, GANG, GROUP 1, ORGANIZATION 1.

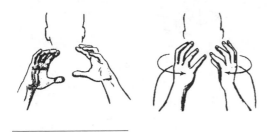

CLASSED *v.* See CLASS.

CLAWS (klôz), *n.* (Indicating the claws.) The open left hand is held palm down. The index finger and thumb of the right hand grasp each fingertip in turn, starting with the left index, and move off a short distance, indicating the extended fingertips or claws.

CLEAN (klēn), *adj.* (Everything is wiped off the hand, to emphasize an uncluttered or clean condition.) The right hand slowly wipes the upturned left palm, from wrist to fingertips. *Cf.* NICE, PLAIN 2, PURE 1, PURITY, SIMPLE 2.

CLEANSER (klenz′ ər), *n.* (The powder and the rubbing.) The signer mimes sprinkling powder into the left palm. The right hand then rubs vigorously back and forth against the left palm.

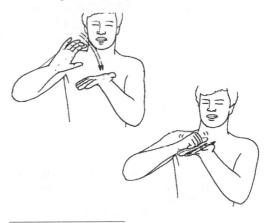

CLEAR (klĭr), *adj.* (Rays of light clearing the way.) Both hands are held at chest height, palms out, all fingertips together. They open into the "5" position in unison, the right hand moving toward the right and the left toward the left. The palms of both hands remain facing out. *Cf.* BRIGHT 1, BRILLIANCE 1, BRILLIANT 2, EVIDENT, EXPLICIT 2, OBVIOUS, PLAIN 1.

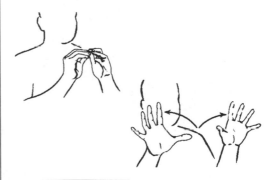

CLEVER (klĕv′ ər), *adj.* (The mind is bright.) The middle finger is placed at the forehead, and then the hand, with an outward flick, turns around so that the palm faces outward. This indicates a brightness flowing from the mind. *Cf.* BRIGHT 3, BRILLIANT 1, INTELLIGENT, SMART.

CLIENT (klī′ ənt), *n*. (The letter "C.") The "C" hands move down the sides of the body, as in INDIVID-UAL 1, *q.v.*

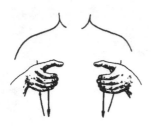

CLIMB 1 (klīm), *v.*, CLIMBED, CLIMBING, *n*. (One hand over the other.) One hand is lifted above the other, as if climbing a pole or tree.

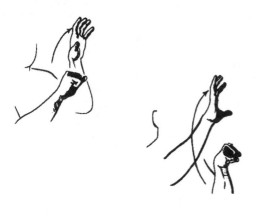

CLIMB 2, *v.* (Climbing up a ladder.) The left "V" hand, palm facing out, serves as the ladder. The right index and middle fingers "walk" up along the back of the left hand, starting at the wrist.

CLOCK (klok), *n*. (A timepiece on the wall.) The signer taps the top of the wrist, indicating a wrist-watch. The index fingers and thumbs are then used to

form a pair of "C"s, and an imaginary clock is held up, as if hanging it on a wall or placing it on a shelf.

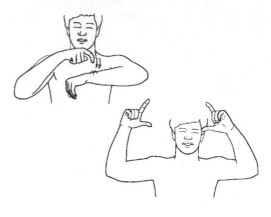

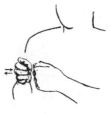

CLOSE 1 (*adj., adv.* klōs; *v.* klōz), CLOSED, CLOSING. (The act of closing.) Both "B" hands, held palms out before the body, come together with some force. *Cf.* SHUT.

CLOSE (TO) 2, *adj.* (One hand is near the other.) The left hand, cupped, fingers together, is held before the chest, palm facing the body. The right hand, also cupped, fingers together, moves a very short distance back and forth, as it is held in front of the left. *Cf.* NEAR 1, NEIGHBOR, NEIGHBORHOOD, VICINI-TY.

CLOSE EYES *v.* (klōs′ īz) (The action.) One hand, held at the eyes in the modified "C" position, with thumb and index finger forming the letter "C," closes so that the index fingers and thumbs come together. The eyes close simultaneously.

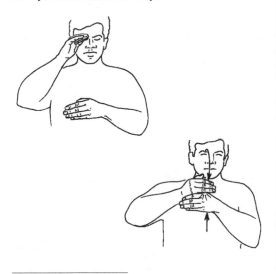

CLOSET 1 (klŏz′ ĭt), *n.*, *v.*, -ETED, -ETING. The extended index and middle fingers of the right hand strike across the back and then the front of the same two fingers of the left hand, which is held with palm facing the chest.

CLOSET 2, *n.* (The hangers.) The right curved index finger is repeatedly hung over the extended left index finger, starting at the lower knuckle and moving successively to the fingertip. *Cf.* HANGER 1.

CLOTH (klôth), *n.* (Plucking the fabric.) The right index and middle fingers and thumb pluck the fabric covering the chest.

CLOTHES (klōz, klōthz), *n. pl.* (Draping the clothes on the body.) With fingertips resting on the chest, both hands move down simultaneously. The action is repeated. *Cf.* CLOTHING, DRESS, FROCK, GARMENT, GOWN, SHIRT, SUIT, WEAR 1.

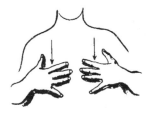

CLOTHESPIN (klōz′ pin), *n.* (The clipping.) The thumb, index, and middle fingers of the downturned right hand clamp down twice on the index finger edge of the left hand. Instead of the clamping, they may slide down.

CLOTHING (klō′ thǐng), *n.* See CLOTHES.

CLOUD(S) (kloud), *n.* (Black objects gathering over the head.) The sign for BLACK is made: the right index finger is drawn over the right eyebrow, from left to right. Both open hands are then rotated alternately before the forehead, outlining the shape of the clouds.

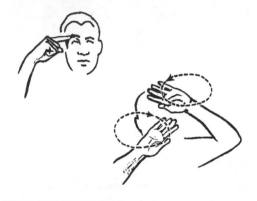

CLOWN (kloun), *n.* (The big nose.) The fingertips of the right claw hand are placed over the nose.

CLUB (klŭb), *n.* (A grouping together.) Both "C" hands, palms facing, are held a few inches apart at chest height. They are swung around in unison, so that the palms now face the body. *Cf.* ASSOCIATION, CIRCLE 2, CLASS, CLASSED, COMPANY 1, GANG, GROUP 1, ORGANIZATION 1.

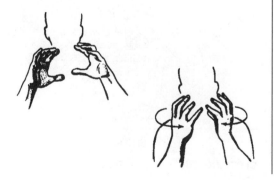

CLUMSINESS (klŭm´ zĭ nĭs), *n.* (Clumsy in gait; all thumbs.) The "3" hands, palms down, move alternately up and down before the body. *Cf.* AWKWARD, AWKWARDNESS, CLUMSY.

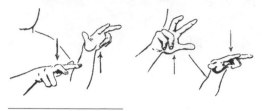

CLUMSY (klŭm´ zĭ), *adj.* See CLUMSINESS.

COAT (kōt), *n.* (The lapels are outlined.) The tips of the "A" thumbs outline the lapels of the coat.

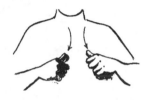

COAX (kōks), *v.,* COAXED, COAXING. (Shaking someone, to implant one's will into another.) Both "A" hands, palms facing, are held before the chest, the left slightly in front of the right. In this position the hands move back and forth a short distance. *Cf.* PERSUADE, PERSUASION, PROD, URGE 2.

COCA-COLA (kō´ kə kō´ lə), *(colloq.)* (A shot in the arm.) The right index finger is thrust into the left upper arm and the thumb wiggles back and forth a number of times, as if implanting a shot in the arm. *Cf.* COKE, DOPE, INOCULATE, MORPHINE, NARCOTICS.

COCAINE 1 (kō kān′), *n.* (The powder is pushed into the nostrils.) The right thumbtip is pressed up against each nostril.

COCAINE 2, *n.* (Inhaling the powder.) The powder is sniffed up through an imaginary straw from the upturned left palm.

COCHLEAR IMPLANT (kok′ le ər im plant), *n.* (The implant's position behind the ear.) The curved right thumb, index, and middle fingers touch the head at a position behind the right ear.

COCOON (kə kōōn′), *n.* (Covering the contents of the cocoon.) The tip of the left thumb protrudes from the tightly cupped right hand.

COERCE 1 (kō ûrs′), *v.,* -ERCED, -ERCING. (Forcing the head to bow.) The right "C" hand pushes down on an imaginary neck. *Cf.* COERCION 1, COMPEL 1, FORCE 1, IMPEL 1.

COERCE 2, *v.* (Pushing something forward.) The open right hand is held palm down at chin level, fingers pointing left. From this position the hand turns to point forward, and moves forcefully forward and away from the body, as if pushing something ahead of it. *Cf.* COERCION 2, FORCE 2.

COERCION 1 (kō ûr′ shən), *n.* See COERCE 1.

COERCION 2, *n.* See COERCE 2.

COFFEE (kôf′ ĭ, kŏf′ ĭ), *n.* (Grinding the coffee beans.) The right "S" hand, palm facing left, rotates in a counterclockwise manner, atop the left "S" hand, palm facing right.

COINCIDE (kō′ in sīd′), v., -CIDED, -CIDING. (A befalling.) Both "D" hands, index fingers pointing away from the body, are simultaneously pivoted over so that the palms face down. Cf. COINCIDENCE, EVENT, HAPPEN 1, INCIDENT, OCCUR, OPPORTUNITY.

COINCIDENCE (kō ĭn′ sə dəns), n. See COINCIDE.

COKE (kōk), (colloq.), n. See COCA-COLA.

COLD 1 (kōld), adj. (The trembling from cold.) Both "S" hands, palms facing, are placed at the sides of the body. In this position the arms and hands shiver. Cf. CHILLY, SHIVER 1, WINTER 1.

COLD 2, n. (Wiping the nose.) The signer makes the motions of wiping the nose several times with an imaginary handkerchief. This is the common cold. Cf. HANDKERCHIEF.

COLLAPSE (kə lăps′), v., -LAPSED, -LAPSING, n. (A collapsing.) Both "5" hands, fingertips joined before the chest, swing down so that the fingertips face down. Cf. BREAKDOWN, CAVE IN.

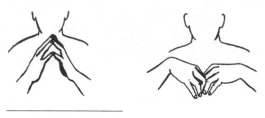

COLLAR (kŏl′ ər), n. (Outlining the collar.) The fingertips of both "Q" hands are placed at either side of the neck. They encircle the neck, coming together under the chin.

COLLECT (kə lĕkt′), v., -LECTED, -LECTING. (Gathering in.) The right "5" hand, its little finger edge touching the upturned left palm, is drawn in an arc toward the body, closing into the "S" position as it sweeps over the base of the left hand. Cf. ACCUMULATE, EARN, SALARY 1, WAGE(S).

COLLEGE (kŏl′ ĭj), n. (Above ordinary school.) The sign for SCHOOL, q.v., is made, but without the clapping of hands. The upper hand swings up in an arc above the lower. The upper hand may form a "C," instead of assuming a clapping position.

COLLIDE (kə lĭd´), *v.,* -LIDED, -LIDING. The fists come together with force. *Cf.* COLLISION, CRASH.

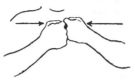

COLLISION (kə lĭzh´ en), *n.* See COLLIDE.

COLOMBIA *n.* (kə lum´ bē a; the letter "C.") The right "C" hand, palm facing forward, makes a counterclockwise circle as it rests on the back of the left hand. A native sign.

COLOR 1 (kŭl´ ər), *n.* The fingertips of the right "5" hand, palm facing the body, are placed against the chin and wiggle back and forth.

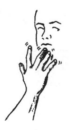

COLOR 2 *(rare), n.* (Mixing the colors on the palette.) The fingertips of the downturned right "B" hand rub against the upturned left palm in a clockwise-counterclockwise fashion.

COLOR 3, *v.* The downturned right "5" hand is held above the upturned left palm. The right fingers, wriggling, are passed back and forth over the left palm, from the base of the hand to the fingertips.

COLUMBUS (kə lum´ bəs), *n.* (The letter "C"; a "name sign.") The thumb of the right "C" hand is placed against the right temple.

COMB (kōm) *n., v.,* COMBED, COMBING. (Act of combing the hair.) The downturned curved fingertips of the right hand, representing the teeth of the comb, are drawn through the hair.

COME 1 (kŭm), *v.,* CAME, COME, COMING. (Movement toward the body.) The index fingers, pointing to each other, are rolled in toward the body.

COME 2, *v*. (A beckoning.) The right index finger makes a natural beckoning movement. *Cf.* BECKON.

COME 3 , *v*. (The natural sign.) The upright hand beckons.

COME ON *v. phrase*. (The natural beckoning motion.) One right-angle hand, held at shoulder level, palm facing the body, is moved toward the body in a beckoning motion, while the signer assumes an appropriately encouraging or anxious expression.

COMET (kom´ it), *n*. (The comet's tail.) The right "C" hand, palm out, describes a broad sweeping arc in the sky as it moves, ending in the "O" position.

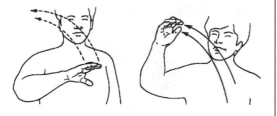

COMFORT (kŭm´ fərt), *n., v.,* -FORTED, -FORTING. (A stroking motion.) Each downturned open hand alternately strokes the back of the other, moving forward from wrist to fingers. *Cf.* COMFORTABLE.

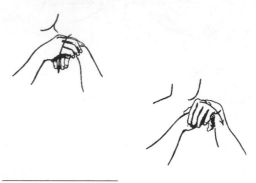

COMFORTABLE (kŭmf´ tə bəl, kŭm´ fər tə bəl), *adj*. See COMFORT.

COMIC (kŏm´ ĭk), *n*. (The nose wrinkles in laughter.) The tips of the right index and middle fingers brush repeatedly off the tip of the nose. *Cf.* COMICAL, FUNNY, HUMOR, HUMOROUS.

COMICAL (kŏm´ ə kəl), *adj*. See COMIC.

COMMA (kŏm´ ə), *n*. (The natural sign.) The right thumb and index finger are held together. In this position they draw a comma in the air before the face.

COMMAND (kə mănd´), *n., v.,* -MANDED, -MANDING. (An issuance from the mouth.) The tip of the index finger of the "D" hand, palm facing the body, is placed at the closed lips. It moves around and out, rather forcefully. *Cf.* DIRECT 2, ORDER 1.

COMMANDMENTS (kə mănd´ mənts), *n. pl.* Hold up the left open hand, palm facing right; place the side of the right "C" hand against the left palm twice, the second time slightly lower than the first.

COMMENCE (kə mĕns´), *v.,* -MENCED, -MENCING. (Turning a key to open up a new venture.) The right index finger, resting between the left index and middle fingers, executes a half turn, once or twice. *Cf.* BEGIN, ORIGIN, START.

COMMEND (kə mĕnd´), *v.,* -MENDED, -MENDING. (Good words coming from the mouth; clapping hands.) The fingertips of the right hand, palm flat and facing the body, are brought up to the lips, so that they touch (part of the sign for GOOD, *q.v.*). The hands are then clapped together several times. *Cf.* APPLAUD, APPLAUSE, CONGRATULATE 1, CONGRATULATIONS 1, PRAISE.

COMMON (kom´ ən), *adj.* (The same all around.) Both downturned "Y" hands execute counterclockwise circles. *Cf.* STANDARD.

COMMON LAW (kom´ ən law), *n.* (Everyday law.) The sign for DAILY is made: the right "A" hand moves forward several times from its initial resting place on the right cheek. This is followed by the sign for LAW: the upright "L" hand, resting palm against palm on the upright left "5" hand, moves down in an arc a short distance, coming to rest on the base of the left palm.

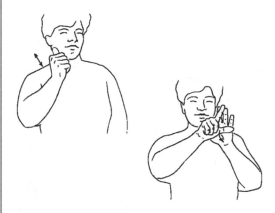

COMMUNITY (kə mū´ nə tĭ), *n.* (A collection of rooftops.) The fingertips of both hands are joined, the hands and arms forming a pyramid. The fingertips separate and rejoin a number of times. Both arms may move a bit from left to right each time the fingertips separate and rejoin. *Cf.* CITY, TOWN.

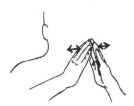

COMPANY 1 (kŭm´ pə nĭ), *n.* (A grouping together.) Both "C" hands, palms facing, are held a few inches apart at chest height. They are swung around in unison, so that the palms now face the body. *Cf.* ASSOCIATION, CIRCLE 2, CLASS, CLASSED, CLUB, GANG, GROUP 1, ORGANIZATION 1.

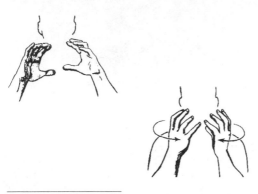

COMPANY 2, *n.* (The abbreviation; a fingerspelled loan sign.) The letters "C-O" are fingerspelled. To avoid misunderstanding, as in "co-worker," the hand may move in a small arc between the "C" and "O."

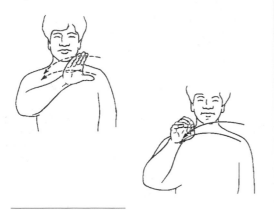

COMPARE (kəm pâr´), *v., -*PARED, -PARING. (Comparing both palms.) Both open hands are held before the body, with palms facing each other and fingers pointing upward. The hands then turn toward the face while the signer looks from one to the other, as if comparing them.

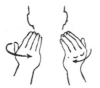

COMPASSION (kəm păsh´ ən), *n.* (Feelings from the heart, conferred on others.) The middle finger of the open right hand moves up the chest over the heart. The same open hand then moves in a small, clockwise circle in front of the right shoulder, with palm facing forward and fingers pointing up. The signer assumes a kindly expression.

COMPETE 1 (kəm pĕt´), *v., -*PETED, -PETING. (Two opponents come together.) Both hands are closed, with thumbs pointing straight up and palms facing the body. From their initial position about a foot apart, the hands are brought together sharply, so that the knuckles strike. The hands, as they are drawn together, also move down a bit, so that they describe a "V." *Cf.* COMPETITION 1, RACE 1, RIVAL 2, RIVALRY 1, VIE 1.

COMPETE 2, *v.* (Opposing objects.) The "A" hands are held side by side before the chest, palms facing each other and thumbs pointing forward. In this position the hands move alternately back and forth, toward and away from the body. *Cf.* COMPETITION 2, RACE 2, RIVAL 3, RIVALRY 2, VIE 2.

COMPETENT (kŏm´ pə tənt), *adj.* (An affirmative movement of the hands, likened to a nodding of the head, to indicate ability or power to accomplish something.) Both "A" hands, held palms down, move down in unison a short distance before the chest. *Cf.* ABILITY, ABLE, CAN, CAPABLE, COULD, MAY 2, POSSIBLE.

COMPETITION 1 (kŏm´ pə tĭsh´ ən), *n.* See COMPETE 1.

COMPETITION 2, *n.* See COMPETE 2.

COMPLAIN (kəm plān´), *v.,* -PLAINED, -PLAINING. (The hand is thrust into the chest to force a complaint out.) The curved fingers of the right hand are thrust forcefully into the chest. *Cf.* COMPLAINT, OBJECT 2, OBJECTION, PROTEST 1.

COMPLAINT (kəm plānt´), *n.* See COMPLAIN.

COMPLETE (kəm plēt´), *v.,* -PLETED, -PLETING. (Wiping off the top of a container, to indicate its condition of fullness.) The downturned open right hand wipes across the index finger edge of the left "S" hand, whose palm faces right. The movement of the right hand is toward the body. *Cf.* FILL 1, FULL.

COMPLEX (kəm pleks´), *adj.* The wriggling fingers indicate the involved nature.) Both downturned "W" hands, fingers facing each other, are moved toward each other while the fingers wriggle, and open and close a bit.

COMPLICATE (kŏm´ plə kāt´), *v.,* -CATED, -CATING. (Scrambling or mixing up.) The downturned right hand is positioned above the upturned left. The fingers of both are curved. Both hands move in opposite horizontal circles. *Cf.* CONFUSE, CONFUSED, CONFUSION, MINGLE 1, MIX, MIXED, MIXED UP, MIX-UP, SCRAMBLE.

COMPOSITION (kom pə zish´ ən), *n.* (Writing down.) Grasping an imaginary pencil, the right hand scribbles across the open left palm. The right thumb and index finger, held apart, then move down the left palm, from the index finger edge to the little finger edge. This second part of the sign is optional.

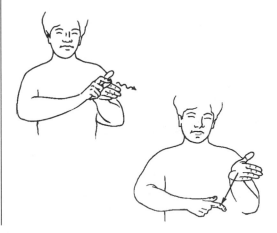

COMPUTER 1 (kəm pyōō′ tər), *n.* The thumb of the right "C" hand is placed on the back of the left hand and moves up the left arm in an arc.

COMPUTER 2, *n.* (Reference to the mind.) The thumb of the right "C" hand touches the forehead or the temple, and the hand twists slightly up and down.

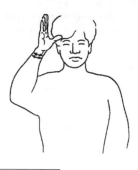

COMPUTER 3, *n.* (The tape in a mainframe drive.) Both index fingers describe clockwise circles.

COMPUTER 4, *n.* Same as COMPUTER 3, using "C" hands.

CONCEITED (kən sē′ tĭd), *(colloq.)*, *adj.* (The natural sign.) Both downturned "L" hands are positioned with index fingers at the temples. They move away

from the head rather slowly, indicating the size or growth of the head. The head is often moved slightly back and forth as the hands move away. An expression of superiority is assumed. *Cf.* BIG-HEADED, BIG SHOT, SWELL-HEADED.

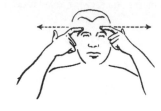

CONCEIVE (kən sēv′), *v.*, -CEIVED, -CEIVING. (A thought coming forward from the mind, modified by the letter "I" for "idea.") With the "I" position on the right hand, palm facing the body, touch the little finger to the forehead, and then move the hand up and away in a circular, clockwise motion. The hand may also be moved up and away without this circular motion. *Cf.* IMAGINATION 1, IMAGINE, THEORY 1, THOUGHT 2.

CONCENTRATE (kŏn′ sən trāt′), *v.*, -TRATED, -TRATING, *n.* (Directing one's attention forward; applying oneself; concentrating.) Both hands, fingers pointing up and together, are held at the sides of the face. They move straight out from the face. *Cf.* ATTEND (TO), ATTENTION, CONCENTRATION, FOCUS, GIVE ATTENTION (TO), MIND 2, PAY ATTENTION (TO).

CONCENTRATION (kŏn′ sən tra′ shən), *n.* See CONCENTRATE.

CONCEPT (kŏn´ sĕpt), *n.* (The letter "C"; an idea popping out of the head.) The right "C" hand is held near the right side of the forehead. It moves up and out a bit.

CONCERN (kən sûrn´), *n., v.,* -CERNED, -CERNING. (A clouding over; a troubling.) Both "B" hands, palms facing each other, are rotated alternately before the forehead. *Cf.* FRET, PROBLEM 1, TROUBLE, WORRIED, WORRY 1.

CONDENSE (kən dĕns´), *v.,* -DENSED, -DENSING. (To squeeze or condense into a small space.) The "C" hands face each other, with the right hand nearer to the body than the left. Both hands draw together and close deliberately, squeezing an imaginary object. *Cf.* ABBREVIATE, BRIEF 2, MAKE BRIEF, SUMMARIZE 1, SUMMARY 1.

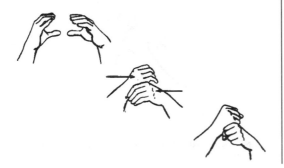

CONDESCEND (kon di send´), *v.* (Looking down upon.) Both downturned "V" hands point somewhat down, indicating the gaze is directed down at someone. To indicate the signer is the subject of condescension, the "V" hands are held at eye level, pointing down toward the signer.

CONDOM 1 (kon´ dəm), *n.* (Slipping on a condom.) The inner edge of the curved right index finger is slipped around the left index finger and moves down.

CONDOM 2, *n.* The same sign as CONDOM 1, but the index and thumb, in the "G" position, slip on the condom.

CONDUCT 1 (*n.* kŏn´ dŭkt; *v.* kən dŭkt´), -DUCTED, -DUCTING. (An activity.) Both open hands, palms down, are swung right and left before the chest. *Cf.* ACT 2, ACTION, ACTIVE, ACTIVITY, DEED, DO, PERFORM 1, PERFORMANCE 1.

CONDUCT 2, *n.* (One hand leads the other.) The right hand grasps the tips of the left fingers and pulls the left hand forward. *Cf.* GUIDE, LEAD.

CONFERENCE (kŏn´ fər əns), *n.* (Assemble all together.) Both "5" hands, palms facing, are held with fingers pointing out from the body. With a sweeping motion they are brought in toward the chest, and all fingertips come together. This is repeated. *Cf.* ASSEMBLE 1, ASSEMBLY, CONVENE, CONVENTION, GATHER 2, GATHERING, MEETING 1.

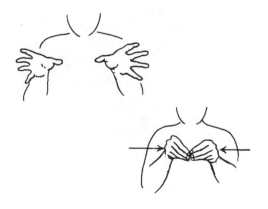

CONFESS (kən fĕs´), *v.*, -FESSED, -FESSING. (Getting something off the chest.) Both hands are held with fingers touching the chest and pointing down. They are then swung up and out, ending with both palms facing up before the body. *Cf.* ADMISSION, ADMIT, CONFESSION 1.

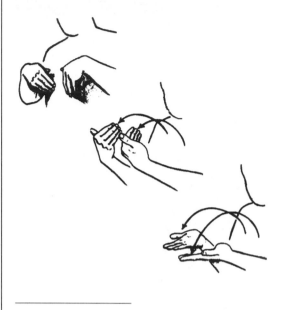

CONFESSION 1 (kən fĕsh´ ən), *n.* See CONFESS.

CONFESSION 2, (*eccles.*), *n.* (The grating through which confession is heard.) The fingers of the right open hand are spread slightly and placed with their backs resting diagonally across the front of the spread fingers of the left open hand, so as to form a grid held just to the side of the face, palms toward the face. *Cf.* CONFESSIONAL.

CONFESSIONAL (kən fĕsh´ ən əl), *adj., n.* See CONFESSION 2.

CONFIDENCE (kŏn′ fə dəns), *n.* (Planting a flag-pole, *i.e.,* planting one's trust.) The "S" hands grasp and plant an imaginary flagpole in the ground. This sign may be preceded by BELIEVE, *q.v. Cf.* TRUST.

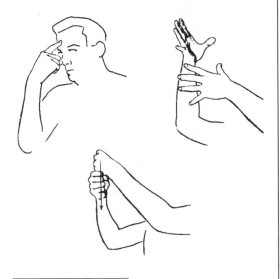

CONFRONT (kən frŭnt′), *v.,* -FRONTED, -FRONTING. (Face to face.) The left hand, fingers together, palm flat and facing the eyes, is held a bit above eye level. The right hand, fingers also together, is held in front of the mouth, with palm facing the left hand. With a sweeping upward movement the right hand moves toward the left, which moves straight up an inch or two at the same time. *Cf.* BEFORE 3, FACE, FACE TO FACE, PRESENCE.

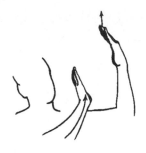

CONFUSE (kən fūz′), *v.,* -FUSED, -FUSING. (Scrambling or mixing up.) The downturned right hand is positioned above the upturned left. The fingers of both are curved. Both hands move in opposite horizontal circles. *Cf.* COMPLICATE, CONFUSED,

CONFUSION, MINGLE 1, MIX, MIXED, MIXED UP, MIX-UP, SCRAMBLE.

CONFUSED (kən fūzd′), *adj.* See CONFUSE.

CONFUSION (kən fū′ zhən), *n.* See CONFUSE.

CONGRATULATE 1 (kən grăch′ ə lāt′), *v.,* -LATED, -LATING. (Good words coming from the mouth; clapping hands.) The fingertips of the right hand, palm flat and facing the body, are brought up to the lips, so that they touch (part of the sign for GOOD, *q.v.*). The hands are then clapped together several times. *Cf.* APPLAUD, APPLAUSE, COMMEND, CONGRATULATIONS 1, PRAISE.

CONGRATULATE 2, *v.* (Shaking the clasped hands in triumph.) The hands are clasped together in front of the face and are shaken vigorously back and forth. The signer smiles. *Cf.* CONGRATULATIONS 2.

CONGRATULATIONS 1 (kən grăch′ ə lă′ shənz), *n. pl.* See CONGRATULATE 1.

CONGRATULATIONS 2, *n. pl.* See CONGRATULATE 2.

CONNECT (kə nĕkt´), *v.*, -NECTED, -NECTING. (Joining together.) Both hands, held in the modified "5" position, palms out, move toward each other. The thumbs and index fingers of both hands then connect. *Cf.* AFFILIATE, ANNEX, ATTACH, BELONG, ENLIST, ENROLL, JOIN, PARTICIPATE, UNITE.

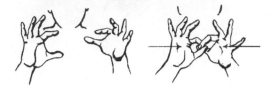

CONNECTION (kə nĕk´ shən), *n.* (The fingers are connected.) The index fingers and thumbs of both hands interlock, and the hands move back and forth from right to left. *Cf.* RELATIONSHIP.

CONQUER (kŏng´ kər), *v.*, -QUERED, -QUERING. (Forcing the head into a bowed position.) The right "S" hand, placed across the left "S" hand, moves over and down a bit. *Cf.* BEAT 2, DEFEAT, OVERCOME, SUBDUE.

CONQUERED *adj.* (The head is forced into a bowed position.) The right "S" hand, palm up, is placed under and across the left "S" hand, whose palm faces down. The right "S" hand moves up and over, toward the body. This sign is used as the passive voice of the verb CONQUER. *Cf.* BEATEN.

CONSCIENCE (kŏn´ shəns), *n.* (A guilty heart.) The side of the right "G" hand strikes against the heart several times.

CONSCIOUS (kŏn´ shəs), *adj.* (Indicating the mind.) The fingertips of the open right hand are placed against the forehead. *Cf.* KNOWING.

CONSENSUS (kən sen´ səs), *n.* (Of the same mind all around.) The sign for AGREE is made: the index finger of the right hand touches the forehead and then both index fingers come together side by side, palms down. Both "Y" hands, palms down, then simultaneously describe a counterclockwise circle.

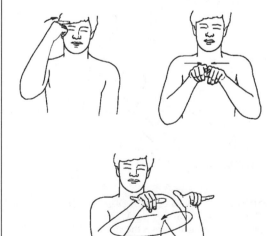

CONSENT (kən sĕnt´), *n., v.,* -SENTED, -SENTING. (Agreement; of the same mind; thinking the same way.) The index finger of the right "D" hand, palm back, touches the forehead (the modified sign for THINK), and then the two index fingers, both in the "D" position, palm down, are brought together so they are side by side, pointing away from the body (the sign for SAME). *Cf.* AGREE.

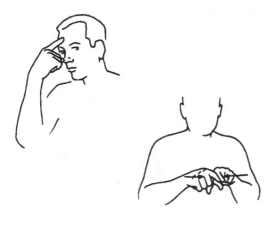

CONSIDER 1 (kən sĭd´ ər), *v.,* -ERED, -ERING. (A thought is turned over in the mind.) The index finger makes a small circle on the forehead. *Cf.* MOTIVE 1, RECKON, SPECULATE 1, SPECULATION 1, THINK, THOUGHT 1, THOUGHTFUL.

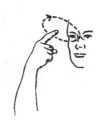

CONSIDER 2, *v.* (Turning thoughts over in the mind.) Both index fingers, pointing to the forehead, describe continuous alternating circles. *Cf.* CONTEMPLATE, PONDER, SPECULATE 2, SPECULATION 2, WEIGHT 2, WONDER 1.

CONSIDER 3, *v.* (The scales move up and down.) The two "F" hands, palms facing each other, move alternately up and down. *Cf.* COURT, EVALUATE 1, IF, JUDGE, JUDGMENT, JUSTICE.

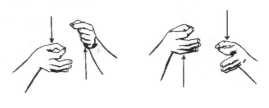

CONSISTENT (kən sĭs´ tənt), *adj.* (Coming together with regular frequency.) Both "D" hands are held with index fingers pointing forward, the right hand above the left. The right "D" hand is brought down on the left several times in rhythmic succession. *Cf.* FAITHFUL, REGULAR.

CONSTELLATION (kon stə lā´ shən), *n.* (Stars in the sky.) The sign for STARS is made: both index fingers, held together and pointing up, move up alternately. The open right hand, palm facing out, then sweeps up and across the sky.

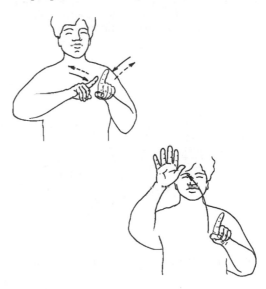

CONSTITUTION (kŏn′ stə tū′ shən, -tōō′-), *n.* (The letter "C.") The right "C" hand moves downward along the left palm, in two stages, from fingertips to wrist.

CONSTRUCT 1 (kən strŭkt′), *v.,* -STRUCTED, -STRUCT-ING. (Piling bricks one on top of another.) The down-turned hands are placed repeatedly atop each other. Each time this is done the arms rise a bit, to indicate the raising of a building. *Cf.* BUILD, CONSTRUCTION.

CONSTRUCT 2, *v.* (Fashioning something with the hands.) The right "S" hand, palm facing left, is placed on top of its left counterpart, whose palm faces right. The hands are twisted back and forth, striking each other slightly after each twist. *Cf.* CRE-ATE 1, DEVISE, MAKE, MANUFACTURE, MEND, PRODUCE 2, REPAIR.

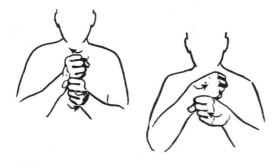

CONSTRUCTION (kən strŭk′ shən), *n.* See CON-STRUCT 1.

CONSUME 1 (kən sōōm′), *v.,* -SUMED, -SUMING. (The natural sign.) The closed right hand goes through the natural motion of placing food in the mouth. This movement is repeated. *Cf.* CONSUMPTION, EAT, FEED 1, FOOD, MEAL.

CONSUME 2, *v.* (To use; the letter "U") The right "U" hand describes a small clockwise circle. *Cf.* USE, USED, USEFUL, UTILIZE, WEAR 2.

CONSUMER 1 (kən sōō′ mər), *n.* (One who buys.) The sign for BUY is made: the upturned right hand, grasping imaginary dollar bills, is positioned in the upturned left palm. The hand moves forward in a small arc, opening up as it does. The sign for INDI-VIDUAL 1 then follows.

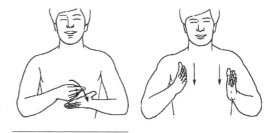

CONSUMER 2, *n.* (One who uses.) The sign for USE is made: the letter "U" describes a small clockwise circle. The sign for INDIVIDUAL 1 then follows.

CONSUMPTION (kən sŭmp´ shən), *n.* See CONSUME 1.

CONTACT 1 (kŏn´ tăkt), *n., v.,* -TACTED, -TACTING. (The natural movement of touching.) The tip of the middle finger of the downturned right "S" hand touches the back of the left hand a number of times. *Cf.* FEEL 1, TOUCH.

CONTACT 2, *v.* (A pinning down.) The left "D" finger represents the one who is caught. The curved index and middle fingers of the right hand, palm facing down, are thrust against the left "D" finger, impaling it. *Cf.* CAUGHT IN THE ACT 1, CORNER 2.

CONTACT LENSES (kon´ takt lenz´ ez), *n.* (Inserting the lens.) Leaning over the upturned index or middle finger, the signer mimes placing a contact lens in the eye.

CONTEMPLATE (kŏn´ təm plāt´, kən tĕm´ plāt), *v.,* -PLATED, -PLATING. (Turning thoughts over in the mind.) Both index fingers, pointing to the forehead, describe continuous alternating circles. *Cf.* CONSIDER 2, PONDER, SPECULATE 2, SPECULATION 2, WEIGH 2, WONDER 1.

CONTEMPT (kən tĕmpt´), *n.* (The gaze is cast downward.) Both "V" hands, side by side and palms facing out, are swept downward so that the fingertips now point down. A haughty expression, or one of mild contempt, is sometimes assumed. *Cf.* LOOK DOWN, SCORN.

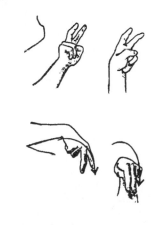

CONTENT (kən tĕnt´), *adj.* (The inner feelings settle down.) Both "B" hands (or "5" hands, fingers together) are placed palms down against the chest, the right above the left. Both move down simultaneously a few inches. *Cf.* CONTENTED, GRATIFY 2, SATISFACTION, SATISFIED, SATISFY 1.

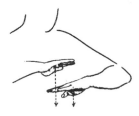

CONTENTED (kən tĕn´ tĭd), *adj.* See CONTENT.

CONTINUE (kən tĭn´ ū), *v.*, -TINUED, -TINUING. (Steady, uninterrupted movement.) The "A" hands are held with palms out, thumbs extended and touching, the right behind the left. In this position the hands move forward in a straight, steady line. *Cf.* ENDURE 2, EVER 1, LAST 3, LASTING, PERMANENT, PERPETUAL, PERSEVERE 3, PERSIST 2, REMAIN, STAY 1, STAY STILL.

CONTRAST (*n.* kŏn´ trăst; *v.* kən trăst´), -TRASTED, -TRASTING. (Separateness.) The tips of the extended index fingers touch before the chest, the right finger pointing left and the left finger pointing right. The fingers then draw apart sharply to either side. *Cf.* OPPOSITE, REVERSE.

CONTRIBUTE (kən trĭb´ ūt), *v.*, -UTED, -UTING. (A giving of something.) Both "A" hands, with index fingers somewhat draped over the tips of the thumbs, are held palms facing in front of the chest. They are pivoted forward and down, in unison, from the wrists. *Cf.* AWARD, GIFT, PRESENT 2.

CONTRITION (kən trish´ ən), *n.* (The heart is circled, to indicate feeling, modified by the letter "S," for SORRY.) The right "S" hand, palm facing the body,

is rotated several times over the area of the heart. *Cf.* APOLOGIZE 1, APOLOGY 1, PENITENT, REGRET, REGRETFUL, REPENT, REPENTANT, RUE, SORROW, SORROWFUL 2, SORRY.

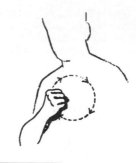

CONTROL 1 (kən trōl´), *v.*, -TROLLED, -TROLLING. (Holding the reins over all.) The "A" hands, palms facing, move alternately back and forth, as if grasping and manipulating reins. The left "A" hand, still in position, swings over so that its palm now faces down. The right hand opens to the "5" position, palm down, and swings over the left which moves slightly to the right. *Cf.* DIRECT 1, GOVERN, MANAGE, MANAGEMENT, MANAGER, OPERATE, REGULATE, REIGN, RULE 1.

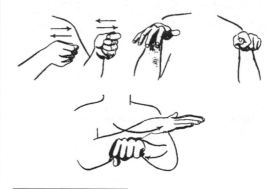

CONTROL 2, *n., v.* (Keeping the feelings down.) The curved fingertips of both hands are placed against the chest. The hands slowly move down as the fingers close into the "S" position. One hand only may also be used. *Cf.* SUPPRESS FEELINGS.

CONTROVERSY (kŏn´ trə vûr´ sĭ), *n.* (An expounding back and forth.) The index fingers here represent the two sides of the argument. First the left index finger is slapped into the open right palm, and then the right makes the same movement into the left palm. This is repeated back and forth several times. *Cf.* ARGUE, ARGUMENT, DEBATE, DISPUTE.

CONVENE (kən vĕn´), *v.,* -VENED, -VENING. (Assemble all together.) Both "5" hands, palms facing, are held with fingers pointing out from the body. With a sweeping motion they are brought in toward the chest, and all fingertips come together. This is repeated. *Cf.* ASSEMBLE 1, ASSEMBLY, CONFERENCE, CONVENTION, GATHER 2, GATHERING, MEETING 1.

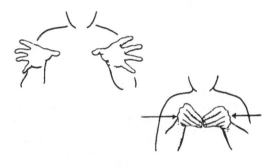

CONVENTION (kən vĕn´ shən), *n.* See CONVENE.

CONVENTIONAL (kən ven´ shən əl), *adj.* (Bound down by custom or habit.) Both "Y" hands are held side by side. They move in a continuous counterclockwise direction.

CONVERSATION 1 (kŏn´ vər sā´ shən), *n.* (Movement forward from, and back to, the mouth.) The tips of both index fingers, held pointing up, move alternately forward from, and back to, the lips. *Cf.* CONVERSE, TALK 3.

CONVERSATION 2, *n.* (Words tossed back and forth.) The open hands are held side by side with palms up, fingers pointing forward and slightly curved. In this position the hands swing back and forth from side to side before the chest. *Cf.* CHAT 1.

CONVERSE (kən vûrs´), *v.,* -VERSED, -VERSING. See CONVERSATION 1.

CONVERT (kən vûrt´), *v.,* -VERTED, -VERTING. (To change positions.) Both "A" hands, thumbs up, are held before the chest, several inches apart. The left hand is pivoted over so that its thumb points to the right. Simultaneously, the right hand is moved up and over the left, describing a small arc, with its thumb pointing to the left. *Cf.* CHANGE 1, MODIFY.

CONVICTION (kən vĭk´ shən), *n.* (A thought clasped onto.) The index finger touches the middle of the forehead (where the thought lies), and then both hands are clasped together. *Cf.* BELIEF, BELIEVE.

CONVINCE (kən vins´), *v.* (The karate chop to the neck wins the prize, *i.e.,* convinces the victim.) One or both upturned open hands mimes a karate chop.

COOK (kŏŏk), *n., v.,* COOKED, COOKING. (Turning over a pancake.)The open right hand rests on the upturned left palm. The right hand flips over and comes to rest with its back on the left palm. This is the action of turning over a pancake. The sign for INDIVIDUAL, for a noun, then follows: both open hands, palms facing each other, move down the sides of the body, tracing its outline to the hips. *Cf.* KITCHEN 1, PANCAKE.

COOKIE (kŏŏk´ ĭ), *n.* (Act of cutting cookies with a cookie mold.) The right hand, in the "C" position, palm down, is placed into the open left palm. It then rises a bit, swings or twists around a little, and in this new position is placed again in the open left palm.

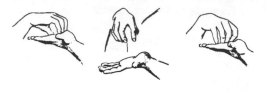

COOL (kŏŏl), *adj., v.,* COOLED, COOLING. (Fanning the face.) Both open hands are held with palms down and fingers spread and pointing toward the face. The hands move up and down as if fanning the face.

COOPERATE (kō ŏp´ ə rāt´), *v.,* -ATED, -ATING. (Joining in movement.) Both "D" hands, thumbs and index fingers interlocked, rotate in a counterclockwise circle in front of the body.

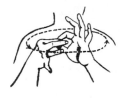

COP (kŏp), *(colloq.), n.* (The letter "C" for "cop"; the shape and position of the badge.) The right "C" hand, palm facing left, is placed against the heart. *Cf.* POLICE, POLICEMAN.

COPULATE (kŏp´ yə lāt´), *v.*, -LATED, -LATING. (The motions of the legs during the sexual act.) The upturned left "V" hand remains motionless, while the downturned right "V" hand comes down repeatedly on the left. *Cf.* FORNICATE, SEXUAL INTERCOURSE.

COPY (kŏp´ ĭ), *n., v.*, COPIED, COPYING. (The natural sign.) The right fingers and thumb close together and move onto the upturned, open left hand, as if taking something from one place to another. *Cf.* DUPLICATE, IMITATE, MIMIC, MODEL.

COPYRIGHT (kop´ ē rīt), *n., v.* (COPY and RIGHT.) The right fingers and thumb close together and move onto the upturned open left hand, as if taking something from one place to another. Next, the sign for RIGHT: the right hand, fingers together and palm facing left, is placed in the upturned left palm, whose fingers point away from the body. The right hand slides straight out along the left palm, over the left fingers, and stops with its heel resting on the left fingertips.

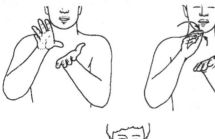

CORDIAL (kôr´ jəl), *adj.* (A crinkling-up of the face.) Both hands, in the "5" position, palms facing back, are placed on either side of the face. The fingers wiggle back and forth, while a pleasant, happy expression is worn. *Cf.* AMIABLE, CHEERFUL, FRIENDLY, JOLLY, PLEASANT.

CORN (kôrn), *n.* (Scraping kernels from the corncob.) The extended left index finger points forward, representing the corncob, while the right thumb and index finger rub back and forth along the finger, as if scraping off kernels.

CORNER 1 (kôr´ nər), *n.* (The natural sign.) Both hands, palms flat and fingers straight, are held in front of the body at right angles to each other with fingertips touching, the left fingertips pointing to the right and the right fingertips pointing forward.

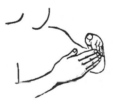

CORNER 2, *v.*, -NERED, -NERING. (A pinning down.) The left "D" finger represents the one who is caught. The curved index and middle fingers of the right hand, palm facing down, are thrust against the left "D" finger, impaling it. *Cf.* CAUGHT IN THE ACT 1, CONTACT 2.

CORN-ON-THE-COB (kôrn, kŏb), *n.* (Act of eating an ear of corn.) The index fingers, touching each other, are brought up against the teeth. Both hands are pivoted around and back several times. One index finger may also be used, instead of two.

CORRECT 1 (kə rĕkt´), *adj.* The right index finger, held above the left index finger, comes down rather forcefully so that the bottom of the right hand comes to rest on top of the left thumb joint. *Cf.* ACCURATE, DECENT, EXACT 2, PROPER, RIGHT 3, SUITABLE.

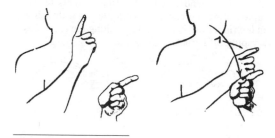

CORRECT 2, *v.*, -RECTED, -RECTING. (A canceling out.) The right index finger makes a cross on the open left palm. *Cf.* CANCEL, CRITICISM, CRITICIZE, FIND FAULT.

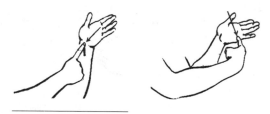

CORRELATION (kôr ə lā´ shən), *n.* (Connection.) The indexes and thumbs of both hands form a link together. Both hands move repeatedly left to right and back.

CORRESPOND (kŏr´ ə spŏnd´), *v.*, -PONDED, -POND-ING. The "AND" hands face each other, one slightly higher than the other. The two hands then move toward and past each other, opening as they do.

CORRIDOR (kôr´ ə dər, kŏr´-), *n.* (The movement.) Both hands, palms facing and fingers together and extended straight out, move in unison away from the body, in a straight or winding manner. *Cf.* HALL, HALLWAY, MANNER 2, METHOD, OPPORTUNITY 3, PATH, ROAD, STREET, TRAIL, WAY 1.

COSMETICS (kŏz mĕt´ ĭks), *n. pl.* (Applying something to the face.) The thumbtip and fingertips of each hand are held together and rotated in small counterclockwise circles on both cheeks simultaneously. *Cf.* MAKE-UP.

COST (kôst, kŏst), *n.*, *v.*, COST, COSTING. (Nicking into one.) The knuckle of the right "X" finger is nicked against the palm of the left hand, held in the "5" position, palm facing right. *Cf.* CHARGE, EXPENSE, FEE, FINE 2, PENALTY, PRICE 2, TAX 1, TAXATION 1, TOLL.

COSTA RICA (kos′ tə rē kə) *n.* (The shape of the North American and South American continents with Panama in between.) The tips of the right "C" hand, palm facing left, rest on the thumb of the left "C" hand, palm facing right. Alternatively, the modified "C" hands may be used, with only thumbs and index fingers forming the "C." In this case, the right index rests on the left thumb. A native sign.

COSTLY (kôst′ lĭ), *adj.* (Throwing away money.) The right "AND" hand lies in the palm of the upturned, open left hand (as if holding money). The right hand then moves up and away from the left, opening abruptly as it does (as if dropping the money it holds). *Cf.* EXPENSIVE.

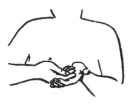

COSTUME (kos′ tōōm), *n.* (The letter "C"; slipping clothes on.) Both "C" hands, palms facing, move down the chest simultaneously. The movement is repeated.

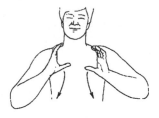

COTTON (kot′ n), *n.* (Picking cotton.) The left hand is held with extended thumb touching fingertips. The right hand closes over the left and pulls away, as if plucking cotton from the plant.

COUGH (kôf), *n.*, *v.* The right claw hand is held with fingertips on the chest. The fingertips alternately open and bend as the signer mimes coughing.

COULD (kŏŏd), *v.* (An affirmative movement of the hands, likened to a nodding of the head, to indicate ability or power to accomplish something.) Both "A" hands, held palms down, move down in unison a short distance before the chest. *Cf.* ABILITY, ABLE, CAN, CAPABLE, COMPETENT, MAY 2, POSSIBLE.

COUNSEL (koun´ səl), *n., v.,* -SELED, -SELING. (Take something, *counsel,* and disseminate it.) The left hand, held limp in front of the body, has its fingers pointing down. The fingers of the right hand, held all together, are placed on top of the left hand, and then move forward, off the left hand, assuming a "5" position, palm down. This may be repeated. *Cf.* ADVICE, ADVISE, COUNSELOR, INFLUENCE 3.

COUNSELOR (koun´ sə lər), *n.* The sign for COUNSEL is made. This is followed by the sign for INDIVIDUAL: both open hands, palms facing each other, move down the sides of the body, tracing its outline to the hips.

COUNT (kount), *v.,* COUNTED, COUNTING. The thumbtip and index fingertip of the right "F" hand move up along the palm of the open left hand, which is held facing right with fingers pointing up.

COUNTRY 1 (kun´ trĭ), *n.* (The elbow reinforcement on the jacket of a "country squire" type; also, a place where one commonly "roughs it," *i.e.,* gets rough elbows.) The open right hand describes a continuous counterclockwise circle on the left elbow.

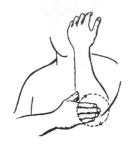

COUNTRY 2, *n.* (An established area.) The right "N" hand, palm down, executes a clockwise circle above the downturned prone left hand. The tips of the "N" fingers then move straight down and come to rest on the back of the left hand. *Cf.* LAND 2, NATION, REPUBLIC.

COURAGE (kûr´ ĭj, kŭr´-), *n.* (Strength emanating from the body.) Both "5" hands are placed palms against the chest. They move out and away, forcefully, closing and assuming the "S" position. *Cf.* BRAVE, BRAVERY, COURAGEOUS, FORTITUDE, HALE, HEALTH, HEALTHY, MIGHTY 2, STRENGTH, STRONG 2, WELL 2.

COURAGEOUS (kə rā´ jəs), *adj.* See COURAGE.

COURT (kôrt), *n.* (The scales move up and down.) The two "F" hands, palms facing each other, move alternately up and down. *Cf.* CONSIDER 3, EVALUATE 1, IF, JUDGE 1, JUDGMENT, JUSTICE.

COURTEOUS (kûr´ ti əs), *adj.* (The ruffled shirt front of a gentleman of old.) The thumb of the right "5" hand is thrust into the chest. The hand then pivots down, with thumb remaining in place. This latter part of the sign, however, is optional. *Cf.* COURTESY, FINE 4, POLITE.

COURTESY (kûr´ tə si), n. See COURTEOUS.

COUSIN 1 (kŭz´ ən), *(f.)*, *n.* (The letter "C" in female position.) The right "C" hand is shaken back and forth next to the right cheek.

COUSIN 2 *(m.)*, *n.* (The letter "C" in male position.) The right "C" hand is shaken back and forth next to the right temple.

COVER 1 (kŭv´ ər), *n., v.,* -ERED, -ERING. (The natural sign.) This sign is used to mean "to cover up something." The right hand, held curved and palm down, slides from fingertips to wrist over the back of the left hand, which is also held curved and palm down.

COVER 2, *n.* (The natural sign.) This sign is used to mean "to place a cover on." The open right hand, held palm down before the chest, moves downward, coming to rest atop the upturned thumb edge of the left "S" hand, as if to cover it.

COVER 3, *v.* (One hand is hidden under the other.) This sign is used to mean "to hide." The thumb of the right "A" hand, whose palm faces left, is placed against the lips. The hand then swings down and under the downturned left hand. The initial contact with the lips is sometimes omitted. *Cf.* HIDE.

COVER 4, *n. v.* (The natural motion.) The signer lifts an imaginary cover and pulls it up over his body.

COW (kou), *n.* (The cow's horns.) The "Y" hands, palms facing away from the body, are placed at the temples, with thumbs touching the head. Both hands are brought out and away simultaneously, in a gentle curve.

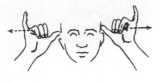

COWBOY 1 (kou′ boi), *n.* (The pistols.) Using both "L" hands, the signer waves them forward and back repeatedly.

COWBOY 2, *n.* (Twirling a lariat.) The signer twirls an imaginary lariat and pulls back. For added effect, the body may bounce up and down slightly, as if on horseback. *Cf.* LARIAT, LASSO.

CRAB 1 (krab), *n.* (The claws.) The indexes and thumbs open and close repeatedly.

CRAB 2, *n.* A variant of CRAB 1. The upturned "V" fingers open and close repeatedly.

CRACKER (krăk′ ər), *n.* The thumb edge of the right fist strikes several times against the left elbow, while the left arm is bent so that the left fist is held against the right shoulder.

CRASH (krăsh), *n.*, *v.*, CRASHED, CRASHING. The fists come together with force. *Cf.* COLLIDE, COLLISION.

CRAVE (krāv), *v.*, CRAVED, CRAVING. (The upper alimentary tract is outlined.) The right "C" hand, palm facing the body, is placed with fingertips touching mid-chest. In this position it moves down a bit. *Cf.* APPETITE, DESIRE 2, STARVATION, STARVE, STARVED, WISH 2.

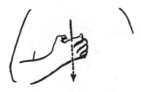

CRAYON (krā′ ən), *n.* (Color and writing.) The sign for COLOR is made: the fingertips of the right "5" hand, palm facing the body, are placed on or just in front of the chin and wiggle back and forth. This is followed by the sign for WRITE: the right hand, holding an imaginary writing implement, "writes" on the palm of the upturned left hand.

CRAZY 1 (krā′ zĭ), *adj.* (Turning of wheels in the head.) The open right hand is held palm down before the face, fingers spread, bent, and pointing toward the forehead. The fingers move in circles before the forehead. *Cf.* INSANE, INSANITY.

CRAZY 2, *adj.* (Turning of wheels in the head.) The right index finger revolves in a clockwise circle at the right temple.

CRAZY FOR *phrase.* (Kissing something to indicate a liking for it.) The back of the fist is kissed.

CRAZY FOR/ABOUT *phrase.* (Something that makes you dizzy.) The right claw hand, facing the signer, shakes from right to left repeatedly. The mouth is usually held open.

CREAM (krēm), *n.* (The motion of "skimming" cream.) The right hand is held slightly cupped and is moved repeatedly across the upturned, open left palm, as if skimming cream from the top of a container of milk.

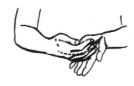

CREATE 1 (krē āt′), *v.,* CREATED, CREATING. (Fashioning something with the hands.) The right "S" hand, palm facing left, is placed on top of its left counterpart, whose palm faces right. The hands are twisted back and forth, striking each other slightly after each twist. *Cf.* CONSTRUCT 2, DEVISE, MAKE, MANUFACTURE, MEND, PRODUCE 2, REPAIR.

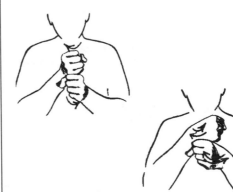

CREATE 2, *v.* (Something springs from the mind, and then the hands go to work to make it.) The right "4" hand, palm facing left, moves up the forehead. The right hand changes to the "S" position, palm facing left, and is placed on top of its left counterpart,whose palm faces right. The hands are twisted back and forth, striking each other slightly after each twist.

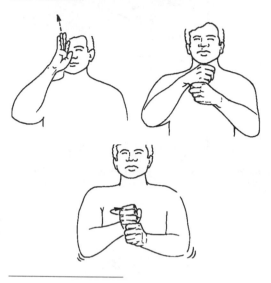

CREDIBLE (krĕd' ə bəl), *adj.* (Fall for something, *i.e.,* swallowing the bait.) The right-angle hand is brought up toward the open mouth.

CREDIT CARD (kred' it kard), *n.* (The credit card machine is used to make an impression on the sales slip.) The left hand is held palm up. The right hand, closed in a fist, is placed with the edge of the little finger on the left palm. The right hand moves back and forth.

CRIB (krib), *n.* (An interlaced support.) The upturned hands are held with fingers interlocked. They separate and move up, forming a cradle or crib.

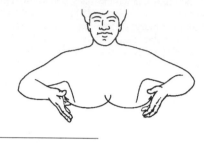

CRICKET (krik' it), *n.* (The natural sign.) The signer mimes swinging a cricket bat.

CRIPPLE (krĭp' əl), *n., v.,* -PLED, -PLING. (The uneven movement of the legs.) The downturned index fingers move alternately up and down. The body sways to and fro a little, keeping time with the movement of the fingers.

CRITICISM (krĭt' ə sĭz' əm), *n.* (A canceling out.) The right index finger makes a cross on the open left palm. *Cf.* CANCEL, CORRECT 2, CRITICIZE, FIND FAULT.

CRITICIZE (krĭt′ ə sīz′), *v.*, -CIZED, -CIZING. See CRITI-CISM.

CROOK (kro͝ok), *n.* (A mustachioed thief.) The fingertips of both "H" hands, palms facing the body, are placed above the lips and are drawn slowly apart, describing a mustache. Sometimes one hand only is used. This is followed by the sign for INDIVIDUAL: both open hands, palms facing each other, move down the sides of the body, tracing its outline to the hips. *Cf.* BANDIT, BURGLAR, BURGLARY, ROB 3, ROBBER, ROBBERY 1, THEFT 3, THIEF 2.

CROSS 1 (krôs), *adj.* (Wrinkling the brow.) The "5" hand is held palm toward the face. The fingers open and close partly, several times, while an angry expression is worn on the face. *Cf.* ANGRY 1, CROSS-NESS, FIERCE, ILL TEMPER, IRRITABLE.

CROSS 2, (*eccles.*), *n.* (The cross on the mountain.) The back of the right "S" hand is struck several times against the back of the left "S" hand to denote something hard, like a ROCK or a MOUNTAIN, *q.v.* The right "C" hand, palm facing out, makes the sign of the cross. *Cf.* CRUCIFIX.

CROSS 3, *v.*, CROSSED, CROSSING. (A crossing over.) The left hand is held before the chest, palm down and fingers together. The right hand, fingers together, glides over the left, with the right little finger touching the top of the left hand. *Cf.* ACROSS, OVER.

CROSS 4, *v.* (Intersecting lines.) The extended index fingers move toward each other at right angles and cross. *Cf.* CROSSING, INTERSECT, INTERSECTION.

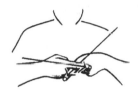

CROSS-COUNTRY SKIING *n.* (The natural movement.) Using a swinging rhythm, the signer takes long sliding strides as the ski poles maneuver back and forth.

CROSSING (krôs′ ĭng), *n.* See CROSS 4.

CROSSNESS *n.* See CROSS 1.

CROWD (kroud), *n.* (Many people spread out.) The downturned claw hands move straight forward. *Cf.* MOB.

CROWDED *adj.* (Squeezed in.) The "5" hands are held about a foot apart in front of the body, fingers pointing forward. The hands are slowly pushed toward each other without touching, as if compressing something into a smaller space. The signer assumes a strained expression.

CROWN (kroun), *n.* (The natural sign.) Both "C" hands, held in a modified position, with middle, ring, and little fingers extended and little finger edges down, are held over the head and slowly lowered, as if placing a crown on the head.

CRUCIFIX (krōō sə fĭks´), *n.* See CROSS 2.

CRUEL 1 (krōō´ əl), *adj.* (Striking down against.) Both "A" or "X" hands are held before the chest, the right above the left. The right hand strikes down and out, hitting the left thumb and knuckles with force. *Cf.* HARM 2, HURT 2, MEAN 1.

CRUEL 2, *adj.* The movements in TEASE 1, *q.v.*, are duplicated, except that the "G" hands are used. *Cf.* TEASE 3.

CRUSH (krush), *v.* (Pressing together.) The heels of both open hands are pressed forcefully together, and the right hand pivots to the right.

CRY (krī), *v.*, CRIED, CRYING. (Tears streaming down the cheeks.) Both index fingers, in the "D" position, move down the cheeks, either once or several times. Sometimes one finger only is used. *Cf.* BAWL 1, TEAR 2, TEARDROP, WEEP.

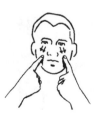

CUBA (kyōō′ bə) *n.* (The cap worn by the militia.) The back of the right open hand is placed against the forehead. A native sign.

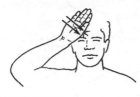

CUP (kŭp), *n.* (The natural sign.) The little finger edge of the right "C" hand rests on the palm of the upturned, open left hand. *Cf.* CUP AND SAUCER.

CUP AND SAUCER (kŭp, sô′ sər), *n. phrase.* See CUP.

CUPBOARD (kub′ ərd), *n.* (Grasping the handles.) The signer mimes opening a pair of cabinet doors by grasping the handles. *Cf.* CABINET 2.

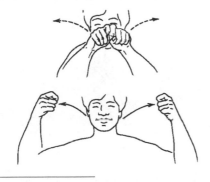

CURAÇAO (kyōōr′ ə sō′), *n.* The right "C" hand, palm facing out and held at chest level, moves to the right and then down a few inches. A native sign.

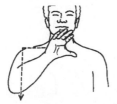

CURIOSITY (kyōōr′ ĭ ŏs′ ə tĭ), *n.* See CURIOUS 3.

CURIOUS 1 (kyōōr′ ĭ əs), *adj.* (Directing the vision from placc to place.) The right "C" hand, palm facing left, moves from right to left across the line of vision, in a series of counterclockwise circles. The signer's gaze remains concentrated and his head turns slowly from right to left. *Cf.* EXAMINE, INVESTIGATE, LOOK FOR, PROBE, SEARCH, SEEK.

CURIOUS 2, *adj.* (Something which distorts the vision.) The "C" hand describes a small arc in front of the face. *Cf.* GROTESQUE, ODD, PECULIAR, QUEER, STRANGE, WEIRD.

CURIOUS 3, *(colloq.), adj.* (The Adam's apple.) The right thumb and index finger pinch the skin over the Adam's apple, while the hand wiggles up and down. *Cf.* CURIOSITY.

CURSE 1 (kûrs), *n., v.,* CURSED, CURSING. (Harsh words and a threatening hand.) The right hand appears to claw words out of the mouth. It ends in the "S" position, above the head, shaking back and forth in a threatening manner. *Cf.* SWEAR 2.

CURSE 2, *n., v.* (Harsh words thrown out.) The right hand, as in CURSE 1, appears to claw words out of the mouth. This time, however, it turns and throws them out, ending in the "5" position. *Cf.* SCREAM, SHOUT.

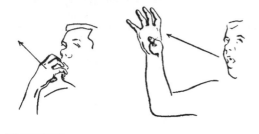

CURSE 3 *(sl.), n., v.* (Curlicues, as one finds in cartoon-type swear words.) The right "Y" hand, palm down, pivots at the wrist along the left "G" hand, from the wrist to the tip of the finger. *Cf.* SWEAR 3.

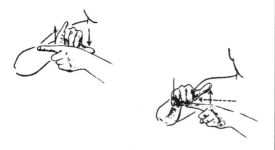

CUSTOM (kŭs´ təm), *n.* (Bound down to custom or habit.) Both "S" hands, palms down, are crossed and brought down in unison before the chest. *Cf.* ACCUSTOM, BOUND, HABIT, LOCKED, PRACTICE 3.

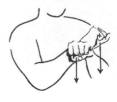

CUT (kŭt), *v.,* CUT, CUTTING. (Cutting the finger with a knife.) The extended right index finger makes a cutting motion across the extended left index finger. Both hands are held palms down.

CUTE 1 (kūt), *adj.* (Titillating to the taste.) The fingertips of the right "U" hand, palm facing the body, brush against the chin a number of times, beginning at the lips. *Cf.* CANDY 1, SUGAR, SWEET.

CUTE 2, *adj.* (Tickling.) The open right hand is held with fingers spread and pointing up, palm facing the chest. In this position the fingertips wiggle up and down, tickling the chin several times.

CYNIC (sĭn′ ĭk), *n*. (The nose is wrinkled in disbelief.) The right "V" hand faces the nose. The index and middle fingers bend as a cynical expression is assumed. This is followed by the sign for INDIVIDUAL: both open hands, palms facing each other, move down the sides of the body, tracing its outline to the hips. *Cf.* CYNICAL, DISBELIEF 1, DON'T BELIEVE, DOUBT 1, INCREDULITY, SKEPTIC 1, SKEPTICAL 1.

CYNICAL (sĭn′ ə kəl), *adj*. See CYNIC. The sign for INDIVIDUAL is omitted.

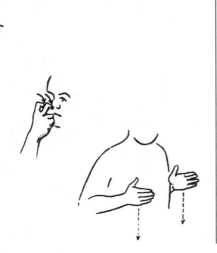

D

DACTYLOLOGY (dăk´ tə lŏl´ ə jĭ), *n.* (The movement of the fingers in fingerspelling.) The right hand, palm out, is moved from left to right, with the fingers wriggling up and down. *Cf.* ALPHABET 1, FINGERSPELLING, MANUAL ALPHABET, SPELL, SPELLING.

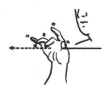

DAD (dăd), (*informal*), *n.* (Derived from the formal sign for FATHER 1, *q.v.* The thumbtip of the right "5" hand touches the right temple a number of times. The other fingers may also wiggle. *Cf.* DADDY, FATHER 2, PAPA, POP 2.

DADDY (dăd´ ĭ), *n.* See DAD.

DAILY (dā´ lĭ), *adj.* (Tomorrow after tomorrow.) The sign for TOMORROW, *q.v.*, is made several times: the right "A" hand moves forward several times from its initial resting place on the right cheek. *Cf.* EVERYDAY.

DAMN! (dam), *interj.* The right "D" hand, palm facing down, is moved forcefully to the right. An expression of annoyance or disapproval is assumed. *Cf.* DARN!

DAMP (dămp), *adj.* (The wetness.) The right fingertips touch the lips, and then the fingers of both hands open and close against the thumbs a number of times. *Cf.* MOIST, WET.

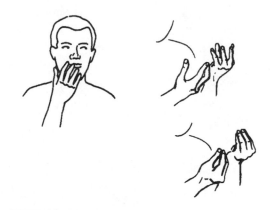

DANCE (dăns, däns), *n., v.,* DANCED, DANCING. (The rhythmic swaying of the feet.) The downturned index and middle fingers of the right "V" hand swing rhythmically back and forth over the upturned left palm. *Cf.* PARTY 2.

DANGER (dān' jər), *n.* (An encroachment; parrying a knife thrust.) The left "A" hand is held palm toward the body, knuckles facing right. The extended thumb of the right "A" hand is brought sharply over the back of the left. *Cf.* DANGEROUS, INJURE 2, PERIL, TRESPASS, VIOLATE.

DANGEROUS *adj.* See DANGER.

DARE (dâr), *n., v.* (The letter "D"; challenge or confront.) Both hands are held in the "D" position, facing each other. The right "D" hand is brought up sharply against the left, and both hands continue away from the body an inch or so.

DARK(NESS) (därk), *adj., n.* (Shutting out the light.) Both open hands are held in front of the face, the right palm over the right eye and the left palm over the left eye. The hands then move toward each other and slightly downward in a short arc, coming to rest one behind the other so that they hide the face.

DARN! (därn), *interj.* The right "D" hand, palm facing down, is moved forcefully to the right. An expression of annoyance or disapproval is assumed. *Cf.* DAMN!

DAUGHTER (dô' tər), *n.* (Female baby.) The FEMALE prefix sign is made: the thumb of the right "A" hand traces a line on the right jaw from just below the ear to the chin. The sign for BABY is then made: the right arm is folded on the left arm. Both palms face up.

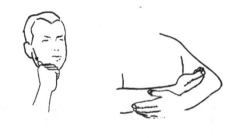

DAY (dā), *n., adj.* (The letter "D"; the course of the sun across the sky.) The left arm, held horizontally, palm down, represents the horizon. The right elbow rests on the back of the left hand, with the right arm in a perpendicular position. The right "D" hand, palm facing left, moves in an arc to the left until it is just above the left elbow.

DEAD (dĕd), *adj.* (Turning over on one's side.) The open hands, fingers pointing ahead, are held side by side, with the right palm down and the left palm up. The two hands reverse their relative positions as they move from the left to the right. *Cf.* DEATH, DIE.

DEAF 1, *adj.* (Deaf and mute.) The tip of the extended right index finger touches first the right ear and then the closed lips.

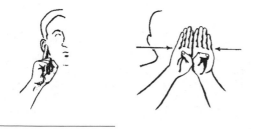

DEAF 2, *adj.* (The ear is shut.) The right index finger touches the right ear. Both "B" hands, palms out, then draw together until their index finger edges touch.

DEATH (dĕth), *n.* See DEAD.

DEBATE (dĭ bāt'), *n., v.,* -BATED, -BATING. (An expounding back and forth.) The index fingers here represent the two sides of the argument. First the left index finger is slapped into the open right palm, and then the right makes the same movement into the left palm. This is repeated back and forth several times. *Cf.* ARGUE, ARGUMENT, CONTROVERSY, DISPUTE.

DEBIT (dĕb' ĭt), *n.* (Pointing to the palm, where the money should be placed.) The index finger of one hand is thrust into the upturned palm of the other several times. *Cf.* ARREARS, DEBT, DUE, OBLIGATION 2, OWE.

DEBT (dĕt), *n.* See DEBIT.

DECAY (dĭ kā'), *v.,* -CAYED, -CAYING. (Fingering the small pieces resulting from the breaking up of something.) The thumbs rub slowly across the fingertips of the upturned hands, from the little fingers to the index fingers, and then continue to the "A" position, palms up. *Cf.* DIE OUT, DISSOLVE, FADE, MELT, ROT.

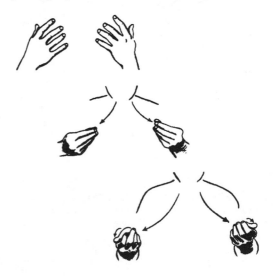

DECEIT (dǐ sēt'), *n.* (Underhandedness.) The right hand, palm down, is held with index and little fingers pointing out. The left hand, in a similar position, is held above the right. The right hand moves forward repeatedly, each time emerging briefly from under the left hand. The positions may be reversed, with the left hand doing the movement, or both hands can move simultaneously. *Cf.* CHEAT, DECEIVE, DECEPTION, DEFRAUD, FRAUD, FRAUDULENT.

DECEIVE (dǐ sēv'), *v.,* -CEIVED, -CEIVING. See DECEIT.

DECENT (dē' sənt), *adj.* The right index finger, held above the left index finger, comes down rather forcefully so that the bottom of the right hand comes to rest on top of the left thumb joint. *Cf.* ACCURATE, CORRECT 1, EXACT 2, PROPER, RIGHT 3, SUITABLE.

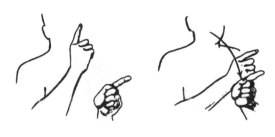

DECEPTION (dǐ sĕp' shən), *n.* See DECEIT.

DECIDE (dǐ sīd'), *v.,* -CIDED, -CIDING. (The mind stops wavering, and the pros and cons are resolved.) The right index finger touches the forehead, the sign for THINK, *q.v.* Both "F" hands, palms facing each other and fingers pointing straight out, then drop down simultaneously. The sign for JUDGE, *q.v.,* explains the rationale behind the movement of the

two hands here. *Cf.* DECISION, DETERMINE, MAKE UP ONE'S MIND, MIND 5, RESOLVE, VERDICT.

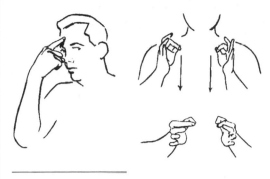

DECISION (dǐ sǐzh' ən), *n.* See DECIDE.

DECLARE (dǐ klâr'), *v.,* -CLARED, -CLARING. (An issuance from the mouth.) Both index fingers are placed at the lips, with palms facing the body. They are rotated once and swung out in arcs, until the left index finger points somewhat to the left and the right index somewhat to the right. Sometimes the rotation of the fingers is omitted in favor of a simple swinging out from the lips. *Cf.* ANNOUNCE, ANNOUNCEMENT.

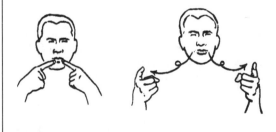

DECLINE (dǐ klīn'), *v.,* -CLINED, -CLINING. (Going down step by step.) The little finger edge of the open right hand is placed on the upper side of the extended left arm, which is held with the open left hand palm down. The right hand moves down along the left arm in a series of short movements. This is the opposite of IMPROVE, *q.v. Cf.* DETERIORATE, DETERIORATION.

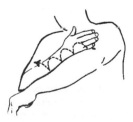

DECLINE IN HEALTH *phrase.* Both upturned thumbs move down in a series of stages.

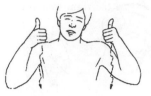

DECORATE 1 (dĕk′ ə rāt′), *v.,* -RATED, -RATING. (The hands describe the flounces of draperies.) Both "C" hands, palms out, are held somewhat above the head. They move out and down in a series of successive arcs.

DECORATE 2, *v.* (Embellishing; adding to.) Both "O" hands, palms facing each other, move alternately back and forth in a curving up and down direction. The fingertips come in contact each time the hands pass each other.

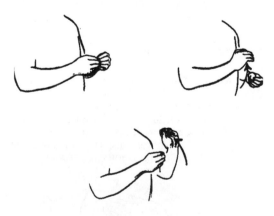

DECREASE (*n.* dē′ krēs; *v.* dĭ krēs′), -CREASED, -CREASING. (The diminishing size or amount.) With palms facing, the right hand is held above the left.

The right hand moves slowly down toward the left, but does not touch it. *Cf.* LESS, REDUCE.

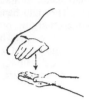

DEDUCT (dĭ dŭkt′), *v.,* -DUCTED, -DUCTING. (Removing.) The right "A" hand, resting in the palm of the left "5" hand, moves slightly up and away, describing a small arc. It is then cast downward, opening into the "5" position, palm down, as if removing something from the left hand and casting it down. *Cf.* ABOLISH, DELETE 1, ELIMINATE, REMOVE, SUBTRACT, SUBTRACTION, TAKE AWAY FROM.

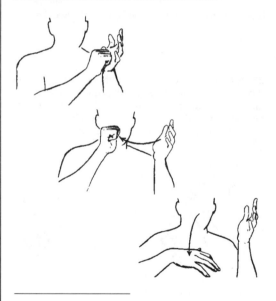

DEED (dēd), *n.* (An activity.) Both open hands, palms down, are swung right and left before the chest. *Cf.* ACT 2, ACTION, ACTIVE, ACTIVITY, CONDUCT 1, DO, PERFORM 1, PERFORMANCE 1.

DEEP (dēp), *adj.* (The "D" hand, movement downward.) The right "D" hand is held with index finger pointing down. In this position it moves down along the left palm, which is held facing right with fingertips pointing forward. *Cf.* DEPTH.

DEER (dĭr), *n.* (The branching of the antlers from the head.) Both hands, in the "5" position, palms up, are placed at the head, thumbs resting on the head above the temples. *Cf.* ANTLERS, ELK, MOOSE.

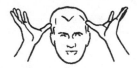

DEFEAT (dĭ fēt'), *v.,* -FEATED, -FEATING. (Forcing the head into a bowed position.) The right "S" hand, placed across the left "S" hand, moves over and down a bit. *Cf.* BEAT 2, CONQUER, OVERCOME, SUBDUE.

DEFEATED *adj.* (Overpowered by great strength.) The right "S" hand (a fist) is held with palm facing the right shoulder. In this position it moves back toward the shoulder, pivoting from the elbow. The left "S" hand, at the same time, is held palm down with knuckles facing right, and is positioned below the right hand and over the right biceps.

DEFECATE (dĕf' ə kāt'), *(sl., vulg.), v.,* -CATED, -CAT-ING. (The passing of fecal material.) The left hand grasps the upturned right thumb. The right hand drops down and the right thumb is exposed. *Cf.* FECES.

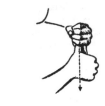

DEFEND (dĭ fĕnd'), *v.,* -FENDED, -FENDING. (Hold down firmly; cover and strengthen.) The "S" hands, downturned, are held side by side in front of the body, the arms almost horizontal, and the left hand in front of the right. Both arms move a short distance forward and slightly downward. *Cf.* DEFENSE, FORTI-FY, GUARD, PROTECT, PROTECTION, SHIELD 1.

DEFENDANT (di fen' dənt), *n.* (One who wards off or shields against.) Both downturned "S" hands, the right above the left, move out sharply a short distance. The sign for INDIVIDUAL 1 then follows.

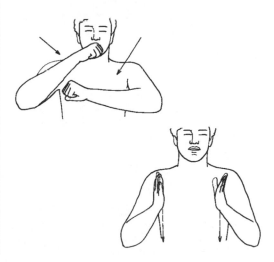

DEFENSE (dĭ fĕns'), *n.* See DEFEND.

DEFER (dĭ fûr'), *v.,* -FERRED, -FERRING. (Putting off; moving things forward repeatedly.) The "F" hands, palms facing and fingers pointing out from the body, are moved forward simultaneously in a series of short movements. *Cf.* DELAY, POSTPONE, PROCRASTINATE, PUT OFF.

DEFICIT (def' ə sit), *n.* (Something is lacking or missing.) The downturned left open hand is held with middle finger hanging down from the rest. The right index finger strikes the left middle finger several times, pushing it back each time toward the left palm, *i.e.,* causing it to be missing.

DEFINE 1 (dĭ fīn'), *v.,* -FINED, -FINING. (Unraveling something to get at its parts.) The "F" hands, palms facing and fingers pointing straight out, are held about an inch apart. They move alternately back and forth a few inches. *Cf.* DESCRIBE 1, DESCRIPTION, EXPLAIN 1.

DEFINE 2, *v.* This is the same sign as for DEFINE 1, except that the "D" hands are used.

DEFLATE (dĭ flāt'), *v.,* -FLATED, -FLATING. (A flattening.) The thumb of the right "C" hand rests on the back of the downturned left "B" hand. The fingers suddenly come down on the right thumb. *Cf.* DEFLATION.

DEFLATION (dĭ flā' shən), *n.* See DEFLATE.

DEFRAUD (dĭ frôd'), *v.,* -FRAUDED, -FRAUDING. (Underhandedness.) The right hand, palm down, is held with index and little fingers pointing out. The left hand, in a similar position, is held above the right. The right hand moves forward repeatedly, each time emerging briefly from under the left hand. The positions may be reversed, with the left hand doing the movement, or both hands can move simultaneously. *Cf.* CHEAT, DECEIT, DECEIVE, DECEPTION, FRAUD, FRAUDULENT.

DEGREE 1 (di grē'), *n.* (A unit of temperature.) The tip of the index finger of the right "D" hand travels up and down the upturned left index finger. *Cf.* TEMPERATURE 2.

DEGREE 2, *n.* (Drawing a percent symbol in the air.) The right "O" hand traces a percent symbol (%) in the air. *Cf.* PERCENT, RATE.

DEGREE 3, *n.* (The rolled up diploma.) With thumbs and index fingers forming circles, both hands, held together initially, separate, describing the shape of a rolled up diploma. *Cf.* DIPLOMA.

DEJECTED (dĭ jĕk' tĭd), *adj.* (The facial features drop.) Both "5" hands, palms facing the eyes and fingers slightly curved, drop simultaneously to a level with the mouth. The head drops slightly as the hands move down, and an expression of sadness is assumed. *Cf.* DEPRESSED 1, GLOOM, GLOOMY, GRAVE 2, GRIEF 1, MELANCHOLY, MOURNFUL, SAD, SORROWFUL 1

DELAY (dĭ lā'), *n., v.,* -LAYED, -LAYING. (Putting off; moving things forward repeatedly.) The "F" hands, palms facing and fingers pointing out from the body, are moved forward simultaneously in a series of short movements. *Cf.* DEFER, POSTPONE, PROCRASTINATE, PUT OFF.

DELEGATE (del' i git), *n.* (The shape of the ribbon hanging down from a delegate's badge.) The right thumb and index finger trace a ribbon hanging down over the chest. The movement is usually repeated.

DELETE 1 (dĭ lēt′), v., -LETED, -LETING. (Removing.) The right "A" hand, resting in the palm of the left "5" hand, moves slightly up and away, describing a small arc. It is then cast downward, opening into the "5" position, palm down, as if removing something from the left hand and casting it down. Cf. ABOLISH, DEDUCT, ELIMINATE, REMOVE, SUBTRACT, SUBTRACTION, TAKE AWAY FROM.

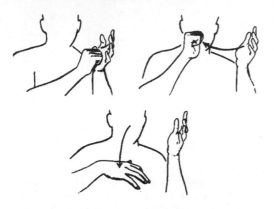

DELETE 2, v. (The printer flicks a piece of type out of the composing stick.) The thumb, positioned initially inside the closed hand, flicks out. The hand moves up a bit as the thumb makes it appearance.

DELICIOUS (dĭ lĭsh′ əs), adj. (Smooth to the taste.) The right middle finger is placed on the lips, and then the hand moves down and out a bit. As it does, the thumb rubs over the middle finger. Both hands may be used.

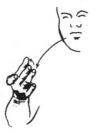

DELIGHT (dĭ līt′), n. (The heart is stirred; the spirits bubble up.) The open right hand, palm facing the body, strikes the heart repeatedly, moving up and off the heart after each strike. Cf. GAIETY, GLAD, HAPPY, JOY, MERRY.

DELIVER (dĭ lĭv′ ər), v., -ERED, -ERING. (Carrying something over.) Both open hands, palms up, move in an arc from left to right, as if carrying something from one point to another. Cf. BRING, CARRY 2.

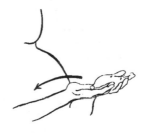

DEMAND (dĭ mănd′, -mänd′), v., -MANDED, -MANDING. (Something specific is moved in toward oneself.) The palm of the left "5" hand faces right. The right index finger is thrust into the left palm, and both hands are drawn sharply in toward the chest. Cf. INSIST, REQUEST 2, REQUIRE.

DEMOCRAT (dĕm′ ə krăt), *n.* (The "D" hand.) The right "D" hand is shaken back and forth several times before the right shoulder.

DEMON (dē′ mən), *n.* (The horns.) With the thumbs resting on the temples, the index and middle fingers of both hands open and close repeatedly. *Cf.* DEVIL, HELL 1, SATAN.

DEMONSTRATE (dĕm′ ən strāt′), *v.,* -STRATED, -STRATING. (Directing the attention to something, and bringing it forward.) The right index finger points into the left palm, held facing out before the body. The left palm moves straight out. *Cf.* DISPLAY, EVIDENCE, EXAMPLE, EXHIBIT, EXHIBITION, ILLUSTRATE, INDICATE, INFLUENCE 2, PRODUCE 1, REPRESENT, SHOW 1, SIGNIFY 1.

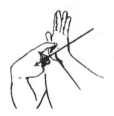

DEMOTE (dĭ′ mōt), *v.,* -MOTED, -MOTING. (Motion downward.) The right-angle hands are held up before the head, fingertips pointing toward each other. From this position, the hands move down in an arc. *Cf.* BASE, LOW, LOWER.

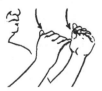

DENTIST (dĕn′ tĭst), *n.* (The teeth.) The index finger touches the lower teeth, and then the sign for INDIVIDUAL 1, *q.v.,* is made. Instead of the latter sign, the sign for DOCTOR, *q.v.,* may be made. Also, instead of the index finger alone, the middle finger and the index may both be used to touch the lower teeth.

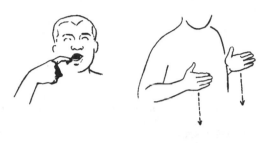

DENY 1 (dĭ nī′), *v.,* -NIED, -NYING. (An emphatic NOT 2, *q.v.*). The thumbs of both "A" hands, positioned under the chin, move out simultaneously, each toward their respective sides of the body. The head may be shaken slightly as the hands move out.

DENY 2, *v.* (Turning down.) The right "A" hand swings down sharply, its thumb pointing down. Both hands are sometimes used here.

DEPART (dǐ part'), v., -PARTED, -PARTING. (Pulling away.) The downturned open hands are held in a line, with fingers pointing to the left, the right hand behind the left. Both hands move in unison toward the right. As they do so, they assume the "A" position. Cf. LEAVE 1, WITHDRAW 1.

DEPEND (dǐ pĕnd'), v., -PENDED, -PENDING. (Hanging onto.) With the right index finger resting across its left counterpart, both hands drop down a bit. Cf. DEPENDABLE, RELY 2.

DEPENDABLE (dǐ pĕn' də bəl), adj. See DEPEND.

DEPOSIT (dǐ pŏz' ĭt), v. (The natural motion.) The downturned "O" hands are brought down and to the left simultaneously from an initial side-by-side position near the right shoulder. Cf. PUT DOWN.

DEPRESSED 1 (dǐ prĕst'), adj. (The facial features drop.) Both "5" hands, palms facing the eyes and fingers slightly curved, drop simultaneously to a level with the mouth. The head drops slightly as the hands move down, and an expression of sadness is assumed. Cf. DEJECTED, GLOOM, GLOOMY, GRAVE 2, GRIEF 1, MELANCHOLY, MOURNFUL, SAD, SORROWFUL 1.

DEPRESSED 2, adj. (The inner feelings are "down.") Both open hands, palms down, fingers pointing down, slide down the chest to waist level.

DEPTH (dĕpth), n. (The "D" hand, movement downward.) The right "D" hand is held with index finger pointing down. In this position it moves down along the left palm, which is held facing right with fingertips pointing forward. Cf. DEEP.

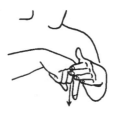

DESCRIBE 1 (dǐ skrīb'), v., -SCRIBED, -SCRIBING. (Unraveling something to get at its parts.) The "F" hands, palms facing and fingers pointing straight out, are held about an inch apart. They move alternately back and forth a few inches. Cf. DEFINE 1, DESCRIPTION, EXPLAIN 1.

DESCRIBE 2, v. (The unraveling or stretching out of words or sentences.) Both open hands are held close to each other, with fingers open and palms facing and almost touching. As the hands are drawn apart, the thumb and index finger of each hand come together to form circles. This is repeated several times. *Cf.* EXPLAIN 2, NARRATE, NARRATIVE, STORY, TALE, TELL ABOUT.

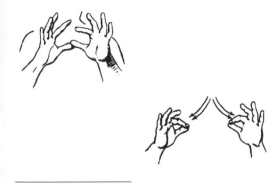

DESCRIBE 3, *v.* (The letter "D"; unraveling something.) The "D" hands, palms facing and index fingers pointing straight forward, are held an inch or two apart. They move alternately forward and back.

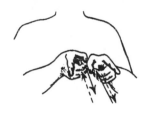

DESCRIPTION (dĭ skrĭp′ shən), *n.* See DESCRIBE.

DESERT (dez′ ərt), *n.* (A dry area.) The downturned curved right index finger draws across the lips, from left to right. The open hands, palms down, then spread forward and apart, indicating an expanse of land.

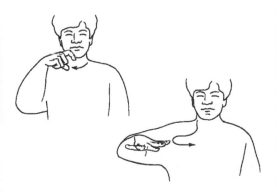

DESIGN (di zīn′), *n., v.* (Drawing and inventing.) The right "I" hand moves across the upturned left palm, from index finger edge to little finger edge, describing a series of curves. Optionally, the signer then places the index finger of the right "4" hand against the forehead and moves straight up.

DESIRE 1 (dĭ zīr′), *n., v.,* -SIRED, -SIRING. (Grasping something and pulling it in.) The upturned "5" hands, held side by side before the chest, close slightly into a grasping position as they move in toward the body. *Cf.* LONG 2, NEED 2, WANT, WILL 2, WISH 1.

DESIRE 2, *v., n.* (The upper alimentary tract is outlined.) The right "C" hand, palm facing the body, is placed with fingertips touching mid-chest. In this position it moves down a bit. *Cf.* APPETITE, CRAVE, STARVATION, STARVE, STARVED, WISH 2.

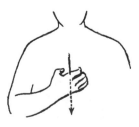

DESPISE (dĭ spīz′), v., -SPISED, -SPISING. (To push away and recoil from; avoid.) The two open hands, palms facing left, are pushed deliberately to the left, as if pushing something away. An expression of disdain or disgust is worn. Cf. ABHOR, AVOID 2, DETEST, HATE, LOATHE.

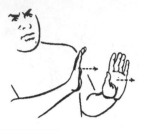

DESPITE (dĭ spīt′), prep., n. Both hands, in the "5" position, are held before the chest, fingertips facing each other. With an alternate back-and-forth movement, the fingertips are made to strike each other. Cf. ANYHOW, ANYWAY, DOESN'T MATTER, HOWEVER 2, INDIFFERENCE, INDIFFERENT, IN SPITE OF, MAKE NO DIFFERENCE, NEVERTHELESS, NO MATTER, WHEREVER.

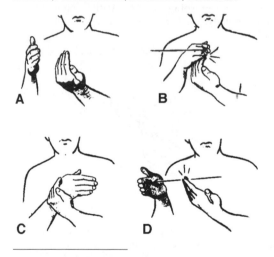

DESSERT (di zûrt′), n. Both hands, held in the "D" position, palms facing, come together once or twice.

DESTROY (dĭ stroi′), v., -STROYED, -STROYING. (Wiping off.) The left "5" hand, palm up, is held slightly above the right "5" hand, held palm down. The right hand swings up, just brushing over the left palm. Both hands close into the "S" position, and the right is brought back with force to its initial position, striking a glancing blow against the left knuckles as it returns. Cf. RUIN.

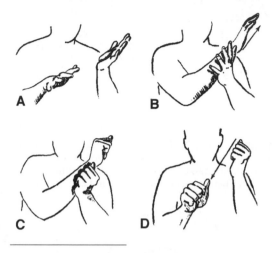

DETACH (dĭ tăch′), v., -TACHED, -TACHING. (An unlocking.) With thumbs and index fingers interlocked initially (the links of a chain), the hands draw apart, showing the break in the chain. Cf. DISCONNECT, PART FROM.

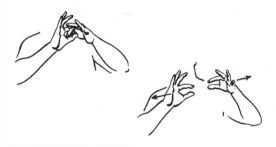

DETECTIVE (dĭ tĕk′ tĭv), n. (The badge.) The right "D" hand circles over the heart.

DETERIORATE (dĭ tĭr′ ĭ ə rāt′), *v.*, -RATED, -RATING. (Going down step by step.) The little finger edge of the open right hand is placed on the upper side of the extended left arm, which is held with the open left hand palm down. The right hand moves down along the left arm in a series of short movements. This is the opposite of IMPROVE, *q.v. Cf.* DECLINE, DETERIORATION.

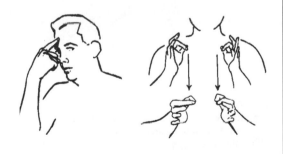

DETERIORATION (dĭ tĭr′ ĭ ə rā′ shən), *n.* See DETERIORATE.

DETERMINE (dĭ tûr′ mĭn), *v.*, -MINED, -MINING. (The mind stops wavering, and the pros and cons are resolved.) The right index finger touches the forehead, the sign for THINK, *q.v.* Both "F" hands, palms facing each other and fingers pointing straight out, then drop down simultaneously. The sign for JUDGE, *q.v.*, explains the rationale behind the movement of the two hands here. *Cf.* DECIDE, DECISION, MAKE UP ONE'S MIND, MIND 5, RESOLVE, VERDICT.

DETEST (dĭ tĕst′), *v.*, -TESTED, -TESTING. (To push away and recoil from; avoid.) The two open hands, palms facing left, are pushed deliberately to the left, as if pushing something away. An expression of disdain or disgust is worn. *Cf.* ABHOR, AVOID 2, DESPISE, HATE, LOATHE.

DEVELOP 1 (dĭ vĕl′ əp), *v.*, -OPED, -OPING. (Flowers or plants emerge from the ground.) The right fingers, pointing up, emerge from the closed left hand, and they spread open as they do. *Cf.* BLOOM, GROW, GROWN, MATURE 1, PLANT 1, RAISE 3, REAR 2, SPRING.

DEVELOP 2, *v.* (The letter "D"; moving upward, as if in growth.) The right "D" hand is placed against the left palm, which is facing right with fingers pointing up. The "D" hand moves straight up to the left fingertips.

DEVIATE 1 (dē′ vĭ āt′), *v.*, -ATED, -ATING. (Going astray.) The open right hand, palm facing left, is placed with its little finger edge resting on the upturned left palm. The right hand curves rather sharply to the left as it moves across the palm. *Cf.* DEVIATION, WRONG 2.

DEVIATE 2, *v.* (The natural motion.) The "G" hands are held side by side and touching, palms down, index fingers pointing forward. Then the right hand moves forward, curving toward the right side as it does. *Cf.* DEVIATION, GO OFF THE TRACK, STRAY.

DEVIATION (dē′ vǐ ā′ shən), *n.* See DEVIATE 1 and 2.

DEVIL (děv′ əl), *n.* (The horns.) With the thumbs resting on the temples, the index and middle fingers of both hands open and close repeatedly. *Cf.* DEMON, HELL 1, SATAN.

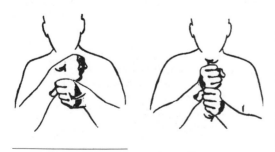

DEVISE (dǐ vīz′), *v.*, -VISED, -VISING. (Fashioning something with the hands.) The right "S" hand, palm facing left, is placed on top of its left counterpart, whose palm faces right. The hands are twisted back and forth, striking each other slightly after each twist. *Cf.* CONSTRUCT 2, CREATE 1, MAKE, MANUFAC-TURE, MEND, PRODUCE 2, REPAIR.

DEVOTION (dǐ vō′ shən), *n.* (Clasping the heart.) The "5" hands are held one atop the other over the heart. Sometimes the "S" hands are used, in which

case they are crossed at the wrists. *Cf.* BELOVED, LOVE, REVERE.

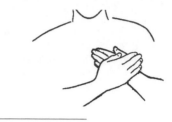

DIAGNOSIS (dī əg nō′ sis), *n.* (Pulling apart to get to the source of the trouble.) The index and middle fingers of both hands are held curved and pointing down. The hands come apart simultaneously a number of times.

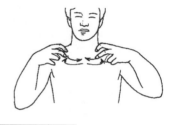

DIALOGUE (dī′ ə lôg, -log), *n.* (Back and forth conversation.) Both upturned index fingers move alternately back and forth in front of the mouth.

DIAMOND (dī′ mənd, dī′ ə-), *n.* (The letter "D"; sparkling with scintillating rays of light.) The right "D" hand is shaken slightly as it is held slightly above the ring finger of the downturned left hand.

DIAPER (dī′ ə pər), *n., v.* (The natural sign.) The thumbs and index and middle fingers of each hand point down and rest on each hip, as the signer mimes the closing of clips to fasten the diaper.

DIARRHEA 1 (dī ə rē′ ə), *n.* (Defecating repeatedly.) The right thumb is drawn repeatedly down and out from the left closed hand.

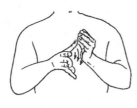

DIARRHEA 2 (Going back and forth to the bathroom.) The upturned thumb goes back and forth from left to right.

DIARRHEA 3 (The bowels in a state of constant movement.) Both hands, with fingertips close to the stomach, palms up, move down repeatedly.

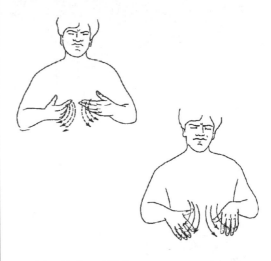

DICTIONARY (dĭk′ shə nĕr′ ĭ), *n.* (Thumbing the pages.) The right "D" hand moves across the left palm quickly, from the fingers to the base, several times, as if thumbing through the pages.

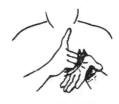

DIE (dī), *v.,* DIED, DYING. (Turning over on one's side.) The open hands, fingers pointing ahead, are held side by side, with the right palm down and the left palm up. The two hands reverse their relative positions as they move from the left to the right. *Cf.* DEAD, DEATH.

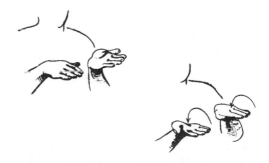

DIE OUT *v. phrase*. (Fingering the small pieces resulting from the breaking up of something.) The thumbs rub slowly across the fingertips of the upturned hands, from the little fingers to the index fingers, and then continue to the "A" position, palms up. *Cf.* DECAY, DISSOLVE, FADE, MELT, ROT.

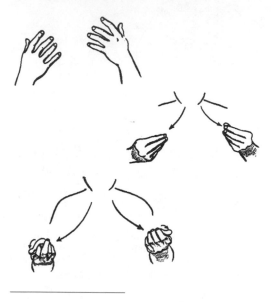

DIFFER (dĭf′ ər), *v.*, -FERED, -FERING. (To think in opposite terms.) The sign for THINK is made: the right index finger touches the forehead. The sign for OPPOSITE is then made: the "D" hands, palms facing the body and index fingers touching, draw apart sharply. *Cf.* DISAGREE.

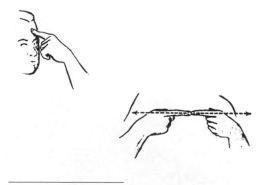

DIFFERENCE (dĭf′ ər əns, dĭf′ rəns,), *n*. (Separated many times; different.) The "D" hands, palms down, are crossed at the index fingers or are held side by side. They separate and return to their initial position

a number of times. *Cf.* ASSORTED, DIFFERENT, DIVERSE 1, DIVERSITY 1, UNLIKE, VARIED.

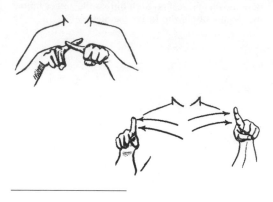

DIFFERENT (dĭf′ ər ənt, dĭf′ rənt), *adj*. See DIFFERENCE.

DIFFICULT 1 (dĭf′ ə kŭlt′), *adj*. (The knuckles are rubbed, to indicate a condition of being worn down.) The knuckles of the curved index and middle fingers of both hands are rubbed up and down against each other. Instead of the up-down rubbing, they may rub against each other in an alternate clockwise-counterclockwise manner. *Cf.* DIFFICULTY, HARD 1, HARDSHIP, POVERTY, PROBLEM 2.

DIFFICULT 2, *adj*. (Striking a hard object.) The curved index and middle fingers of the right hand, whose palm faces the body or the left, are brought down sharply against the back of the downturned left "S" hand. *Cf.* HARD 2.

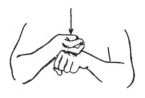

DIFFICULTY (dĭf′ ə kŭl′ tĭ, -kəl tĭ), *n*. See DIFFICULT 1.

DIG (dĭg), *v.,* DUG, DIGGING. (The natural motion.) Both hands, in the "A" position, right hand facing up and left hand facing down, grasp an imaginary shovel. They go through the natural movements of shoveling earth—first digging in and then tossing the earth aside. *Cf.* SHOVEL 1.

DIGRESS (di gres'), *v.* (Moving off the track.) Both "S" hands are held at chest height, palms facing each other. The right index finger shoots out as the right hand crosses over the left.

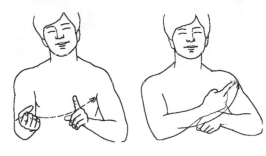

DILIGENCE (dĭl' ə jəns), *n.* (Rubbing the hands together in zeal or ambition.) The open hands are rubbed vigorously back and forth against each other. *Cf.* AMBITIOUS, ANXIOUS, DILIGENT, EAGER, EAGERNESS, ENTHUSIASM, ENTHUSIASTIC, INDUSTRIOUS, METHODIST, ZEAL, ZEALOUS.

DILIGENT (dĭl' ə jənt), *adj.* See DILIGENCE.

DINOSAUR (dī' nə sôr), *n.* (The swinging neck.) The right arm is held upright, with the hand facing forward, all fingers touching the thumb. The hand swivels from right to left in a slow, deliberate move-ment. The cupped left hand may be used to support the right elbow.

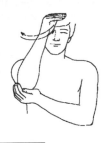

DIPLOMA (di plŏ' mə), *n.* (The rolled up diploma.) With thumbs and index fingers forming circles, both hands, held together initially, separate, describing the shape of a rolled up diploma. *Cf.* DEGREE 3.

DIRECT 1 (dĭ rĕkt', dī-), *v.,* -RECTED, -RECTING. (Holding the reins over all.) The "A" hands, palms facing, move alternately back and forth, as if grasping and manipulating reins. The left "A" hand, still in position, swings over so that its palm now faces down. The right hand opens to the "5" position, palm down, and swings over the left which moves slightly to the right. *Cf.* CONTROL 1, GOVERN, MANAGE, MANAGEMENT, MANAGER, OPERATE, REGULATE, REIGN, RULE 1.

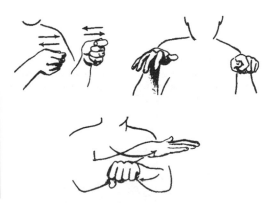

DIRECT 2, v. (An issuance from the mouth.) The tip of the index finger of the "D" hand, palm facing the body, is placed at the closed lips. It moves around and out, rather forcefully. *Cf.* COMMAND, ORDER 1.

DIRECTION (di rek′ shən), n. The "D" letters; one hand follows the other.) The right "D" hand is positioned behind its left counterpart, and both hands move forward together.

DIRT (dûrt), n. (Fingering the soil.) Both hands, held upright before the body, finger imaginary pinches of soil. *Cf.* GROUND, SOIL 1.

DIRTY (dûr′ tĭ), *adj.* (A modification of the pig's snout groveling in a trough.) The downturned right hand is placed under the chin. Its fingers, pointing left, wiggle repeatedly. *Cf.* FILTHY, SOIL 2.

DISAGREE (dĭs′ ə grē′), v., -GREED, -GREEING. (To think in opposite terms.) The sign for THINK is made: the right index finger touches the forehead. The sign for OPPOSITE is then made: the "D" hands, palms facing the body and index fingers touching, draw apart sharply. *Cf.* DIFFER.

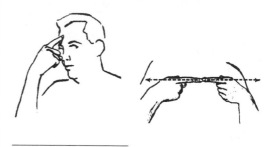

DISAPPEAR (dĭs′ ə pir′), v., -PEARED, -PEARING. (A disappearance.) The right open hand, palm facing the body, is held by the left hand and is drawn down and out, ending in a position with fingers drawn together. The left hand, meanwhile, may close into a position with fingers also drawn together. *Cf.* ABSENCE, ABSENT, GONE 1, VANISH.

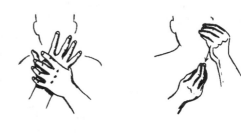

DISAPPOINT (dĭs′ ə point′), v., -pointed, -pointing. (The feelings sink.) The middle fingers of both "5" hands, one above the other, rest on the heart. They both move down a few inches.

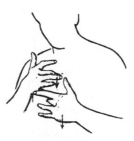

DISAPPOINTED *adj.* (Something sour or bitter.) The right index finger is brought sharply up against the lips, while the mouth is puckered up as if tasting something sour. *Cf.* BITTER, DISAPPOINTMENT, SOUR.

DISAPPOINTMENT (dĭs´ ə point´ mənt), *n.* See DIS-APPOINTED.

DISBELIEF 1 (dĭs bĭ lēf´), *n.* (The nose is wrinkled in disbelief.) The right "V" hand faces the nose. The index and middle fingers bend as a cynical expression is assumed. *Cf.* CYNIC, CYNICAL, DON'T BELIEVE, DOUBT 1, INCREDULITY, SKEPTIC 1, SKEPTICAL 1.

DISBELIEF 2, *n.* (The wavering.) The downturned "S" hands swing alternately up and down. *Cf.* DOUBT 2, DOUBTFUL, WAVER 2.

DISCARD (*v.* dĭs kärd´; *n.* dĭs´ kärd), -CARDED, -CARDING. (To throw something aside.) Both "S" hands are held with palms facing at chest level and then thrown down and to the left, opening into the

"5" position. *Cf.* ABANDON, CAST OFF, FORSAKE 2, LEAVE 2, LET ALONE, NEGLECT.

DISCHARGE (dĭs chärj´), *v.,* -CHARGED, -CHARGING. ("Getting the axe"; the head is chopped off.) The upturned open right hand is swung sharply over the index finger edge of the left "S" hand, whose palm faces right. *Cf.* EXPEL, FIRE 2.

DISCO (dĭs´ kō), *n.* (The natural sign.) The signer mimes dancing to a disco beat.

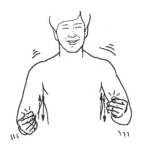

DISCONNECT (dĭs´ kə nĕkt´), *v.,* -NECTED, -NECTING. (An unlocking.) With thumbs and index fingers interlocked initially (the links of a chain), the hands draw apart, showing the break in the chain. *Cf.* DETACH, PART FROM.

DISCONTENTED (dĭs´ kən tĕn´ tĭd), *adj.* (NOT, SATISFIED.) The sign for NOT 1 is made: the crossed downturned open hands draw apart. The sign for SATISFIED then follows: the downturned "B" hands, the right above the left, are positioned on the chest. They move straight down simultaneously. *Cf.* DISSATISFACTION, DISSATISFIED.

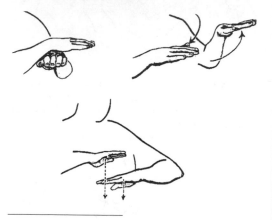

DISCOURAGE (dĭs kûr´ ĭjd), *v.,* -AGED, -AGING. (Throwing up the hands in a gesture of surrender.) Both "A" hands are held palms down before the chest and then thrown up in unison, ending in the "5" position. *Cf.* FORFEIT, GIVE UP, RELINQUISH, RENOUNCE, RENUNCIATION, SURRENDER, YIELD.

DISCOURSE (*n.* dĭs´ kôrs, dĭs kôrs´; *v.* dĭs kôrs´), -COURSED, -COURSING. (Words tumbling from the mouth.) The right index finger, pointing left, describes a continuous small circle in front of the mouth. *Cf.* HEARING, MAINTAIN 2, MENTION, REMARK, SAID, SAY, SPEAK, SPEECH 1, STATE 1, TALK 1, TELL, VERBAL.

DISCOVER (dĭs kŭv´ ər), *v.,* -ERED, -ERING. (The natural motion of selecting something from the hand.) The thumb and index fingers of the outstretched right hand grasp an imaginary object on the upturned left palm. The right hand then moves straight up. *Cf.* DISCOVERY, FIND, PICK 1, SELECT 1.

DISCOVERY (dĭs kŭv´ ə rĭ), *n.* See DISCOVER.

DISCUSS (dĭs kŭs´), *v.,* -CUSSED, -CUSSING. (Expounding one's points.) The right "D" hand is held with the palm facing the body. It moves down repeatedly so that the side of the index finger strikes the upturned left palm. *Cf.* DISCUSSION.

DISCUSSION (dĭs kŭsh´ ən), *n.* See DISCUSS.

DISEASE (dĭ zēz´), *n., v.,* -EASED, -EASING. (The sick parts of the anatomy are indicated.) The right middle finger rests on the forehead, and its left counterpart is placed against the stomach. The signer assumes an expression of sadness or physical distress. *Cf.* ILL, ILLNESS, SICK.

DISGUST (dĭs gŭst'), *n., v.,* -GUSTED, -GUSTING. (Turning the stomach.) The fingertips of the curved right hand describe a continuous circle on the stomach. The signer assumes an exaggerated expression of disgust. *Cf.* DISGUSTED, DISGUSTING, MAKE ME DISGUSTED, MAKE ME SICK, NAUSEA, NAUSEATE, NAUSEOUS, OBNOXIOUS, REVOLTING.

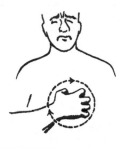

DISGUSTED (dĭs gŭs' tĭd), *adj.* See DISGUST.

DISGUSTING (dĭs gŭs' tĭng), *adj.* See DISGUST.

DISH (dĭsh), *n.* (The finger touches a brittle substance.) The index finger is brought up to touch the exposed front teeth. *Cf.* CHINA 4, GLASS 1, PLATE 1, PORCELAIN.

DISHWASHER (dĭsh' wôsh ər), *n.* (The action of the water inside the machine.) Both hands, in the claw position, palms facing and one above the other, move back and forth in opposite clockwise/counterclockwise motions.

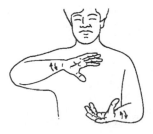

DISHWASHING (dĭsh' wŏsh ĭng -wôsh-), *n.* (The natural sign.) The downturned right "5" hand describes a clockwise circle as it moves over the upturned left "5" hand. *Cf.* WASH DISHES.

DISOBEDIENCE (dĭs´ ə bē´ dĭ əns), *n.* See DISOBEY.

DISOBEY (dĭs´ ə bā´), *v.,* -BEYED, -BEYING. (Turning the head.) The right "S" hand, held up with its palm facing the body, swings sharply around to the palm-out position. The head meanwhile moves slightly toward the left. *Cf.* DISOBEDIENCE, REBEL.

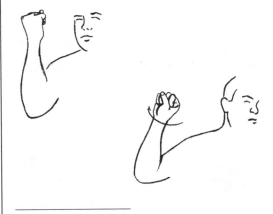

DISPLAY (dĭs plā'), *v.,* -PLAYED, -PLAYING. (Directing the attention to something, and bringing it forward.) The right index finger points into the left palm, held facing out before the body. The left palm moves straight out. *Cf.* DEMONSTRATE, EVIDENCE, EXAMPLE, EXHIBIT, EXHIBITION, ILLUSTRATE, INDICATE, INFLUENCE 2, PRODUCE 1, REPRESENT, SHOW 1, SIGNIFY 1.

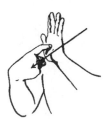

DISPOSE (dĭs pōz'), v., -POSED, -POSING, n. (The feelings of the heart move toward a specific object.) The tip of the right middle finger touches the heart. The open right hand, palm facing the body, then moves away from the heart toward the palm of the open left hand. Cf. DISPOSED TO, INCLINATION, INCLINE, INCLINED, TEND, TENDENCY.

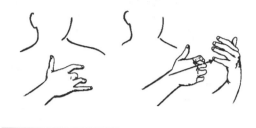

DISPOSED TO (dĭs pōzd'), adj. phrase. See DISPOSE.

DISPUTE (dĭs pūt'), n., v., -PUTED, -PUTING. (An expounding back and forth.) The index fingers here represent the two sides of the argument. First the left index finger is slapped into the open right palm, and then the right makes the same movement into the left palm. This is repeated back and forth several times. Cf. ARGUE, ARGUMENT, CONTROVERSY, DEBATE.

DISREGARD (dĭs' rĭ gärd'), v., -GARDED, -GARDING. (Thumbing the nose.) The index finger of the right "B" hand is placed under the tip of the nose. From this position the right hand moves straight forward, away from the face. Cf. IGNORE.

DISRUPT (dĭs rŭpt'), v., -RUPTED, -RUPTING. (Obstruct, bother.) The left hand, fingers together and palm flat, is held before the body, facing somewhat down. The little finger side of the right hand, held with palm flat, makes one or several up-down chopping motions against the left hand, between its thumb and index finger. Cf. ANNOY, ANNOYANCE, BOTHER, DISTURB, HINDER, HINDRANCE, IMPEDE, INTERCEPT, INTERFERE, INTERFERENCE, INTERFERE WITH, INTERRUPT, MEDDLE 1, OBSTACLE, OBSTRUCT, PREVENT, PREVENTION.

DISSATISFACTION (dĭs' săt ĭs făk' shən), n. (NOT, SATISFIED.) The sign for NOT 1 is made: the crossed downturned open hands draw apart. The sign for SATISFIED then follows: the downturned "B" hands, the right above the left, are positioned on the chest. They move straight down simultaneously. Cf. DISCONTENTED, DISSATISFIED.

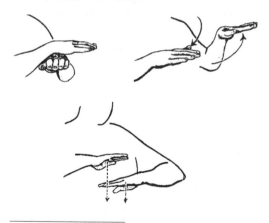

DISSATISFIED (dĭs săt' ĭs fĭd'), adj. See DISSATISFACTION.

DISSOLVE (dĭ zŏlv'), v., -SOLVED, -SOLVING. (Fingering the small pieces resulting from the breaking up of something.) The thumbs rub slowly across the fingertips of the upturned hands, from the little fingers to the index fingers, and then continue to the

"A" position, palms up. *Cf.* DECAY, DIE OUT, FADE, MELT, ROT.

INTERRUPT, MEDDLE 1, OBSTACLE, OBSTRUCT, PREVENT, PREVENTION.

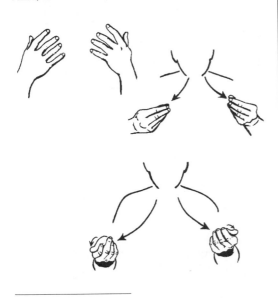

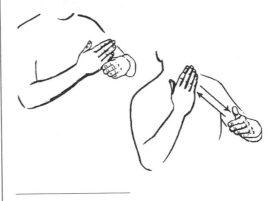

DISTRIBUTE (dĭs trĭb′ ūt), *v.*, -UTED, -UTING. (Giving out widely.) The "AND" hands are held with palms up and fingertips touching each other, the right fingertips pointing left and the left fingertips pointing right. From this position, the hands sweep forward and curve to either side, opening, palms up, as they do.

DIVE (dīv), *v.*, DIVED or DOVE, DIVED, DIVING. (The natural motion.) The extended right index and middle fingertips are placed on the back of the same two fingers of the left hand, which is held palm down in front of the body. From this position the right hand moves upward and back in an arc, as if diving off the left hand.

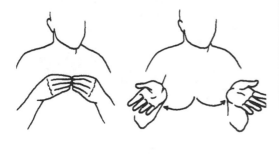

DISTURB (dĭs tûrb′), *v.*, -TURBED, -TURBING. (Obstruct, bother.) The left hand, fingers together and palm flat, is held before the body, facing somewhat down. The little finger side of the right hand, held with palm flat, makes one or several up-down chopping motions against the left hand, between its thumb and index finger. *Cf.* ANNOY, ANNOYANCE, BOTHER, DISRUPT, HINDER, HINDRANCE, IMPEDE, INTERCEPT, INTERFERE, INTERFERENCE, INTERFERE WITH,

DIVERSE 1 (dĭ vûrs′, dī-, dī′ vûrs), *adj.* (Separated many times; different.) The "D" hands, palms down, are crossed at the index fingers or are held side by side. They separate and return to their initial position a number of times. *Cf.* ASSORTED, DIFFERENCE, DIFFERENT, DIVERSITY 1, UNLIKE, VARIED.

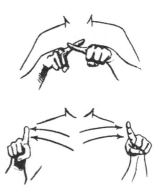

DIVERSE 2, *adj.* (The fingertips indicate many things.) Both hands, in the "D" position, palms out and index fingertips touching, are drawn apart. As they move apart, the index fingers wiggle up and down. *Cf.* DIVERSITY 2, VARIOUS, VARY.

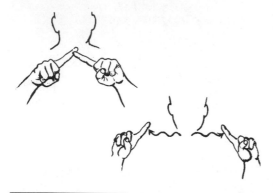

DIVERSITY 1 (dĭ vûr′ sə tĭ, dī-), *n.* See DIVERSE 1.

DIVERSITY 2, *n.* See DIVERSE 2.

DIVIDE (dĭ vīd′), *v.,* -VIDED, -VIDING. (A splitting apart or dividing.) The two hands are crossed, with the right little finger resting on the left index finger. Both hands are dropped down and separated simultaneously, so that the palms face down. *Cf.* DIVISION, SHARE 2.

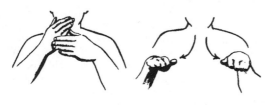

DIVIDEND 1 (dĭv′ ə dĕnd′), *n.* (A regular taking in.) The outstretched open left hand, held palm facing right, moves in toward the body, assuming the "A" position, palm still facing right. This is repeated several times. *Cf.* INCOME, SUBSCRIBE, SUBSCRIPTION.

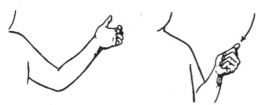

DIVIDEND 2, *n.* The right fingers trace a continuous circle in the upturned left palm.

DIVISION (dĭ vĭzh′ ən), *n.* See DIVIDE.

DIVORCE 1 (dĭ vōrs′), *n., v.,* -VORCED, -VORCING. (The hands are moved apart.) Both hands, in the "A" position, thumbs up, are held together, with knuckles touching. With a deliberate movement they come apart. *Cf.* APART, PART 3, SEPARATE 1.

DIVORCE 2, *n., v.* (The hands, locked in marriage, come apart.) The clasped hands draw apart, into the "A" position, palms facing each other.

DIVORCE 3, *n., v.* (The letter "D"; a separating.) The "D" hands, palms facing and fingertips touching, draw apart.

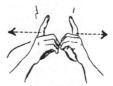

DIZZY (dĭz′ ĭ), *adj.* (Images swinging around before the eyes.) The right "5" hand, palm facing the body and fingers somewhat curved, swings around in a continuous counterclockwise circle before the eyes.

DO (dōō), *v.,* DOES, DID, DONE, DOING. (An activity.) Both open hands, palms down, are swung right and left before the chest. *Cf.* ACT 2, ACTION, ACTIVE, ACTIVITY, CONDUCT 1, DEED, PERFORM 1, PERFORMANCE 1.

DO AS ONE WISHES *phrase.* (Think for yourself.) The sign for THINK is made: the right index finger touches the center of the forehead. The SELF sign follows: the upturned right thumb moves straight forward from the signer toward the person addressed. *Cf.* UP TO YOU.

DOCTOR (dŏk′ tər), *n.* (The letter "M," from "M.D."; feeling the pulse.) The fingertips of the right "M" hand lightly tap the left pulse a number of times.

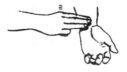

DOESN'T MATTER *v. phrase.* Both hands, in the "5" position, are held before the chest, fingertips facing each other. With an alternate back-and-forth movement, the fingertips are made to strike each other. *Cf.* ANYHOW, ANYWAY, DESPITE, HOWEVER 2, INDIFFERENCE, INDIFFERENT, IN SPITE OF, MAKE NO DIFFERENCE, NEVERTHELESS, NO MATTER, WHEREVER.

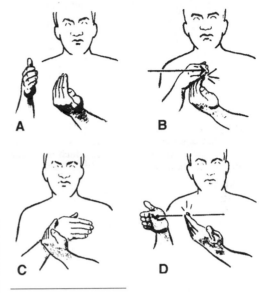

DOG (dôg), *n.* (Patting the knee and snapping the fingers to beckon the dog.) The right hand pats the right knee, and then the fingers are snapped.

DOLL (dŏl), *n.* (Pulling the nose.) The right "X" finger, resting on the nose, pulls the head with it as it moves down slightly. It does not leave its position on the nose.

DOLLAR(S) (dŏl′ ər), *n.* (The natural sign; drawing a bill from a billfold.) The right thumb and index finger trace the outlines of a bill on the upturned left palm. Or, the right thumb and fingers may grasp the base of the open left hand, which is held palm facing right and fingers pointing forward; the right hand, in this position, then slides forward along and off the left hand, as if drawing bills from a billfold.

DOLPHIN (dol′ fin), *n.* (The diving.) The right "B" hand makes a series of undulating dive movements in front of the downturned left arm, which represents the surface of the water.

DOMINICAN REPUBLIC *n.* (də min′ i ken re pub′ lik) (The initials.) The right "D" is placed at the right temple, and then it moves down to chin level, changing to the letter "R."

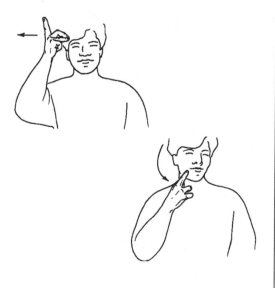

DONE (dŭn), *v.* (Shaking the hands to rid them of something.) The upright "5" hands, palms facing each other, are suddenly and quickly swung around to a palm-out position. *Cf.* END 3, FINISH.

DONKEY (dŏng′ kǐ), *n.* (The donkey's broad ear; the animal is traditionally a stubborn one.) The open hand, or the "B" hand, is placed at the side of the head, with palm out and fingers pointing straight up. The hand moves forward and back, pivoting at the wrist, as in the case of a donkey's ears flapping. Both hands may also be used, at either side of the head. *Cf.* MULE, MULISH, OBSTINATE, STUBBORN.

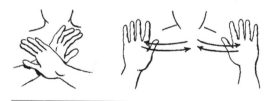

DO NOT 1, *v. phrase.* (The natural sign.) The crossed "5" hands, palms facing out (or down), separate and recross quickly and repeatedly. The head is usually shaken simultaneously. This sign is from NOT 1, *q.v. Cf.* DON'T 1.

DO NOT 2, *v. phrase.* The thumb of the right "A" hand is placed under the chin. From this position it is flicked outward in an arc. This sign is a variant of DO NOT 1. *Cf.* DON'T 2.

DON'T 1 (dŏnt) *v.* See DO NOT 1.

DON'T 2, *v.* See DO NOT 2.

DON'T BELIEVE *v. phrase.* (The nose is wrinkled in disbelief.) The right "V" hand faces the nose. The index and middle fingers bend as a cynical expression is assumed. *Cf.* CYNIC, CYNICAL, DISBELIEF 1, DOUBT 1, INCREDULITY, SKEPTIC 1, SKEPTICAL 1.

DON'T CARE 1, *(colloq.), v. phrase.* (Wiping the nose, *i.e.,* "Keeping the nose clean" or not becoming involved.) The downturned right "D" hand, index finger touching the nose, is suddenly flung down and to the right.

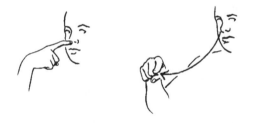

DON'T CARE 2, *(colloq.), v. phrase.* The thumb of the right "Y" hand touches the right ear. The right "Y" hand is then flung down and to the right. *Cf.* DON'T CARE FOR, DON'T LIKE.

DON'T CARE FOR *(colloq.), v. phrase.* See DON'T CARE 2.

DON'T KNOW *v. phrase.* (Knowledge is lacking.) The sign for KNOW is made: the right fingertips tap the forehead several times. The right hand is then flung over to the right, ending in the "5" position, palm out.

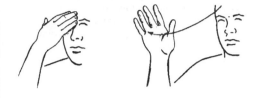

DON'T LIKE *(colloq.), v. phrase.* See DON'T CARE 2.

DON'T WANT *v. phrase.* (The hands are shaken, indicating a wish to rid them of something.) The "5" hands, palms facing the body, suddenly swing around to the palms-down position.

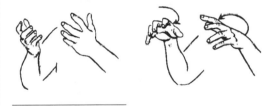

DOOR (dōr), *n.* (The opening and closing of the door.) The "B" hands, palms out and edges touching, are drawn apart and then come together again. *Cf.* DOORWAY, OPEN THE DOOR.

DOORKNOB (dōr′ nob), *n.* (The natural sign.) The signer mimes twisting a doorknob.

DOORWAY (dôr′ wā′), *n.* See DOOR.

DOPE (dōp), *(colloq.), n.* (A shot in the arm.) The right index finger is thrust into the left upper arm and the thumb wiggles back and forth a number of times, as if implanting a shot in the arm. *Cf.* COCA-COLA, COKE, INOCULATE, MORPHINE, NARCOTICS.

DOUBT 1 (dout), *n., v.,* DOUBTED, DOUBTING. (The nose is wrinkled in disbelief.) The right "V" hand faces the nose. The index and middle fingers bend as a cynical expression is assumed. *Cf.* CYNIC, CYNICAL, DISBELIEF 1, DON'T BELIEVE, INCREDULITY, SKEPTIC 1, SKEPTICAL 1.

DOUBT 2, *n., v.* (The wavering.) The downturned "S" hands swing alternately up and down. *Cf.* DISBELIEF 2, DOUBTFUL, WAVER 2.

DOUBTFUL (dout′ fəl), *adj.* See DOUBT 2.

DOWN (doun), *prep.* (The natural sign.) The right hand, pointing down, moves down an inch or two.

DRAMA (dra′ mə, drăm′ ə), *n.* (Motion or movement, modified by the letter "A" for "act.") Both "A" hands, palms out, are held at shoulder height and rotate alternately toward the head. *Cf.* ACT 1, ACTOR, ACTRESS, PERFORM 2, PERFORMANCE 2, PLAY 2, SHOW 2.

DRAW (drô), *v.,* DREW, DRAWN, DRAWING. (Drawing on the hand.) The little finger of the right hand, representing a pencil, traces a curved line in the upturned left palm. *Cf.* ART.

DRAWBRIDGE (drô′ brij), *n.* (The opening of the bridge.) Both hands are held palms down, fingertips touching. They sweep up in individual arcs, miming the opening of a drawbridge.

DRAWER (drôr), *n.* (The natural sign.) The upturned hands grasp imaginary drawer pulls and pull the drawer toward the body.

DREAD (drĕd), *v.*, DREADED, DREADING. (The hands attempt to ward off something which causes fear.) The "5" hands, right behind left, move downward before the body, in a wavy motion. *Cf.* FEAR 2, TERROR 2, TIMID.

DREADFUL (drĕd′ fəl), *adj.* (Throwing out the hands.) Both hands, their fingertips touching their respective thumbs, are held, palms facing each other, near the temples. They are thrown out before the face, assuming "5" positions, palms still facing. *Cf.* AWFUL, TERRIBLE, TRAGEDY 1, TRAGIC.

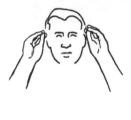

DREAM (drĕm), *n.*, *v.*, DREAMED, DREAMT, DREAMING. (A thought wanders off into space.) The right curved index finger opens and closes quickly as it leaves its initial position on the forehead and moves up into the air.

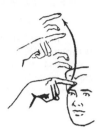

DRESS (drĕs), *n.*, *v.*, DRESSED, DRESSING. (Draping the clothes on the body.) With fingertips resting on the chest, both hands move down simultaneously. The action is repeated. *Cf.* CLOTHES, CLOTHING, FROCK, GARMENT, GOWN, SHIRT, SUIT, WEAR 1.

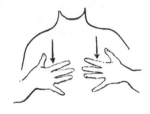

DRINK (drĭngk), *n.*, *v.*, DRANK, DRUNK, DRINKING. (The natural sign.) An imaginary glass is tipped at the open lips.

DRIVE (drīv), *v.*, DROVE, DRIVEN, DRIVING, *n.* (The steering wheel.) The hands grasp an imaginary steering wheel and manipulate it. *Cf.* AUTOMOBILE, CAR.

DRIVE TO (drīv to), *v.* (The steering wheel moves forward.) Holding an imaginary steering wheel, the hands move straight forward. *Cf.* GO BY CAR.

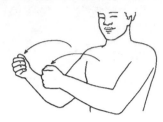

DROP (drŏp), *v.*, DROPPED, DROPPING. (The natural sign.) The downturned right closed hand, held at shoulder height, drops down, opening into the downturned "5" position.

DROWN 1 (droun), *v.* (The legs go under.) The index and middle fingers of the right "V" hand, palm facing the body, are drawn down between the index and middle fingers of the downturned left "4" hand. The right index finger alone may be substituted for the "V" fingers.

DROWN 2, *v.* (The downward movement.) The downturned right hand, fingers touching thumb, is thrust down into the cup formed by the open left hand. The right hand continues straight down through this cup.

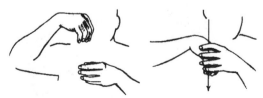

DRUG (drŭg), *n.* (Mixing of medicine; rolling a pill.) The ball of the middle fingertip of the right "5" hand describes a small counterclockwise circle in the upturned left palm. *Cf.* MEDICINE.

DRUM (drŭm), *n., v.*, DRUMMED, DRUMMING. (The natural sign.) The hands play an imaginary drum.

DRUNK (drŭngk), *adj.* (The act of drinking.) The thumbtip of the right "Y" hand is tilted toward the mouth, as if it were a drinking glass or bottle. The signer tilts his head back slightly, as if drinking. *Cf.* BEER, DRUNKARD, DRUNKENNESS, INTOXICATE, INTOXICATION, LIQUOR 2.

DRUNKARD (drŭngk′ ərd), *n.* See DRUNK.

DRUNKENNESS (drŭngk′ ən nĭs), *n.* See DRUNK.

DRY (drī), *adj., v.*, DRIED, DRYING. (A dryness, indicated by a wiping of the lips.) The "X" finger is drawn across the lips, from left to right, as if wiping them. *Cf.* BORE, DULL 2.

DRYER (drī′ ər), *n.* (The circular movement.) The sign for DRY is made: the downturned curved index finger is wiped across the lips. The right index finger then twirls around in a cup formed by the left "C" hand.

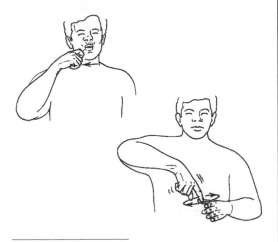

DUCK (dŭk), *n.* (The broad bill.) The right hand is held with its back resting against the mouth. The thumb, index and middle fingers come together repeatedly, indicating the opening and closing of a broad bill.

DUCKLING (dŭk′ ling), *n.* (A small duck.) The sign for DUCK is made: the right hand is held with the back of the hand resting against the mouth. The thumb and index and middle fingers open and close together, depicting the broad bill of the duck. The cupped hands then come together, indicating a small item within.

DUE (dū, dōō), *adj.* (Pointing to the palm, where the money should be placed.) The index finger of one hand is thrust into the upturned palm of the other several times. *Cf.* ARREARS, DEBIT, DEBT, OBLIGATION 2, OWE.

DULL 1 (dŭl), *adj.* (Knocking the head to indicate its empty state.) The "S" hand, palm facing the body, knocks against the forehead. *Cf.* DUMB 1, DUNCE, STUPID 1.

DULL 2, *adj.* See DRY.

DUMB 1 (dŭm), *adj.* See DULL 1.

DUMB 2, *(colloq.)*, *adj.* (The thickness of the skull is indicated, to stress intellectual density.) With the thumb of the right "C" hand grasped by the closed left hand, the right hand is swung away from the body, describing a small arc as it moves. The space between the curved right fingers and the closed left hand indicates the thickness of the skull. *Cf.* MORON, STUPID 2, THICK-SKULLED, UNSKILLED.

DUMBFOUNDED 1 (dŭm found' ed), *adj.* (The mind is frozen; the thought is frozen.) The index finger of the right "D" hand, palm facing the body, touches the forehead (modified THINK sign, *q.v.*). Both hands, in the "5" position, palms down, are then suddenly and deliberately dropped down in front of the body. A look of surprise is assumed at this point, and the head jerks back slightly. *Cf.* AT A LOSS, SHOCKED 1.

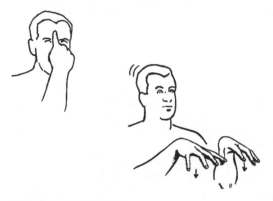

DUMBFOUNDED 2, *(colloq.)*, *adj.* (The mouth drops open.) The fingertips of both "V" hands are held curved and touching before the body, one hand above the other. Then the hands are suddenly drawn apart, and at the same instant the mouth drops open and the eyes open wide. *Cf.* OPEN-MOUTHED, SPEECHLESS, SURPRISE 2.

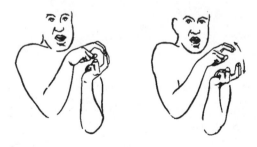

DUMMY (dum' ə), *n.* The thumb of the right "C" hand is placed inside the closed left hand. Pivoting on the thumb, the right hand moves up and over the back of the left.

DUNCE (dŭns), *n.* See DULL 1.

DUPLICATE (*adj.*, *n.* dū' plə kĭt, dōō'-; *v.* dū' plə kāt', dōō'-), -CATED, -CATING. (The natural sign.) The right fingers and thumb close together and move onto the upturned, open left hand, as if taking something from one place to another. *Cf.* COPY, IMITATE, MIMIC, MODEL.

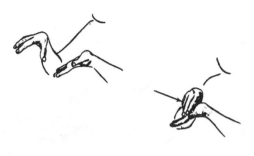

DURING (dyŏŏr' ĭng, dōŏr'-), *prep.* (Parallel time.) Both "D" hands, palms down, move forward in unison, away from the body. They may move straight forward or may follow a slight upward arc. *Cf.* MEANTIME, WHILE.

DUSTPAN (dust' pan), *n.* (The sweeping.) The upturned left hand is the dustpan. The little finger edge of the right hand repeatedly "sweeps" dust into the left.

EACH (ĕch), *adj.* (Peeling off, one by one.) The left "A" hand is held palm facing the right. The knuckles of the right "A" hand are drawn repeatedly down the left thumb, from its tip to its base. *Cf.* EVERY.

EACH OTHER *pron. phrase.* (Mingling with.) Both hands are held in modified "A" positions, thumbs out. The left hand is positioned with its thumb pointing straight up, and the right hand, with its thumb pointing down, revolves above the left thumb in a clockwise direction. *Cf.* ASSOCIATE, FELLOWSHIP, MINGLE 2, MUTUAL, ONE ANOTHER.

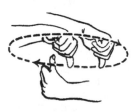

EAGER (ē' gər), *adj.* (Rubbing the hands together in zeal or ambition.) The open hands are rubbed vigorously back and forth against each other. *Cf.* AMBITIOUS, ANXIOUS, DILIGENCE, DILIGENT, EAGERNESS, ENTHUSIASM, ENTHUSIASTIC, INDUSTRIOUS, METHODIST, ZEAL, ZEALOUS.

EAGERNESS *n.* See EAGER.

EAGLE (ē' gəl), *n.* (The hooked beak and the wings.) The index finger of the right "X" hand is placed on the nose, either facing out or across it. The hands and arms then flap slowly, in imitation of the bird's majestic flight.

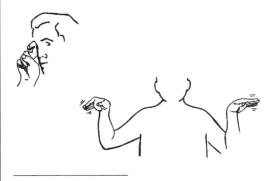

EAR (ir), *n.* (The natural sign.) The right index finger touches the right ear.

EARACHE (ĭr' āk´), *n.* (A stabbing pain in the ear.) The sign for EAR is made, followed by the sign for ACHE: the "D" hands, index fingers pointing to each other and palms facing the body, are rotated in elliptical fashion before the chest—simultaneously but in opposite directions.

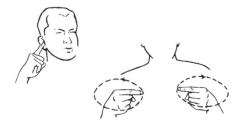

EARLY (ûr′ lē), *adj.* The middle finger of the down-turned right hand rests on the back of the downturned left hand. The top hand moves forward, while the middle finger is drawn back against the palm.

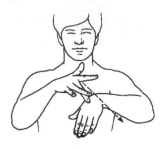

EARN (ûrn), *v.*, EARNED, EARNING. (Gathering in.) The right "5" hand, its little finger edge touching the upturned left palm, is drawn in an arc toward the body, closing into the "S" position as it sweeps over the base of the left hand. *Cf.* ACCUMULATE, COLLECT, SALARY 1, WAGE(S).

EARRING 1 (ĭr′ rĭng′), *n.* (The natural sign.) The right thumb and index finger press the right ear lobe.

EARRING 2, *n.* (The natural sign.) The signer squeezes the earlobe, which may also be shaken slightly.

EARTH (ûrth), *n.* (The earth and its axes are indicated.) The downturned left "S" hand indicates the earth. The thumb and index finger of the downturned right "5" hand are placed at each edge of the left. In this position the right hand swings back and forth, while maintaining contact with the left. *Cf.* GEOGRAPHY, GLOBE 1, PLANET 1.

EARTHQUAKE (ûrth′ kwāk′), *n.* (Earth, noise.) The sign for EARTH 1 is made. This is followed by the sign for NOISE. After placing the index finger on the ear, both hands assume the "S" position, palms down. They move alternately back and forth forcefully.

EASTER (ēs′ tər), *n.* (The letter "E.") The right "E" hand, pivoted at the wrist, is shaken slightly.

EASY 1 (ē′ zǐ), *adj.* (The fingertips are easily moved.) The right fingertips brush repeatedly over their upturned left counterparts, causing them to move. *Cf.* SIMPLE 1.

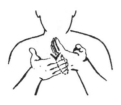

EASY 2, *(loc., colloq.), adj.* (Rationale obscure.) The thumb and index finger of the right "F" hand are placed on the chin.

EAT (ēt), *v.,* ATE, EATEN, EATING. (The natural sign.) The closed right hand goes through the natural motion of placing food in the mouth. This movement is repeated. *Cf.* CONSUME 1, CONSUMPTION, FEED 1, FOOD, MEAL.

EAVESDROP 1 (ēvz′ drop), *v.* (Information is pulled into the eye.) The hand is held with thumb below the eye, index and middle fingers pointing forward. The index and middle fingers repeatedly move in and out, as if bringing something into the eye. This is a culturally related sign, taking into account that deaf people gather information with their eyes rather than their ears.

EAVESDROP 2 , *v.* (Information is pulled into the ear.) The same hand position as in EAVESDROP 1, above. The thumbtip is placed on the ear, and the index and middle fingers move in and out, as if bringing something into the ear.

ECCENTRIC (ĭk sĕn′ trĭk), *adj.* -TRICALLY, *adv.* (Something which distorts the vision.) The "C" hand describes a small arc in front of the face.

ECONOMIC (ek ə nom′ ik), *adj.* (The "E" hand; money.) The back of the upturned right "E" hand is brought down twice on the upturned left open hand.

ECUADOR (ek′ wə dôr) *n.* The right "E" hand makes a clockwise circle at the right temple. A native sign.

EDITING (video or film), *phrase.* (The snipping in the cutting room.) The signer mimes snipping film with both hands working simultaneously.

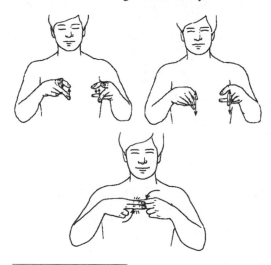

EDUCATE (ĕj′ о̄о̄ kāt′), *v., -CATED, -CATING.* (Giving forth from the mind.) The fingertips of each hand are placed on the temples. They then swing out and open into the "5" position. *Cf.* INDOCTRINATE, INDOCTRINATION, INSTRUCT, INSTRUCTION, TEACH.

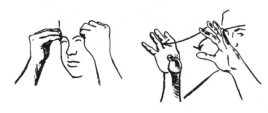

EFFEMINATE (i fem′ ə nit), *adj.* (The mincing gestures.) Both "F" hands, palms out, are held at shoul-

der height. The signer moves them alternately forward and back, while the shoulders keep pace with the forward-and-back movements. *Cf.* GAY 4, HOMOSEXUAL 4.

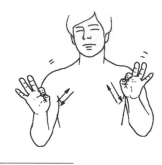

EFFORT 1 (ĕf′ ərt), *n.* (Trying to push through.) The "A" hands, palms facing before the body, are swung around and a bit down, so that the palms now face out. The movement indicates an attempt to push through a barrier. *Cf.* ATTEMPT 1, ENDEAVOR, PERSEVERE 1, PERSIST 1, TRY 1.

EFFORT 2, *n.* (Trying to push through, using the "T" hands, for "try.") This is the same sign as EFFORT 1, except that the "T" hands are employed. *Cf.* ATTEMPT 2, PERSEVERE 2, TRY 2.

EFFORT 3, *n.* (The letter "E"; attempting to break through.) Both "E" hands move forward simultaneously, describing a small, downturned arc.

EGG (ĕg), *n.* (Act of breaking an egg into a bowl.) The right "H" hand is brought down on the left "H" hand, and then both hands are pivoted down and slightly apart. *Cf.* HATCH.

EGOTISM 1 (ē' gə tĭz´ əm, ĕg' ə-), *n.* (The self is carried uppermost.) The right "A" hand, thumb up, is brought up against the chest, from waist to breast. *Cf.* SELF 2.

EGOTISM 2, *n.* (Repeated "I"s.) The "I" hands are alternately swung in toward and away from the chest. The movement is repeated a number of times.

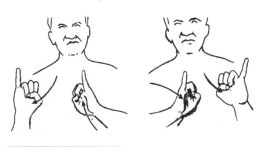

EGOTISM 3, *(colloq.), n.* (A big "I.") The right "I" hand, palm facing left, rests on the chest. The left hand, wrapped loosely around the right little finger, is drawn straight up, as if to extend the right little finger.

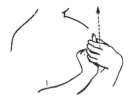

EITHER 1 (ē' thər) *or esp. Brit.,* ī' thər), *conj.* (Selection between two or among multiple choices.) The left "L" hand is held palm facing the body and thumb pointing straight up. The right index finger touches the left thumbtip and then the left index fingertip.

EITHER 2, *adj.* (Making a choice.) The left "V" hand faces the body. The right thumb and index finger close first over the left index fingertip and then over the left middle fingertip. *Cf.* CHOICE.

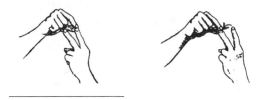

EITHER 3, *conj.* (Considering one thing against another.) The "A" hands, palms facing and thumbs pointing straight up, move alternately up and down before the chest. *Cf.* OR, WHETHER, WHICH.

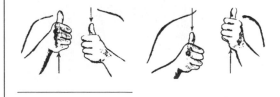

EJACULATE 1 (i jak' yə lāt), *v., n.* (The pulsing of the penis during release.) The left index finger, representing the penis, is positioned at the base of the right "E" or "S" hand, whose palm faces left. The fingers of the right hand open and close twice, as the two hands, connected, move forward an inch or so. This sign is used for male ejaculation. *Cf.* EJACULATION 1, SEMEN, SPERM.

EJACULATE 2, *v.*, *n.* (Pulsation within the vagina.) The left hand grasps the right wrist as the right fingers are thrown open repeatedly. *Cf.* EJACULATION 2.

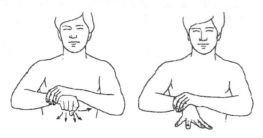

EJACULATION 1 (i jak yə lā′ shən), *n.* See EJACULATE 1.

EJACULATION 2, *n.* See EJACULATE 2.

ELBOW (el′ bō), *n.* (The elbow is pointed to.) The signer touches his elbow.

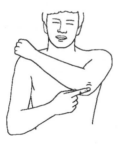

ELECT (ĭ lĕkt′), *n.*, *v.*, -LECTED, -LECTING. (Placing a ballot in a box.) The right hand, holding an imaginary ballot between the thumb and index finger, places it into an imaginary box formed by the left "O" hand, palm facing right. *Cf.* ELECTION, VOTE 1.

ELECTION (ĭ lĕk′ shən), *n.* See ELECT.

ELECTRIC (ĭ lĕk′ trĭk), *adj.* (The points of the electrodes.) The "X" hands are held palms facing the body, thumb edges up. The knuckles of the index fingers touch each other repeatedly. *Cf.* ELECTRICITY, PHYSICS.

ELECTRICITY (ĭ lĕk′ trĭs′ ə tĭ), *n.* See ELECTRIC.

ELECTRIC OUTLET (out′ lət), *n.* (Plugging in.) Both "V" hands, palms facing each other, are held before the body. The right "V" hand, representing the prongs of a plug, is brought into an interlocking position with the left. *Cf.* ELECTRIC PLUG.

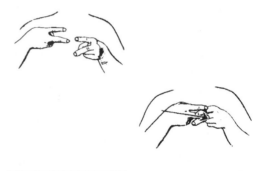

ELECTRIC PLUG (plŭg), *n.* See ELECTRIC OUTLET.

ELECTRON (i lek′ tron), *n.* (The letter "E"; circling.) The right "E" makes a circle around the left fist.

ELEGANT (el′ ə gənt), *adj.* (The feelings are titillated.) With the thumb resting on the upper part of the chest, the fingers are wiggled back and forth. *Cf.* FINE 1, GRAND 2, GREAT 4, SPLENDID 2, SWELL 2, WONDERFUL 2.

ELEMENTARY (el ə men′ tər ē), *adj.* (The letter "E"; something basic, *i.e.*, necessary to support one's knowledge.) The upturned right thumb is placed underneath the downturned left palm. The thumb makes a continuous counterclockwise circle.

ELEPHANT (ĕl′ ə fənt), *n.* (The movement of the trunk.) The cupped downturned right hand is placed with its back resting on the nose. The hand moves down, out, and around, imitating the motion of the trunk in bringing food up to the mouth. The hand may also be moved in random undulations.

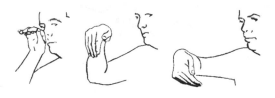

ELEVATOR 1 (ĕl′ ə vā′ tər), *n.* (A rising platform.) With the downturned right "V" fingers standing on the upturned left palm, the left hand rises straight up.

ELEVATOR 2, *n.* (The letter "E"; the rising.) The right "E" hand, palm facing left and thumb edge up, rises straight up.

ELIMINATE (ĭ lĭm ə nāt′), *v.*, -NATED, -NATING. (Scratching something out and throwing it away.) The fingertips of the open right hand scratch downward across the palm of the upright left hand. In one continuous motion, the right hand then closes as if holding something, and finally opens again forcefully and motions as if throwing something away. *Cf.* ABOLISH, DEDUCT, DELETE 1, REMOVE, SUBTRACT, SUBTRACTION, TAKE AWAY FROM.

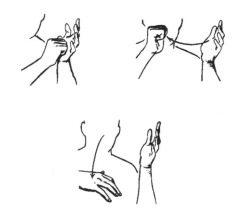

ELK (ĕlk), *n.* (The branching of the antlers from the head.) Both hands, in the "5" position, palms up, are placed at the head, thumbs resting on the head above the temples. *Cf.* ANTLERS, DEER, MOOSE.

ELSE (els), *adj.* (Moving over to *another* position.) The right "A" hand, thumb up, is pivoted from the wrist and swung over to the right, so that the thumb now points to the right. *Cf.* ANOTHER, OTHER.

EMANCIPATE (ĭ măn′ sə pāt′), *v.,* -PATED, -PATING. (Breaking the bonds.) The "S" hands, crossed in front of the body, swing apart and face out. *Cf.* FREE 1, FREEDOM, INDEPENDENCE, INDEPENDENT 1, LIBERATION, REDEEM 1, RELIEF, RESCUE, SAFE, SALVATION, SAVE 1.

EMBARRASS (ĕm băr′ əs), *v.,* -RASSED, -RASSING. (The red rises in the cheeks.) The sign for RED is made: the tip of the right index finger of the "D" hand moves down over the lips, which are red. Both hands are then placed palms facing the cheeks, and move up along the face, to indicate the rise of color. *Cf.* BLUSH, EMBARRASSED, FLUSH, MORTIFICATION.

EMBARRASSED *adj.* See EMBARRASS.

EMBRACE (ĕm brās′), *v.,* -BRACED, -BRACING, *n.* (The natural sign.) The arms clasp the body in a natural hugging position. *Cf.* HUG.

EMERGENCY (i mûr′ jən sē), *n., adj.* (The flashing light.) The right "E" hand is positioned above the head. It rotates in imitation of a flashing emergency light.

EMOTION 1 (ĭ mō′ shən), *n.* (The welling up of feelings or emotions in the heart.) The right middle finger, touching the heart, moves up an inch or two a number of times. *Cf.* FEEL 2, FEELING, MOTIVE 2, SENSATION, SENSE 2.

EMOTION 2, *n.* (The letter "E"; that which moves about in the chest, *i.e.,* the heart.) The "E" hands, palms facing in, are positioned close to the chest. Both hands describe alternate circles, the left hand clockwise and the right hand counterclockwise. The right hand alone may be used.

EMPEROR (ĕm′ pər ər), *n.* (The letter "E"; the sash worn by royalty.) The right "E" hand, palm facing left, moves down in an arc from the left shoulder to the right hip.

EMPHASIS (ĕm′ fə sĭs), *n.* (Pressing down to emphasize.) The right thumb is pressed down deliberately against the upturned left palm. Both hands move forward a bit. *Cf.* EMPHASIZE, EMPHATIC, STRESS.

EMPHASIZE (ĕm′ fə sīz′), *v.,* -SIZED, -SIZING. See EMPHASIS.

EMPHATIC (ĕm făt′ ĭk), *adj.* See EMPHASIS.

EMPTY (ĕmp′ tĭ), *adj.* (Devoid of everything on the surface.) The middle finger of the downturned right "5" hand sweeps over the back of the downturned left "A" or "S" hand, from wrist to knuckles, and continues beyond a bit. *Cf.* BARE, NAKED, NUDE, OMISSION, VACANCY, VACANT, VOID.

ENCOUNTER (ĕn koun′ tər), *v.,* -TERED, -TERING. (A coming together of two persons.) Both "D" hands, palms facing each other, are brought together. *Cf.* MEET.

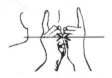

ENCOURAGE (ĕn kûr′ ĭj), *v.,* -AGED, -AGING. (Pushing forward.) Both "5" hands are held, palms out, the right fingers facing right and the left fingers left. The hands move straight forward in a series of short movements. *Cf.* MOTIVATE, MOTIVATION, URGE 1.

ENCYCLOPEDIA (en sī klə pē′ dē ə), *n.* (The letter "E"; turning the pages.) The upturned left hand indicates the open page. The right "E" hand, palm down, repeatedly brushes against the left palm, from fingertips to heel.

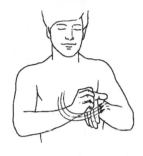

END 1 (ĕnd), *n., v.,* ENDED, ENDING. (The little, *i.e.,* LAST, fingers are indicated.) With the hands in the "I" position, the tip of the right little finger strikes the tip of its left counterpart. *Cf.* EVENTUALLY, FINAL 1, FINALLY 1, LAST 1, LASTLY, ULTIMATE, ULTIMATELY.

END 2, *n., v.* (A single little, *i.e.,* LAST, finger is indicated.) The tip of the index finger of the right "D" hand strikes the tip of the little finger of the left "I" hand. *Cf.* FINAL 2, FINALLY 2, LAST 2, LASTLY.

END 3, *n., v.* (Shaking the hands to rid them of something.) The upright "5" hands, palms facing each other, are suddenly and quickly swung around to a palm-out position. *Cf.* DONE, FINISH.

ENDEAVOR (ĭn dĕv' ər), *n.* (Trying to push through.) The "A" hands, palms facing before the body, are swung around and a bit down, so that the palms now face out. The movement indicates an attempt to push through a barrier. *Cf.* ATTEMPT 1, EFFORT 1, PERSEVERE 1, PERSIST 1, TRY 1.

ENDORSE 1 (ĕn dôrs'), *v., -DORSED, -DORSING.* (Holding up.) The right "S" hand pushes up the left "S" hand. *Cf.* MAINTENANCE, SUPPORT 1, SUSTAIN, SUSTENANCE, UPHOLD.

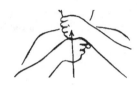

ENDORSE 2, *v.* (One hand upholds the other.) Both hands, in the "S" position, are held palms facing the body, the right under the left. The right hand pushes up the left in a gesture of support. *Cf.* ADVOCATE, SUPPORT 2.

ENDORSE 3, *v.* ("Second"—two fingers.) The right "L" hand, held somewhat above the head, index finger pointing straight up, pivots forward a bit, so that the index finger now points forward. Used in parliamentary procedure. *Cf.* SECOND 2.

ENDURE 1 (ĕn dyŏŏr', -dŏŏr'), *v., -DURED, -DURING.*

(A clenching of the fists; the rise and fall of pain.) Both "S" hands, tightly clenched, revolve about each other, slowly and deliberately, while a pained expression is worn. *Cf.* SUFFER 1, TOLERATE 2.

ENDURE 2, *v.* (Steady, uninterrupted movement.) The "A" hands are held with palms out, thumbs extended and touching, the right behind the left. In this position the hands move forward in a straight, steady line. *Cf.* CONTINUE, EVER 1, LAST 3, LASTING, PERMANENT, PERPETUAL, PERSEVERE 3, PERSIST 2, REMAIN, STAY 1, STAY STILL.

ENEMY (ĕn' ə mĭ), *n.* (At sword's point.) The two index fingers, after pointing to each other, are drawn sharply apart. This is followed by the sign for INDIVIDUAL: both open hands, palms facing each other, move down the sides of the body, tracing its outline to the hips. *Cf.* FOE, OPPONENT, RIVAL 1.

ENERGY (ĕn' ər jē), *n.* (The letter "E"; power or muscle.) The left arm, fist closed, is extended, palm up. The right "E" hand, palm down, describes an arc over the upper muscle area.

ENGAGED (ĕn gājd'), *adj.* (The letter "E"; the ring finger.) The right "E" hand moves in a clockwise circle over the downturned left hand, and then comes to rest on the left ring finger.

ENGINE (ĕn' jən), *n.* (The meshing gears.) With the knuckles of both hands interlocked, the hands pivot up and down, imitating the meshing of gear teeth. *Cf.* FACTORY, MACHINE, MACHINERY, MECHANIC 1, MECHANISM, MOTOR 1.

ENGLAND (ĭng' glənd), *n.* (The English are supposed to be handshakers.) The right hand grasps and shakes the left. *Cf.* BRITAIN, BRITISH, ENGLISH, GREAT BRITAIN.

ENGLISH (ĭng' glĭsh), *adj.* See ENGLAND.

ENJOY (ĕn joi'), *v.*, -JOYED, -JOYING. (A pleasurable feeling on the heart.) The open right hand is circled on the chest, over the heart. *Cf.* APPRECIATE, ENJOYMENT, GRATIFY 1, LIKE 3, PLEASE, PLEASURE, WILLING 2.

ENJOYMENT (ĕn joi' mənt), *n.* See ENJOY.

ENLIST (ĕn lĭst'), *v.*, -LISTED, -LISTING. (Joining together.) Both hands, held in the modified "5" position, palms out, move toward each other. The thumbs and index fingers of both hands then connect. *Cf.* AFFILIATE, ANNEX, ATTACH, BELONG, CONNECT, ENROLL, JOIN, PARTICIPATE, UNITE.

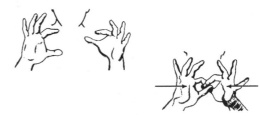

ENOUGH (ĭ nŭf'), *adj.* (A full cup.) The left hand, in the "S" position, is held palm facing right. The right "5" hand, palm down, is brushed outward several times over the top of the left, indicating a wiping off of the top of a cup. *Cf.* ABUNDANCE, ABUNDANT, ADEQUATE, AMPLE, PLENTY, SUBSTANTIAL, SUFFICIENT.

ENRAGE (ĕn rāj'), *v.*, -RAGED, -RAGING. (A violent welling-up of the emotions.) The curved fingers of the right hand are placed in the center of the chest, and fly up suddenly and violently. An expression of anger is worn. *Cf.* ANGER, ANGRY 2, FURY, INDIGNANT, INDIGNATION, IRE, MAD, RAGE.

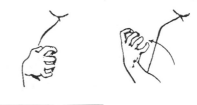

ENROLL (ĕn rōl'), *v.*, -ROLLED, -ROLLING. See ENLIST.

ENTER (ĕn′ tər), *v.*, -TERED, -TERING. (Going in.) The downturned open right hand sweeps under its downturned left counterpart. *Cf.* ENTRANCE.

ENTHUSIASM (ĕn thōō′ zĭ ăz′ əm), *n.* (Rubbing the hands together in zeal or ambition.) The open hands are rubbed vigorously back and forth against each other. *Cf.* AMBITIOUS, ANXIOUS, DILIGENCE, DILIGENT, EAGER, EAGERNESS, ENTHUSIASTIC, INDUSTRIOUS, METHODIST, ZEAL, ZEALOUS.

ENTHUSIASTIC (ĕn thōō′ zĭ ăs′ tĭk), *adj.* See ENTHUSIASM.

ENTIRE (ĕn tīr′), *adj.* (Encompassing; a gathering together.) Both hands are held in the right angle position, palms facing the body, and the right hand in front of the left. The right hand makes a sweeping outward movement around the left, and comes to rest with the back of the right hand resting in the left palm. *Cf.* ALL, UNIVERSAL, WHOLE.

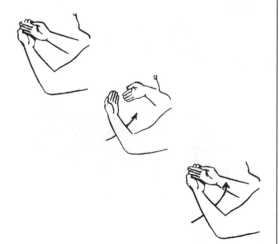

ENTRANCE (ĕn trans′), *n.* See ENTER.

ENTREAT (ĕn trēt′), *v.*, -TREATED, -TREATING. (An act of supplication.) With the right hand clasped over the left, both hands are shaken gently before the body. The eyes often are directed upward. *Cf.* BEG 2, IMPLORE, PLEA, PLEAD, SUPPLICATION.

ENVELOPE (en′ və lōp), *n.* (Licking the flap.) The shape of the envelope is indicated with the curved thumbs and index fingers, which move apart to show the length. The tongue then emerges and licks back and forth against the flap.

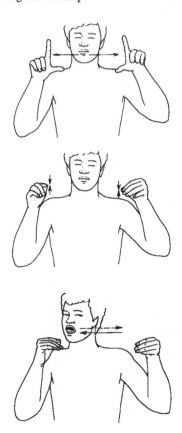

ENVIOUS (ĕn' vĭ əs), *adj.* (Biting the finger to suppress the feelings.) The tip of the index finger is bitten. The tip of the little finger is sometimes used. *Cf.* ENVY, JEALOUS, JEALOUSY.

ENVIRONMENT (ĕn vī' rən mənt), *n.* (The letter "E"; encircling the individual, represented by the index finger.) The right "E" hand travels around the upright left index finger.

ENVY (en' vĭ), *n.* See ENVIOUS.

EPIDEMIC (ep ə dem' ik), *n.* (Sickness spreads.) The sign for SICK is made: the right middle finger rests on the forehead and its left counterpart on the stomach. Both hands are then held palms down, in the modified "O" position. The hands move out and spread apart, with fingers opening wide.

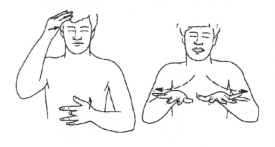

EPILEPSY (ep' ə lep sē), *n.* (The body shakes in a fit.) The right hand, palm up, index and middle fingers curved, is placed in the upturned left palm. The right hand's index and middle fingers open and close

slightly as the two fingers tremble. *Cf.* FIT, SEIZURE.

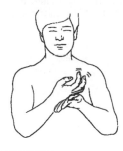

EPILOGUE (ep' ə lôg), *n.* (The letter "E"; coming to the end.) The right "E" hand moves along the index finger edge of the left and drops down over the left fingertips.

EPISCOPAL (ĭ pĭs' kə pəl), *adj.* (The surplice sleeve.) The left arm is held horizontally, the right index finger describes an arc under it, from wrist to elbow.

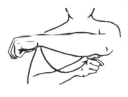

EQUAL (ē' kwəl), *adj., n., v.,* -QUALED, -QUALING. (Sameness is stressed.) The downturned "B" hands, held at chest height, are brought together repeatedly, so that the index finger edges or fingertips come into contact. *Cf.* EQUIVALENT, EVEN, FAIR, LEVEL·

EQUATOR (i kwā′ tər), *n*. (The letter "E"; circling the globe.) The right "E" hand describes a circle around the left fist, which represents the planet.

EQUIVALENT (ĭ kwĭv′ ə lənt), *adj*. See EQUAL.

ERECTION (i rek′ shən), *n*. (The arm portrays the erection of the penis.) The left hand grasps the right arm or the crook of the right elbow as the right "S" hand moves up in an arc from a horizontal position.

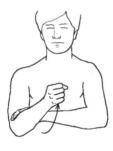

ERROR (ĕr′ ər), *n*. (Rationale obscure; the thumb and little finger are said to represent, respectively, right and wrong, with the head poised between the two.) The right "Y" hand, palm facing the body, is brought up to the chin. *Cf*. MISTAKE, WRONG 1.

ESCALATOR (es′ kə lā tər), *n*. (Standing on moving stairs.) The right index and middle fingers "stand" on the left hand, which is held either up or down. The

left hand moves up at an angle, carrying the right hand with it.

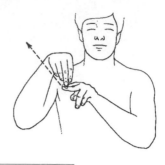

ESCAPE (ĕs kāp′), *v*., -CAPED, -CAPING. (Emerging from a hiding place.) The downturned right "D" hand is positioned under the downturned open left hand. The right "D" hand suddenly emerges and moves off quickly to the right. *Cf*. FLEE.

ESKIMO (es′ kə mō), *n*. (The letter "E"; the fur hood.) The "E" hand, palm facing out, describes a circle over the head, from left to right.

ESTABLISH (ĕs tăb′ lĭsh), *v*., -LISHED, -LISHING. (To set up.) The right "A" hand, thumb up and palm facing left, comes down to rest on the back of the downturned left "S" hand. Before doing so, the right "A" hand may describe a clockwise circle above the left hand, but this is optional. *Cf*. FOUND, FOUNDED.

ETERNITY (ĭ tûr′ nə tĭ), *n.* (Around the clock and ahead into the future.) The right index finger, pointing forward, traces a clockwise circle in the air. The downturned right "Y" hand then moves forward, either in a straight line or in a slight downward curve. *Cf.* EVER 2, EVERLASTING, FOREVER.

ETHICS (eth′ iks), *n.* (The letter "E"; having to do with the heart or character.) The right "E" hand, palm facing the signer, describes a counterclockwise circle over the heart.

EVADE (ĭ vād′), *v.,* -VADED, -VADING. (Ducking back and forth, away from something.) Both "A" hands, thumbs pointing straight up, are held some distance before the chest, with the left hand in front of the right. The right hand, swinging back and forth, moves away from the left and toward the chest. *Cf.* AVOID 1, EVASION, SHIRK, SHUN.

EVALUATE 1 (ĭ văl′ yŏŏ āt′), *v.,* -ATED, -ATING. (The scales move up and down.) The two "F" hands, palms facing each other, move alternately up and down. *Cf.* CONSIDER 3, COURT, IF, JUDGE 1, JUDGMENT, JUSTICE.

EVALUATE 2, *v.* (The letter "E"; weighing up and down.) The "E" hands, palms facing out from the body, move alternately up and down.

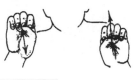

EVALUATE 3, *v.* (Weighing.) Both "E" hands, palms out, move alternately up and down.

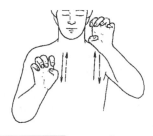

EVASION (ĭ vā′ zhən), *n.* See EVADE.

EVEN (ē′ vən), *adj.* (Sameness is stressed.) The downturned "B" hands, held at chest height, are brought together repeatedly, so that the index finger edges or fingertips come into contact. *Cf.* EQUAL, EQUIVALENT, FAIR, LEVEL.

EVENT (ĭ vĕnt′), *n.* (A befalling.) Both "D" hands, index fingers pointing away from the body, are simultaneously pivoted over so that the palms face down. *Cf.* COINCIDE, COINCIDENCE, HAPPEN 1, INCIDENT, OCCUR, OPPORTUNITY 4.

EVENTUALLY (ĭ vĕn′ chŏŏ ə lĭ), *adv.* (The little, *i.e.,* LAST, fingers are indicated.) With the hands in the "I" position, the tip of the right little finger strikes the tip of its left counterpart. The right index finger may be used instead of the right little finger. *Cf.* END 1, FINAL 1, FINALLY 1, LAST 1, ULTIMATE, ULTIMATELY.

EVER 1 (ĕv′ ər), *adv.* (Steady, uninterrupted movement.) The "A" hands are held with palms out, thumbs extended and touching, the right behind the left. In this position the hands move forward in a straight, steady line. *Cf.* CONTINUE, ENDURE 2, LAST 3, LASTING, PERMANENT, PERPETUAL, PERSEVERE 3, PERSIST 2, REMAIN, STAY 1, STAY STILL.

EVER 2, *adv.* (Around the clock and ahead into the future.) The right index finger, pointing forward, traces a clockwise circle in the air. The downturned right "Y" hand then moves forward, either in a straight line or in a slight downward curve. *Cf.* ETERNITY, EVERLASTING, FOREVER.

EVERLASTING (ĕv′ ər lăs′ tĭng, -läs′-), *adj.* See EVER 2.

EVER SINCE (ĕv′ ər sĭns), *phrase.* (From a point up and over.) In the "D" position, palms down, both index fingers touch the right shoulder and then are brought up and over, ending in a palm-up position, pointing straight ahead of the body. *Cf.* ALL ALONG, ALL THE TIME, SINCE 1, SO FAR, THUS FAR.

EVERY (ĕv′ rĭ), *adj.* (Peeling off, one by one.) The left "A" hand is held palm facing the right. The knuckles of the right "A" hand are drawn repeatedly down the left thumb, from its tip to its base. *Cf.* EACH.

EVERYDAY (ĕv′ rĭ dā′), *adj.* (Tomorrow after tomorrow.) The sign for TOMORROW, *q.v.,* is made several times: the right "A" hand moves forward several times from its initial resting place on the right cheek. *Cf.* DAILY.

EVERY YEAR (yĭr), *phrase.* (Several years brought forward.) This sign is actually a modification of the sign for YEAR, *q.v.* The ball of the right "S" hand, moving straight out from the body, palm facing left, glances over the thumb side of the left "S" hand, which is held palm facing right. As this contact is made, the right index finger is flung straight out, and the right hand, in this new position, continues forward. This is repeated several times, to indicate several years. *Cf.* ANNUAL, YEARLY.

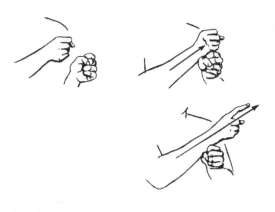

EVIDENCE (ĕv′ ə dəns), *n., v.,* -DENCED, -DENCING. (Directing the attention to something, and bringing it forward.) The right index finger points into the left palm, held facing out before the body. The left palm moves straight out. *Cf.* DEMONSTRATE, DISPLAY, EXAMPLE, EXHIBIT, EXHIBITION, ILLUSTRATE, INDICATE, INFLUENCE 2, PRODUCE 1, REPRESENT, SHOW 1, SIGNIFY 1.

EVIDENT (ev′ ə dənt), *adj.* (Rays of light clearing the way.) Both hands are held at chest height, palms out, all fingertips together. They open into the "5" position in unison, the right hand moving toward the right and the left toward the left. The palms of both hands remain facing out. *Cf.* CLEAR, OBVIOUS, PLAIN 1.

EXACT 1 (ĭg zăkt′), *adj.* (The fingers come together precisely.) The thumb and index finger of each hand, palms facing, the right above the left, form circles. They are brought together with a deliberate movement, so that the fingers and thumbs now touch. Sometimes the right hand, before coming together with the left, executes a slow clockwise circle above the left. *Cf.* EXACTLY, EXPLICIT 1, PRECISE, SPECIFIC 1.

EXACT 2, *adj.* The right index finger, held above the left index finger, comes down rather forcefully so that the bottom of the right hand comes to rest on top of the left thumb joint. *Cf.* ACCURATE, CORRECT 1, DECENT, PROPER, RIGHT 3, SUITABLE.

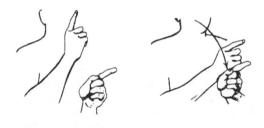

EXACTLY (ĭg zăkt′ lĭ), *adv.* See EXACT 1.

EXAGGERATE (ĭg zăj′ ə rāt′), (*sl.*), *v.,* -ATED, -ATING. (Stretching out one's words.) The left "S" hand, palm facing right, is held before the mouth. Its right counterpart, palm facing left, is moved forward in a series of short up-and-down arcs.

EXAMINATION 1 (ĭg zăm´ ə nā´ shən), *n.* (A series of questions spread out on a page.) Both "D" hands, palms down, simultaneously execute a single circle, the right hand moving in a clockwise direction and the left in a counterclockwise direction. Upon completion of the circle, both hands open into the "5" position and move straight down a short distance. (The hands actually draw question marks in the air.) *Cf.* QUIZ 1, TEST.

EXAMINATION 2, *n.* (Firing questions.) The index fingers of both "D" hands repeatedly curve and straighten out as the hands are alternately flung forward and back, as if firing questions. *Cf.* ASK 3, INQUIRE 3, INTERROGATE 1, INTERROGATION 1, QUERY 1, QUESTION 3, QUIZ 3.

EXAMINE (ĭg zăm´ ĭn), *v.,* -INED, -INING. (Directing the vision from place to place.) The right "C" hand, palm facing left, moves from right to left across the line of vision, in a series of counterclockwise circles. The signer's gaze remains concentrated and his head turns slowly from right to left. *Cf.* CURIOUS 1, INVESTIGATE, LOOK FOR, PROBE, SEARCH, SEEK.

EXAMPLE (ĭg zăm´ pəl, -zăm´-), *n., v.,* -PLED, -PLING. (Directing the attention to something, and bringing it forward.) The right index finger points into the left palm, held facing out before the body. The left palm moves straight out. *Cf.* DEMONSTRATE, DISPLAY, EVI-

DENCE, EXHIBIT, EXHIBITION, ILLUSTRATE, INDICATE, INFLUENCE 2, PRODUCE 1, REPRESENT, SHOW 1, SIGNIFY 1.

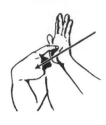

EXCELLENT (ĕk´ sə lənt), *adj.* (The hands gesture toward the heavens.) The "5" hands, palms out and arms raised rather high, are positioned somewhat above the line of vision. The arms move abruptly forward and up once or twice. An expression of pleasure or surprise is usually assumed. *Cf.* GRAND 1, GREAT 3, MARVELOUS, SPLENDID 1, SWELL 1, WONDER 2, WONDERFUL 1.

EXCEPT (ĭk sĕpt´), *prep., conj.* (Selecting a particular item from among several.) The index finger and thumb of the right hand grasp and pull up the left index finger. *Cf.* EXCEPTION, SPECIAL.

EXCEPTION (ĭk sĕp´ shən), *n.* See EXCEPT.

EXCHANGE (ĭks chānj′), *v.,* -CHANGED, -CHANGING. (Exchanging places.) The right "A" hand, positioned above the left "A" hand, swings down and under the left, coming up a bit in front of it. *Cf.* INSTEAD OF 1, REPLACE, SUBSTITUTE, TRADE.

EXCITE (ĭk sīt′), *v.,* -CITED, -CITING. (The heart beats violently.) Both middle fingers move up alternately to strike the heart sharply. *Cf.* EXCITEMENT, EXCITING, THRILL 1.

EXCITEMENT (ĭk sīt′ mənt), *n.* See EXCITE.

EXCITING (ĭk sī′ tĭng), *adj.* See EXCITE.

EXCUSE (*n.* ĭk skūs′; *v.* ĭk skūz′), -CUSED, -CUSING. (A wiped-off and cleaned slate.) The right hand wipes off the left palm several times. *Cf.* APOLOGIZE 2, APOLOGY 2, FORGIVE, PARDON, PAROLE.

EXHIBIT (ĭg zĭb′ ĭt), *v.,* -ITED, -ITING. (Directing the attention to something, and bringing it forward.) The right index finger points into the left palm, held facing out before the body. The left palm moves straight out. *Cf.* DEMONSTRATE, DISPLAY, EVIDENCE, EXAMPLE, EXHIBITION, ILLUSTRATE, INDICATE, INFLUENCE 2, PRODUCE 1, REPRESENT, SHOW 1, SIGNIFY 1.

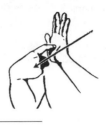

EXHIBITION (ĕk′ sə bĭsh′ ən), *n.* See EXHIBIT.

EXPAND (ĭk spănd′), *v.,* -PANDED, -PANDING. (A large amount.) The "5" hands face each other, fingers curved and touching. They move apart rather quickly. *Cf.* GREAT 2, INFINITE, LOT, MUCH.

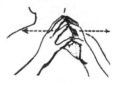

EXPECT (ĭk spĕkt′), *v.,* -PECTED, -PECTING. (A thought awaited.) The tip of the right index finger, held in the "D" position, palm facing the body, is placed on the forehead (modified THINK, *q.v.*). Both hands then assume right angle positions, fingers facing, with the left hand held above left shoulder level and the right before the right breast. Both hands, held thus, wave to each other several times. *Cf.* ANTICIPATE, ANTICIPATION, HOPE.

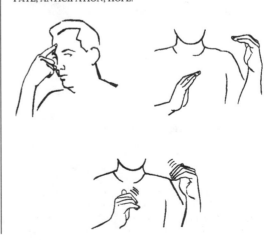

EXPEL (ĭk spĕl′), v., -PELLED, -PELLING. ("Getting the axe"; the head is chopped off.) The upturned open right hand is swung sharply over the index finger edge of the left "S" hand, whose palm faces right. *Cf.* DISCHARGE, FIRE 2.

EXPENSE (ĭk spĕns′), n. (Nicking into one.) The knuckle of the right "X" finger is nicked against the palm of the left hand, held in the "5" position, palm facing right. *Cf.* CHARGE, COST, FEE, FINE 2, PENALTY, PRICE 2, TAX 1, TAXATION 1, TOLL.

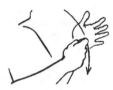

EXPENSIVE (ĭk spĕn′ sĭv), adj. (Throwing away money.) The right "AND" hand lies in the palm of the upturned, open left hand (as if holding money). The right hand then moves up and away from the left, opening abruptly as it does (as if dropping the money it holds). *Cf.* COSTLY.

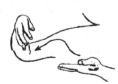

EXPERIENCE 1 (ĭk spĭr′ ĭ əns), n. (A sharp-edged hand.) The right hand grasps the little finger edge of the left firmly. As it leaves this position, moving down and out, it assumes the "A" position, palm facing left. *Cf.* ADEPT, EXPERT, SHARP, SKILL, SKILLFUL.

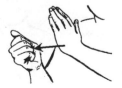

EXPERIENCE 2, n. (White hair.) The right fingertips gently pull the hair of the right temple. The movement is repeated.

EXPERIENCE SOMETHING *phrase.* (Coming in contact; finish, meaning "to have done so.") The sign for TOUCH is made: the tip of the middle finger of the downturned right "5" hand touches the back of the downturned left hand. This is followed by the sign for FINISH: the upright "5" hands, palms facing each other, are suddenly and quickly swung around to a palm-out position. One hand only may also be used.

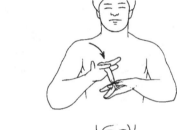

EXPERIMENT (ĭk spĕr′ ə mənt), n., v. (The "E" letters; manipulating the test tubes.) Both "E" hands, palms out, make a series of alternating circles, the right in a counterclockwise manner, and the left in a clockwise fashion. The movement looks like pouring out the contents of test tubes.

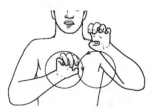

EXPERT (*n.* ĕks' pûrt; *adj.* ĭk spûrt'). See EXPERIENCE 1.

EXPLAIN 1 (ĭk splān'), *v.*, -PLAINED, -PLAINING. (Unraveling something to get at its parts.) The "F" hands, palms facing and fingers pointing straight out, are held about an inch apart. They move alternately back and forth a few inches. *Cf.* DEFINE 1, DESCRIBE 1, DESCRIPTION.

EXPLAIN 2, *v.* (The unraveling or stretching out of words or sentences.) Both open hands are held close to each other, with fingers open and palms facing and almost touching. As the hands are drawn apart, the thumb and index finger of each hand come together to form circles. This is repeated several times. *Cf.* DESCRIBE 2, NARRATE, NARRATIVE, STORY, TALE, TELL ABOUT.

EXPLICIT 1 (ĭk splĭs' ĭt), *adj.* (The fingers come together precisely.) The thumb and index finger of each hand, palms facing, the right above the left, form circles. They are brought together with a deliberate movement, so that the fingers and thumbs now touch. Sometimes the right hand, before coming together with the left, executes a slow clockwise circle above the left. *Cf.* EXACT 1, EXACTLY, PRECISE, SPECIFIC 1.

EXPLICIT 2, *adj.* (Rays of light clearing the way.) Both hands are held at chest height, palms out, all fingertips together. They open into the "5" position in unison, the right hand moving toward the right and the left toward the left. The palms of both hands remain facing out. *Cf.* BRIGHT 1, BRILLIANCE 1, BRILLIANT 2, CLEAR, OBVIOUS, PLAIN 1.

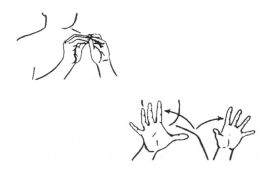

EXPRESS (ĭk spres'), *v.* (Getting something out of the system.) Both "S" (or "E") hands, palms facing up, are positioned on the chest. They move forward simultaneously in an arc, opening into the "5" position.

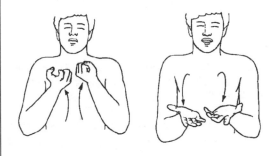

EXPRESSIVE (ĭk spres' iv), *adj.* (Coming out from within.) The upturned clenched fists are positioned side by side at the upper chest. They move out and forward, opening to the upturned "5" position.

EXTRAVAGANT (ĭk străv′ ə gənt), *adj.* (Repeated giving forth.) The back of the upturned right hand, thumb touching fingertips, is placed in the upturned left palm. The right hand moves off and away from the left once or several times, each time opening into the "5" position, palm up. *Cf.* SPEND 1, SQUANDER 1, WASTE 1.

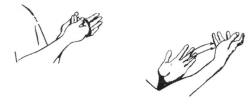

EXULTATION (ĕg′ zŭl tā′ shən), *n.* (Waving a flag.) The right "A" hand goes through the natural movement of waving a flag in circular fashion. Preceding this, the right hand may go through the motion of grabbing the flagstaff out of the left hand. *Cf.* TRIUMPH 1, VICTORY 2, WIN 2.

EYE (ī) *n., v.,* EYED, EYEING or EYING. (The natural sign.) The right index finger touches the lower lid of the right eye.

EYEBROW (ī′ brou), *n.* (Tracing the eyebrow.) The right index finger runs along the eyebrow, from left to right.

EYEGLASSES (ī′ glăs′ əs), *n. pl.* (The shape.) The thumb and index finger of the right hand, placed flat against the right temple, move back toward the right ear, tracing the line formed by the eyeglass frame. *Cf.* GLASSES.

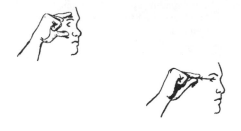

EYELASHES (ī′ lash ez), *n.* (The shape.) Both downturned "4" hands are held at the eyes, fingers pointing forward. The hands move slightly forward, in an upturned arc.

EYES ROLLING AROUND (*colloq.*), *v. phrase.* (The natural sign.) Both "F" hands, palms facing, are held at eye level. They execute a series of small circular movements before the eyes.

F

FACE (fās), *v.*, FACED, FACING. (Face to face.) The left hand, fingers together, palm flat and facing the eyes, is held a bit above eye level. The right hand, fingers also together, is held in front of the mouth, with palm facing the left hand. With a sweeping upward movement the right hand moves toward the left, which moves straight up an inch or two at the same time. *Cf.* BEFORE 3, CONFRONT, FACE TO FACE, PRESENCE.

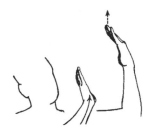

FACE TO FACE *phrase.* See FACE.

FACTORY (făk′ tə rĭ), *n.* (The meshing gears.) With the knuckles of both hands interlocked, the hands pivot up and down, imitating the meshing of gear teeth. *Cf.* ENGINE, MACHINE, MACHINERY, MECHANIC 1, MECHANISM, MOTOR 1.

FADE (fād), *v.*, FADED, FADING. (Fingering the small pieces resulting from the breaking up of something.) The thumbs rub slowly across the fingertips of the upturned hands, from the little fingers to the index fingers, and then continue to the "Λ" position, palms up. *Cf.* DECAY, DIE OUT, DISSOLVE, MELT, ROT.

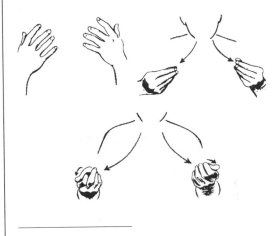

FAHRENHEIT (far′ ən hīt), *n.* (The letter "F"; rise and fall of temperature.) The thumb and index finger of the right "F" hand move up and down the upturned left index finger.

FAIL (fāl), *v.*, FAILED, FAILING. (A sliding.) The right "V" hand, palm up, slides along the upturned left palm, from its base to its fingertips.

FAINT (fānt), *adj.* (The knees buckle.) The right "V" hand is placed with fingertips resting in the upturned left palm. The knuckles of the "V" fingers buckle a bit. This motion may be repeated. *Cf.* FEEBLE, FRAIL, WEAK, WEAKNESS.

FAIR (fâr), *adj.* (Sameness is stressed.) The down-turned "B" hands, held at chest height, are brought together repeatedly, so that the index finger edges or fingertips come into contact. *Cf.* EQUAL, EQUIVALENT, EVEN, LEVEL.

FAITHFUL (fāth′ fəl), *adj.* (Coming together with regular frequency.) Both "D" hands are held with index fingers pointing forward, the right hand above the left. The right "D" hand is brought down on the left several times in rhythmic succession. *Cf.* CONSISTENT, REGULAR.

FAKE (fāk), *v.*, FAKED, FAKING. (A double face, *i.e.*, a mask covers the face.) The right hand is placed over the back of the left hand and pushes it down and a bit in toward the body. *Cf.* BLUFF, HUMBUG, HYPOCRITE, IMPOSTOR.

FALL 1 (fôl), *n.* (The falling of leaves.) The left arm, held upright with palm facing back, represents a tree trunk. The right hand, fingers together and palm down, moves down along the left arm, from the back of the wrist to the elbow, either once or several times. This represents the falling of leaves from the tree branches, indicated by the left fingers.

FALL 2, *n., v.,* FELL, FALLEN, FALLING. (Falling on one's side.) The downturned index and middle fingers of the right "V" hand are placed in a standing position on the upturned left palm. The right "V" hand flips over, coming to rest palm up on the upturned left palm.

FALL FOR *v.* (Swallowing the bait.) The mouth is held wide open. The right hand, fingers pointing to the rear of the signer, moves as if to enter the mouth, but brushes the right cheek as it passes to the rear. This sign is used in the context of someone who has been duped, or has proved gullible.

FALSE (fôls), *adj.* (Words diverted instead of coming straight, or truthfully, out.) The index finger of the right "D" hand, pointing to the left, moves along the lips from right to left. *Cf.* FALSEHOOD, LIAR, LIE 1.

FALSEHOOD (fôls′ hŏŏd), *n.* See FALSE.

FAME (fām), *n.* (One's fame radiates far and wide.) The extended index fingers rest on the lips (or on the temples). Moving in small, continuous spirals, they move up and to either side of the head. *Cf.* FAMOUS, PROMINENT, RENOWNED.

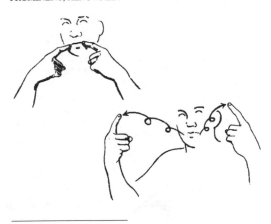

FAMILIAR (fə mil′ yər), *adj.* (Patting the head to indicate something of value inside.) The right fingers pat the forehead several times. *Cf.* KNOW.

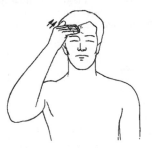

FAMILY (făm′ ə lĭ), *n.* (The letter "F"; a circle or group.) The thumb and index fingers of both "F" hands are in contact, palms facing. The hands swing open and around, coming together again at their little finger edges, palms now facing the body.

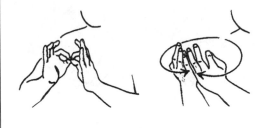

FAMOUS (fā′ məs), *adj.* See FAME.

FAN 1 (fan), *n.* (Electric; blowing on the face.) The sign for ELECTRIC is made. The knuckles of both bent index fingers come together several times, indicating the electrodes coming in contact. The right index finger, pointing at the face, makes a clockwise circle and then the right hand moves toward the face, fingers spread open. The sign for ELECTRIC may be omitted.

FAN 2, *n., v.* (Fanning oneself.) The signer, grasping an imaginary fan, mimes fanning the face.

FAR (fär), *adj.* (Moving beyond, *i.e.,* the concept of distance or "farness.") The "A" hands are held together, thumbs pointing away from the body. The right hand moves straight ahead in a slight arc. The left hand does not move. *Cf.* REMOTE.

FAR-FETCHED (fär' fecht) *adj.* (The imagination is in a whirl.) The right "4" hand, index finger touching the right temple as in a salute, moves away and somewhat upwards, in a continuous clockwise spiral.

FARM (färm), *(sl.),* *n.* (The stubbled beard commonly associated with an uncouth backwoods type.) The open right "5" hand is placed with thumb resting on the left side of the chin. The hand moves over to the right side of the chin, with the thumb always in contact with it.

FART 1 (färt), *v., n., sl.* (The escaping gas.) The right index finger, pointing up, moves suddenly

forward from a position between two fingers of the downturned open left hand.

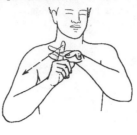

FART 2, *v., n., sl.* (Gas escaping.) The right hand, fingers and thumbs touching, is held under the left elbow. The right hand opens and closes quickly.

FASCINATE (făs' ə nāt'), *v.,* -NATED, -NATING. (Drawing one out.) The index and middle fingers of both hands, one above the other, are placed on the middle part of the chest. Both hands move forward simultaneously. As they do, the index and middle fingers of each hand come together. *Cf.* INTEREST 1, INTERESTED 1, INTERESTING 1.

FAST (făst), *adj.* (A quick movement.) The thumbtip of the upright right hand is flicked quickly off the tip of the curved right index finger, as if shooting marbles. *Cf.* IMMEDIATELY, QUICK, QUICKNESS, SPEED, SPEEDY, SWIFT.

FAT 1 (făt), *adj.* (The swollen cheeks.) The cheeks are puffed out and the open "C" hands, positioned at either cheek, move away to their respective sides. *Cf.* STOUT.

FAT 2, *n.* (The drippings from a fleshy, *i.e.,* animal, substance. Used, however, to indicate both organic and inorganic types of oil.) The right thumb and middle finger grasp the fleshy part of the open left hand. The right hand moves straight down. This is repeated once or twice. *Cf.* FATTY, GRAVY, GREASE, GREASY, OIL 2, OILY.

FATHER 1 (fä′ t͟hər), *n.* (Male who holds the baby.) The sign for MALE, *q.v.,* is made: the thumb and extended fingers of the right hand are brought up to grasp an imaginary cap brim, representing the tipping of caps by men in olden days. Both hands are then held open with palms facing up, as if holding a baby. This is the formal sign.

FATHER 2, *(informal), n.* (Derived from the formal sign for FATHER 1, *q.v.*) The thumbtip of the right "5" hand touches the right temple a number of times.

The other fingers may also wiggle. *Cf.* DAD, DADDY, PAPA, POP 2.

FATTY (făt′ ĭ), *adj.* (The from a fleshy, *i.e.,* animal, substance. Used, however, to indicate both organic and inorganic types of oil.) The right thumb and middle finger grasp the fleshy part of the open left hand. The right hand moves straight down. This is repeated once or twice. *Cf.* FAT 2, GRAVY, GREASE, GREASY, OIL 2, OILY.

FAULT (fôlt), *n.* (The blame is firmly placed.) The right "A" hand, thumb pointing up, is brought down firmly against the back of the left hand, held palm down; the right thumb is then directed toward the person or object to blame. When personal blame is acknowledged, the thumb is brought in to the chest. *Cf.* ACCUSE, BLAME, GUILTY 1.

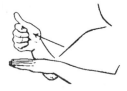

FAVORITE 1 (fā′ vər it), *adj.* (To the taste.) The middle finger is placed against the lips and the signer assumes an expression indicating pleasure.

FAVORITE 2, *adj.* (Hooked on to; a good friend.) Both index fingers interlock and move down forcefully an inch or two. The lips are held together tightly and an expression of pleasure is shown. *Cf.* GOOD FRIEND.

FAVORITE 3, *adj.* (Kissing, to indicate a high approval rating.) The back of either fist is kissed, and an expression of pleasure is shown. *Cultural note:* this sign is considered overused by many deaf people. To them it indicates a lack of discrimination (everything is a "favorite").

FAX 1 (faks), *n., v.* (The paper coming out.) The downturned left hand undulates a little as it moves under and out of the downturned right hand.

FAX 2, *n., v.* (A fingerspelled loan sign.) The signer fingerspells "F-A-X."

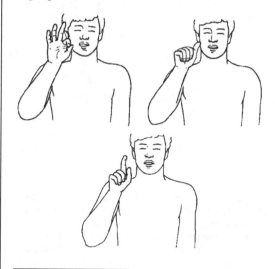

FEAR 1 (fĭr), *n., v.,* FEARED, FEARING. (The heart is suddenly covered with fear.) Both hands, fingers together, are placed side by side, palms facing the chest. They quickly open and come together over the heart, one on top of the other. *Cf.* AFRAID, FRIGHT, FRIGHTEN, SCARE(D), TERROR 1.

FEAR 2, *n., v.* (The hands attempt to ward off something which causes fear.) The "5" hands, right behind left, move downward before the body, in a wavy motion. *Cf.* DREAD, TERROR 2, TIMID.

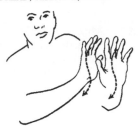

FEAST (fēst), *n.* (Stuffing food into the mouth.) Both closed hands come to the mouth in alternate continuous circles. *Cf.* BANQUET.

FEASTDAY (fēst′ dā), *n.* (CARE, DAY.) The sign for CARE 1 is made: the "K" hands are crossed, the right above the left, little finger edges down. In this position they describe a small clockwise circle in front of the chest. This is followed by the sign for DAY: the left arm, held horizontally, palm down, represents the horizon. The right elbow rests on the back of the left hand, with the right arm in a perpendicular position. The right "D" hand, palm facing left, moves in an arc to the left until it is just above the left elbow.

FECES (fē′ sēz), *(sl., vulg.), n.* (The passing of fecal material.) The left hand grasps the upturned right

thumb. The right hand drops down and the right thumb is exposed. *Cf.* DEFECATE.

FEE (fē), *n.* (Nicking into one.) The knuckle of the right "X" finger is nicked against the palm of the left hand, held in the "5" position, palm facing right. *Cf.* CHARGE, COST, EXPENSE, FINE 2, PENALTY, PRICE 2, TAX 1, TAXATION 1, TOLL.

FEEBLE (fē′ bəl), *adj.* (The knees buckle.) The right "V" hand is placed with fingertips resting in the upturned left palm. The knuckles of the "V" fingers buckle a bit. This motion may be repeated. *Cf.* FAINT, FRAIL, WEAK, WEAKNESS.

FEED 1 (fēd), *v.,* FED, FEEDING. (The natural sign.) The closed right hand goes through the natural motion of placing food in the mouth. This movement is repeated. *Cf.* CONSUME 1, CONSUMPTION, EAT, FOOD, MEAL.

FEED 2, *v.* (Placing food before someone; the action of placing food in someone's mouth.) The upturned hands, holding imaginary pieces of food, the right behind the left, move forward simultaneously, in a gesture of placing food in someone's mouth.

FEEDBACK (fēd' bak), *n.* (The letters "F" and "B"; back and forth.) Both "F" hands are positioned in front of the face, the left facing in and the right facing out. They move in and out alternately, changing from "F" to "B" each time.

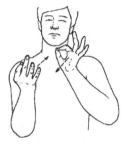 

FEEL 1 (fēl), *v.*, FELT, FEELING. (The natural movement of touching.) The tip of the middle finger of the downturned right "5" hand touches the back of the left hand a number of times. *Cf.* CONTACT 1, TOUCH.

FEEL 2, *v.* (The welling up of feelings or emotions in the heart.) The right middle finger, touching the heart, moves up an inch or two a number of times. *Cf.* EMOTION 1, FEELING, MOTIVE 2, SENSATION, SENSE 2.

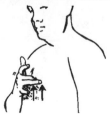

FEELING (fē' lĭng), *n.* See FEEL 2.

FEEL TOUCHED (tŭcht), *v. phrase.* (A piercing of the heart.) The tip of the middle finger of the right "5" hand is thrust against the heart. The head, at the same time, moves abruptly back a very slight distance. *Cf.* TOUCHED, TOUCHING.

FELLOWSHIP (fĕl' ō shĭp'), *n.* (Mingling with.) Both hands are held in modified "A" positions, thumbs out. The left hand is positioned with its thumb pointing straight up, and the right hand, with its thumb pointing down, revolves above the left thumb in a clockwise direction. *Cf.* ASSOCIATE, EACH OTHER, MINGLE 2, MUTUAL, ONE ANOTHER.

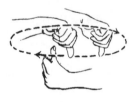

FEMALE (fē' māl), *n., adj.* (The bonnet string used by women of old.) The right "A" hand's thumb moves down along the line of the right jaw, from ear almost to chin. This outlines the string used to tie ladies' bonnets in olden days. This is a root sign to modify many others. *Viz:* FEMALE plus BABY: DAUGHTER; FEMALE plus SAME: SISTER; etc.

FERRIS WHEEL (fer′ is), *n.* (The circling seat.) The downturned right index and middle fingers are draped over the downturned left thumb, which is held rigid. Both hands, thus held, execute a series of large clockwise forward circles, imitating the action of a ferris wheel.

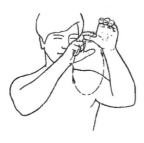

FETTER (fĕt′ ər), *n., v.,* -TERED, -TERING. (The course of the chain or shackle around the ankles.) The right "X" finger describes a half-circle around the left wrist, and then the hands are switched and the movement repeated with the left "X" finger and the right wrist. Both hands, in the "S" position, palms down, are then crossed.

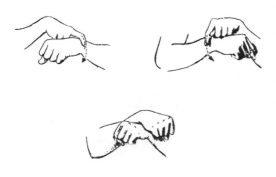

FEVER (fē′ vər), *n.* (The rise and fall of the mercury in the thermometer.) The index finger of the right "D" hand, pointing left, moves slowly up and down the index finger of the left "D" hand, which is held pointing up. *Cf.* TEMPERATURE, THERMOMETER.

FEW (fū), *adj.* (The fingers are presented in order, to convey the concept of "several.") The right "A" hand is held palm facing up. One by one the fingers open, beginning with the index finger and ending with the little finger. Some use only the index and middle fingers. *Cf.* SEVERAL.

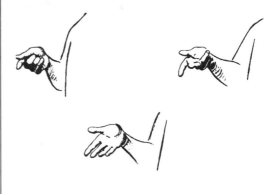

FEW SECONDS AGO, A *adv. phrase.* (Time moved backward a bit.) The right "D" hand, palm facing the body, is placed in the palm of the left hand, which is facing right. The right hand swings back a bit toward the body, with the index finger describing an arc. *Cf.* JUST A MOMENT AGO, WHILE AGO, A 2.

FIB (fĭb), *n.* (The words are deflected from their normal straight path from the lips.) The right "D" hand, palm facing left, moves quickly in front of the lips, from right to left.

FIDELITY (fĭ dĕl′ ə tĭ, fə-), *n.* (Coming forth directly from the lips; true.) The index finger of the right "D" hand, palm facing left, is placed against the lips. It moves up an inch or two and then describes a small arc forward and away from the lips. *Cf.* ABSOLUTE, ABSOLUTELY, ACTUAL, ACTUALLY, AUTHENTIC, CERTAIN, CERTAINLY, FRANKLY, GENUINE, INDEED, POSITIVE 1, POSITIVELY, REAL, REALLY, SINCERE 2, SURE, SURELY, TRUE, TRULY, TRUTH, VALID, VERILY.

FIELD 1 (fēld), *n.* (A straight, *i.e.,* special, path.) The hands are held in the "B" position, one above the other, with left palm facing right and right palm facing left. The little finger edge of the right hand moves straight forward along the index finger edge of the left. *Cf.* IN THE FIELD OF, SPECIALIZE, SPECIALTY.

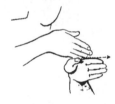

FIELD 2, *n.* (The letter "F"; straight line denotes a specific "line" or area of pursuit.) The thumb edge of the right "F" hand moves forward along the outstretched left index finger. *Cf.* PROFESSION 1.

FIELD 3, *n.* (The letter "F"; outlining the space.) Both downturned "F" hands, thumbs and index fingers touching, are held several inches in front of the chest. They describe a circle as they separate and move in toward the chest.

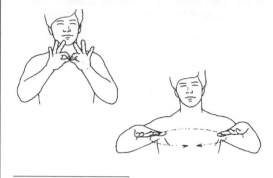

FIERCE (fĭrs), *adj.* (Wrinkling the brow.) The "5" hand is held palm toward the face. The fingers open and close partly, several times, while an angry expression is worn on the face. *Cf.* ANGRY 1, CROSS 1, CROSSNESS, ILL TEMPER, IRRITABLE.

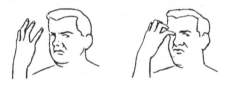

FIGHT 1 (fīt), *n., v.,* FOUGHT, FIGHTING. (The fists in combat.) The "S" hands, palms facing, swing down simultaneously toward each other. They do not touch, however.

FIGHT 2, *n., v.* (The natural sign.) Both clenched fists go through the circular motions of boxing. *Cf.* BOX 2.

Figure   199   **Filmstrip**

FIGURE 1 (fĭg′ yər), *n., v.,* -URED, -URING. (A multiplying.) The "V" hands, palms facing the body, alternately cross and separate, several times. *Cf.* ARITHMETIC, MULTIPLY 1.

FIGURE 2, *n., v.* (Contours are indicated or outlined.) Both "A" hands, held about a foot apart before the face, with palms facing each other, move down simultaneously in a wavy, undulating motion. *Cf.* FORM 1, IMAGE, SCULPT, SCULPTURE, SHAPE, STATUE.

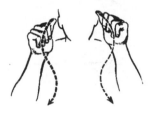

FILE (fīl), *n., v.* (Standing up files in proper order.) The left "5" hand, fingers spread, faces right. The open or "B" right hand, palm facing the signer, moves down repeatedly between the different fingers of the left hand.

FILL 1 (fĭl), *v.* FILLED, FILLING. (Wiping off the top of a container, to indicate its condition of fullness.) The downturned open right hand wipes across the index

finger edge of the left "S" hand, whose palm faces right. The movement of the right hand is toward the body. *Cf.* COMPLETE, FULL.

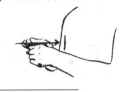

FILL 2 , *v.* (Fill to the brim.) The left hand is held palm facing the body. The little finger edge of the downturned right hand moves up the left, from little finger edge to index.

FILM (fĭlm), *n.* (The frames of the film speeding through the projector.) The left "5" hand, palm facing right and thumb pointing up, is the projector. The right "5" hand is placed against the left, and moves back and forth quickly. *Cf.* MOTION PICTURE, MOVIE(S), MOVING PICTURE.

FILMSTRIP (fĭlm′ strĭp), *n.* (A strip of movie film.) The sign for MOVIE is made: the left "5" hand is held palm facing right. The right "5" or "F" hand is placed on the left palm and moves back and forth quickly. The right thumb and index then move straight down the left palm.

FILTHY (fĭl′ thĭ), *adj.* (A modification of the pig's snout groveling in a trough.) The downturned right hand is placed under the chin. Its fingers, pointing left, wiggle repeatedly. *Cf.* DIRTY, SOIL 2.

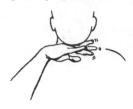

FINAL 1 (fī′ nəl), *adj.* (The little, *i.e.*, LAST, fingers are indicated.) With the hands in the "I" position, the tip of the right little finger strikes the tip of its left counterpart. *Cf.* END 1, EVENTUALLY, FINALLY 1, LAST 1, LASTLY, ULTIMATE, ULTIMATELY.

FINAL 2, *adj.* (A single little, *i.e.*, LAST, finger is indicated.) The tip of the index finger of the right "D" hand strikes the tip of the little finger of the left "I" hand. *Cf.* END 2, FINALLY 2, LAST 2, LASTLY.

FINALLY 1 (fī′ nə lĭ), *adv.* See FINAL 1.

FINALLY 2, *adv.* See FINAL 2.

FINANCE (fi nans′), *v.* (PAY and SUPPORT.) The sign for PAY: the right index finger, resting in the upturned left palm, flicks forward. This is followed

by the sign for SUPPORT: the right "S" hand pushes up its left counterpart.

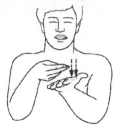

FINANCES (fĭ năn′ səs, fī′ năn səs), *n. pl.* (Slapping of paper money in the palm.) The upturned right hand, grasping some imaginary bills, is brought down into the upturned left palm a number of times. *Cf.* FUNDS, MONEY 1.

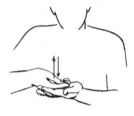

FIND (fīnd), *n., v.,* FOUND, FINDING. (The natural motion of selecting something from the hand.) The thumb and index fingers of the outstretched right hand grasp an imaginary object on the upturned left palm. The right hand then moves straight up. *Cf.* DISCOVER, DISCOVERY, PICK 1, SELECT 1.

FIND FAULT (fôlt), *v. phrase.* (A canceling out.) The right index finger makes a cross on the open left palm. *Cf.* CANCEL, CORRECT 2, CRITICISM, CRITICIZE.

FINE 1 (fīn), *adj., interj.* (The feelings are titillated.) With the thumb resting on the upper part of the chest, the fingers are wiggled back and forth. *Cf.* ELEGANT, GRAND 2, GREAT 4, SPLENDID 2, SWELL 2, WONDERFUL 2.

FINE 2, *n., v.,* FINED, FINING. (Nicking into one.) The knuckle of the right "X" finger is nicked against the palm of the left hand, held in the "5" position, palm facing right. *Cf.* CHARGE, COST, EXPENSE, FEE, PENALTY, PRICE 2, TAX 1, TAXATION 1, TOLL.

FINE 3, *adj.* (The fineness of sand or dust.) The index finger and thumb of the right "F" hand rub each other, as if fingering sand or dust.

FINE 4, *adj.* (The ruffled shirt front of a gentleman of old.) The thumb of the right "5" hand is thrust into the chest. The hand then pivots down, with thumb remaining in place. This latter part of the sign, however, is optional. *Cf.* COURTEOUS, COURTESY, POLITE.

FINGER (fing′ gər), *n.* (Indicating a finger.) The right index finger and thumb grasp the left index finger and shake it very slightly.

FINGERSPELLING (fing′ ger spĕl ĭng), *n.* (The movement of the fingers in fingerspelling.) The right hand, palm out, is moved from left to right, with the fingers wriggling up and down. *Cf.* ALPHABET 1, DACTYLOLOGY, MANUAL ALPHABET, SPELL, SPELLING.

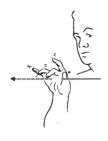

FINISH (fĭn′ ĭsh), *(colloq.), n., v.,* -ISHED, -ISHING. (Shaking the hands to rid them of something.) The upright "5" hands, palms facing each other, are suddenly and quickly swung around to a palm-out position. *Cf.* DONE, END 3.

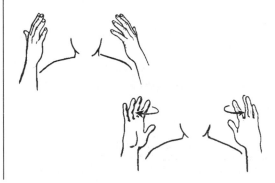

FINLAND (fin′ lənd) *n*. The curved index finger taps the chin twice. This is a native Finnish sign.

FIRE 1 (fīr), *n*., *v*., FIRED, FIRING. (The leaping of flames.) The "5" hands are held with palms facing the body. They move up and down alternately, while the fingers wiggle. *Cf*. BURN, FLAME, HELL 2.

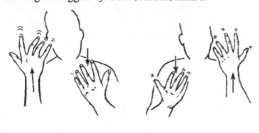

FIRE 2 , *v*. ("Getting the axe"; the head is chopped off.) The upturned open right hand is swung sharply over the index finger edge of the left "S" hand, whose palm faces right. *Cf*. DISCHARGE, EXPEL.

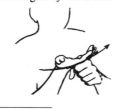

FIRE FIGHTER (fīr′ fī tər), *n*. (The shield on the hat.) The right "B" hand, palm out, is placed above the forehead.

FIREPLACE (fīr′ plās), *n*. (FIRE; the shape of the mantel.) The sign for FIRE is made: the upturned wriggling fingers, hands facing the signer, move alternately up and down in imitation of the flames. The downturned open hands, held together, move apart and then down, palms now facing each other, to describe the sides of the mantel.

FIRST (fûrst), *adj*. (The first finger is indicated.) The right index finger touches the upturned left thumb.

FISH (fĭsh), *n*. (The natural motion.) The open right hand, palm facing left and fingers pointing forward, represents the fish. The open left hand, palm facing right and fingers also pointing forward, is positioned behind the right hand so that its fingertips rest against the base of the right hand. The right hand flaps back and forth, from right to left, moving very slightly forward meanwhile. The left hand remains in contact with the right, but its only movement is forward. The left hand may also be dispensed with.

FIT (fit), *n*. (The body shakes in a fit.) The right hand, palm up, index and middle fingers curved, is placed in the upturned left palm. The right hand's index and middle fingers open and close slightly as the two fingers tremble. *Cf.* EPILEPSY, SEIZURE.

FIVE OF US *n. phrase.* ("Five," all in a circle.) The right "5" hand swings in an arc from right shoulder to left shoulder.

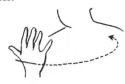

FLAME (flām), *n., v.,* FLAMED, FLAMING. (The leaping of flames.) The "5" hands are held with palms facing the body. They move up and down alternately, while the fingers wiggle. *Cf.* BURN, FIRE 1, HELL 2.

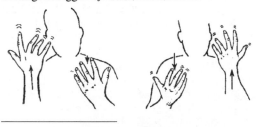

FLAT (flat), *adj.* (The flatness is indicated.) Both open hands are positioned with palms down, right on top of left. The right hand moves off straight to the right.

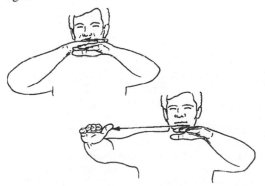

FLATBED PRESS (flăt bĕd prĕs), *(voc.)*. (The natural motion of feeding sheets of paper into the flatbed press.) The downturned open hands, held side by side, move over to the right, grasp an imaginary sheet of paper, and, moving to the left, feed it into the press. The movement is usually repeated.

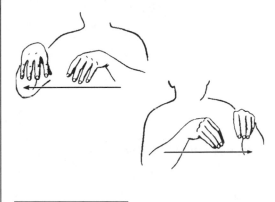

FLATTER 1 (flăt′ ər), *v.,* -TERED, -TERING. (Blinding one with sparkling words.) The downturned open hands are joined at the thumbtips. The fingers wiggle at random. Sometimes the hands sway up and down alternately, but in any case the thumbtips remain in contact at all times. *Cf.* FLATTERY 1.

FLATTER 2, *v.* (All eyes are directed to the signer, the one being flattered.) The "V" hands, palms facing the body, wave back and forth before the face. *Cf.* FLATTERY 2.

FLATTER 3, *v.* (Massaging the ego.) The fingertips of the right hand, pointing forward or left, brush back and forth against the upright left index finger. This sign is used to indicate flattery of someone.

FLATTERY 1 (flăt′ ə rĭ), *n.* See FLATTER 1.

FLATTERY 2, *n.* See FLATTER 2.

FLAT TIRE *n.* (The natural sign.) The right hand, palm down and fingers pointing forward, is placed with thumb on top of left hand. The right hand closes down suddenly on the right thumb, imitating a flat tire.

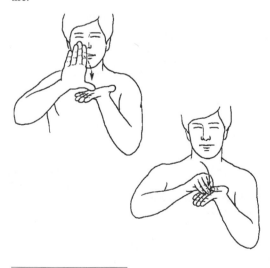

FLEE (flē), *v.,* fled, fleeing. (Emerging from a hiding place.) The downturned right "D" hand is positioned under the downturned open left hand. The

right "D" hand suddenly emerges and moves off quickly to the right. *Cf.* ESCAPE.

FLESH (flĕsh), *n.* (The fleshy part of the hand.) The right index finger and thumb squeeze the fleshy part of the open left hand, between thumb and index finger. *Cf.* BEEF, MEAT.

FLIER (flī′ ər), *n.* (An individual who flies a plane.) The sign for either AIRPLANE 1 or AIRPLANE 2 is made, and this is followed by the sign for INDIVIDUAL: both open hands, palms facing each other, move down the sides of the body, tracing its outline to the hips. *Cf.* AVIATOR, PILOT.

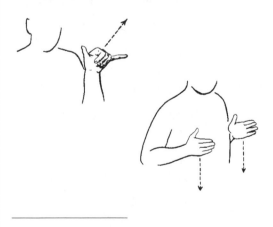

FLIGHT ATTENDANT (flīt ə ten′ dənt) *n.* (A person who flies and serves food.) The downturned open right hand, with thumb, little finger, and (optionally) index fingers extended, moves forward above the head, as an airplane in flight. Both upturned hands then mime serving a succession of dishes to some-one. The sign for INDIVIDUAL 1 then follows.

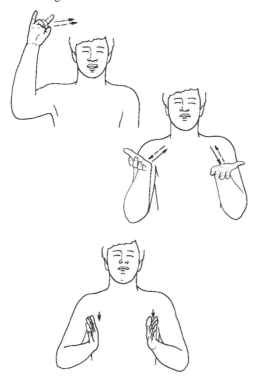

FLIRT 1 (flûrt), v., FLIRTED, FLIRTING. (Dazzling one by using scintillating looks.) The "5" hands, thumbs touching, swing alternately up and down. The fingers sometimes wiggle, as in FLATTER 1, *q.v.*

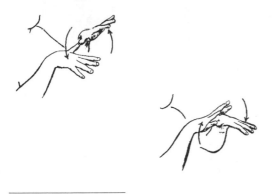

FLIRT 2, *v.* (Dazzling someone with the wiggling fingers.) Both downturned "5" hands are held thumb to thumb, and the fingers wiggle while the signer

assumes a flirtatious look.

FLIRT 3, *v.* (Fanning someone.) The hands are held as in FLIRT 1, but the signer moves them alternately up and down while maintaining contact between the two thumbs. As before, a flirtatious look is assumed.

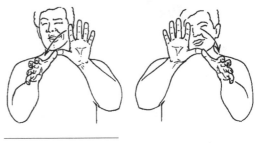

FLOAT 1 (flōt), *n., v.,* FLOATED, FLOATING. (Resting on an object which bobs up and down on the water.) Both hands are held in the palms-down position. The right index and middle fingers rest on their left counterparts. The left hand moves forward in a series of bobbing movements, carrying the right hand along with it.

FLOAT 2, *n., v.* (Prone on a floating object.) The downturned right open hand rests on the downturned left hand. Both hands move forward in a series of bobbing actions.

FLOOR (flôr), *n.* (Boards arranged side by side.) The downturned open hands, fingers together, are held side by side at the left side of the body. They separate and come together repeatedly as they move toward the right.

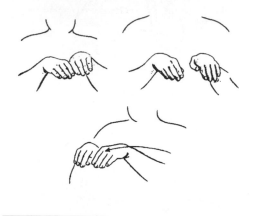

FLOUR (flour), *n.* (The sign for WHITE; feeling the flour.) The sign for WHITE is made: the right "5" hand is placed at mid-chest, palm facing the body. It moves off the chest, closing into the "O" position, palm still facing the body. The right hand then fingers an imaginary pinch of flour.

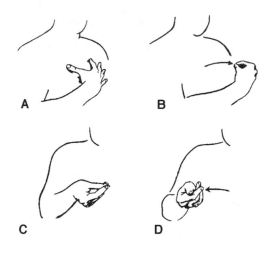

A

B

C

D

FLOWER (flou' ər), *n.* (The natural motion of smelling a flower.) The right hand, grasping an imaginary flower, holds it first against the right

nostril and then against the left.

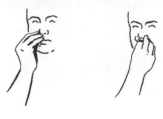

FLUNK (flŭngk), *v.,* FLUNKED, FLUNKING. The right "F" hand strikes forcefully against the open left palm, which faces right with fingers pointing forward.

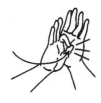

FLUSH (flŭsh), *v.,* FLUSHED, FLUSHING. (The red rises in the cheeks.) The sign for RED is made: the tip of the right index finger of the "D" hand moves down over the lips, which are red. Both hands are then placed palms facing the cheeks, and move up along the face, to indicate the rise of color. *Cf.* BLUSH, EMBARRASS, EMBARRASSED, MORTIFICATION.

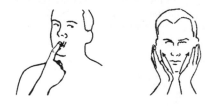

FLUTE (flōōt), *n.* (Playing the instrument.) The signer mimes playing a flute.

FLY 1 (flī), *v.,* FLEW, FLOWN, FLYING. (The wings of the airplane.) The "Y" hand, palm down and drawn up near the shoulder, moves forward, up and away from the body. Either hand may be used. *Cf.* AIR-PLANE, PLANE 1.

FLY 2, *v., n.* (The wings and fuselage of the airplane.) The hand assumes the same position as in FLY 1, but the index finger is also extended, to represent the fuselage of the airplane. Either hand may be used, and the movement is the same as in FLY 1. *Cf.* PLANE 2.

FLY A KITE *phrase.* (Holding the kite string.) Looking up, the signer pulls on an imaginary string several times. Both hands may be used. *Cf.* KITE.

FLY TO HERE *v. phrase.* (The aircraft comes to the signer.) With the right thumb and index and little fingers extended and pointing to the signer, the hand moves up in an arc toward the chest. It stops short of touching.

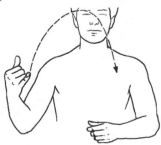

FOCUS (fō′ kəs), *n., v.,* -CUSED, -CUSING. (Directing one's attention forward; applying oneself; concentrating.) Both hands, fingers pointing up and together, are held at the sides of the face. They move straight out from the face. *Cf.* ATTEND (TO), ATTENTION, CONCENTRATE, CONCENTRATION, GIVE ATTENTION (TO), MIND 2, PAY ATTENTION (TO).

FOE (fō), *n.* (At sword's point.) The two index fingers, after pointing to each other, are drawn sharply apart. This is followed by the sign for INDIVIDUAL: both open hands, palms facing each other, move down the sides of the body, tracing its outline to the hips. *Cf.* ENEMY, OPPONENT, RIVAL 1.

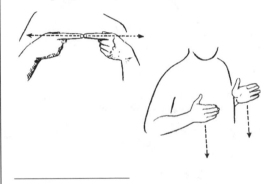

FOLLOW (fŏl′ō), *v.,* -LOWED, -LOWING. (One hand follows the other.) The "A" hands are used, thumbs pointing up. The right is positioned a few inches behind the left. The left hand moves straight forward, while the right follows behind in a series of wavy movements. *Cf.* FOLLOWING, SEQUEL.

FOLLOWING (fŏl′ ō ĭng), *adj.* See FOLLOW.

FOLLY (fŏl′ ĭ), *n*. (Thoughts flickering back and forth.) The right "Y" hand, thumb almost touching the forehead, is shaken back and forth across the forehead several times. *Cf.* FOOLISH, NONSENSE, RIDICULOUS, SILLY, TRIFLING.

FOOD (fo͞od), *n*. (The natural sign.) The closed right hand goes through the natural motion of placing food in the mouth. This movement is repeated. *Cf.* CONSUME 1, CONSUMPTION, EAT, FEED 1, MEAL.

FOOL AROUND (fo͞ol ə rownd′) *v*. (Frivolous activity.) Both "Y" hands, swiveling at the wrists, move alternately back and forth. This sign is derived from the verb PLAY.

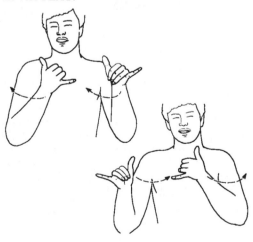

FOOLISH (fo͞o′lĭsh), *adj*. (Thoughts flickering back and forth.) The right "Y" hand, thumb almost

touching the forehead, is shaken back and forth across the forehead several times. *Cf.* FOLLY, NONSENSE, RIDICULOUS, SILLY, TRIFLING.

FOOT 1 (fo͝ot), *n*. (The length is indicated.) The "A" hands, palms down and thumbtips touching, are held before the chest. They separate until they are about a foot apart.

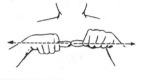

FOOT 2, *n*. (The measurement.) The left hand is held palm down. The heel of the right "F" hand is placed on the left wrist, and then moves in an arc to the left fingertips.

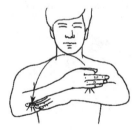

FOOTBALL 1 (fo͝ot′ bôl′), *n*. (The teams lock in combat.) The "5" hands, facing each other, are interlocked suddenly. They are drawn apart and the action is repeated.

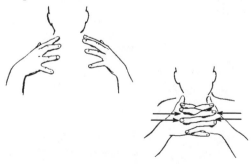

FOOTBALL 2, *n.* (The shape of the ball.) The "5" hands face each other, the right fingers in contact with their left counterparts. The hands are drawn apart into the "O" position, palms facing each other.

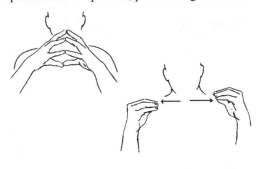

FOR 1 (fôr), *prep.* (The thoughts are directed outward, toward a specific goal or purpose.) The right index finger, resting on the right temple, leaves its position and moves straight out in front of the face. *Cf.* TO 2.

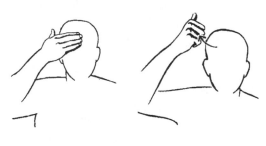

FOR 2, *prep.* (A thought or knowledge uppermost in the mind.) The fingers of the right hand or the index finger are placed on the center of the forehead, and then the hand is brought strongly up above the head, assuming the "A" position, with thumb pointing up. *Cf.* BECAUSE.

FORBID 1 (fər bĭd'), *v.,* -BADE or -BAD, -BIDDEN or -BID, -BIDDING. (A modification of LAW, *q.v.;* "against the law.") The downturned right "D" or "L"

hand is thrust forcefully into the left palm. *Cf.* BAN, FORBIDDEN 1, PROHIBIT.

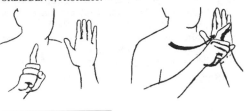

FORBID 2, *v.* (The letter "F"; the same sign as above.) The right "F" hand makes the same sign as in FORBID 1. *Cf.* FORBIDDEN 2.

FORBIDDEN 1 (fər bĭd' ən), *v.* See FORBID 1.

FORBIDDEN 2, *adj.* See FORBID 2.

FORCE 1 (fôrs), *v.,* FORCED, FORCING. (Forcing the head to bow.) The right "C" hand pushes down on an imaginary neck.

FORCE 2, *v.* (Pushing something forward.) The open right hand is held palm down at chin level, fingers pointing left. From this position the hand turns to point forward, and moves forcefully forward and away from the body, as if pushing something ahead of it.

FORECAST (fōr′ kăst′, -käst′), v., -CAST or -CASTED, -CASTING. (The vision is directed forward, into the distance.) The right "V" fingertips are placed under the eyes, with palm facing the body. The hand is then swung around and forward, moving under the downturned prone left hand and continuing forward and upward. Cf. FORESEE, FORETELL, PERCEIVE 2, PREDICT, PROPHECY, PROPHESY, PROPHET, VISION 2.

FORESEE (fōr sē′), v., -SAW, -SEEN, -SEEING. See FORECAST.

FOREST (fôr′ ĭst), n. (A series of trees.) The open right "5" hand is raised, with elbow resting on the back of the left hand, as in TREE, q.v. As the right hand swings around and back a number of times, pivoting at the wrist, the left arm carries the right arm from left to right.

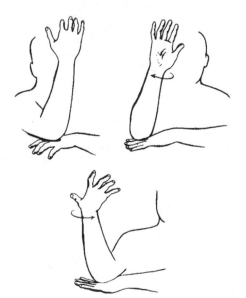

FORETELL (fōr tĕl′), v., -TOLD, -TELLING. See FORECAST.

FOREVER (fōr ĕv′ ər), adv. (Around the clock and ahead into the future.) The right index finger, pointing forward, traces a clockwise circle in the air. The downturned right "Y" hand then moves forward, either in a straight line or in a slight downward curve. Cf. ETERNITY, EVER 2, EVERLASTING.

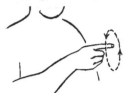 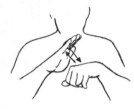

FOREWARN (fōr wôrn′), v., -WARNED, -WARNING. (Tapping one to draw attention to danger.) The right hand taps the back of the left several times. Cf. ADMONISH, CAUTION, WARN.

FORFEIT (fôr′ fĭt), n. (Throwing up the hands in a gesture of surrender.) Both "A" hands are held palms down before the chest and then thrown up in unison, ending in the "5" position. Cf. DISCOURAGE, GIVE UP, RELINQUISH, RENOUNCE, RENUNCIATION, SURRENDER, YIELD.

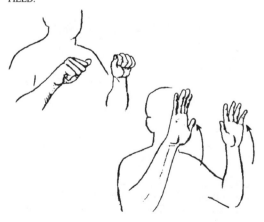

FORGET 1 (fər gĕt′), v., -GOT, -GOTTEN, -GETTING. (Wiping knowledge from the mind.) The right hand, fingers pointing left, rests on the forehead. It moves off to the right, assuming the "A" position, thumb up and palm facing the signer's rear.

FORGET 2, v. (The thought is gone.) The sign for THINK is made: the index finger makes a small circle on the forehead. This is followed by the sign for GONE 1: the right open hand, palm facing the body, is held by the left hand and is drawn down and out, ending in a position with fingers drawn together. The left hand, meanwhile, has closed into a position with fingers also drawn together.

FORGIVE (fər gĭv′), v., -GAVE, -GIVEN, -GIVING. (A wiped-off and cleaned slate.) The right hand wipes off the left palm several times. Cf. APOLOGIZE 2, APOLOGY 2, EXCUSE, PARDON, PAROLE.

FORK (fôrk), n., v., FORKED, FORKING. (The natural

sign.) The downturned fingertips of the right "V" hand are thrust repeatedly into the upturned left palm.

FORM 1 (fôrm), n. (Contours are indicated or outlined.) Both "A" hands, held about a foot apart before the face, with palms facing each other, move down simultaneously in a wavy, undulating motion. Cf. FIGURE 2, IMAGE, SCULPT, SCULPTURE, SHAPE, STATUE.

FORM 2 (The letters "F"; outlining the shape.) Both "F" hands, palms facing out, outline the shape of a piece of paper.

FORMERLY (fôr′ mər lĭ), adv. (Something past, behind.) The upraised right hand, in the "5" position with palm facing the body, is held just above the right shoulder and is thrown back over it. Cf. AGO, ONCE UPON A TIME, PAST, PREVIOUS, PREVIOUSLY, WAS, WERE.

FORMULA (fôr′ myə lə), *n.* (The letter "F"; something spelled out to be seen.) The left palm faces forward or slightly to the right. The right "F" hand is placed at the left fingertips, and then moves down to the base of the left hand.

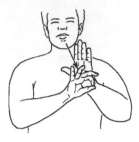

FORNICATE (fôr′ nə kāt′), *v.*, -CATED, -CATING. (The motions of the legs during the sexual act.) The upturned left "V" hand remains motionless, while the downturned right "V" hand comes down repeatedly on the left. *Cf.* COPULATE, SEXUAL INTERCOURSE.

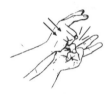

FORSAKE 1 (fôr sāk′), *v.*, -SOOK, -SAKEN, -SAKING. (Wiping knowledge from the mind.) The right hand, fingers pointing left, rests on the forehead. It moves off to the right, assuming the "A" position, thumb up and palm facing the signer' rear. *Cf.* FORGET 1.

FORSAKE 2, *v.* (To throw something aside.) Both "S" hands are held with palms facing at chest level and then thrown down and to the left, opening into the "5" position. *Cf.* ABANDON, CAST OFF, DISCARD, LEAVE 2, LET ALONE, NEGLECT.

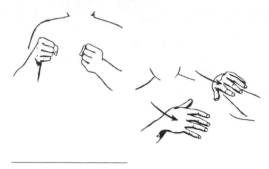

FORTIFY (fôr′ tə fī′), *v.*, -FIED, -FYING. (Hold down firmly; cover and strengthen.) The "S" hands, downturned, are held side by side in front of the body, the arms almost horizontal, and the left hand in front of the right. Both arms move a short distance forward and slightly downward. *Cf.* DEFEND, DEFENSE, GUARD, PROTECT, PROTECTION, SHIELD 1.

FORTITUDE (fôr′ tə tūd′, -tōōd′), *n.* (Strength emanating from the body.) Both "5" hands are placed palms against the chest. They move out and away, forcefully, closing and assuming the "S" position. *Cf.* BRAVE, BRAVERY, COURAGE, COURAGEOUS, HALE, HEALTH, HEALTHY, MIGHTY 2, STRENGTH, STRONG 2, WELL 2.

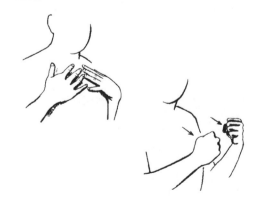

FOUND (found), *v.*, FOUNDED, FOUNDING. (To set up.) The right "A" hand, thumb up and palm facing left, comes down to rest on the back of the downturned left "S" hand. Before doing so, the right "A" hand may describe a clockwise circle above the left hand, but this is optional. *Cf.* ESTABLISH, FOUNDED.

FOUNDATION (foun dā′ shən), *n.* (The area below.) Both hands, in the "5" position, palms down, are held before the chest, the right under the left. The right hand moves under the left in a counterclockwise fashion. *Cf.* BACKGROUND 1, BASIS, BELOW 1, BOTTOM.

FOUNDED *v.* See FOUND.

FOUR (fōr), *adj.* (The natural sign.) Four fingers are displayed.

FOUR OF US *n. phrase.* ("Four"; an encompassing movement.) The right "4" hand, palm facing the body, moves from the right shoulder to the left shoulder.

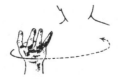

FOX (fŏks), *n.* (The letter "F"; the pointed snout.) The tip of the nose is placed in the circle formed by the right "F" hand, which swings back and forth a short distance. *Cf.* FOXY.

FOXY (fŏk′ sĭ), *adj.* See FOX.

FRACTURE (frăk′ chər), *n., v.*, -TURED, -TURING. (The natural sign.) The hands grasp an imaginary object and break it in two. *Cf.* BREAK.

FRAGRANT (frā′ grənt), *adj.* (Bringing something up to the nose.) The upturned right hand moves slowly up to and past the nose, and the signer breathes in as the hand sweeps by. *Cf.* ODOR, SCENT, SMELL.

FRAIL (frāl), *adj.* (The knees buckle.) The right "V" hand is placed with fingertips resting in the upturned left palm. The knuckles of the "V" fingers buckle a bit. This motion may be repeated. *Cf.* FAINT, FEEBLE, WEAK, WEAKNESS.

FRAME (frām), *n., v.,* FRAMED, FRAMING. (The frame is outlined.) The downturned index finger and thumb of each hand outline the square shape of a frame.

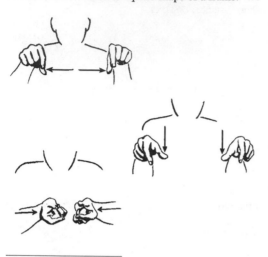

FRANK (frăngk), *adj.* (The letter "H," for HONEST; a straight and true path.) The index and middle fingers of the right "H" hand, whose palm faces left, move straight forward along the upturned left palm. *Cf.* HONEST, HONESTY, SINCERE 1.

FRANKFURTER 1 (frăngk' fər tər), *n.* (The shape.) The "C" hands are held side by side, palms out, thumbs and index fingers touching. They change to the "S" position as they are drawn apart. *Cf.* HOT DOG 1.

FRANKFURTER 2 (The shape in a roll or bun.) The left hand is held with the fingers pointing up. The

right index finger is placed between the thumb and the other fingers. *Cf.* HOT DOG 2.

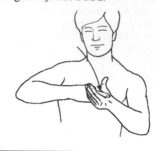

FRANKLY (frăngk' lĭ), *adv.* (Coming forth directly from the lips; true.) The index finger of the right "D" hand, palm facing left, is placed against the lips. It moves up an inch or two and then describes a small arc forward and away from the lips. *Cf.* ABSOLUTE, ABSOLUTELY, ACTUAL, ACTUALLY, AUTHENTIC, CERTAIN, CERTAINLY, FIDELITY, GENUINE, INDEED, POSITIVE 1, POSITIVELY, REAL, REALLY, SINCERE 2, SURE, SURELY, TRUE, TRULY, TRUTH, VALID, VERILY.

FRAUD (frôd), *n.* (Underhandedness.) The right hand, palm down, is held with index and little fingers pointing out. The left hand, in a similar position, is held above the right. The right hand moves forward repeatedly, each time emerging briefly from under the left hand. The positions may be reversed, with the left hand doing the movement, or both hands can move simultaneously. *Cf.* CHEAT, DECEIT, DECEIVE, DECEPTION, DEFRAUD, FRAUDULENT.

FRAUDULENT (frô' jə lənt), *adj.* See FRAUD.

FREE 1 (frē), *adj., v.,* FREED, FREEING. (Breaking the bonds.) The "S" hands, crossed in front of the body, swing apart and face out. *Cf.* EMANCIPATE, FREEDOM, INDEPENDENCE, INDEPENDENT 1, LIBERATION, REDEEM 1, RELIEF, RESCUE, SAFE, SALVATION, SAVE 1.

FREE 2, *adj., v.* (The letter "F.") The "F" hands make the same sign as in FREE 1.

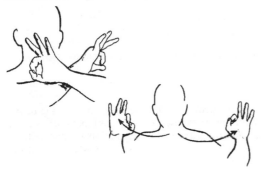

FREEDOM (frē' dəm), *n.* See FREE 1.

FREEWAY (frē' wā), *n.* (Traffic flowing in opposite directions.) The downturned "4" hands pass each other as the right moves repeatedly to the left and the left repeatedly to the right. The downturned "V" hands are often used instead of the "4"s. *Cf.* HIGHWAY.

FREEZE (frēz), *v.,* FROZE, FROZEN, FREEZING. (The stiff fingers.) The fingers of the "5" hands, held palms down, stiffen and contract. *Cf.* FROZEN, ICE.

FREQUENT (*adj.* frē' kwənt; *v.* frĭ kwĕnt'), -QUENTED, -QUENTING. The left hand, open in the "5" position, palm up, is held before the chest. The right hand, in the right-angle position, fingers pointing up, arches over and into the left palm. This is repeated several times. *Cf.* OFTEN.

FRESHMAN (fresh' mən), *n., adj.* (The first year after the preparatory year at Gallaudet University.) The right index finger touches the ring finger of the other hand.

FRET (frĕt), *n., v.,* FRETTED, FRETTING. (A clouding over; a troubling.) Both "B" hands, palms facing each other, are rotated alternately before the forehead. *Cf.* CONCERN, PROBLEM 1, TROUBLE, WORRIED, WORRY 1.

FREUD (froid), *n.* (The letter "F"; PSYCHOLOGY.) The right hand forms the letter "F." The little finger edge is thrust twice into the open left hand, its palm facing out, between thumb and index finger. This is the sign for PSYCHOLOGY, shaping the Greek letter "psi." Strictly speaking, Freud was not a psychologist but a psychoanalytic psychiatrist. This so-called "name sign" applies nevertheless.

FRIEND (frĕnd), *n.* (Locked together in friendship.) The right and left hands are interlocked at the index fingers. The hands separate, change their relative positions, and come together again as before. *Cf.* FRIENDSHIP.

FRIENDLY (frĕnd′ lĭ), *adj.* (A crinkling-up of the face.) Both hands, in the "5" position, palms facing back, are placed on either side of the face. The fingers wiggle back and forth, while a pleasant, happy expression is worn. *Cf.* AMIABLE, CHEERFUL, CORDIAL, JOLLY, PLEASANT.

FRIENDSHIP (frĕnd′ shĭp), *n.* See FRIEND.

FRIGHT (frīt), *n.* (The heart is suddenly covered with fear.) Both hands, fingers together, are placed side by side, palms facing the chest. They quickly open and come together over the heart, one on top of the other. *Cf.* AFRAID, FEAR 1, FRIGHTEN, SCARE(D), TERROR 1.

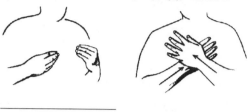

FRIGHTEN (frī′ tən), *v.*, -TENED, -TENING. See FRIGHT.

FROCK (frŏk), *n.* (Draping the clothes on the body.) With fingertips resting on the chest, both hands move down simultaneously. The action is repeated. *Cf.* CLOTHES, CLOTHING, DRESS, GARMENT, GOWN, SHIRT, SUIT, WEAR 1.

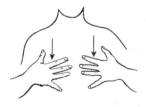

FROM (frŏm), *prep.* (The "away from" action is indicated.) The knuckle of the right "X" finger is placed against the base of the left "D" or "X" finger, and then moved away in a slight curve toward the body.

FROM TIME TO TIME *adv. phrase.* (Forward in slow, deliberate movements.) The right hand, palm facing the signer, fingers pointing left, makes a series of small forward movements, describing a small arc each time. *Cf.* NOW AND THEN, ONCE IN A WHILE 2.

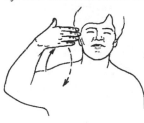

FROZEN (frō' zən), *adj.* (The stiff fingers.) The fingers of the "5" hands, held palms down, stiffen and contract. *Cf.* FREEZE, ICE, RIGID.

FRUSTRATED (frŭs' trāt ĭd), *adj.* (Coming up against a wall; a door is slammed in the face.) The open right hand is brought up sharply, and its back strikes the mouth and nose. The head moves back a bit at the same time.

FULL (fŏŏl), *adj.* (Wiping off the top of a container, to indicate its condition of fullness.) The downturned open right hand wipes across the index finger edge of the left "S" hand, whose palm faces right. The movement of the right hand is toward the body. *Cf.* COMPLETE, FILL 1.

FUN (fŭn), *n.* (The wrinkled nose—indicative of laughter or fun.) The index and middle fingers of the right "U" hand, whose palm faces the body, are placed on the nose. The right hand swings down in an arc and, palm down, the "U" fingers strike their left counterparts on the downturned left "U" hand, and either stop at that point or continue on.

FUND (fund), *v.* (Support from money.) The sign for MONEY 1 is made: the upturned right hand, grasping some imaginary bills, is brought down into the upturned left palm. The right "S" hand then pushes up the left "S" hand.

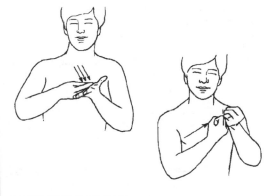

FUNDAMENTAL (fun' də men' təl), *adj.* (The letter "F"; basic or underlying.) The right "F" moves in a continuous clockwise circle under the downturned left hand.

FUNDRAISING *v. phrase.* (Money is raised.) The sign for MONEY 1 is made: the upturned right hand, grasping some imaginary bills, is brought down into the upturned left palm a number of times. Both upturned open hands then move up together.

FUNDS (fŭndz), *n. pl.* (Slapping of paper money in the palm.) The upturned right hand, grasping some imaginary bills, is brought down into the upturned left palm a number of times. *Cf.* FINANCES, MONEY 1.

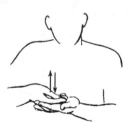

FUNNY (fŭn′ ĭ), *adj.* (The nose wrinkles in laughter.) The tips of the right index and middle fingers brush repeatedly off the tip of the nose. *Cf.* COMIC, COMICAL, HUMOR, HUMOROUS.

FUR (fûr), *n.* (Fingering the fur.) The downturned right hand repeatedly fingers imaginary fur covering the back of the downturned left hand.

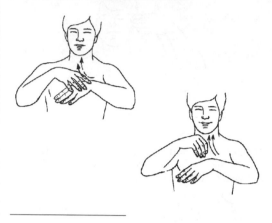

FURY (fyo͝or′ ĭ), *n.* (A violent welling-up of the emotions.) The curved fingers of the right hand are placed in the center of the chest, and fly up suddenly and violently. An expression of anger is worn. *Cf.* ANGER, ANGRY 2, ENRAGE, INDIGNANT, INDIGNATION, IRE, MAD, RAGE.

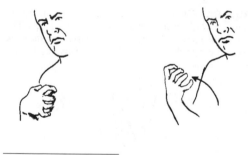

FUTURE (fū′ chər), *n.* (Something ahead or in the future.) The upright, open right hand, palm facing left, moves straight out and slightly up from a position beside the right temple. *Cf.* IN THE FUTURE, LATER 2, LATER ON, SHALL, WILL 1, WOULD.

G

GAIETY (gā′ ə tĭ), *n.* (The heart is stirred; the spirits bubble up.) The open right hand, palm facing the body, strikes the heart repeatedly, moving up and off the heart after each strike. *Cf.* DELIGHT, GLAD, HAPPY, JOY, MERRY.

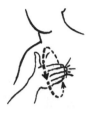

GAIN 1 (gān), *v.*, GAINED, GAINING. (Adding on.) The index and middle fingers of the right "H" hand, palm up, are swung up and over until they come to rest on the index and middle fingers of the left "H" hand, held palm down. *Cf.* ADD 3, ADDITION, INCREASE, ON TO, RAISE 2.

GAIN 2, *n., v.* (To get a profit; a coin popped into the vest pocket.) The sign for GET is made: both outstretched hands, held in a grasping "5" position, close into "S" positions, with the right on top of the left. At the same time both hands are drawn in to the body. The thumb and index finger of the right hand, holding an imaginary coin, are then popped into an imaginary vest or breast pocket. Note: the sign for GET is sometimes omitted. *Cf.* PROFIT.

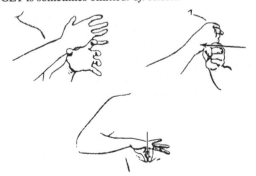

GALLEY (găl′ ĭ), *(voc.)*, *n.* (The shape of the galley or of the galley proof.) Both downturned open hands rest on the edges of an imaginary galley frame. The left hand moves forward, tracing the elongated shape of the frame.

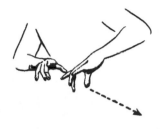

GALLOP (gal′ əp), *v., n.* (The horse's legs.) Both "V" hands, palms down, are held one before the other, fingers curved down. Both hands move forward in unison in a series of circles. Each time they rise, the curved fingers close up, opening again as they fall.

GAMBLE (gam′ bəl), *n., v.* (Throwing the dice.) The signer grasps imaginary dice in the closed fist, shakes them up, and throws them out.

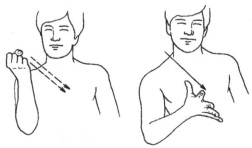

GAME (gām), *n., v.,* GAMED, GAMING. (Two individuals pitted against each other.) The hands are held in the "A" position, thumbs pointing straight up, palms facing the body. They come together forcefully, moving down a bit as they do, and the knuckles of one hand strike those of the other. *Cf.* CHALLENGE, OPPORTUNITY 2, VERSUS.

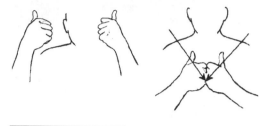

GANG (găng), *n.* (A grouping together.) Both "C" hands, palms facing, are held a few inches apart at chest height. They are swung around in unison, so that the palms now face the body. *Cf.* ASSOCIATION, CIRCLE 2, CLASS, CLASSED, CLUB, COMPANY 1, GROUP 1, ORGANIZATION 1.

GARDEN (gär' dən), *n.* (The letter "G"; an area.) The right "G" hand circles counterclockwise around the downturned open left hand.

GARLIC (gär' lik), *n.* (Garlic breath.) The right hand, in the claw position, fingers placed at the open

mouth, spins forward.

GARMENT (gär' mənt), *n.* (Draping the clothes on the body.) With fingertips resting on the chest, both hands move down simultaneously. The action is repeated. *Cf.* CLOTHES, CLOTHING, DRESS, FROCK, GOWN, SHIRT, SUIT, WEAR 1.

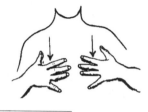

GAS (găs), *n.* (The act of pouring gasoline into an automobile tank.) The thumb of the right "A" hand is placed into the hole formed by the left "O" hand. *Cf.* GASOLINE.

GASOLINE (găs' ə lēn´, găs ə lēn'), *n.* See GAS.

GATE (gāt), *n.* (The natural sign.) The fingertips of both open hands touch each other before the body, palms toward the chest, thumbs pointing upward. Then the right fingers swing forward and back to their original position several times, imitating the movement of a gate opening and closing.

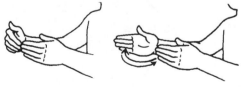

GATHER 1 (găth′ ər), v., -ERED, -ERING. (A gathering together.) The right "5" hand, fingers curved and palm facing left, sweeps across and over the upturned left palm, several times, in a circular movement. Cf. GATHERING TOGETHER.

GATHER 2, v. (Assemble all together.) Both "5" hands, palms facing, are held with fingers pointing out from the body. With a sweeping motion they are brought in toward the chest, and all fingertips come together. This is repeated. Cf. ASSEMBLE 1, ASSEMBLY, CONFERENCE, CONVENE, CONVENTION, GATHERING, MEETING 1.

GATHERING (găth′ ər ĭng), n. See GATHER 2.

GATHERING TOGETHER phrase. See GATHER 1.

GAY 1 (gā), n., adj. (Homosexual.) The tips of the "G" fingers are placed on the chin. Cf. HOMOSEXUAL 1.

GAY 2, n., adj. (Supposedly a code originally.) The signer pulls the ear lobe. Cf. HOMOSEXUAL 2.

GAY 3, n., adj. (Mutual masturbation.) Both fists, palms facing down, come together repeatedly. Cf. HOMOSEXUAL 3.

GAY 4, n., adj. (An effeminate gesture.) Both "F" hands, palms out, are held at shoulder height. The signer moves them alternately forward and back, while the shoulders keep pace with the forward-and-back movements. Cf. EFFEMINATE, HOMOSEXUAL 4.

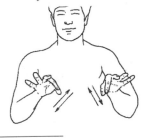

GAZE (gāz), v., GAZED, GAZING, n. (The vision is directed forward.) The tips of the right "V" fingers point to the eyes. The right hand is then swung around and forward a bit. Cf. LOOK AT, OBSERVE, WITNESS.

GENERAL (jen′ ər əl), *n.* (The insignia of rank.) The right "G" hand is placed on the right shoulder and moves down an inch or two.

GENERATION (jĕn′ ə rā′ shən), *n.* (Persons descending, one after another, from an original or early person.) The downturned cupped hands are positioned one above the other at the right shoulder. They roll over each other as they move alternately downward and a bit away from the body. This sign is used only when talking about people.

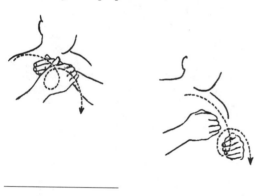

GENEROUS (jĕn′ ər əs), *adj.* (The heart rolls out.) Both right-angle hands roll over each other as they move down and away from their initial position at the heart. *Cf.* KIND 1, MERCY 1.

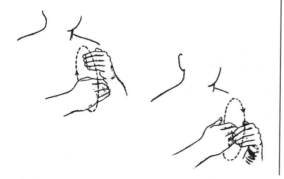

GENTLEMAN (jĕn′ təl mən), *n.* (A fine or polite man.) The MALE prefix sign is made: the right hand grasps the edge of an imaginary cap. The sign for POLITE is then made: the thumb of the right "5" hand is placed slowly and deliberately on the right side of the chest.

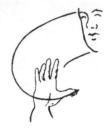

GENUINE (jĕn′ yo͞o ĭn), *adj.* (Coming forth directly from the lips; true.) The index finger of the right "D" hand, palm facing left, is placed against the lips. It moves up an inch or two and then describes a small arc forward and away from the lips. *Cf.* ABSOLUTE, ABSOLUTELY, ACTUAL, ACTUALLY, AUTHENTIC, CERTAIN, CERTAINLY, FIDELITY, FRANKLY, INDEED, POSITIVE 1, POSITIVELY, REAL, REALLY, SINCERE 2, SURE, SURELY, TRUE, TRULY, TRUTH, VALID, VERILY.

GEOGRAPHY (jĭ ŏg′ rə fĭ), *n.* (The earth and its axis are indicated.) The downturned left "S" hand indicates the earth. The thumb and index finger of the downturned right "5" hand are placed at each edge of the left. In this position the right hand swings back and forth, while maintaining contact with the left. *Cf.* EARTH, GLOBE 1, PLANET 1.

GERBIL (jûr′ bil), *n.* (The letter "G"; MOUSE.) The back of the right "G" hand brushes the nose several times.

GET (gĕt), *v., GOT, GOTTEN, GETTING.* (A grasping and bringing forward to oneself.) Both hands, in the "5" position, fingers curved, are crossed at the wrists, with the left palm facing right and the right palm facing left. They are brought in toward the chest, while closing into a grasping "S" position. *Cf.* ACQUIRE, OBTAIN, PROCEDURE, RECEIVE.

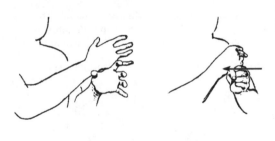

GET AWAY *phrase, interj.* (Shooing someone away with a wave of the hand.) The downturned right hand is flung away to the right. The signer usually assumes an expression of annoyance.

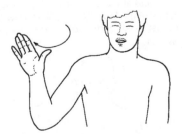

GET IN FRONT OF *phrase.* (The movement.) Both "A" hands are placed with the right behind the left. The right hand moves ahead, passing the left, and positions itself in front of the left.

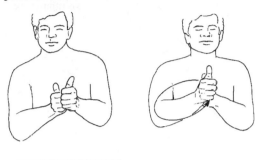

GET UP (ŭp), *v. phrase.* (Getting onto one's feet.) The upturned index and middle fingers of the right hand, representing the legs, are swung up and over in an arc, coming to rest in the upturned left palm. *Cf.* ARISE 2, RISE 1, RISE 1, STAND 2, STAND UP.

GHOST (gōst), *n.* (Something thin and filmy, *i.e.,* ephemeral.) The hands are held palms facing, with one above the other and index fingers and thumbs touching and almost connected. As the upper hand moves straight up, the index fingers and thumbs of both hands slowly come together, giving the impression of drawing out a thread or other thin substance. *Cf.* SOUL, SPIRIT.

GIFT (gĭft), *n.* (A giving of something.) Both "A" hands, with index fingers somewhat draped over the tips of the thumbs, are held palms facing in front of the chest. They are pivoted forward and down, in unison, from the wrists. *Cf.* AWARD, CONTRIBUTE, PRESENT 2.

GIGGLE (gĭg' əl), *n., v.* (The mouth contorts repeatedly in laughter.) Both index fingers, at each corner of the mouth, move back quickly and repeatedly, as if forcing the mouth to open in laughter.

GILLS (gĭlz), *n.* (The fluttering movement.) Both hands are placed at either side of the throat, fingertips touching the throat. They flip open and shut repeatedly, imitating the fluttering movement of gills.

GIRL (gûrl), *n.* (A female who is small.) The FEMALE root sign is given: the thumb of the right "A" hand moves down along the line of the right jaw, from ear almost to chin. This outlines the string used to tie ladies' bonnets in olden days. The downturned open right hand is then held at waist level, indicating the short height of the female.

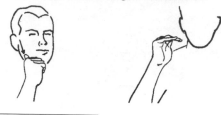

GIVE (gĭv), *v.,* GAVE, GIVEN, GIVING. (Holding something and extending it toward someone.) The right "O" hand is held before the right shoulder and then moved outward in an arc, away from the body.

GIVE ASSISTANCE (ə sĭs' təns), *v. phrase.* (Helping up; supporting.) The left "S" hand, thumb side up, rests in the open right palm. In this position the left hand is pushed up a short distance by the right. *Cf.* AID, ASSIST, ASSISTANCE, BENEFIT 1, BOOST, HELP.

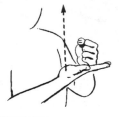

GIVE ATTENTION (TO) (ə tĕn' shən), *v. phrase.* (Directing one's attention forward; applying oneself; concentrating.) Both hands, fingers pointing up and together, are held at the sides of the face. They move straight out from the face. *Cf.* ATTEND (TO), ATTENTION, CONCENTRATE, CONCENTRATION, FOCUS, MIND 2, PAY ATTENTION (TO).

GIVE ME (mē), *v. phrase.* (Extending the hand toward oneself.) This sign is a reversal of GIVE.

GIVE UP (gĭv ŭp′), *v. phrase.* (Throwing up the hands in a gesture of surrender.) Both "A" hands are held palms down before the chest and then thrown up and back in unison, ending in the "5" position. The head moves back a little as the hands are thrown up. *Cf.* DISCOURAGE, FORFEIT, RELINQUISH, RENOUNCE, RENUNCIATION, SURRENDER, YIELD.

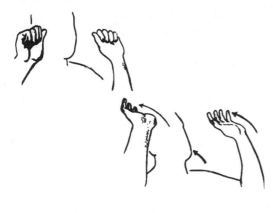

GLACIER (glă′ shər), *n.* (The movement forward.) The downturned claw hands move very slowly forward.

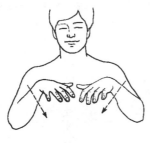

GLAD (glăd), *adj.* (The heart is stirred; the spirits bubble up.) The open right hand, palm facing the body, strikes the heart repeatedly, moving up and off the heart after each strike. *Cf.* DELIGHT, GAIETY, HAPPY, JOY, MERRY.

GLASS 1 (glăs, gläs), *n.* (The finger touches a brittle substance.) The index finger is brought up to touch the exposed front teeth. *Cf.* CHINA 4, DISH, PLATE 1, PORCELAIN.

GLASS 2, *n.* (The shape of a drinking glass.) The little finger edge of the right "C" hand rests in the upturned left palm. The right hand moves straight up a few inches, tracing the shape of a drinking glass.

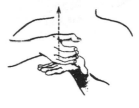

GLASSES (glăs′ əs), *n. pl.* (The shape.) The thumb and index finger of the right hand, placed flat against the right temple, move back toward the right ear, tracing the line formed by the eyeglass frame. *Cf.* EYEGLASSES.

GLISTEN (glis′ ən), *v.*, -TENED, -TENING. (Reflected glistening of light rays.) The left hand, held supinely before the chest, palm down, represents the object from which the rays glisten. The right hand, in the "5" position, touches the back of the left lightly and moves up toward the right, pivoting slightly at the wrist, with fingers wiggling. *Cf.* BRIGHT 2, SHINE, SHINING.

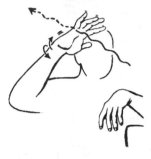

GLOBE 1 (glŏb), *n.* (The earth and its axis are indicated.) The downturned left "S" hand indicates the earth. The thumb and index finger of the downturned right "5" hand are placed at each edge of the left. In this position the right hand swings back and forth, while maintaining contact with the left. *Cf.* EARTH, GEOGRAPHY, PLANET 1.

GLOBE 2, *n.* (The letter "W," for WORLD, in orbit.) The right "W" hand makes a complete circle around the left "W" hand and comes to rest on the thumb edge of the left "W" hand. The left hand frequently assumes the "S" position instead of the "W," to represent the stationary sun. *Cf.* WORLD.

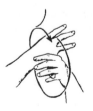

GLOOM (glo͞om), *n.* (The facial features drop.) Both "5" hands, palms facing the eyes and fingers slightly curved, drop simultaneously to a level with the mouth. The head drops slightly as the hands move down, and an expression of sadness is assumed. *Cf.* DEJECTED, DEPRESSED 1, GLOOMY, GRAVE 2, GRIEF 1, MELANCHOLY, MOURNFUL, SAD, SORROWFUL 1.

GLOOMY (glo͞o′ mĭ), *adj.* See GLOOM.

GLORIOUS (glôr′ ĭ əs), *adj.* See GLORY.

GLORY (glôr′ ĭ), *n.* (The letter "G"; scintillating or shining.) The right "G" hand moves in a clockwise circle, or is simply held stationary, above the downturned left "S" or "A" hand. The right hand then opens into the "5" position, palm facing the left hand, and moves up in a deliberate wavy motion. *Cf.* GLORIOUS.

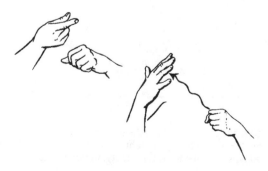

GLUE (glo͞o), *n., v.* (Squeezing a tube of glue; indicating the stickiness.) The right hand squeezes an imaginary tube, pressing its contents onto the upturned left palm. The right hand, using the thumb and finger, then demonstrates the stickiness by touching the left palm and then indicating the difficulty in separating the finger from the thumb.

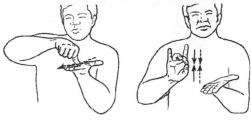

GO 1 (gō), *v.,* WENT, GONE, GOING. (Continuous motion forward.) With palms facing each other, the index fingers of the "D" hands revolve around each other as both hands move forward.

GO 2, *interj., v.* (The natural sign.) The right index finger is flung out, as a command to go. A stern expression is usually assumed.

GO AHEAD (ə hĕd′), *v. phrase.* (Moving forward.) Both right-angle hands, palms facing each other and knuckles facing forward, move forward simultaneously. *Cf.* PROCEED, RESUME.

GOAL (gōl), *n.* (A thought directed upward, toward a goal.) The index finger of the right "D" hand touches the forehead, and then moves up to the index finger of the left "D" hand, which is held above eye level. The two index fingers stop just short of touching. *Cf.* AIM, AMBITION, OBJECTIVE, PERSEVERE 4, PURPOSE 2.

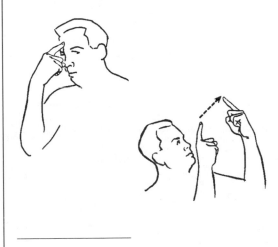

GO AS A GROUP *phrase.* (Many people, forming a circle, move forward.) Both "C" hands, palms facing each other and fingers facing forward, form a circle or a ball and move forward in unison.

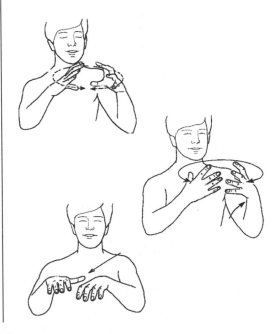

GO BY BOAT *phrase.* (The boat moves forward.) With upright cupped hands held side by side, both hands move straight forward.

GO BY CAR *phrase.* (The steering wheel moves forward.) Holding an imaginary steering wheel, the hands move straight forward. *Cf.* DRIVE TO.

GO BY TRAIN *phrase.* (The train moves forward.) The downturned right index and middle fingers, placed on top of their left counterparts, move suddenly forward.

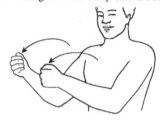

GOD (gŏd), *n.* (A motion indicating the One above.) The right open hand, palm facing left, swings up above the head, and is then moved down in a slight curve, an inch or two. Meanwhile, the signer looks up while making the sign. *Cf.* LORD 2.

GODFATHER (gŏd' fä ŧhər), *n.* (Second father.) The right "2" hand is twisted around (SECOND), and then the signer makes the sign for FATHER 2: the tip of the thumb of the right "5" hand is placed against the right forehead or temple. The signer may make the two signs in reverse order.

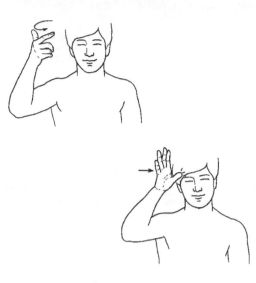

GODMOTHER (gŏd' muŧh ər), *n.* (Second mother.) The right "2" hand is twisted around (SECOND), and then the signer makes the sign for MOTHER 2: the tip of the thumb of the right "5" hand is placed against the right cheek. The signer may make the two signs in reverse order.

GOLD (gōld), *n.* (Yellow earrings, *i.e.,* gold, which was discovered in California.) The earlobe is pinched, and then the sign for YELLOW is made: the "Y" hand, pivoted at the wrist, is shaken back and forth repeatedly. *Cf.* CALIFORNIA.

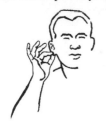

GONE 1 (gôn, gŏn), *adj.* (A disappearance.) The right open hand, palm facing the body, is held by the left hand and is drawn down and out, ending in a position with fingers drawn together. The left hand, meanwhile, may close into a position with fingers also drawn together. *Cf.* ABSENCE, ABSENT, DISAPPEAR, VANISH.

GONE 2, *(sl.), adj.* (A disappearance into the distance. The narrowing perspective is the main feature here.) The right "L" hand, resting on the back of the downturned left hand, moves straight forward suddenly. As it does, the index finger and thumb come together.

GONORRHEA (gon ə rē′ ə), *n.* (The penis is infected, *i.e.,* covered with the disease.) The right claw hand is brought down on the tip of the left index.

Cf. CLAP. Although this is essentially a male sign, it may also be used in a nongender-specific context.

GOOD 1 (gŏŏd), *adj.* (Tasting something, approving it, and offering it forward.) The fingertips of the right "5" hand are placed at the lips. The right hand then moves out and into a palm-up position on the upturned left palm. *Cf.* WELL 1.

GOOD 2, *adj.* (Thumbs up.) One or both thumbs are held up. *Cf.* GOOD LUCK.

GOODBYE (gŏŏd′ bī′), *interj.* (A wave of the hand.) The right open hand waves back and forth several times. *Cf.* HELLO, SO LONG.

GOOD FRIEND (go͝od frĕnd) *n.* (Hooked on to.) Both index fingers interlock and move down forcefully an inch or two. The lips are held together tightly and an expression of pleasure is shown. *Cf.* FAVORITE 2.

GOOD LUCK *phrase.* (Thumbs up!) The right "A" hand is held with thumb pointing straight up. The hand moves forward and out about an inch. This may be repeated. *Cf.* GOOD 2.

GO OFF THE TRACK *v. phrase.* (The natural motion.) The "G" hands are held side by side and touching, palms down, index fingers pointing forward. Then the right hand moves forward, curving toward the right side as it does. *Cf.* DEVIATE 2, STRAY.

GOOSE BUMPS (*colloq.*), *n.* (Fingertips indicate where the bumps appear.) The downturned right claw hand moves up the back of the left arm.

GO TO BED *v. phrase.* (Laying the head on the pillow.) The head is placed on its side, in the open palm, and the eyes are closed.

GOVERN (gŭv′ ərn), *v.,* -ERNED, -ERNING. (Holding the reins over all.) The "A" hands, palms facing, move alternately back and forth, as if grasping and manipulating reins. The left "A" hand, still in position, swings over so that its palm now faces down. The right hand opens to the "5" position, palm down, and swings over the left which moves slightly to the right. *Cf.* CONTROL 1, DIRECT 1, MANAGE, MANAGEMENT, MANAGER, OPERATE, REGULATE, REIGN, RULE 1.

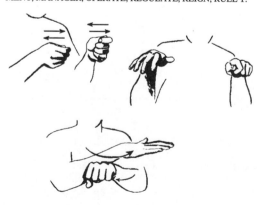

GOVERNMENT (gŭv′ ərn mənt, -ər-), *n.* (The head indicates the head or seat of government.) The right index finger, pointing toward the right temple, describes a small clockwise circle and comes to rest on the right temple. *Cf.* CAPITAL.

GO WITH *phrase.* (Going forward together.) Both "A" hands, knuckles and thumbs touching, move forward in unison. *Cf.* ACCOMPANY 2.

GOWN (goun), *n.* (Draping the clothes on the body.) With fingertips resting on the chest, both hands move down simultaneously. The action is repeated. *Cf.* CLOTHES, CLOTHING, DRESS, FROCK, GARMENT, SHIRT, SUIT, WEAR 1.

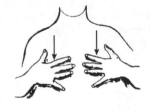

GRAB (grăb), *v.,* GRABBED, GRABBING, *n.* (Grasping something and holding it down.) Both hands, palms down, quickly close into the "S" position, the right on top of the left. *Cf.* CAPTURE, CATCH 2, GRASP, SEIZE.

GRADE (grād), *n.* (The letter "G"; the level.) Both "G" hands, palms facing out, move apart, indicating a level or stage.

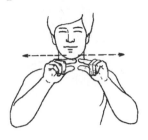

GRADUATE 1 (*n.* grăj′ ठठ ĭt; *v.* grăj′ ठठ āt′), -ATED, -ATING. (The letter "G"; the ribbon around the diploma.) The right "G" hand makes a single clockwise circle, and drops down into the upturned left palm.

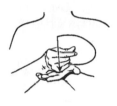

GRADUATE 2, *adj.* (Fingers represent a total of seven years of college.) The left "5" hand is held palm facing the chest. The right "2" hand, palm also facing the chest, is placed across the left, so that the index and middle fingers are next to the left thumb, making a total of seven fingers presented. This sign is traditionally used at Gallaudet University, where the first five fingers represent years at school, with the little finger corresponding to the preparatory year and the remaining four signifying freshman through senior years. Thus the two extra fingers added on will be the two extra years beyond senior year required in most cases for a master's degree. This sign is today applicable to any graduate school or program.

GRAM (gram), *n.* (The letter "G"; weighing.) The right "G" fingers rock back and forth on the extended left index.

GRAND 1 (grănd), *adj.* (The hands gesture toward the heavens.) The "5" hands, palms out and arms raised rather high, are positioned somewhat above the line of vision. The arms move abruptly forward and up once or twice. An expression of pleasure or surprise is usually assumed. *Cf.* EXCELLENT, GREAT 3, MARVELOUS, SPLENDID 1, SWELL 1, WONDER 2, WONDER-FUL 1.

GRAND 2, *adj., interj.* (The feelings are titillated.) With the thumb resting on the upper part of the chest, the fingers are wiggled back and forth. *Cf.* ELEGANT, FINE 1, GREAT 4, SPLENDID 2, SWELL 2, WONDERFUL 2.

GRANDDAUGHTER (grăn' dô tər), *n.* (The letter "G"; DAUGHTER.) The "G" is formed with the right hand. The sign for DAUGHTER is then made: the FEMALE prefix sign is formed, with the thumb of the right hand tracing a line on the right jaw from

just below the ear to the chin. The right upturned arm then rests on its left counterpart, as if holding a baby.

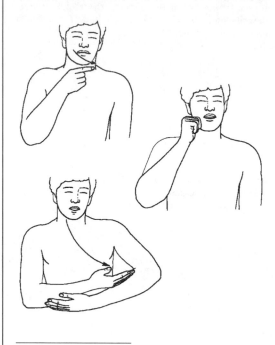

GRANDFATHER 1 (grănd' fä´ thər), *n.* (A male baby-holder; a predecessor.) The sign for FATHER 2 is made: the thumbtip of the right "5" hand touches the right temple a number of times. Then both open hands, palms up, are extended in front of the chest, as if supporting a baby. From this position they sweep over the left shoulder. The whole sign is smooth and continuous.

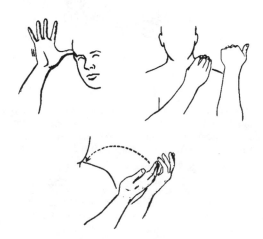

GRANDFATHER 2, *n.* (A variation of GRANDFA-THER 1.) The "A" hands are held with the left in front of the right, and the right thumb positioned against the forehead. Both hands open into the "5" position, so that the right little finger touches or almost touches the left thumb. Both hands may, as they open, move forward an inch or two.

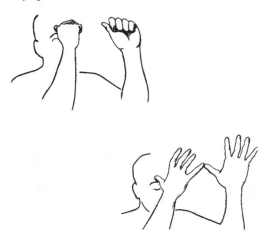

GRANDMOTHER 1 (grănd' mŭťh´ ər), *n.* (Same rationale as for GRANDFATHER 1.) The sign for MOTHER 2 is made: the thumb of the right "5" hand rests on the right cheek or on the right chin bone. The rest of the sign follows that for GRANDFA-THER 1.

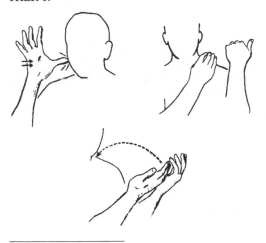

GRANDMOTHER 2, *n.* (A variation of GRAND-MOTHER 1.) The "A" hands are positioned as in GRANDFATHER 2 but with the right thumb on the right cheek. They open in the same manner as in GRANDFATHER 2.

GRANDSON (grănd' sun), *n.* (The letter "G"; SON.) The "G" is formed with the right hand. The sign for SON is then made: the MALE prefix sign is formed, the thumb and extended fingers of the right hand are brought up to grasp an imaginary cap brim. The right upturned arm then rests on its left counterpart, as if holding a baby.

GRANT 1 (grănt, gränt), *v.*, GRANTED, GRANTING. (A permissive upswinging of the hands, as if giving in.) Both hands, palms facing and fingers pointing away from the body, are held at chest level, almost a foot apart. With an upward movement, using their wrists as pivots, the hands sweep up until the fingers point almost straight up. *Cf.* ALLOW, LET, LET'S, LET US, MAY 3, PERMISSION 1, PERMIT 1, TOLERATE 1.

GRANT 2, *v.* The modified "O" hand, little finger edge down, moves forward and down in an arc before the body, as if giving something to someone.

GRAPES (grăps), *n. pl.* (A clump of the fruit is outlined.) The curved right fingertips move along the back of the downturned open left hand, from wrist to knuckles, in a series of short, up-down, curved movements, outlining a clump of grapes.

GRAPH (graf), *n.* (Drawing the lines of a graph.) The right "G" hand traces the imaginary up-down lines of a graph in the air.

GRASP (grăsp, gräsp), *v.*, GRASPED, GRASPING. See GRAB.

GRASS 1 (gras), *n.* (The letter "G"; growing.) The index and thumb of the right "G" hand is pushed up

through the left hand, which forms a cup.

GRASS 2 (Blades of grass obscuring the view; or the smell of new-mown grass.) The open right hand, palm facing the signer, moves up in front of the lips and nose. The movement is usually repeated.

GRASSHOPPER (gras' hop' ər), *n.* (The jumping.) The right index and middle fingers execute a series of jumping motions as they move up the downturned left arm.

GRATEFUL (grāt′ fəl), *adj.* (Expressions from the heart and mouth.) The open right hand is placed against the mouth, the open left hand against the heart. Both move forward, away from the body, simultaneously.

GRATIFY 1 (grăt′ ə fi′), *v.*, -FIED, -FYING. (A pleasurable feeling on the heart.) The open right hand is circled on the chest, over the heart. *Cf.* APPRECIATE, ENJOY, ENJOYMENT, LIKE 3, PLEASE, PLEASURE, WILLING 2.

GRATIFY 2, *v.* (The inner feelings settle down.) Both "B" hands (or "5" hands, fingers together) are placed palms down against the chest, the right above the left. Both move down simultaneously a few inches. *Cf.* CONTENT, CONTENTED, SATISFACTION, SATISFIED, SATISFY 1.

GRAVE 1 (grāv), *n.* (The mound of a grave.) The downturned open hands, slightly cupped, are held side by side. They describe an arc as they are drawn in toward the body. *Cf.* BURY 1, CEMETERY.

GRAVE 2, *adj.* (The facial features drop.) Both "5" hands, palms facing the eyes and fingers slightly curved, drop simultaneously to a level with the mouth. The head drops slightly as the hands move down, and an expression of sadness is assumed. *Cf.* DEJECTED, DEPRESSED 1, GLOOM, GLOOMY, GRIEF 1, MELANCHOLY, MOURNFUL, SAD, SORROWFUL 1.

GRAVITY (grav′ ə tē), *n.* (The letter "G"; dropping down.) The right "G" hand, positioned under the downturned left palm, drops straight down.

GRAVY (grā′ vĭ), *n.* (The drippings from a fleshy, *i.e.,* animal, substance. Used, however, to indicate both organic and inorganic types of oil.) The right thumb and middle finger grasp the fleshy part of the open left hand. The right hand moves straight down. This is repeated once or twice. *Cf.* FAT 2, FATTY, GREASE, GREASY, OIL 2, OILY.

GRAY 1 (grā), *(rare), adj.* (Mixing of colors, in this case black and white, to produce the necessary shade.) The fingertips of the open right hand describe a continuous clockwise circle in the upturned left palm. *Cf.* GREY.

GRAY 2, *(loc.), adj.* (Rationale unknown.) The right "O" hand traces an S-curve in the air as it moves down before the body. *Cf.* GREY.

GRAY 3, *adj.* (Intermingling of colors, in this case black and white.) The open "5" hands, fingers pointing to one another and palms facing the body, alternately swing in toward and out from the body. Each time they do so, the fingers of one hand pass through the spaces between the fingers of the other. *Cf.* GREY.

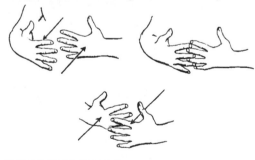

GRAY 4, *adj.* (The letter "G"; modified sign for BLACK.) The right "G" hand, fingers pointing left, moves across the brow from left to right.

GREASE (*n.* grēs; *v.* grēs, grēz), *n., v.,* GREASED, GREASING. (The drippings from a fleshy, *i.e.,* animal, substance. Used, however, to indicate both organic and inorganic types of oil.) The right thumb and middle finger grasp the fleshy part of the open left hand. The right hand moves straight down. This is repeated once or twice. *Cf.* FAT 2, FATTY, GRAVY, GREASY, OIL 2, OILY.

GREASY (grē′ sĭ, -zĭ), *adj.* See GREASE.

GREAT 1 (grāt), *adj.* (A delineation of something big, modified by the letter "L," which stands for LARGE.) Both "L" hands, palms facing out, are placed before the face, and separate rather widely. *Cf.* BIG 1, LARGE.

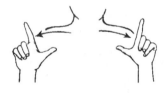

GREAT 2, *adj.* (A large amount.) The "5" hands face each other, fingers curved and touching. They move apart rather quickly. *Cf.* EXPAND, INFINITE, LOT, MUCH.

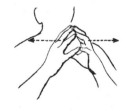

GREAT 3, *adj.* (The hands gesture toward the heavens.) The "5" hands, palms out and arms raised rather high, are positioned somewhat above the line of vision. The arms move abruptly forward and up once or twice. An expression of pleasure or surprise is usually assumed. *Cf.* EXCELLENT, GRAND 1, MARVELOUS,

SPLENDID 1, SWELL 1, WONDER 2, WONDERFUL 1.

GREAT 4, *adj., interj.* (The feelings are titillated.) With the thumb resting on the upper part of the chest, the fingers are wiggled back and forth. *Cf.* ELEGANT, FINE 1, GRAND 2, SPLENDID 2, SWELL 2, WONDERFUL 2.

GREAT BRITAIN (brĭt ən), *n.* (The English are supposed to be handshakers.) The right hand grasps and shakes the left. *Cf.* BRITAIN, BRITISH, ENGLAND, ENGLISH.

GREAT GRANDFATHER (grāt′ grănd′ fä′ t͟hər), *n.* (A male holder of a baby, two predecessors removed.) The sign for GRANDFATHER 1, *q.v.*, is made, except that the hands swing over the left shoulder in two distinct steps.

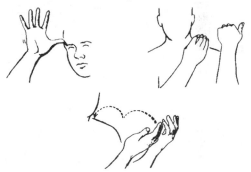

GREAT GRANDMOTHER (grāt′ grănd′ mŭt͟h′ ər), *n.* (Same rationale as for GREAT GRANDFATHER.) The sign for GRANDMOTHER 1, *q.v.*, is made, followed by the same end-sign as employed for GREAT GRANDFATHER.

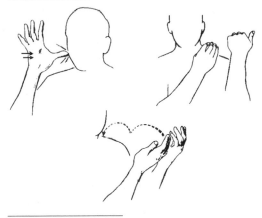

GREAT GRANDPARENTS *n.* See GREAT GRANDFATHER.

GREEDY 1 (grē′ dĭ), *adj.* (Pulling things toward oneself.) Both prone open or "V" hands are held in front of the body with fingers bent. The hands are then drawn quickly and forcefully inward, as if raking things toward oneself. *Cf.* SELFISH 1, STINGY 1, TIGHTWAD 1.

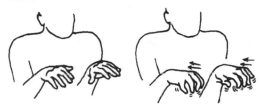

GREEDY 2, *adj.* (Scratching the palm in greed.) The right fingers scratch the upturned left palm several times. A frowning expression is often used. *Cf.* SELFISH 2, STINGY 2, TIGHTWAD 2.

GREEDY 3, *adj.* (Scratching in greed.) The down-turned "3" hands, held side by side, make a scratching motion as they move in toward the body. *Cf.* SELFISH 3, STINGY 3.

GREY (grā), *adj.* See GRAY 1, 2, or 3.

GRIEF 1 (grēf), *n.* (The facial features drop.) Both "5" hands, palms facing the eyes and fingers slightly curved, drop simultaneously to a level with the mouth. The head drops slightly as the hands move down, and an expression of sadness is assumed. *Cf.* DEJECTED, DEPRESSED 1, GLOOM, GLOOMY, GRAVE 2, MELANCHOLY, MOURNFUL, SAD, SORROWFUL 1.

GRIEF 2, *n.* (Wringing the heart.) Both clenched hands, held at the heart with knuckles touching, go through back-and-forth wringing motions. A sad expression is usually assumed. *Cf.* GRIEVE.

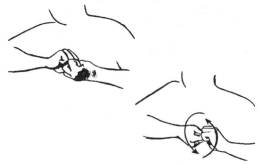

GRIEVE (grēv), *v.*, GRIEVED, GRIEVING. See GRIEF 2.

GRIMACE (grĭ mās´, grĭ´ məs), *n., v.*, -MACED, -MAC-ING. (The facial features are distorted.) The "X" hands are moved alternately up and down in front of the face, whose features are distorted with a pronounced frown. *Cf.* HOMELY 1, UGLINESS 1, UGLY 1.

GROTESQUE (grō tĕsk´), *adj.* (Something which distorts the vision.) The "C" hand describes a small arc in front of the face. *Cf.* CURIOUS 2, ODD, PECULIAR, QUEER, STRANGE, WEIRD.

GROUND (ground), *n.* (Fingering the soil.) Both hands, held upright before the body, finger imaginary pinches of soil. *Cf.* DIRT, SOIL 1.

GROUP 1 (groop), *n.* (A grouping together.) Both "C" hands, palms facing, are held a few inches apart at chest height. They are swung around in unison, so that the palms now face the body. *Cf.* ASSOCIATION, CIRCLE 2, CLASS, CLASSED, CLUB, COMPANY 1, GANG, ORGANIZATION 1.

GROUP 2, *n.* (The letter "G.") The sign for GROUP 1 is made, using the "G" hands.

 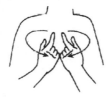

GROVEL (gruv′ əl), *v.* (Walk on knees.) The knuckles of the right index and middle fingers "walk" on the upturned left palm.

GROW (grō), *v.,* GREW, GROWN, GROWING. (Flowers or plants emerge from the ground.) The right fingers, pointing up, emerge from the closed left hand, and they spread open as they do. *Cf.* BLOOM, DEVELOP 1, GROWN, MATURE 1, PLANT 1, RAISE 3, REAR 2, SPRING.

GROWL 1 (groul), *n., v.* (Sound coming out of the throat.) The right claw hand, palm facing the signer, is positioned at the throat. The fingers wriggle as the hand moves forward from the throat. The signer assumes a threatening countenance, baring the teeth.

GROWL 2, *n., v.* (The threatening face and bared teeth.) With both claw hands facing forward, the signer assumes a threatening countenance and bares the teeth.

GROWN (grōn), *adj.* See GROW.

GUARANTEE (găr′ ən tē′), *n., v.,* -TEED, -TEEING. (The arm is raised.) The right index finger is placed at the lips. The right arm is then raised, palm out and elbow resting on the back of the left hand. *Cf.* LOYAL, OATH, PLEDGE, PROMISE 1, SWEAR 1, SWORN, TAKE OATH, VOW.

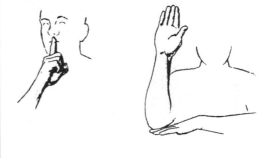

GUARD (gärd), *v.,* GUARDED, GUARDING. (Hold down firmly; cover and strengthen.) The "S" hands, downturned, are held side by side in front of the body, the arms almost horizontal, and the left hand in front of the right. Both arms move a short distance forward and slightly downward. *Cf.* DEFEND, DEFENSE, FORTIFY, PROTECT, PROTECTION, SHIELD 1.

GUATEMALA (gwä´ tə mä´ lä) *n.* The open right hand rubs the stomach in a counterclockwise direction. A native sign.

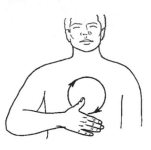

GUESS 1 (gĕs), *n., v.,* GUESSED, GUESSING. (A thought comes into view.) The index finger of the right "D" hand is placed at mid-forehead, pointing straight up. The slightly cupped right hand, palm facing left, then swings around so that the palm is toward the face.

GUESS 2, *n., v.* (A thought is grasped.) The right fingertip touches the forehead; then the right hand

makes a quick grasping movement in front of the head, ending in the "S" position.

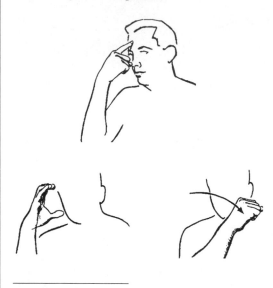

GUESS 3, *v.* (Weighing one thing against another.) The upturned open hands move alternately up and down. *Cf.* MAY 1, MAYBE, MIGHT 2, PERHAPS, POSSIBILITY, POSSIBLY, PROBABLE, PROBABLY, SUPPOSE.

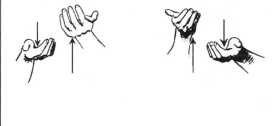

GUIDE (gīd), *n., v.,* GUIDED, GUIDING. (One hand leads the other). The right hand grasps the tips of the left fingers and pulls the left hand forward. *Cf.* CONDUCT 2, LEAD.

GUILTY 1 (gĭl′tĭ), *adj.* (The blame is firmly placed.) The right "A" hand, thumb pointing up, is brought down firmly against the back of the left hand, held palm down; the right thumb is then directed toward the person or object to blame. When personal blame is acknowledged, the thumb is brought in to the chest. *Cf.* ACCUSE, BLAME, FAULT.

GUILTY 2, *adj.* (The "G" hand; a guilty heart.) The index finger edge of the right "G" hand taps the chest over the heart.

GUINEA PIG *n.* (The letter "G"; PIG.) The right "G" hand brushes the tip of the nose twice, then the sign for PIG is made: the downturned right prone hand is placed under the chin, fingers pointing forward. The hand swings alternately up and down.

GUM (gum), *n.* (The chewing motion.) The thumb of the right "A" hand, held against the right cheek, swivels forward and back several times. Alternatively, the tips of the right "V" hand are placed at the right cheek and move in and out. *Cf.* CHEWING GUM.

GYMNASTICS (jim nas′ tiks), *n.* (The body movement.) The right index and middle fingers rest in the upturned left palm. The right hand leaves the left, assuming a palm-up position. The index and middle fingers swing in the air in a clockwise circle, and then the two fingers "land" again in the left palm. *Cf.* ACROBAT.

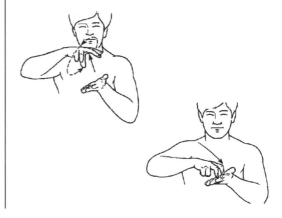

H

HABIT (hăb′ ĭt), *n.* (Bound down to custom or habit.) Both "S" hands, palms down, are crossed and brought down in unison before the chest. *Cf.* ACCUSTOM, BOUND, CUSTOM, LOCKED, PRACTICE 3.

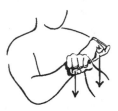

HAIFA (hī′ fə) *n.* (Apparently something to do with an army camp or base located there.) The signer executes a salute. A native sign.

HAIR (hâr), *n.* (The natural sign.) A lock of hair is grasped by the right index finger and thumb.

HAIRCUT (hâr′ kut), *n.* (The scissors at both sides of the head.) The two "V" hands, palms facing the sides

of the head, open and close repeatedly as the hands move alternately back and forth. *Cf.* BARBER.

HAIRDRESSER (hâr′ drĕs′ ər), *n.* (Working on the hair.) The "S" hands, palms out, are positioned above the head. They move alternately toward and away from the head, as if pulling locks of hair. This sign is followed by the sign for INDIVIDUAL: both open hands, palms facing each other, move down the sides of the body, tracing its outline to the hips.

HAIR DRYER (hâr′ drī′ ər), *n.* (Holding the machine above the head.) The right "L" hand, thumb pointing up, aims the index finger at the hair as the hand moves at random over the head.

HAITI (hä′ tē) *n.* The right "H" hand moves repeatedly across the line of vision of the right eye. A native sign.

HALE (hāl), *adj.* (Strength emanating from the body.) Both "5" hands are placed palms against the chest. They move out and away, forcefully, closing and assuming the "S" position, *Cf.* BRAVE, BRAVERY, COURAGE, COURAGEOUS, FORTITUDE, HEALTH, HEALTHY, MIGHTY 2, STRENGTH, STRONG 2, WELL 2.

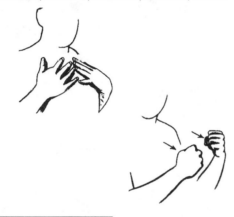

HALF (haf), *adj.* (Indicating half a finger.) The right index finger moves across the midpoint of the left index finger.

HALL (hôl), *n.* (The movement.) Both hands, palms facing and fingers together and extended straight out, move in unison away from the body, in a straight or winding manner. *Cf.* CORRIDOR, HALLWAY, MANNER 2, METHOD, OPPORTUNITY 3, PATH, ROAD, STREET, TRAIL, WAY 1.

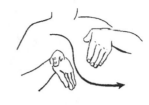

HALLOWED (hăl′ ŏd, hăl′ ŏ ĭd), *adj.* (Made holy.) The sign for MAKE is made: the right "S" hand, palm facing left, is placed on top of its left counterpart, whose palm faces right. The hands are twisted back and forth, striking each other slightly after each twist. This is followed by the sign for HOLY: the right "H" hand makes a clockwise circular movement, and is then opened and wiped across the open left palm.

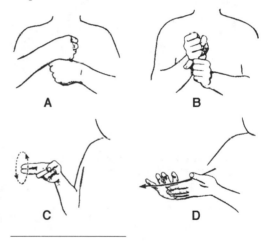

HALLWAY (hôl′ wā′), *n.* See HALL.

HALT (hôlt), *v.,* HALTED, HALTING. (A stopping or cutting short.) The little finger edge of the right hand is thrust abruptly into the upturned left palm, indicating a cutting short. *Cf.* STOP.

HAMBURGER (hăm′ bûr′ gər), *n.* (Making patties.) Both open hands go through the motions of forming patties.

if cutting off the left hand; and for the plural the action is repeated with the hands switched.

HAMMER (hăm′ ər), *n., v.,* -MERED, -MERING. (The natural sign.) The right hand, grasping an imaginary hammer, swings down toward the left fist, which represents the object being hammered. The right hand does not touch the left, however. The action is usually repeated.

 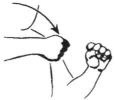

HAMSTER (ham′ stər), *n.* (The letter "H"; a rodent or rat.) The right "H" fingers brush repeatedly across the tip of the nose.

HANDCUFF (hand′ kuf), *v., n.* (Placing handcuffs on the wrists.) The right index and thumb, forming a "C," close over the left wrist. The left hand then does the same to the right.

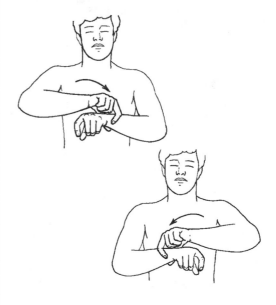

HAND (hănd), *n.* (The natural sign.) The prone right hand is drawn over the back of the prone left hand. For the plural, the action is repeated with the hands switched. The little finger edge of the right hand may instead be drawn across the back of the left wrist, as

HANDKERCHIEF (hăng′ kər chĭf, -chēf′), *n.* (Wiping the nose.) The signer makes the motions of wiping the nose several times with an imaginary handkerchief. This is the common cold. *Cf.* COLD 2.

HANG 1 (hăng), *v.*, HUNG, HANGED, HANGING. (The natural sign.) The curved right index finger "hangs" on the extended left index finger. *Cf.* SUSPEND.

HANG 2, *v.* (Hanging by the throat.) The thumb of the "Y" hand is placed at the right side of the neck, and the head hangs toward the left, as if it were caught in a noose. *Cf.* SCAFFOLD.

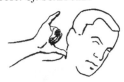

HANG 3, *v.* (The hanger attached to the closet pole.) The right curved index finger is draped over the horizontal left index finger. The sign may be repeated a number of times, or the right index finger may slide along the left toward the tip.

HANGER 1 (hang′ ər), *n.* (The hangers.) The right curved index finger is repeatedly hung over the extended left index finger, starting at the lower knuckle and moving successively to the fingertip. *Cf.* CLOSET 2.

HANGER 2, *n. (loc.)* (Clothing hanging from the hanger.) The right "Y" hand, palm facing the body, is positioned under the chin.

HANGER 3, *n., loc.* (The curved hook.) The knuckle of the curved right index finger is placed beneath the chin.

HAPPEN 1 (hăp′ ən), *v.*, -ENED, -ENING. (A befalling.) Both "D" hands, index fingers pointing away from the body, are simultaneously pivoted over so that the palms face down. *Cf.* COINCIDE, COINCIDENCE, EVENT, INCIDENT, OCCUR, OPPORTUNITY 4.

HAPPEN 2, *v.* The same sign as for HAPPEN 1, except that the "H" hands are used.

HAPPY (hăp′ ĭ), *adj.* (The heart is stirred; the spirits bubble up.) The open right hand, palm facing the body, strikes the heart repeatedly, moving up and off the heart after each strike. *Cf.* DELIGHT, GAIETY, GLAD, JOY, MERRY.

HARD 1 (härd), *adj.* (The knuckles are rubbed, to indicate a condition of being worn down.) The knuckles of the curved index and middle fingers of both hands are rubbed up and down against each other. Instead of the up-down rubbing, they may rub against each other in an alternate clockwise-counterclockwise manner. *Cf.* DIFFICULT 1, DIFFICULTY, HARDSHIP, POVERTY, PROBLEM 2.

HARD 2, *adj.* (Striking a hard object.) The curved index and middle fingers of the right hand, whose palm faces the body or the left, are brought down sharply against the back of the downturned left "S" hand. *Cf.* DIFFICULT 2.

HARD OF HEARING *adj. phrase.* (The "H" is indicated twice.) The right "H" hand drops down an inch or so, rises, moves in a short arc to the right, and drops down an inch or so again.

HARDSHIP (härd′ shĭp), *n.* See HARD 1.

HARM 1 (härm), *n.* (A stabbing pain.) The "D" hands, index fingers pointing to each other, are rotated in elliptical fashion before the chest—simultaneously but in opposite directions. *Cf.* ACHE, HURT 1, INJURE 1, INJURY, PAIN, SIN, WOUND.

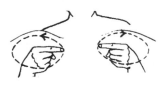

HARM 2, *v.*, HARMED, HARMING. (Striking down against.) Both "A" or "X" hands are held before the chest, the right above the left. The right hand strikes down and out, hitting the left thumb and knuckles with force. *Cf.* CRUEL 1, HURT 2, MEAN 1.

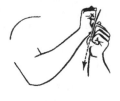

HARVEST 1 (här′ vĕst), *v.*, -VESTED, -VESTING. (Gathering in the harvest.) The right open hand sweeps across the upturned left palm and closes into the "A" position, as if gathering up some stalks. *Cf.* REAP 1.

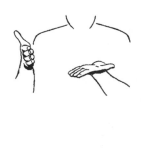

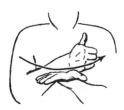

HARVEST 2, *v.* (The cutting.) The left hand grasps the heads of imaginary wheat stalks. The upturned right hand, imitating a sickle blade, then swings in to cut the stalks. *Cf.* REAP 2.

HASIDIC (has' i dik) *adj.* (The *pais,* or sidecurls worn by ultra-orthodox Jewish males.) The signer twirls an imaginary curl hanging down on the side of the head. *Cf.* ORTHODOX 2.

HASTE (hāst), *n.* (Letter "H"; quick movements.) The "H" hands, palms facing each other and held about six inches apart, shake alternately up and down. One hand alone may be used. *Cf.* HURRY.

HAT (hăt), *n.* (The natural sign.) The right hand pats the head.

HATCH (hach), *v.* (Cracking the shell.) The right "H" hand is brought down on the left "H" hand, and

then both hands are pivoted down and slightly apart. *Cf.* EGG.

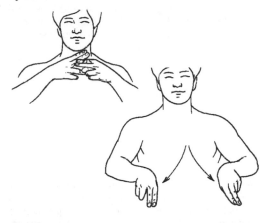

HATCHET (hach' it), *n.* (The chopping.) The left arm is held straight up from the bent elbow. The little finger edge of the upturned right hand (or "H" hand) then makes a series of chopping movements against the left elbow. *Cf.* AXE.

HATE (hāt), *n., v.,* HATED, HATING. (To push away and recoil from; avoid.) The two open hands, palms facing left, are pushed deliberately to the left, as if pushing something away. An expression of disdain or disgust is worn. *Cf.* ABHOR, AVOID 2, DESPISE, DETEST, LOATHE.

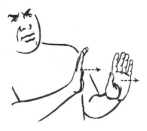

HAVE (hăv), v., HAS, HAD, HAVING. (The act of bringing something over to oneself.) The right-angle hands, palms facing and thumbs pointing up, are swept toward the body until the fingertips come to rest against the middle of the chest. *Cf.* POSSESS.

HAVE TO v. *phrase*. (Being pinned down.) The right hand, in the "X" position, palm down, moves forcefully up and down once or twice. An expression of determination is frequently assumed. *Cf.* MUST, NECESSARY 1, NECESSITY, NEED 1, OUGHT TO, SHOULD, VITAL 2.

HAWAII (hə wä′ ē, hə wĭ′ yə), *n.* ("H"; beautiful.) The right "H" hand makes a counterclockwise circle around the face. This movement is from the sign for BEAUTIFUL.

HAY (hā), *n.* (Blades of grass obscuring the view, or the smell of newly mown hay.) The open right hand, palm facing the signer, moves up in front of the lips and nose. The movement is usually repeated. *Cf.* GRASS.

HAYLOFT (ha′ lôft), *n.* (Stuffing the hay.) The sign for HAY, above, is made, followed by the right hand stuffing imaginary hay into a cup formed by the left hand.

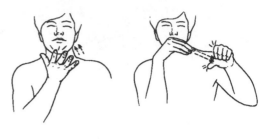

HAYSTACK (hā′ stak), *n.* (A pile of hay or grass.) The sign for HAY, above, is made. The downturned cupped hands, held together, then move down and apart, describing a mound or pile.

HE (hē), *pron.* (Pointing at a male.) The MALE prefix sign is made: the right hand grasps an imaginary cap brim. The right index finger then points at an imaginary male. If in context the gender is clear, the prefix sign is usually omitted. *Cf.* HIM 1.

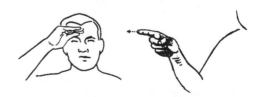

HEAD (hĕd), *n.* (The head is indicated.) The tips of the fingers of the right right-angle hand are placed at the right temple, and then move down in an arc to the right jaw.

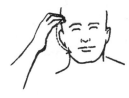

HEADACHE (hĕd' āk´), *n.* (A stabbing pain in the head.) The index fingers, pointing to each other, move back and forth on the forehead.

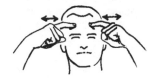

HEADLINE (hed' līn), *n.* (A banner across a newspaper.) The right curved index and thumb sweep across an imaginary newspaper page, from left to right.

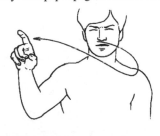

HEALTH (hĕlth), *n.* (Strength emanating from the body.) Both "5" hands are placed palms against the chest. They move out and away, forcefully, closing and assuming the "S" position. *Cf.* BRAVE, BRAVERY, COURAGE, COURAGEOUS, FORTITUDE, HALE, HEALTHY, MIGHTY 2, STRENGTH, STRONG 2, WELL 2.

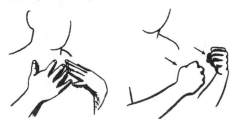

HEALTHY (hĕl' thĭ), *adj.* See HEALTH.

HEAR (hĭr), *v.,* HEARD (hûrd), HEARING. (Cupping the hand at the ear.) The right hand is placed, usually slightly cupped, behind the right ear. *Cf.* LISTEN.

HEARING (hĭr' ĭng), *pron.* (Words tumbling from the mouth, indicating the old association of being able to hear with being able to speak.) The right index finger, pointing left, describes a continuous small circle in front of the mouth. *Cf.* DISCOURSE, MAINTAIN 2, MENTION, REMARK, SAID, SAY, SPEAK, SPEECH 1, STATE, STATEMENT, TALK 1, TELL, VERBAL.

HEARING AID 1, *n.* (Behind the ear.) The right curved index finger is hooked onto the right ear, fingertip facing either forward or backward.

HEARING AID 2, *n.* (The wire leading down from the hearing aid.) The thumb and index finger trace an imaginary wire leading down from the ear to the chest.

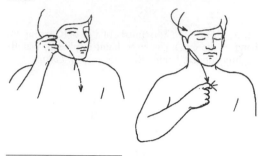

HEART (härt), *n.* (The natural sign.) The index fingers trace a heart at the appropriate spot on the chest.

HEART ATTACK (ə tăk'). (The heart is struck.) The sign for HEART 1 is made. Then the closed right fist strikes the open left palm, which faces right.

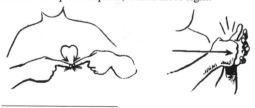

HEARTBEAT (härt' bēt'), *n.* (The natural sign.) The right fist beats rhythmically against the heart.

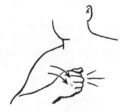

HEAT (hēt), *v.*, HEATED, HEATING. (The action of flames under a pot or pan.) The upturned left hand is

the pot. The fingers of the upturned right hand, held underneath the left hand, wiggle in imitation of the action of flames.

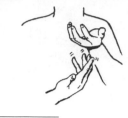

HEAVEN (hěv' ən), *n.* (Entering heaven through a break in the clouds.) Both open hands, fingers straight and pointing up, move upward in an arc on either side of the head. Just before they touch above the head, the right hand, palm down, sweeps under the left and moves up, its palm now facing out. *Cf.* SKY.

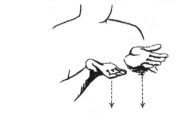

HEAVY (hěv' ĭ), *adj.* (The hands drop under a weight.) The upturned "5" hands, held before the chest, suddenly drop a short distance. *Cf.* WEIGHTY.

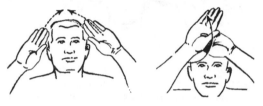

HEBREW (hē' brōō), *n., adj.* (The beard of the old Jewish patriarchs.) The fingers and thumb of each hand are placed at the chin and stroke an imaginary beard. *Cf.* JEW, JEWISH.

HEIGHT 1 (hīt), *n.* (The height is indicated.) The index finger of the right "D" hand moves straight up against the palm of the left "5" hand. *Cf.* TALL 1.

HEIGHT 2, *n.* (The height is indicated.) The right right-angle hand, palm facing the left, is held at the height the signer wishes to indicate. *Cf.* BIG 2, HIGH 3, TALL 2.

HELICOPTER (hel′ ə kop′ tər), *n.* (The rotor.) The downturned left "5" hand is placed on the upturned right index and trembles or quivers as the right index pushes it up.

HELL 1 (hĕl), *n.* (The devil; pointing down.) The sign for DEVIL is made: with the thumbs resting on the temples, the index and middle fingers of both hands open and close repeatedly. The right index

finger, pointing down, then moves straight down a few inches. The pointing may be omitted. *Cf.* DEMON, DEVIL, SATAN.

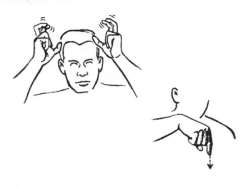

HELL 2, *n.* (The leaping of flames.) The "5" hands are held with palms facing the body. They move up and down alternately, while the fingers wiggle. *Cf.* BURN, FIRE 1, FLAME.

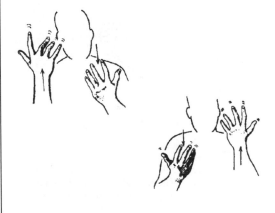

HELL 3, *n.* (The letter "H.") The right "H" hand, palm facing the body, moves sharply in an arc to the right.

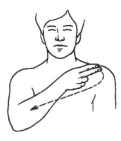

HELLO (hĕ lō′), *interj* (A wave of the hand.) The right open hand waves back and forth several times. *Cf.* GOODBYE, SO LONG.

HELP (hĕlp), *n., v.,* HELPED, HELPING. (Helping up; supporting.) The left "S" hand, thumb side up, rests in the open right palm. In this position the left hand is pushed up a short distance by the right. *Cf.* AID, ASSIST, ASSISTANCE, GIVE ASSISTANCE.

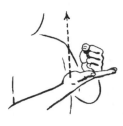

HENPECK (hĕn′ pĕk′), *v.,* -PECKED, -PECKING. (The hen's beak pecks.) The index finger and thumb of the right hand, held together, are brought against the index finger of the left "D" hand a number of times. *Cf.* NAG, PICK ON.

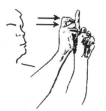

HER 1 (hûr), *pron.* (Pointing at a female.) The FEMALE prefix sign is made: the right "A" hand's thumb moves down along the line of the right jaw, from ear almost to chin. The right index finger then points at an imaginary female. If in context the gender is clear, the prefix sign is usually omitted. *Cf.* SHE. For the possessive sense of this pronoun, see HERS.

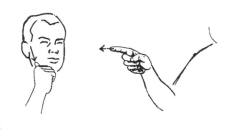

HER 2, *pron.* (honorific) (The shape or presence of the person in question.) The upturned open hand, fingers pointing toward the female person in question, moves down a few inches. Roughly equivalent to the English gloss "that's her, in person."

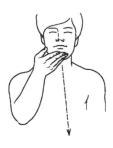

HERE (hĭr), *adv.* The open "5" hands, palms up and fingers slightly curved, move back and forth in front of the body, the right hand to the right and the left hand to the left. *Cf.* WHERE 2.

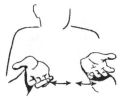

HERESY (hĕr′ ə sĭ), N. (ARCH.) (False faith.) The sign for FALSE 2 is made: the index finger of the right "D" hand, pointing to the left, moves along the lips from right to left. This is followed by the sign for FAITH: the index finger touches the forehead, and then the "S" hands grasp and plant an imaginary flagpole in the ground.

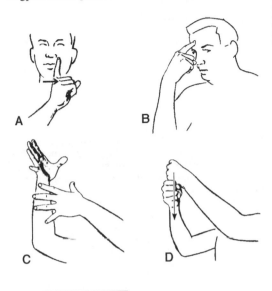

HERETIC (hĕr′ ə tĭk), n. (False believer.) The sign for FALSE 2, as in HERESY, is made. This is followed by the sign for BELIEVE: the index finger touches the middle of the forehead, and then both hands are clasped together. This is followed by the sign for INDIVIDUAL: both open hands, palms facing each other, move down the sides of the body, tracing its outline to the hips.

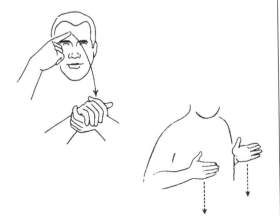

HERITAGE (hĕr′ ə tĭj), n. (The "H" hands; rolling down from the past into the present.) The "H" hands, palms down, are positioned over the shoulder, one atop the other, but not touching. They roll down over each other as they move down and forward. See also GENERATION.

HERMIT (hûr′ mĭt), (colloq.), n. (A lone person with himself.) The "I" hands, palms facing the body, touch repeatedly along their little finger edges.

HERMIT CRAB n. (The shape and function.) The downturned bent left "V" fingers creep forward as they pull the right hand, the shell, along.

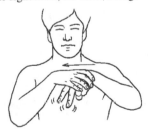

HEROIN (her′ ō in), n. (Jabbing in the needle.) The right fist grasps an imaginary needle and jabs it into the crook of the left elbow.

HERS (hûrz), *pron.* (Belonging to a female.) The FEMALE prefix sign is made. The open right hand, palm facing out, then moves straight forward a few inches. If in context the gender is clear, the prefix sign is usually omitted.

HERSELF (hər sĕlf'), *pron.* (The thumb indicates an individual who is stressed above others.) The FEMALE prefix sign is made. The right "A" hand, thumb upturned, then moves forward an inch or two, either once or twice. If in context the gender is clear, the prefix sign is usually omitted.

HESITATE (hĕz' ə tāt'), *v.*, -TATED, -TATING. (A faltering gesture.) The right "D" hand, palm facing left, moves forward in steps, an inch or so at a time. Each time it moves forward the head nods slightly.

HETEROSEXUAL (het ər ə sek' shoo əl), *adj.* (Straight) The upright right arm, palm facing left, moves straight forward in an arc. *Cf.* STRAIGHT 2.

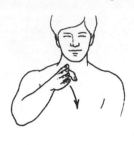

HEY! (hā), *interj.* (Waving for attention.) The open hand waves vigorously, with fingers pointing either up or at the person being addressed. This of course takes into account that deaf people communicate visually.

HIDE (hīd), *v.*, HID, HIDDEN, HIDING. (One hand is hidden under the other.) The thumb of the right "A" hand, whose palm faces left, is placed against the lips. The hand then swings down and under the downturned left hand. The initial contact with the lips is sometimes omitted. *Cf.* COVER 3.

HIGH 1 (hī), *adj.* (Something high up.) Both hands, in the right angle position, are held before the face, about a foot apart, palms facing. They are raised abruptly about a foot, in a slight outward curving movement. *Cf.* ADVANCED, PROMOTE, PROMOTION.

HIGH 2, *adj.* (Indicating height.) The right "A" hand, held with thumb pointing upward, moves straight up above the right shoulder. *Cf.* SUPERIOR 1.

HIGH 3, *adj.* (The height is indicated.) The right right-angle hand, palm facing the left, is held at the height the signer wishes to indicate. *Cf.* BIG 2, HEIGHT 2, TALL 2.

HIGH 4, *adj.* (The letter "H"; the natural movement.) The right "H" hand, palm facing the body, is moved up about a foot, to a position somewhat above the head.

HIGHBROW (hī' brou'), *(colloq.)*, *n.*, *adj.* (The natural sign.) The wide open right "C" hand is placed with thumb against the forehead, and palm facing left. The position of the hand thus indicates the height of the brow.

HIGH SCHOOL (The letters "H" and "S.") The letters "H" and "S" are fingerspelled.

HIGHWAY (hī' wā), *n.* (Traffic flowing in opposite directions.) The downturned "4" hands pass each other as the right moves repeatedly to the left and the left repeatedly to the right. The downturned "V" hands are often used instead of the "4"s. *Cf.* FREEWAY.

HILL 1 (hĭl), *n.* (A rocky mound.) The sign for ROCK is made: the back of the right "S" hand is struck several times against the back of the left "S" hand. Both "5" hands, palms down, then move in a wavy, undulating manner either from left to right or from right to left. The sign for ROCK is frequently omitted.

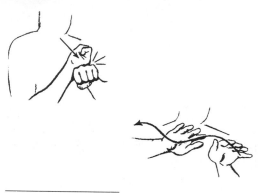

HILL 2, *n.* (The shape.) With the right downturned hand positioned above its left counterpart, a hill is described by moving the right hand up and forward in a hump or arc.

HIM 1 (hĭm), *pron.* (Pointing at a male.) The MALE prefix sign is made: the right hand grasps an imaginary cap brim. The right index finger then points at an imaginary male. If in context the gender is clear, the prefix sign is usually omitted. *Cf.* HE.

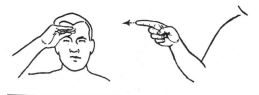

HIM 2, *pron.* (honorific) (The shape or presence of the person in question.) The upturned open hand, fingers pointing toward the male person in question,

moves down a few inches. Roughly equivalent to the English gloss "that's him, in person."

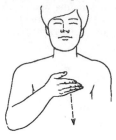

HIMSELF (hĭm sĕlf'), *pron.* (The thumb indicates an individual who is stressed above others.) The MALE prefix sign is made. The right "A" hand, thumb upturned, then moves forward an inch or two, either once or twice. If in context the gender is clear, the prefix sign is usually omitted.

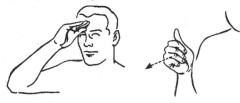

HINDER (hĭn' dər), *v.,* -DERED, -DERING. (Obstruct, block.) The left hand, fingers together and palm flat, is held before the body, facing somewhat down. The little finger side of the right hand, held with palm flat, makes one or several up-down chopping motions against the left hand, between its thumb and index finger. *Cf.* ANNOY, ANNOYANCE, BOTHER, DISRUPT, DISTURB, HINDRANCE, IMPEDE, INTERCEPT, INTERFERE, INTERFERENCE, INTERFERE WITH, INTERRUPT, MEDDLE 1, OBSTACLE, OBSTRUCT, PREVENT, PREVENTION.

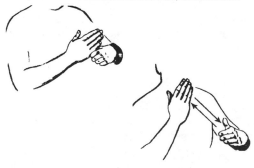

HINDRANCE (hĭn' drəns), *n.* See HINDER.

HINGE (hĭnj), *n.* (The natural sign.) The hands are joined at the fingertips, and are positioned at right angles to each other, with the fingertips pointing away from the body. The hands come together and separate again, always with fingertips in contact. This imitates the action of a hinge.

HISTORY (hĭs′ tə rĭ), *n.* (The letter "H"; moving down toward the present from the past.) The right "H" hand, palm facing left, swings down in an arc, from its initial position a bit above shoulder height.

HIT 1 (hĭt), *n., v.,* HIT, HITTING. (The natural sign.) The right "S" hand strikes its knuckles forcefully against the open left palm, which is held facing right. *Cf.* POUND 2, PUNCH 1, STRIKE 1.

HIPPOPOTAMUS (hĭp′ ə pot′ ə məs), *n.* (The large mouth opens.) Both "C" hands are placed on top of each other, fingertips pointing forward. The hands pivot wide open and close again. Another way to make this sign is with the extended index and little fingers of each hand, with the same open-and-close movement as before. The fingers here represent the teeth.

HIT 2, *n., v.* (Hitting the ball with a baseball bat.) The signer mimes hitting a ball with a baseball bat. *Cf.* BASEBALL.

HIS (hĭz), *poss. pron.* (Belonging to a male.) The MALE prefix sign is made. The open right hand, palm facing out, then moves straight forward a few inches. If in context the gender is clear, the prefix sign is usually omitted.

HITCH (hĭch), *n., v.,* HITCHED, HITCHING. (Hooking on to something and pulling.) With index fingers interlocked, the right hand pulls the left hand from left to right. *Cf.* HOOK, PULL 2, TOW.

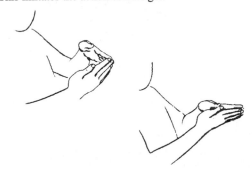

HIT THE NAIL ON THE HEAD *colloq. phrase.* (Hitting the mark.) The right fist hits the left index finger on the side.

HOCKEY (hok' ē), *n.* (The hockey stick.) The knuckle of the curved right index finger strikes against the upturned left palm, from fingertips to base, as if hitting a hockey puck.

HOE 1 (hō), *n., v.,* HOED, HOEING. (The natural sign.) The fingertips of the right right-angle hand are thrust repeatedly into the upturned left palm. The right hand is pulled back and a bit down before it is thrust into the palm again. This is the characteristic motion of the hoe as it tills the soil.

HOE 2, *n., v.* (Cutting a chunk of earth from a mound.) The right "C" hand digs repeatedly into the left palm, which is held either up or facing right.

HOLD (hōld), *n., v.,* HELD, HOLDING. (The gripping is emphasized.) Both "S" hands, one resting on the other, tremble slightly as they grip an imaginary object.

HOLDUP (hōld' ŭp'), *(colloq.), n.* (The guns.) Both "L" hands, palms facing each other, thumbs pointing straight up, are thrown forward slightly, as if presenting a pair of revolvers. *Cf.* ROBBERY 2.

HOLE (hōl), *n.* (The natural sign.) The left index finger and thumb form a circle. The right index finger is placed on this circle and traces its outline.

HOLIDAY (hŏl' ə dā'), *n.* (A position of idleness.) With thumbs tucked in the armpits, the remaining fingers of both hands wiggle. *Cf.* IDLE, LEISURE, RETIRE, VACATION.

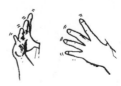

HOLY (hō′ lē), *adj.* (The letter "H"; cleanliness or purity.) The right "H" hand makes a clockwise circular movement, and is then opened and wiped across the open left palm.

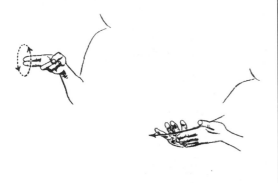

HOME (hōm), *n.* (A place where one eats and sleeps.) The closed fingers of the right hand are placed against the lips (the sign for EAT), and then, opening into a flat palm, against the right cheek (resting the head on a pillow, as in SLEEP). The head leans slightly to the right, as if going to sleep in the right palm, during this latter movement.

HOMELY 1 (hōm′ lĭ), *adj.* (The facial features are distorted.) The "X" hands are moved alternately up and down in front of the face, whose features are distorted with a pronounced frown. *Cf.* GRIMACE, UGLINESS 1, UGLY 1.

HOMELY 2, *adj.* In this variant of HOMELY 1, the "X" hands, palms down, move back and forth in a horizontal direction in front of the face, whose features are distorted with a pronounced frown. *Cf.* UGLINESS 2, UGLY 2.

HOMOSEXUAL 1 (hō′ mə sek′ shoo əl), *n., adj.* The tips of the "G" fingers are placed on the chin. *Cf.* GAY 1.

HOMOSEXUAL 2, *n., adj.* (Supposedly a code originally.) The signer pulls the ear lobe. *Cf.* GAY 2.

HOMOSEXUAL 3, *n., adj.* (Mutual masturbation.) Both fists, palms facing down, come together repeatedly. *Cf.* GAY 3.

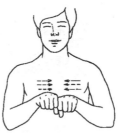

HOMOSEXUAL 4, *n., adj.* (An effeminate gesture.) Both "F" hands, palms out, are held at shoulder height. The signer moves them alternately forward and back, while the shoulders keep pace with the forward-and-back movements. *Cf.* EFFEMINATE, GAY 4.

HONDURAS (hon dŏŏr' əs), *n.* The downturned right "V" hand moves down an inch or two on the right side of the body, as if putting something into a side pocket. A native sign.

HONEST (ŏn' ĭst), *adj.* (The letter "H" for HONEST; a straight and true path.) The index and middle fingers of the right "H" hand, whose palm faces left, move straight forward along the upturned left palm. *Cf.* FRANK, HONESTY, SINCERE 1.

HONESTY (ŏn' ĭs tĭ), *n.* See HONEST.

HONEY 1 (hun' ē), *n.* (Wiping the lips.) The upturned right index finger is swept across the mouth, from left to right.

HONEY 2, *n.* (Wiping the lips.) With right index and little fingers extended, the signer wipes the lips from left to right, and then throws the hand down.

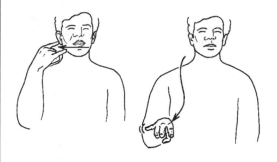

HONG KONG (hong' kong', hông' kông'), *n.* The closed hand is held in front of the mouth, palm facing out. The hand is thrown forward twice, each time with the fingers opening.

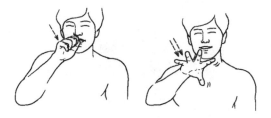

HONOR (ŏn' ər), n., v., -ORED, -ORING. (The letter "H"; a gesture of respect.) The right "H" hand, palm facing left, swings down in an arc from its initial position in front of the forehead. The head bows slightly during this movement of the hand. Cf. HONORARY.

HONORARY (ŏn' ə rĕr´ ĭ), adj. See HONOR.

HOOK (hŏŏk), n. (Hooking on to something and pulling.) With index fingers interlocked, the right hand pulls the left hand from left to right. Cf. HITCH, PULL 2, TOW.

HOPE (hōp), n., v., HOPED, HOPING. (A thought awaited.) The tip of the right index finger, held in the "D" position, palm facing the body, is placed on the forehead (modified THINK, q.v.). Both hands then assume right angle positions, fingers facing, with the left hand held above left shoulder level and the right before the right breast. Both hands, held thus, wave to each other several times. Cf. ANTICIPATE, ANTICIPATION, EXPECT.

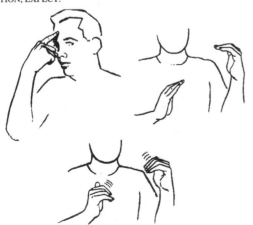

HOPSCOTCH (hop' skoch), n. (The movement of the feet or legs.) The index and middle fingers, placed on the heel of the left hand, "run" forward about half the distance between the heel and the fingertips. The "running" fingers then execute a series of short jumps forward until they reach the fingertips.

HORDES (hôrdz), n. (Many people coming together in one place.) The downturned "5" hands, fingers wriggling, come toward each other until the fingertips almost touch.

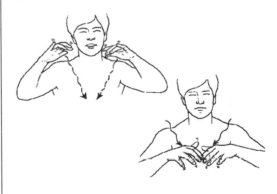

HORNY 1 (hôr' nē), adj., sl. (The horns.) One or both index fingers are placed at the top of the forehead, pointing out.

HORNY 2, *adj., sl.* (The pulse in the throat.) The right hand, index and little fingers extended and palm facing out, is held at the right side of the throat. The index finger repeatedly strikes the side of the throat.

HORROR (hôr′ ər), *n.* (A threatening gesture, much used in childhood.) Both claw hands, palms out, are positioned in front of the face. The signer's teeth are bared, or the mouth is held open.

HORSE (hôrs), *n.* (The ears.) The "U" hands are placed palms out at either side of the head. The index and middle fingers move forward and back repeatedly, imitating the movement of a horse's ears.

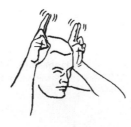

HORSEBACK (hôrs′ băk′), *n.* (Mounted on horseback.) The right index and middle fingers straddle the left hand, which is held palm facing right.

The left hand moves in a rhythmic up-down motion, carrying the right hand with it.

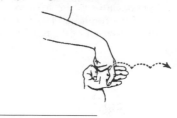

HOSPITAL 1 (hŏs′ pĭ təl), *n.* (The letter "H"; the red cross on the sleeve.) The index and middle fingers of the right "H" hand trace a cross on the upper part of the left arm.

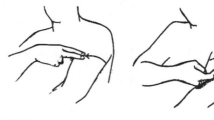

HOSPITAL 2, *n.* (The wide, bird-like hood worn by the French nursing sisters.) The right "B" hand, palm facing the left, swings over from the left side of the forehead to the right side.

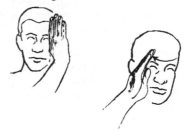

HOT (hŏt), *adj.* (Removing hot food from the mouth.) The cupped hand, palm facing the body, moves up in front of the slightly open mouth. It is then flung down to the palm-down position.

HOT DOG 1 (hŏt′ dôg), *(colloq.)*. (The shape.) The "C" hands are held side by side, palms out, thumbs and index fingers touching. They change to the "S" position as they are drawn apart. *Cf.* FRANKFURTER 1.

HOT DOG 2, *n.* (The shape in a roll or bun.) The left hand is held with the fingers pointing up. The right index finger is placed between the thumb and the other fingers. *Cf.* FRANKFURTER 2.

HOT ROD (hŏt′ rŏd), *n.* (The stick shift.) The signer mimes shifting automobile gears violently, while holding the top of the steering wheel in the other hand. The body may show bouncing as the car takes off.

HOUR (our), *n.* (The minute hand completes a circle around the clock's face.) The left "5" hand, palm facing right and fingers pointing forward or upward, is the clock's face. The right "D" hand is placed against it so that the right index finger points straight up.

The right hand, always in contact with the left palm, executes a full clockwise circle, tracing the movement of the minute hand.

HOUSE (hous), *n.* (The shape of the house.) The open hands are held with fingertips touching, so that they form a pyramid a bit above eye level. From this position, the hands separate and move diagonally downward for a short distance; then they continue straight down a few inches. This movement traces the outline of a roof and walls. *Cf.* RESIDENCE 1.

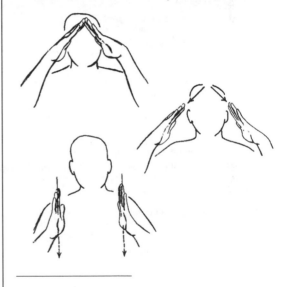

HOW (hou), *adv.* (The hands come into view, to reveal something.) The right-angle hands, palms down and knuckles touching, swing up and open to the palms-up position. *Cf.* MANNER 1.

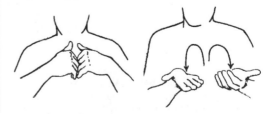

HOW ARE YOU? *phrase.* (What are your feelings?) Both middle fingers quickly sweep up and out from the chest. The eyebrows are raised in inquiry. *Cf.* WHAT'S NEW? 2

HOWEVER 1 (hou ĕv′ ər), *conj.* (A divergence or a difference; the opposite of same.) The index fingers of both "D" hands, palms facing down, are crossed near their tips. The hands are drawn apart. *Cf.* BUT, ON THE CONTRARY 1.

HOWEVER 2, *conj.* Both hands, in the "5" position, are held before the chest, fingertips facing each other. With an alternate back-and-forth movement, the fingertips are made to strike each other. *Cf.* ANYHOW, ANYWAY, DESPITE, DOESN'T MATTER, INDIFFERENCE, INDIFFERENT, IN SPITE OF, MAKE NO DIFFERENCE, NEVERTHELESS, NO MATTER, WHEREVER.

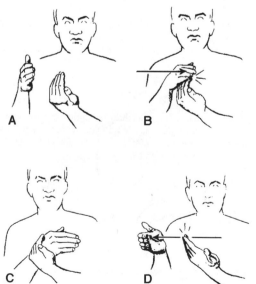

A   B

C   D

HOW MANY? *interrogative phrase.* (Throwing up a number of things before the eyes; a display of fingers to indicate a question of how many or how much.) The right hand, palm up, is held before the chest, all fingers touching the thumb. The hand is tossed straight up, while the fingers open to the "5" position. *Cf.* AMOUNT 2, HOW MUCH?

HOW MUCH? *interrogative phrase.* See HOW MANY?

HOW MUCH MONEY? *interrogative.* (Amount of money is indicated.) The sign for MONEY is made: the upturned right hand, grasping some imaginary bills, is brought down into the upturned left palm a number of times. The right hand then moves straight up, opening into the "5" position, palm up. *Cf.* PRICE 1, WHAT IS THE PRICE?

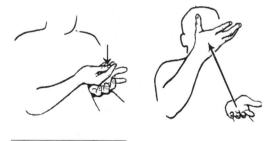

HUG (hŭg), *v.,* HUGGED, HUGGING, *n.* (The natural sign.) The arms clasp the body in a natural hugging position. *Cf.* EMBRACE.

HUH? (hu), *interj.* (Throwing out a question.) The downturned curved right index finger is thrown out and forward very slightly, while the signer follows the finger with a very slight forward movement of the body. An expression of inquiry or perplexity is assumed.

HUMANITY (hū măn' ə tĭ), *n.* (People, indicated by the rotating "P" hands.) The "P" hands, side by side, are moved alternately toward the body in continuous counterclockwise circles. *Cf.* PEOPLE, PUBLIC.

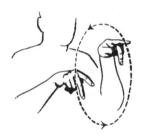

HUMBLE 1 (hŭm' bəl, ŭm'-), *adj.* (The head bows; a turtle's head retreats into its shell; an act of humility.) The index finger edge of the right "B" hand, palm facing left, is placed at the lips. The right "B" hand is then brought down and under the downturned open left hand. The head, at the same time, bows.

HUMBLE 2, *adj.* Same as HUMBLE 1, but only the right hand is used.

HUMBUG (hŭm' bŭg), *n.* (A double face, *i.e.*, a mask covers the face.) The right hand is placed over the back of the left hand and pushes it down and a bit in toward the body. *Cf.* BLUFF, FAKE, HYPOCRITE, IMPOSTOR.

HUMOR (hū' mər, ū´-), *n.* (The nose wrinkles in laughter.) The tips of the right index and middle fingers brush repeatedly off the tip of the nose. *Cf.* COMIC, COMICAL, FUNNY, HUMOROUS.

HUMOROUS (hū' mər əs, ū´-), *adj.* See HUMOR.

HUNDRED (hŭn′ drəd), *n., adj.* (The Roman "C," *centum,* for "hundred.") The letter "C" is formed. This is preceded by a "1" for a simple hundred, or by whatever number of hundreds one wishes to indicate.

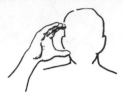

HUNT (hŭnt), *n., v.,* HUNTED, HUNTING. (Firing a rifle.) The left hand grasps the barrel of an imaginary rifle, while the right hand grasps the base, its thumb extended upward to represent the sight, and index finger wiggling back and forth, as if pulling the trigger. At the same time, both hands make short back-and-forth movements, as if the rifle is firing.

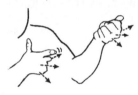

HURRY (hûr′ ĭ), *v.,* -RIED, -RYING. (Letter "H"; quick movements.) The "H" hands, palms facing each other and held about six inches apart, shake alternately up and down. One hand alone may be used. *Cf.* HASTE.

HURT 1 (hûrt), *v.,* HURT, HURTING, *n.* (A stabbing pain.) The "D" hands, index fingers pointing to each other, are rotated in elliptical fashion before the chest—simultaneously but in opposite directions. *Cf.* ACHE, HARM 1, INJURE 1, INJURY, PAIN, SIN, WOUND.

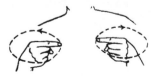

HURT 2, *v., n.* (Striking down against.) Both "A" or "X" hands are held before the chest, the right above the left. The right hand strikes down and out, hitting the left thumb and knuckles with force. *Cf.* CRUEL 1, HARM 2, MEAN 1.

HUSBAND (hŭz′ bənd), *n.* (A male joined in marriage.) The MALE prefix sign is formed: the right hand grasps the brim of an imaginary cap. The hands are then clasped together.

HYMN (hĭm), *n.* (The letter "H.") The right "H" hand is waved back and forth, to and from the open palm of the left hand, in a series of elongated figure-eights.

HYPOCRITE (hĭp′ ə krĭt), *n.* (A double face, *i.e.,* a mask covers the face.) The right hand is placed over the back of the left hand and pushes it down and a bit in toward the body. *Cf.* BLUFF, FAKE, HUMBUG, IMPOSTOR.

HYSTERECTOMY (his tə rek′ tə mē), *n.* (WOMAN, CUT, REMOVE.) The sign for WOMAN is made: the thumb of the open "5" hand leaves the chin and moves down to the chest. Next is the sign for CUT, as in operation: the right thumb slashes across the belly. This is followed by REMOVE: the right hand makes a grasping movement from the palm of the left hand and is thrown down.

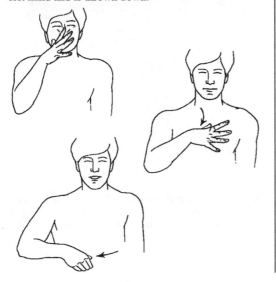

I 1 (ī), *pron.* (The letter "I," held to the chest.) The right "I" hand is held with its thumb edge to the chest and little finger pointing up.

I 2, *pron.* (The natural sign.) The signer points to himself. *Cf.* ME.

ICE (īs), *n., v.,* ICED, ICING. (The stiff fingers.) The fingers of the "5" hands, held palms down, stiffen and contract. *Cf.* FREEZE, FROZEN, RIGID.

ICE CREAM 1 (crēm), *n.* (The eating action.) The upturned left palm represents a dish or plate. The curved index and middle fingers of the right hand represent the spoon. They are drawn up repeatedly from the left palm to the lips. *Cf.* SPOON.

ICE CREAM 2, *n.* (The natural sign.) The signer goes through the act of licking an imaginary ice cream cone.

IDENTICAL (ī děn′ tə kəl), *adj.* (Matching fingers are brought together.) The outstretched index fingers are brought together, either once or several times. *Cf.* ALIKE, LIKE 2, SAME 1, SIMILAR, SUCH.

IDIOM (ĭd′ ē əm), *n.* (The "I" letters; quotation marks.) Both "I" hands, palms out, move apart. The signer then curves the index and middle fingers of each hand, describing a pair of quotation marks in the air.

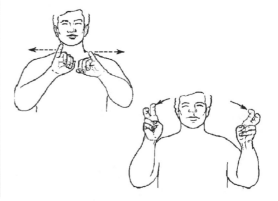

IDLE (ī′ dəl), *adj.* (A position of idleness.) With thumbs tucked in the armpits, the remaining fingers of both hands wiggle. *Cf.* HOLIDAY, LEISURE, RETIRE, VACATION.

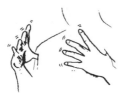

IF (ĭf), *conj.* (The scales move up and down.) The two "F" hands, palms facing each other, move alternately up and down. *Cf.* CONSIDER 3, COURT, EVALUATE 1, JUDGE 1, JUDGMENT, JUSTICE.

IGNORANT (ĭg′ nə rənt), *adj.* (The head is struck to emphasize its emptiness or lack of knowledge.) The back of the right "V" hand strikes the forehead once or twice. Two fingers represent prison bars across the mind—the mind is imprisoned.

IGNORE (ĭg nôr′), *v.,* -NORED, -NORING. (Thumbing the nose.) The index finger of the right "B" hand is placed under the tip of the nose. From this position the right hand moves straight forward, away from the face. *Cf.* DISREGARD.

ILL (il), *adj., n., adv.* (The sick parts of the anatomy are indicated.) The right middle finger rests on the forehead, and its left counterpart is placed against the stomach. The signer assumes an expression of sadness or physical distress. *Cf.* DISEASE, ILLNESS, SICK.

ILLNESS (il′ nĭs), *n.* See ILL.

ILL TEMPER (tĕm′ pər). (Wrinkling the brow.) the "5" hand is held palm toward the face. The fingers open and close partly, several times, while an angry expression is worn on the face. *Cf.* ANGRY 1, CROSS 1, CROSSNESS, FIERCE, IRRITABLE.

ILLUSTRATE (ĭl′ ə strāt′, ĭ lŭs′ trāt), *v.*, -TRATED, -TRATING. (Directing the attention to something, and bringing it forward.) The right index finger points into the left palm, held facing out before the body. The left palm moves straight out. *Cf.* DEMONSTRATE, DISPLAY, EVIDENCE, EXAMPLE, EXHIBIT, EXHIBITION, INDICATE, INFLUENCE 2, PRODUCE 1, REPRESENT, SHOW 1, SIGNIFY 1.

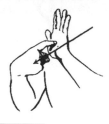

IMAGE (ĭm′ ĭj), *n.* (Contours are indicated or outlined.) Both "A" hands, held about a foot apart before the face, with palms facing each other, move down simultaneously in a wavy, undulating motion. *Cf.* FIGURE 2, FORM 1, SCULPT, SCULPTURE, SHAPE, STATUE.

IMAGINATION 1 (ĭ măj′ ə nā′ shən), *n.* (A thought coming forward from the mind, modified by the letter "I" for "idea.") With the "I" position on the right hand, palm facing the body, touch the little finger to the forehead, and then move the hand up and away in a circular, clockwise motion. The hand may also be moved up and away without this circular motion. *Cf.* CONCEIVE, IMAGINE, THEORY 1, THOUGHT 2.

IMAGINATION 2, *n.* (The "I" letters; thoughts wandering off into the air.) Both "I" hands are positioned near their respective temples. They move forward and up, describing a series of circles.

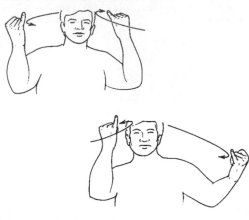

IMAGINE (ĭ măj′ in), *v.*, -INED, -INING. See IMAGINATION 1.

IMITATE (ĭm′ ə tāt′), *v.*, -TATED, -TATING. (The natural sign.) The right fingers and thumb close together and move onto the upturned, open left hand, as if taking something from one place to another. *Cf.* COPY, DUPLICATE, MIMIC, MODEL.

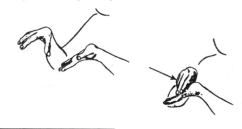

IMMEDIATELY (ĭ mē′ dĭ ĭt lĭ), *adv.* (A quick movement.) The thumbtip of the upright right hand is flicked quickly off the tip of the curved right index finger, as if shooting marbles. *Cf.* FAST, QUICK, QUICKNESS, SPEED, SPEEDY, SWIFT.

IMPAIRED (ĭm pârd'), *adj.* (The letter "I"; held back or impeded.) The right little finger is brought into the space between the left thumb and index finger.

IMPEDE (ĭm pēd'), *v.*, -PEDED, -PEDING. (Obstruct, block.) The left hand, fingers together and palm flat, is held before the body, facing somewhat down. The little finger side of the right hand, held with palm flat, makes one or several up-down chopping motions against the left hand, between its thumb and index finger. *Cf.* ANNOY, ANNOYANCE, BOTHER, DISRUPT, DISTURB, HINDER, HINDRANCE, INTERCEPT, INTERFERE, INTERFERENCE, INTERFERE WITH, INTERRUPT, MEDDLE 1, OBSTACLE, OBSTRUCT, PREVENT, PREVENTION.

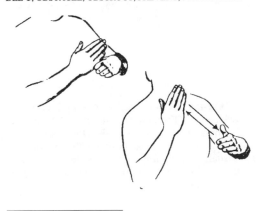

IMPLORE (ĭm plôr'), *v.*, -PLORED, -PLORING. (An act of supplication.) With the right hand clasped over the left, both hands are shaken gently before the body. The eyes often are directed upward. *Cf.* BEG 2, ENTREAT, PLEA, PLEAD, SUPPLICATION.

IMPLY (ĭm plī'), *v.*, -PLIED, -PLYING. (Relative standing of one's thoughts.) A modified sign for THINK is made: the right index finger touches the middle of the forehead. The tips of the right "V" hand, palm down, are then thrust into the upturned left palm (as in STAND, *q.v.*). The right "V" hand is then re-thrust into the upturned left palm, with right palm now facing the body. *Cf.* INTEND, INTENT, INTENTION, MEAN 2, MEANING, MOTIVE 3, PURPOSE 1, SIGNIFICANCE 2, SIGNIFY 2, SUBSTANCE 2.

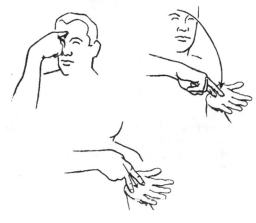

IMPORTANT (ĭm pôr' tənt), *adj.* Both "F" hands, palms facing each other, move apart, up, and together in a smooth elliptical fashion, coming together at the tips of the thumbs and index fingers of both hands. *Cf.* SIGNIFICANCE 1, SIGNIFICANT, VALUABLE, VALUE, VITAL 1, WORTH, WORTHWHILE, WORTHY.

IMPOSSIBLE (ĭm pŏs' ə bəl), *(loc.)*, *adj.* The downturned right "Y" hand is placed in the upturned left palm a number of times. The up-down movement is very slight.

IMPOSTOR (ĭm pŏs' tər), *n.* (A double face, *i.e.,* a mask covers the face.) The right hand is placed over the back of the left hand and pushes it down and a bit in toward the body. *Cf.* BLUFF, FAKE, HUMBUG, HYPOCRITE.

IMPOTENCE 1 (ĭm' pə təns), *n.* (No erection.) The sign for NO 1 is made: both "O" hands are held facing each other. They are then drawn apart, while the signer's head shakes slightly in negation. This is followed by ERECTION: the left hand grasps the right arm or the crook of the right elbow as the right "S" hand moves up in an arc. *Cf.* IMPOTENT 1.

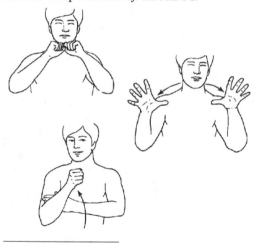

IMPOTENCE 2, *n. sl.* (The penis is limp.) The right hand is held in the downturned "X" position. *Cf.* IMPOTENT 2.

IMPOTENT 1 (ĭm' pə tent), *adj.* See IMPOTENCE 1.

IMPOTENT 2, *adj.* See IMPOTENCE 2.

IMPROVE (ĭm prōōv'), *v.,* -PROVED, -PROVING. (Moving up.) The little finger edge of the right hand rests on the back of the downturned left hand. It moves up the left arm in successive stages, indicating improvement or upward movement.

IN (ĭn), *prep., adv., adj.* (The natural sign.) The fingers of the right hand are thrust into the left. *Cf.* INSIDE, INTO, WITHIN.

IN A FEW DAYS *adv. phrase.* (Several TOMORROWS ahead.) The thumb of the right "A" hand is positioned on the right cheek. One by one, the remaining fingers appear, starting with the index finger. Usually, when all five fingers have been presented, the hand moves forward a few inches, to signify the concept of the future.

IN A FEW YEARS *adv. phrase.* (Few, years, future.) The sign for FEW is made. This is followed by the sign for YEAR: the right "S" hand, palm facing left, is positioned atop the left "S" hand, whose palm faces right. The right "S" hand describes a complete circle around the left and comes to rest in its original position. Finally, the sign for FUTURE is made.

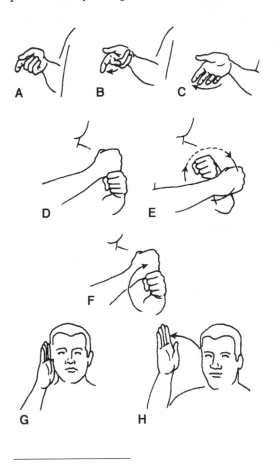

IN A WEEK *adv. phrase.* (A week around the corner.) The upright, right "D" hand is placed palm-to-palm against the left "5" hand, whose palm faces right. The right "D" hand moves along the left palm from base to fingertips and then curves to the left, around the left fingertips.

INCH (inch), *n.* (The length of the thumb's first joint.) The upturned left thumb is crooked. The thumb and index finger of the right hand rest on the tip and first joint of the left thumb, to indicate its length.

INCIDENT (ĭn′ sə dənt), *n.* (A befalling.) Both "D" hands, index fingers pointing away from the body, are simultaneously pivoted over so that the palms face down. *Cf.* COINCIDE, COINCIDENCE, EVENT, HAPPEN 1, OCCUR, OPPORTUNITY 4.

INCLINATION (ĭn′ klə nā′ shən), *n.* (The feelings of the heart move toward a specific object.) The tip of the right middle finger touches the heart. The open right hand, palm facing the body, then moves away from the heart toward the palm of the open left hand. *Cf.* DISPOSE, DISPOSED TO, INCLINE, INCLINED, TEND, TENDENCY.

INCLINE (ĭn klīn′), *v.*, -CLINED, -CLINING. See INCLINATION.

INCLINED (ĭn klīnd′), *adj.* See INCLINATION.

INCLUDE (ĭn klo͞od′), *v.*, -CLUDED, -CLUDING. (All; the whole.) The left hand is held in the "C" position, fingers pointing right. The right hand, in the "5" position, fingers facing out from the body, palm down, is held above the left. With a horizontal swing to the right, the right hand describes an arc, as the fingers close and are thrust into the left "C" hand, which closes over it. *Cf.* INCLUSIVE, WHOLE (THE).

INCLUSIVE (ĭn klo͞o′ sĭv), *adj.* See INCLUDE.

INCOME (ĭn′ kŭm), *n.* (A regular taking in.) The outstretched open left hand, held palm facing right, moves in toward the body, assuming the "A" position, palm still facing right. This is repeated several times. *Cf.* DIVIDEND 1, SUBSCRIBE, SUBSCRIPTION.

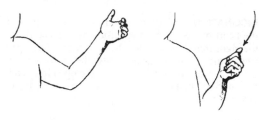

INCREASE (*n.* ĭn′ krēs; *v.* ĭn krēs′) -CREASED, -CREASING. (Adding on.) The index and middle fingers of the right "H" hand, palm up, are swung up and over until they come to rest on the index and middle fingers of the left "H" hand, held palm down. *Cf.* ADD 3, ADDITION, GAIN 1, ON TO, RAISE 2.

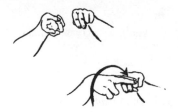

INCREDULITY (ĭn′ krə dū′ lə tĭ, -do͞o′-), *n.* (The nose is wrinkled in disbelief.) The right "V" hand faces the nose. The index and middle fingers bend as a cynical expression is assumed. *Cf.* CYNIC, CYNICAL, DISBELIEF 1, DON'T BELIEVE, DOUBT 1, SKEPTIC 1, SKEPTICAL 1.

INDECISION (ĭn′ dĭ sĭzh′ ən), *n.* (On a fence.) The index and middle fingers of the right hand, palm down, straddle the index finger edge of the left "B" hand, which is held palm facing right. In this position the right hand rocks deliberately back and forth, from left to right. *Cf.* UNCERTAIN, UNSURE, WAVER 1.

INDEED (ĭn dēd′), *adv., interj.* (Coming forth directly from the lips; true.) The index finger of the right "D" hand, palm facing left, is placed against the lips. It moves up an inch or two and then describes a small arc forward and away from the lips. *Cf.* ABSOLUTE, ABSOLUTELY, ACTUAL, ACTUALLY, AUTHENTIC, CERTAIN, CERTAINLY, FIDELITY, FRANKLY, GENUINE, POSITIVE 1, POSITIVELY, REAL, REALLY, SINCERE 2, SURE, SURELY, TRUE, TRULY, TRUTH, VALID, VERILY.

INDEPENDENCE (ĭn´ dĭ pĕn´ dəns), *n.* (Breaking the bonds.) The "S" hands, crossed in front of the body, swing apart and face out. *Cf.* EMANCIPATE, FREE 1, FREEDOM, INDEPENDENT 1, LIBERATION, REDEEM 1, RELIEF, RESCUE, SAFE, SALVATION, SAVE 1.

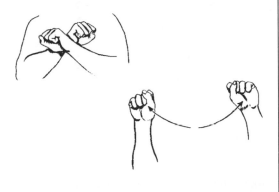

INDEPENDENT 1 (ĭn´ dĭ pĕn´ dənt), *adj.* See INDE-PENDENCE.

INDEPENDENT 2, *adj.* (Initialized version.) As in INDEPENDENCE, the hands swing apart and face out, but here both hands form the letter "I."

INDIAN 1 (ĭn´ dĭ ən), *n., adj.* (The feathered head-dress.) The right thumb and index fingers, holding an imaginary feather, are placed first on the tip of the nose and then under the right ear or on the right side of the head. *Cf.* NATIVE AMERICAN 1.

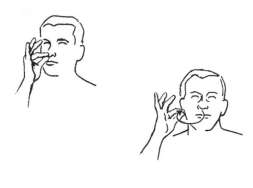

INDIAN 2, *n., adj.* (The characteristic motions during dancing.) The right "5" hand is placed behind the head, fingers pointing upward to indicate the feath-ers. The left hand touches the open lips repeatedly. *Cf.* NATIVE AMERICAN 2.

INDICATE (ĭn´ də kāt´), *v.,* -CATED, -CATING. (Directing the attention to something, and bringing it forward.) The right index finger points into the left palm, held facing out before the body. The left palm moves straight out. *Cf.* DEMONSTRATE, DISPLAY, EVI-DENCE, EXAMPLE, EXHIBIT, EXHIBITION, ILLUSTRATE, INFLUENCE 2, PRODUCE 1, REPRESENT, SHOW 1, SIGNIFY 1.

INDIFFERENCE (ĭn dĭf′ ər əns), *n.* Both hands, in the "5" position, are held before the chest, fingertips facing each other. With an alternate back-and-forth movement, the fingertips are made to strike each other. *Cf.* ANYHOW, ANYWAY, DESPITE, DOESN'T MATTER, HOWEVER 2, INDIFFERENT, IN SPITE OF, MAKE NO DIFFERENCE, NEVERTHELESS, NO MATTER, WHEREVER.

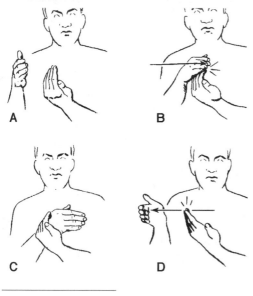

A   B

C   D

INDIFFERENT (ĭn dĭf′ ər ənt), *adj.* See INDIFFERENCE.

INDIGNANT (ĭn dĭg′ nənt), *adj.* (A violent welling-up of the emotions.) The curved fingers of the right hand are placed in the center of the chest, and fly up suddenly and violently. An expression of anger is worn. *Cf.* ANGER, ANGRY 2, ENRAGE, FURY, INDIGNATION, IRE, MAD, RAGE.

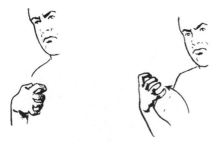

INDIGNATION (ĭn′ dĭg nā′ shən), *n.* See INDIGNANT

INDIVIDUAL 1 (ĭn′ də vĭj′ ŏŏ əl), *n.* (The shape of an individual.) Both open hands, palms facing each other, move down the sides of the body, tracing its outline to the hips. This is an important suffix sign, that changes a verb to a noun. *e.g.,* TEACH, *v.,* becomes TEACHER, *n.,* by the addition of this sign.

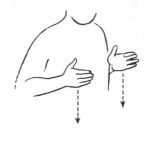

INDIVIDUAL 2, *n.* (The "I" hands; the outline of a person.) The "I" hands, palms facing and little fingers pointing out, are held before the body. They are drawn down a few inches, outlining the shape of an imaginary person standing before the signer.

INDOCTRINATE (ĭn dŏk′ trĭ nāt′), *v.,* -NATED, -NATING. (Giving forth from the mind.) The fingertips of each hand are placed on the temples. They then swing out and into the "5" position. *Cf.* EDUCATE, INDOCTRINATION, INSTRUCT, INSTRUCTION, TEACH.

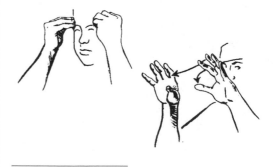

INDOCTRINATION *n.* See INDOCTRINATE.

INDULGENCE (ĭn dŭl′ jəns), *(eccles.)*, *n.* (The "P" refers to "Purgatory.") The tip of the middle finger of the right "P" hand executes a continuous clockwise circle on the upturned left palm.

INDUSTRIOUS (ĭn dŭs′ trĭ əs), *adj.* (Rubbing the hands together in zeal or ambition.) The open hands are rubbed vigorously back and forth against each other. *Cf.* AMBITIOUS, ANXIOUS, DILIGENCE, DILIGENT, EAGER, EAGERNESS, ENTHUSIASM, ENTHUSIASTIC, METHODIST, ZEAL, ZEALOUS.

INEXPENSIVE (ĭn′ ĭk spĕn′ sĭv), *adj.* (A small amount of money.) The sign for MONEY is made: the upturned right hand, grasping some imaginary bills, is brought down into the upturned left palm a number of times. The downturned cupped right hand is then positioned over the upturned cupped left hand. The right hand descends a short distance but does not touch the left.

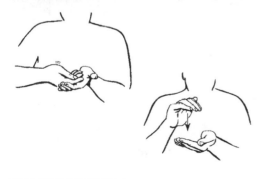

INFANT (ĭn′ fənt), *n.* (The rocking of the baby.) The arms are held with one resting on the other, as if cradling a baby. They rock from side to side. *Cf.* BABY.

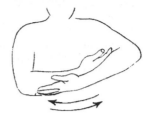

INFERIOR (ĭn fîr′ ē ər), *adj.* (The letter "I"; underneath.) The right little finger executes a clockwise circle underneath the downturned left palm.

INFINITE (ĭn′ fə nĭt), *adj.* (A large amount.) The "5" hands face each other, fingers curved and touching. They move apart rather quickly. *Cf.* EXPAND, GREAT 2, LOT, MUCH.

INFLATION (in flā′ shən), *n.* (The letter "I"; spiraling upwards.) The base of the right "I" hand rests on the left hand. It spirals upward.

INFLUENCE 1 (ĭn′ flōō əns), *n., v.,* -ENCED, -ENCING. (Rays of influence emanating from a given source.) All the right fingertips, including the thumb, are positioned on the tip of the upturned thumb of the left "A" hand. The right hand, opening into the downturned "5" position, moves forward from its initial position. Instead of its initial position on the left thumb, the right hand is frequently placed on the back of the downturned left "S" hand, moving forward.

INFLUENCE 2, *n., v.* (Directing the attention to something, and bringing it forward.) The right index finger points into the left palm, held facing out before the body. The left palm moves straight out. *Cf.* DEMONSTRATE, DISPLAY, EVIDENCE, EXAMPLE, EXHIBIT, EXHIBITION, ILLUSTRATE, INDICATE, PRODUCE 1, REPRESENT, SHOW 1, SIGNIFY 1.

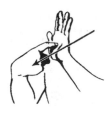

INFLUENCE 3, *n., v.* (Take something, *influence,* and disseminate it.) The left hand, held limp in front of the body, has its fingers pointing down. The fingers of the right hand, held all together, are placed on the top of the left hand, and then move forward, off the left hand, assuming a "5" position, palm down. Essentially similar to second part of INFLUENCE 1. *Cf.* ADVICE, ADVISE, COUNSEL, COUNSELOR.

INFORM (ĭn fôrm′), *v.,* -FORMED, -FORMING. (Taking knowledge from the mind and giving it out to all.) The fingertips are positioned on either side of the forehead. Both hands then swing down and out, opening into the upturned "5" position. *Cf.* INFORMATION, LET KNOW, NOTIFY.

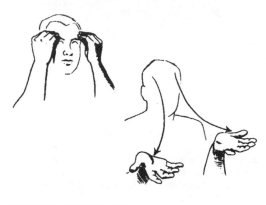

INFORMATION (ĭn fər mā′ shən), *n.* See INFORM.

INJECTION (ĭn jĕk′ shən), *n.* (The natural sign.) The right hand goes through the motions of injecting a substance into the upper left arm. *Cf.* SHOT, SHOT IN THE ARM.

INJURE 1, (ĭn′ jər), *v.,* -JURED, -JURING. (A stabbing pain.) The "D" hands, index fingers pointing to each other, are rotated in elliptical fashion before the chest—simultaneously but in opposite directions. *Cf.* ACHE, HARM 1, HURT 1, INJURY, PAIN, SIN, WOUND.

INJURE 2, *v.* (An encroachment; parrying a knife thrust.) The left "A" hand is held palm toward the body, knuckles facing right. The extended thumb of the right "A" hand is brought sharply over the back of the left. *Cf.* DANGER, DANGEROUS, PERIL, TRESPASS, VIOLATE.

INJURY (ĭn′ jə rĭ), *n.* See INJURE 1.

INJUSTICE (ĭn jŭs′ tĭs), *n.* (Not, justice.) The sign for NOT 1 is made: the downturned open hands are crossed. They are drawn apart rather quickly. This is followed by the sign for JUSTICE: the two "F" hands, palms facing each other, move alternately up and down.

INK 1 (ĭngk), *n.* (The letter "I"; dipping the pen and shaking off the excess ink.) The little finger of the right "I" hand is dipped into the hole formed by the left "O" hand, held thumb side up. The right hand then emerges and shakes off the imaginary ink from the little finger.

INK 2, *n.* (The letter "I"; dipping the pen; writing.) The little finger of the right "I" hand is drawn along the right eyebrow, from left to right. This is a modified sign for BLACK, *q.v.* The same finger is then "dipped into the inkwell," as explained in INK 1. Finally the right hand, holding an imaginary pen, writes on the upturned left palm.

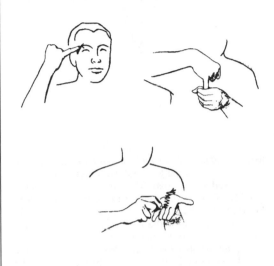

IN-LAW (ĭn′ lô′), *n.* (See material pertaining to each word.) The sign for IN is made: the fingers of the right hand are thrust into the left. This is followed by the sign for LAW: the upright right "L" hand, resting palm against palm on the upright left "5" hand, moves down in an arc a short distance, coming to rest on the base of the left palm.

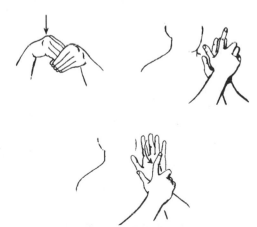

INNER FEELINGS *n.* (Things within.) The left "C" hand is held near the base of the throat, palm facing the body. The right hand, fingers closed, is stuffed into the left. This sign should be made a bit slowly and deliberately.

INNOCENT 2, *adj., n.* Both open hands, palms facing out, are held in front of the mouth, with the ring fingers bent against the palm. Both hands move out and away from the mouth, describing arcs. *Cf.* NAIVE 2.

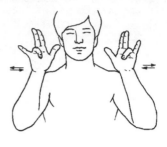

INNOCENCE (ĭn′ ə səns), *n.* (Not to blame.) The sign for NOT is made: the downturned open hands are crossed at the wrists. They are drawn apart rather quickly. This is followed by the sign for BLAME: the right "A" hand, thumb pointing up, is brought down firmly against the back of the left hand, held palm down; the right thumb is then directed toward the person or object to blame. When personal blame is acknowledged, the thumb is brought in to the chest. The two signs are sometimes presented in reverse order. *Cf.* INNOCENT 1.

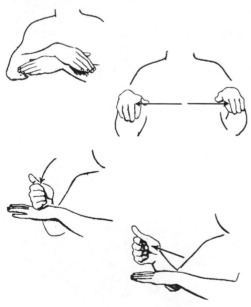

INOCULATE (ĭ nŏk′ yə lāt′), *(colloq.), v.,* -LATED, -LATING. (A shot in the arm.) The right index finger is thrust into the left upper arm and the thumb wiggles back and forth a number of times, as if implanting a shot in the arm. *Cf.* COCA-COLA, COKE, DOPE, MORPHINE, NARCOTICS.

INQUIRE 1 (ĭn kwīr′), *v.,* -QUIRED, -QUIRING. (Pray tell.) Both hands, held upright about a foot in front of the chest, with palms facing and fingers pointing straight up, are positioned about a foot apart. Moving toward the chest, they come together until they touch, as if in prayer. *Cf.* ASK 1, REQUEST 1.

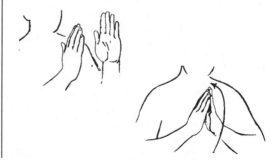

INNOCENT 1 (ĭn′ ə sənt), *adj.* See INNOCENCE.

INQUIRE 2, *(colloq.)*, *v.* (Fire a question.) The right hand, held in a modified "S" position with palm facing out, assumes a position with the thumb resting on the fingernail of the index finger. The index finger is flicked out and forward, usually directed at the person being asked a question. *Cf.* ASK 2, INTERROGATE 2, INTERROGATION 2, QUERY 2, QUESTION 2, QUIZ 2.

INQUIRE 3, *v.* (Firing questions.) The index fingers of both "D" hands repeatedly curve and straighten out as the hands are alternately flung forward and back, as if firing questions. *Cf.* ASK 3, EXAMINATION 2, INTERROGATE 1, INTERROGATION 1, QUERY 1, QUESTION 3, QUIZ 3.

INSANE (ĭn sān′), *adj.* (Turning of wheels in the head.) The open right hand is held palm down before the face, fingers spread, bent, and pointing toward the forehead. The fingers move in circles before the forehead. *Cf.* CRAZY 1, INSANITY.

INSANITY (ĭn săn′ ə tĭ), *n.* See INSANE.

INSECT (ĭn′ sĕkt), *(sl.)*, *n.* (The quivering antennae.) The thumb of the "3" hand rests against the nose, and the index and middle fingers bend slightly and straighten again a number of times.

INSENSATE (ĭn sĕn′ sāt), *adj.* (The slapping indicates the feelings of the heart are being tested.) The right hand rests on the heart. It then swings off and down, palm upturned, its fingertips slapping against the left palm as it moves down. An expression of contempt is often assumed.

INSIDE *(prep., adv.* ĭn′ sīd′; *adj.* ĭn′ sīd′). (The natural sign.) The fingers of the right hand are thrust into the left. *Cf.* IN, INTO, WITHIN.

INSIST (ĭn sĭst′), *v.*, -SISTED, -SISTING. (Something specific is moved in toward oneself.) The palm of the left "5" hand faces right. The right index finger is thrust into the left palm, and both hands are drawn sharply in toward the chest. *Cf.* DEMAND, REQUEST 2, REQUIRE.

INSPIRE (ĭn spīr′), *v.* (The feelings well up.) Both hands, fingers touching thumbs, are placed against the chest, with palms facing the body. They slide up the chest, opening into the "5" position.

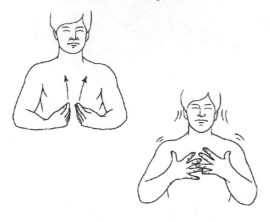

IN SPITE OF (spīt), *prep. phrase.* Both hands, in the "5" position, are held before the chest, fingertips facing each other. With an alternate back-forth movement, the fingertips are made to strike each other. *Cf.* ANYHOW, ANYWAY, DESPITE, DOESN'T MATTER, HOWEVER 2, INDIFFERENCE, INDIFFERENT, MAKE NO DIFFERENCE, NEVERTHELESS, NO MATTER, WHEREVER.

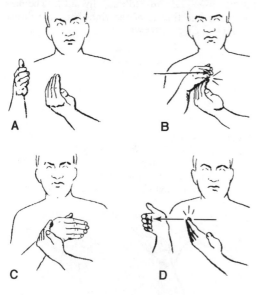

INSTALL (ĭn stôl′), *v.,* -STALLED, -STALLING. (Placing into.) The right hand, fingers touching the thumb, is

placed into the left "C" hand, whose palm faces out or toward the right.

INSTEAD OF 1 (ĭn stĕd′), *prep. phrase.* (Exchanging places.) The right "A" hand, positioned above the left "A" hand, swings down and under the left, coming up a bit in front of it. *Cf.* EXCHANGE, REPLACE, SUBSTITUTE, TRADE.

INSTEAD OF 2, *prep. phrase.* This is the same sign as for INSTEAD OF 1, except that "F" hands are used.

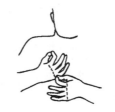
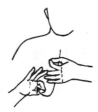

INSTITUTE (ĭn′ stə tūt′, -tōōt′), *n.* (The letter "I"; establishment on a firm base.) The right "I" hand is placed so that its base rests on the back of the down-turned left "S" hand. The movement is repeated, involving a slight up-down motion. Sometimes the right hand executes a small clockwise circle before coming to rest on the left. In this case the motion is not repeated. *Cf.* INSTITUTION.

INSTITUTION (ĭn´ stə tū´ shən), *n*. See INSTITUTE.

INSTRUCT (ĭn strŭkt´), *v., -*STRUCTED, -STRUCTING. (Giving forth from the mind.) The fingertips of each hand are placed on the temples. They then swing out and open into the "5" position. *Cf.* EDUCATE, INDOC-TRINATE, INDOCTRINATION, INSTRUCTION, TEACH.

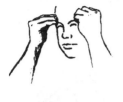

INSTRUCTION (ĭn strŭk´ shən), *n*. See INSTRUCT.

INSTRUCTOR (ĭn strŭk´ tər), *n*. The sign for INSTRUCT is made. This is followed by the sign for INDIVIDUAL: both open hands, palms facing each other, move down the sides of the body, tracing its outline to the hips. *Cf.* TEACHER.

INSULT 1 (*n*. ĭn´ sŭlt; *v*. ĭn sŭlt´) -SULTED, -SULTING. (A puncturing.) The right index finger is thrust quickly and deliberately between the index and mid-dle fingers of the left "V" hand, which is held palm facing right.

INSULT 2, *v*. (A slap in the face.) The right hand slaps the back of the left a glancing blow, and its momentum continues it beyond the left hand.

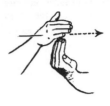

INSULT 3, *n., v*. (The thrust of a foil or épée.) The right index finger is thrust quickly forward and a bit up, in imitation of a fencing maneuver.

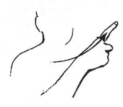

INSULT 4, *v.,* (Directing a barrage of insults or ripostes.) Both index fingers, pointing out from the body, execute continuous alternate forward move-ments.

INSURANCE (ĭn shŏŏr´ əns), *n*. (The letter "I.") The right "I" hand, palm out, is shaken slightly.

INTELLIGENT (in tĕl' ə jənt), *adj.* (The mind is bright.) The middle finger is placed at the forehead, and then the hand, with an outward flick, turns around so that the palm faces outward. This indicates a brightness flowing from the mind. *Cf.* BRIGHT 3, CLEVER, SMART.

with palm flat, makes one or several up-down chopping motions against the left hand, between its thumb and index finger. *Cf.* ANNOY, ANNOYANCE, BOTHER, DISRUPT, DISTURB, HINDER, HINDRANCE, IMPEDE, INTERFERE, INTERFERENCE, INTERFERE WITH, INTERRUPT, MEDDLE 1, OBSTACLE, OBSTRUCT, PREVENT, PREVENTION.

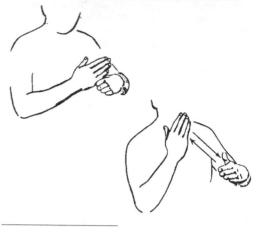

INTEND (in tĕnd'), *v.,* -TENDED, -TENDING. (Relative standing of one's thoughts.) A modified sign for THINK is made: the right index finger touches the middle of the forehead. The tips of the right "V" hand, palm down, are then thrust into the upturned left palm (as in STAND, *q.v.*). The right "V" hand is then re-thrust into the upturned left palm, with right palm now facing the body. *Cf.* IMPLY, INTENT, INTENTION, MEAN 2, MEANING, MOTIVE 3, PURPOSE 1, SIGNIFICANCE 2, SIGNIFY 2, SUBSTANCE 2.

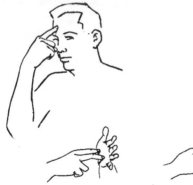

INTENT (in tĕnt'), *n.* See INTEND.

INTENTION (in tĕn' shən), *n.* See INTEND.

INTERCEPT (in' tər sĕpt'), *v.,* -CEPTED, -CEPTING. (Obstruct, block.) The left hand, fingers together and palm flat, is held before the body, facing somewhat down. The little finger side of the right hand, held

INTEREST 1 (in' tər ist, -trist), *n., v.,* -ESTED, -ESTING. (Drawing one out.) The index and middle fingers of both hands, one above the other, are placed on the middle part of the chest. Both hands move forward simultaneously. As they do, the index and middle fingers of each hand come together. *Cf.* FASCINATE, INTERESTED 1, INTERESTING 1.

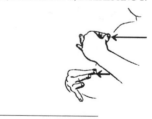

INTEREST 2, *n., v.* (The tongue is pulled out, causing the mouth to gape.) The curved open right hand is placed at the mouth, with index finger and thumb poised as if to grasp the tongue. The hand moves straight out, assuming the "A" position. *Cf.* INTERESTED 2, INTERESTING 2.

INTERESTED 1 (ĭn′ tər ĭs tĭd, -trĭs tĭd, -tə rĕs′ tĭd), *adj.* See INTEREST 1.

INTERESTED 2, *adj.* See INTEREST 2.

INTERESTING 1 (ĭn′ tər ĭs tĭng, -trĭs tĭng, -tə rĕs′ tĭng), *adj.* See INTEREST 1.

INTERESTING 2, *adj.* See INTEREST 2.

INTERFERE (ĭn′ tər fîr′), *v.,* -FERED, -FERING. (Obstruct, block.) The left hand, fingers together and palm flat, is held before the body, facing somewhat down. The little finger side of the right hand, held with palm flat, makes one or several up-down chopping motions against the left hand, between its thumb and index finger. *Cf.* ANNOY, ANNOYANCE, BOTHER, DISRUPT, DISTURB, HINDER, HINDRANCE, IMPEDE, INTERCEPT, INTERFERENCE, INTERFERE WITH, INTERRUPT, MEDDLE 1, OBSTACLE, OBSTRUCT, PREVENT, PREVENTION.

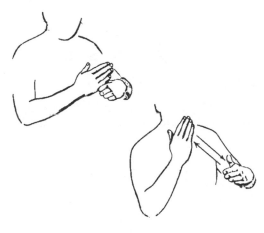

INTERFERENCE (ĭn′ tər fîr′ əns), *n.* See INTERFERE.

INTERFERE WITH *v. phrase.* See INTERFERE

INTERPRET (ĭn tûr′ prĭt), *v.,* -PRETED, -PRETING. (Changing one language to another.) The "F" hands are held palms facing and thumbs and index fingers in contact with each other. The hands swing around each other, reversing their relative positions.

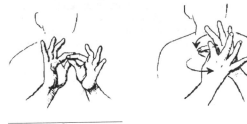

INTERROGATE 1 (ĭn tĕr′ ə gāt′), *v.,* -GATED, -GATING. (Firing questions.) The index fingers of both "D" hands repeatedly curve and straighten out as the hands are alternately flung forward and back, as if firing questions. *Cf.* ASK 3, EXAMINATION 2, INQUIRE 3, INTERROGATION 1, QUERY 1, QUESTION 3, QUIZ 3.

INTERROGATE 2, *(colloq.), v.* (Fire a question.) The right hand, held in a modified "S" position with palm facing out, assumes a position with the thumb resting on the fingernail of the index finger. The index finger is flicked out and forward, usually directed at the person being asked a question. *Cf.* ASK 2, INQUIRE 2, INTERROGATION 2, QUERY 2, QUESTION 2, QUIZ 2.

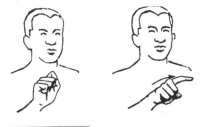

INTERROGATION 1 (ĭn tĕr′ ə gā′ shən), *n.* See INTERROGATE 1.

INTERROGATION 2, *(colloq.), n.* See INTERROGATE 2.

INTERRUPT (ĭn´ tə rŭpt´), v., -RUPTED, -RUPTING. (Obstruct, block.) The left hand, fingers together and palm flat, is held before the body, facing somewhat down. The little finger side of the right hand, held with palm flat, makes one or several up-down chopping motions against the left hand, between its thumb and index finger. *Cf.* ANNOY, ANNOYANCE, BOTHER, DISRUPT, DISTURB, HINDER, HINDRANCE, IMPEDE, INTERCEPT, INTERFERE, INTERFERENCE, INTERFERE WITH, MEDDLE 1, OBSTACLE, OBSTRUCT, PREVENT, PREVENTION.

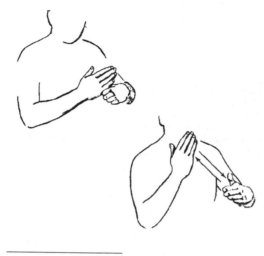

INTERSECT (ĭn´ tər sĕkt´), v., -SECTED, -SECTING. (Intersecting lines.) The extended index fingers move toward each other at right angles and cross. *Cf.* CROSS 4, CROSSING, INTERSECTION.

INTERSECTION (ĭn´ tər sĕk shən), n. See INTERSECT.

IN THE FIELD OF prep. phrase. (A straight, i.e., special, path.) The hands are held in the "B" position, one above the other, with left palm facing right and right palm facing left. The little finger edge of the right hand moves straight forward along the index finger edge of the left. *Cf.* FIELD 1, SPECIALIZE, SPECIALTY.

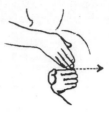

IN THE FUTURE adv. phrase. (Something ahead or in the future.) The upright, open right hand, palm facing left, moves straight out and slightly up from a position beside the right temple. *Cf.* FUTURE, LATER 2, LATER ON, SHALL, WILL 1, WOULD.

INTO (ĭn´ tōō), prep. (The natural sign.) The fingers of the right hand are thrust into the left. *Cf.* IN, INSIDE, WITHIN.

INTOXICATE (ĭn tŏk´ sə kāt´), v., -CATED, -CATING. (The act of drinking.) The thumbtip of the right "Y" hand is tilted toward the mouth, as if it were a drinking glass or bottle. The signer tilts his head back slightly, as if drinking. *Cf.* BEER, DRUNK, DRUNKARD, DRUNKENNESS, INTOXICATION, LIQUOR 2.

INTOXICATION (ĭn tŏk´ sə ka´ shən), n. See INTOXICATE.

IN TWO WEEKS *adv. phrase.* (In a week, two.) The upright, right "2" hand is placed palm-to-palm against the left "5" hand, whose palm faces right. The right hand moves along the left palm from base to fingertips and then curves to the left, around the left fingertips. (This is the same sign as for IN A WEEK except the "2" hand is used here.)

INVENT (ĭn vĕnt'), *v.,* -VENTED, -VENTING. (Something emerges from the head and is grasped.) The index finger edge of the right "5" hand moves up the forehead until it is above the head.

INVESTIGATE (ĭn vĕs' tə gāt), *v.,* -GATED, -GATING. (Directing the vision from place to place.) The right "C" hand, palm facing left, moves from right to left across the line of vision, in a series of counter-clockwise circles. The signer's gaze remains concentrated and his head turns slowly from right to left. *Cf.* CURIOUS 1, EXAMINE, LOOK FOR, PROBE, SEARCH, SEEK.

INVITE (ĭn vīt'), *v.,* -VITED, -VITING. (Opening or leading the way toward something.) The open right hand, held up before the body, sweeps down in an arc and over toward the left side of the chest, ending in the palm-up position. Reversing the movement gives the passive form of the verb, except that the hand does

not arc upward but rather simply moves outward in a small arc from the body. *Cf.* USHER, WELCOME.

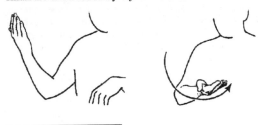

INVITED *passive voice of the verb* INVITE. The upturned right hand, touching the chest, moves straight forward and away from the body.

INVOLVE (ĭn vŏlv'), *v.,* -VOLVED, -VOLVING. (Immersed in something.) The downturned right "5" hand moves in a clockwise circle above the cupped left "C" hand. Then the right fingers are thrust into the cupped left "C" hand, which closes over the right fingers.

ION (ī' ən), *n.* (The letter "I"; circling.) The right "I" hand makes a clockwise circle around the left fist.

IRE (īr), *n.* (A violent welling-up of the emotions.) The curved fingers of the right hand are placed in the center of the chest, and fly up suddenly and violently. An expression of anger is worn. *Cf.* ANGER, ANGRY 2, ENRAGE, FURY, INDIGNANT, INDIGNATION, MAD, RAGE.

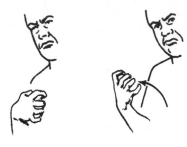

IRELAND (īr′ lənd), *n.* (A modified version of the sign for POTATO, *i.e.,* IRISH potato.) The downturned right "V" hand, poised over the downturned left "S" hand, executes a clockwise circle; then the "V" fingers stab the back of the left "S" hand. *Cf.* IRISH.

IRISH (ī′ rĭsh), *n., adj.* See IRELAND.

IRON (ī′ ərn), *v.,* IRONED, IRONING. (The act of pressing with an iron.) The right hand goes through the motion of swinging an iron back and forth over the upturned left palm. *Cf.* PRESS.

IRONY (ī′ rə nē), *n.* (Masking or in an underhanded way.) Both downturned hands are held in front of the face, the right above the left, and both hands displaying index and little fingers only. The right hand, with a flourish, descends, crossing the left arm. Meanwhile the left arm has moved to the right.

IRRITABLE (ĭr′ ə tə bəl), *adj.* (Wrinkling the brow.) The "5" hand is held palm toward the face. The fingers open and close partly, several times, while an angry expression is worn on the face. *Cf.* ANGRY 1, CROSS 1, CROSSNESS, FIERCE, ILL TEMPER.

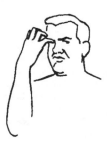

ISRAEL (iz′ rē əl) *n.* (The letter "I"; the beard worn by many Jewish males.) The right little finger, pointing straight up, moves down the left side of the mouth and then makes the same movement down the right side of the mouth.

IT (ĭt), *pron.* The right little finger is thrust into the upturned left palm.

ITALY 1 (ĭt′ ə lĭ), *n.* (The letter "I"; the cross, signifying the Vatican.) The right "I" finger traces a small cross on the forehead.

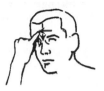

ITALY 2, *(loc.)*, *n.* (A characteristic Italian gesture.) The thumb and index finger of the right "F" hand are placed against the right cheek, while the hand trembles.

J

JAIL (jāl), *n., v.,* JAILED, JAILING. (The crossed bars.) The "4" hands, palms facing the body, are crossed at the fingers. *Cf.* PRISON.

JAM (jăm), *n.* (Spreading the letter "J.") The little finger of the right "J" hand moves twice across the upturned left palm, toward the base of the left hand. *Cf.* JELLY.

JAMAICA (jə mā′ kə) *n.* (The shape of the island.) The left hand is held downturned at chest level. The right hand, fingers together, runs along the right side of the left hand, around the fingertips, and along the little finger edge.

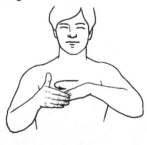

JAPAN 1 (jə păn′), *n.* (The letter "J"; the slanting eyes.) The right little finger is placed at the corner of the right eye, pulling it back slightly into a slant. Both little fingers may also be used, involving both eyes. Although this is an old and well-established sign, today it is considered derogatory and offensive in light of heightened sensitivity to differences in race and ethnicity. See JAPAN 2. *Cf.* JAPANESE.

JAPAN 2, *n.* (The shape of the islands on the map.) With hands facing the body, the index fingers and thumbs form a triangle. They come apart, moving in a slight upward arc, and close, so that the index fingers now touch their respective thumbs.

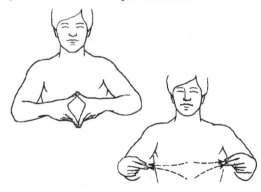

JAPANESE (jăp′ ə nēz′, -nēs′), *adj., n.* The sign for JAPAN 1 is made. This is followed by the sign for INDIVIDUAL: both open hands, palms facing each other, move down the sides of the body, tracing its outline to the hips. *Cf.* JAPAN 1.

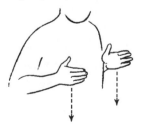

JEALOUS (jĕl′ əs), *adj.* (Biting the finger to suppress the feelings.) The tip of the index finger is bitten. The tip of the little finger is sometimes used. *Cf.* ENVIOUS, ENVY, JEALOUSY.

JEALOUSY (jĕl′ ə sĭ), *n.* See JEALOUS.

JELLY (jĕl′ ĭ), *n.* See JAM.

JERUSALEM (jĭ rōō′ sə ləm), *(eccles.), (rare), n.* (The holy city.) The sign for HOLY is made: the right "H" hand moves in a small clockwise circle several times. The right palm then wipes the upturned left palm. This is followed by the sign for CITY: the fingertips of both hands are joined, the hands and arms forming a pyramid. The fingertips separate and rejoin a number of times. Both arms may move a bit from left to right each time the fingertips separate and rejoin.

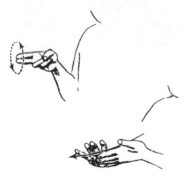

JESUS (jē′ zəs), *n.* (The marks of the crucifixion.) Both "5" hands are used. The left middle finger touches the right palm, and then the right middle finger touches the left palm.

JEW (jōō), *n.* (The beard of the old Jewish patriarchs.) The fingers and thumb of each hand are placed at the chin, and stroke an imaginary beard. *Cf.* HEBREW, JEWISH.

JEWISH (jōō′ ĭsh), *adj.* See JEW.

JOB (job), *n.* (Striking an anvil.) Both "S" hands are held palms down. The right hand strikes against the back of the left a number of times. *Cf.* LABOR, OCCUPATION, TASK, TOIL, TRAVAIL, VOCATION, WORK.

JOIN (join), *v.*, JOINED, JOINING. (Joining together.) Both hands, held in the modified "5" position, palms out, move toward each other. The thumbs and index fingers of both hands then connect. *Cf.* AFFILIATE, ANNEX, ATTACH, BELONG, CONNECT, ENLIST, ENROLL, PARTICIPATE, UNITE.

JOLLY (jŏl′ ĭ), *adj.* (A crinkling-up of the face.) Both hands, in the "5" position, palms facing back, are placed on either side of the face. The fingers wiggle back and forth, while a pleasant, happy expression is worn. *Cf.* AMIABLE, CHEERFUL, CORDIAL, FRIENDLY, PLEASANT.

JOURNEY 1 (jûr′ nĭ), *n., v.*, -NEYED, -NEYING. (Moving around from place to place.) Both "D" hands are held palms facing, the index fingers pointing to each other. In this position the hands describe a series of small counterclockwise circles as they move in random fashion from right to left. *Cf.* TRAVEL 1, TRIP 1.

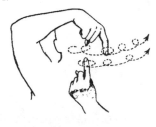

JOURNEY 2, *n., v.* A variation of JOURNEY 1, but using only the right hand. *Cf.* TRAVEL 2, TRIP 2.

JOURNEY 3, *n., v.* A variation of JOURNEY 1 and JOURNEY 2, but using the downturned curved "V" fingers. *Cf.* TRANSIENT, TRAVEL 3, TRIP 3.

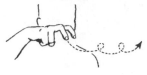

JOY (joi), *n.* (The heart is stirred; the spirits bubble up.) The open right hand, palm facing the body, strikes the heart repeatedly, moving up and off the heart after each strike. *Cf.* DELIGHT, GAIETY, GLAD, HAPPY, MERRY.

JUDGE 1 (jŭj), *n., v.*, JUDGED, JUDGING. (The scales move up and down.) The two "F" hands, palms facing each other, move alternately up and down. *Cf.* CONSIDER 3, COURT, EVALUATE 1, IF, JUDGMENT, JUSTICE.

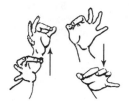

JUDGE 2, *n.* (Judge, individual.) The sign for JUDGE 1 is made. This is followed by the sign for INDIVIDUAL: both open hands, palms facing each other, move down the sides of the body, tracing its outline to the hips. *Cf.* REFEREE, UMPIRE.

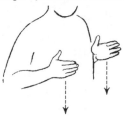

JUDGMENT (jŭj′ mənt), *n*. See JUDGE 1.

JUGGLE (jug′ əl), *v*. (The natural movement.) The signer mimes juggling several objects.

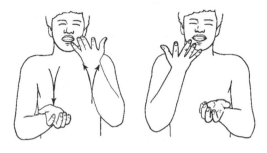

JUMP (jump), *v*., JUMPED, JUMPING. (The natural sign.) The bent right index and middle fingers rest on the upturned left palm. The right hand rises suddenly, as if the fingers have jumped up. The fingers usually remain bent, but they may also straighten out as the hand rises. The motion may also be repeated.

JUMP ROPE (jump rōp) *v. phrase*. (The natural movement.) The signer mimes jumping rope.

JUMP START *v. phrase*. (Placing the cables on the battery terminals.) Using the downturned "V" hands,

the signer mimes clamping them on the terminals of a car battery.

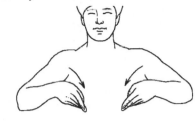

JUNIOR (jōōn′ yər), *n*. (College student.) The left index finger taps the palm of the right hand.

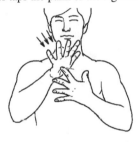

JUST A MOMENT AGO *adv. phrase*. (Time moved backward a bit.) The right "D" hand, palm facing the body, is placed in the palm of the left hand, which is facing right. The right hand swings back a bit toward the body, with the index finger describing an arc. *Cf.* FEW SECONDS AGO, A; WHILE AGO, A 2.

JUSTICE (jŭs′ tĭs), *n*. (The scales move up and down.) The two "F" hands, palms facing each other, move alternately up and down. *Cf.* CONSIDER 3, COURT, EVALUATE 1, IF, JUDGE 1, JUDGMENT.

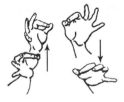

KANGAROO (kang gə rōō′), *n.* (The shape and movement.) The vertical right arm represents the kangaroo's body; the index and little fingers, the ears; and the thumb touching the middle and ring fingers, the snout. With the upturned cupped left hand resting on the right arm near the elbow, to represent the pouch, the signer executes a series of short forward jumping motions.

KARATE (kä rä′ tä), *n.* (The chopping motions.) Using both hands and arms, the signer mimes the chopping motions of karate.

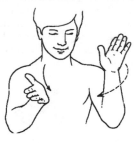

KEEP (kēp), *v.,* KEPT, KEEPING. (Slow, careful movement.) The "K" hands are crossed, the right above the left, little finger edges down. In this position the hands are moved up and down a short distance. *Cf.* CARE 2, CAREFUL 2, MAINTAIN 1, MIND 3, PRESERVE, RESERVE 2, TAKE CARE OF 2.

KEEP A SECRET *colloq. phrase.* (Squeezing the mouth shut.) The right "S" hand is placed thumb side against the lips. It swings to the palm-down position, held tightly against the lips.

KEEP QUIET 1, *v. phrase.* (The natural sign.) The index finger is placed forcefully against the closed lips. The signer frowns or looks stern. *Cf.* KEEP STILL 1.

KEEP QUIET 2, *v. phrase.* (The mouth is sealed; the sign for QUIET.) The downturned open hands are crossed at the lips with the left in front of the right. Both hands are drawn apart and down rather forcefully, while the signer frowns or looks stern. *Cf.* KEEP STILL 2.

KEEP STILL 1, *v. phrase.* See KEEP QUIET 1.

KEEP STILL 2, *v. phrase.* See KEEP QUIET 2.

KERCHIEF (kûr′ chif), *n.* (Tying the kerchief over the head.) The signer mimes placing a kerchief over the head and tying it under the chin.

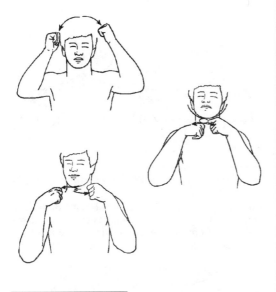

KEY (kē), *n.* (The turning of the key.) The right hand, holding an imaginary key, twists it in the open left palm, which is facing right. *Cf.* LOCK 1.

KEYBOARD 1 (kē′ bôrd), *n.* (The shape and function.) The signer types on an imaginary keyboard, and then the downturned index fingers trace a rectangle, indicating the shape of the keyboard.

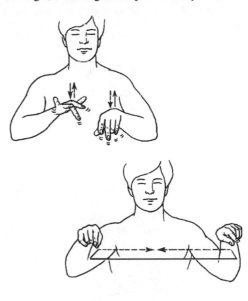

KEYBOARD 2, *n.* (A fingerspelled loan sign.) The letters "K-B" are fingerspelled.

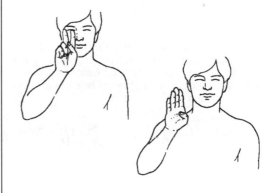

KICK (kĭk), *n., v.,* KICKED, KICKING. (The natural sign.) The right "B" hand, palm facing the body and fingers pointing down, swings in an arc to the left, striking the side of the left "S" hand, held palm facing up.

KID (kĭd), *(colloq.)*, *n.* (The running nose.) The index and little fingers of the right hand, held palm down, are extended, pointing to the left. The index finger is placed under the nose and the hand trembles somewhat.

KIKE (kīk), *n. sl.* (A disparaging and offensive sign for a person of Jewish descent.) The heel of the open right hand rests on the chin and the hand swivels forward and back, pivoted at the wrist.

KILL (kĭl), *v.,* KILLED, KILLING. (Thrusting a dagger and twisting it.) The outstretched right index finger is passed under the downturned left hand. As it moves under the left hand, the right wrist twists in a clockwise direction. *Cf.* MURDER, SLAY.

KILOGRAM (kil′ ə gram), *n.* (The letter "K"; weighing.) The right "K" hand is balanced back and forth as it rests on the index finger of the left "G" hand.

KILOMETER (kil′ ə mē tər), *n.* (The "K" and the "M.") Both hands are first held in the "K" position. They change to the "M" position, side by side, and move apart.

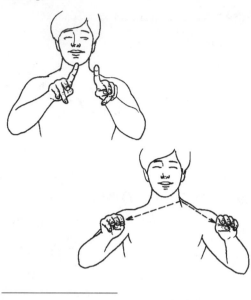

KIND 1 (kīnd), *adj.* (The heart rolls out.) Both right-angle hands roll over each other as they move down and away from their initial position at the heart. *Cf.* GENEROUS, MERCY 1.

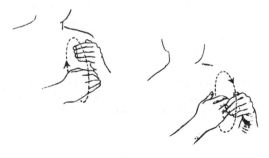

KIND 2, *n.* (The letter "K"; the wholeness or global characteristic.) The right "K" hand revolves once around the left "K" hand. This is used to describe a class or group.

KINDERGARTEN (kin′ dər gär tən), *n.* (The letter "K"; SCHOOL.) The right hand makes a "K" and shakes it back and forth. The right open hand then comes down on the left palm, clapping several times.

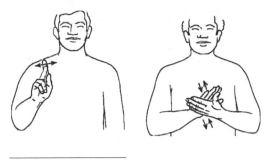

KING (kĭng), *n.* (The letter "K"; the royal sash.) The right "K" hand moves from the left shoulder to the right hip.

KISS (kĭs), *n., v.,* KISSED, KISSING. (Lips touch lips.) With fingers touching their thumbs, both hands are brought together. They tremble slightly, indicating the degree of intensity of the kiss.

KITCHEN 1 (kĭch′ ən), *n.* (Turning over a pancake.) The open right hand rests on the upturned left palm. The right hand flips over and comes to rest with its back on the left palm. This is the action of turning over a pancake. Then the sign for ROOM is made: the open hands, palms facing and fingers pointing out, are dropped an inch or two simultaneously. They then shift their relative positions so that both palms face the body, with one hand in front of the other. In this new position they again drop an inch or two simultaneously.

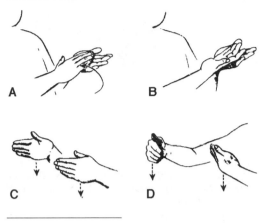

KITCHEN 2, *n.* (The letter "K.") The right "K" hand is placed palm down on the upturned left palm. It flips over to the palm-up position, and comes to rest again on the upturned left palm, as if flipping over a pancake.

KITE (kɪt), *n.* (Holding the kite string.) Looking up, the signer pulls on an imaginary string several times. Both hands may be used. *Cf.* FLY A KITE.

KNEE (nē), *n.* The signer points to the knee.

KNEEL (nēl), *v.*, KNELT or KNEELED, KNEELING. (Kneeling in church.) The knuckles of the right index and middle fingers are placed in the upturned left palm. The action may be repeated. *Cf.* PROTESTANT.

KNIFE 1 (nīf), *n.* (Shaving or paring.) The edge of the right "H" hand, resting on the edge of its left counterpart, moves forward several times, as if shaving layers of flesh.

KNIFE 2, *n.* (A variation of KNIFE 1.) The index fingers are used here, in the same manner as above.

KNIFE 3, *n.* (The cutting.) The right index finger cuts back and forth across the midpoint of its left counterpart.

KNIT (nĭt), *n.*, *v.*, KNITTED or KNIT, KNITTING. (The knitting.) The index fingers, pointing forward,

are rubbed back and forth against each other. *Cf.* SOCK(S), STOCKING(S).

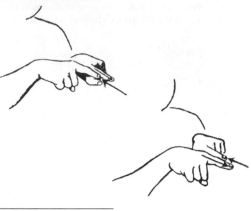

KNOCK (nŏk), *v.*, KNOCKED, KNOCKING. (The natural sign.) The right knuckles knock against the palm of the left hand, which is facing right.

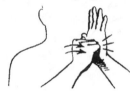

KNOT (nŏt), *n.*, *v.*, KNOTTED, KNOTTING. (The act of tying.) Both hands, in the "A" position, go through the natural hand-over-hand motions of tying and drawing out a knot. *Cf.* BIND, TIE 1.

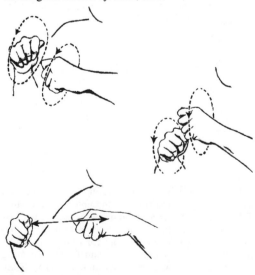

KNOW (nō), *v.,* KNEW, KNOWN, KNOWING. (Patting the head to indicate something of value inside.) The right fingers pat the forehead several times. *Cf.* FAMILIAR, KNOWING, KNOWLEDGE, RECOGNIZE.

KNOWING (nō′ ĭng), *adj.* See KNOW.

KNOWLEDGE (nŏl′ ĭj), See KNOW.

KNOW NOTHING 1, *phrase.* (Zero in the head.) The right "O" hand, palm facing left, is brought up sharply to the forehead.

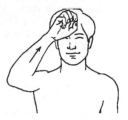

KNOW NOTHING 2, *phrase.* (A variation of above.) The right "O" hand swings back and forth at the forehead.

KNOW WELL *phrase.* (Tapping the mind emphatically.) The fingertips strike the forehead repeatedly, as the signer assumes an expression of intensity.

L

LABOR (lā′ bər), *n., v.,* -BORED, -BORING. (Striking an anvil.) Both "S" hands are held palms down. The right hand strikes against the back of the left a number of times. *Cf.* JOB, OCCUPATION, TASK, TOIL, TRAVAIL, VOCATION, WORK.

LADY (lā′ dǐ), *n.* (A female with a ruffled bodice; *i.e.,* an elegantly dressed woman, a lady.) The FEMALE root sign is made: the thumb of the right "A" hand moves down along the right jaw, from ear almost to chin. The thumbtip of the right "5" hand, palm facing left, is then placed on the chest, with the other fingers pointing up. Pivoted at the thumb, the hand swings down a bit, so that the other fingers are now pointing out somewhat.

LAMP (lămp), *n.* (The rays come out.) The downturned "8" hand, positioned at the chin, flicks open a number of times. *Cf.* LIGHT 3.

LAND 1 (lănd), *n.* (An expanse of ground.) The sign for SOIL 1 is made: both hands, held upright before the body, finger imaginary pinches of soil. The downturned open right "5" hand then sweeps in an arc from right to left.

LAND 2, *n.* (An established area.) The right "N" hand, palm down, executes a clockwise circle above the downturned prone left hand. The tips of the "N" fingers then move straight down and come to rest on the back of the left hand. *Cf.* COUNTRY 2, NATION, REPUBLIC.

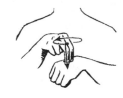

LANGUAGE 1 (lăng′ gwĭj), *n.* (A series of letters spelled out on the printed page.) The downturned "F" hands are positioned with thumbs and index fingertips touching. The hands move straight apart to either side in a wavy motion. *Cf.* SENTENCE.

LANGUAGE 2, *n*. (The letter "L.") The sign for LANGUAGE 1 is made, but with the "L" hands.

LANGUAGE OF SIGNS *n*. (LANGUAGE 1 and hand/arm movements.) The "D" hands, palms facing and index fingers pointing back toward the face, describe a series of continuous counterclockwise circles toward and away from the face, imitating the foot motions in bicycling. This is followed by the sign for LANGUAGE 1. *Cf*. SIGN LANGUAGE, SIGNS.

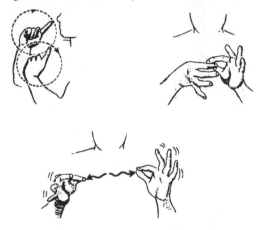

LARGE (lärj), *adj*. (A delineation of something big, modified by the letter "L," which stands for LARGE.) Both "L" hands, palms facing out, are placed before the face, and separate rather widely. *Cf*. BIG 1, GREAT 1.

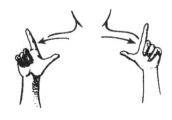

LARIAT (lar′ ē ət), *n*. (Twirling a lariat.) The signer twirls an imaginary lariat and pulls back. For added

effect, the body may bounce up and down slightly, as if on horseback. *Cf*. COWBOY 2, LASSO.

LASSO (lăs′ ȯ), *n*. See LARIAT.

LAST 1 (lăst), *adj*. (The little, *i.e.*, LAST, fingers are indicated.) With the hands in the "I" position, the tip of the right little finger strikes the tip of its left counterpart. The right index finger may be used instead of the right little finger. *Cf*. END 1, EVENTUALLY, FINAL 1, FINALLY 1, LASTLY, ULTIMATE, ULTIMATELY.

LAST 2, *adj*. (A single little, *i.e.*, LAST, finger is indicated.) The tip of the index finger of the right "D" hand strikes the tip of the little finger of the left "I" hand. *Cf*. END 2, FINAL 2, FINALLY 2, LASTLY.

LAST 3, *v*. (Steady, uninterrupted movement.) The "A" hands are held with palms out, thumbs extended and touching, the right behind the left. In this position the hands move forward in a straight, steady line. *Cf*. CONTINUE, ENDURE 2, EVER 1, LASTING, PERMANENT, PERPETUAL, PERSEVERE 3, PERSIST 2, REMAIN, STAY 1, STAY STILL.

LASTING (lăs′ tĭng), *adj.* See LAST 3.

LASTLY (lăst′ lĭ), *adv.* See LAST 1, 2.

LATE (lāt), *adj.* (Hanging back.) The "5" hand and forearm, hanging loosely and straight down from the elbow, move back and forth under the armpit. *Cf.* NOT DONE, NOT YET, TARDY.

LATER 1 (lā′ tər), *adj.* (A moving on of the minute hand of the clock.) The right "L" hand, its thumb thrust into the palm of the left and acting as a pivot, moves forward a short distance. *Cf.* AFTER A WHILE, AFTERWARD, SUBSEQUENT, SUBSEQUENTLY.

LATER 2, *adj., adv.* (Something ahead or in the future.) The upright, open right hand, palm facing left, moves straight out and slightly up from a position beside the right temple. *Cf.* FUTURE, IN THE FUTURE, LATER ON, SHALL, WILL 1, WOULD.

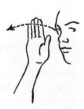

LATER ON *adv. phrase.* See LATER 2.

LATIN (lăt′ ən), *(rare), n., adj.* (The Roman nose with the "L" initial.) The thumbtip of the right "L" hand, palm facing left, moves down in an arc from mid-forehead to the tip of the nose.

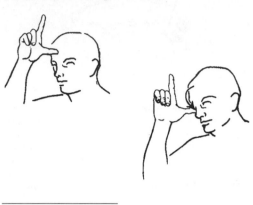

LAUGH (lăf), *n., v.,* LAUGHED, LAUGHING. (The natural sign.) The fingers of both "D" hands move repeatedly up along the jawline, or up from the corners of the mouth. The signer meanwhile laughs. *Cf.* LAUGHTER 1.

LAUGHTER 1 (lăf′ tər), *n.* See LAUGH.

LAUGHTER 2, *(colloq.), n.* (The shaking of the stomach.) The cupped hands, held at stomach level, palms facing the body, move alternately up and down, describing short arcs. The signer meanwhile laughs.

LAUGHTER 3, *(colloq.),* *n.* (Literally, rolling in the aisles; the legs are doubled up and the body rolls on the floor.) With index and middle fingers crooked, and its little finger edge or back resting on the upturned left palm, the right hand moves in a continuous counterclockwise circle in the left palm. The signer meanwhile laughs.

LAW (lô), *n.* (A series of LAWS as they appear on the printed page.) The upright right "L" hand, resting palm against palm on the upright left "5" hand, moves down in an arc a short distance, coming to rest on the base of the left palm. *Cf.* ATTORNEY, LAWYER, LEGAL.

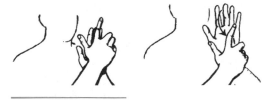

LAWYER (lô′ yər), *n.* The sign for LAW is made. The sign for INDIVIDUAL is then added: both hands, fingers together, are placed at either side of the chest and are moved down to waist level. *Cf.* ATTORNEY, LAW, LEGAL.

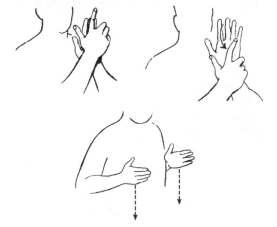

LAZINESS (lā′ zĭ nĭs), *n.* (The initial "L" rests against the body; the concept of inactivity.) The right "L" hand is placed against the left shoulder once or a number of times. The palm faces the body. *Cf.* LAZY.

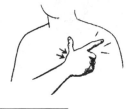

LAZY (lā′ zĭ), *adj.* See LAZINESS.

LEAD (lēd), *v.,* LED, LEADING, *n.* (One hand leads the other.) The right hand grasps the tips of the left fingers and pulls the left hand forward. *Cf.* CONDUCT 2, GUIDE.

LEAF (lēf), *n.* The left "5" hand, palm out, is the tree. The right thumb and index finger trace the shape of a leaf from one of the outstretched left fingers.

LEAN (lēn), *adj.* (The sunken cheeks.) The fingertips of both hands run down either side of the face. The cheeks meanwhile are sucked in a bit.

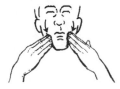

LEAP (lēp), *v.* (The movement.) The downturned right index and middle fingers stand on the left hand. They "jump" forward and out.

LEARN (lûrn), *v.,* LEARNED, LEARNING. (Taking knowledge from a book and placing it in the head.) The downturned fingers of the right hand are placed on the upturned left palm. They close, and then the hand rises and the right fingertips are placed on the forehead.

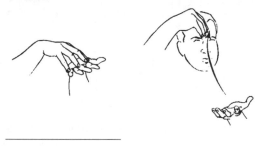

LEAST (lēst), *adj.* (A small amount; the superlative degree.) The slightly cupped hands, palms facing, are brought together until they almost touch, and then the right thumb is brought up sharply to a position above the head.

LEATHER (leŧh′ ər), *n., adj.* (The letter "L"; worn on or covering the body.) The thumb of the right "L" hand is placed on the chest and moves down an inch or two several times.

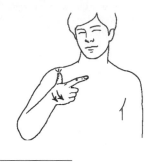

LEAVE 1 (lēv), *v.,* LEFT, LEAVING. (Pulling away.) The downturned open hands are held in a line, with fingers pointing to the left, the right hand behind the left. Both hands move in unison toward the right. As they do so, they assume the "A" position. *Cf.* DEPART, WITHDRAW 1.

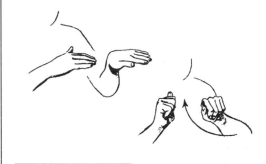

LEAVE 2, *v.* (To throw something aside.) Both "S" hands are held with palms facing at chest level and then thrown down and to the left, opening into the "5" position. *Cf.* ABANDON, CAST OFF, DISCARD, FORSAKE 2, LET ALONE, NEGLECT.

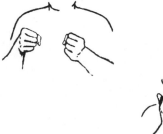

LEAVE COLLEGE *phrase.* (A form of escaping.) The right index finger is positioned on the tip of any of the five fingers of the upturned left hand, from the little finger to the thumb. The right index moves suddenly forward and out. From the thumb, the leaving occurs at the senior year; from the ring finger, at the freshman level. The little finger is reserved for the so-called "prep" year in some schools designed to admit a heterogeneous student body needing extensive pre-freshman orientation.

LECTURE (lek′ chər), *n., v.,* -TURED, -TURING. (A gesture of an orator.) The right open hand, palm facing left, is held above and to the right of the head. It pivots on the wrist, forward and backward, several times. *Cf.* ORATE, SPEECH 2, TALK 2, TESTIMONY 1.

LEFT (lĕft), *adj.* (The remainder is left behind.) The "5" hands, palms facing each other and fingers pointing forward, are dropped simultaneously a few inches, as if dropping something on the table. *Cf.* REMAINDER.

LEGAL (lē′ gəl), *adj.* (A series of LAWS as they appear on the printed page.) The upright right "L" hand, resting palm against palm on the upright left "5" hand, moves down in an arc, a short distance, coming to rest on the base of the left palm. *Cf.* ATTORNEY, LAW, LAWYER.

LEGISLATURE (lĕj′ ĭs lā′ chər), *n.* (The letter "L"; possibly the Roman toga.) The thumb of the right "L" hand moves from the left shoulder to the right shoulder.

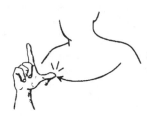

LEISURE (lē′ zhər, lĕzh′ ər), *n.* (A position of idleness.) With thumbs tucked in the armpits, the remaining fingers of both hands wiggle. *Cf.* HOLIDAY, IDLE, RETIRE, VACATION.

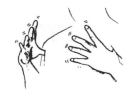

LEMON (lĕm′ ən), *n.* (Yellow and sour.) The sign for YELLOW, is made: the right "Y" hand shakes back and forth, pivoted at the wrist. The sign for SOUR is then made: the right index finger is brought sharply up against the lips, while the mouth is puckered up as if tasting something sour.

LEMONADE (lĕm ən ād′), *n.* (The "L," for LEMON; something sour is brought to the lips.) The thumbtip of the right "L" hand is brought sharply up to the lips, and then the signer mimes drinking from a glass.

LEND 1 (lĕnd), *v.*, LENT, LENDING. (Something kept, *i.e.*, in one's custody, is moved forward to other, temporary, ownership.) The crossed "K" hands, for KEEP, *q.v.*, are moved forward simultaneously, in a short arc. *Cf.* LOAN 1.

LEND 2, *v.* The side of the right index finger is brought up against the right side of the nose. *Cf.* LOAN 2.

LENGTH (lengkth), *n.* (The distance is traced.) The right index finger traces a long line along the upturned left arm from wrist almost to shoulder. *Cf.* LONG.

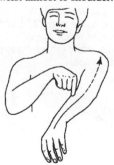

LEOTARDS (lē′ ə tärdz), *n.* (Drawing up the tight garment.) The signer mimes struggling into a very tight garment. *Cf.* TIGHTS.

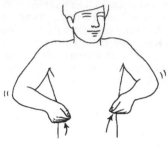

LESBIAN (lez′ bē ən), *n., adj.* (The letter "L.") The right "L" hand is held palm facing the body, index finger pointing left. In this position the hand is placed against the chin.

LESS (lĕs), *adj.* (The diminishing size or amount.) With palms facing, the right hand is held above the left. The right hand moves slowly down toward the left, but does not touch it. *Cf.* DECREASE, REDUCE.

LESSON (lĕs′ ən), *n.* (A section of a page.) The upturned open left hand represents the page. The little finger edge of the right-angle hand is placed on the left palm near the fingertips. It moves up and over, in an arc, to the base of the left palm.

LESS THAN *adj. phrase.* (Something below.) Both downturned open hands are positioned with right below left. The right hand moves down a few inches, and the left remains stationary.

LET (lĕt), *v.*, LET, LETTING, *n.* (A permissive upswinging of the hands, as if giving in.) Both hands, palms facing and fingers pointing away from the body, are held at chest level, almost a foot apart. With an upward movement, using their wrists as pivots, the hands sweep up until the fingers point almost straight up. *Cf.* ALLOW, GRANT 1, LET'S, LET US, MAY 3, PERMISSION 1, PERMIT 1, TOLERATE 1.

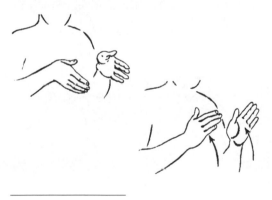

LET ALONE *v. phrase.* (To throw something aside.) Both "S" hands are held with palms facing at chest level and then thrown down and to the left, opening into the "5" position. *Cf.* ABANDON, CAST OFF, DISCARD, FORSAKE 2, LEAVE 2, NEGLECT.

LET KNOW *v. phrase.* (Taking knowledge from the mind and giving it out to all.) The fingertips are positioned on either side of the forehead. Both hands then swing down and out, opening into the upturned "5" position. *Cf.* INFORM, INFORMATION, NOTIFY.

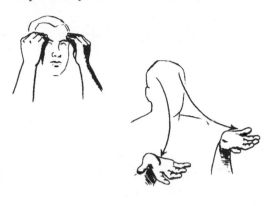

LET'S (lĕts); **LET US** *v. phrase.* See LET.

LETTER (lĕt' ər), *n.* (The stamp is affixed.) The right thumb is placed on the tongue, and is then pressed into the open left palm. *Cf.* MAIL 1.

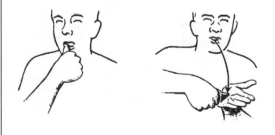

LETTUCE (lĕt' ĭs), *n.* (A "head" of lettuce; the upturned fingers represent the leaves.) The base of the right "5" hand strikes the right side of the head a number of times.

LEVEL (lĕv′ əl), *adj., n., v.,* -ELED, -ELING. (Sameness is stressed.) The downturned "B" hands, held at chest height, are brought together repeatedly, so that the index finger edges or fingertips come into contact. *Cf.* EQUAL, EQUIVALENT, EVEN, FAIR.

LIAR (lī′ ər), *n.* (Words diverted instead of coming straight, or truthfully, out.) The index finger of the right "D" hand, pointing to the left, moves along the lips from the right to left. *Cf.* FALSE, FALSEHOOD, LIE 1.

LIBERATION (lĭb′ ər ā′ shən), *n.* (Breaking the bonds.) The "S" hands, crossed in front of the body, swing apart and face out. *Cf.* EMANCIPATE, FREE 1, FREEDOM, INDEPENDENCE, INDEPENDENT 1, REDEEM 1, RELIEF, RESCUE, SAFE, SALVATION, SAVE 1.

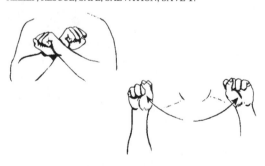

LIBRARY (lī′ brĕr′ ĭ), *n.* (The initial "L.") The right "L" hand, palm out, describes a small clockwise circle.

LICENSE 1 (lī′ səns), *n., v.,* -CENSED, -CENSING. (Affixing a seal.) The little finger edge of the right "S" hand strikes the palm of the upturned left "5" hand.

LICENSE 2, *(loc.), n.* (The "L" hands outline the dimensions of the license form.) The "L" hands, palms out, touch at the thumbtips several times.

LICK (lĭk), *v., n.* (The action of the tongue.) The right index and middle fingers, held together, sweep up and down twice on the outstretched left palm.

LID (lĭd), *n.* (Covering something.) The cupped left hand represents a can or a jar. The downturned right hand, fingers somewhat curved, comes down on the left, lifting off an imaginary lid.

LIE 1 (līe), *n., v.,* LIED, LYING. (Words diverted instead of coming straight, or truthfully, out.) The index finger of the right "D" hand, pointing to the left, moves along the lips from right to left. *Cf.* FALSE, FALSE-HOOD, LIAR.

LIE 2, *n., v.* (Same rationale as in LIE 1 but more emphatic, as indicated by several fingers.) The index finger edge of the downturned "B" hand moves along the lips (or under the chin) from right to left.

LIE DOWN *v.* LAY, LAIN, LYING. (The prone position of the legs, in lying down.) The index and middle fingers of the right "V" hand, palm facing up, are placed in the upturned left palm and slide down an inch or two toward the fingertips. *Cf.* RECLINE.

LIFE 1 (līf), *n.* (The fountain [of LIFE, *q.v.*] wells up from within the body.) The upturned thumbs of the "A" hands move in unison up the chest. *Cf.* ADDRESS, ALIVE, LIVE 1, LIVING, RESIDE.

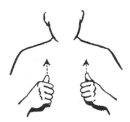

LIFE 2, *n.* (Same rationale as for LIFE 1 with the initials "L.") The upturned thumbs of the "L" hands move in unison up the chest. *Cf.* LIVE 2.

LIFT (līft), *v.* (Raising something up.) Both upturned open hands move up simultaneously.

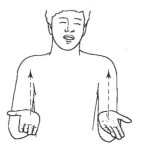

LIGHT 1 (līt), *n.* (The candle flame and the rays of light.) The index finger of the "D" hand is placed on the pursed lips, as if blowing out a candle. The right hand is then raised above the head, with the fingertips and thumbtip touching, and palm facing out. The hand then moves down and a bit forward, opening into the "5" position, palm down. (The "candle" part of this sign is frequently omitted.)

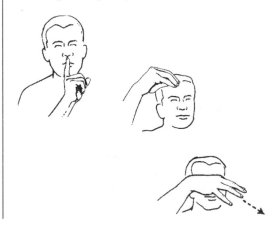

LIGHT 2, *adj.* (Easily lifted.) The open hands, palms up, move up and down together in front of the body, as if lifting something very light.

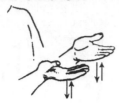

LIGHT 3, *n.* (The rays come out.) The downturned "8" hand, positioned near the temple, flicks open a number of times.

LIGHT 4, *n.* (The rays come out.) *Cf.* LAMP.

LIKE 1 (līk), *v.,* LIKED, LIKING. (Drawing out the feelings.) The thumb and index finger of the right open hand, held an inch or two apart, are placed at midchest. As the hand moves straight out from the chest the two fingers come together.

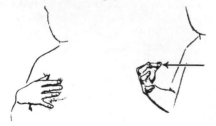

LIKE 2, *adj., n.* (Matching fingers are brought together.) The outstretched index fingers are brought together, either once or several times. *Cf.* ALIKE, IDENTICAL, SAME 1, SIMILAR, SUCH.

LIKE 3, *v.* (A pleasurable feeling on the heart.) The open right hand is circled on the chest, over the heart. *Cf.* APPRECIATE, ENJOY, ENJOYMENT, GRATIFY 1, PLEASE, PLEASURE, WILLING 2.

LIMIT (lĭm′ ĭt), *n., v.,* LIMITED, LIMITING. (The upper and lower limits are defined.) The right-angle hands, palms facing, are held before the body, the right above the left. They swing out 45 degrees simultaneously, pivoted from their wrists. *Cf.* CAPACITY, RESTRICT.

LIMOUSINE (lĭm′ ə zēn′), *n.* (The elongated chassis.) The "C" hands, left palm facing right and right palm facing left, are joined as if holding a telescope, with the right hand in front of the left. The right hand moves straight forward about 6 inches. The left hand remains in position. Sometimes both hands close into the "S" position as the right hand moves forward.

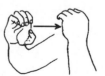

LINCOLN (lĭng′ kən), *n.* (The initial "L" at the head, probably to denote the head of the country—the president.) The right "L" hand, palm facing out, is placed with the thumbtip resting on the right temple.

LION (lī′ ən), *n.* (The mane.) The downturned "C" hand (or "5" hand with fingers somewhat curved) moves straight back over the head in a wavy motion.

LIPREADING (lĭp′ rēd′ ĭng) *n.* (Reading the lips—the lines of vision, represented by the two fingers, scan the lips.) The right "V" hand, palm facing the body, is placed in front of the face, with slightly curved index and middle fingers directly in front of the lips. The right hand moves in a small counter-clockwise circle around the lips. *Cf.* ORAL, READ LIPS, SPEECHREADING.

LIQUOR 1 (lĭk′ ər), *n.* (The size of the jigger is indicated.) The right hand, with index and little fingers extended and the remaining fingers held against the palm by the thumb, strikes the back of the downturned "S" hand several times. *Cf.* ALCOHOL, WHISKEY.

LIQUOR 2, *n.* (The act of drinking.) The thumbtip of the right "Y" hand is tilted toward the mouth, as if it were a drinking glass or bottle. The signer tilts his head back slightly, as if drinking. *Cf.* BEER, DRUNK, DRUNKARD, DRUNKENNESS, INTOXICATE, INTOXICATION.

LISTEN (lĭs′ ən), *v.,* -TENDED, -TENING. (Cupping the hand at the ear.) The right hand is placed, usually slightly cupped, behind the right ear. *Cf.* HEAR.

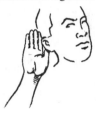

LITTLE 1 (lĭt′ əl), *adj.* (Indicating a small size or amount.) The open hands are held facing each other, one facing down and the other facing up. In this position the top hand moves down toward the bottom hand but does not quite touch it. The space between the hands shows the small size or amount.

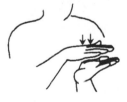

LITTLE 2, *adj., adv., n.* (A small or tiny movement.) The right thumbtip is flicked off the index finger several times, as if shooting marbles, although the movement is not so pronounced.

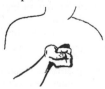

LIVE 1 (lĭv), *v.*, LIVED, LIVING. (The fountain [of LIFE, *q.v.*] wells up from within the body.) The upturned thumbs of the "A" hands move in unison up the chest. *Cf.* ADDRESS, ALIVE, LIFE 1, LIVING, RESIDE.

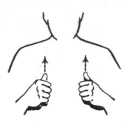

LIVE 2, *v.* See LIFE 2.

LIVER (lĭv′ ər), *n.* (The liver is indicated.) The middle finger of the right "5" hand, palm facing the body, is brought against the body, in the area of the liver, a number of times.

LIVING (lĭv′ ĭng), *adj.* See LIVE 1.

LIVING ROOM *n.* (Fine room.) The downturned "5" hand is placed with the thumb touching the chest. It moves repeatedly up and out an inch or two, returning each time to its initial position. This is followed by the sign for ROOM: the open hands, palms facing and fingers pointing out, are dropped an inch or two simultaneously. They then shift their relative positions so that both palms face the body, with one hand, in front of the other. In this new position they

again drop an inch or two simultaneously. The "R" hands may be substituted for the open hands.

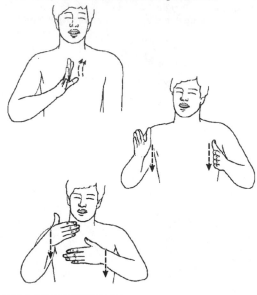

LOAN 1 (lōn), *n.* (Something kept, *i.e.*, in one's custody, is moved forward to other, temporary, ownership.) The crossed "K" hands, for KEEP, *q.v.*, are moved forward simultaneously, in a short arc. *Cf.* LEND 1.

LOAN 2, *(loc.), (colloq.), n., v.*, LOANED, LOANING. The side of the right index finger is brought up against the right side of the nose. *Cf.* LEND 2.

LOATHE (lōth), *v.*, LOATHED, LOATHING. (To push away and recoil from; avoid.) The two open hands, palms facing left, are pushed deliberately to the left, as if pushing something away. An expression of disdain or disgust is worn. *Cf.* ABHOR, AVOID 2, DESPISE, DETEST, HATE.

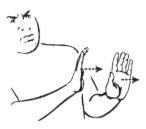

LOCATION (lō kā′ shən), *n.* (The letter "P"; a circle or square is indicated, to show the locale or place.) The "P" hands are held side by side before the body, with middle fingertips touching. From this position, the hands separate and outline a circle (or a square), before coming together again closer to the body. *Cf.* PLACE 1, POSITION.

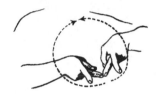

LOCK 1 (lŏk), *n., v.,* LOCKED, LOCKING. (The turning of the key.) The right hand, holding an imaginary key, twists it in the open left palm, which is facing right. *Cf.* KEY.

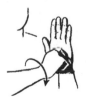

LOCK 2, *(loc.), v.* (Bind down.) The right "S" hand, palm down, makes a clockwise circle and comes down on the back of the left "S" hand, also held palm down.

LOCKED *(loc.), adj.* (Bound down to custom or habit.) Both "S" hands, palms down, are crossed and brought down in unison before the chest. *Cf.* ACCUSTOM, BOUND, CUSTOM, HABIT, PRACTICE 3.

LOCK HORNS *sl. phrase.* (Clashing or banging together.) Both downturned "Y" hands, representing horns, come together forcefully.

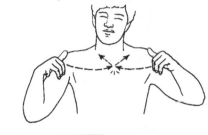

LONE (lōn), *adj.* (One, wandering around in a circle.) The index finger, pointing straight up, palm facing the body (the number *one*), is rotated before the face in a counterclockwise direction. *Cf.* ALONE, ONLY, SOLE.

LONELY 1 (lōn′ lĭ), *adj.* ("Oneness"; quietness.) The index finger of the right "1" hand moves straight down across the lips once or twice. *Cf.* LONESOME.

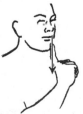

LONELY 2, *(colloq.), adj.* ("I" signs; *i.e.,* alone with oneself.) Both "I" hands are held facing the body, the little fingers upright and held an inch or two apart. The little fingers come together and separate repeatedly.

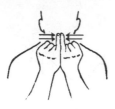

LONESOME (lŏn′ səm), *adj.* See LONELY 1.

LONG 1 (lông, lŏng), *adj. n., adv.* (The distance is traced.) The right index finger traces a long line along the upturned left arm from wrist almost to shoulder.

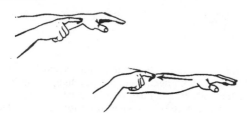

LONG 2, *v.,* LONGED, LONGING. (Grasping something and pulling it in.) The upturned "5" hands, held side by side before the chest, close slightly into a grasping position as they move in toward the body. *Cf.* DESIRE 1, NEED 2, WANT, WILL 2, WISH 1.

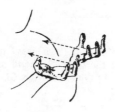

LOOK 1 (lo͝ok), *v.,* LOOKED, LOOKING. (The eyesight is directed forward.) The right "V" hand, palm facing the body, is placed so that the fingertips are just under the eyes. The hand swings around and out, so

that the fingertips are now pointing forward. *Cf.* PERCEIVE 1, PERCEPTION, WATCH 2.

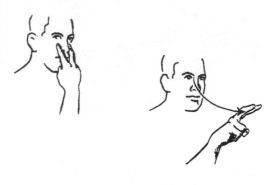

LOOK 2, *v.* (Something presented before the eyes.) The open right hand, palm flat and facing out, with fingers together and pointing up, is positioned at shoulder level. Pivoting from the wrist, the hand is swung around so that the palm now faces the eyes. Sometimes the eyes glance at the newly presented palm. *Cf.* APPARENT, APPARENTLY, APPEAR 1, SEEM.

LOOK AT *v. phrase.* (The vision is directed forward.) The tips of the right "V" fingers point to the eyes. The right hand is then swung around and forward a bit. *Cf.* GAZE, OBSERVE, WITNESS.

LOOK DOWN *v. phrase.* (The gaze is cast down-ward.) Both "V" hands, side by side and palms facing out, are swept downward so that the fingertips now point down. A haughty expression, or one of mild contempt, is sometimes assumed. *Cf.* CONTEMPT, SCORN.

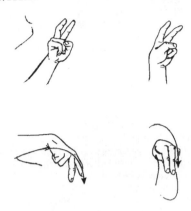

LOOK FOR *v. phrase.* (Directing the vision from place to place; the French *chercher.*) The right "C" hand, palm facing left, moves from right to left across the line of vision, in a series of counterclockwise circles. The signer's gaze remains concentrated and his head turns slowly from right to left. *Cf.* CURIOUS 1, EXAMINE, INVESTIGATE, PROBE, SEARCH, SEEK.

LOOK UP *v.* (Thumbing through pages.) The downturned right thumb "digs" into the upturned left palm a number of times. *Cf.* PAGE.

LORD 1 (lôrd), *n.* (The ribbon worn across the chest by nobles; the initial "L.") The right "L" hand, palm facing out, moves down across the chest from left shoulder to right hip.

LORD 2, *n.* (A motion indicating the One above.) The right open hand, palm facing left, swings up above the head, and is then moved down in a slight curve, an inch or two. Meanwhile, the signer looks up while making the sign. *Cf.* GOD.

LOSE (lōōz), *v.,* LOST, LOSING. (Dropping something.) Both hands, with fingers touching their respective thumbs, are held palms up and with the backs of the fingers almost touching or in contact with one another. The hands drop into an open position, with fingers pointing down. *Cf.* LOST.

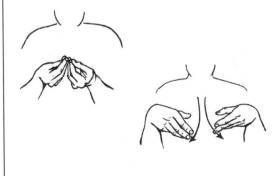

LOSE COMPETITION *v. phrase.* (Being pinned down to the mat, as in a wrestling match.) The downturned right "3" or "V" hand is slapped into the upturned left palm.

LOST (lôst, lŏst), *adj.* See LOSE.

LOT (lŏt), *n.* (A large amount.) The "5" hands face each other, fingers curved and touching. They move apart rather quickly. *Cf.* EXPAND, GREAT 2, INFINITE, MUCH.

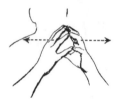

LOUD (loud), *adj.* (Something heard which shakes the surrounding area.) The right index finger touches the ear. The "5" hands, palms down, then move sharply in front of the body, in quick alternate motions, first away from and then back to the body. *Cf.* LOUDLY, LOUD NOISE.

LOUDLY (loud' lǐ), *adv.* See LOUD.

LOUD NOISE *n. phrase.* See LOUD.

LOUSY (lou' zǐ), *(sl.)*, *adj.* (A modification of the sign for spitting or thumbing the nose.) The right "3" hand is held with thumbtip against the nose. Then it is thrown sharply forward, and an expression of contempt is assumed. *Cf.* ROTTEN.

LOVE (lŭv), *n.*, *v.*, LOVED, LOVING. (Clasping the heart.) The "5" hands are held one atop the other over the heart. Sometimes the "S" hands are used, in which case they are crossed at the wrists. *Cf.* BELOVED, DEVOTION, REVERE.

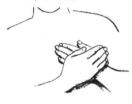

LOVER (lŭv' ər), *(colloq.)*, *n.* (Heads nodding toward each other.) The "A" hands are placed together before the body with thumbs up. The thumbs wiggle up and down. *Cf.* BEAU, MAKE LOVE 1, SWEETHEART 1.

LOW (lō), *adj.*, *n.* (Motion downward.) The right-angle hands are held up before the head, fingertips pointing toward each other. From this position, the hands move down in an arc. *Cf.* BASE, DEMOTE, LOWER.

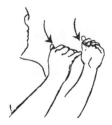

LOWER (lō′ ər), v., -ERED, -ERING. See LOW.

LOYAL (loi′ əl), adj. (The arm is raised.) The right index finger is placed at the lips. The right arm is then raised, palm out and elbow resting on the back of the left hand. Cf. GUARANTEE, OATH, PLEDGE, PROMISE 1, SWEAR 1, SWORN, TAKE OATH, VOW.

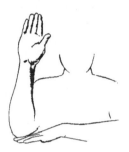

LUGGAGE (lŭg′ ĭj), n. (The natural sign.) The down-turned right "S" hand grasps an imaginary piece of luggage and shakes it up and down slightly, as if testing its weight. Cf. BAGGAGE, SUITCASE, VALISE.

LYRIC (lir′ ik), n. (The letter "L"; rhythmic movement to represent music.) The left hand is held in a downturned horizontal position. The right hand, in the "L" position, moves rhythmically back and forth over the left. Alternatively, the back-and-forth movement may be in the shape of a continuous figure 8.

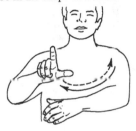

MACHINE (mə shĕn´), *n.* (The meshing gears.) With the knuckles of both hands interlocked, the hands pivot up and down, imitating the meshing of gear teeth. *Cf.* ENGINE, FACTORY, MACHINERY, MECHANIC 1, MECHANISM, MOTOR 1.

MACHINERY (mə shē´ nə rĭ), *n.* (The meshing gears.) With the knuckles of both hands interlocked, the hands pivot up and down, imitating the meshing of gear teeth. *Cf.* ENGINE, FACTORY, MACHINE, MECHANIC 1, MECHANISM, MOTOR 1.

MAD (măd), *adj.* (A violent welling-up of the emotions.) The curved fingers of the right hand are placed in the center of the chest, and fly up suddenly and violently. An expression of anger is worn. *Cf.* ANGER, ANGRY 2, ENRAGE, FURY, INDIGNANT, INDIGNATION, IRE, RAGE.

MAGAZINE (măg´ ə zēn´, măg´ ə zēn´), *n.* (A book with a narrow spine.) The left hand, fingers together, is held upright, palm facing right. The right hand wraps around the lower edge of the left and travels up to the little finger. This denotes a narrow object. The sign for BOOK is then made: the hands are placed together, palm to palm, and then opened, as if opening a book. Sometimes this latter sign is omitted. *Cf.* BOOKLET, MANUAL, PAMPHLET.

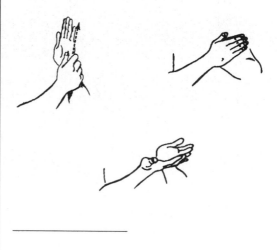

MAID (mād), *n.* (Passing the dishes, one by one.) The upturned "5" hands move alternately toward and away from the chest. *Cf.* SERVANT, SERVE 2, SERVICE, WAITER, WAITRESS.

318

MAIL 1 (māl), *n.* (The stamp is affixed.) The right thumb is placed on the tongue, and is then pressed into the open left palm. *Cf.* LETTER.

MAIL 2, *v.*, MAILED, MAILING. (Sending a letter.) The sign for LETTER is made: the right thumbtip is licked and placed against the upturned left palm. The right hand, palm out and fingers touching thumb, is then thrown forward, opening into the "5" position, palm out.

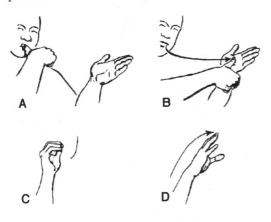

A   B

C   D

MAINTAIN 1 (mǎn tān'), *v.*, -TAINED, -TAINING. (Slow, careful movement.) The "K" hands are crossed, the right above the left, little finger edges down. In this position the hands are moved up and down a short distance. *Cf.* CARE 2, CAREFUL 2, KEEP, MIND 3, PRESERVE, RESERVE 2, TAKE CARE OF 2.

MAINTAIN 2, *v.* (Words tumbling from the mouth.) The right index finger, pointing left, describes a continuous small circle in front of the mouth. *Cf.* DISCOURSE, HEARING, MENTION, REMARK, SAID, SAY, SPEAK, SPEECH 1, STATE, STATEMENT, TALK 1, TELL, VERBAL.

MAINTENANCE (mǎn' tə nəns), *n.* (Holding up.) The right "S" hand pushes up the left "S" hand. *Cf.* ENDORSE 1, SUPPORT 1, SUSTAIN, SUSTENANCE, UPHOLD.

MAKE (māk), *v.*, MADE, MAKING, *n.* (Fashioning something with the hands.) The right "S" hand, palm facing left, is placed on top of its left counterpart, whose palm faces right. The hands are twisted back and forth, striking each other slightly after each twist. *Cf.* CONSTRUCT 2, CREATE 1, DEVISE, MANUFACTURE, MEND, PRODUCE 2, REPAIR.

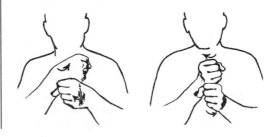

MAKE BRIEF *v. phrase.* (To squeeze or condense into a small space.) The "C" hands face each other, with the right hand nearer to the body than the left. Both hands draw together and close deliberately, squeezing an imaginary object. *Cf.* ABBREVIATE, BRIEF 2, CONDENSE, SUMMARIZE 1, SUMMARY 1.

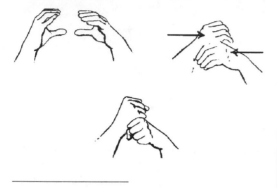

MAKE FUN OF *v. phrase.* (Derision; poking or prodding.) Both hands are held closed except for index and little fingers, which extend straight out from the body. The right hand is brought up and its index fingertip pulls the right corner of the mouth into a slight smile. Both hands then move forward simultaneously in a series of short jabbing motions, the right somewhat behind the left. An expression of disdain is assumed during this sign. The first part of the sign, pulling the mouth into a smile, is frequently omitted. *Cf.* MOCK, RIDICULE.

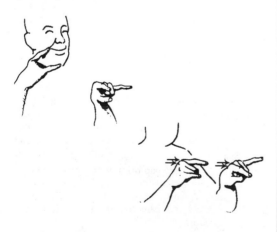

MAKE LOVE 1, *(colloq.), v. phrase.* (Heads nodding toward each other.) The "A" hands are placed together before the body with thumbs up. The thumbs

wiggle up and down. *Cf.* BEAU, LOVER, SWEETHEART 1.

MAKE LOVE 2, *(sl.), v. phrase.* (Necks interlocked.) The "S" hands, palms facing, are crossed at the wrists. They swing up and down while the wrists remain in contact. *Cf.* NECKING, PETTING.

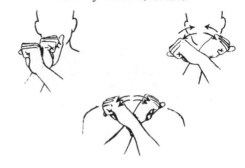

MAKE ME DISGUSTED *v. phrase.* (Turning the stomach.) The fingertips of the curved right hand describe a continuous circle on the stomach. The signer assumes an exaggerated expression of disgust. *Cf.* DISGUST, DISGUSTED, DISGUSTING, MAKE ME SICK, NAUSEA, NAUSEATE, NAUSEOUS, OBNOXIOUS, REVOLTING.

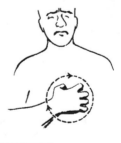

MAKE ME SICK *v. phrase.* See MAKE ME DISGUSTED.

MAKE NO DIFFERENCE *v. phrase.* Both hands, in the "5" position, are held before the chest, fingertips facing each other. With an alternate back-and-forth movement, the fingertips are made to strike each other. *Cf.* ANYHOW, ANYWAY, DESPITE, DOESN'T

MATTER, HOWEVER 2, INDIFFERENCE, INDIFFERENT, IN SPITE OF, NEVERTHELESS, NO MATTER, WHEREVER.

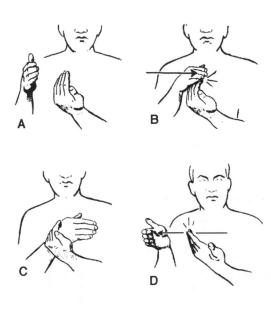

A   B

C   D

MAKE RESPONSE *v. phrase.* (Directing a reply from the mouth to someone.) The tip of the right index finger, held in the "D" position, palm facing the body, is placed on the lips, while the left "D" hand, palm also facing the body, is held about a foot in front of the right hand. The right index finger, swinging around, moves toward and stops in a pointing position a few inches from the left index fingertip. *Cf.* ANSWER, REPLY 1, RESPOND, RESPONSE 1.

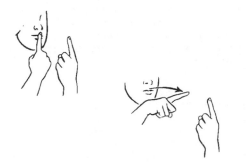

MAKEUP (māk′ ŭp), *n.* (Applying something to the face.) The thumbtip and fingertips of each hand are held together and rotated in small counterclockwise circles on both cheeks simultaneously. *Cf.* COSMETICS.

MAKE UP ONE'S MIND *v. phrase.* (The mind stops wavering, and the pros and cons are resolved.) The right index finger touches the forehead, the sign for THINK, *q.v.* Both "F" hands, palms facing each other and fingers pointing straight out, then drop down simultaneously. The sign for JUDGE, *q.v.,* explains the rationale behind the movement of the two hands here. *Cf.* DECIDE, DECISION, DETERMINE, MIND 5, RESOLVE, VERDICT.

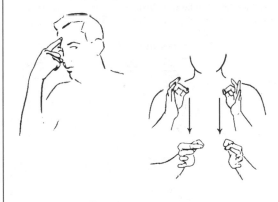

MALE (māl), *n., adj.* (The man's cap.) The thumb and extended fingers of the right hand are brought up to grasp an imaginary cap brim, representing the tipping of caps by men in olden days. This is a root sign used to modify many others. *Viz.:* MALE plus BABY: SON; MALE plus SAME: BROTHER; etc. *Cf.* MAN, MANKIND.

MAMA (mä′ mə), *n.* (Familiar derivation of the more formal MOTHER, *q.v.*) The thumb of the right "5" hand touches the right cheek repeatedly.

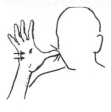

MAN (măn), *n.* See MALE.

MANAGE (măn′ ĭj), *v.*, -AGED, -AGING. (Holding the reins over all.) The "A" hands, palms facing, move alternately back and forth, as if grasping and manipulating reins. The left "A" hand, still in position, swings over so that its palm now faces down. The right hand opens to the "5" position, palm down, and swings over the left which moves slightly to the right. *Cf.* CONTROL 1, DIRECT 1, GOVERN, MANAGE-MENT, MANAGER, OPERATE, REGULATE, REIGN, RULE 1.

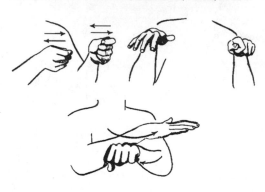

MANAGEMENT (măn′ ĭj mənt), *n.* The sign for MANAGE is made. This is followed by the sign for -MENT: the downturned right "M" hand moves down along the left palm, which is facing away from the body.

MANAGER (măn′ ĭj ər), *n.* The sign for MANAGE, *q.v.*, is made. This is followed by the sign for INDI-VIDUAL: both open hands, palms facing each other, move down the sides of the body, tracing its outline to the hips.

MANKIND (măn′ kīnd′), *n.* See MALE.

MANNER 1 (măn′ ər), *n.* (The hands come into view, to reveal the "how" of something.) The right-angle hands, palms down and knuckles touching, swing up and open to the palms-up position. *Cf.* HOW.

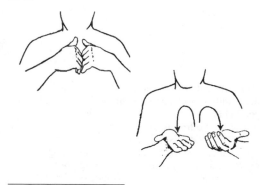

MANNER 2, *n.* (The movement.) Both hands, palms facing and fingers together and extended straight out, move in unison away from the body, in a straight or winding manner. *Cf.* CORRIDOR, HALL, HALLWAY, METHOD, OPPORTUNITY 3, PATH, ROAD, STREET, TRAIL, WAY 1.

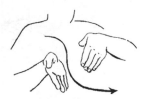

MANUAL (măn′ yŏŏ əl), *n.* (A book with a narrow spine.) The left hand, fingers together, is held upright, palm facing right. The right hand wraps around the lower edge of the left and travels up to the little finger. This denotes a narrow object. The sign for BOOK, is then made: the hands are placed together, palm to palm, and then opened, as if opening a book. Sometimes this latter sign is omitted. *Cf.* BOOKLET, MAGAZINE, PAMPHLET.

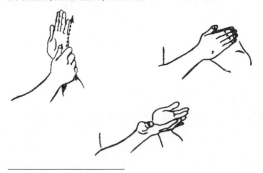

MANUAL ALPHABET (The movement of the fingers in fingerspelling.) The right hand, palm out, is moved from left to right, with the fingers wriggling up and down. *Cf.* ALPHABET 1, DACTYLOLOGY, FINGER-SPELLING, SPELL, SPELLING.

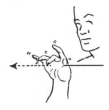

MANUFACTURE (măn′ yə făk′ chər), *n., v.,* -TURED, -TURING. (Fashioning something with the hands.) The right "S" hand, palm facing left, is placed on top of its left counterpart, whose palm faces right. The hands are twisted back and forth, striking each other slightly after each twist. *Cf.* CONSTRUCT 2, CREATE 1, DEVISE, MAKE, MEND, PRODUCE 2, REPAIR.

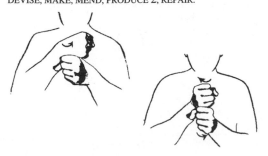

MANY (mĕn′ ĭ), *adj.* (*Many* fingers are indicated.) The upturned "S" hands are thrown up, opening into the "5" position, palms up. This may be repeated. *Cf.* MULTIPLE, NUMEROUS, PLURAL, QUANTITY.

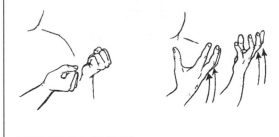

MARBLE (mär′ bəl), *n.* (Flicking a marble ball, as in a child's game.) The signer uses the thumb to "flick" a marble ball forward. The action is repeated. This sign is used for both the ball and the stone used in building and sculpture.

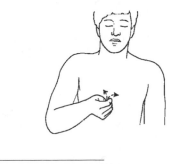

MARCH (märch), *v.,* MARCHED, MARCHING. (A column of marchers, one behind the other.) The down-turned open hands, fingers pointing down, are held one behind the other. Pivoted from the wrists, they move rhythmically forward and back in unison. *Cf.* PARADE.

MARIJUANA (mar ə wä′ nə), *n.* (The act of smoking marijuana.) The signer mimes holding the marijuana cigarette to the lips and inhaling deeply. *Cf.* POT.

MARRIAGE (măr′ ĭj), *n.* (A clasping of hands, as during the wedding ceremony.) The hands are clasped together, the right on top of the left. *Cf.* MARRY.

MARRY (măr′ ĭ), *v.*, -RIED, -RYING. See MARRIAGE.

MASK (mask), *n., v.* (Covering the face.) The cupped hands, palms facing the body and fingers pointing up, shield the eyes and then move back to cover the rest of the face.

MATCH (măch), *n.* (The natural sign.) The right hand, grasping an imaginary match, strikes it against the open left palm, which is facing right.

MATHEMATICS (măth′ ə măt′ ĭks), *n.* (Calculation; the "X" movement, with the letter "M.") Both "M" hands, fingertips facing and palms facing the body, are crossed repeatedly.

MATURE 1 (mə tyo͞or′, -to͞or′), *v.*, -TURED, -TURING. (Flowers or plants emerge from the ground.) The right fingers, pointing up, emerge from the closed left hand, and they spread open as they do. *Cf.* BLOOM, DEVELOP 1, GROW, GROWN, PLANT 1, RAISE 3, REAR 2, SPRING.

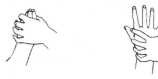

MATURE 2, *adj., n.* (Growing up.) The index finger edge of the right "M" hand, palm facing down, moves up the outstretched upright left palm.

MAXIMUM (mak′ sə məm), *adj.* Both hands, in the "M" position, are held palms down, fingertips touching. The right hand rises above the left.

MAY 1 (mā), *v.* (Weighing one thing against another.) The upturned open hands move alternately up and down. *Cf.* GUESS 3, MAYBE, MIGHT 2, PERHAPS, POSSIBILITY, POSSIBLY, PROBABLE, PROBABLY, SUPPOSE.

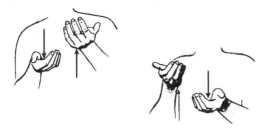

MAY 2, *v.* (An affirmative movement of the hands, likened to a nodding of the head, to indicate ability or power to accomplish something.) Both "A" hands, held palms down, move down in unison a short distance before the chest. *Cf.* ABILITY, ABLE, CAN, CAPABLE, COMPETENT, COULD, POSSIBLE.

MAY 3, *v.* (A permissive upswinging of the hands, as if giving in.) Both hands, palms facing and fingers pointing away from the body, are held at chest level, almost a foot apart. With an upward movement, using their wrists as pivots, the hands sweep up until the fingers point almost straight up. *Cf.* ALLOW, GRANT 1, LET, LET'S, LET US, PERMISSION 1, PERMIT 1, TOLERATE 1.

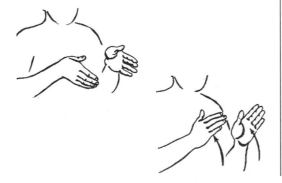

MAYBE (mā' bǐ, -bē), *adv.* See MAY 1.

MAYONNAISE (mā ə nāz'), *n.* (The letter "M"; spreading.) The downturned right "M" hand "spreads" the mayonnaise on the upturned left palm.

MCDONALD'S (mək don' əldz), *loc.* (The letter "M"; the arches of the well-known hamburger place.) The right "M" hand describes one or two arches along the back of the downturned left hand.

ME (mē; *unstressed* mǐ), *pron.* (The natural sign.) The signer points to himself. *Cf.* I 2.

MEADOW (mĕd′ ō), *n.* (Outlining the space.) Both downturned "M" hands, index fingers touching, are held several inches in front of the chest. They describe a circle as they separate and move in toward the chest.

MEAL (mēl), *n.* (The natural sign.) The closed right hand goes through the natural motion of placing food in the mouth. This movement is repeated. *Cf.* CONSUME 1, CONSUMPTION, EAT, FEED 1, FOOD.

MEAN 1 (mēn), *adj.* (Striking down against.) Both "A" or "X" hands are held before the chest, the right above the left. The right hand strikes down and out, hitting the left thumb and knuckles with force. *Cf.* CRUEL 1, HARM 2, HURT 2.

MEAN 2, *v.,* MEANT, MEANING. (Relative standing of one's thoughts.) A modified sign for THINK is made: the right index finger touches the middle of the forehead. The tips of the right "V" hand, palm down, are then thrust into the upturned left palm (as in STAND, *q.v.*). The right "V" hand is then re-thrust into the upturned left palm, with right palm now

facing the body. *Cf.* IMPLY, INTEND, INTENT, INTENTION, MEANING, MOTIVE 3, PURPOSE 1, SIGNIFICANCE 2, SIGNIFY 2, SUBSTANCE 2.

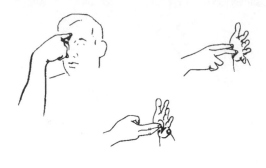

MEANING (mē′ nǐng), *n.* See MEAN 2.

MEANTIME (mēn′ tīm′), *n., adv.* (Parallel time.) Both "D" hands, palms down, move forward in unison, away from the body. They may move straight forward or may follow a slight upward arc. *Cf.* DURING, WHILE.

MEASURE (mĕzh′ ər), *n., v.,* -URED, -URING. (The act of measuring a short distance.) Both "Y" hands, palms out and thumbs touching, rotate back and forth. Alternatively, the hands, in this same position, separate and come together repeatedly.

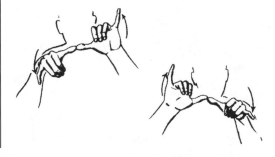

MEAT (mēt), *n.* (The fleshy part of the hand.) The right index finger and thumb squeeze the fleshy part of the open left hand, between thumb and index finger. *Cf.* BEEF, FLESH.

MECHANIC 1 (mə kăn′ ĭk), *n.* (The meshing gears.) With the knuckles of both hands interlocked, the hands pivot up and down, imitating the meshing of gear teeth. This may be followed by the sign for INDIVIDUAL 1, *q.v. Cf.* ENGINE, FACTORY, MACHINE, MACHINERY, MECHANISM, MOTOR 1.

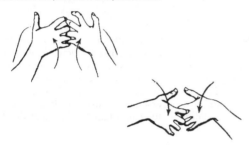

MECHANIC 2, *n.* (The natural movement.) The index finger of the right hand is grasped by the outstretched index and middle fingers of the left hand. The left hand executes a series of up-and-down movements, as if manipulating a wrench. This is followed by the sign for INDIVIDUAL: both open hands, palms facing each other, move down the sides of the body, tracing its outline to the hips.

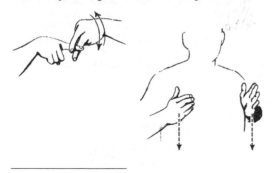

MECHANISM (mĕk′ ə nĭz′ əm), *n.* See MECHANIC 1.

MEDAL (mĕd′ əl), *n.* (The medal hanging from the left side of the chest.) The right index and middle fingers, held together and pointing straight down, are brought against the left side of the chest, either once or twice.

MEDDLE 1 (mĕd′ əl), *v.,* -DLED, -DLING. (Obstruct, block.) The left hand, fingers together and palm flat, is held before the body, facing somewhat down. The little finger side of the right hand, held with palm flat, makes one or several up-down chopping motions against the left hand, between its thumb and index finger. *Cf.* ANNOY, ANNOYANCE, BOTHER, DISRUPT, DISTURB, HINDER, HINDRANCE, IMPEDE, INTERCEPT, INTERFERE, INTERFERENCE, INTERFERE WITH, INTERRUPT, OBSTACLE, OBSTRUCT, PREVENT, PREVENTION.

MEDDLE 2, *v.* (The nose is poked into something.) The sign for NOSE is formed by touching the tip of the nose with the index finger. The sign for IN, INTO follows: the right hand, fingertips touching the thumb, is thrust into the left "C" hand, which closes a bit over the right fingers as they enter.

MEDICINE (mĕd′ ə sən), *n.* (Mixing of medicine; rolling a pill.) The ball of the middle fingertip of the right "5" hand describes a small counterclockwise circle in the upturned left palm. *Cf.* DRUG.

MEDITATE 1 (mĕd′ ə tāt), *v.* (Think deep.) The sign for THINK is made: the right index finger describes a small continuous counterclockwise circle on the forehead. This is followed by DEEP: the downturned right index finger moves straight down the left palm, which is held forward or to the right.

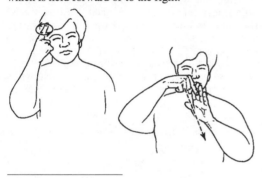

MEDITATE 2, *v.* (The letter "M"; THINK.) The right "M" hand executes a continuous counterclockwise circle on the forehead.

MEET (mēt), *v.,* MET, MEETING. (A coming together of two persons.) Both "D" hands, palms facing each other, are brought together. *Cf.* ENCOUNTER.

MEETING 1 (mē′ tǐng), *n.* (Assemble all together.) Both "5" hands, palms facing, are held with fingers pointing out from the body. With a sweeping motion they are brought in toward the chest, and all fingertips come together. This is repeated. *Cf.* ASSEMBLE 1, ASSEMBLY, CONFERENCE, CONVENE, CONVENTION, GATHER 2, GATHERING.

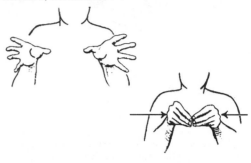

MEETING 2, *(loc.), n.* (A random coming together of different persons.) The "D" hands, facing each other and touching at the thumbs, are held with right palm facing the body and left palm facing away from the body. They pivot around so that their relative positions are now reversed. This may be done several times. In addition, the hands may be separated slightly during the pivoting, but they must come together at the end of this movement.

MELANCHOLY (mĕl′ ən kŏl′ ǐ), *n.* (The facial features drop.) Both "5" hands, palms facing the eyes and fingers slightly curved, drop simultaneously to a level with the mouth. The head drops slightly as the hands move down, and an expression of sadness is assumed. *Cf.* DEJECTED, DEPRESSED 1, GLOOM, GLOOMY, GRAVE 2, GRIEF 1, MOURNFUL, SAD, SORROWFUL 1.

MELON (mĕl′ ən), *n.* (Sounding for ripeness.) The right middle finger is flicked once or twice against the back of the downturned left hand.

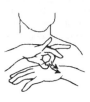

MELT (mĕlt), *v.,* MELTED, MELTING. (Fingering the small pieces resulting from the breaking up of something.) The thumbs rub slowly across the fingertips of the upturned hands, from the little fingers to the index fingers, and then continue to the "A" position, palms up. *Cf.* DECAY, DIE OUT, DISSOLVE, FADE, ROT.

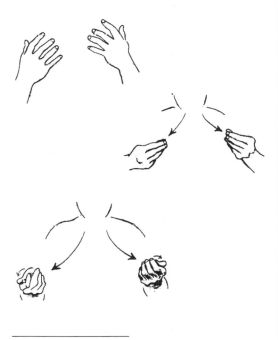

MEMBER 1 (mĕm′ bər), *n.* (Linked together.) The sign for JOIN is made: both hands, held in the modified "5" position, palms out, move toward each other. The thumbs and index fingers of both hands then connect. This is followed by the sign for INDIVIDUAL: both open hands, palms facing each other,

move down the sides of the body, tracing its outline to the hips.

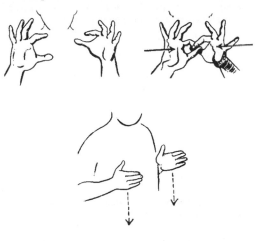

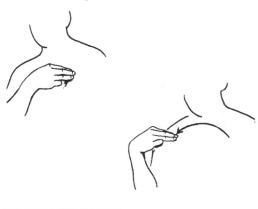

MEMBER 2, *n.* The right "M" hand, palm facing the body and fingers pointing left, moves from the left shoulder to the right.

MEMORIAL (mə môr′ ē əl), *n.* (Looking back.) The right "M" hand, positioned near the right temple, moves straight back over the shoulder.

MEMORIZE (mĕm′ ə rīz′), v., -RIZED, -RIZING. (Holding on to knowledge.) The open right hand is placed on the forehead. Then as it is removed straight forward, it is clenched into a fist.

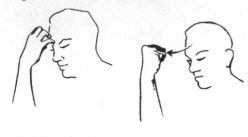

MEMORY (mĕm′ ə rĭ), n. (Knowledge which remains.) The sign for KNOW is made: the right fingertips are placed on the forehead. The sign for REMAIN then follows: the "A" hands are held with palms toward the body, thumbs extended and touching, the right behind the left. In this position the hands move forward in a straight, steady line, or straight down. Cf. RECALL 2, RECOLLECT 2, REMEMBER.

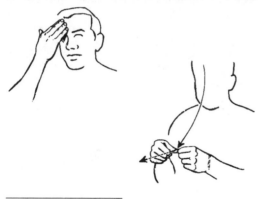

MEND (mĕnd), v., MENDED, MENDING. (Fashioning something with the hands.) The right "S" hand, palm facing left, is placed on top of its left counterpart, whose palm faces right. The hands are twisted back and forth, striking each other slightly after each twist. Cf. CONSTRUCT 2, CREATE 1, DEVISE, MAKE, MANUFACTURE, PRODUCE 2, REPAIR.

MENOPAUSE (men′ ə pôz), n. (OLD; MENSTRUATION; STOP.) The sign for OLD: the hand pulls down on an imaginary beard. For MENSTRUATION, the right "A" hand, palm facing left, is brought against the right cheek twice. For STOP, the little finger edge of the open right hand is brought sharply down on the upturned left palm.

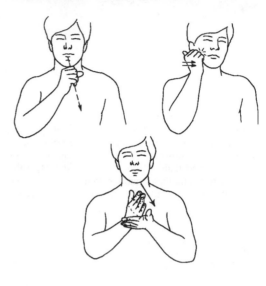

MENSTRUATE (mĕn′ strŏŏ āt′), v., -ATED, -ATING. (Blotting the brow.) The knuckle edge of the right "A" hand is pressed twice against the right cheek.

-MENT condition. suffix. The downturned right "M" hand moves down along the left palm, which is facing away from the body.

MENTAL (mĕn′ təl), *adj.* (Patting the head to indicate something of value inside.) The right fingers pat the forehead several times. *Cf.* MIND 1, SENSE 1.

MENTALLY LIMITED *adj.* (The limits, upper and lower, of the mind.) The signer touches the forehead with the right index finger. The two hands are then held palms facing down, the right positioned an inch or so above the left. Both hands move straight forward a short distance.

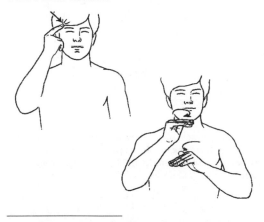

MENTION (mĕn′ shən), *v.*, -TIONED, -TIONING. (Words tumbling from the mouth.) The right index finger, pointing left, describes a continuous small circle in front of the mouth. *Cf.* DISCOURSE, HEARING, MAINTAIN 2, REMARK, SAID, SAY, SPEAK, SPEECH 1, STATE, STATEMENT, TALK 1, TELL, VERBAL.

MERCHANT (mûr′ chənt), *n.* (Transferring ownership.) The sign for SALE is formed: the downturned hands, each with fingers grasping an imaginary object, pivot out from the wrists, away from the body. The sign for INDIVIDUAL is then made: both open hands, palms facing each other, move down the sides of the body, tracing its outline to the hips. *Cf.* SALESMAN, SELLER, VENDER.

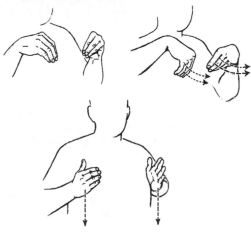

MERCY 1 (mûr′ sĭ), *n.* (The heart rolls out.) Both right-angle hands roll over each other as they move down and away from their initial position at the heart. *Cf.* GENEROUS, KIND 1.

MERCY 2, *n.* (Feelings from the heart, conferred on others.) The middle fingertip of the open right hand touches the chest over the heart. The same open hand then moves in a small, clockwise circle before the right shoulder, with palm facing forward and fingers pointing up. *Cf.* PITY, SYMPATHY 2.

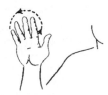

MERGE (mûrj), *v.*, MERGED, MERGING. (The natural sign.) Both open hands are held with palms toward the chest, fingertips pointing toward each other, thumbs pointing up. The hands then move toward each other until their fingers "merge."

MERRY (mĕr′ ĭ), *adj.* (The heart is stirred; the spirits bubble up.) The open right hand, palm facing the body, strikes the heart repeatedly, moving up and off the heart after each strike. *Cf.* DELIGHT, GAIETY, GLAD, HAPPY, JOY.

MERRY-GO-ROUND (mer′ ē gō round), *n.* (Seated and riding in a circle.) The right curved index and middle fingers are placed atop their left counterparts, and both hands make a horizontal counterclockwise circle.

MESSAGE (mĕs′ ĭj), *(rare), n.* (Word, carry.) The sign for WORD is formed: the right index fingertip and thumbtip are held about an inch apart and placed on the side of the outstretched left index finger, which represents the length of a sentence. This is followed by the sign for CARRY: both open hands, palms up, move in an arc from left to right, as if carrying something from one point to another.

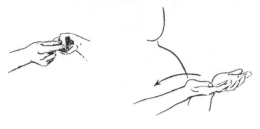

MESSIAH (mə sī′ ə), *n.* (The letter "M"; from the heart.) The right "M" hand, placed at the heart, moves down and out, away from the chest, or down to the right hip.

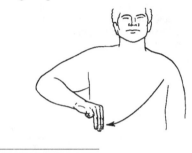

METAL 1 (mĕt′ əl), *n.* (Hammering on metal.) The little finger edge of the right "S" hand is brought down forcefully against the back of the prone, open left hand several times.

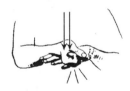

METAL 2, *n.* (A hard substance.) The right "S" hand moves up from the chest to strike the bottom of the chin several times, and continues forward in a short arc after each blow.

METER (mē′ tər), *n.* (Measuring.) Both "M" hands, palms out and hands touching, move apart a short distance.

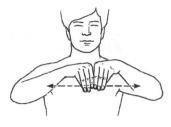

METHOD (mĕth′ əd), *n.* (The movement.) Both hands, palms facing and fingers together and extended straight out, move in unison away from the body, in a straight or winding manner. *Cf.* CORRIDOR, HALL, HALLWAY, MANNER 2, OPPORTUNITY 3, PATH, ROAD, STREET, TRAIL, WAY 1.

METHODIST (mĕth′ əd ĭst), *n., adj.* (Rubbing the hands together in zeal or ambition.) The open hands are rubbed vigorously back and forth against each other. *Cf.* AMBITIOUS, ANXIOUS, DILIGENCE, DILIGENT, EAGER, EAGERNESS, ENTHUSIASM, ENTHUSIASTIC, INDUSTRIOUS, ZEAL, ZEALOUS.

ME TOO *(colloq.).* (Two figures are compared, back and forth.) The right "Y" hand, palm facing left, is moved alternately toward and away from the body. *Cf.* SAME 2.

MEXICO (mĕk′ sə kō), *n.* (The sombrero.) Both index fingers describe the wide brim of a sombrero.

MICROPHONE (mī′ krə fōn), *n.* (Holding a microphone.) The signer mimes holding a microphone in front of the face.

MIDDAY (mĭd′ dā′), *n.* (The sun is directly overhead.) The right "B" hand, palm facing left, is held upright in a vertical position, its elbow resting on the back of the open left hand. *Cf.* NOON.

MIDDLE (mĭd′ əl), *adj.* (The natural sign.) The downturned right fingers describe a small clockwise circle and come to rest in the center of the upturned left palm. *Cf.* CENTER, CENTRAL.

MIDNIGHT (mĭd′ nīt′), *n.* (The sun is directly opposite the NOON position, *q.v.*) The right "B" hand is held fingers pointing straight down and palm facing left. The left hand, representing the horizon, is held open and fingers together, palm down, its little finger edge resting against the right arm near the crook of the elbow.

MIGHT 1 (mīt), *n.* (Flexing the muscles.) With fists clenched, palms facing back, the signer raises both arms and shakes them once, with force. *Cf.* MIGHTY 1, POWER 1, POWERFUL 1, STRONG 1, STURDY, TOUGH 1.

MIGHT 2, *v.* (Weighing one thing against another.) The upturned open hands move alternately up and down. *Cf.* GUESS 3, MAY 1, MAYBE, PERHAPS, POSSIBILITY, POSSIBLY, PROBABLE, PROBABLY, SUPPOSE.

MIGHT 3, *n.* (The curve of the flexed biceps is indicated.) The left hand, clenched into a fist, is held up, palm facing the body. The index finger of the right "D" hand moves in an arc over the left biceps muscle, from shoulder to crook of the elbow. *Cf.* POWER 2, POWERFUL 2.

MIGHTY 1 (mī′ tĭ), *adj.* See MIGHT 1.

MIGHTY 2, *adj.* (Strength emanating from the body.) Both "5" hands are placed palms against the chest. They move out and away, forcefully, closing and assuming the "S" position. *Cf.* BRAVE, BRAVERY, COURAGE, COURAGEOUS, FORTITUDE, HALE, HEALTH, HEALTHY, STRENGTH, STRONG 2, WELL 2.

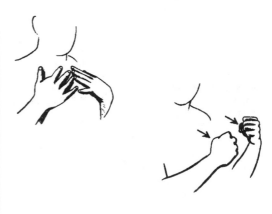

MILK (mĭlk), *n., v.,* MILKED, MILKING. (The act of milking a cow.) Both hands, alternately grasping and releasing imaginary teats, move alternately up and down before the body.

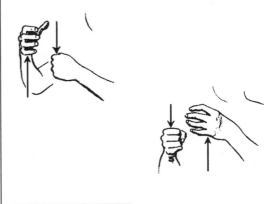

MILLIGRAM (mĭl′ ə gram), *n.* (The letters "M" and "G"; weighing on a beam balance.) The right "M" hand, positioned on the knuckle of the left index finger, moves forward toward the left index finger-tip, while changing to the "G."

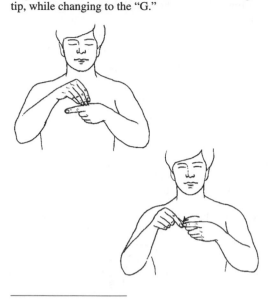

MILLIMETER (mil′ ə mē tər), *n.* (The letters "M.") Both "M" hands are held with index fingers touching. They move apart a short distance, dropping down slightly as they do.

MILLION (mĭl′ yən), *n., adj.* (A thousand thousands.) The fingertips of the right "M" hand, palm down, are thrust twice into the upturned left palm, first at the base of the palm and then near the base of the left fingers. (The "M" stands for *mille*, the Latin word for *thousand*.)

MIMIC (mĭm′ ĭk), *v.,* -ICKED, -ICKING, *n.* (The natural sign.) The right fingers and thumb close together and move onto the upturned, open left hand, as if taking something from one place to another. *Cf.* COPY, DUPLICATE, IMITATE, MODEL.

MIND 1 (mīnd), *n.* (Patting the head to indicate something of value inside.) The right fingers pat the forehead several times. *Cf.* MENTAL, SENSE 1.

MIND 2, *n.* (Directing one's attention forward; applying oneself; concentrating.) Both hands, fingers pointing up and together, are held at the sides of the face. They move straight out from the face. *Cf.* ATTEND (TO), ATTENTION, CONCENTRATE, CONCENTRATION, FOCUS, GIVE ATTENTION (TO), PAY ATTENTION (TO).

MIND 3, *v.* (Slow, careful movement.) The "K" hands are crossed, the right above the left, little finger edges down. In this position the hands are moved up and down a short distance. *Cf.* CARE 2, CAREFUL 2, KEEP, MAINTAIN 1, PRESERVE, RESERVE 2, TAKE CARE OF 2.

MIND 4, *v.*, MINDED, MINDING. (The hands are thrown open as an act of obeisance.) Both "A" hands, palms facing, are positioned at either side of the head. They are thrown open and out, ending in the "5" position, palms up. The head is bowed slightly at the same time. *Cf.* OBEDIENCE, OBEDIENT, OBEY.

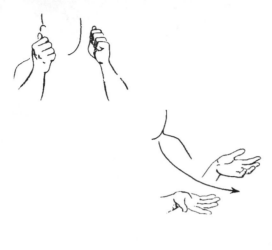

MIND 5, *n.* (The mind stops wavering, and the pros and cons are resolved.) The right index finger touches the forehead, the sign for THINK, *q.v.* Both "F" hands, palms facing each other and fingers pointing straight out, then drop down simultaneously. The sign for JUDGE, *q.v.,* explains the rationale behind the movement of the two hands here. *Cf.* DECIDE, DECISION, DETERMINE, MAKE UP ONE'S MIND, RESOLVE, VERDICT.

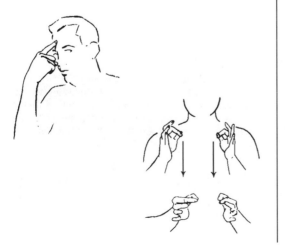

MINE (mīn), *pron.* (Pressing something to one's bosom.) The "5" hand is brought up against the chest. *Cf.* MY.

MINGLE 1 (mǐng′ gəl), *v.*, -GLED, -GLING. (Scrambling or mixing up.) The downturned right hand is positioned above the upturned left. The fingers of both are curved. Both hands move in opposite horizontal circles. *Cf.* COMPLICATE, CONFUSE, CONFUSED, CONFUSION, MIX, MIXED, MIXED UP, MIX-UP, SCRAMBLE.

MINGLE 2, *v.* (Mingling with.) Both hands are held in modified "A" positions, thumbs out. The left hand is positioned with its thumb pointing straight up, and the right hand, with its thumb pointing down, revolves above the left thumb in a clockwise direction. *Cf.* ASSOCIATE, EACH OTHER, FELLOWSHIP, MUTUAL, ONE ANOTHER.

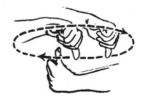

MINIMUM (min′ ə məm), *adj., n.* (The space limitations; the letter "M.") Both "M" hands are held one above the other, palms facing down. The top hand moves down to rest on the back of the bottom hand.

MINISTER (mĭn' ĭs tər), *n.* (Placing morsels of wisdom, or food for thought, into the mind.) The right hand, palm out, with thumb and index finger touching, is moved forward and slightly downward a number of times from its initial position near the right temple. This is followed by the sign for INDIVIDUAL: both open hands, palms facing each other, move down the sides of the body, tracing its outline to the hips. *Cf.* PASTOR, PREACHER.

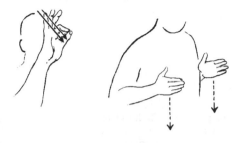

MINUTE (mĭn' ĭt), *n.* (The minute hand of a clock.) The right "D" hand is held with its index finger edge against the palm of the left "5" hand, which faces right. The right index finger moves forward in a short arc. *Cf.* MOMENT.

MIRROR (mĭr' ər), *n.* (A glass object through which one views oneself.) The sign for GLASS is made: the tip of the right index finger is brought up against the exposed front teeth. The open curved right hand is then held palm opposite the face. The hand, pivoting from the wrist, moves back and forth a bit, as if focusing the facial image in its center. Meanwhile, the eyes are directed to the center of the palm. (The sign for GLASS is frequently omitted.)

MISSING (mĭs' ĭng), *adj.* The extended right index finger strikes against the downturned middle finger of the left hand, which is held with palm down and other fingers pointing right.

MISSION (mĭsh' ən), *n.* (The letter "M.") The right downturned "M": hand swings from the right shoulder to the left.

MISTAKE (mĭs tāk'), *n.* (Rationale obscure; the thumb and little finger are said to represent, respectively, right and wrong, with the head poised between the two.) The right "Y" hand, palm facing the body, is brought up to the chin. *Cf.* ERROR, WRONG 1.

MISUNDERSTAND (mĭs' ŭn dər stănd'), *v.*, -STOOD, -STANDING. (The thought is twisted around.) The right "V" hand is positioned with index and middle fingers touching the right side of the forehead. The hand swings around so that the palm now faces out, with the two fingers still on the forehead.

MITTEN (mit′ n), *n.* (The shape is outlined.) The upright left hand is outlined by the right index finger, which moves along the edge from thumb to below the little finger. The outline may also start at the little finger edge and move along to the thumb.

MIX (mĭks), *n., v.,* MIXED, MIXING. (Scrambling or mixing up.) The downturned right hand is positioned above the upturned left. The fingers of both are curved. Both hands move in opposite horizontal circles. *Cf.* COMPLICATE, CONFUSE, CONFUSED, CONFUSION, MINGLE 1, MIXED, MIXED UP, MIX-UP, SCRAMBLE.

MIXED (mĭkst), *adj.* See MIX.

MIXED UP *adj. phrase.* See MIX.

MIXER (mik′ sər), *n.* (The mixing motion.) Both claw hands, facing, are held one atop the other. They twist back and forth repeatedly.

MIX-UP (mĭks′ ŭp′), *n.* See MIX.

MOB (mob), *n.* (Many people spread out.) The downturned claw hands move straight forward. *Cf.* CROWD.

MOCK (mŏk), *v.,* MOCKED, MOCKING. (Derision; poking or prodding.) Both hands are held closed except for index and little fingers, which extend straight out from the body. The right hand is brought up and its index fingertip pulls the right corner of the mouth into a slight smile. Both hands then move forward simultaneously in a series of short jabbing motions, the right somewhat behind the left. An expression of disdain is assumed during this sign. The first part of the sign, pulling the mouth into a smile, is frequently omitted. *Cf.* MAKE FUN OF, RIDICULE.

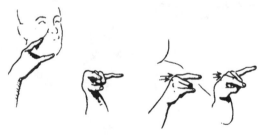

MODEL (mŏd′ əl), *n., adj., v.,* -ELED, -ELING. (The natural sign.) The right fingers and thumb close together and move onto the upturned, open left hand, as if taking something from one place to another. *Cf.* COPY, DUPLICATE, IMITATE, MIMIC.

MODERN (mod′ ərn), *adj.* (A new leaf is turned.) With both hands held palm up before the body, the right hand sweeps in an arc into the left, and continues up a bit.

MODIFY (mŏd′ ə fī′), *v.,* -FIED, -FYING. (To change positions.) Both "A" hands, thumbs up, are held before the chest, several inches apart. The left hand is pivoted over so that its thumb points to the right. Simultaneously, the right hand is moved up and over the left, describing a small arc, with its thumb pointing to the left. *Cf.* CHANGE 1, CONVERT.

MOIST (moist), *adj.* (The wetness.) The right fingertips touch the lips, and then the fingers of both hands open and close against the thumbs a number of times. *Cf.* DAMP, WET.

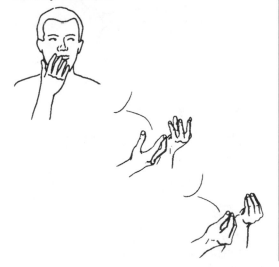

MOLECULE (mol′ ə kyōōl), *n.* (The letter "M"; around the world.) The right "M" hand makes a circle around the left fist.

MOMENT (mō′ mənt), *n.* (The minute hand of a clock.) The right "D" hand is held with its index finger edge against the palm of the left "5" hand, which faces right. The right index finger moves forward in a short arc. *Cf.* MINUTE.

MONEY 1 (mŭn′ ĭ), *n.* (Slapping of paper money in the palm.) The upturned right hand, grasping some imaginary bills, is brought down into the upturned left palm a number of times. *Cf.* FINANCES, FUNDS.

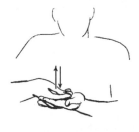

MONEY 2, *n.* (Fingering the money.) The thumb rubs over the index and middle fingers of the upturned hand, as if fingering money.

MONK (mungk), *n.* (The hood.) The downturned cupped or "M" hands outline the shape of a hood as it comes up over the head.

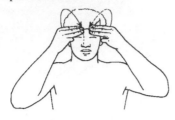

MONKEY (mŭng′ kĭ), *n.* (The scratching of apes.) Both hands go through the natural motion of scratching the sides of the chest.

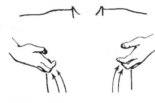

MONOTONOUS (mə nŏt′ ə nəs), *adj.* (The nose is pressed, as if to a grindstone wheel.) The right index finger touches the tip of the nose, as a bored expression is assumed. The right hand is sometimes pivoted back and forth slightly, as the fingertip remains against the nose. *Cf.* BORING 1, TEDIOUS.

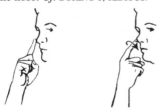

MONSTER (mon′ stər), *n.* (The characteristic gestures of children trying to frighten others.) Both claw hands are held palms out in a threatening way. The signer grimaces and shows the teeth.

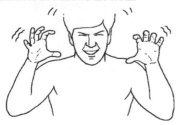

MONTH (mŭnth), *n.* (The tip and three joints represent the four weeks of a month.) The extended right index finger moves down along the upturned, extended left index finger.

MONTHLY (mŭnth′ lĭ), *adj., adv.* (Month after month.) The sign for MONTH is made several times. *Cf.* RENT.

MOON (mōōn), *n.* (The face only.) The right "C" hand indicates the face of the moon.

MOOSE (mōōs), *n.* (The branching of the antlers from the head.) Both hands, in the "5" position, palms up, are placed at the head, thumbs resting on the head above the temples. *Cf.* ANTLERS, DEER, ELK.

MORE (mōr), *adj., n., adv.* (One hand is added to the other; an addition.) Both hands, palms facing, are held fingers together, the left a bit above the right. The right hand is brought up to the left until their fingertips touch.

MORE THAN (mor than) *adj.* (Above the limit.) Both downturned hands are held horizontally, right above left. The right hand, with a slight flourish, moves up above the left.

MORNING (môr' nĭng), *n.* (The sun comes over the horizon.) The little finger edge of the left hand rests in the crook of the right elbow. The left arm, held horizontally, represents the horizon. The open right hand, fingers together and pointing up, with palm facing the body, rises slowly to an almost upright angle.

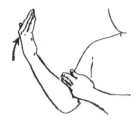

MORON (môr' ŏn), *(colloq.)*, *n.* (The thickness of the skull is indicated, to stress intellectual density.) With the thumb of the right "C" hand grasped by the closed left hand, the right hand is swung away from the body, describing a small arc as it moves. The space between the curved right fingers and the closed left hand indicates the thickness of the skull. *Cf.* DUMB 2, STUPID 2, THICK-SKULLED, UNSKILLED.

MORPHINE (môr' fēn), *n.* (A shot in the arm) The right index finger is thrust into the left upper arm and the thumb wiggles back and forth a number of times,

as if implanting a shot in the arm. *Cf.* COCA-COLA, COKE, DOPE, INOCULATE, NARCOTICS.

MORTIFICATION (môr´ tə fə kā' shən), *n.* (The red rises in the cheeks.) The sign for RED is made: the tip of the right index finger of the "D" hand moves down over the lips, which are red. Both hands are then placed palms facing the cheeks, and move up along the face, to indicate the rise of color. *Cf.* BLUSH, EMBARRASS, EMBARRASSED, FLUSH.

 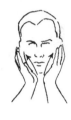

MOSCOW (mos' kou), *n.* The knuckles of the right "A" hand slap the right cheek twice. A native sign.

MOSES 1 (mō' zis), *n.* (The letter "M"; the ten commandments.) The downturned right "M" hand is positioned with index finger edge against the outstretched left palm, near the fingertips. The "M" moves down in an arc to the heel of the left hand.

MOSES 2, *n. arch.* (The veil said to have been worn by Moses to shield the populace from the brilliant rays of light surrounding his face upon his return from talking with God.) The two "F" hands mime lifting up a veil and placing it in front of the face and fastening it behind. This sign, rarely seen today, is often mistaken for a pair of horns, implying that Moses was a horned and therefore evil man.

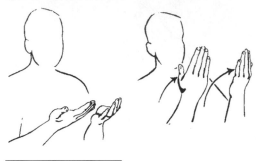

MOTHER 1 (mŭth′ ər), *n.* (A female who carries a baby.) The FEMALE root sign is made: the thumb of the right "A" hand moves down along the line of the right jaw, from ear almost to chin. Both hands are then held open and palms facing up, as if holding a baby. This is the formal sign.

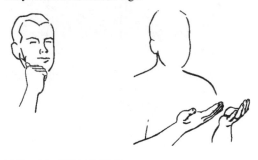

MOTHER 2, *(colloq.), n.* (Derived from the FEMALE root sign.) The thumb of the right "5" hand rests on the right cheek or on the right chin bone. The other fingers wiggle slightly. Or the thumb is thrust repeatedly into the right side of the face, and the rest of the hand remains open and in the "5" position, palm facing out. This latter modification is used for MAMA.

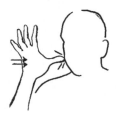

MOTION (mō′ shən), *n.* (An offering; a presenting.) Both hands, slightly cupped, palms up, are held close to the chest. They move up and out in unison, describing a very slight arc. *Cf.* OFFER, OFFERING, PRESENT 1, PROPOSE, SUGGEST.

MOTION PICTURE (The frames of the film speeding through the projector.) The left "5" hand, palm facing right and thumb pointing up, is the projector. The right "5" hand is placed against the left, and moves back and forth quickly. *Cf.* FILM, MOVIE(S), MOVING PICTURE.

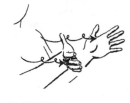

MOTIVATE (mō′ tə vāt′), *v.,* -VATED, -VATING. (Pushing forward.) Both "5" hands are held, palms out, the right fingers facing right and the left fingers left. The hands move straight forward in a series of short movements. *Cf.* ENCOURAGE, MOTIVATION, URGE 1.

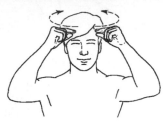

MOTIVATION (mō′ tə vā′ shən), *n.* See MOTIVATE.

MOTIVE 1 (mō′ tĭv), *n.* (A thought is turned over in the mind.) The index finger makes a small circle on the forehead. *Cf.* CONSIDER 1, RECKON, SPECULATE 1,

SPECULATION 1, THINK THOUGHT 1, THOUGHTFUL.

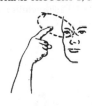

MOTIVE 2, *n., adj.* (The welling up of feelings or emotions in the heart.) The right middle finger, touching the heart, moves up an inch or two a number of times. *Cf.* EMOTION 1, FEEL 2, FEELING, SENSATION, SENSE 2.

MOTIVE 3, *n., adj.* (Relative standing of one's thoughts.) A modified sign for THINK is made: the right index finger touches the middle of the forehead. The tips of the right "V" hand, palm down, are then thrust into the upturned left palm (as in STAND, *q.v.*). The right "V" hand is then re-thrust into the upturned left palm, with right palm now facing the body. *Cf.* IMPLY, INTEND, INTENT, INTENTION, MEAN 2, MEANING, PURPOSE 1, SIGNIFICANCE 2, SIGNIFY 2, SUBSTANCE 2.

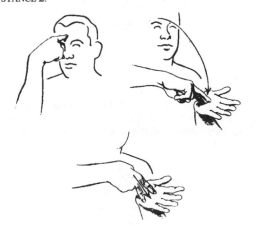

MOTOR 1 (mō′ tər), *n.* (The meshing gears.) With the knuckles of both hands interlocked, the hands pivot up and down, imitating the meshing of gear teeth. *Cf.* ENGINE, FACTORY, MACHINE, MACHINERY, MECHANIC 1, MECHANISM.

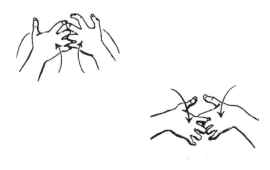

MOTOR 2 *n.* (The pistons moving.) Both upturned fists move alternately up and down.

MOTORCYCLE (mō′ tər sī′ kəl), *n.* (Manipulating the handles.) The "S" hands, spread apart, grasp and manipulate the handle bars of an imaginary motorcycle.

MOUNTAIN (moun′ tən), *n.* (An undulating pile of rocks.) The sign for ROCK is made: the back of the upturned right "S" hand strikes the back of the downturned left "S" hand twice. The downturned "5" hands then move from left to right in wavy, up-down movements.

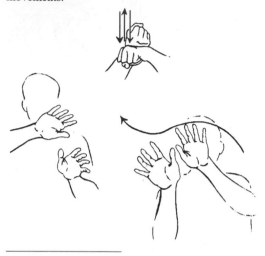

MOURNFUL (mōrn′ fəl), *adj.* (The facial features drop.) Both "5" hands, palms facing the eyes and fingers slightly curved, drop simultaneously to a level with the mouth. The head drops slightly as the hands move down, and an expression of sadness is assumed. *Cf.* DEJECTED, DEPRESSED 1, GLOOM, GLOOMY, GRAVE 2, GRIEF 1, MELANCHOLY, SAD, SORROWFUL 1.

MOUSE (mous), *n.* (The twitching nose.) The index finger brushes across the tip of the nose several times.

MOVE (mōōv), *n., v.,* MOVED, MOVING. (Moving from one place to another.) The downturned hands, fingers touching their respective thumbs, move in unison from left to right. *Cf.* PLACE 2, PUT.

MOVIE(S) (mōō′ vǐ), *n.* (The frames of the film speeding through the projector.) The left "5" hand, palm facing right and thumb pointing up, is the projector. The right "5" hand is placed against the left, and moves back and forth quickly. *Cf.* FILM, MOTION PICTURE, MOVING PICTURE.

MOVING PICTURE See MOVIE(S).

MOW (mō), *v.* (The clipping blades.) The downturned right "5" hand rests on its downturned left counterpart. Both hands move quickly back and forth over each other, imitating opposite moving blades for cutting grass or hair.

MUCH (mŭch), *adj., adv.* (A large amount.) The "5" hands face each other, fingers curved and touching. They move apart rather quickly. *Cf.* EXPAND, GREAT 2, INFINITE, LOT.

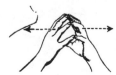

MUG (mug), *n.* (Holding the handle and tipping the mug to the mouth.) The little finger of the right "Y" hand rests on the upturned left palm. The "Y" hand moves up to the mouth, as if tipping the contents of the mug into the mouth.

MULE (mūl), *n.* (The donkey's broad ear; the animal is traditionally a stubborn one.) The open hand, or the "B" hand, is placed at the side of the head, with palm out and fingers pointing straight up. The hand moves forward and back, pivoting at the wrist, as in the case of a donkey's ears flapping. Both hands may also be used, at either side of the head. *Cf.* DONKEY, MULISH, OBSTINATE, STUBBORN.

MULISH (mū' lĭsh), *adj.* See MULE.

MULL OVER *v. phrase.* (Many thoughts turn over in the mind.) The right hand makes a continuous counterclockwise circle in front of the head. Meanwhile, the fingers wriggle continuously.

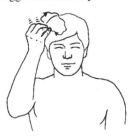

MULTIPLE (mŭl' tə pəl), *adj.* (Many fingers are indicated.) The upturned "S" hands are thrown up, opening into the "S" position, palms up. This may be repeated. *Cf.* MANY, NUMEROUS, PLURAL, QUANTITY.

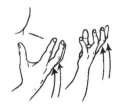

MULTIPLY 1 (mŭl' tə plī'), *v.,* -PLIED, -PLYING. (A multiplying.) The "V" hands, palms facing the body, alternately cross and separate, several times. *Cf.* ARITHMETIC, FIGURE 1.

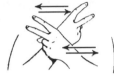

MULTIPLY 2, *v.* (A variation of MULTIPLY 1.) The same sign as MULTIPLY 1 except that the index fingers are used instead of the "V" fingers.

MUMMY (mum' ē), *n.* (The crossed hands in the coffin.) The signer, with eyes closed, crosses the arms on the chest.

MURDER (mûr′ dər), *n.* (Thrusting a dagger and twisting it.) The outstretched right index finger is passed under the downturned left hand. As it moves under the left hand, the right wrist twists in a clockwise direction. *Cf.* KILL, SLAY.

MUSCLE (mus′ əl), *n.* (Pointing to the muscle.) The signer flexes the left arm and points to the biceps muscle.

MUSEUM (myōō zē′ əm), *n.* (The letter "M"; a house or building.) With both hands forming the letter "M," the signer traces the outline of the roof and walls.

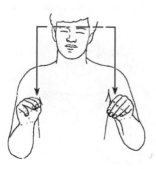

MUSHROOM (mush′ rōōm), *n.* (The stem and cap.) The downturned right claw hand is positioned on top of the left index finger.

MUSIC (mū′ zĭk), *n.* (A rhythmic, wavy movement of the hand, to indicate a melody; the movement of a conductor's hand in directing a musical performance.) The right "5" hand, palm facing left, is waved back and forth next to the left hand, in a series of elongated figure-eights. *Cf.* SING, SONG.

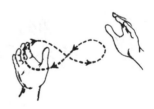

MUST (mŭst), *aux. v.* (Being pinned down.) The right hand, in the "X" position, palm down, moves forcefully up and down once or twice. An expression of determination is frequently assumed. *Cf.* HAVE TO, NECESSARY 1, NECESSITY, NEED 1, OUGHT TO, SHOULD, VITAL 2.

MUTUAL (mū′ chŏŏ əl), *adj.* (Mingling with.) Both hands are held in modified "A" positions, thumbs out. The left hand is positioned with its thumb pointing straight up, and the right hand, with its thumb pointing down, revolves above the left thumb in a clockwise direction. *Cf.* ASSOCIATE, EACH OTHER, FELLOWSHIP, MINGLE 2, ONE ANOTHER.

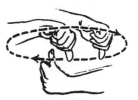

MY (mī), *pron.* (Pressing something to one's bosom.)

The "5" hand is brought up against the chest. *Cf.* MINE.

MYSELF (mī sĕlf′), *pron.* (The thumb represents the self.) The upturned thumb of the right "A" hand is brought up against the chest.

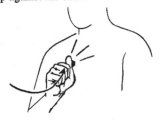

N

NAG (năg), *v.*, NAGGED, NAGGING. (The hen's beak pecks.) The index finger and thumb of the right hand, held together, are brought against the index finger of the left "D" hand a number of times. *Cf.* HENPECK, PICK ON.

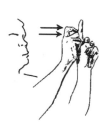

NAIL POLISH (pŏl′ ĭsh), *n.* (The natural sign.) The fingertips of the right "U" hand, held palm down, are brushed repeatedly over the fingernail of the left middle or index finger.

NAIVE 1 (nä ēv′), *adj.* Both "N" hands are placed at the lips. They move forward and out, away from the lips.

NAIVE 2, *adj.* Both open hands, palms facing out, are held in front of the mouth, with the ring fingers bent against the palm. Both hands move out and away from the mouth, describing arcs. *Cf.* INNOCENT 2.

NAKED (nā′ kĭd), *adj.* (Devoid of everything on the surface.) The middle finger of the downturned right "5" hand sweeps over the back of the downturned left "A" or "S" hand, from wrist to knuckles, and continues beyond a bit. *Cf.* BARE, EMPTY, NUDE, OMISSION, VACANCY, VACANT, VOID.

NAME (nām), *n., v.,* NAMED, NAMING. (The "X" used by illiterates in writing their names. This sign is indicative of widespread illiteracy when the language of signs first began to evolve as an instructional medium in deaf education.) The right "H" hand, palm facing left, is brought down on the left "H" hand, palm facing right.

NAMED *v.* (NAME, indicating who is named.) The sign for NAME is made: the right "H" hand, palm facing left, is brought down on the left "H" hand, palm facing right. The hands, in this position, move forward a few inches. *Cf.* CALLED.

NAP 1 (năp), *v.*, NAPPED, NAPPING, *n.* (The eyes are closed.) The fingers of the right open hand, facing the forehead, are placed on the forehead. The hand moves down and away from the head, with the fingers closing so that they all touch. The eyes meanwhile close, and the head bows slightly, as in sleep. *Cf.* ASLEEP, SLEEP 1.

NAP 2, *n.*, *v.* (A short sleep.) The sign for SLEEP is made: the open hand, palm facing the signer, is placed in front of the eyes. It moves down a bit, while the fingers come together. The eyes close as the hand moves down. The sign for SHORT follows: the index and middle fingers of the right "H" hand are placed across the top of the index and middle fingers of the left "H" hand, and move a short distance back and forth, along the length of the left index finger.

NARCOTICS (när kŏt' iks), *(colloq.)*, *n. pl.* (A shot in the arm.) The right index finger is thrust into the left upper arm and the thumb wiggles back and forth a number of times, as if implanting a shot in the arm. *Cf.* COCA-COLA, COKE, DOPE, INOCULATE, MORPHINE.

NARRATE (nă rāt', năr' āt), *v.*, -RATED, -RATING. (The unraveling or stretching out of words or sentences.) Both open hands are held close to each other, with fingers open and palms facing and almost touching. As the hands are drawn apart, the thumb and index finger of each hand come together to form circles. This is repeated several times. *Cf.* DESCRIBE 2, EXPLAIN 2, NARRATIVE, STORY, TALE, TELL ABOUT.

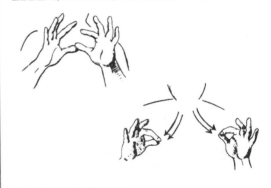

NARRATIVE (năr' ə tĭv), *n.* See NARRATE.

NATION (nā' shən), *n.* (An established area.) The right "N" hand, palm down, executes a clockwise circle above the downturned prone left hand. The tips of the "N" fingers then move straight down and come to rest on the back of the left hand. *Cf.* COUNTRY 2, LAND 2, REPUBLIC.

NATIVE AMERICAN 1 (năt′ iv ə mĕr′ i kən), *n., adj.* (The feathered headdress.) The right thumb and index fingers, holding an imaginary feather, are placed first on the tip of the nose and then under the right ear or on the right side of the head. *Cf.* INDIAN 1.

NATIVE AMERICAN 2, *n., adj.* (The characteristic motions during dancing.) The right "5" hand is placed behind the head, fingers pointing upward to indicate the feathers. The left hand touches the open lips repeatedly. *Cf.* INDIAN 2.

NAUGHT 1 (nôt), *n.* (The zeros.) Both "O" hands, palms facing, are thrown out and down into the "5" position. *Cf.* NONE 1, NOTHING 1.

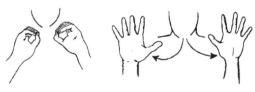

NAUGHT 2, *n.* (The zeros.) In this variant of NAUGHT 1, both "O" hands, palms facing, move back and forth a number of times, the right hand to the right and the left hand to the left. *Cf.* NOTHING 2.

NAUSEA (nô′ shə, -shĭ ə, -sĭ ə), *n.* (Turning the stomach.) The fingertips of the curved right hand describe a continuous circle on the stomach. The signer assumes an exaggerated expression of disgust. *Cf.* DISGUST, DISGUSTED, DISGUSTING, MAKE ME DISGUSTED, MAKE ME SICK, NAUSEATE, NAUSEOUS, OBNOXIOUS, REVOLTING.

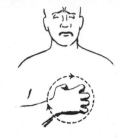

NAUSEATE *v.,* -ATED, -ATING. See NAUSEA.

NAUSEOUS (nô′ shəs, -shĭ əs), *adj.* See NAUSEA.

NEAR 1 (nĭr), *adv., prep.* (One hand is near the other.) The left hand, cupped, fingers together, is held before the chest, palm facing the body. The right hand, also cupped, fingers together, moves a very short distance back and forth, as it is held in front of the left. *Cf.* CLOSE (TO) 2, NEIGHBOR, NEIGHBORHOOD, VICINITY.

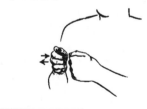

NEAR 2, *adv., prep.* (Coming close to.) Both hands are held in the right angle position, fingers facing each other, with the right hand held between the left hand and the chest. The right hand slowly moves toward the left. *Cf.* APPROACH, TOWARD 2.

NEARLY (nǐr′ lǐ), *adv.* The left hand is held at chest level in the right angle position, with fingers pointing up and the back of the hand facing right. The right fingers are swept up along the back of the left hand. *Cf.* ABOUT 2, ALMOST.

NECESSARY 1 (nĕs′ ə sĕr′ ĭ), *adj.* (Being pinned down.) The right hand, in the "X" position, palm down, moves forcefully up and down once or twice. An expression of determination is frequently assumed. *Cf.* HAVE TO, MUST, NECESSITY, NEED 1, OUGHT TO, SHOULD, VITAL 2.

NECESSARY 2, *adj.* (The letter "N"; a forceful movement of the hand.) The "N" hand is thrust straight down a few inches.

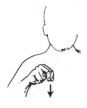

NECESSITY (nə sĕs′ ə tǐ), *n.* See NECESSARY.

NECKING (nĕk′ ing), *(sl.), n.* (Necks interlocked.) The "S" hands, palms facing, are crossed at the wrists. They swing up and down while the wrists remain in contact. *Cf.* MAKE LOVE 2, PETTING.

NECKTIE (nĕk′ tǐ), *n.* (The natural motion.) The "H" hands go through the natural hand-over-hand motions of tying a knot in a necktie at the throat. The right "H" hand then moves down the front of the chest to indicate the fall of the tie. *Cf.* TIE 2.

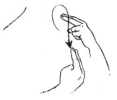

NEE (nā), *adj.* (Presenting the baby from womb to hand; a coming out from the womb to the waiting hand. Referring to birth name.) The upturned right hand is brought forward from the stomach to the upturned left palm. *Cf.* BIRTH 1, BORN 1.

NEED 1 (nēd), *n., v.,* NEEDED, NEEDING. (Being pinned down.) The right hand, in the "X" position, palm down, moves forcefully up and down once or twice. An expression of determination is frequently assumed. *Cf.* HAVE TO, MUST, NECESSARY 1, NECESSITY, OUGHT TO, SHOULD, VITAL 2.

NEED 2, *n.* (Grasping something and pulling it in.) The upturned "5" hands, held side by side before the chest, close slightly into a grasping position as they move in toward the body. *Cf.* DESIRE 1, LONG 2, WANT, WILL 2, WISH 1.

NEEDLE 1 (nē′ dəl), *n.* (The sewing; the length is indicated.) The sign for SEW is made: the right hand, grasping an imaginary needle, goes through the natural motion of hand-stitching on the open left palm. The thumb and index finger of the right hand are then placed on the side of the left index finger, at the tip and third knuckle, to indicate the length of the needle.

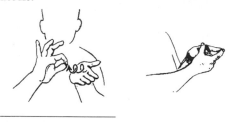

NEEDLE 2, *n.* (The natural sign.) The signer mimes threading a needle and pulling the thread through the hole.

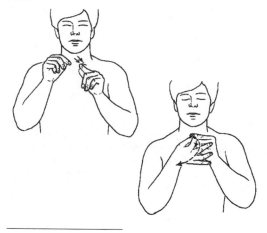

NEGLECT (nĭ glĕkt′), *v.,* -GLECTED, -GLECTING. (To throw something aside.) Both "S" hands are held with palms facing at chest level and then thrown down and to the left, opening into the "5" position. *Cf.* ABANDON, CAST OFF, DISCARD, FORSAKE 2, LEAVE 2, LET ALONE.

NEIGHBOR (nā′bər), *n.* (One who is near.) The sign for NEAR is made: the left hand, cupped, fingers together, is held before the chest, palm facing the body. The right hand, also cupped, fingers together, moves a very short distance back and forth, as it is held in front of the left. This is followed by the sign for INDIVIDUAL: both open hands, palm facing each other, move down the sides of the body, tracing its outline to the hips. *Cf.* CLOSE (TO) 2, NEAR 1, NEIGHBORHOOD, VICINITY.

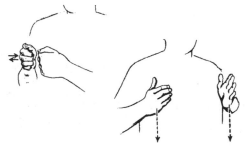

NEIGHBORHOOD (nā′ bər hŏŏd′), *n.* See NEIGHBOR. The sign is repeated on both sides of the body, and the sign for INDIVIDUAL 1 is omitted.

NEPHEW (nĕf′ ū), *n.* (The initial "N"; the upper or masculine portion of the head.) The right "N" hand, held near the right temple, shakes slightly or pivots at the wrist.

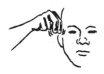

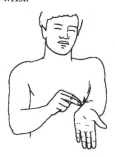

NERVE (nûrv), *n.* (Tracing a nerve along the arm.) The right "N" moves along the outstretched left arm from elbow to wrist.

NERVOUS (nûr′ vəs), *adj.* (The trembling fingers.) Both "5" hands, held palm down, tremble noticeably.

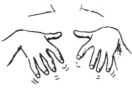

NET (net), *n.* (The shape.) The upturned cupped hands are held with fingertips interlocked. They move apart and up, outlining a net.

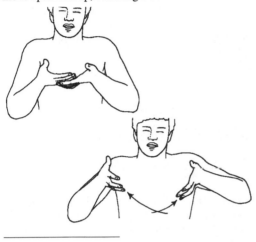

NETWORK(ING) (net′ wûrk), *n., v.* (Remaining in contact.) The middle fingers of both "5" hands touch and both hands move together in a large counterclockwise circle.

NEUROTIC (nŏŏ rot′ ik), *adj.* (The letter "N"; something to do with the mind.) The tips of the right "N" hand are placed against the right temple. The hand may shake very slightly.

NEVER (nĕv′ ər), *adv.* The open right hand, fingers together and palm facing out, moves in a short arc from left to right, and then straight down. The movement is likened to forming a question mark or an "S" in the air.

NEVERTHELESS (nĕv′ ər thə lĕs′), *adv.* Both hands, in the "5" position, are held before the chest, fingertips facing each other. With an alternate back-and-forth movement, the fingertips are made to strike each other. *Cf.* ANYHOW, ANYWAY, DESPITE, DOESN'T MATTER, HOWEVER 2, INDIFFERENCE, INDIFFERENT, IN SPITE OF, MAKE NO DIFFERENCE, NO MATTER, WHEREVER.

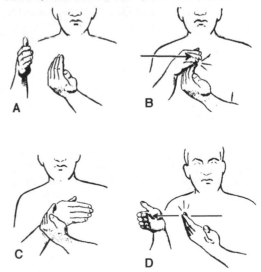

NEW (nū, nōō), *adj.* (Turning over a new leaf.) With both hands held palm up before the body, the right hand sweeps in an arc into the left, and continues up a bit. *Cf.* NEWS.

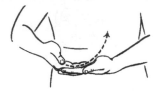

NEW ORLEANS (ôr′ lĭ ənz; *older:* ôr lĕnz′), *n.* (The letter "O"; a modified sign for NEW, *q.v.*) The thumb side of the downturned right "O" hand brushes down twice across the left palm which is facing right.

NEWS (nūz, nōōz), *n.* See NEW.

NEWSPAPER (nūz′ pā′ pər, nōōz′-, nūs′-, nōōs′-), *n.* (The action of the press.) The right "5" hand, held palm down, fingers pointing left, is brought down twice against the upturned left "5" hand, whose fingers point right. *Cf.* PAPER, PUBLISH.

NEXT 1 (nĕkst), *adj.* The index finger of the right hand is placed across the index finger of the left "L" hand. The right hand then flips over, around the tip of the left index finger and up against its underside.

NEXT 2, *adj., adv.* The left hand is lifted over the right and placed down in front of the right palm.

NEXT 3, *adj., v.* The right open hand is held with palm toward the body, fingers pointing left. In this position the right hand moves forward and back against the back of the left open hand, which is also held with palm toward the body, fingers pointing right.

NEXT WEEK *adv. phrase.* The upright, right "D" hand is placed palm-to-palm against the left "5" hand, whose palm faces right. The right "D" hand moves along the left palm from base to fingertips and then beyond in an arc.

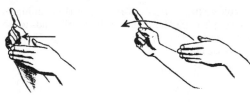

NEXT YEAR *adv. phrase.* (A year in the future.) The right "S" hand, palm facing left, is brought forcefully down to rest on the upturned thumb edge of the left "S" hand, which is held with palm facing right. (*Cf.* YEAR.) From this position the right hand moves forward with index finger extended and pointing ahead.

NIBBLE (nib′ əl), v., n (Small bites.) The right fingertips make a series of small "bites" against the index finger edge of the downturned left hand.

NICARAGUA (nik ə rä′ gwə), n. (The letter "N.") The right hand, forming the letter "N," taps the left shoulder twice. A native sign.

NICE (nīs), adj. (Everything is wiped off the hand, to emphasize an uncluttered or clean condition.) The right hand slowly wipes the upturned left palm, from wrist to fingertips. Cf. CLEAN, PLAIN 2, PURE 1, PURITY, SIMPLE 2.

NIECE (nēs), n. (The initial "N"; the lower or feminine portion of the head.) The right "N" hand, held near the right side of the jaw, shakes slightly, or pivots at the wrist.

NIGHT (nīt), n. (The sun drops beneath the horizon.) The left hand, palm down, is positioned at chest height. The downturned right hand, held an inch or so above the left, moves over the left hand in an arc, as the sun setting beneath the horizon.

NIGHTMARE (nīt′ mâr), n. (Bad dream.) The sign for BAD is made: the tips of the right "B" hand are placed at the lips and then the hand is thrown down. This is followed by the sign for DREAM: the right curved index finger opens and closes quickly and continuously as it leaves its initial position on the forehead and moves up into the air.

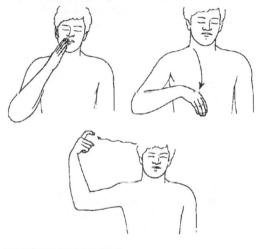

NIPPLES (nip′ əlz), n. (The shape and position.) The right "F" hand is placed first at the right nipple and then at the left.

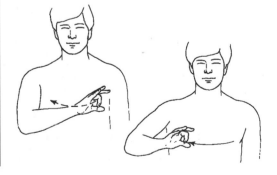

NO 1 (nō), *adv., adj.* (The letter "O.") Both "O" hands are held facing each other in front of the face. They are then drawn apart slowly, the right hand moving to the right and the left hand moving to the left.

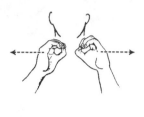

NO 2, *interj.* (The letters "N" and "O.") The index and middle fingers of the right "N" hand are held raised, and are then lowered against the extended right thumb, in a modified "O" position.

NO GOOD (nō gŏŏd'), *phrase.* (A fingerspelled loan sign.) The letters "N-G" are fingerspelled.

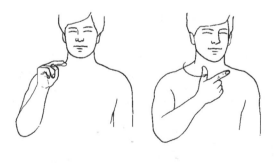

NOISE (noiz), *n.* (A shaking which disturbs the ear.) After placing the index finger on the ear, both hands assume the "S" position, palms down. They move

alternately back and forth, forcefully. *Cf.* NOISY, THUNDER.

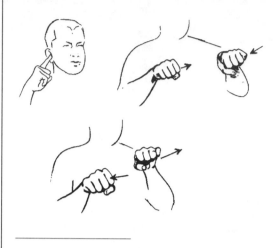

NOISY (noi' zĭ), *adj.* See NOISE.

NO MATTER *phrase.* Both hands, in the "5" position, are held before the chest, fingertips facing each other. With an alternate back-and-forth movement, the fingertips are made to strike each other. *Cf.* ANYHOW, ANYWAY, DESPITE, DOESN'T MATTER, HOWEVER 2, INDIFFERENCE, INDIFFERENT, IN SPITE OF, MAKE NO DIFFERENCE, NEVERTHELESS, WHEREVER.

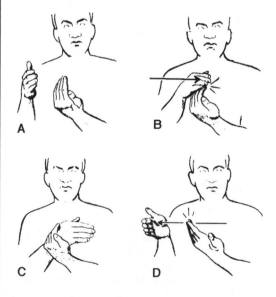

NOMINATE (nom′ ə nāt), *v*. (The "N" letters; offering something up front.) The "N" hands, palms up, move forward alternately, tracing continuous elliptical paths.

NONE 1 (nŭn), *adj*. (The zeros.) Both "O" hands, palms facing, are thrown out and down into the "5" position. *Cf.* NAUGHT 1, NOTHING 1.

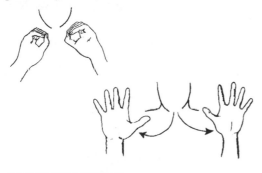

NONE 2, *adj*. (The "O" hands.) Both "O" hands are crossed at the wrists before the chest, thumb edges toward the body. From this position the hands draw apart, the right hand moving to the right and the left hand to the left.

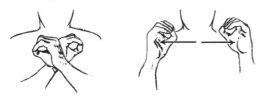

NONE 3, *n., adj*. (Blowing away.) The thumb and index finger of each hand come together to form circles in front of the mouth, as if holding something. The signer then blows on the hands, whereupon they move abruptly away from the face and open into the

"5" position, palms out, showing that whatever they held is gone.

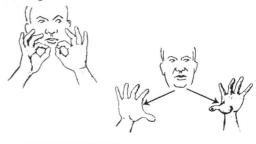

NONSENSE (nŏn′ sĕns), *n*. (Thoughts flickering back and forth.) The right "Y" hand, thumb almost touching the forehead, is shaken back and forth across the forehead several times. *Cf.* FOLLY, FOOLISH, RIDICULOUS, SILLY, TRIFLING.

NOODLE (nōōd′ 1), *n*. (The "N;" lifting the noodles from the plate. Both "N" hands mime forks lifting a pile of noodles from a plate.

NOON (nōōn), *n*. (The sun is directly overhead.) The right "B" hand, palm facing left, is held upright in a vertical position, its elbow resting on the back of the open left hand. *Cf.* MIDDAY.

NORM (nôrm), *n*. (The letter "N"; going through the range, from top to bottom.) The right "N" hand is positioned against the fingertips of the outstretched left palm. It moves down to the base of the left hand.

NORMAL DISTRIBUTION (nôr′ məl dis trə byōō′ shən), *n*. (The typical statistical curve.) Both down-turned "N" hands, held side by side, move apart and down, tracing a curve in the air.

NORWAY (nôr′ wā), *n*. (The letter "N"; the stream-ing of the flag.) The right hand, forming an "N" (or a modified "H") makes a wavy movement across the chest, from left to right.

NOSY (nō′ zī), *(sl.)*, *adj*. (A big nose.) The right index finger, after resting on the tip of the nose, moves forward and then back to the nose, in an oval, as if tracing a long extension of the nose.

NOT 1 (not), *adv*. (Crossing the hands—a negative gesture.) The downturned open hands are crossed. They are drawn apart rather quickly. *Cf.* UN-.

NOT 2, *adv*. The right "A" hand is placed with the tip of the upturned thumb under the chin. The hand draws out and forward in a slight arc.

NOT DONE *phrase*. (Hanging back.) The "5" hand and forearm, hanging loosely and straight down from the elbow, move back and forth under the armpit. *Cf.* LATE, NOT YET, TARDY.

NOTHING 1 (nŭth′ ĭng), *n*. (The zeros.) Both "O" hands, palms facing, are thrown out and down into the "5" position. *Cf.* NAUGHT 1, NONE 1.

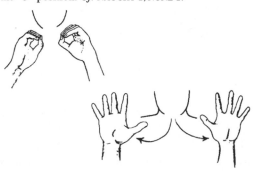

NOTHING 2, *n.* (The zeros.) Both "O" hands, palms facing, move back and forth a number of times, the right hand to the right and the left hand to the left. *Cf.* NAUGHT 2.

NOTICE (nō′ tis), *n.* (Posted on the wall.) The thumbs mime pinning thumbtacks into the wall to hold up a four-cornered sheet of paper.

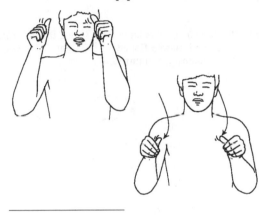

NOTIFY (nō′ tə fī′), *v.*, -FIED, -FYING. (Taking knowledge from the mind and giving it out to all.) The fingertips are positioned on either side of the forehead. Both hands then swing down and out, opening into the upturned "5" position. *Cf.* INFORM, INFORMATION, LET KNOW.

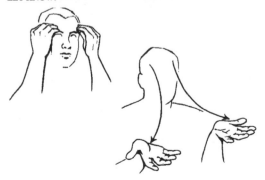

NOT YET *phrase.* (Hanging back.) The "5" hand and forearm, hanging loosely and straight down from the elbow, move back and forth under the armpit. *Cf.* LATE, NOT DONE, TARDY.

NOW (nou), *adv.* (Something right in front of you.) The upturned right-angle hands drop down rather sharply. The "Y" hands may also be used. *Cf.* PRESENT 3.

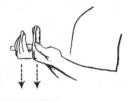

NOW AND THEN *adv. phrase.* (Forward in slow, deliberate movements.) The right hand, palm facing the signer, fingers pointing left, makes a series of small forward movements, describing a small arc each time. *Cf.* FROM TIME TO TIME, ONCE IN A WHILE 2.

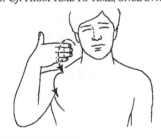

NUCLEAR (noo′ klē ər), *adj.* (The letter "N"; around the world.) The right "N" hand makes a circle around the left "S" hand.

NUDE (nūd, no͞od), *adj.* (Devoid of everything on the surface.) The middle finger of the downturned right "5" hand sweeps over the back of the down-turned left "A" or "S" hand, from wrist to knuckles, and continues beyond a bit. *Cf.* BARE, EMPTY, NAKED, OMISSION, VACANCY, VACANT, VOID.

NUMEROUS (nū' mər əs, no͞o'-), *adj.* (Many fingers are indicated.) The upturned "S" hands are thrown up, opening into the "5" position, palms up. This may be repeated. *Cf.* MANY, MULTIPLE, PLURAL, QUANTITY.

 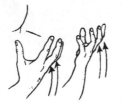

NUN (nŭn), *n.* (The veil.) Both open hands, palms facing the head and fingers pointing up, are moved down along either side of the head, as if tracing the outline of a nun's hood.

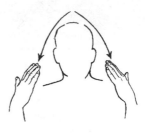

NURSE (nûrs), *n.* (The letter "N"; taking the pulse.) The index and middle fingers of the right "N" hand are placed against the upturned left wrist.

OATH (ōth), *n.* (The arm is raised.) The right index finger is placed at the lips. The right arm is then raised, palm out and elbow resting on the back of the left hand. *Cf.* GUARANTEE, LOYAL, PLEDGE, PROMISE 1, SWEAR 1, SWORN, TAKE OATH, VOW.

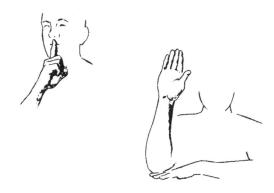

OBEDIENCE (ō bē′ dǐ əns), *n.* (The hands are thrown open as an act of obeisance.) Both "A" hands, palms facing, are positioned at either side of the head. They are thrown open and out, ending in the "5" position, palms up. The head is bowed slightly at the same time. *Cf.* MIND 4, OBEDIENT, OBEY.

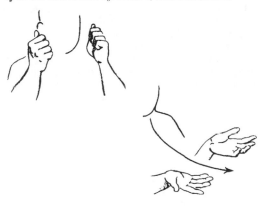

OBEDIENT (ō bē′ dǐ ənt), *adj.* See OBEDIENCE.

OBEY (ō bā′), *v.*, OBEYING, OBEYED. See OBEDIENCE.

OBJECT 1 (ŏb′ jĭkt), *n.* (Something shown in the hand.) The outstretched right hand, palm up and held before the chest, is dropped slightly and brought over a bit to the right. *Cf.* SUBSTANCE 1, THING.

OBJECT 2 (əb jĕkt′), *v.*, -JECTED, -JECTING. (The hand is thrust into the chest to force a complaint out.) The curved fingers of the right hand are thrust forcefully into the chest. *Cf.* COMPLAIN, COMPLAINT, OBJECTION, PROTEST 1.

OBJECTION (əb jĕk′ shən), *n.* See OBJECT 2.

OBJECTIVE (əb jĕk′ tĭv), *n.* (A thought directed upward, toward a goal.) The index finger of the right "D" hand touches the forehead, and then moves up to the index finger of the left "D" hand, which is held above eye level. The two index fingers stop just short of touching. *Cf.* AIM, AMBITION, GOAL, PERSEVERE 4, PURPOSE 2.

OBLIGATION 1 (ŏb′ lə gā′ shən), *n.* (Something which weighs down or burdens one with responsibility.) The fingertips of both hands, placed on the right shoulder, bear down. *Cf.* RELY 1, RESPONSIBILITY 1, RESPONSIBLE 1.

OBLIGATION 2, *n.* (Pointing to the palm, where the money should be placed.) The index finger of one hand is thrust into the upturned palm of the other several times. *Cf.* ARREARS, DEBIT, DEBT, DUE, OWE.

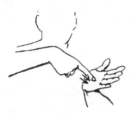

OBNOXIOUS (əb nŏk′ shəs), adj. (Turning the stomach.) The fingertips of the curved right hand describe a continuous circle on the stomach. The signer assumes an exaggerated expression of disgust. *Cf.* DISGUST, DISGUSTED, DISGUSTING, MAKE ME DISGUSTED, MAKE ME SICK, NAUSEA, NAUSEATE, NAUSEOUS, REVOLTING.

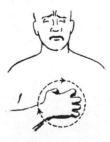

OBSERVE 1 (əb zûrv′), *v.,* -SERVED, -SERVING. (The vision is directed forward.) The tips of the right "V" fingers point to the eyes. The right hand is then swung around and forward a bit. *Cf.* GAZE, LOOK AT, WITNESS.

OBSERVE 2, *v.* (The vision is directed all over.) Both "V" hands, pointing out, are moved alternately in circular directions.

OBSTACLE (ŏb′ stə kəl), *n.* (Obstruct, block.) The left hand, fingers together and palm flat, is held before the body, facing somewhat down. The little finger side of the right hand, held with palm flat, makes one or several up–down chopping motions against the left hand, between its thumb and index finger. *Cf.* ANNOY, ANNOYANCE, BOTHER, DISRUPT, DISTURB, HINDER, HINDRANCE, IMPEDE, INTERCEPT, INTERFERE, INTERFERENCE, INTERFERE WITH, INTERRUPT, MEDDLE 1, OBSTRUCT, PREVENT, PREVENTION.

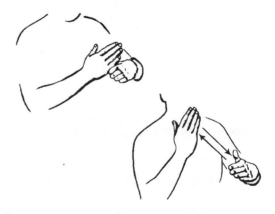

OBSTINATE (ŏb′ stə nĭt), *adj.* (The donkey's broad ear; the animal is traditionally a stubborn one.) The open hand, or the "B" hand, is placed at the side of the head, with palm out and fingers pointing straight up. The hand moves forward and back, pivoting at the wrist, as in the case of a donkey's ears flapping. Both hands may also be used, at either side of the head. *Cf.* DONKEY, MULE, MULISH, STUBBORN.

_____

OBSTRUCT (əb strŭkt′), *v.,* -STRUCTED, -STRUCTING. See OBSTACLE.

_____

OBTAIN (əb tān′), *v.,* -TAINED, -TAINING. (A grasping and bringing forward to oneself.) Both hands, in the "5" position, fingers curved, are crossed at the wrists, with the left palm facing right and the right palm facing left. They are brought in toward the chest, while closing into a grasping "S" position. *Cf.* ACQUIRE, GET, PROCURE, RECEIVE.

_____

OBVIOUS (ŏb′ vĭ əs), *adj.* (Rays of light clearing the way.) Both hands are held at chest height, palms out, all fingertips together. They open into the "5" position in unison, the right hand moving toward the right and the left toward the left. The palms of both

hands remain facing out. *Cf.* BRIGHT 1, BRILLIANCE 1, BRILLIANT 2, CLEAR, EVIDENT, EXPLICIT 2, PLAIN 1.

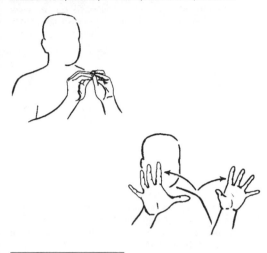

_____

OCCASIONAL (ə kā′ zhən əl), *adj.* (The "1" finger is brought up very slowly.) The right index finger, resting in the open left palm, which is facing right, swings up slowly from its position to one in which it is pointing straight up. The movement is repeated slowly, after a pause. *Cf.* OCCASIONALLY, ONCE IN A WHILE 1, SELDOM, SOMETIME(S).

_____

OCCASIONALLY (ə kā′ zhən ə lĭ), *adv.* See OCCASIONAL.

_____

OCCUPATION (ŏk′ yə pā′ shən), *n.* (Striking an anvil.) Both "S" hands are held palms down. The right hand strikes against the back of the left a number of times. *Cf.* JOB, LABOR, TASK, TOIL, TRAVAIL, VOCATION, WORK.

OCCUR (ə kûr'), *v.*, -CURRED, -CURRING. (A befalling.) Both "D" hands, index fingers pointing away from the body, are simultaneously pivoted over so that the palms face down. *Cf.* COINCIDE, COINCIDENCE, EVENT, HAPPEN 1, INCIDENT, OPPORTUNITY 4.

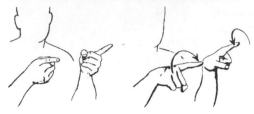

OCTOPUS (ok' tə pəs), *n.* (The shape and swimming motion.) The left downturned cupped hand rests on the back of the downturned right hand. The right hand makes a series of undulating up-down motions, with fingers wriggling all the time.

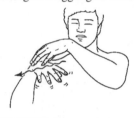

ODD (ŏd), *adj.* (Something which distorts the vision.) The "C" hand describes a small arc in front of the face. *Cf.* CURIOUS 2, GROTESQUE, PECULIAR, QUEER, STRANGE, WEIRD.

ODOR (ō' dər), *n.* (Bringing something up to the nose.) The upturned right hand moves slowly up to and past the nose, and the signer breathes in as the hand sweeps by. *Cf.* FRAGRANT, SCENT, SMELL.

OFF (ôf), *adv., prep.* The fingers of the downturned, open right hand rest on the back of the fingers of the downturned, open left hand. Then the right hand moves up and forward, turning so that its palm faces the body.

OFFER (ôf' ər), *v.*, -FERED, -FERING. (An offering; a presenting.) Both hands, slightly cupped, palms up, are held close to the chest. They move up and out in unison, describing a very slight arc. *Cf.* MOTION, OFFERING, PRESENT 1, PROPOSE, SUGGEST.

OFFERING (ôf' ər ĭng), *n.* See OFFER.

OFFICER (ôf' ə sər, ôf' ə-), *n.* (The epaulets.) The fingertips of the downturned right "5" hand strike the right shoulder twice. *Cf.* CAPTAIN.

OFF THE SUBJECT *phrase.* (Deviating.) The left index finger is held either straight up or pointing forward. The right index finger moves sharply off to the left, striking the left index finger as it does.

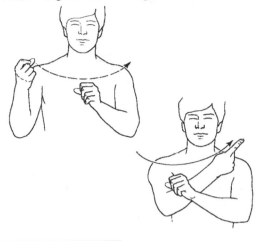

OFTEN (ôf′ ən, ŏf′ ən), *adv.* The left hand, open in the "5" position, palm up, is held before the chest. The right hand, in the right-angle position, fingers pointing up, arches over and into the left palm. This is repeated several times. *Cf.* FREQUENT.

OH! (ō), *interj.* (A fingerspelled loan sign.) The signer, assuming an expression of surprise or sudden understanding, fingerspells "O-H" in a slow and deliberate manner, throwing the hand out for the "H."

OIL 1 (oil), *(colloq.), v.,* OILED, OILING. (The oil can.) The curved right "V" fingers grasp the crown of an imaginary oil can, and the right thumb moves in and out repeatedly, as if pressing the bottom of the can.

OIL 2, *n.* (The drippings from a fleshy, *i.e.,* animal, substance. Used, however, to indicate both organic and inorganic types of oil.) The right thumb and middle finger grasp the fleshy part of the open left hand. The right hand moves straight down. This is repeated once or twice. *Cf.* FAT 2, FATTY, GRAVY, GREASE, GREASY, OILY.

OILY (oi′ lĭ), *adj.* See OIL 2.

OINTMENT (oint′ mənt), *n.* (Rubbing on the skin.) The signer mimes taking a dab of ointment from a jar and rubbing it on the back of the hand.

O.K. 1 (ō′ kā′), *adj., adv.* (A straightening out.) The right hand, fingers together and palm facing left, is placed in the upturned left palm, whose fingers point away from the body. The right hand slides straight out along the left palm, over the left fingers, and stops with its heel resting on the left fingertips. *Cf.* ALL RIGHT, PRIVILEGE, RIGHT 1, RIGHTEOUS, YOU'RE WELCOME 2.

O.K. 2 (*adj., adv.* ŏ´ kā´; *v., n.* ŏ´ kā´), *(colloq.),* *phrase.* The letters "O" and "K" are fingerspelled.

OLD (ōld), *adj.* (The beard of an old man.) The right hand grasps an imaginary beard at the chin and pulls it downward. *Cf.* AGE.

OLYMPICS (ō lĭm´ pĭkz), *n.* (The interlocking circles of the Olympic logo.) The thumbs and index fingers of both hands interlock several times.

OMISSION (ō mĭsh´ ən), *n.* (Devoid of everything on the surface.) The middle finger of the downturned right "5" hand sweeps over the back of the down

turned left "A" or "S" hand, from wrist to knuckles, and continues beyond a bit. *Cf.* BARE, EMPTY, NAKED, NUDE, VACANCY, VACANT, VOID.

ON (ŏn, ôn), *prep.* (Placing one hand on the other.) The right hand is placed on the back of the downturned left hand.

ONCE (wŭns), *adv.* (The "1" finger jumps up.) The right index finger (the "1" finger) touches the left palm, which is facing right. It is then brought up sharply, so that it points straight up.

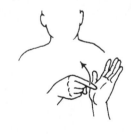

ONCE IN A WHILE 1, *adv. phrase.* (The "1" finger is brought up very slowly.) The right index finger, resting in the open left palm, which is facing right, swings up slowly from its position to one in which it is pointing straight up. The movement is repeated slowly, after a pause. *Cf.* OCCASIONAL, OCCASIONALLY, SELDOM, SOMETIME(S).

ONCE IN A WHILE 2, *phrase.* (Forward in slow, deliberate movements.) The right hand, palm facing the signer, fingers pointing left, makes a series of small forward movements, describing a small arc each time. *Cf.* FROM TIME TO TIME, NOW AND THEN.

ONCE UPON A TIME *adv. phrase.* (Something past, behind.) The upraised right hand, in the "5" position with palm facing the body, is held just above the right shoulder and is thrown back over it. *Cf.* AGO, FORMERLY, PAST, PREVIOUS, PREVIOUSLY, WAS, WERE.

ONE ANOTHER *pron. phrase.* (Mingling with.) Both hands are held in modified "A" positions, thumbs out. The left hand is positioned with its thumb pointing straight up, and the right hand, with its thumb pointing down, revolves above the left thumb in a clockwise direction. *Cf.* ASSOCIATE, EACH OTHER, FELLOWSHIP, MINGLE 2, MUTUAL.

ONE MORE *colloq. phrase.* (One finger beckons.) The right hand is held palm up, with the index finger making very small and rapid beckoning movements.

ONE-TO-ONE *phrase.* (The natural sign.) The "D" hands, palms facing, are brought together a number of times.

ONION 1 (ŭn′ yən), *n.* (The rubbing of the eye, which is irritated by the onion.) The knuckle of the right "X" finger is placed just beside the right eye. The right hand pivots back and forth at the wrist.

ONION 2, *n.* (Same rationale as in ONION 1.) The knuckles of the right "S" hand, positioned as in ONION 1, execute the same pivoting movement.

ONLY (ōn′ lĭ), *adv.* (One, wandering around in a circle.) The index finger, pointing straight up, palm facing the body (the number *one*), is rotated before the face in a counterclockwise direction. *Cf.* ALONE, LONE, SOLE.

ONLY ONE *phrase.* (Emphasizing the "1" finger.) The "1" hand, palm out, swings around emphatically, moving slightly upward at the same time.

ON THE CONTRARY 1, *adv. phrase.* (A divergence or a difference; the opposite of same.) The index fingers of both "D" hands, palms facing down, are crossed near their tips. The hands are drawn apart. *Cf.* BUT, HOWEVER 1.

ON THE CONTRARY 2, *adv. phrase.* (Opposites.) With index fingertips touching initially, both hands move away from each other.

ON TO (tōō), *phrase.* (Adding on.) The index and middle fingers of the right "H" hand, palm up, are swung up and over until they come to rest on the index and middle fingers of the left "H" hand, held palm down. *Cf.* ADD 3, ADDITION, GAIN 1, INCREASE, RAISE 2.

OPEN 1 (ō′ pən), *adj., v.,* opened, opening. (The natural sign.) The "B" hands, palms out, are held with index finger edges touching. They swing apart so that the palms now face each other.

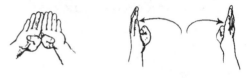

OPEN 2, *adj., v.* (The natural sign.) Here the "B" hands move straight apart, with palms still facing out. See OPEN 1.

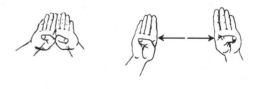

OPEN 3, *v.* (Opening a jar.) The signer mimes struggling with and then opening a jar.

OPEN-EYED (ō′ pən ĭd′), *(colloq.), adj.* (The eyes pop open.) The "S" hands, palms facing each other, are held before the eyes. They suddenly open into the "C" position, with the eyes wide open. *Cf.* SHOCKED 2, SURPRISED.

OPEN-MOUTHED (ō′ pən mouŧhd′, -mouŧht′), *(colloq.), adj.* (The mouth drops open.) The fingertips of both "V" hands are held curved and touching before the body, one hand above the other. Then the hands are suddenly drawn apart, and at the same instant the mouth drops open and the eyes open wide. *Cf.* DUMB-FOUNDED 2, SPEECHLESS, SURPRISE 2.

OPEN THE DOOR *v. phrase.* (The opening and closing of the door.) The "B" hands, palms out and edges touching, are drawn apart and then come together again. *Cf.* DOOR, DOORWAY.

OPEN THE WINDOW *phrase.* (The opening of the window.) With both palms facing the body, the little finger edge of the right hand rests atop the index finger edge of the left hand. The right hand then moves straight up. *Cf.* WINDOW.

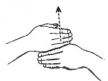

OPERA 1 (op′ ər ə), *n.* (The rhythmic movement.) The right "5" hand, palm facing left, is waved back and forth over the downturned left hand. The mouth may be held open in song. *Cf.* SING, SONG.

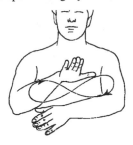

OPERA 2, *n.* (A variation of OPERA 1, above.) The letter "O" is substituted for the "5."

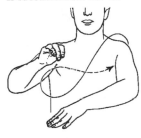

OPERATE (ŏp′ ə rāt′), *v.,* -ATED, -ATING. (Holding the reins over all.) The "A" hands, palms facing, move alternately back and forth, as if grasping and manipulating reins. The left "A" hand, still in position, swings over so that its palm now faces down. The right hand opens to the "5" position, palm down, and swings over the left, which moves slightly to the right. *Cf.* CONTROL 1, DIRECT 1, GOVERN, MANAGE, MANAGEMENT, MANAGER, REGULATE, REIGN, RULE 1.

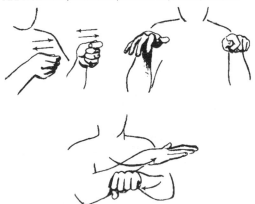

OPERATION 1 (ŏp′ ə rā′ shən), *n.* (The action of the scalpel.) The thumb of the right "A" hand is drawn straight down across the upright left palm. *Cf.* SURGERY.

OPERATION 2, *n.* (The action of a scalpel.) The thumbtip of the right "A" hand, palm facing down, moves a short distance across the lower chest or stomach region.

OPINION (ə pǐn′ yən), *n.* (The "O" hand, circling in the head.) The right "O" hand circles before the forehead several times.

OPPONENT (ə pǒ′ nənt), *n.* (At sword's point.) The two index fingers, after pointing to each other, are drawn sharply apart. This is followed by the sign for INDIVIDUAL: both open hands, palms facing each other, move down the sides of the body, tracing its outline to the hips. *Cf.* ENEMY, FOE, RIVAL 1.

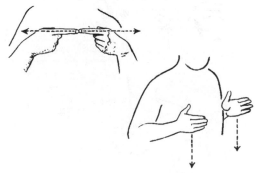

OPPORTUNITY 1 (ŏp′ ər tū′ nə tǐ), *n.* Both hands, slightly cupped, palms up, are held close to the chest. They move up and out in unison, describing an arc.

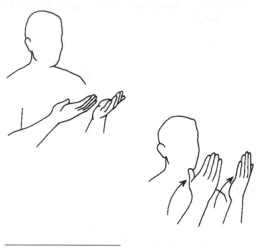

OPPORTUNITY 2, *n.* (Two individuals pitted against each other.) The hands are held in the "A" position, thumbs pointing straight up, palms facing the body. They come together forcefully, moving down a bit as they do, and the knuckles of one hand strike those of the other. *Cf.* CHALLENGE, GAME, VERSUS.

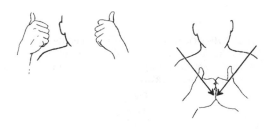

OPPORTUNITY 3, *n.* (The movement.) Both hands, palms facing and fingers together and extended straight out, move in unison away from the body, in a straight or winding manner. *Cf.* CORRIDOR, HALL, HALLWAY, MANNER 2, METHOD, PATH, ROAD, STREET, TRAIL, WAY 1.

OPPORTUNITY 4, *n.* (A befalling.) Both "D" hands, index fingers pointing away from the body, are simultaneously pivoted over so that the palms face down. *Cf.* COINCIDE, COINCIDENCE, EVENT, HAPPEN 1, INCIDENT, OCCUR.

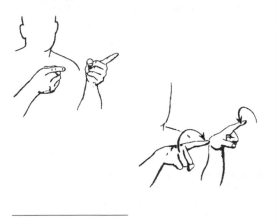

OPPORTUNITY 5, *n.* (The letters "O" and "P"; pushing through.) Both "O" hands are held palms down, side by side. They swing up a bit as they assume the "P" position.

OPPOSE (ə′ pōz), *v.*, OPPOSED, OPPOSING. (Opposed to; restraint.) The tips of the right fingers, held together, are thrust purposefully into the open left palm, whose fingers are also together and pointing forward. *Cf.* AGAINST.

OPPOSITE (ŏp′ ə zĭt), *adj., n.* (Separateness.) The tips of the extended index fingers touch before the chest, the right finger pointing left and the left finger pointing right. The fingers then draw apart sharply to either side. *Cf.* CONTRAST, REVERSE.

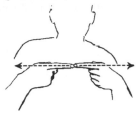

OR (ôr; *unstressed* ər), *conj.* (Considering one thing against another.) The "A" hands, palms facing and thumbs pointing straight up, move alternately up and down before the chest. *Cf.* EITHER 3, WHETHER, WHICH.

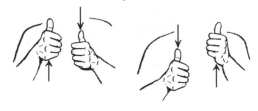

ORAL (ōr′ əl), *adj.* (Reading the lips—the lines of vision, represented by the two fingers, scan the lips.) The right "V" hand, palm facing the body, is placed in front of the face, with slightly curved index and middle fingers directly in front of the lips. The right hand moves in a small counterclockwise circle around the lips. *Cf.* LIPREADING, READ LIPS, SPEECHREADING.

ORANGE 1 (ôr′ ĭnj, ŏr′-), *n., adj.* (The action of squeezing an orange to get its juice into the mouth.) The right "C" hand is held at the mouth. It opens and closes deliberately, as if squeezing an orange.

ORANGE 2, *n.* (The peeling of the fruit.) The thumbtip of the right "Y" hand moves over the back of the left "S" hand, which is held palm down or palm facing the body.

ORANGE 3, *n., adj.* Both "Y" hands are held before the body, palms facing each other. In this position the hands alternate in drawing imaginary circles in the air with the little fingers. This sign is used for both the color and the fruit.

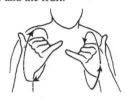

ORATE (ō rāt′, ōr′ āt), *v.*, ORATED, ORATING. (A gesture of an orator.) The right open hand, palm facing left, is held above and to the right of the head. It pivots on the wrist, forward and backward, several times. *Cf.* LECTURE, SPEECH 2, TALK 2, TESTIMONY 1.

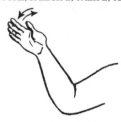

ORATOR (ôr′ ə tər, ŏr′-), *n.* (The characteristic waving of the speaker's hand as he makes his point.) The sign for ORATE is made. This is followed by the sign for INDIVIDUAL: both open hands, palms facing each other, move down the sides of the body, tracing its outline to the hips. *Cf.* SPEAKER.

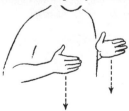

ORBIT (ôr′ bĭt), n., v., -BITED, -BITING. (Encircling the planet.) The left hand, in the "S" position, knuckles facing right, is encircled by the right index finger, which travels in a clockwise direction. It makes one revolution and comes to rest atop the left hand. *Cf.* ALL YEAR, ALL YEAR 'ROUND, AROUND THE WORLD.

ORDER 1 (ôr′ dər), *n., v.,* -DERED, -DERING. (An issuance from the mouth.) The tip of the index finger of the "D" hand, palm facing the body, is placed at the closed lips. It moves around and out, rather forcefully. *Cf.* COMMAND, DIRECT 2.

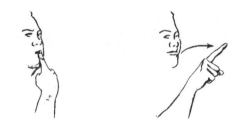

ORDER 2, *(rare), n.* (Something you write and give to someone.) The sign for WRITE is made: the right index finger and thumb, grasping an imaginary pen, write across the open left palm. This is followed by the sign for GIVE: both hands are held palms down, about a foot apart, thumbs resting on fingertips. The hands are extended forward in a slight arc, opening to the "5" position as they do.

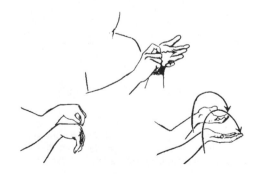

ORDER 3, *n., v.* (Placing things in order.) The hands, palms facing, fingers together and pointing away from the body, are positioned at the left side and held about a foot apart. With a slight up-down motion, as if describing waves, the hands travel in unison from left to right. *Cf.* ARRANGE, ARRANGEMENT, PLAN 1, PREPARE 1, PROGRAM 1, PROVIDE 1, PUT IN ORDER, READY 1.

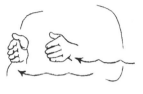

ORDERLY (ôr′ dər li), *adj.* (In order, *i.e.,* equally spaced or arranged.) Both open hands, palms facing each other and fingers pointing away from the body, move in unison, in a series of short arcs, from left to right. This is essentially the same as ORDER 3.

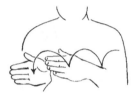

ORGANIZATION 1 (ôr′ gən ə zā′ shən), *n.* (A grouping together.) Both "C" hands, palms facing, are held a few inches apart at chest height. They are swung around in unison, so that the palms now face the body. *Cf.* ASSOCIATION, CIRCLE 2, CLASS, CLASSED, CLUB, COMPANY 1, GANG, GROUP 1.

ORGANIZATION 2, *n.* (The letter "O"; a group or class.) Both "O" hands are held with palms facing out and thumb edges touching. The hands swing apart, around, and come together again with little finger edges touching.

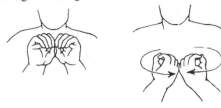

ORIGIN (ôr′ ə jĭn, ŏr′-), *n.* (Turning a key to open up a new venture.) The right index finger, resting between the left index and middle fingers, executes a half turn, once or twice. *Cf.* BEGIN, COMMENCE, START.

ORPHAN (ôr′ fən), *n.* (The letter "O"; female and male.) The right "O" hand is placed first at the chin and then at the temple.

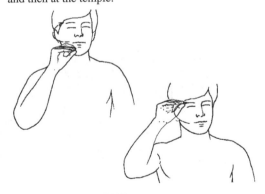

ORTHODOX 1 (ôr′ thə doks), *adj.* (Adhering to a strict and straight line.) The right index and thumb, forming an "F," move forward along the upturned left palm.

ORTHODOX 2, *adj.* (The *pais,* or sidecurls, worn by ultra-orthodox Jewish males.) The signer twirls an imaginary curl hanging down the side of the head. *Cf.* HASIDIC.

OSAKA (ō′ sä kä), *n.* The right "U" hand, palm facing out, is placed at the forehead, like a salute. It moves very slightly back and forth. A native sign.

OTHER (ŭth′ ər), *adj.* (Moving over to another position.) The right "A" hand, thumb up, is pivoted from the wrist and swung over to the right, so that the thumb now points to the right. *Cf.* ANOTHER, ELSE.

OUGHT TO (ôt), *aux. v.* (Being pinned down.) The right hand, in the "X" position, palm down, moves forcefully up and down once or twice. An expression of determination is frequently assumed. *Cf.* HAVE TO, MUST, NECESSARY 1, NECESSITY, NEED 1, SHOULD, VITAL 2.

OUR (our), *pron.* (An encompassing, including oneself and others.) The right hand, palm facing left, is placed at the right shoulder. It swings around to the left shoulder, its palm now facing right.

OURSELVES (our sĕlvz′), *pron. pl.* (An encompassing; the thumb representing *self, i.e.,* oneness.) The right "A" hand, thumb held straight up, is placed at the right shoulder. It executes the same movement as in OUR.

OUT (out), *adv.* (The natural motion of withdrawing, *i.e.,* taking *out,* of the hand.) The downturned open right hand, grasped loosely by the left, is drawn up and out of the left hand's grasp. As it does so, the fingers come together with the thumb. The left hand, meanwhile, closes into the "O" position, palm facing right.

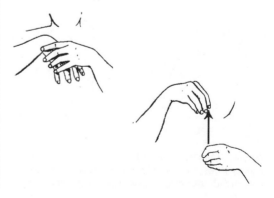

OUTFIT (out' fit), *n.* (Matching top and bottom.) The thumb of the right "Y" hand is placed at midchest, and then the hand travels down so that the little finger of the same "Y" hand touches the trousers or skirt.

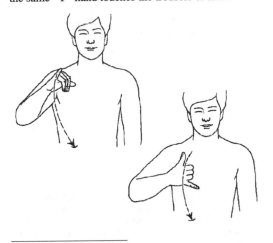

OVEN (ŭv' ən), *n.* (Placing the bread in the oven.) The upturned right "B" hand, representing the bread, is thrust slowly forward under the downturned left hand, representing the oven. *Cf.* BAKE.

OVER (ō' vər), *prep.* (A crossing over.) The left hand is held before the chest, palm down and fingers together. The right hand, fingers together, glides over the left, with the right little finger touching the top of the left hand. *Cf.* ACROSS, CROSS 3.

OVER AGAIN *phrase.* (Turning over a new leaf.) The left hand, in the "5" position, palm up, is held before the chest. The right hand, in the right-angle position, fingers pointing up, arches up and over into the left palm.

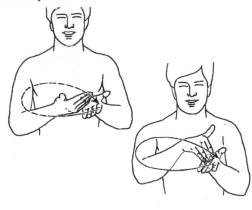

OVERALLS (ō' vər ôlz), *n.* (The clips at the shoulders, holding up the garment.) Both hands are positioned with index and middle fingers and thumbs all pointing down. The hands trace a pair of imaginary suspenders up along the chest, and the fingers close against their respective thumbs.

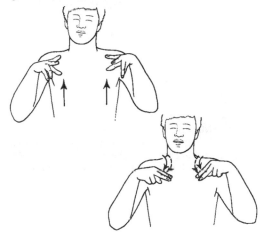

OVERCOME (ō' vər kŭm'), *v.,* -CAME, -COME, -COMING. (Forcing the head into a bowed position.) The right "S" hand, placed across the left "S" hand, placed across the left "S" hand, moves over and down a bit. *Cf.* BEAT 2, CONQUER, DEFEAT, SUBDUE.

OVERHEAD PROJECTOR *n.* (Projecting something behind a speaker.) The right hand, thumb resting against all the other fingers, moves over the right shoulder, as all fingers open into the "5" position.

OVER MY HEAD *sl. phrase.* Both index fingers flick out as the "S" hands, palms facing backwards, are thrown over the head.

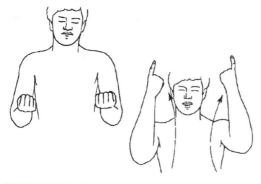

OVERSPEND (ō vər spend'), *v.* (Throwing money randomly into the air.) Both hands, closed into fists, palms facing the chest, move alternately up into the air, index fingers flicking out. *Cf.* SPEND 2, SQUANDER 2.

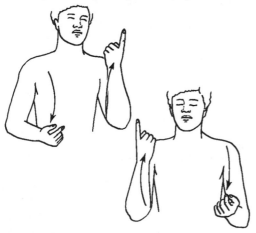

OVERWHELMED (ō vər hwelmd'), *adj.* (Over one's head.) Both downturned hands, fingers pointing back, move backwards over the head.

OWE (ō), *v.*, OWED, OWING. (Pointing where the money should be placed.) The index finger of one hand is thrust into the upturned palm of the other several times. *Cf.* ARREARS, DEBIT, DEBT, DUE, OBLIGATION 2.

OWN (ōn), *v., adj.* (Holding something to oneself.) The downturned right hand, fingers open, is brought up to the chest, where the fingers come together.

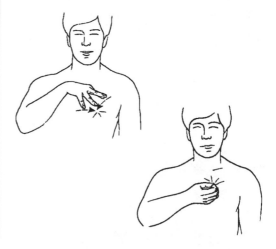

OXYGEN (ok′ sə jin), *n.* (The symbol for oxygen.) The signer fingerspells "O-2," dropping the hand a bit for the "2."

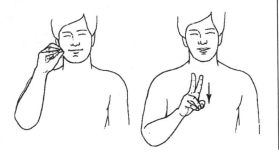

OYSTER (ois′ tər), *n.* (The shucking movement.) The upturned right open hand's little finger edge is wedged between the downturned left thumb and index. The right hand rocks back and forth, attempting to gain entry into the shell.

P

PACKAGE (păk' ĭj), *n., v.,* -AGED, -AGING. (The dimensions are indicated.) The open hands, palms facing and fingers pointing out, are dropped an inch or two simultaneously. They then shift their relative positions so that both palms face the body, with one hand in front of the other. In this new position they again drop an inch or two simultaneously. *Cf.* BOX 1, ROOM 1, SQUARE, TRUNK.

PAGE (pāj), *n.* (Thumbing through pages.) The downturned right thumb "digs" into the upturned left palm a number of times. *Cf.* LOOK UP.

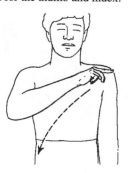

PAGEANT (paj' ənt), *n.* (The sash worn by a contestant.) The curved thumb and index finger of the right hand trace an imaginary ribbon from the left shoulder to the right side of the waist. The letter "P" may be substituted for the thumb and index.

PAIL (pāl), *n.* (The shape and grasping the handle.) The left hand holds an imaginary pail. The right index finger describes a downturned arc as it moves from the left wrist to the elbow.

PAIN (pān), *n.* (A stabbing pain.) The "D" hands, index fingers pointing to each other, are rotated in elliptical fashion before the chest—simultaneously but in opposite directions. *Cf.* ACHE, HARM 1, HURT 1, INJURE 1, INJURY, SIN, WOUND.

PAINT 1 (pānt), *n., v.,* PAINTED, PAINTING. (The action of the brush.) The hands are held open with palms facing each other. The right hand, representing a wide brush, sweeps back and forth over the left palm, as if spreading paint on it. (This sign is used in the sense of painting a large area such as a wall.)

PAINT 2, *n., v.* (The action of a small brush.) The tips of the fingers of the right "H" hand are swept back and forth repeatedly over the left palm, as if spreading paint on it with a small or narrow brush. (This sign is used in reference to fine art painting.)

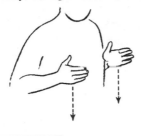

PAINTER 1 (pān' tər), *n.* The sign for PAINT 1 is made, followed by the sign for INDIVIDUAL: both open hands, palms facing each other, move down the sides of the body, tracing its outline to the hips.

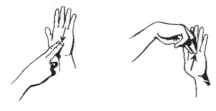

PAINTER 2, *n.* The sign for PAINT 2 is made, followed by the sign for INDIVIDUAL, as in PAINTER 1.

PAJAMAS (pə jä' məz), *n.* (A fingerspelled loan sign.) The signer fingerspells "P-J."

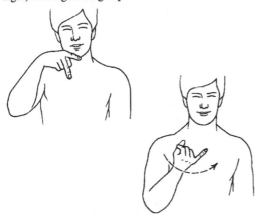

PAL (pal), *n.* The right index finger and thumb form a "C." The right thumbtip moves across the chin, from left to right.

PALACE (pal' is), *n.* (The elaborate roofline.) The downturned "P" hands trace an elaborate roofline, moving in stages down and apart.

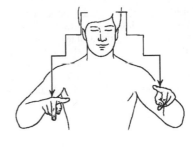

PALE (pāl) *adj., v.,* PALED, PALING. The sign for WHITE is made: the fingertips of the "5" hand are placed against the chest. The hand moves straight out from the chest, while the fingers and thumb all come together. Then both hands, fingers spread, rise up and over the cheeks.

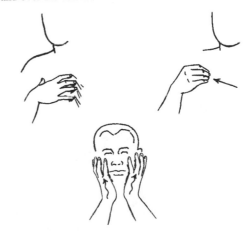

PALERMO (pä ler′ mō), *n.* (Stealing something.) The downturned right "3" or claw-shaped hand, held near the right hip, swivels twice in a clockwise manner, as if picking up something surreptitiously. This sign is highly derogatory, for it implies that all natives of this city are thieves. It should not normally be used. *Cf.* SICILY.

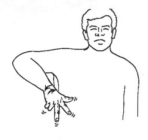

PAMPHLET (pam′ flit), *n.* (A book with a narrow spine.) The left hand, fingers together, is held upright, palm facing right. The right hand wraps around the lower edge of the left and travels up to the little finger. This denotes a narrow object. The sign for BOOK is then made: the hands are placed together, palm to palm, and then opened, as if opening a book. Sometimes this latter sign is omitted. *Cf.* BOOKLET, MAGAZINE, MANUAL.

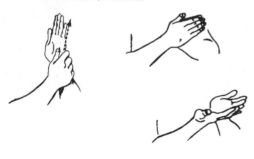

PAN (pan), *n.* (Manipulating the handle.) The signer grasps the handle of an imaginary pan and moves it forward and back quickly a number of times.

PANAMA (pan′ ə mä), *n.* (The letter "P"; the crossing of the canal.) The right "P" hand crosses over the back of the loosely held downturned left hand.

PANCAKE (pǎn′ kāk′), *n.* (Turning over a pancake.) The open right hand rests on the upturned left palm. The right hand flips over and comes to rest with its back on the left palm. This is the action of turning over a pancake.

PANDA (pan′ də), *n.* (The letter "P"; emphasizing the panda's markings.) The right "P" hand makes a counterclockwise circle around the face.

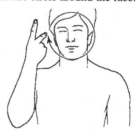

PANTIES (pan′ tēz), *n.* (The elastic waist.) Grasping an imaginary waistline, the signer mimes stretching it open and closed.

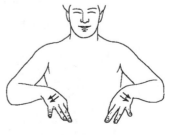

PANTS (pănts), *n. pl.* (The natural sign.) The open hands are drawn up along the thighs, starting at the knees.

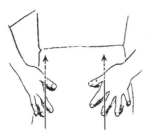

PAPA (pä′ pə), *n.* (Derived from the formal sign for FATHER 1, *q.v.*) The thumbtip of the right "5" hand touches the right temple a number of times. The other fingers may also wiggle. *Cf.* DAD, DADDY, FATHER 2, POP 2.

PAPER (pä′ pər), *n.* (The action of the press.) The right "5" hand, held palm down, fingers pointing left, is brought down twice against the upturned left "5" hand, whose fingers point right. *Cf.* NEWSPAPER, PUBLISH.

PAPER BAG (pä′ pər bag), *n.* (The material and the shape.) The sign for PAPER: the heels of both hands come together several times. The signer next traces the bottom and sides of a paper bag, using

the "C" hands, palms facing.

PAPER CLIP (pä′ pər klip), *n.* (Affixing the clip.) Using the downturned right index finger and thumb, the signer slides an imaginary paper clip over the fingers of the left hand.

PARADE (pə rād′), *n., v.,* -RADED, -RADING. (A column of marchers, one behind the other.) The downturned open hands, fingers pointing down, are held one behind the other. Pivoted from the wrists, they move rhythmically forward and back in unison. *Cf.* MARCH.

PARALLELOGRAM (par ə lel′ ə gram), *n.* With the left hand in the "P" position and the right in the "R" position, the signer traces a rectangle in the air.

PARANOID (par ə noid'), *adj.* (The letter "P"; picking at the mind.) The middle finger of the right "P" hand scratches repeatedly against the right temple.

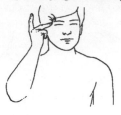

PARASITE (par' ə sīt), *n.* (Attaching to something and tugging on it.) The extended right thumb, index, and middle fingers grasp the extended left index and middle fingers. In this position the right hand pulls at the left several times.

PARDON (pär' dən), *n.* (A wiped-off and cleaned slate.) The right hand wipes off the left palm several times. *Cf.* APOLOGIZE 2, APOLOGY 2, EXCUSE, FORGIVE, PAROLE.

PARENTS 1 (pâr' əntz), *n.* (Mother and father.) Using the right "5" hand, the right thumbtip first touches the right side of the chin, then moves up to touch the right temple.

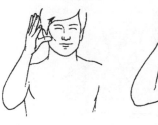 

PARENTS 2, *n.* Same as for PARENTS 1 above, but the letter "P" is used.

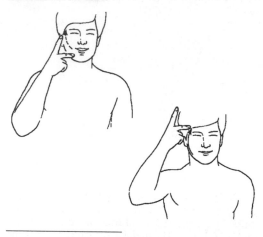

PARK (pärk), *arch., loc.* (The windows in the head of the Statue of Liberty.) The curved fingers of the right hand repeatedly touch the forehead as the hand moves from left to right. This sign was once popular with New York deaf children since a class outing to the Statue of Liberty was considered a treat, on a par with a visit to the local park or zoo.

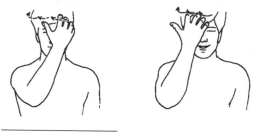

PARLIAMENT (pär' lə mənt), *n.* (The letter "P"; the Roman toga fastened at the shoulders.) The right "P" hand moves from left shoulder to right.

PAROLE (pə rōl'), *n., v.,* -ROLED, -ROLING. See PARDON.

PARROT (par' ət), *n.* (The curved beak.) The curved index finger moves away from and down from the nose.

PART 1 (pärt), *n., adj.* (Cutting off or designating a part.) The little finger edge of the open right hand moves straight down the middle of the upturned left palm. *Cf.* PIECE, PORTION, SECTION, SHARE 1, SOME.

PART 2, *n., adj.* (Separating to classify.) Both hands, in the right angle position, are placed palms down before the body, knuckles to knuckles. They pull apart or separate, once or a number of times. *Cf.* SEPARATE 2.

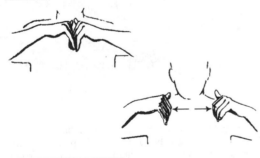

PART 3, *n., adj.* (The hands are moved apart.) Both hands, in the "A" position, thumbs up, are held together, with knuckles touching. With a deliberate movement they come apart. *Cf.* APART, DIVORCE 1, SEPARATE 1.

PART FROM *v. phrase.* (An unlocking.) With thumbs and index fingers interlocked initially (the links of a chain), the hands draw apart, showing the break in the chain. *Cf.* DETACH, DISCONNECT.

PARTICIPATE (pär tĭs' ə pāt'), *v.,* -PATED, -PATING. (Joining together.) Both hands, held in the modified "5" position, palms out, move toward each other. The thumbs and index fingers of both hands then connect. *Cf.* AFFILIATE, ANNEX, ATTACH, BELONG, CONNECT, ENLIST, ENROLL, JOIN, UNITE.

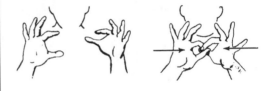

PARTNER (pärt' nər), *n.* (Sharing.) The little finger edge of the right hand sweeps back and forth over the index finger edge of the left hand. This is followed by the sign for INDIVIDUAL.

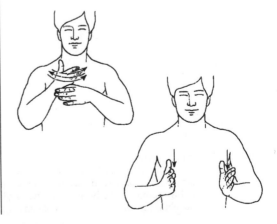

PARTY 1 (pär' tǐ), *n.* (The swinging of tambourines.) Both open hands, held somewhat above the head, are pivoted back and forth repeatedly, as if swinging a pair of tambourines.

PARTY 2, *n.* (The rhythmic swaying of the feet.) The downturned index and middle fingers of the right "V" hand swing rhythmically back and forth over the upturned left palm. *Cf.* DANCE.

PASS (păs), *v.,* PASSED, PASSING. (One hand passes the other.) Both "A" hands, palms facing each other, are held before the body, the right behind the left. The right hand moves forward, its knuckles brushing those of the left, and continues forward a bit beyond the left.

PASS BY (păs bī), *v. phrase.* (The fingers pass each other.) The right "D" hand, palm facing away from the body, moves forward a bit. At the same time the left "D" hand, palm facing the body, moves toward the body a bit. The action involves both hands passing

each other as they move in opposite directions.

PASSION (păsh' ən), *n.* (The alimentary canal—the area of hunger and hunger gratification—is indicated.) The fingertips of the right "C" hand move slowly and deliberately down the middle of the chest once or twice. The eyes are usually narrowed and the teeth clenched.

PASSOVER (pas' ō vər), *n.* (The letter "P"; passing over.) The right "P" hand passes over the downturned left hand.

PAST (păst), *adj., n., adv.* (Something past, behind.) The upraised right hand, in the "5" position with palm facing the body, is held just above the right shoulder and is thrown back over it. *Cf.* AGO, FORMERLY, ONCE UPON A TIME, PREVIOUS, PREVIOUSLY, WAS, WERE.

PASTE (pāst), *n., v.* (Spreading the paste.) The downturned "H" hand spreads the paste over the thumb and index fingers of the left fist or "O" hand.

PASTOR (păs′ tər), *n.* (Placing morsels of wisdom, or food for thought, into the mind.) The right hand, palm out, with thumb and index finger touching, is moved forward and slightly downward a number of times from its initial position near the right temple. This is followed by the sign for INDIVIDUAL: both open hands, palms facing each other, move down the sides of the body, tracing its outline to the hips. *Cf.* MINISTER, PREACHER.

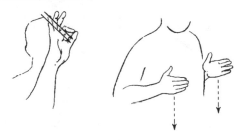

PAT (pat), *n., v.* (The natural sign.) The signer's right hand pats the left shoulder several times.

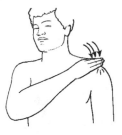

PATH (păth), *n.* (The winding movement.) Both hands, palms facing and fingers together and extended straight out, move in unison away from the body,

in a winding manner. *Cf.* CORRIDOR, HALL, HALLWAY, MANNER 2, METHOD, OPPORTUNITY 3, ROAD, STREET, TRAIL, WAY 1.

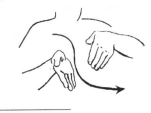

PATIENCE (pā′ shəns), *n.* The thumb of the right "A" hand is drawn down across the lips. This is frequently followed by the sign for SUFFER 1: both "S" hands, tightly clenched, revolve about each other, slowly and deliberately, while a pained expression is worn. *Cf.* PATIENT 1.

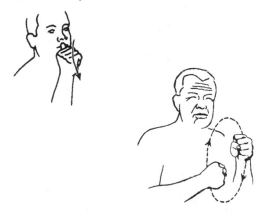

PATIENT 1 (pā′ shənt), *n.* See PATIENCE.

PATIENT 2, *n.* (The letter "P"; the red cross on the hospital gown's sleeve.) The thumb and middle fingers of the right "P" hand trace a small cross on the upper left arm.

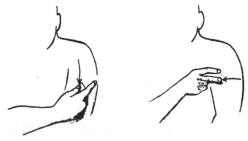

PATRONIZE (pā′ trən īz), v. (Offering unwanted sympathy.) The middle fingers of both "5" hands move forward in small circles together. The signer's expression is one of condescension. This sign indicates patronizing someone. To be patronized, the hands swing around so that the middle fingers point to the signer. The same expression is used.

PAY 1 (pā), v., PAID, PAYING. (Giving forth of money.) The right index finger, resting in the upturned left palm, swings forward and up a bit.

PAY 2 v. (Peeling off a bill.) The right hand, grasping several imaginary bills, "peels off" one as it moves forward.

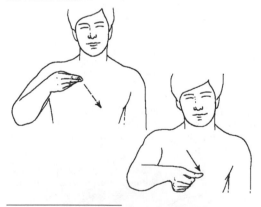

PAY ATTENTION (TO) v. phrase. (Directing one's attention forward; applying oneself; concentrating.) Both hands, fingers pointing up and together, are held at the sides of the face. They move straight out from the face. Cf. ATTEND (TO), ATTENTION, CONCEN-TRATE, CONCENTRATION, FOCUS, GIVE ATTENTION (TO), MIND 2.

PAY TO v. See PAY 1.

PEACE (pēs), n. (The hands are clasped as a gesture of harmony or peace; the opening signifies quiet or calmness.) The hands are clasped both ways, and then open and separate, assuming the "5" position, palms down.

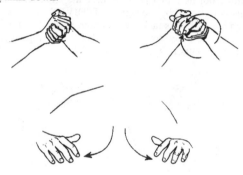

PEACOCK (pē′ kok), n. (The letter "P"; the fan tail.) The right "P" hand is first positioned at the left elbow; then it moves down the arm, opening into a wide fan, with fingers spread apart.

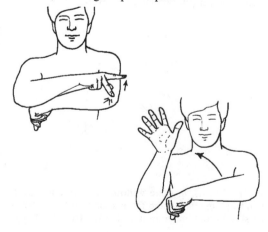

PECULIAR (pǐ kūl′ yər), *adj.* (Something which distorts the vision.) The "C" hand describes a small arc in front of the face. *Cf.* CURIOUS 2, GROTESQUE, ODD, QUEER, STRANGE, WEIRD.

PEER (pǐr), *n.* (Equal in height or status.) The right-angle hands, palms down, are held at about eye level, one in front of the other. The hand in front moves straight forward a short distance, away from the face, while the other hand remains stationary. This sign is used to indicate an equal, never a member of the nobility.

PENALTY (pěn′ əl tǐ), *n.* (Nicking into one.) The knuckle of the right "X" finger is nicked against the palm of the left hand, held in the "5" position, palm facing right. *Cf.* CHARGE, COST, EXPENSE, FEE, FINE 2, PRICE 2, TAX 1, TAXATION 1, TOLL.

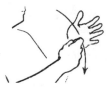

PENGUIN (pen′ gwin), *n.* (The characteristic gait.) Both downturned hands, fingers touching, are held at

the sides of the body. The signer rocks alternately back and forth.

PENIS (pē′ nis), *n.* (The letter "P," for "pee.") The middle finger of the right "P" hand is placed on the tip of the nose.

PENITENT (pěn′ ə tənt), *adj.* (The heart is circled, to indicate feeling, modified by the letter "S," for SORRY.) The right "S" hand, palm facing the body, is rotated several times over the area of the heart. *Cf.* APOLOGIZE 1, APOLOGY 1, CONTRITION, REGRET, REGRETFUL, REPENT, REPENTANT, RUE, SORROW, SORROWFUL 2, SORRY.

PENNY (pěn′ ǐ), *n.* (The Lincoln head.) The right index finger touches the right temple and moves up and away quickly. This is "one cent." For two cents, the "2" hand is used, etc. *Cf.* CENT, CENTS.

PENNY-PINCHING (pen' ē pinch ing), *adj.* (Holding onto money tightly.) The signer makes a tight fist, shaking it slightly. *Cf.* TIGHTFISTED.

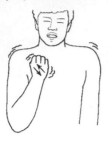

PEOPLE (pē' pəl), *n. pl.* (The letter "P" in continuous motion, to indicate plurality.) The "P" hands, side by side, are moved alternately toward the body in continuous counterclockwise circles. *Cf.* HUMANITY, PUBLIC.

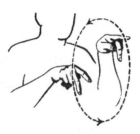

PERCEIVE 1 (pər sēv'), *v.*, -CEIVED, -CEIVING. (The eyesight is directed forward.) The right "V" hand, palm facing the body, is placed so that the fingertips are just under the eyes. The hand swings around and out, so that the fingertips are now pointing forward. *Cf.* LOOK 1, PERCEPTION, WATCH 2.

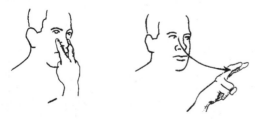

PERCEIVE 2, *v.* (The vision is directed forward, into the distance.) The right "V" fingertips are placed under the eyes, with palm facing the body. The hand is then swung around and forward, moving under the

downturned prone left hand and continuing forward and upward. *Cf.* FORECAST, FORESEE, FORETELL, PREDICT, PROPHECY, PROPHESY, PROPHET, VISION 2.

PERCENT (pər sěnt'), *n.* (Drawing a percent symbol in the air.) The right "O" hand traces a percent symbol (%) in the air. *Cf.* DEGREE 2, RATE.

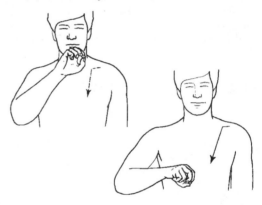

PERCEPTION (pər sěp' shən), *n.* See PERCEIVE 1.

PERFECT (*adj., n.* pûr' fĭkt; *v.* pər fěkt'), -FECTED, -FECTING. (The letter "P"; the hands come into precise contact.) The "P" hands face each other. The right executes a clockwise circle above the stationary left, and then moves down so that the thumb and middle fingers of each hand come into precise contact.

PERFORM 1 (pər fôrm′), v., -FORMED, -FORMING. (An activity.) Both open hands, palms down, are swung right and left before the chest. Cf. ACT 2, ACTION, ACTIVE, ACTIVITY, CONDUCT 1, DEED, DO, PERFORMANCE 1.

PERFORM 2, v. (Motion or movement, modified by the letter "A" for "act.") Both "A" hands, palms out, are held at shoulder height and rotate alternately toward the head. Cf. ACT 1, ACTOR, ACTRESS, DRAMA, PERFORMANCE 2, PLAY 2, SHOW 2.

PERFORMANCE 1 (pər fôr′ məns), n. See PERFORM 1.

PERFORMANCE 2, n. See PERFORM 2.

PERFUME (pər fyōōm′), n. (Dabbing perfume on the neck.) The right thumb lightly touches the right side of the neck several times.

PERHAPS (pər hăps′), adv. (Weighing one thing against another.) The upturned open hands move alternately up and down. Cf. GUESS 3, MAY 1, MAYBE, MIGHT 2, POSSIBILITY, POSSIBLY, PROBABLE, PROBABLY, SUPPOSE.

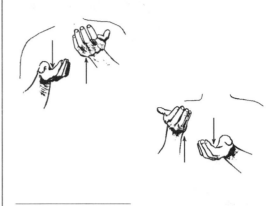

PERIL (pĕr′ əl), n. (An encroachment; parrying a knife thrust.) The left "A" hand is held palm toward the body, knuckles facing right. The extended thumb of the right "A" hand is brought sharply over the back of the left. Cf. DANGER, DANGEROUS, INJURE 2, TRESPASS, VIOLATE.

PERMANENT (pûr′ mə nənt), adj. (Steady, uninterrupted movement.) The "A" hands are held with palms out, thumbs extended and touching, the right behind the left. In this position the hands move forward in a straight, steady line. Cf. CONTINUE, ENDURE 2, EVER 1, LAST 3, LASTING, PERPETUAL, PERSEVERE 3, PERSIST 2, REMAIN, STAY 1, STAY STILL.

PERMISSION 1 (pər mĭsh' ən), *n.* (A permissive upswinging of the hands, as if giving in.) Both hands, palms facing and fingers pointing away from the body, are held at chest level, almost a foot apart. With an upward movement, using their wrists as pivots, the hands sweep up until the fingers point almost straight up. *Cf.* ALLOW, GRANT 1, LET, LET'S, LET US, MAY 3, PERMIT 1, TOLERATE 1.

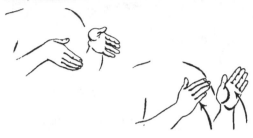

PERMISSION 2, *n.* (The "P" hands are used.) The same sign as in PERMISSION 1 is used, except with the "P" hands. *Cf.* PERMIT 2.

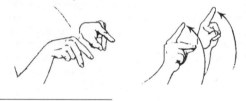

PERMIT 1 (pər mit'), *v.*, -MITTED, -MITTING. See PERMISSION 1.

PERMIT 2, *n., v.* See PERMISSION 2.

PERPENDICULAR 1 (pûr pən dik' yə lər), *adj.* (The letter "P.") The right index finger touches the middle finger of the left "P" hand.

PERPENDICULAR 2, *adj.* (The shape.) The little finger edge of the right hand rests upright and perpendicular in the upturned left palm. It may wave back and forth slightly, as if achieving balance.

PERPETUAL (pər pĕch' ŏŏ əl), *adj.* (Steady, uninterrupted movement.) The "A" hands are held with palms out, thumbs extended and touching, the right behind the left. In this position the hands move forward in a straight, steady line. *Cf.* CONTINUE, ENDURE 2, EVER 1, LAST 3, LASTING, PERMANENT, PERSEVERE 3, PERSIST 2, REMAIN, STAY 1, STAY STILL.

PERSEVERE 1 (pûr' sə vĭr'), *v.*, -VERED, -VERING. (Trying to push through.) The "A" hands, palms facing before the body, are swung around and a bit down, so that the palms now face out. The movement indicates an attempt to push through a barrier. *Cf.* ATTEMPT 1, EFFORT 1, ENDEAVOR, PERSIST 1, TRY 1.

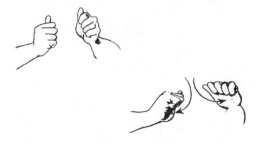

PERSEVERE 2, *v.* (Trying to push through, using the "T" hands, for "try.") This is the same sign as PER-SEVERE 1, except that the "T" hands are employed. *Cf.* ATTEMPT 2, EFFORT 2, TRY 2.

PERSEVERE 3, *v.* (Steady, uninterrupted move-ment.) The "A" hands are held with palms out, thumbs extended and touching, the right behind the left. In this position the hands move forward in a straight, steady line. *Cf.* CONTINUE, ENDURE 2, EVER 1, LAST 3, LASTING, PERMANENT, PERPETUAL, PERSIST 2, REMAIN, STAY 1, STAY STILL.

PERSEVERE 4, *v.* (A thought directed upward, toward a goal.) The index finger of the right "D" hand touches the forehead, and then moves up to the index finger of the left "D" hand, which is held above eye level. The two index fingers stop just short of touching. *Cf.* AIM, AMBITION, GOAL, OBJECTIVE, PUR-POSE 2.

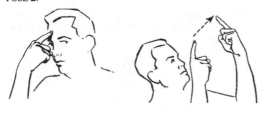

PERSIST 1 (pər sĭst′, -zĭst′), *v.,* -SISTED, -SISTING. (Trying to push through.) The "A" hands, palms fac-ing before the body, are swung around and a bit down, so that the palms now face out. The movement indicates an attempt to push through a barrier. *Cf.* ATTEMPT 1, EFFORT 1, ENDEAVOR, PERSEVERE 1, TRY 1.

PERSIST 2, *v.* (Steady, uninterrupted movement.) The "A" hands are held with palms out, thumbs extended and touching, the right behind the left. In this position the hands move forward in a straight, steady line. *Cf.* CONTINUE, ENDURE 2, EVER 1, LAST 3, LASTING, PERMANENT, PERPETUAL, PERSEVERE 3, REMAIN, STAY 1, STAY STILL.

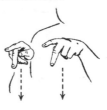

PERSON (pûr′ sən), *n.* (The letter "P"; an individual is indicated.) The "P" hands, side by side, move straight down a short distance, as if outlining the sides of an unseen individual.

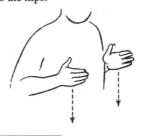

"PERSON" ENDING Both open hands, palms facing each other, move down the sides of the body, tracing its outline to the hips.

PERSONAL (pûr′ sən əl), *adj.* (The lips are sealed, as in a secret or something personal.) The back of the right thumb is pressed against the lips.

PERSONAL COMPUTER *n.* (A fingerspelled loan sign.) The signer fingerspells "P-C."

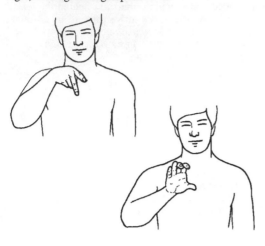

PERSPIRATION 1 (pûr' spə rā' shən), *n.* See PER-SPIRE 1.

PERSPIRATION 2, *n.* See PERSPIRE 2.

PERSPIRE 1 (pər spīr'), *v.,* -SPIRED, -SPIRING. (Wiping the brow.) The bent right index finger is drawn across the forehead from left to right and then shaken to the side, as if getting rid of the sweat. *Cf.* PERSPIRATION 1, SWEAT 1.

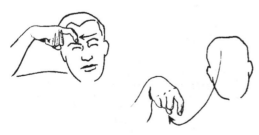

PERSPIRE 2, *v.* (Perspiration dripping from the brow.) The index finger edge of the open right hand wipes across the brow, and the same open hand then continues forcefully downward off the brow, its fingers wiggling, as if shaking off the perspiration gathered. *Cf.* PERSPIRATION 2, SWEAT 2.

PERSUADE (pər swād'), *v.,* -SUADED, -SUADING. (Shaking someone, to implant one's will into another.) Both "A" hands, palms facing, are held before the chest, the left slightly in front of the right. In this position the hands move back and forth a short distance. *Cf.* COAX, PERSUASION, PROD, URGE 2.

PERSUASION (pər swā' zhən), *n.* See PERSUADE.

PERU (pə rōo'), *n.* (Possibly to do with native headdress.) The middle finger of the right "P" hand taps the forehead several times. A native sign.

PET (pĕt), *n., adj., v.,* PETTED, PETTING. (Stroking a person or the head of a pet.) The right hand strokes the back of the left several times. *Cf.* STROKE 2, TAME.

PETTING (pĕt′ ĭng), *(sl.)*, *v.* (Necks interlocked.) The "S" hands, palms facing, are crossed at the wrists. They swing up and down while the wrists remain in contact. *Cf.* MAKE LOVE 2, NECKING.

PETTY (pĕt′ ĭ), *adj.* (Indicating a small mass.) The extended right thumb and index finger are held slightly spread. They are then moved slowly toward each other until they almost touch. *Cf.* SLIGHT, SMALL 1, TINY.

PHARAOH (fâr′ ō), *n.* (The "P"; the headdress.) Both "P" hands trace the shape of the headdress down the sides of the head.

PHEW! *interj.* The "5" hand, palm facing the body, is shaken up and down several times.

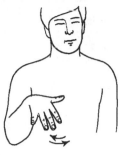

PHILADELPHIA (fĭl′ ə dĕl′ fĭ ə), *n.* The right "P" hand moves down in a quick, curved, right–left–right manner.

PHONE (fōn), *n., v.,* PHONED, PHONING. (The natural sign.) The right "Y" hand is placed at the right side of the head with the thumb touching the ear and the little finger touching the lips. This is the more modern telephone receiver. *Cf.* TELEPHONE.

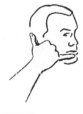

PHOOEY! *interj.* (A look of derision.) With a look of derision, the signer throws one hand down and out, as if ridding himself of something. *Cf.* BAH!

PHOTOGRAPH (fō' tə grăf'), *n., v.,* -GRAPHED, -GRAPHING. (Recording an image.) The right "C" hand is held in front of the face, with thumb edge near the face and palm facing left. The hand is then brought sharply around in front of the open left hand and is struck firmly against the left palm, which is held facing forward with fingers pointing up. *Cf.* PICTURE.

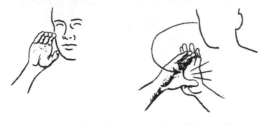

PHYSICAL 1 (fĭz' ə kəl), *adj.* (The body is indicated.) One or both hands are placed against the chest and then are removed and replaced at a point a bit below the first. *Cf.* BODY.

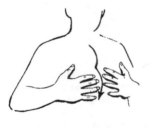

PHYSICAL 2, *adj.* (The "P" letters; indicating the body.) The downturned "P" hands are positioned at chest height on the body. They move down in an arc to the waist.

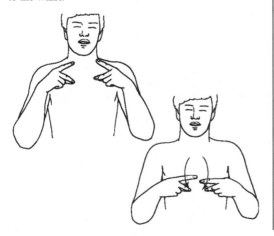

PHYSICS (fĭz' ĭks), *n.* (The points of the electrodes.) The "X" hands are held palms facing the body, thumb edges up. The knuckles of the index fingers touch each other repeatedly. *Cf.* ELECTRIC, ELECTRICITY.

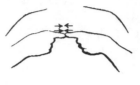

PIANO (pĭ ăn' ō), *n.* (The natural sign.) The downturned hands go through the natural movements involved in manipulating a piano keyboard.

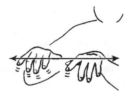

PICK 1 (pĭk), *v.,* PICKED, PICKING. (The natural motion of selecting something from the hand.) The thumb and index fingers of the outstretched right hand grasp an imaginary object on the upturned left palm. The right hand then moves straight up. *Cf.* DISCOVER, DISCOVERY, FIND, SELECT 1.

PICK 2, *v.* (The natural sign.) The fingertips and thumbtip of the downturned open right hand come together, and the hand moves up a short distance, as if picking something. *Cf.* PICK UP 2, SELECT 3.

PICKLE (pĭk′ əl), *n., v.,* -LED, -LING. (Something sour or bitter.) The right index finger is brought sharply up against the lips, while the mouth is puckered up as if tasting something sour. The thumb and index finger may then indicate the length of the pickle.

PICK ON (pĭk), *v. phrase.* (The hen's beak pecks.) The index finger and thumb of the right hand, held together, are brought against the index finger of the left "D" hand a number of times. *Cf.* HENPECK, NAG.

PICK UP 1, *v. phrase.* (To take up.) Both hands, held palms down in the "5" position, are at chest level. With a grasping upward movement, both close into "S" positions before the face. *Cf.* ASSUME, TAKE UP.

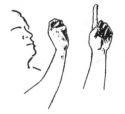

PICK UP 2, *v. phrase.* See PICK 2.

PICTURE (pĭk′ chər), *n., v.,* -TURED, -TURING. (Recording an image.) The right "C" hand is held in front of the face, with thumb edge near the face and palm facing left. The hand is then brought sharply around in front of the open left hand and is struck firmly against the left palm, which is held facing forward with fingers pointing up. *Cf.* PHOTOGRAPH.

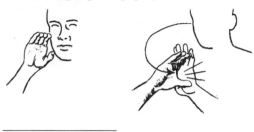

PIE (pī), *n.* (Slicing a wedge-shaped piece of pie.) The upturned left hand represents the pie. The little finger edge of the open right hand goes through the motions of slicing a wedge-shaped piece from the pie.

PIECE (pēs), *n., v.,* PIECED, PIECING. (Cutting off or designating a part.) The little finger edge of the open right hand moves straight down the middle of the upturned left palm. *Cf.* PART 1, PORTION, SECTION, SHARE 1, SOME.

PIG 1 (pĭg), *n.* (The snout digs into the trough.) The downturned right prone hand is placed under the chin, fingers pointing forward. The hand, in this position, swings alternately up and down.

PIG 2, *n.* (Same rationale as for PIG 1.) The sign for PIG 1 is repeated, except that the fingers point to the left.

PILGRIM (pil′ grim), *n.* (The letter "P"; the wide collar.) Both "P" hands trace a wide collar around the neck, beginning in the back and moving around to the front.

PILOT (pī′ lət), *n.* (An individual who flies a plane.) The sign for either AIRPLANE 1 or AIRPLANE 2 is made, and this is followed by the sign for INDIVIDUAL: both open hands, palms facing each other, move down the sides of the body, tracing its outline to the hips. *Cf.* AVIATOR, FLIER.

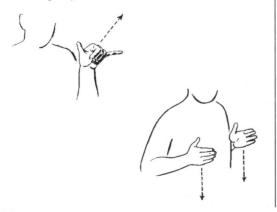

PINEAPPLE (pīn′ ap əl), *n.* (The "P"; chewing.) The middle fingertip of the right "P" hand is placed against the cheek. The hand swivels back and forth. Alternately, the "P" may move in a continuous counterclockwise circle against the cheek.

PINWHEEL (pin′ hwēl), *n.* (The whirling around.) With the index finger thrust into the palm of the other "5" hand, the "5" hand moves very rapidly back and forth, imitating a spinning pinwheel.

PIONEER (pī ə nir′), *n.* (The first finger, *i.e.,* first explorers.) The middle finger of the right "P" hand touches the tip of the left thumb, the hand's first finger.

PITY (pĭt' ĭ), *n., v.,* PITIED, PITYING. (Feelings from the heart, conferred on others.) The middle fingertip of the open right hand touches the chest over the heart. The same open hand then moves in a small, clockwise circle before the right shoulder, with palm facing forward and fingers pointing up. *Cf.* MERCY 2, SYMPATHY 2.

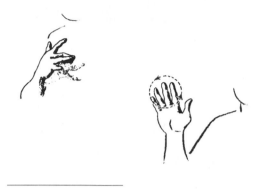

PIZZA 1 (pēt' sə), *n.* (Eating a slice.) The signer mimes eating a slice of pizza.

PIZZA 2, *n.* (The letter "P"; the drawing of a "Z" in the air.) The right "P" hand draws a "Z" in the air.

PIZZA 3, *n.* (The double "Z" in the spelling.) The curved index and middle fingers draw a "Z" in the air.

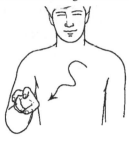

PLACE 1 (plās), *n.* (The letter "P"; a circle or square is indicated, to show the locale or place.) The "P" hands are held side by side before the body, with middle fingertips touching. From this position, the hands separate and outline a circle (or a square), before coming together again closer to the body. *Cf.* LOCATION, POSITION.

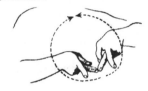

PLACE 2, *n., v.,* PLACED, PLACING. (Moving from one place to another.) The downturned hands, fingers touching their respective thumbs, move in unison from left to right. *Cf.* MOVE, PUT.

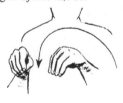

PLACEMENT (plās' mənt), *n.* (Putting an object firmly in place.) The right hand, held in a fist, moves firmly forward and down.

PLAGIARISM (plā' jə riz em), *n.* (The letter "P"; steal.) The right hand, forming a "P," makes a small clockwise circle, and then the curved index and middle fingers close over an imaginary object under the left elbow and move up toward the right.

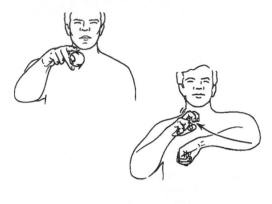

PLAIN 1 (plān), *adj.* (Rays of light clearing the way.) Both hands are held at chest height, palms out, all fingertips together. They open into the "5" position in unison, the right hand moving toward the right and the left toward the left. The palms of both hands remain facing out. *Cf.* BRIGHT 1, BRILLIANCE 1, BRILLIANT 2, CLEAR, EVIDENT, EXPLICIT 2, OBVIOUS.

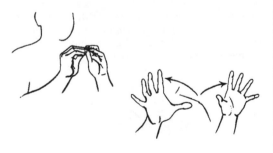

PLAIN 2, *adj.* (Everything is wiped off the hand, to emphasize an uncluttered or clean condition.) The right hand slowly wipes the upturned left palm, from wrist to fingertips. *Cf.* CLEAN, NICE, PURE 1, PURITY, SIMPLE 2.

PLAIN 3, *n.* (The letters "P"; the space.) Both "P" hands draw a circle toward the chest.

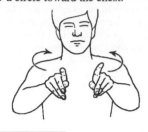

PLAINTIFF (plān' tif), *n.* (Voicing one's feelings or objections.) The sign for COMPLAIN is made: the right claw hand, palm facing the body, is thrust twice into midchest. The sign for INDIVIDUAL 1 then follows.

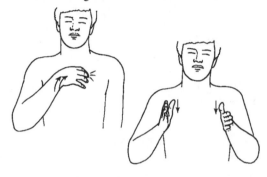

PLAN 1 (plăn), *n., v.,* PLANNED, PLANNING. (Placing things in order.) The hands, palms facing, fingers together and pointing away from the body, are positioned at the left side and held about a foot apart. With a slight up–down motion, as if describing waves, the hands travel in unison from left to right. *Cf.* ARRANGE, ARRANGEMENT, ORDER 3, PREPARE 1, PROGRAM 1, PROVIDE 1, PUT IN ORDER, READY 1.

PLAN 2, *n., v.* (The initial "P.") PLAN 1 is repeated, except with the "P" hands, palms down.

PLANE 1 (plăn), *n.* (The wings of the airplane.) The "Y" hand, palm down and drawn up near the shoulder, moves forward, up and away from the body. Either hand may be used. *Cf.* AIRPLANE, FLY 1.

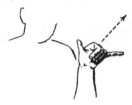

PLANE 2, *n.* (The wings and fuselage of the airplane.) The hand assumes the same position as in PLANE 1, but the index finger is also extended, to represent the fuselage of the airplane. Either hand may be used, and the movement is the same as in PLANE 1. *Cf.* FLY 2.

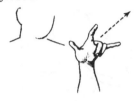

PLANET 1 (plăn′ ĭt), *n.* (The earth and its axis are indicated.) The downturned left "S" hand indicates the earth. The thumb and index finger of the downturned right "5" hand are placed at each edge of the left. In this position the right hand swings back and forth, while maintaining contact with the left. *Cf.* EARTH, GEOGRAPHY, GLOBE 1.

PLANET 2, *n.* (The letter "P"; around the world.) The right "P" hand moves around the left fist.

PLANT 1 (plănt), *n.* (Flowers or plants emerge from the ground.) The right fingers, pointing up, emerge from the closed left hand, and they spread open as they do. *Cf.* BLOOM, DEVELOP 1, GROW, GROWN, MATURE 1, RAISE 3, REAR 2, SPRING.

PLANT 2, *v.*, PLANTED, PLANTING. (Placing the seed into the ground.) The right hand, holding some imaginary seeds, is thrust into the cupped left hand.

PLASTIC (plăs′ tik), *n., adj.* (Pliable.) The right hand grasps the middle finger of the left "P" hand and bends it back and forth.

PLATE 1 (plāt), *n.* (The material and shape.) The sign for GLASS or PORCELAIN is made: the index finger is brought up to touch the exposed front teeth. The downturned index fingers then describe the circular shape of the plate. *Cf.* CHINA 4, DISH, GLASS 1, PORCELAIN.

Plate 400 **Playhouse**

PLATE 2, *n.* (The shape.) The downturned thumbs and index fingers are held in a curve as they outline the edge of a plate.

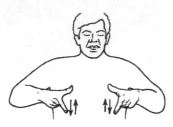

PLATEAU (pla tō'), *n.* (The flatness.) The right "P" hand, palm down, moves in a counterclockwise circle.

PLATTER (plat' ər), *n.* (The shape and function.) Both upturned hands, side by side, describe a circle as they move outward from the body.

PLAY 1 (plā), *v.,* PLAYED, PLAYING. (Shaking tambourines.) The "Y" hands, held aloft, are shaken back and forth, pivoted at the wrists.

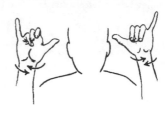

PLAY 2, *n.* (Motion or movement, modified by the letter "A" for "act.") Both "A" hands, palms out, are held at shoulder height and rotate alternately toward the head. *Cf.* ACT 1, ACTOR, ACTRESS, DRAMA, PERFORM 2, PERFORMANCE 2, SHOW 2.

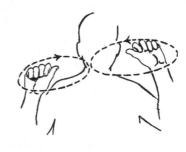

PLAYER (plā' ər), *n.* The sign for PLAY 1 is made, followed by the sign for INDIVIDUAL: both open hands, palms facing each other, move down the sides of the body, tracing its outline to the hips.

PLAYHOUSE (plā hous), *n.* (PLAY and HOUSE.) The sign for PLAY: both "A" hands, palms out, are held at shoulder height and rotate alternately toward the head. This is followed by HOUSE: both hands, fingertips touching, form a sloping roof. They move down, separate, and indicate the walls. The sign for PLAY 1 may also be made by shaking both "Y" hands back and forth.

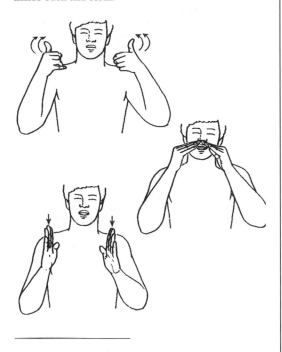

PLAYING CARDS *n. pl.* (The action of dealing out cards.) The signer goes through the motions of dealing out imaginary playing cards. *Cf.* CARD PLAYING, CARDS.

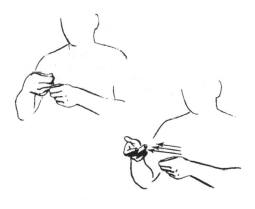

PLAYWRIGHT (plā′ rīt), *n.* (One who writes plays.) The sign for PLAY 1, as above, is made, followed by the sign for WRITE: the right hand moves an imaginary pencil over the upturned left palm. Optionally,

the sign for INDIVIDUAL 1 may be added.

PLEA (plē), *n.* (An act of supplication.) With the right hand clasped over the left, both hands are shaken gently before the body. The eyes often are directed upward. *Cf.* BEG 2, ENTREAT, IMPLORE, PLEAD, SUPPLICATION.

PLEAD (plēd), *v.*, PLEADED, PLEADING. See PLEA.

PLEASANT (plĕz′ ənt), *adj.* (A crinkling-up of the face.) Both hands, in the "5" position, palms facing back, are placed on either side of the face. The fingers wiggle back and forth, while a pleasant, happy expression is worn. *Cf.* AMIABLE, CHEERFUL, CORDIAL, FRIENDLY, JOLLY.

PLEASE (plēz), *v.*, PLEASED, PLEASING. (A pleasurable feeling on the heart.) The open right hand is circled on the chest, over the heart. *Cf.* APPRECIATE, ENJOY, ENJOYMENT, GRATIFY 1, LIKE 3, PLEASURE, WILLING 2.

PLEASURE (plĕzh′ ər), *n.* See PLEASE.

PLEDGE (plĕj), *n., v.,* PLEDGED, PLEDGING. (The arm is raised.) The right index finger is placed at the lips. The right arm is then raised, palm out and elbow resting on the back of the left hand. *Cf.* GUARANTEE, LOYAL, OATH, PROMISE 1, SWEAR 1, SWORN, TAKE OATH, VOW.

PLENTY (plĕn′ tĭ), *n., adj., adv.* (A full cup.) The left hand, in the "S" position, is held palm facing right. The right "5" hand, palm down, is brushed outward several times over the top of the left, indicating a wiping off of the top of a cup. *Cf.* ABUNDANCE, ABUNDANT, ADEQUATE, AMPLE, ENOUGH, SUBSTANTIAL, SUFFICIENT.

PLOW (plou), *n.* (The action of the plow's blade in making a furrow.) The open right hand is placed

upright in a perpendicular position on the upturned left palm, with the little finger edge resting in the palm. The right hand moves forward along the left palm. As it does so, it swings over to a palm-down position, and moves off a bit to the right.

PLOWER (plou′ər), *n.* The sign for PLOW is made. This is followed by the sign for INDIVIDUAL: both open hands, palms facing each other, move down the sides of the body, tracing its outline to the hips.

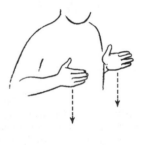

PLUM (plum), *n.* (The texture, likened to a smooth cheek.) The thumb and index and middle fingers, held apart, are placed at the cheek. They move away and back repeatedly. Each time they move off, the three fingers come together.

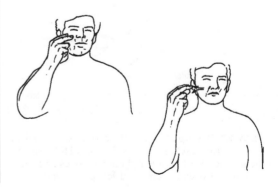

PLURAL (plŏŏr′ əl), *adj.* (Many fingers are indicated.) The upturned "S" hands are thrown up, opening into the "5" position, palms up. This may be repeated. *Cf.* MANY, MULTIPLE, NUMEROUS, QUANTITY.

PLUS (plŭs), *prep., n.* (A mathematical symbol.) The two index fingers are crossed at right angles. *Cf.* ADD 2, ADDITION, POSITIVE 2.

POISON (poi′ zən), *n.* (The crossed bones.) Both "S" hands are crossed and held against the chest. The signer bares the teeth, in imitation of a skull.

POKER (pō′ kər), *n.* The slightly curved left index finger, pointing slightly up and out, moves in and out from the body, an inch or so.

POLAR BEAR *n.* (A white bear.) The sign for BEAR is made: both claw hands, crossed, scratch the shoulders several times. This is followed by WHITE: the right "5" hand is placed against the chest, palm facing the body. The hand moves forward once or twice; each time the fingertips come together.

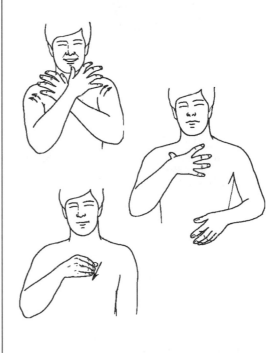

POLICE (pə lēs′), *n., v.,* -LICED, -LICING. (The letter "C" for "cop"; the shape and position of the badge.) The right "C" hand, palm facing left, is placed against the heart. *Cf.* COP, POLICEMAN.

POLICEMAN (pə lēs′ mən), *n.* See POLICE.

POLICY (pŏl' ə sē), *n.* (The letter "P"; the law, as spelled out on the outstretched page.) The right "P" hand rests on the fingertips of the outstretched left palm. The right hand moves down to the heel of the left palm.

POLISH (pŏl' ĭsh), *(voc.), n., v.,* -ISHED, -ISHING. (The act of rubbing.) The right knuckles rub briskly against the outstretched left palm. *Cf.* RUB, SANDPA-PER, SHINE SHOES.

POLITE (pə līt'), *adj.* (The ruffled shirt front of a gentleman of old.) The thumb of the right "5" hand is thrust into the chest. The hand then pivots down, with thumb remaining in place. This latter part of the sign, however, is optional. *Cf.* COURTEOUS, COURTESY, FINE 4.

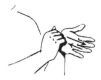

POLITICAL (pə lĭt' i kəl), *adj.* (The letter "P"; at the head.) The right "P" hand, held facing the side of the head, makes a clockwise circle and comes to rest with the little finger touching the right temple.

POLLUTE 1 (pə lōōt'), *v.* (Spreading poison.) The middle finger of the right "P" hand makes a small clockwise circle in the upturned left palm. This is a sign for POISON. The downturned hands then spread out in a counterclockwise arc.

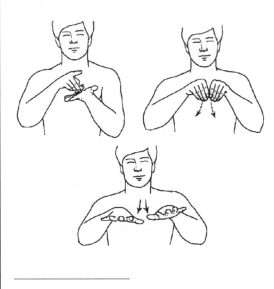

POLLUTE 2, *v.* (Spreading dirt.) The downturned open hand is placed under the chin, where the fingers wriggle. This is the sign for DIRT. The downturned hand then spreads out in a counterclockwise arc.

POLO (pō' lō), *n.* (The polo playing.) The signer, holding a pair of imaginary reins and moving as if on horseback, swings an imaginary polo mallet, hitting a ball on the ground.

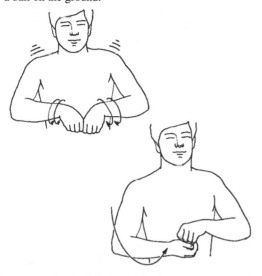

PONCE (pôn´ sā), *n.* (The letter "P"; the Arawak Indian headdress.) The right "P" hand is placed at the forehead and moves back over the head. A native sign.

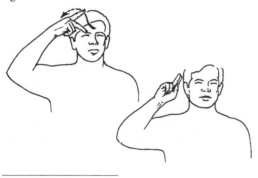

POND (pŏnd), *n.* (The letter "P"; the space and shimmering water.) The right "P" hand describes a counterclockwise circle, while the hand trembles slightly, as if reflecting the shimmering water.

PONDER (pŏn´ dər), *v.,* -DERED, -DERING. (Turning thoughts over in the mind.) Both index fingers, pointing to the forehead, describe continuous alternating circles. *Cf.* CONSIDER 2, CONTEMPLATE, SPECULATE 2, SPECULATION 2, WEIGH 2, WONDER 1.

POOL (pōol), *n.* (The game of pool.) The signer, hunched over an imaginary cue stick, mimes striking the ball. *Cf.* BILLIARDS.

POOR (pŏŏr), *adj.* (Ragged elbows.) The open right hand is placed at the left elbow. It moves down and off, closing into the "O" position. *Cf.* POVERTY 1.

POP 1 (pŏp), *n.* (Corking a bottle.) The left "O" hand is held with thumb edge up, representing a bottle. The thumb and index finger of the right "5" hand represent a cork, and are inserted into the circle formed by the "O" hand. The palm of the open right hand then strikes down on the upturned edge of the "O" hand, as if forcing the cork into the bottle. *Cf.* SODA POP, SODA WATER.

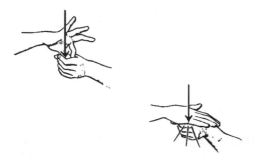

POP 2, *(informal), n.* (Derived from the formal sign for FATHER 1, *q.v.*) The thumbtip of the right "5" hand touches the right temple a number of times. The other fingers may also wiggle. *Cf.* DAD, DADDY, FATHER 2, PAPA.

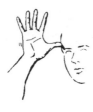

POPCORN (pŏp' kôrn), *n.* (The popping.) The index fingers alternately flick up.

POPSICLE (pŏp' si kəl), *n.* (Licking the popsicle.) The index and middle fingers of either hand, held together, are brought up repeatedly to the outstretched tongue.

POPULATION (pŏp yə lā' shən), *n.* (Running through many individuals.) The left "5" hand is held palm facing the body. The right "P" hand sweeps over the outstretched left fingers, starting at the little finger.

POP UP *(colloq.), v.* (Popping up before the eyes.) The right index finger, pointing up, pops up between the index and middle fingers of the left hand, whose palm faces down. *Cf.* APPEAR 2, RISE 2.

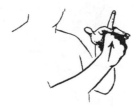

PORCELAIN (pôr′ sə lĭn, pôrs′ lĭn), *n.* (The finger touches a brittle substance.) The index finger is brought up to touch the exposed front teeth. *Cf.* CHINA 4, DISH, GLASS 1, PLATE 1.

PORCUPINE (pôr′ kyə pīn), *n.* (The outstretched quills.) The right "S" hand rests on the back of the left "S" hand. The right hand, moving down to the fingers of the left, opens wide, the fingers representing outstretched quills.

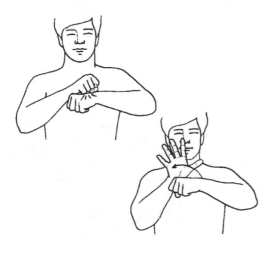

PORTION (pôr′ shən), *n.* (Cutting off or designating a part.) The little finger edge of the open right hand moves straight down the middle of the upturned left palm. *Cf.* PART 1, PIECE, SECTION, SHARE 1, SOME.

PORTUGAL (pôr′ chə gəl), *n.* (The coastline looks like a human profile.) The right index finger moves down the face, from forehead to chin, tracing the outline of the features. A native sign.

POSITION (pə zĭsh′ ən), *n.* (The letter "P"; a circle or square is indicated, to show the locale or place.) The "P" hands are held side by side before the body, with middle fingertips touching. From this position, the hands separate and outline a circle (or a square), before coming together again closer to the body. *Cf.* LOCATION, PLACE 1.

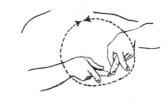

POSITIVE 1 (pŏz′ ə tĭv), *adj.* (Coming forth directly from the lips; true.) The index finger of the right "D" hand, palm facing left, is placed against the lips. It moves up an inch or two and then describes a small arc forward and away from the lips. *Cf.* ABSOLUTE, ABSOLUTELY, ACTUAL, ACTUALLY, AUTHENTIC, CERTAIN, CERTAINLY, FIDELITY, FRANKLY, GENUINE, INDEED, POSITIVELY, REAL, REALLY, SINCERE 2, SURE, SURELY, TRUE, TRULY, TRUTH, VALID, VERILY.

POSITIVE 2, *adj.* (A mathematical symbol.) The two index fingers are crossed at right angles in the sign for PLUS. *Cf.* ADD 2, ADDITION, PLUS.

POSITIVELY *adv.* See POSITIVE 1.

POSSESS (pə zĕs'), *v.*, -SESSED, -SESSING. (The act of bringing something over to oneself.) The right-angle hands, palms facing and thumbs pointing up, are swept toward the body until the fingertips come to rest against the middle of the chest. *Cf.* HAVE.

POSSIBILITY (pŏs' ə bĭl' ə tĭ), *n.* (Weighing one thing against another.) The upturned open hands move alternately up and down. *Cf.* GUESS 3, MAY 1, MAYBE, MIGHT 2, PERHAPS, POSSIBLY, PROBABLE, PROBABLY, SUPPOSE.

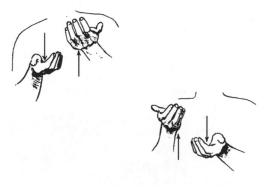

POSSIBLE (pŏs' ə bəl), *adj.* (An affirmative movement of the hands, likened to a nodding of the head, to indicate ability or power to accomplish something.) Both "A" hands, held palms down, move down in unison a short distance before the chest. *Cf.* ABILITY, ABLE, CAN, CAPABLE, COMPETENT, COULD, MAY 2.

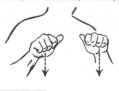

POSSIBLY (pŏs' ə blĭ), *adv.* See POSSIBILITY.

POST OFFICE *n.* (A fingerspelled loan sign.) The signer fingerspells "P-O."

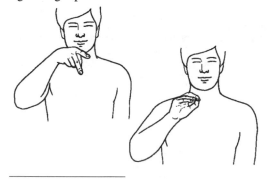

POSTPONE (pōst pōn'), *v.*, -PONED, -PONING. (Putting off; moving things forward repeatedly.) The "F" hands, palms facing and fingers pointing out from the body, are moved forward simultaneously in a series of short movements. *Cf.* DEFER, DELAY, PROCRASTINATE, PUT OFF.

POT (pŏt), *n. sl.* (The act of smoking marijuana.) The signer mimes holding the marijuana cigarette to the lips and inhaling deeply. *Cf.* MARIJUANA.

POTATO (pə tā′ tō), *n.* (The fork is thrust into the potato.) The downturned left "S" hand represents the potato. The slightly bent fingers of the right "V" hand are thrust repeatedly against the back of the left hand.

POTATO CHIP (pə tā′ tō chĭp) *n.* (Breaking a chip with the teeth.) The sign for POTATO is made: the downturned right index and middle fingers are thrust repeatedly onto the left fist. The signer then mimes breaking a potato chip with the teeth.

POUND 1 (pound), *n.* (The balancing of the scale is described.) The fingers of the right "H" hand are centered on the left index finger and rocked back and forth. *Cf.* SCALE 1, WEIGH 1, WEIGHT.

POUND 2, *v.,* POUNDED, POUNDING. (The natural sign.) The right "S" hand strikes its knuckles forcefully against the open left palm, which is held facing right. *Cf.* HIT 1, PUNCH 1, STRIKE 1.

POVERTY (pŏv′ ər tĭ), *n.* (The knuckles are rubbed, to indicate a condition of being worn down.) The knuckles of the curved index and middle fingers of both hands are rubbed up and down against each other. Instead of the up–down rubbing, they may rub against each other in an alternate clockwise–counterclockwise manner. *Cf.* DIFFICULT 1, DIFFICULTY, HARD 1, HARDSHIP, PROBLEM 2.

POWDER (pou′ dər) *n., v.* (Sprinkling powder or talc on the body.) The signer shakes an imaginary powder container on the chest.

POWER 1 (pou′ ər), *n.* (Flexing the muscles.) With fists clenched, palms facing back, the signer raises both arms and shakes them once, with force. *Cf.* MIGHT 1, MIGHTY 1, POWERFUL 1, STRONG 1, STURDY, TOUGH 1.

POWER 2, *n.* (The curve of the flexed biceps is indicated.) The left hand, clenched into a fist, is held up, palm facing the body. The index finger of the right "D" hand moves in an arc over the left biceps muscle, from the shoulder to the crook of the elbow. *Cf.* MIGHT 3, POWERFUL 2.

POWERFUL 1 (pou′ ər fəl), *adj*. See POWER 1.

POWERFUL 2, *adj*. See POWER 2.

PRACTICE 1 (prăk′ tĭs), *n.*, *v.*, -TICED, -TICING. (Polishing or sharpening up.) The knuckles of the downturned right "A" hand are rubbed briskly back and forth over the side of the hand and index finger of the left "D" hand. *Cf.* TRAIN 2.

PRACTICE 2, *(rare)*, *v*. (Same rationale as for PRACTICE 1.) The knuckles of both "A" hands, palms facing, sweep past each other repeatedly, coming in contact each time they do.

PRACTICE 3, *n., v*. (Bound down to custom or habit.) Both "S" hands, palms down, are crossed and brought down in unison before the chest. *Cf.* ACCUSTOM, BOUND, CUSTOM, HABIT, LOCKED.

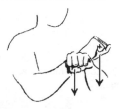

PRAISE (prāz), *n., v.*, PRAISED, PRAISING. (Good words coming from the mouth; clapping hands.) The fingertips of the right hand, palm flat and facing the body, are brought up to the lips so that they touch (part of the sign for GOOD, *q.v.*). The hands are then clapped

together several times. *Cf.* APPLAUD, APPLAUSE, COMMEND, CONGRATULATE 1, CONGRATULATIONS 1.

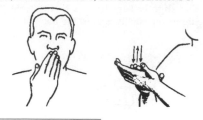

PRAM (pram), *n*. (Rocking back and forth.) The signer mimes grasping a pram's handle and rocking it back and forth. *Cf.* CARRIAGE.

PREACH (prēch), *v.*, PREACHED, PREACHING. (Placing morsels of wisdom, or food for thought, into the mind.) The right hand, palm out, with thumb and index finger touching, is moved forward and slightly downward a number of times from its initial position near the right temple. *Cf.* SERMON.

PREACHER (prē′ chər), *n*. The sign for PREACH is made. This is followed by the sign for INDIVIDUAL: both open hands, palms facing each other, move down the sides of the body, tracing its outline to the hips. *Cf.* MINISTER, PASTOR.

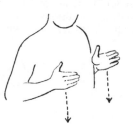

PRECISE (prĭ sīs′), *adj.* (The fingers come together precisely.) The thumb and index finger of each hand, palms facing, the right above the left, form circles. They are brought together with a deliberate movement, so that the fingers and thumbs now touch. Sometimes the right hand, before coming together with the left, executes a slow clockwise circle above the left. *Cf.* EXACT 1, EXACTLY, EXPLICIT 1, SPECIFIC 1.

PREDICT (prĭ dĭkt′), *v.,* -DICTED, -DICTING. (The vision is directed forward, into the distance.) The right "V" fingertips are placed under the eyes, with palm facing the body. The hand is then swung around and forward, moving under the downturned prone left hand and continuing forward and upward. *Cf.* FORECAST, FORESEE, FORETELL, PERCEIVE 2, PROPHECY, PROPHESY, PROPHET, VISION 2.

PREFER (prĭ fûr′), *v.,* -FERRED, -FERRING. (More good.) The fingertips of one hand are placed at the lips, as if tasting something (see GOOD). Then the hand is moved up to a position just above the head, where it assumes the "A" position, thumb up. *Cf.* BETTER.

PREGNANT 1 (preg′ nənt), *adj.* One or both open hands are placed on the stomach and move forward an inch or two, to indicate the swollen belly.

PREGNANT 2, *adj.* (Same as PREGNANT 1.) The hands interlock.

PREGNANT 3, *adj.* (Impaled by a fork-like implement, *i.e,* "stuck.") The index and middle fingers are thrust quickly into the throat. This would refer to an unwanted pregnancy, *i.e.,* "stuck with it."

PREPARE 1 (pri pâr'), *v.*, -PARED, -PARING. (Placing things in order.) The hands, palms facing, fingers together and pointing away from the body, are positioned at the left side and held about a foot apart. With a slight up–down motion, as if describing waves, the hands travel in unison from left to right. *Cf.* ARRANGE, ARRANGEMENT, ORDER 3, PLAN 1, PROGRAM 1, PROVIDE 1, PUT IN ORDER, READY 1.

PREPARE 2, *v.* (The "R" hands, for READY.) The "R" hands are held side by side before the body, palms up and fingers pointing outward. The hands then turn toward each other and over, so that the palms face down and fingers point toward each other. *Cf.* READY 2.

PREPARE 3, *v.* (Set out.) The "A" hands are crossed, with the right resting on top of the left. The right palm faces left and the left palm faces right. Both hands suddenly open and swing apart to the palm-down position. *Cf.* READY 4.

PRESENCE (prĕz' əns), *n.* (Face to face.) The left hand, fingers together, palm flat and facing the eyes, is held a bit above eye level. The right hand, fingers also together, is held in front of the mouth, with palm facing the left hand. With a sweeping upward movement the right hand moves toward the left, which

moves straight up an inch or two at the same time. *Cf.* CONFRONT, FACE, FACE TO FACE.

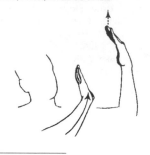

PRESENT 1 (prĕz' ənt), *n.* (An offering; a presenting.) Both hands, slightly cupped, palms up, are held close to the chest. They move up and out in unison, describing a very slight arc. *Cf.* MOTION, OFFER, OFFERING, PROPOSE, SUGGEST.

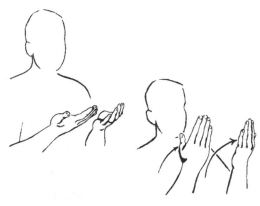

PRESENT 2 (*n.* prĕz' ənt; *v.* pri zĕnt'), -SENTED, -SENTING. (A giving of something.) Both "A" hands, with index fingers somewhat draped over the tips of the thumbs, are held palms facing in front of the chest. They are pivoted forward and down in unison, from the wrists. *Cf.* AWARD, CONTRIBUTE, GIFT.

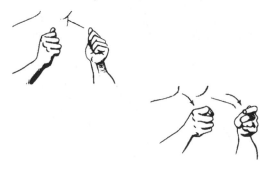

PRESENT 3, *adj.* (Something right in front of you.) The upturned right-angle hands drop down rather sharply. The "Y" hands may also be used. *Cf.* NOW.

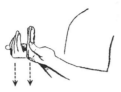

PRESERVE (prĭ zûrv'), *v.,* -SERVED, -SERVING. (Slow, careful movement.) The "K" hands are crossed, the right above the left, little finger edges down. In this position the hands are moved up and down a short distance. *Cf.* CARE 2, CAREFUL 2, KEEP, MAINTAIN 1, MIND 3, RESERVE 2, TAKE CARE OF 2.

PRESIDENT (prĕz' ə dənt), *n.* The "C" hands, held palms out at either temple, are drawn out and up from the head into the "S" position.

PRESS (prĕs), *v.,* PRESSED, PRESSING. (The act of pressing with an iron.) The right hand goes through the motion of swinging an iron back and forth over the upturned left palm. *Cf.* IRON.

PRESSURE (presh' ər), *n.* (Pushing down.) The left index finger, pointing forward, is pushed down by the downturned right hand. The signer assumes an expression of intensity.

PRETTY (prĭt' ĭ), *adj.* (Literally, a good face.) The right hand, fingers closed over the thumb, is placed at or just below the lips (indicating a tasting of something GOOD, *q.v.*). It then describes a counterclockwise circle around the face, opening into the "5" position, to indicate the whole face. At the completion of the circling movement the hand comes to rest in its initial position, at or just below the lips. *Cf.* BEAUTIFUL, BEAUTY.

PRETZEL (pret′ səl), *n.* (The shape.) Both "R" hands trace the twisted shape of a pretzel.

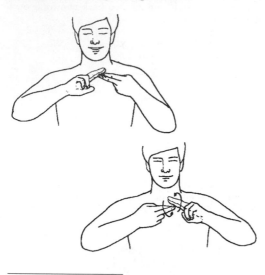

PREVENT (prĭ vĕnt′), *v.*, -VENTED, -VENTING. (Obstruct, block.) The left hand, fingers together and palm flat, is held before the body, facing somewhat down. The little finger side of the right hand, held with palm flat, makes one or several up-down chopping motions against the left hand, between its thumb and index finger. *Cf.* ANNOY, ANNOYANCE, BOTHER, DISRUPT, DISTURB, HINDER, HINDRANCE, IMPEDE, INTERCEPT, INTERFERE, INTERFERENCE, INTERFERE WITH, INTERRUPT, MEDDLE 1, OBSTACLE, OBSTRUCT, PREVENTION.

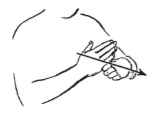

PREVENTION (prĭ vĕn′ shən), *n.* See PREVENT.

PREVIOUS (prē′ vĭ əs), *adj.* (Something past, behind.) The upraised right hand, in the "5" position with palm facing the body, is held just above the right shoulder and is thrown back over it. *Cf.* AGO,

FORMERLY, ONCE UPON A TIME, PAST, PREVIOUSLY, WAS, WERE.

PREVIOUSLY *adv.* See PREVIOUS.

PRICE 1 (prīs), *n., v.,* PRICED, PRICING. (Amount of money is indicated.) The sign for MONEY is made: the upturned right hand, grasping some imaginary bills, is brought down into the upturned left palm a number of times. The right hand then moves straight up, opening into the "5" position, palm up. *Cf.* HOW MUCH MONEY?, WHAT IS THE PRICE?

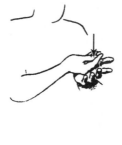

PRICE 2, *n., v.* (Nicking into one.) The knuckle of the right "X" finger is nicked against the palm of the left hand, held in the "5" position, palm facing right. *Cf.* CHARGE, COST, EXPENSE, FEE, FINE 2, PENALTY, TAX 1, TAXATION 1, TOLL.

PRIDE (prīd), *n., v.,* PRIDED, PRIDING. (The feelings rise up.) The thumb of the right "A" hand, palm down, moves up along the right side of the chest. A haughty expression is assumed. *Cf.* PROUD.

PRIEST (prēst), *n.* (The ecclesiastical collar.) The thumbs and index fingers of both hands indicate the shape of the collar as they move around the neck, coming together in front of the throat. Sometimes only one hand is used.

PRINCE (prins), *n.* (The male root sign; tracing the royal sash.) The right hand grasps an imaginary cap brim, and then the signer, using the right "P" hand, traces an imaginary sash from left shoulder to right hip.

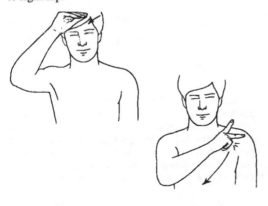

PRINCESS (prin' sis), *n.* (The female root sign; tracing the royal sash.) The right thumb moves down the

line of the right jaw, and then, as above for PRINCE, the royal sash is traced.

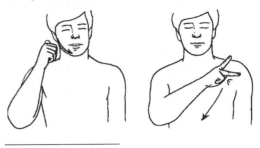

PRINCIPAL (prin' sə pəl), *n.* (The letter "P"; one who rules over others.) The downturned, right "P" hand is swung from right to left over the back of the prone left hand.

PRINCIPLE (prin' sə pəl), *n.* (A collection or listing is indicated by the open palm, representing a page.) The right "P" hand is placed against the upper part of the open left hand, which faces right, fingers pointing upward. The right "P" hand swings down to the lower part of the left palm.

PRINT 1 (print), *v.,* PRINTED, PRINTING. (Placing type in a printer's stick.) The upturned, left "5" hand represents the printer's stick. The right index finger and thumb close over an imaginary piece of type and place it in the left palm.

PRINT 2, *v.*, PRINTED, PRINTING. (The act of printing block letters.) The right index finger traces letters in the upturned left palm.

PRIORITY (prī ôr′ ə tē), *n.* (The letter "P"; touching the first finger.) The middle finger of the right "P" hand touches the left thumbtip.

PRISON (priz′ ən), *n.* (The crossed bars.) The "4" hands, palms facing the body, are crossed at the fingers. *Cf.* JAIL.

PRIVACY (prī′ və sĭ), *n.* (The sealing of the lips; keeping the words back.) The back of the thumb of the right "A" hand is placed firmly against the closed lips. The thumb, in this position, may move off the lips slightly and return again to the lips. As an optional addition, the thumb may swing down under the downturned cupped left hand, after being placed on the lips as above. *Cf.* PRIVATE 1, SECRET.

PRIVATE 1 (prī′ vĭt), *adj.* See PRIVACY.

PRIVATE 2, *(colloq.), adj.* (Closed.) Both open hands are held before the body, fingers pointing out, right palm facing left and left facing right. The right hand, held above the left, comes down against the index finger edge of the left a number of times.

PRIVATE 3, *n.* (The stripe on the uniform sleeve.) The right index finger traces the shape of the private's stripe on the left sleeve.

PRIVATE CONVERSATION *(colloq. phrase).* (Small give-and-take from the mouth.) The index and middle fingers of the right or left "V" hand move alternately back and forth on the lips.

PRIVILEGE (prĭv′ ə lĭj), *n.* (A straightening out.) The right hand, fingers together and palm facing left, is placed in the upturned left palm, whose fingers point away from the body. The right hand slides straight out along the left palm, over the left fingers, and stops with its heel resting on the left fingertips. *Cf.* ALL RIGHT, O.K. 1, RIGHT 1, RIGHTEOUS, YOU'RE WELCOME 2.

PROBABLE (prŏb′ ə bəl), *adj.* (Weighing one thing against another.) The upturned open hands move alternately up and down. *Cf.* GUESS 3, MAY 1, MAYBE, MIGHT 2, PERHAPS, POSSIBILITY, POSSIBLY, PROBABLY, SUPPOSE.

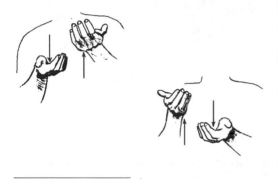

PROBABLY (prŏ′ ə blĭ), *adv.* See PROBABLE.

PROBE (prŏb), *v.*, PROBED, PROBING, *n.* (Directing the vision from place to place.) The right "C" hand, palm facing left, moves from right to left across the line of vision, in a series of counterclockwise circles. The signer's gaze remains concentrated and his head turns slowly from right to left. *Cf.* CURIOUS 1, EXAMINE, INVESTIGATE, LOOK FOR, SEARCH, SEEK.

PROBLEM 1 (prŏb′ ləm), *n.* (A clouding over; a troubling.) Both "B" hands, palms facing each other, are rotated alternately before the forehead. *Cf.* CONCERN, FRET, TROUBLE, WORRIED, WORRY 1.

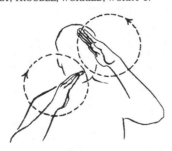

PROBLEM 2, *n.* (The knuckles are rubbed, to indicate a condition of being worn down.) The knuckles of the curved index and middle fingers of both hands are rubbed up and down against each other. Instead of the up–down rubbing, they may rub against each other in an alternate clockwise–counterclockwise manner. *Cf.* DIFFICULT 1, DIFFICULTY, HARD 1, HARDSHIP, POVERTY.

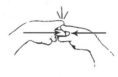 

PROBLEM 3, *n.* (Coming to grips.) The curved index and middle fingers of both hands, palms facing the body, are brought sharply into an interlocking position. The action may be repeated, this time with the wrists first twisted slightly in opposite directions.

PROCEED (prə sēd′), *v.*, -CEEDED, -CEEDING. (Moving forward.) Both right-angle hands, palms facing each other and knuckles facing forward, move forward simultaneously. *Cf.* GO AHEAD, RESUME.

PROCRASTINATE (prŏ krăs′ tə nāt′), *v.*, -NATED, -NATING. (Putting off; moving things forward repeatedly.) The "F" hands, palms facing and fingers pointing out from the body, are moved forward simultaneously in a series of short movements. *Cf.* DEFER, DELAY, POSTPONE, PUT OFF.

PROCURE (prō kyŏŏr'), *v.*, -CURED, -CURING. (A grasping and bringing forward to oneself.) Both hands, in the "5" position, fingers curved, are crossed at the wrists, with the left palm facing right and the right palm facing left. They are brought in toward the chest, while closing into a grasping "S" position. *Cf.* ACQUIRE, GET, OBTAIN, RECEIVE.

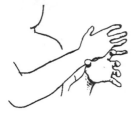

PROD (prŏd), *v.*, PRODDED, PRODDING. (Shaking someone, to implant one's will into another.) Both "A" hands, palms facing, are held before the chest, the left slightly in front of the right. In this position the hands move back and forth a short distance. *Cf.* COAX, PERSUADE, PERSUASION, URGE 2.

PRODUCE 1 (*n.* prŏd' ūs; *v.* prə dūs'), -DUCED, -DUC-ING. (Directing the attention to something, and bring-ing it forward.) The right index finger points into the left palm, held facing out before the body. The left palm moves straight out. *Cf.* DEMONSTRATE, DISPLAY, EVIDENCE, EXAMPLE, EXHIBIT, EXHIBITION, ILLUSTRATE, INDICATE, INFLUENCE 2, REPRESENT, SHOW 1, SIGNIFY 1.

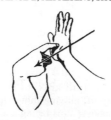

PRODUCE 2, *v.* (Fashioning something with the hands.) The right "S" hand, palm facing left, is placed on top of its left counterpart, whose palm faces right. The hands are twisted back and forth, striking each other slightly after each twist. *Cf.*

CONSTRUCT 2, CREATE 1, DEVISE, MAKE, MANUFACTURE, MEND, REPAIR.

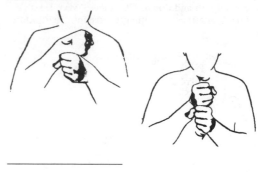

PRODUCER (prə dōō' sər), *n.* (One who makes.) Both "P" hands are crossed, the right above the left. The hands are twisted back and forth, striking each other after each twist. The sign for INDIVIDUAL 1 then follows.

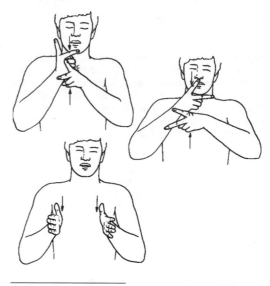

PRODUCT (prŏd' əkt), *n.* The same sign as PRO-DUCER, but the INDIVIDUAL 1 sign is omitted.

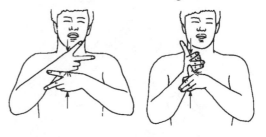

PRODUCTION (prə duk′ shən), *n.* The "P"s; making or fashioning something.) Both "P" hands are held one on top of the other, palms facing the signer, with the right fingertips pointing left and left fingertips pointing right. They turn forward repeatedly, so that the fingertips are now facing forward. The movement is repeated several times.

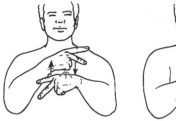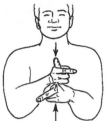

PROFESSION 1 (prə fĕsh′ ən), *n.* (The letter "F"; straight line denotes a specific "line" or area of pursuit.) The thumb edge of the right "F" hand moves forward along the outstretched left index finger. *Cf.* FIELD 2.

PROFESSION 2, *n.* (The letter "P"; the field or line.) The middle finger of the right "P" hand moves forward along the line of the outstretched, left index finger.

PROFIT (prŏf′ ĭt), *n., v.,* -FITED, -FITTING. (To get a profit; a coin popped into the vest pocket.) The sign for GET is made: both outstretched hands, held in a grasping "5" position, close into "S" positions, with the right on top of the left. At the same time both hands are drawn in to the body. The thumb and index finger of the right hand, holding an imaginary coin,

are then popped into an imaginary vest or breast pocket. *Note:* the sign for GET is sometimes omitted. *Cf.* GAIN 2.

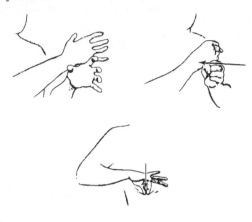

PROGRAM 1 (prō′ grăm, -grəm), *n.* (Placing things in order.) The hands, palms facing, fingers together and pointing away from the body, are positioned at the left side and held about a foot apart. With a slight up–down motion, as if describing waves, the hands travel in unison from left to right. *Cf.* ARRANGE, ARRANGEMENT, ORDER 3, PLAN 1, PREPARE 1, PROVIDE 1, PUT IN ORDER, READY 1.

PROGRAM 2, *n.* (The letter "P"; a listing on both sides of the page.) The thumb side of the right "P" hand is placed against the palm of the open left hand, which is facing right. The right "P" hand moves down the left palm. The left hand then swings around so that its palm faces the body. The right "P" hand then moves over and down the back of the left hand.

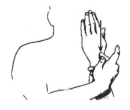

PROGRESS (*n.* prŏg′ rĕs; *v.* prə grĕs′), -GRESSED, -GRESSING. (Moving forward, step by step.) Both hands, in the right angle position, palms facing, are held before the chest, a few inches apart, with the right hand slightly behind the left. The right hand is brought up, over and forward, so that it is now ahead of the left. The left hand then follows suit, so that it is now ahead of the right. *Cf.* ADVANCE.

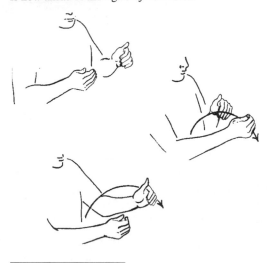

PROGRESSIVE (prə gres′ iv), *adj.* (Step by step.) Both right-angle hands are held facing the body, the right in front of the left. The hands move forward in stages, with one jumping over the other each time.

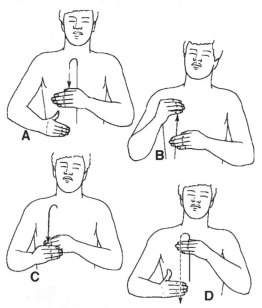

PROHIBIT (prō hĭb′ ĭt), *v.,* -ITED, -ITING. (A modification of LAW, *q.v.;* "against the law.") The down-turned right "D" or "L" hand is thrust forcefully into the left palm. *Cf.* BAN, FORBID 1, FORBIDDEN 1.

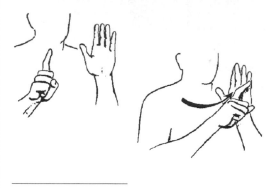

PROJECT (proj′ ekt), *n.* (The letters "P" and "J.") The middle finger of the right "P" hand moves down the left palm, held facing the body. Then the right "J" hand moves down the back of the left hand.

PROLOGUE (prō′ lôg), *n.* (The "P"s; bringing together or introducing.) Both "P" hands are held side by side, palms up and fingertips facing each other. The hands are swung toward each other, stopping just before they touch.

PROMINENT (prŏm' ə nənt), *adj.* (One's fame radiates far and wide.) The extended index fingers rest on the lips (or on the temples). Moving in small, continuous spirals, they move up and to either side of the head. *Cf.* FAME, FAMOUS, RENOWNED.

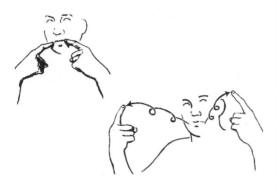

PROMISCUOUS 1 (prə mis' kyo͞o əs), *adj.* (Traveling from one person to the next.) The left "5" hand faces down or right. The bent right index and middle fingers move in small jumps from left to right.

PROMISCUOUS 2, *adj., sl.* (One whose legs are separated.) Both "X" hands, palms down, move up to the palms out position. This sign is used only for a female.

PROMISE 1 (prŏm' ĭs), *n., v.,* -ISED, -ISING. (The arm is raised.) The right index finger is placed at the lips. The right arm is then raised, palm out and elbow resting on the back of the left hand. *Cf.* GUARANTEE, LOYAL, OATH, PLEDGE, SWEAR 1, SWORN, TAKE OATH, VOW.

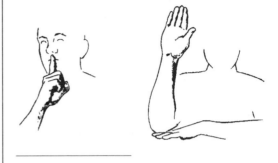

PROMISE 2, *n., v.* (Sealing the word.) The right index finger is placed at the lips, as in PROMISE 1. The open right hand is then brought down against the upturned left hand.

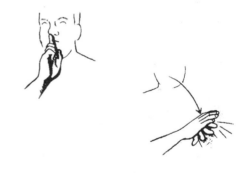

PROMISE 3, *n., v.* (A variation of PROMISE 2.) The right index finger is placed at the lips, as in PROMISE 1. The open right hand is then brought down against the thumb side of the left "S" hand.

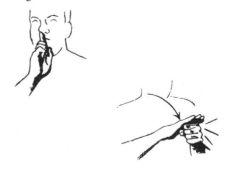

PROMOTE (prə mōt'), *v.*, -MOTED, -MOTING. (Something high up.) Both hands, in the right angle position, are held before the face, about a foot apart, palms facing. They are raised abruptly about a foot, in a slight outward curving movement. *Cf.* ADVANCED, HIGH 1, PROMOTION.

PROMOTION (prə mō' shən), *n.* See PROMOTE.

PROOF (prōōf), *n.* (Laying out the proof for all to see.) The back of the open right hand is placed with a flourish on the open left palm. The index finger may first touch the lips. *Cf.* PROVE.

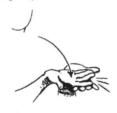

PROPER (prŏp' ər), *adj.* The right index finger, held above the left index finger, comes down rather forcefully so that the bottom of the right hand comes to rest on top of the left thumb joint. *Cf.* ACCURATE, CORRECT 1, DECENT, EXACT 2, RIGHT 3, SUITABLE.

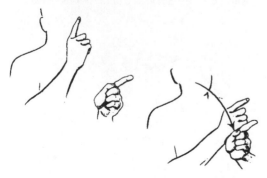

PROPHECY (prŏf' ə sī), *n.* (The vision is directed forward, into the distance.) The right "V" fingertips are placed under the eyes, with palm facing the body. The hand is then swung around and forward, moving under the downturned prone left hand and continuing forward and upward. *Cf.* FORECAST, FORESEE, FORETELL, PERCEIVE 2, PREDICT, PROPHESY, PROPHET, VISION 2.

PROPHESY (prŏf' ə sī), *v.*, -SIED, -SYING. See PROPHECY.

PROPHET (prŏf' it), *n.* See PROPHECY.

PROPORTION (prə pōr' shən), *n.* (In proportion.) Both "D" or "P" hands, palms facing down, are held before the body. They describe a short arc from right to left and, while unnecessary, they may return to their original position. *Cf.* THEREFORE 1, THUS.

PROPOSE (prə pōz'), *v.*, -POSED, -POSING. (An offering; a presenting.) Both hands, slightly cupped, palms up, are held close to the chest. They move up and out in unison, describing a very slight arc. *Cf.* MOTION, OFFER, OFFERING, PRESENT 1, SUGGEST.

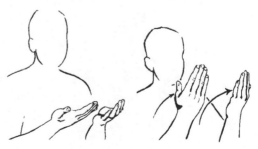

PROSE (prōz), *n.* (The letter "P"; writing.) The right "P" hand, held above the upturned left, moves toward the right. Optionally, the right hand may wriggle slightly as it moves toward the right.

PROSPER (prŏs' pər), *v.*, -PERED, -PERING. (Penetrating the heights.) The "D" hands, palms back, are held at each side of the head, near the temples. With a pivoting motion of the wrists, the hands swing up and around, simultaneously, to a position above the head, with palms facing out. *Cf.* ACCOMPLISH, ACHIEVE, SUCCEED, SUCCESS, SUCCESSFUL, TRIUMPH 2.

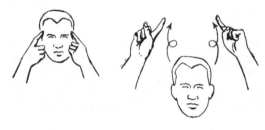

PROSTITUTE (prŏs' tə tūt'), *n.* (The blood rushes up the cheek in shame—several times for emphasis.) The curved back of the right hand, placed against the right cheek, moves up and off the cheek several times. *Cf.* WHORE.

PROTECT (prə tĕkt'), *v.*, -TECTED, -TECTING. (Hold down firmly; cover and strengthen.) The "S" hands, downturned, are held side by side in front of the body, the arms almost horizontal, and the left hand in front of the right. Both arms move a short distance forward and slightly downward. *Cf.* DEFEND, DEFENSE, FORTIFY, GUARD, PROTECTION, SHIELD 1.

PROTECTION (prə tĕk' shən), *n.* See PROTECT.

PROTEST 1 (*n.* prō' tĕst; *v.* prə tĕst'), -TESTED, -TESTING. (The hand is thrust into the chest to force a complaint out.) The curved fingers of the right hand are thrust forcefully into the chest. *Cf.* COMPLAIN, COMPLAINT, OBJECT 2, OBJECTION.

PROTEST 2, *n.*, *v.* (Turning one's head away in protest.) The right "S" hand, palm facing back, is held at forehead level. It swings forcefully around to the palm-forward position. This sign is used to indicate organized activity, as in "protesting the company's new policy."

PROTESTANT (prŏt′ ĭs tənt), *n., adj.* (Kneeling in church.) The knuckles of the right index and middle fingers are placed in the upturned left palm. The action may be repeated. *Cf.* KNEEL.

PROTON (prō′ ton), *n.* (The letter "P"; around the world.) The right "P" hand makes a circle around the left fist.

PROUD (proud), *adj.* (The feelings rise up.) The thumb of the right "A" hand, palm down, moves up along the right side of the chest. A haughty expression is assumed. *Cf.* PRIDE.

PROVE (prōōv), *v.*, PROVED, PROVEN, PROVING. See PROOF.

PROVIDE 1 (prə vīd′), *v.*, -VIDED, -VIDING. (Placing things in order.) The hands, palms facing, fingers together and pointing away from the body, are positioned at the left side and held about a foot apart. With a slight up–down motion, as if describing waves, the hands travel in unison from left to right. *Cf.* ARRANGE, ARRANGEMENT, ORDER 3, PLAN 1,

PREPARE 1, PROGRAM 1, PUT IN ORDER, READY 1.

PROVIDE 2, *v.* (Handing over.) The "AND" hands are held upright with palms toward the body. From this position they swing forward and down, opening up as if giving something out.

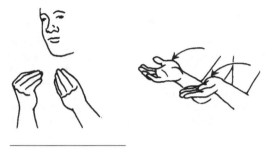

PSEUDONYM (sōō′ də nim), *n.* (False name.) The right hand is held in the "P" position. The upturned right index finger then brushes the tip of the nose (FALSE). Optionally the sign for NAME is then made: the index and middle fingers of the right "H" hand come down on top of their left counterparts.

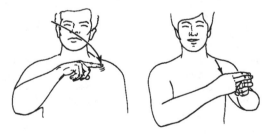

PSYCHIATRIST (sī kī′ ə trĭst), *n.* (The letter "P"; the pulse, which the doctor feels.) The thumb and middle finger of the right "P" hand twice touch the pulse of the upturned left hand.

PSYCHOLOGY (sī kŏl′ ə jĭ), *n.* (The Greek letter Ψ, "psi," symbol of psychology.) The little finger edge of the open right hand is thrust into the open left hand, between thumb and index finger. The action is usually repeated.

PSYCHOSIS (sī kō′ sis), *n.* (The mind collapses or breaks down.) The right index touches the forehead and then both hands, palms down, fingers slightly interlocked, "collapse" downward.

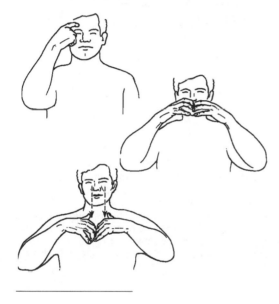

PUBLIC (pŭb′ lĭk), *adj., n.* (People, indicated by the rotating "P" hands.) The "P" hands, side by side, are moved alternately toward the body in continuous counterclockwise circles. *Cf.* HUMANITY, PEOPLE.

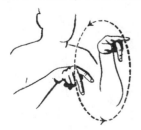

PUBLIC RELATIONS *n.* (The abbreviation; a finger-spelled loan sign.) The letters "P" and "R" are fingerspelled. This may be confused with "Puerto Rico," so one must rely on context.

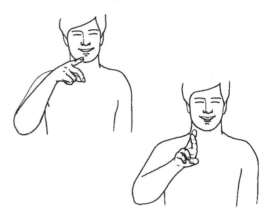

PUBLISH (pŭb′ lĭsh), *v.,* -LISHED, LISHING. (The action of the press.) The right "5" hand, held palm down, fingers pointing left, is brought down twice against the upturned left "5" hand, whose fingers point right. *Cf.* NEWSPAPER, PAPER.

PUERTO RICO (pwer′ tō rē′ kō), *n.* (The letters.) The signer makes the letters "P" and "R" on the back of the downturned left hand. A native sign.

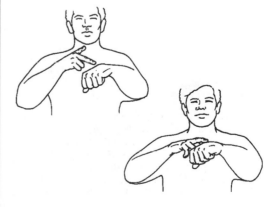

PULL 1 (pŏŏl), *v.*, PULLED, PULLING. (The natural action.) Both open hands, the right palm up and the left palm down, grasp an imaginary pole and pull it toward the body.

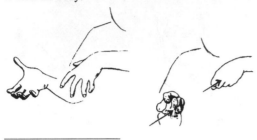

PULL 2, *v.* (Hooking on to something and pulling.) With index fingers interlocked, the right hand pulls the left hand from left to right. *Cf.* HITCH, HOOK, TOW.

PUMPKIN (pŭmp′ kĭn), *n.* (The yellow object is defined.) The sign for YELLOW is made: the right "Y" hand, palm facing the body, shakes slightly, pivoting at the wrist. Then the open "5" hands, fingers curved and palms facing, are held before the body to define the shape of the pumpkin.

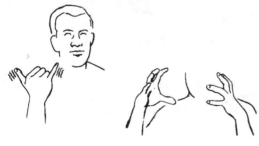

PUNCH 1 (pŭnch), *n., v.*, PUNCHED, PUNCHING. (The natural sign.) The right "S" hand strikes its knuckles forcefully against the open left palm, which is held facing right. *Cf.* HIT 1, POUND 2, STRIKE 1.

PUNCH 2, *n., v.* (The natural sign.) The right fist strikes the chin.

PUNISH (pŭn′ ĭsh), *v.*, -ISHED, -ISHING. (A striking movement.) The right index finger strikes the left elbow with a glancing blow.

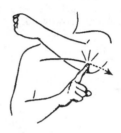

PUPIL 1 (pū′ pəl), *n.* (One who learns.) The sign for LEARN is made: the downturned fingers of the right hand are placed on the upturned left palm. They close, and then the hand rises and the right fingertips are placed on the forehead. This is followed by the sign for INDIVIDUAL: both open hands, palms facing each other, move down the sides of the body, tracing its outline to the hips. *Cf.* SCHOLAR, STUDENT 1.

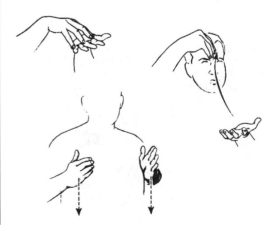

PUPIL 2, *n.* (One who studies.) The sign for STUDY is made: the upturned left hand represents a page. The right fingers wiggle as they move back and forth a short distance above the left hand. This is followed by the sign for INDIVIDUAL, as in PUPIL 1.

PURCHASE (pûr′ chəs), *n., v.,* -CHASED, -CHASING. (Giving out money.) The sign for MONEY is made: the upturned right hand, grasping some imaginary bills, is brought down into the upturned left palm, and then the right hand moves forward and up in a small arc. *Cf.* BUY.

PURE 1 (pyo͝or), *adj.* (Everything is wiped off the hand, to emphasize an uncluttered or clean condition.) The right hand slowly wipes the upturned left palm, from wrist to fingertips. *Cf.* CLEAN, NICE, PLAIN 2, PURITY, SIMPLE 2.

PURE 2, *n.* (The letter "P," for PURE, passed over the palm to denote CLEAN.) The right "P" hand moves forward along the palm of the upturned left hand, which is held flat, with fingers pointing forward.

PURITAN (pyo͝or′ ə tən), *n.* (The letter "P"; wiping off the hand.) The right "P" hand sweeps over the upturned left palm. The sign for INDIVIDUAL 1 then follows.

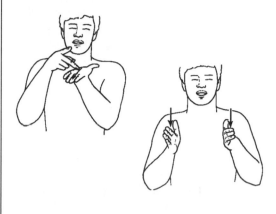

PURITY (pyo͝or′ ə tĭ), *n.* See PURE 1.

PURPOSE 1 (pûr′ pəs), *n.* (Relative standing of one's thoughts.) A modified sign for THINK is made: the right index finger touches the middle of the forehead. The tips of the right "V" hand, palm down, are then thrust into the upturned left palm (as in STAND, *q.v.*). The right "V" hand is then re-thrust into the upturned left palm, with right palm now facing the body. *Cf.* IMPLY, INTEND, INTENT, INTENTION, MEAN 2, MEANING, MOTIVE 3, SIGNIFICANCE 2, SIGNIFY 2, SUBSTANCE 2.

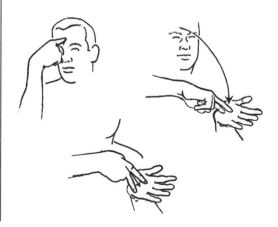

PURPOSE 2, *n.* (A thought directed upward, toward a goal.) The index finger of the right "D" hand touches the forehead, and then moves up to the index finger of the left "D" hand, which is held above eye level. The two index fingers stop just short of touching. *Cf.* AIM, AMBITION, GOAL, OBJECTIVE, PERSEVERE 4.

PURSUE (pər sōō'), *v.*, -SUED, -SUING. (The natural sign.) The "A" hands are held in front of the body, with the thumbs facing forward, the right palm facing left and the left palm facing right. The left hand is held slightly ahead of the right; it then moves forward in a straight line while the right hand follows after, executing a circular motion or swerving back and forth, as if in pursuit. *Cf.* CHASE.

PUSHCART (pŏŏsh' kärt), *n.* (Holding the handles and moving forward.) Grasping an imaginary pair of handles and lifting with effort, the signer moves slightly forward. *Cf.* WHEELBARROW.

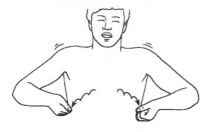

PUT (pŏŏt), *v.*, PUT, PUTTING. (Moving from one place to another.) The downturned hands, fingers touching their respective thumbs, move in unison from left to right. *Cf.* MOVE, PLACE 2.

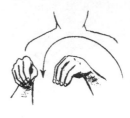

PUT DOWN *v. phrase.* (The natural motion.) The downturned "O" hands are brought down and to the left simultaneously from an initial side-by-side position near the right shoulder. *Cf.* DEPOSIT 1.

PUT IN ORDER *v. phrase.* (Placing things in order.) The hands, palms facing, fingers together and pointing away from the body, are positioned at the left side and held about a foot apart. With a slight up–down motion, as if describing waves, the hands travel in unison from left to right. *Cf.* ARRANGE, ARRANGEMENT, ORDER 3, PLAN 1, PREPARE 1, PROGRAM 1, PROVIDE 1, READY 1.

PUT OFF *v. phrase.* (Putting off; moving things forward repeatedly.) The "F" hands, palms facing and fingers pointing out from the body, are moved forward simultaneously in a series of short movements. *Cf.* DEFER, DELAY, POSTPONE, PROCRASTINATE.

PUZZLE (puz′ əl), *n*. (Manipulating the pieces.) The downturned fingers of both hands manipulate the pieces of a jigsaw puzzle.

PYRAMID (pir′ ə mid), *n*. (The shape.) Both downturned "B" hands, held far apart, move up toward the head, describing a pyramid.

Q

QUAKE (kwāk), *(colloq.), v.,* QUAKED, QUAKING. (The legs tremble.) Both "D" hands, index fingers pointing down, are held side by side to represent the legs. The hands tremble.

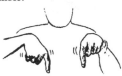

QUANTITY (kwŏn′ tə tĭ), *n.* (Many fingers are indicated.) The upturned "S" hands are thrown up, opening into the "5" position, palms up. This may be repeated. *Cf.* MANY, MULTIPLE, NUMEROUS, PLURAL.

QUARREL (kwôr′ əl, kwŏr′-), *n., v.* -RELED, -RELING. (Repeated rejoinders.) Both "D" hands are held with index fingers pointing toward each other. The hands move up and down alternately, each pivoting in turn at the wrist.

QUART (kwôrt), *n.* The "Q" hand, palm down, shakes slightly.

QUEEN (kwēn), *n.* (The letter "Q"; the royal sash.) The right "Q" hand, palm down, moves from left shoulder to right hip, tracing the sash worn by royalty.

QUEER (kwĭr), *adj.* (Something which distorts the vision.) The "C" hand describes a small arc in front of the face. *Cf.* CURIOUS 2, GROTESQUE, ODD, PECULIAR, STRANGE, WEIRD.

QUERY 1 (kwĭr′ ĭ), *n., v.,* -RIED, -RYING. (Firing questions.) The index fingers of both "D" hands repeatedly curve and straighten out as the hands are alternately flung forward and back, as if firing questions. *Cf.* ASK 3, EXAMINATION 2, INQUIRE 3, INTERROGATE 1, INTERROGATION 1, QUESTION 3, QUIZ 3.

QUERY 2, *(colloq.), n.* (Fire a question.) The right hand, held in a modified "S" position with palm facing out, assumes a position with the thumb resting on the fingernail of the index finger. The index finger is flicked out and forward, usually directed at the person being asked a question. *Cf.* ASK 2, INQUIRE 2,

INTERROGATE 2, INTERROGATION 2, QUESTION 2, QUIZ 2.

QUESTION 1 (kwĕs' chən), *n.* (The natural sign.) The right index finger draws a question mark in the air. *Cf.* QUESTION MARK.

QUESTION 2, *n.* See QUERY 2.

QUESTION 3, *n.* See QUERY 1.

QUESTION MARK *n.* See QUESTION 1.

QUICK (kwĭk), *adj.* (A quick movement.) The thumbtip of the upright right hand is flicked quickly off the tip of the curved right index finger, as if shooting marbles. *Cf.* FAST, IMMEDIATELY, QUICKNESS, SPEED, SPEEDY, SWIFT.

QUICKNESS *n.* See QUICK.

QUIET 1 (kwī' ət), *n., adj., interj., v.,* QUIETED, QUIET-ING. (The natural sign.) The index finger is brought up against the pursed lips. *Cf.* BE QUIET 1, SILENCE 1, SILENT, STILL 2.

QUIET 2, *n., adj., interj., v.* (Quiet and peace.) The open hands are crossed before the mouth, the right palm facing left, left facing right. Then both hands, held palms down, move down from the mouth, curving outward to either side of the body. *Cf.* BE QUIET 2, BE STILL, CALM, SILENCE 2.

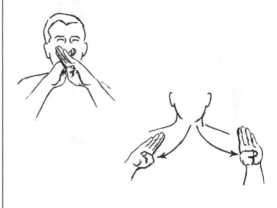

QUIT (kwĭt), *v.,* QUIT, QUITTING. (Pulling out.) The index and middle fingers of the right "H" hand are grasped by the left hand. The right hand pulls out of the left. *Cf.* RESIGN, WITHDRAW 2.

QUIZ 1 (kwĭz), *v.,* QUIZZED, QUIZZING, *n.* (A series of questions, spread out on a page.) Both "D" hands, palms down, simultaneously execute a single circle, the right hand moving in a clockwise direction and the left in a counterclockwise direction. Upon completion of the circle, both hands open into the "5" position and move straight down a short distance. (The hands actually draw question marks in the air.) *Cf.* EXAMINATION 1, TEST.

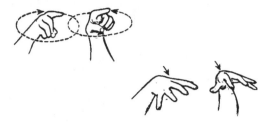

QUIZ 2, *(colloq.), v., n.* (Fire a question.) The right hand, held in a modified "S" position with palm facing out, assumes a position with the thumb resting on the fingernail of the index finger. The index finger is flicked out and forward, usually directed at the person being asked a question. *Cf.* ASK 2, INQUIRE 2, INTERROGATE 2, INTERROGATION 2, QUERY 2, QUESTION 2.

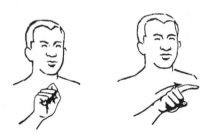

QUIZ 3, *v., n.* (Firing questions.) The index fingers of both "D" hands repeatedly curve and straighten out as the hands are alternately flung forward and back, as if firing questions. *Cf.* ASK 3, EXAMINATION 2, INQUIRE 3, INTERROGATE 1, INTERROGATION 1, QUERY 1, QUESTION 3.

QUOTATION (kwō tā′ shən), *n.* (The quotation marks are indicated.) The curved index and middle fingers of both hands, held palms out, move slightly to either side of the body, as if drawing quotation marks in the air. *Cf.* CAPTION 1, QUOTE, SO-CALLED, SUBJECT, THEME, TITLE, TOPIC.

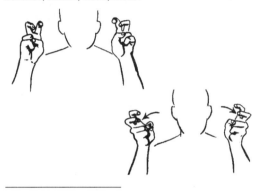

QUOTE (kwōt), *n., v.,* QUOTED, QUOTING. See QUOTATION.

R

RABBI (răb′ ĭ), *n.* (The letter "R"; the prayer shawl or tallith.) Both upright "R" hands trace the fall of the shawl down the sides of the chest.

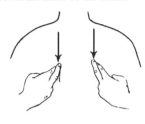

RABBIT (răb′ ĭt), *n.* (The movement of the ears.) Both "U" hands are placed at either side of the head, palms facing back. The index and middle fingers, joined together, move forward and back repeatedly, imitating a rabbit's ears.

RACE 1 (rās), *n., v.,* RACED, RACING. (Two opponents come together.) Both hands are closed, with thumbs pointing straight up and palms facing the body. From their initial position about a foot apart, the hands are brought together sharply, so that the knuckles strike. The hands, as they are drawn together, also move down a bit, so that they describe a "V." *Cf.* COMPETE 1, COMPETITION 1, RIVAL 2, RIVALRY 1, VIE 1.

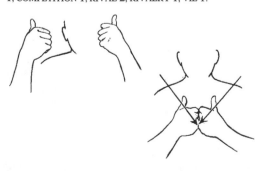

RACE 2, *n., v.* (Opposing objects.) The "A" hands are held side by side before the chest, palms facing each other and thumbs pointing forward. In this position the hands move alternately back and forth, toward and away from the body. *Cf.* COMPETE 2, COMPETITION 2, RIVAL 3, RIVALRY 2, VIE 2.

RACE 3, *n., v.* (The changing fortunes of competitors.) The "A" hands are held facing each other, thumbs pointing up in front of the body. Both hands are moved alternately backward and forward past each other several times. *Cf.* RIVAL 4, RIVALRY 3, VIE 3.

RACKET (rak′ it), *n.* (Holding the racket.) The signer goes through the motions of manipulating a tennis racket. *Cf.* TENNIS.

RADIOACTIVE (ra´ dĕ ō ak´ tiv), *adj.* (The "R" and "A" letters; moving away.) The right "R" hand moves away from the left "A" hand, as if tracing the rays.

RAFT (raft), *n.* (Floating along on top of a support.) With the right hand resting on the left, both hands "float" away.

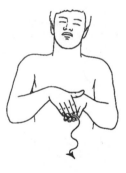

RAGE (rāj), *n., v.,* RAGED, RAGING. (A violent welling-up of the emotions.) The curved fingers of the right hand are placed in the center of the chest, and fly up suddenly and violently. An expression of anger is worn. *Cf.* ANGER, ANGRY 2, ENRAGE, FURY, INDIGNANT, INDIGNATION, IRE, MAD.

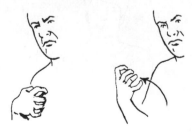

RAILROAD 1 (rāl´ rōd´), *n.* (Running along the tracks.) The "V" hands are held palms down. The right "V" fingers move over the backs of the downturned left "V" fingers from base to tips. *Cf.* TRAIN 1, TRANSPORTATION 2.

RAILROAD 2, *n.* (The letter "R.") The right "R" hand, palm down, moves down an inch or two, and moves to the right in a small arc.

RAINBOW (rān´ bō´), *n.* (Tracing the colors across the sky.) The right "4" hand, palm facing the signer, describes an arc in the air, from left to right.

RAISE 1 (rāz), *n., v.,* RAISED, RAISING. (Getting onto one's feet.) The upturned index and middle fingers of the right hand, representing the legs, are swung up and over in an arc, coming to rest in the upturned left palm. *Cf.* ARISE 2, GET UP, RISE 1, STAND 2, STAND UP.

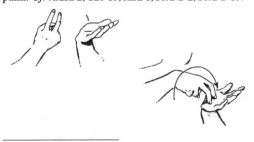

RAISE 2, *n., v.* (Adding on.) The index and middle fingers of the right "H" hand, palm up, are swung up and over until they come to rest on the index and middle fingers of the left "H" hand, held palm down. *Cf.* ADD 3, ADDITION, GAIN 1, INCREASE, ON TO.

RAISE 3, *n., v.* (Flowers or plants emerge from the ground.) The right fingers, pointing up, emerge from the closed left hand, and they spread open as the blooms do. *Cf.* BLOOM, DEVELOP 1, GROW, GROWN, MATURE 1, PLANT 1, REAR 2, SPRING.

RAISE 4, *v.* (To bring up, say, a child.) The downturned, open left hand slowly rises straight up, indicating the growth of a child. The right hand may also be used.

RAISINS (rā' zənz), *n.* (The letter "R"; a cluster of grapes.) The right "R" fingers move down the back of the prone left hand, tapping as they go.

RAMP (ramp), *n.* (The incline.) The downturned right hand, fingers pointing forward, moves up an imaginary incline. Both hands may also be used, with one leading the other.

RANCH (ranch), *n.* (The letter "R"; the stubbled chin of a rough cowboy.) The right "R" hand, palm facing left, slides from the left chin to the right.

RAPE 1 (rāp), *n., v. vulg.* (Pulling the legs apart and penetrating the victim.) The signer mimes pulling a victim's legs apart forcefully. The right "S" hand then moves down and forward in an arc. This rather coarse sign is not used in polite conversation. The first part of the sign, involving the legs, is often omitted.

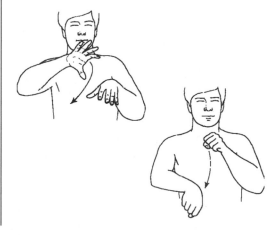

RAPE 2, *n., v.* (An assault involving the wringing the neck.) Both "S" hands are held palms facing forward. The right "S" brushes against the left "S" as it twists and moves forward. This is a more socially acceptable sign than RAPE 1.

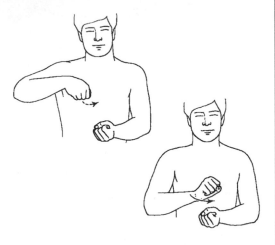

RASH (rash), *n.* (Spots on the body.) Both claw hands make dots all over the chest and/or face.

RAT (răt), *n.* (The twitching nose.) The tips of the right "R" fingers brush the tip of the nose several times.

RATE (rāt), *n.* (Drawing a percent symbol in the air.) The right "O" hand traces a percent symbol (%) in the air. *Cf.* DEGREE 2, PERCENT.

REACTION 1 (rĭ ăk'shən), *n.* (The letter "R"; coming out of the mouth.) Both "R" hands are held before the face, with the right "R" hand at the lips and behind the left "R" hand. Both hands move forward simultaneously, describing a small upward arc. *Cf.* REPLY 2, REPORT, RESPONSE 2.

REACTION 2, *n.* (The "R"; moving apart.) Both "R" hands, fingers touching at the tips, move apart.

READ 1 (rēd), *v.,* READ, READING. (The eyes scan the page.) The left hand is held before the body, palm up and fingers pointing to the right. This represents the page. The right "V" hand then moves down as if scanning the page.

READ 2, *v.* (The eyes scan a page.) The index and middle fingers of the right "V" hand represent the eyes and follow imaginary lines on the left palm, which represents the page of a book.

READ 3, *v.* (Reading a book.) The open hands support an imaginary book. The signer, looking at the book, moves his head repeatedly from left to right as if reading.

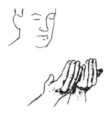

READ LIPS *v. phrase.* (Reading the lips—the lines of vision, represented by the two fingers, scan the lips.) The right "V" hand, palm facing the body, is placed in front of the face, with slightly curved index and middle fingers directly in front of the lips. The right hand moves in a small counterclockwise circle around the lips. *Cf.* LIPREADING, ORAL, SPEECHREADING.

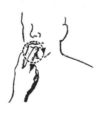

READY 1 (rĕd′ ĭ), *adj., v.,* READIED, READYING. (Placing things in order.) The hands, palms facing, fingers together and pointing away from the body, are positioned at the left side and held about a foot apart. With a slight up–down motion, as if describing waves, the hands travel in unison from left to right.

Cf. ARRANGE, ARRANGEMENT, ORDER 3, PLAN 1, PREPARE 1, PROGRAM 1, PROVIDE 1, PUT IN ORDER.

READY 2, *adj.* (The "R" hands.) The "R" hands are held side by side before the body, palms up and fingers pointing outward. The hands then turn toward each other and over, so that the palms face down and fingers point toward each other. *Cf.* PREPARE 2.

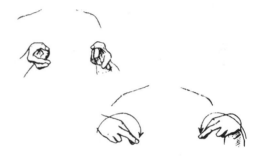

READY 3, *adj., adv.* (The "R" hands.) The same sign as for READY 1, *q.v.,* is made, except that the "R" hands are used. With palms facing down, they move simultaneously from left to right.

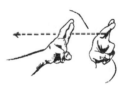

READY 4, *adj., v.* (Set out.) The "A" hands are crossed, with the right resting on top of the left. The right palm faces left and the left palm faces right. Both hands suddenly open and swing apart to the palm-down position. *Cf.* PREPARE 3.

REAL (rē′ əl, rēl), *adj.* (Coming forth directly from the lips; true.) The index finger of the right "D" hand, palm facing left, is placed against the lips. It moves up an inch or two and then describes a small arc forward and away from the lips. *Cf.* REALLY, SURE, SURELY, TRUE, TRULY, TRUTH.

REALIZE (rē′ ə līz′), *v.*, -IZED, -IZING. (Knowing and understanding.) The sign for KNOW is made: the right fingers pat the forehead several times. This is followed by the sign for UNDERSTAND: the curved index finger of the right hand, palm facing the body, is placed with the fingernail resting on the middle of the forehead. It suddenly flicks up into the "D" position.

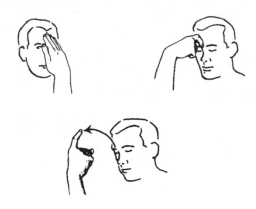

REALLY (rē′ ə lǐ, rē′ lǐ), *adv.* See REAL.

REAP 1 (rēp), *v.*, REAPED, REAPING. (Gathering in the harvest.) The right open hand sweeps across the upturned left palm and closes into the "A" position,

as if gathering up some stalks. *Cf.* HARVEST 1.

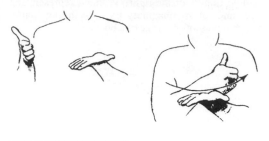

REAP 2, *v* . (The cutting.) The left hand grasps the heads of imaginary wheat stalks. The upturned right hand, imitating a sickle blade, then swings in to cut the stalks. *Cf.* HARVEST 2.

REAR 1 (rĭr), *n.* (The natural sign.) The right hand moves over the right shoulder to tap the back.

REAR 2, *v.* (Flowers or plants emerge from the ground.) The right fingers, pointing up, emerge from the closed left hand, and they spread open as they do. *Cf.* BLOOM, DEVELOP 1, GROW, GROWN, MATURE 1, PLANT 1, RAISE 3, SPRING.

REASON (rē′ zən), *n.* (The letter "R"; the thought.) The fingertips of the right "R" hand describe a small counterclockwise circle in the middle of the forehead.

REBEL (*adj., n.* rĕb′ əl; *v.* rĭ bĕl′), -BELLED, -BELLING. (Turning the head.) The right "S" hand, held up with its palm facing the body, swings sharply around to the palm-out position. The head meanwhile moves slightly toward the left. *Cf.* DISOBEDIENCE, DISOBEY.

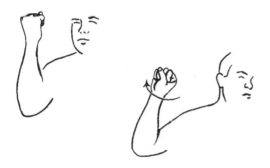

RECALL 1 (rĭ kôl′), *v.,* -CALLED, -CALLING. (Bringing something back from the past.) The right open hand reaches back over the right shoulder as if to grasp something, and then brings the imaginary thing before the face with the closed "AND" hand. *Cf.* RECOLLECT 1.

RECALL 2, *v.* (Knowledge which remains.) The sign for KNOW is made: the right fingertips are placed on the forehead. The sign for REMAIN then follows: the "A" hands are held with palms toward the body, thumbs extended and touching, the right behind the left. In this position the hands move forward in a straight, steady line, or straight down. *Cf.* MEMORY, RECOLLECT 2, REMEMBER.

RECEIVE (rĭ sēv′), *v.,* -CEIVED, -CEIVING. (A grasping and bringing forward to oneself.) Both hands, in the "5" position, fingers curved, are crossed at the wrists, with the left palm facing right and the right palm facing left. They are brought in toward the chest, while closing into a grasping "S" position. *Cf.* ACQUIRE, GET, OBTAIN, PROCURE.

 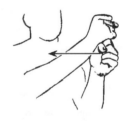

RECEIVE REGULARLY *phrase.* (Pulling in repeatedly.) The right claw hand, held above the side of the head, palm facing left, is pulled down repeatedly, closing into the "S" shape each time. This is an appropriate sign for "subscription," "benefits," such as Social Security, and "earnings" or "salary."

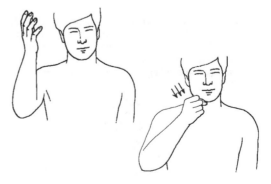

RECENT (rē' sənt), *adj.* (The slight movement represents a slight amount of time.) With the closed right hand held with knuckles against the right cheek, the thumbtip flicks off the tip of the curved index finger a number of times. The eyes squint a bit and the lips are drawn out in a slight smile. The hand remains against the cheek during the flicking movement. Sometimes, instead of the flicking movement, the tip of the curved index finger scratches slightly up and down against the cheek. In this case, the palm faces back toward the shoulder. The same expression is used as in the flicking movement. *Cf.* RECENTLY, WHILE AGO, A 1.

RECENTLY *adv.* See RECENT.

RECITATION (rĕs´ ə tā' shən), *n.* (Studying back and forth.) This sign is derived from the sign for STUDY, *q.v.* The right-angle hands face each other, with the right hand facing left and the left hand facing right. They move alternately forward and back, with fingers wiggling.

RECKLESS (rĕk' lĭs), *adj.* (The vision is sidetracked, causing one to lose sight of the object in view.) The right "V" hand, representing the vision, is held in front of the face, palm facing left. The hand, pivoted at the wrist, moves back and forth a number of times. *Cf.* CARELESS.

RECKON (rĕk' ən), *v.*, -ONED, -ONING. (A thought is turned over in the mind.) The index finger makes a small circle on the forehead. *Cf.* CONSIDER 1, MOTIVE 1, SPECULATE 1, SPECULATION 1, THINK, THOUGHT 1, THOUGHTFUL.

RECLINE (rĭ klīn'), *v.*, -CLINED, -CLINING. (The prone position of the legs, in lying down.) The index and middle fingers of the right "V" hand, palm facing up, are placed in the upturned left palm and slide down an inch or two toward the fingertips. *Cf.* LIE DOWN.

RECOGNIZE (rĕk' əg nīz´), *v.*, -NIZED, -NIZING. (Patting the head to indicate something of value inside.) The right fingers pat the forehead several times. *Cf.* KNOW, KNOWING, KNOWLEDGE.

RECOLLECT 1 (rĕk ə lĕkt'), *v.*, -LECTED, -LECTING. (Bringing something back from the past.) The right open hand reaches back over the right shoulder as if to grasp something, and then brings the imaginary thing before the face with the closed "AND" hand. *Cf.* RECALL 1.

RECOLLECT 2, *v*. (Knowledge which remains.) The sign for KNOW is made: the right fingertips are placed on the forehead. The sign for REMAIN then follows: the "A" hands are held with palms toward the body, thumbs extended and touching, the right behind the left. In this position the hands move forward in a straight, steady line, or straight down. *Cf.* MEMORY, RECALL 2, REMEMBER.

RECORD (rek′ ərd), *n*. (The letter "P"; revolving record table.) The right "R" hand, fingers pointing down, makes a series of large clockwise circles in the upturned left palm.

RECTANGLE (rek′ tang´ gəl), *n*. (The letter "R"; the shape.) Both "R" hands describe a rectangle in the air.

RED (rĕd), *adj., n*. (The lips, which are red, are indicated.) The tip of the right index finger moves down

across the lips. The "R" hand may also be used.

REDEEM 1 (rĭ dēm′), *v., -DEEMED, -DEEMING*. (Breaking the bonds.) The "S" hands, crossed in front of the body, swing apart and face out. *Cf.* EMANCIPATE, FREE 1, FREEDOM, INDEPENDENCE, INDEPENDENT 1, LIBERATION, RELIEF, RESCUE, SAFE, SALVATION, SAVE 1.

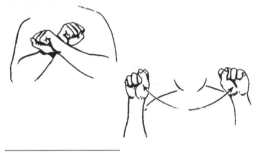

REDEEM 2, *v*. (The "R" hands.) The sign for REDEEM 1 is made with the "R" hands.

REDEEMER (rĭ dē′ mər), *n*. (One who redeems.) The sign for REDEEM 1 or 2 is made. This is followed by the sign for INDIVIDUAL: both open hands, palms facing each other, move down the sides of the body, tracing its outline to the hips.

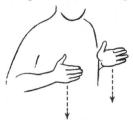

REDUCE (rĭ dūs′, -dōōs′), *v.*, -DUCED, -DUCING. (The diminishing size or amount.) With palms facing, the right hand is held above the left. The right hand moves slowly down toward the left, but does not touch it. *Cf.* DECREASE, LESS.

REFER (rĭ fûr′), *v.*, -FERRED, -FERRING. (The letter "R," transferring.) The fingertips of the right "R" hand touch the palm of the open left hand, which is held with palm facing right, fingers pointing upward. From this position the right hand moves backward, off the left palm.

REFEREE (rĕf′ ə rē′), *n.* (Judge, individual.) The sign for JUDGE is formed: the two "F" hands, palms facing each other, move alternately up and down. This is followed by the sign for INDIVIDUAL: both open hands, palms facing each other, move down the sides of the body, tracing its outline to the hips. *Cf.* JUDGE 2, UMPIRE.

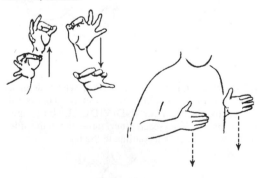

REFLECT (ri flekt′), *v.* (The image reflects back.) The right "R" fingers, held up, touch the outstretched left palm, and move forward slowly and deliberately. The signer may cause the right hand to tremble

slightly as it moves forward.

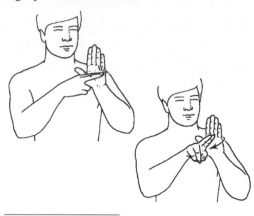

REFRIGERATOR 1 (ri frij′ ə rā´ tər), *n.* (ELECTRIC, *i.e.,* an ice box operated by electricity.) Both bent index fingers strike each other repeatedly at the knuckles. The movement pertains to the contact between the electrodes. This sign, though archaic in concept, is still widely used today.

REFRIGERATOR 2, *n.* (A fingerspelled loan word.) The signer fingerspells "R-E-F."

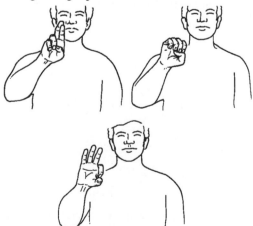

REFUGE (rĕf′ ūj), *n*. (A shield.) The "S" hands are held before the chest, the left behind the right, and are pushed slightly away from the body. Then the right hand opens, palm facing out, and moves clockwise as if shielding the left fist. *Cf*. SHELTER, SHIELD 2.

REFUSE (rĭ fūz′), *v*., -FUSED, -FUSING. (Holding back.) The right "A" hand, palm facing left, moves up sharply to a position above the right shoulder. *Cf*. WON'T.

REGION (rē′ jən), *n*. (The "R" letters; a space is outlined.) Both downturned "R" hands, touching, execute a circle by moving apart and in toward the chest.

REGRESSION (ri gresh′ ən), *n*. The letter "R"; declining or going down.) The right "R" hand runs down the outstretched downturned left arm in a series of small steps.

REGRET (rĭ grĕt′), *n*., *v*., -GRETTED, -GRETTING. (The heart is circled, to indicate feeling, modified by the letter "S," for SORRY.) The right "S" hand, palm facing the body, is rotated several times over the area of the heart. *Cf*. APOLOGIZE 1, APOLOGY 1, CONTRITION, PENITENT, REGRETFUL, REPENT, REPENTANT, RUE, SORROW, SORROWFUL 2, SORRY.

REGRETFUL (rĭ grĕt′ fəl), *adj*. See REGRET.

REGULAR (rĕg′ yə lər), *adj*. (Coming together with regular frequency.) Both "D" hands are held with index fingers pointing forward, the right hand above the left. The right "D" hand is brought down on the left several times in rhythmic succession as both hands move forward. *Cf*. CONSISTENT, FAITHFUL.

REGULATE (rĕg′ yə lāt′), *v*., -LATED, -LATING. (Holding the reins over all.) The "A" hands, palms facing, move alternately back and forth, as if grasping and manipulating reins. The left "A" hand, still in position, swings over so that its palm now faces down. The right hand opens to the "5" position, palm down, and swings over the left, which moves slightly to the right. *Cf*. CONTROL 1, DIRECT 1, GOVERN, MANAGE, MANAGEMENT, MANAGER, OPERATE, REIGN, RULE 1.

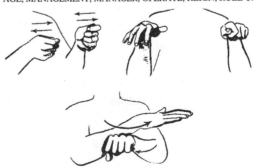

REGULATION(S) (rĕg´ yə lā´ shən), *n.* (The letter "R"; the listing.) The upright, open left hand, fingers together and palm facing out, represents a piece of paper on which are listed the rules or regulations. The right "R" hand is placed upright against the tips of the left fingers, and then it moves down in an arc to a position against the base of the left hand. *Cf.* RULE(S) 2.

REHABILITATION (re´ hə bĭl´ ə tā´ shən), *n.* (The letter "R"; one hand helps or supports the other.) The right "R" hand rests with its base or side in the upturned left palm. The left hand pushes up the right a short distance.

REIGN (rān), *n.* See REGULATE.

REINFORCE (rē´ ĭn fōrs´), *v.*, -FORCED, -FORCING. (The letter "R"; pushing up, *i.e.*, assisting or reinforcing.) The right "R" hand, palm facing down, pushes up the left "S" hand, which is facing right.

REINS (rānz), *n. pl.* (Holding the reins.) The hands grasp and manipulate imaginary reins.

REJECT (*n.* rē´ jĕkt; *v.* rĭ jĕkt´), -JECTED, -JECTING. (The act of rejecting or sending off.) The downturned, right right-angle hand is positioned just above the base of the upturned, open left hand. The right hand sweeps forward in an arc over the left, and its fingertips brush sharply against the left palm. *Cf.* REJECTION.

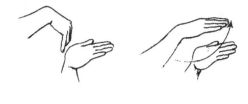

REJECTION (rĭ jĕk´ shən), *n.* See REJECT.

REJOICE (rĭ jois´), *v.*, -JOICED, -JOICING. (Waving of flags.) Both upright hands, grasping imaginary flags, wave them in small circles. *Cf.* CELEBRATE, CELEBRATION, CHEER, VICTORY 1, WIN 1.

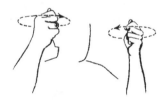

RELAPSE (rĭ lăps´), *n., v.*, -LAPSED, -LAPSING. (Going down.) The little finger edge of the open right hand is placed at the elbow of the downturned left arm. The right hand travels down the left arm in one sweeping movement, or in short stages. This is the opposite of IMPROVE, *q.v.*

RELATION (rĭ lā′ shən), *(rare), n.* (A variation of the COUSIN sign, *q.v.*) The right "C" hand, held near the right temple, wiggles down to shoulder level.

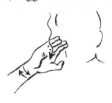

RELATIONSHIP (rĭ lā′ shən shĭp′), *n.* (The fingers are connected.) The index fingers and thumbs of both hands interlock, and the hands move back and forth from right to left. *Cf.* CONNECTION.

RELATIVE (rĕl′ ə tĭv), *n.* (Touching one another, as members of a family.) The "D" hands, palms facing the body and index fingers pointing toward each other, swing alternately up and down. Each time they pass each other, the index fingertips come into mutual contact.

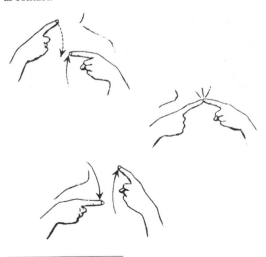

RELAX 1 (rĭ lăks′), *v.*, -LAXED, -LAXING. (The folded arms; a position of rest.) With palms facing the body,

the arms are folded across the chest. *Cf.* REST 1, RESTFUL 1.

RELAX 2, *n.* (The "R" hands.) The sign for REST 1, *q.v.*, is made, but with the crossed "R" hands. *Cf.* REST 2, RESTFUL 2.

RELAY (rē′ lā), *n., v.* (Back and forth movement.) Both "R" hands pass each other repeatedly as they move back and forth.

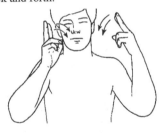

RELIEF (rĭ lēf′), *n.* (Breaking the bonds.) The "S" hands, crossed in front of the body, swing apart and face out. *Cf.* EMANCIPATE, FREE 1, FREEDOM, INDEPENDENCE, INDEPENDENT 1, LIBERATION, REDEEM 1, RESCUE, SAFE, SALVATION, SAVE 1.

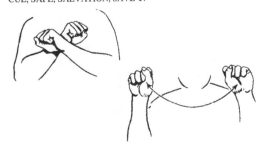

RELINQUISH (rĭ lǐng' kwǐsh), *v.*, -QUISHED, -QUISH-ING. (Throwing up the hands in a gesture of surrender.) Both "A" hands are held palms down before the chest and then thrown up in unison, ending in the "5" position. *Cf.* DISCOURAGE, FORFEIT, GIVE UP, RENOUNCE, RENUNCIATION, SURRENDER, YIELD.

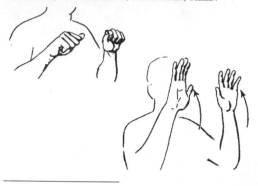

RELY 1 (rĭ lī'), *v.*, -LIED, -LYING. (Something which weighs down or burdens one with responsibility.) The fingertips of both hands, placed on the right shoulder, bear down. *Cf.* OBLIGATION, RESPONSIBILITY 1, RESPONSIBLE 1.

RELY 2, *v.* (Hanging on to.) With the right index finger resting across its left counterpart, both hands drop down a bit. *Cf.* DEPEND, DEPENDABLE.

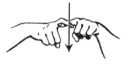

REMAIN (rĭ mān'), *v.*, -MAINED, -MAINING. (Steady, uninterrupted movement.) The "A" hands are held with palms out, thumbs extended and touching, the right behind the left. In this position the hands move forward in a straight, steady line. *Cf.* CONTINUE, ENDURE 2, EVER 1, LAST 3, LASTING, PERMANENT, PERPETUAL, PERSEVERE 3, PERSIST 2, STAY 1, STAY STILL.

REMAINDER (rĭ mān' dər), *n.* (The remainder is left behind.) The "5" hands, palms facing each other and fingers pointing forward, are dropped simultaneously a few inches, as if dropping something on the table. *Cf.* LEFT.

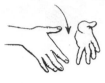

REMARK (rĭ märk'), *v.*, -MARKED, -MARKING. (Words tumbling from the mouth.) The right index finger, pointing left, describes a continuous small circle in front of the mouth. *Cf.* DISCOURSE, HEARING, MAINTAIN 2, MENTION, SAID, SAY, SPEAK, SPEECH 1, STATE, STATEMENT, TALK 1, TELL, VERBAL.

REMEMBER (rĭ mĕm' bər), *v.*, -BERED, -BERING. (Knowledge which remains.) The sign for KNOW is made: the right fingertips are placed on the forehead. The sign for REMAIN then follows: the "A" hands are held with palms toward the body, thumbs extended and touching, the right behind the left. In this position the hands move forward in a straight, steady line, or straight down. *Cf.* MEMORY, RECALL 2, RECOLLECT 2.

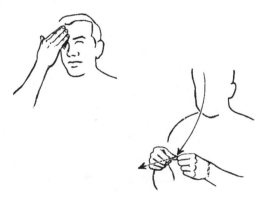

REMIND (rĭ mīnd'), (colloq.), v., -MINDED, -MINDING. (Bring up to mind.) The index finger swings up quickly to the forehead. As it touches the forehead, the head tilts back. The eyes are sometimes opened wide for emphasis.

REMOTE (rĭ mōt'), adj. (Moving beyond, i.e., the concept of distance or "farness.") The "A" hands are held together, thumbs pointing away from the body. The right hand moves straight ahead in a slight arc. The left hand does not move. Cf. FAR.

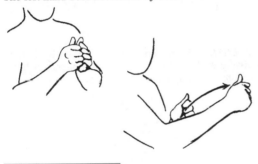

REMOVE (rĭ mōōv'), v., -MOVED, -MOVING. (Removing.) The right "A" hand, resting in the palm of the left "5" hand, moves slightly up and away, describing a small arc. It is then cast downward, opening into the "5" position, palm down, as if removing something from the left hand and casting it down. Cf. ABOLISH, DEDUCT, DELETE 1, ELIMINATE, SUBTRACT, SUBTRACTION, TAKE AWAY FROM.

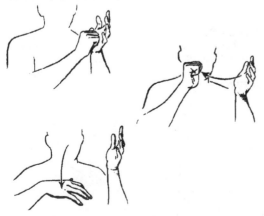

RENOUNCE (rĭ nouns'), v., -NOUNCED, -NOUNCING. (Throwing up the hands in a gesture of surrender.) Both "A" hands are held palms down before the chest and then thrown up in unison, ending in the "5" position. Cf. DISCOURAGE, FORFEIT, GIVE UP, RELINQUISH, RENUNCIATION, SURRENDER, YIELD.

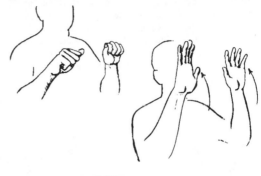

RENOWNED (rĭ nound'), adj. (One's fame radiates far and wide.) The extended index fingers rest on the lips (or on the temples). Moving in small, continuous spirals, they move up and to either side of the head. Cf. FAME, FAMOUS, PROMINENT.

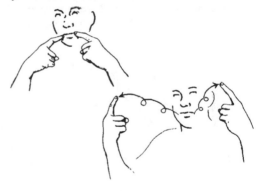

RENT (rent), n., v. (Monthly.) The sign for MONTH is made: the extended right index finger moves down along the upturned extended left index finger. This movement is repeated several times. Cf. MONTHLY.

RENUNCIATION (rĭ nŭn´ sĭ ā´ shən, -shĭ-), *n.* See RENOUNCE.

REPAIR (rĭ pâr´), *v.,* -PAIRED, -PAIRING. (Fashioning something with the hands.) The right "S" hand, palm facing left, is placed on top of its counterpart, whose palm faces right. The hands are twisted back and forth, striking each other slightly after each twist. *Cf.* CONSTRUCT 2, CREATE 1, DEVISE, MAKE, MANUFACTURE, MEND, PRODUCE 2.

REPAIR WHAT WAS SAID (Grammatical device in ASL.) The right index finger is brought firmly up against the tightly closed lips. The eyes may be closed and the head may shake slightly. The English gloss here may be "Excuse me, I didn't mean that;" "Let me correct myself." Also known as "repairs" in ASL grammar.

REPEAT (rĭ pēt´), *v.,* -PEATED, -PEATING. The left hand, open in the "5" position, palm up, is held before the chest. The right hand, in the right angle position, fingers pointing up, arches over and into the left palm. *Cf.* AGAIN.

REPEATEDLY *adv.* (Repeating over and over again.) The sign for REPEAT is made several times.

REPENT (ri pent´), *v.,* -PENTED, -PENTING. (The heart is circled, to indicate feeling, modified by the letter "S," for SORRY.) The right "S" hand, palm facing the body, is rotated several times over the area of the heart. *Cf.* APOLOGIZE 1, APOLOGY 1, CONTRITION, PENITENT, REGRET, REGRETFUL, REPENTANT, RUE, SORROW, SORROWFUL 2, SORRY.

REPENTANCE (ri pen´ təns), *n.* (The "R" letters, twisting the heart.) Both "R" hands, fingers touching, execute a twisting motion at the heart.

REPENTANT (ri pen´ tənt), *adj.* See REPENT.

REPLACE (rĭ plās´), *v.,* -PLACED, -PLACING. (Exchanging places.) The right "A" hand, positioned above the left "A" hand, swings down and under the left, coming up a bit in front of it. *Cf.* EXCHANGE, INSTEAD OF 1, SUBSTITUTE, TRADE.

REPLY 1 (rĭ plī'), *n., v.,* -PLIED, -PLYING. (Directing a reply from the mouth to someone.) The tip of the right index finger, held in the "D" position, palm facing the body, is placed on the lips, while the left "D" hand, palm also facing the body, is held about a foot in front of the right hand. The right index finger, swinging around, moves toward and stops in a pointing position a few inches from the left index fingertip. *Cf.* ANSWER, MAKE RESPONSE, RESPOND, RESPONSE 1.

REPLY 2, *v.* (The letter "R"; coming out of the mouth.) Both "R" hands are held before the face, with the right "R" hand at the lips and behind the left "R" hand. Both hands move forward simultaneously, describing a small upward arc. *Cf.* REACTION 1, REPORT, RESPONSE 2.

REPORT (rĭ pôrt'), *v.,* -PORTED, -PORTING. See REPLY 2.

REPRESENT (rĕp' rĭ zĕnt'), *v.,* -SENTED, -SENTING. (Directing the attention to something, and bringing it forward.) The right index finger points into the left palm, held facing out before the body. The left palm moves straight out. *Cf.* DEMONSTRATE, DISPLAY, EVIDENCE, EXAMPLE, EXHIBIT, EXHIBITION, ILLUSTRATE, INDICATE, INFLUENCE 2, PRODUCE 1, SHOW 1, SIGNIFY 1.

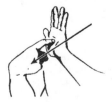

REPRESENTATIVE (rĕp rĭ zĕn' tə tiv), *n.* (The letter "R"; to show.) The right "R" hand, placed in the left palm, is pushed forward by the palm. The sign for INDIVIDUAL 1 usually then follows.

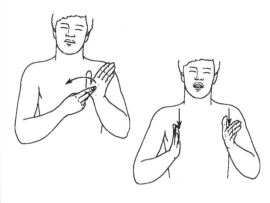

REPRIMAND (rĕp' rə mănd'), *n., v.,* -MANDED, -MANDING. (A scolding with the finger.) The right index finger shakes back and forth in a natural scolding movement. *Cf.* REPROVE, SCOLD 1.

REPROVE (rĭ prōōv'), *v.,* -PROVED, -PROVING. See REPRIMAND.

REPUBLIC (ri pub' lik), *n.* (The letter "R"; NATION.) The tips of the right "R" fingers make a clockwise circle above the downturned left hand and come down to rest on the back of the left fist. *Cf.* COUNTRY 2, LAND 2, NATION.

REQUEST 1 (rĭ kwĕst′), n., v., -QUESTED, -QUESTING. (Pray tell.) Both hands, held upright about a foot in front of the chest, with palms facing and fingers pointing straight up, are positioned about a foot apart. Moving toward the chest, they come together until they touch, as if in prayer. Cf. ASK 1, INQUIRE 1.

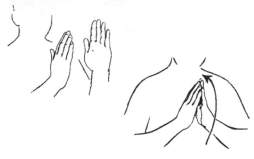

REQUEST 2, n., v. (Something specific is moved in toward oneself.) The palm of the left "5" hand faces right. The right index finger is thrust into the left palm, and both hands are drawn sharply in toward the chest. Cf. DEMAND, INSIST, REQUIRE.

REQUIRE (rĭ kwīr′), v., -QUIRED, -QUIRING. See REQUEST 2.

RESCUE (rĕs′ kū), v., -CUED, -CUING, n. (Breaking the bonds.) The "S" hands, crossed in front of the body, swing apart and face out. Cf. EMANCIPATE, FREE 1, FREEDOM, INDEPENDENCE, INDEPENDENT 1, LIBERATION, REDEEM 1, RELIEF, SAFE, SALVATION, SAVE 1.

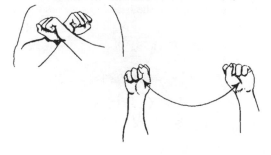

RESERVATION (rĕz′ ər vā′ shən), n. (Binding the hands down.) The downturned, right "S" hand makes a single, clockwise circle and comes down to rest on the back of the downturned, left "S" hand. Cf. RESERVE 1.

RESERVE 1 (rĭ zûrv′), v. -SERVED, -SERVING. See RESERVATION 1.

RESERVE 2, v. (Slow, careful movement.) The "K" hands are crossed, the right above the left, little finger edges down. In this position the hands are moved up and down a short distance. Cf. CARE 2, CAREFUL 2, KEEP, MAINTAIN 1, MIND 3, PRESERVE, TAKE CARE OF 2.

RESERVE 3, v. (Holding back.) The right "V" fingers are tapped once or twice across the back of their left counterparts. Both palms face the chest. Cf. SAVE 2, STORE.

RESIDE (rĭ zīd′), v. -SIDED, -SIDING. (A place where one lives.) The "A" hands, thumbs up, are placed on either side of the body, at waist level. They slide up the body in unison, to chest level. This is the sign for

LIFE or LIVE, indicating an upsurging of life. *Cf.* ADDRESS, ALIVE, LIFE 1, LIVE 1, LIVING.

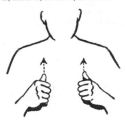

RESIDENCE 1 (rĕz′ ə dəns), *n.* (The shape of the building.) The open hands are held with fingertips touching, so that they form a pyramid a bit above eye level. From this position, the hands separate and move diagonally downward for a short distance; then they continue straight down a few inches. This movement traces the outline of a roof and walls. *Cf.* HOUSE.

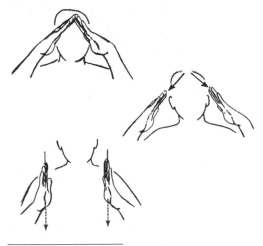

RESIDENCE 2, *n.* (The letter "R"; LIVE.) Both "R" hands move up together against the body. This is an initialized version of LIVE.

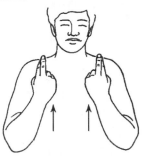

RESIGN (rĭ zīn′), *v.,* -SIGNED, -SIGNING. (Pulling out.) The index and middle fingers of the right "H" hand are grasped by the left hand. The right hand pulls out of the left. *Cf.* QUIT, WITHDRAW 3.

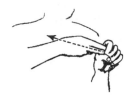

RESOLVE (rĭ zŏlv′), *v.,* -SOLVED, -SOLVING, *n.* (The mind stops wavering, and the pros and cons are resolved.) The right index finger touches the forehead, the sign for THINK, *q.v.* Both "F" hands, palms facing each other and fingers pointing straight out, then drop down simultaneously. The sign for JUDGE, *q.v.,* explains the rationale behind the movement of the two hands here. *Cf.* DECIDE, DECISION, DETERMINE, MAKE UP ONE'S MIND, MIND 5, VERDICT.

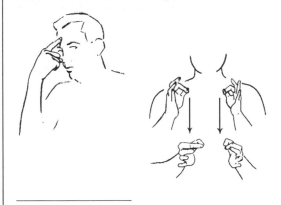

RESPECT (rĭ spĕkt′), *n., v.,* -SPECTED, -SPECTING. (The letter "R"; bowing the head.) The right "R" hand swings up in an arc toward the head, which bows somewhat as the hand moves up toward it. The hand's movement is sometimes reversed, moving down and away from the head in an arc, while the head bows.

RESPIRATION (rĕs′ pə rā′ shən), *n*. (The rise and fall of the chest in respiration.) The hands, folded over the chest, move forward and back to the chest, to indicate the breathing. *Cf.* BREATH, BREATHE.

RESPOND (rĭ spŏnd′), *v*., -PONDED, -PONDING. (Directing a reply from the mouth to someone.) The tip of the right index finger, held in the "D" position, palm facing the body, is placed on the lips, while the left "D" hand, palm also facing the body, is held about a foot in front of the right hand. The right index finger, swinging around, moves toward and stops in a pointing position a few inches from the left index fingertip. *Cf.* ANSWER, MAKE RESPONSE, REPLY 1, RESPONSE 1.

RESPONSE 1 (rĭ spŏns′), *n*. See RESPOND.

RESPONSE 2, *n*. (The letter "R"; coming out of the mouth.) Both "R" hands are held before the face, with the right "R" hand at the lips and behind the left "R" hand. Both hands move forward simultaneously, describing a small upward arc. *Cf.* REACTION 1, REPLY 2, REPORT.

RESPONSIBILITY 1 (rĭ spŏn′ sə bĭl′ ə tĭ), *n*. (Something which weighs down or burdens one with responsibility.) The fingertips of both hands, placed on the right shoulder, bear down. *Cf.* OBLIGATION, RELY 1, RESPONSIBLE 1.

RESPONSIBILITY 2, *n*. (Something which weighs down or burdens, modified by the letter "R," for "responsibility.") The "R" hands bear down on the right shoulder in the same manner as RESPONSIBILITY 1. *Cf.* RESPONSIBLE 2.

RESPONSIBLE 1 (rĭ spŏn′ sə bəl), *adj*. See RESPONSIBILITY 1.

RESPONSIBLE 2, *adj*. See RESPONSIBILITY 2.

REST 1 (rĕst), *n*. (The folded arms; a position of rest.) With palms facing the body, the arms are folded across the chest. *Cf.* RELAX 1, RESTFUL 1.

REST 2, *n.* (The "R" hands.) The sign for REST 1 is made, but with the crossed "R" hands. *Cf.* RELAX 2, RESTFUL 2.

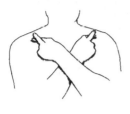

RESTFUL 1 (rĕst′ fəl), *adj.* See REST 1.

RESTFUL 2, *adj.* See REST 2.

RESTRICT (rĭ strĭkt′), *v., -STRICTED, -STRICTING.* (The upper and lower limits are defined.) The right-angle hands, palms facing, are held before the body, the right above the left. They swing out 45 degrees simultaneously, pivoted from their wrists. *Cf.* CAPACITY, LIMIT.

RESUME (rĭ zōōm′), *v., -SUMED, -SUMING.* (Moving forward.) Both right-angle hands, palms facing each other and knuckles facing forward, move forward simultaneously. *Cf.* GO AHEAD, PROCEED.

RÉSUMÉ (rĕz′ ŏŏ mā), *n.* (The letter "R"; the shape of a piece of paper.) Both "R" hands trace the top and sides of an imaginary piece of paper.

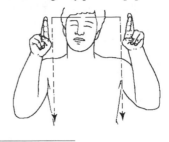

RETALIATE (rĭ tăl′ ĭ āt′), *v., -ATED, -ATING.* (Birds pecking back and forth at each other.) The right index finger and thumb, pressed together, strike their counterparts with force. *Cf.* RETALIATION, REVENGE.

RETALIATION (rĭ tăl′ ĭ ā′ shən), *n.* See RETALIATE.

RETIRE (rĭ tīr′), *v., -TIRED, -TIRING.* (A position of idleness.) With thumbs tucked in the armpits, the remaining fingers of both hands wiggle. *Cf.* HOLIDAY, IDLE, LEISURE, VACATION.

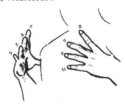

REVENGE (rĭ vĕnj′), *n., v., -VENGED, -VENGING.* (Birds pecking back and forth at each other.) The right index finger and thumb, pressed together, strike their left counterparts with force. *Cf.* RETALIATE, RETALIATION.

REVERE (rǐ vǐr'), *v.*, -VERED, -VERING. (Clasping the heart.) The "5" hands are held one atop the other over the heart. Sometimes the "S" hands are used, in which case they are crossed at the wrists. *Cf.* BELOVED, DEVOTION, LOVE.

REVERSE (rǐ vûrs'), *adj., n., v.*, -VERSED, -VERSING. (Separateness.) The tips of the extended index fingers touch before the chest, the right finger pointing left and the left finger pointing right. The fingers then draw apart sharply to either side. *Cf.* CONTRAST, OPPOSITE.

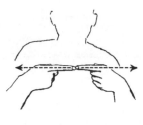

REVERSE ROLES *phrase.* (Changing places.) The right "V" hand, palm up, fingers pointing left, turns over to the palm down position.

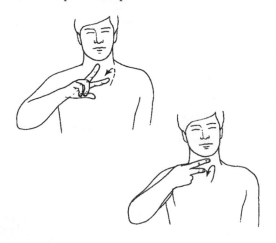

REVOLTING (rǐ vōl' tǐng), *adj.* (Turning the stomach.) The fingertips of the curved right hand describe a continuous circle on the stomach. The signer assumes an exaggerated expression of disgust. *Cf.* DISGUST, DISGUSTED, DISGUSTING, MAKE ME DISGUSTED, MAKE ME SICK, NAUSEA, NAUSEATE, NAUSEOUS, OBNOXIOUS.

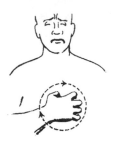

REVOLUTION 1 (rev´ ə lōō' shən), *n.* (The letter "R"; a whirlwind.) Both "R" hands, fingertips pointing at each other, are held with the right above the left. The "R" fingers spin around each other in a sudden and dramatic movement.

REVOLUTION 2, *n.* (The letter "R"; turning around or rebelling.) The upturned right "R" hand, held palm back at shoulder height, twists around suddenly with a dramatic flourish to the palm out position.

RHINOCEROS (rī nos′ ər əs), *n.* (The horn.) The right "I" hand, palm facing left and thumb tucked under the fingers, is placed on the nose. The hand moves forward and up in an arc, tracing the characteristic shape of the horn.

RHYTHM (rith′ əm), *n.* (The letter "R"; the rhythmic beat.) The right "R" hand taps the left wrist in a rhythmic fashion.

RICH (rĭch), *adj.* (A pile of money.) The sign for MONEY is made: the back of the upturned right hand, whose thumb and fingertips are all touching, is placed in the upturned left palm. The right hand then moves straight up, as it opens into the "5" position, palm facing down and fingers somewhat curved. *Cf.* WEALTH, WEALTHY.

RIDICULE (rĭd′ ə kūl′), *n., v,* -CULED, -CULING. (Derision; poking or prodding.) Both hands are held closed except for index and little fingers, which extend straight out from the body. The right hand is brought up and its index fingertip pulls the right corner of the mouth into a slight smile. Both hands then move forward simultaneously in a series of short jabbing motions, the right somewhat behind the left. An expression of disdain is assumed during this sign. The first part of the sign, pulling the mouth into a smile, is frequently omitted. *Cf.* MAKE FUN OF, MOCK.

RIDICULOUS (rĭ dĭk′ yə ləs), *adj.* (Thoughts flickering back and forth.) The right "Y" hand, thumb almost touching the forehead, is shaken back and forth across the forehead several times. *Cf.* FOLLY, FOOLISH, NONSENSE, SILLY, TRIFLING.

RIFLE (rī′ fəl), *n.* (Shooting a gun.) The left "S" hand is held above the head as if holding a gun barrel. At the same time the right "L" hand is held below the left hand, its index finger moving back and forth, as if pulling a trigger.

RIGHT 1 (rīt), *adj.* (A straightening out.) The right hand, fingers together and palm facing left, is placed in the upturned left palm, whose fingers point away from the body. The right hand slides straight out along the left palm, over the left fingers, and stops with its heel resting on the left fingertips. *Cf.* ALL RIGHT, O.K. 1, PRIVILEGE, RIGHTEOUS, YOU'RE WELCOME 2.

RIGHT 2, *adj., adv.* (The letter "R"; the movement.) The right "R" hand moves toward the right.

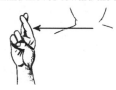

RIGHT 3, *adj., adv.* The right index finger, held above the left index finger, comes down rather forcefully so that the bottom of the right hand comes to rest on top of the left thumb joint. *Cf.* ACCURATE, CORRECT 1, DECENT, EXACT 2, PROPER, SUITABLE.

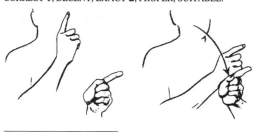

RIGHTEOUS (rī' chəs), *adj.* See RIGHT 1.

RIGID (rĭj'ĭd), *adj.* (The stiff fingers.) The fingers of the "5" hands, held palms down, stiffen and contract. *Cf.* FREEZE, FROZEN, ICE.

RING (rĭng), *n.* (The natural sign.) The index finger and thumb of the open right hand go through the motions of slipping a ring on the left ring finger.

RIP OFF (rĭp' ôf'), *v., sl.* (A magician's trick of flipping a coin into the sleeve, and thus cheating someone.) The middle finger of the right downturned hand rests on the upturned left palm. The finger makes a swift backward movement, closing against the right palm. The movement is sometimes repeated. *Cf.* TAKE ADVANTAGE OF.

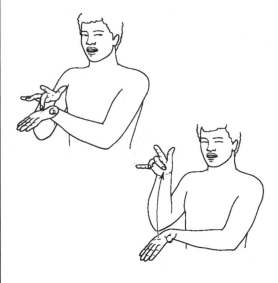

RISE 1 (rīz), *v.*, ROSE, RISEN, RISING, *n.* (Getting onto one's feet.) The upturned index and middle fingers of the right hand, representing the legs, are swung up and over in an arc, coming to rest in the upturned left palm. *Cf.* ARISE 2, GET UP, RAISE 1, STAND 2, STAND UP.

RISE 2, *v., n.* (Popping up before the eyes.) The right index finger, pointing up, pops up between the index and middle fingers of the left hand, whose palm faces down. *Cf.* APPEAR 2, POP UP.

RISE 3, *v., n.* (Rising up.) Both upturned hands, held at chest level, rise in unison, to about shoulder height. *Cf.* ARISE 1.

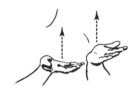

RIVAL 1 (rī′ vəl), *n., adj., v.,* -VALED, -VALING. (At sword's point.) The two index fingers, after pointing to each other, are drawn sharply apart. This is followed by the sign for INDIVIDUAL: both open hands, palms facing each other, move down the sides of the body, tracing its outline to the hips. *Cf.* ENEMY, FOE, OPPONENT.

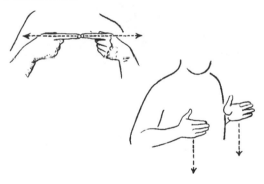

RIVAL 2, *v.* (Two opponents come together.) Both hands are closed, with thumbs pointing straight up and palms facing the body. From their initial position about a foot apart, the hands are brought together sharply, so that the knuckles strike. The hands, as

they are drawn together, also move down a bit, so that they describe a "V." *Cf.* COMPETE 1, COMPETITION 1, RACE 1, RIVALRY 1, VIE 1.

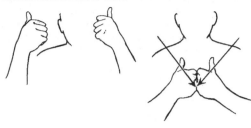

RIVAL 3, *n., v.* (Opposing objects.) The "A" hands are held side by side before the chest, palms facing each other and thumbs pointing forward. In this position the hands move alternately back and forth, toward and away from the body. *Cf.* COMPETE 2, COMPETITION 2, RACE 2, RIVALRY 2, VIE 2.

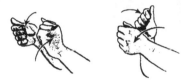

RIVAL 4, *n., v.* (The changing fortunes of competitors.) The "A" hands are held facing each other, thumbs pointing up in front of the body. Both hands are moved alternately backward and forward past each other several times. *Cf.* RACE 3, RIVALRY 3, VIE 3.

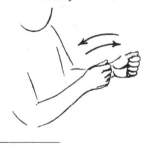

RIVALRY 1 (rī′ vəl rĭ), *n.* See RIVAL 2.

RIVALRY 2, *n.* See RIVAL 3.

RIVALRY 3, *n.* See RIVAL 4.

ROAD (rōd), *n.* (The winding movement.) Both hands, palms facing and fingers together and extended straight out, move in unison away from the body, in a winding manner. *Cf.* CORRIDOR, HALL, HALLWAY, MANNER 2, METHOD, OPPORTUNITY 3, PATH, STREET, TRAIL, WAY 1.

ROAM (rōm), *v.*, ROAMED, ROAMING. (Random movement.) The right "D" hand, palm facing left, moves to and fro from right to left. *Cf.* WANDER.

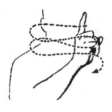

ROAR (rôr), *n., v.* (Miming making a roar.) Both claw hands, palms facing, and one on top of the other, open up in front of the mouth. Meanwhile the signer makes a silent roar, baring the teeth.

ROB 1 (rŏb), *v.*, ROBBED, ROBBING. (The hand, partly concealed, takes something surreptitiously.) The index and middle fingers of the right hand, somewhat curved, are placed under the left elbow. As they move slowly along the left forearm toward the left

wrist, they close a bit. *Cf.* ROBBERY 1, STEAL 1, THEFT 1, THIEF 1, THIEVERY.

ROB 2, *(colloq.), v.* (A sly, underhanded movement.) The right open hand, palm down, is held under the left elbow. Beginning with the little finger, the right hand closes finger by finger into the "A" position, as if wrapping itself around something, and moves to the right. *Cf.* ROBBERY 1, STEAL 2, THEFT 2.

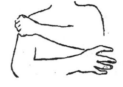
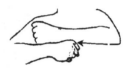

ROB 3, *v.* (A mustachioed thief.) The fingertips of both "H" hands, palms facing the body, are placed above the lips and are drawn slowly apart, describing a mustache. Sometimes one hand only is used. *Cf.* BANDIT, BURGLAR, BURGLARY, CROOK, ROBBER, ROBBERY 1, THEFT 3, THIEF 2.

ROB 4, *v.* (Brandishing handguns.) The signer mimes brandishing a pair of guns.

ROBBER (rŏb′ ər), *n.* The sign ROB 1, 2, or 3 is used. This is followed by the sign for INDIVIDUAL: both open hands, palms facing each other, move down the sides of the body, tracing its outline to the hips.

ROBBERY 1 (rŏb′ ə rĭ), *n.* See ROB 1, 2, or 3.

ROBBERY 2, *(colloq.), n.* (The guns.) Both "L" hands, palms facing each other, thumbs pointing straight up, are thrown forward slightly, as if presenting a pair of revolvers. *Cf.* HOLDUP.

ROBOT (rō′ bət), *n.* (The robot's mechanical gait.) The signer mimes the mechanical walk of a fiction-type robot, with the stiff movements of the hands and legs.

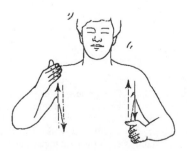

ROCK 1 (rŏk), *n.* (The hardness is indicated by the striking of the fists.) The back of the right "S" hand is struck several times against the back of the left "S" hand. *Cf.* STONE 1.

ROCK 2, *n.* (A hard, unyielding substance.) The back of the right "S" hand strikes the bottom of the chin twice. *Cf.* STONE 2.

ROCKET (rŏk′ ĭt), *n.* (A rocket takes off from its pad.) The downturned right "R" hand (for ROCKET) is placed so that its index and middle fingers rest on the back of the downturned left "S" hand. The right hand moves quickly forward off the left hand. The "R" hand may also point up and move off the left hand from this position.

ROCKING CHAIR 1, *n.* (A rocking chair.) The "L" hands, palms facing each other and about two feet apart, are held before the chest. They arc up and down toward the shoulders a number of times. The body is sometimes rocked back and forth in time with the movement of the hands.

ROCKING CHAIR 2, *n.* (The "R" hands; retire or loaf.) The thumbs of both "R" hands are tucked into the armpits and the signer imitates the forward backward motion of a rocking chair.

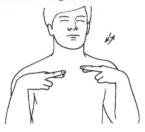

ROLE (rōl), *n.* (The "R"; placing someone in the center of a frame.) The right "R" hand makes a counterclockwise circle in front of the forward facing left palm, and comes to rest in the palm's center.

ROLLER COASTER (rō' lər kō stər), *n.* (The undulating movement.) The downturned right hand mimes the movement of a roller coaster, climbing to the top, speeding down, and veering off suddenly to change direction.

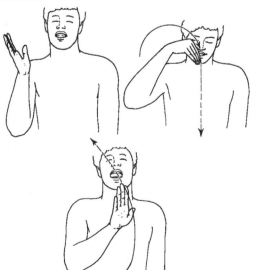

ROOM 1 (rōōm, rŏŏm), *n.* (The dimensions are indicated.) The open hands, palms facing and fingers pointing out, are dropped an inch or two simultaneously. They then shift their relative positions so that both palms face the body, with one hand in front of the other. In this new position they again drop an inch or two simultaneously. *Cf.* BOX 1, PACKAGE, SQUARE, TRUNK.

ROOM 2, *n.* (The "R" hands.) This is the same sign as for ROOM 1, except that the "R" hands are used.

ROOMY (rōō' mē), *adj.* (Lots of elbow room.) The "S" hands, palms facing, are positioned at chest height. As the elbows move apart the palms move down.

ROOSTER (rōōs' tər), *n.* (The pecking beak and the comb of the cock.) The "Q" hand's back is placed against the lips, and the thumb and index fingers open and close, representing a beak. The thumb of the right "3" hand is then thrust against the forehead a couple of times, representing the comb.

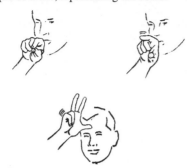

ROSH HASHANAH (rosh hə shä′ nə), *n.* (Blowing the shofar or ram's horn.) The thumb of the "Y" hand touches the lips and the signer pretends to blow.

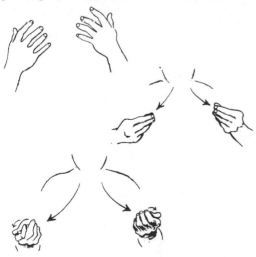

ROT (rŏt), *v.,* ROTTED, ROTTING, *n.* (Fingering the small pieces resulting from the breaking up of something.) The thumbs rub slowly across the fingertips of the upturned hands, from the little fingers to the index fingers, and then continue to the "A" position, palms up. *Cf.* DECAY, DIE OUT, DISSOLVE, FADE, MELT.

ROTTEN (rŏt′ ən), *adj.* (A modification of the sign for spitting or thumbing the nose.) The right "3" hand is held with thumbtip against the nose. Then it is thrown sharply forward, and an expression of contempt is assumed. *Cf.* LOUSY.

ROUGH (rŭf), *adj.* (The "roughness," in the form of ridges, described.) The tips of the curved right fingers trace imaginary ridges over the upright left palm, from the base of the hand to the fingertips. The action is repeated several times. *Cf.* RUDE, RUDENESS, SCOLD 2.

ROUND (round), *adj.* (The shape.) The curved open hands are held with fingertips touching, as if holding a ball. *Cf.* BALL.

RUB (rŭb), *v.,* RUBBED, RUBBING. (The act of rubbing.) The right knuckles rub briskly against the outstretched left palm. *Cf.* POLISH, SANDPAPER, SHINE SHOES.

RUBBER (rŭb′ ər), *n.* (The pliability.) The side of the right "X" finger moves up and down on the right cheek. The mouth is held open, and may engage in a chewing motion, keeping time with the right "X" finger.

RUDE (rōōd), *adj.* (The "roughness," of words is described.) The tips of the curved right fingers trace imaginary ridges over the upright left palm, from the base of the hand to the fingertips. The action is repeated several times. *Cf.* ROUGH, RUDENESS, SCOLD 2.

RUDENESS (rōōd′ nĭs), *n.* See RUDE.

RUE (rōō), *v.*, RUED, RUING, *n.* (The heart is circled, to indicate feeling, modified by the letter "S," for SORRY.) The right "S" hand, palm facing the body, is rotated several times over the area of the heart. *Cf.* APOLOGIZE 1, APOLOGY 1, CONTRITION, PENITENT, REGRET, REGRETFUL, REPENT, REPENTANT, SORROW, SORROWFUL 2, SORRY.

RUG (rug), *n.* (The "R"; covering a flat surface.) The right "R" hand is placed on the upturned left palm, with the right thumb underneath the left hand. The right hand moves straight forward from the heel.

RUIN (rōō′ ĭn), *n.* (Wiping off.) The left "5" hand, palm up, is held slightly above the right "5" hand, held palm down. The right hand swings up, just brushing over the left palm. Both hands close into the "S" position, and the right is brought back with force to its initial position, striking a glancing blow against the left knuckles as it returns. *Cf.* DESTROY.

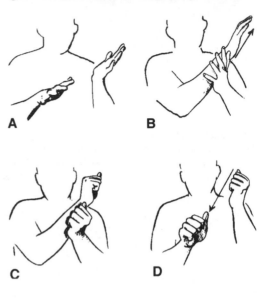

A   B

C   D

RULE 1 (rōōl), *n.*, *v.*, RULED, RULING. (Holding the reins over all.) The "A" hands, palms facing, move alternately back and forth, as if grasping and manipulating reins. The left "A" hand, still in position, swings over so that its palm now faces down. The right hand opens to the "5" position, palm down, and swings over the left, which moves slightly to the right. *Cf.* CONTROL 1, DIRECT 1, GOVERN, MANAGE, MANAGEMENT, MANAGER, OPERATE, REGULATE, REIGN.

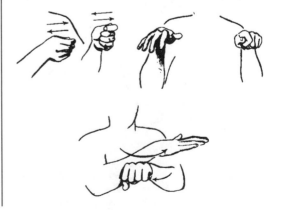

RULE(S) 2, *n.* (The letter "R"; the listing.) The upright, open left hand, fingers together and palm facing out, represents a piece of paper on which are listed the rules or regulations. The right "R" hand is placed upright against the tips of the left fingers, and then it moves down in an arc to a position against the base of the left hand. *Cf.* REGULATION(S).

RUN 1 (rŭn), *v.,* RAN, RUN, RUNNING. The open left hand is held pointing out, palm down. The open right hand is held beneath it, facing up. The right hand is thrown forward rather quickly so the palm brushes repeatedly across the palm of the left.

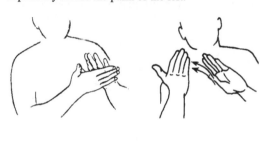

RUN 2, *v.* (A turning wheel, as in a machine that is running.) The upturned, open right hand moves in a counterclockwise circle on the palm of the downturned, open left hand.

RUN AWAY *v. phrase.* (Slipping out and away.) The right index finger is held pointing upward between the index and middle fingers of the prone left hand. From this position the right index finger moves to the

right, slipping out of the grasp of the left fingers and away from the left hand. *Cf.* SLIP AWAY.

RUN OFF (rŭn' ôf´), *v.* (Moving forward suddenly and quickly.) The upturned right palm slaps against the downturned left palm and shoots forward.

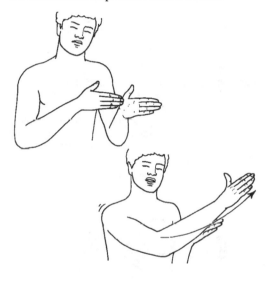

RUSSIA (rush' ə), *n.* The right index fingertip travels across the lips from left to right and is then thrown down. This is a native sign.

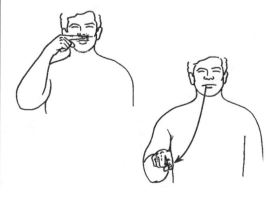

S

SACRIFICE (săk′ rə fĭs′), *n., v.,* -FICED, -FICING. (An offering.) The outstretched hands, palms up, move upward gracefully. The head turns upward at the same time.

SAD (săd), *adj.* (The facial features drop.) Both "5" hands, palms facing the eyes and fingers slightly curved, drop simultaneously to a level with the mouth. The head drops slightly as the hands move down, and an expression of sadness is assumed. *Cf.* DEJECTED, DEPRESSED 1, GLOOM, GLOOMY, GRAVE 2, GRIEF 1, MELANCHOLY, MOURNFUL, SORROWFUL 1.

SAFE (sāf), *adj., n.* (Breaking the bonds.) The "S" hands, crossed in front of the body, swing apart and face out. *Cf.* EMANCIPATE, FREE 1, FREEDOM, INDEPENDENCE, INDEPENDENT 1, LIBERATION, REDEEM 1, RELIEF, RESCUE, SALVATION, SAVE 1.

SAFETY PIN (sāf′ tē pin), *n.* (Closing the pin.) The right index and thumb come together against the left chest.

SAID (sĕd), *v.* (Words tumbling from the mouth.) The right index finger, pointing left, describes a continuous small circle in front of the mouth. *Cf.* DISCOURSE, HEARING, MAINTAIN 2, MENTION, REMARK, SAY, SPEAK, SPEECH 1, STATE 1, TALK 1, TELL, VERBAL.

SAILOR (sā′ lər), *n.* (The bell bottoms.) Both hands, fingers pointing straight down, indicate the flare of bell bottom pants, first above the left leg and then the right.

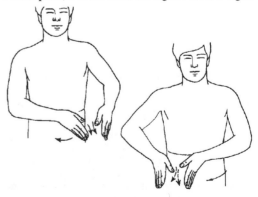

SAINT (sānt), *(eccles.), n.* (Cleanliness or purity, defined by the letter "S.") The right "S" hand is wiped across the open left palm.

ST. LOUIS (sānt' lōō is), *n.* (The arch.) The left arm is outstretched, palm down. The right "S" hand is placed at the left elbow. It travels up and over in a distinct arch, changing to an "L" as it does, and coming to rest on the back of the left hand. The left arm sometimes faces up instead of down.

SALARY 1 (săl' ə rĭ), *n.* (Gathering in.) The right "5" hand, its little finger edge touching the upturned left palm, is drawn in an arc toward the body, closing into the "S" position as it sweeps over the base of the left hand. *Cf.* ACCUMULATE, COLLECT, EARN, WAGE(S).

SALARY 2, *n.* (EARN, MONEY.) The sign for EARN is made: the right "5" hand, its little finger edge resting on the upturned left palm, moves toward the left and closes into the "S" position. This is followed by MONEY: the upturned right fingertips, grasping a wad of imaginary dollar bills, slaps down on the left palm.

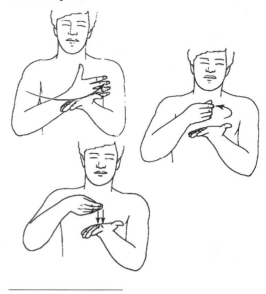

SALE (sāl), *n.* (Transferring ownership of an object.) Both "AND" hands, fingers touching their respective thumbs, are held palms down before the body. The hands are pivoted simultaneously outward and away from the body, once or several times. *Cf.* SELL, VEND.

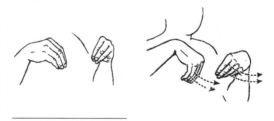

SALOON (sə lōōn'), *n.* (Raising the beer stein or mug.) The thumb of the right "A" or "Y" hand is brought up to the mouth. *Cf.* BAR.

SALT 1 (sôlt), *n.* (The act of tapping the salt from a knife edge.) Both "H" hands, palms down, are held before the chest. The fingers of the right "H" hand tap those of the left several times.

SALT 2, *n.* (Tasting the salt.) The tips of the right "H" hand are placed against the lips. The rest of this sign is exactly like SALT 1.

SALVATION (săl vā′ shən), *n.* (Breaking the bonds.) The "S" hands, crossed in front of the body, swing apart and face out. *Cf.* EMANCIPATE, FREE 1, FREEDOM, INDEPENDENCE, INDEPENDENT 1, LIBERATION, REDEEM 1, RELIEF, RESCUE, SAFE, SAVE 1.

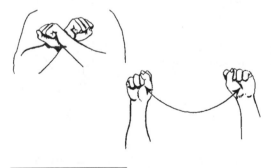

SAME 1 (săm), *adj.* (Matching fingers are brought together.) The outstretched index fingers are brought together, either once or several times. *Cf.* ALIKE, IDENTICAL, LIKE 2, SIMILAR, SUCH.

SAME 2, *(colloq.), adj.* (Two figures are compared, back and forth.) The right "Y" hand, palm facing left, is moved alternately toward and away from the body. *Cf.* ME TOO.

SAME 3, *adj.* (Parallel movement.) Both downturned "Y" hands, held a few inches apart, move simultaneously from left to right. *Cf.* UNIFORM, UNIFORMLY.

SAME AS *phrase.* (A likeness; a sameness.) Both index fingers, held together at one side of the body near waist level, point forward. As they travel to the other side of the body they separate an inch or two and come together again. *Cf.* ACCORDING (TO), ALSO, AS, TOO.

SAME TIME *adv. phrase.* (Time is the same.) The downturned curved right index finger taps the back of the left wrist, and then both hands, in the downturned "Y" position, separate quickly. *Cf.* SIMULTANEOUSLY.

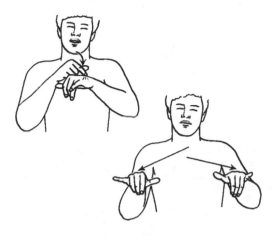

SAMPLE (săm′ pəl), *n.* (The letter "S"; something shown or pushed forward.) The left "5" hand pushes the right "S" hand forward.

SANCTUARY (sangk′ chōō er′ ē), *n.* (The letter "S"; describing an area.) Both downturned "S" hands describe a circle as they are drawn in toward the chest.

SAND (sand), *n.* (Trickling.) The right fist is held above the upturned left palm and, trembling slightly, pretends to trickle sand on it.

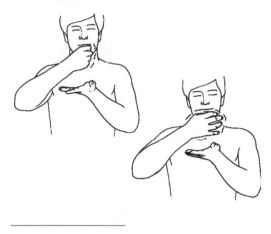

SANDAL (săn′ dəl), *n.* (The crossed straps or thongs.) The downturned right "4" hand crosses the downturned left hand from little finger edge to thumb. It then turns around to the palm up position and crosses the left hand from wrist to fingertips.

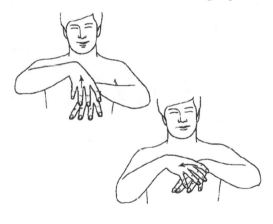

SANDALS (săn′ dəls), *n. pl.* (The thong between the toes.) The left "5" hand is held palm down. The index finger traces the course of an imaginary thong between the left index and middle fingers.

SANDPAPER (sănd′ pa′ pər), *(voc.)*, *n.* (The act of rubbing.) The right knuckles rub briskly against the outstretched left palm. *Cf.* POLISH, RUB, SHINE SHOES.

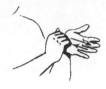

SANDWICH 1 (sănd′ wĭch, săn′-), *n.* (The two pieces of bread.) With the fingertips of both hands facing the body, one hand is placed atop the other and both are brought up to the mouth, which opens slightly.

SANDWICH 2, *n.* (In between slices.) The fingers of the upturned right hand are tucked between the middle and third fingers of the left hand, whose palm faces the signer. The motion may be repeated.

SAN FRANCISCO (săn′ frən sĭs′ kō), *n.* The initials "S" and "F" are formed. During the formation of the "F," the hand may be moved slightly to the right.

SAN JUAN (sän hwän′), *n.* (The letters.) The right "J" hand makes a series of quick clockwise movements.

SATAN (sā′ tən), *n.* (The horns.) With the thumbs resting on the temples, the index and middle fingers of both hands open and close repeatedly. *Cf.* DEMON, DEVIL, HELL 1.

SATIRE (sat′ īr), *n.* (The letter "S"; going under or around that which would point out the truth or the actual.) The right "S" hand makes a small clockwise circle, and then both hands assume a shape involving the outstretched index and little fingers. The right hand goes under the left.

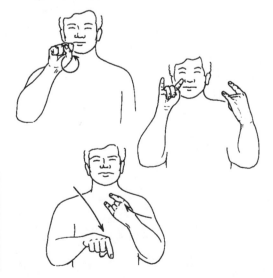

SATISFACTION (săt′ ĭs făk′ shən), *n.* (The inner feelings settle down.) Both "B" hands (or "5" hands, fingers together) are placed palms down against the chest, the right above the left. Both move down simultaneously a few inches. *Cf.* CONTENT, CONTENTED, GRATIFY 2, SATISFIED, SATISFY 1.

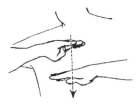

SATISFIED (săt′ ĭs fīd), *adj.* See SATISFACTION.

SATISFY 1 (săt′ ĭs fī), *v.,* -FIED, -FYING. See SATISFACTION.

SATISFY 2, *v.* This is the same sign as for SATISFY 1 but with only one hand used.

SATURDAY (săt′ ər dǐ), *n.* The "S" hand, held before the body, is rotated clockwise.

SAVE 1 (sāv), *v.,* SAVED, SAVING. (Breaking the bonds.) The "S" hands, crossed in front of the body, swing apart and face out. *Cf.* EMANCIPATE, FREE 1, FREEDOM, INDEPENDENCE, INDEPENDENT 1, LIBERATION, REDEEM 1, RELIEF, RESCUE, SAFE, SALVATION.

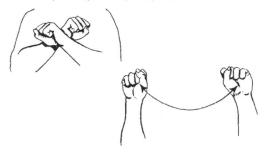

SAVE 2, *v.* (Holding back.) The right "V" fingers are tapped once or twice across the back of their left counterparts. Both palms face the chest. *Cf.* RESERVE 3, STORE.

SAW 1 (sô), *n., v.,* SAWED, SAWN, SAWING. (The sawing of wood.) The little finger edge of the open right hand moves back and forth in a sawing motion over the back of the downturned left hand. *Cf.* WOOD.

SAW 2, *(voc.), n., v.* (Act of holding a saw.) The right hand grasps an imaginary saw and moves back and forth over the downturned left hand.

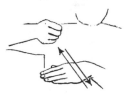

SAY (sā), *v.,* SAID, SAYING. (Words tumbling from the mouth.) The right index finger, pointing left, describes a continuous small circle in front of the mouth. *Cf.* DISCOURSE, HEARING, MAINTAIN 2, MENTION, REMARK, SAID, SPEAK, SPEECH 1, STATE 1, TALK 1, TELL, VERBAL.

SCAFFOLD (skăf' əld, -ōld), *n.* (Hanging by the throat.) The thumb of the right "Y" hand is placed at the right side of the neck, and the head hangs toward the left, as if it were caught in a noose. *Cf.* HANG 2.

SCALE 1 (skāl), *n.* (The balancing of the scale is described.) The fingers of the right "H" hand are centered on the left index finger and rocked back and forth. *Cf.* POUND 1, WEIGH 1, WEIGHT.

SCALE 2, *n., v.* (The scales.) Both open hands, held palms down in front of the body, move alternately up and down, imitating a pair of scales.

SCAPULAR (skăp' yə lər), *(eccles.), n.* (The garment is described.) The index fingers are drawn from the shoulders to a point where they come together at the center of the chest.

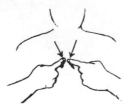

SCARE(D) (skâr), *v.,* SCARED, SCARING, *n.* (The heart is suddenly covered with fear.) Both hands, fingers together, are placed side by side, palms facing the chest. They quickly open and come together over the heart, one on top of the other. *Cf.* AFRAID, FEAR 1, FRIGHT, FRIGHTEN, TERROR 1.

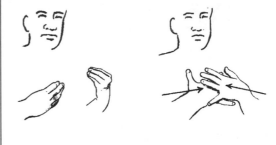

SCENE (sēn), *n.* (The letter "S"; a portion of a playscript.) The right "S" hand is placed at the top of the outstretched left palm. It moves down to the base of the palm.

SCENT (sĕnt), *n.* (Bringing something up to the nose.) The upturned right hand moves slowly up to and past the nose, and the signer breathes in as the hand sweeps by. *Cf.* FRAGRANT, ODOR, SMELL.

SCHEDULE (skej′ ool), *n.* (Making boxes to indicate dates on a calendar.) The right "4" hand, palm facing the left palm, moves down, turns over, and moves forward along the left palm, from the heel to the fingertips.

SCHIZOPHRENIA (skit′ sŏ frē′ nē ə), *n.* (The letter "S"; the zigzag movement depicts the splitting of the head, *i.e.,* a split personality.) The right "S" hand is placed on the upturned open left palm or on the forehead. The "S" hand opens into the "B" position, little finger edge resting on the left palm. It moves down the palm in a zigzag manner.

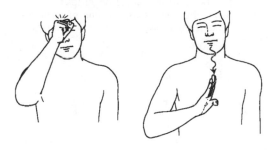

SCHOLAR (skŏl′ ər), *n.* (One who learns.) The sign for LEARN is made: the downturned fingers of the right hand are placed on the upturned left palm. They close, and then the hand rises and the right fingertips are placed on the forehead. This is followed by the sign for INDIVIDUAL: both open hands, palms facing each other, move down the sides of the body, tracing its outline to the hips. *Cf.* PUPIL 1, STUDENT 1.

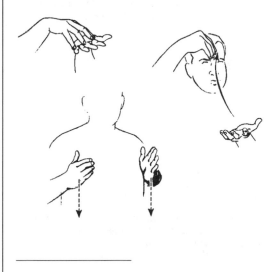

SCHOOL (skool), *n.* (The teacher's hands are clapped for attention.) The hands are clapped together several times.

SCIENCE 1 (sī′ əns), *n.* (Pouring alternately from test tubes.) The upright thumbs of both "A" hands swing over alternately in elliptical fashion, as if pouring out the contents of a pair of test tubes. *Cf.* CHEMISTRY 1.

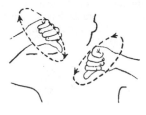

SCIENCE 2 *(arch.), n.* (Deep wisdom.) The right index finger circles in front of the forehead, and is then moved down and thrust between the extended and loosely parted fingers of the downturned left hand, to indicate that wisdom goes deep.

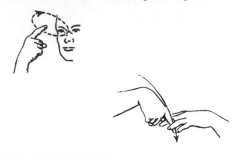

SCISSORS (sĭz′ ərz), *n., pl.* or *sing.* (The natural sign.) The index and middle fingers, forming a "V," open and close like scissors.

SCOLD 1 (skōld), *v.,* SCOLDED, SCOLDING. (A scolding with the finger.) The right index finger shakes back and forth in a natural scolding movement. *Cf.* REPRIMAND, REPROVE.

SCOLD 2, *(colloq.), v.* (Rough language.) The tips of the curved right fingers trace imaginary ridges over the upright left palm, from the base of the hand to the fingertips. The action is repeated several times. *Cf.* ROUGH, RUDE, RUDENESS.

SCOLD 3, *(sl.), v.* (The opening and closing of the barking dog's mouth.) The hands are positioned palm against palm before the body, with the fingertips pointing forward. With the bases of the hands always touching and serving as a hinge, the hands open and close repeatedly, with the stress on the opening movement, which is sudden and abrupt. *Cf.* BARK.

SCOLD 4, *(sl.), v.* (Big, *i.e.,* curse, words tumble out.) The right "Y" hand moves forward in a wavy manner along the left index finger, which is pointing forward. The action is repeated several times. The wide space between the thumb and little finger of the "Y" hand represents the length of the words, and the forward movement the tumbling out of the words in anger.

SCORN (skôrn), *n.* (The gaze is cast downward.) Both "V" hands, side by side and palms facing out, are swept downward so that the fingertips now point down. A haughty expression, or one of mild contempt, is sometimes assumed. *Cf.* CONTEMPT, LOOK DOWN.

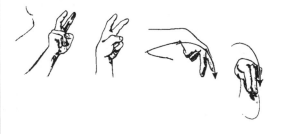

SCOT 1 (skŏt), *n.* (The crossing of the plaid pattern is indicated on the hand.) The outstretched fingers of the open right hand, palm down, are brought over the back of the downturned left hand, from the little finger side to the thumb side. The right hand then turns to the palm-up position and is drawn along the left hand, back to back, from wrist to fingertips. *Cf.* SCOTCH 1, SCOTLAND 1, SCOTTISH 1.

SCOT 2, *n.* (The plaid.) The "5" hands are held with palms toward the chest, the right fingers resting across the back of the left fingers, to represent "plaid." The hands then drop away toward either side. *Cf.* SCOTCH 2, SCOTLAND 2, SCOTTISH 2.

SCOT 3, *n.* (Plaid.) The four fingers of the right "B" hand, held slightly spread, trace a set of imaginary parallel lines across the left arm just below the shoulder. The hand is then turned over, and the backs of the fingers trace another set of parallel lines downward across the first set, completing an imaginary plaid pattern. *Cf.* SCOTCH 3, SCOTLAND 3, SCOTTISH 3.

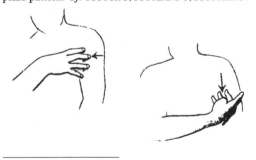

SCOTCH 1 (skŏch), *n., adj.* See SCOT 1.

SCOTCH 2, *n., adj.* See SCOT 2.

SCOTCH 3, *n., adj.* See SCOT 3.

SCOTCH TAPE *n., v.* (Spreading the tape.) Both downturned thumbs, tips touching, move apart in opposite directions, as if smoothing on a piece of tape.

SCOTLAND 1 (skŏt′ lənd), *n.* See SCOT 1.

SCOTLAND 2, *n.* See SCOT 2.

SCOTLAND 3, *n.* See SCOT 3.

SCOTTISH 1 (skŏt′ ish), *adj.* See SCOT 1.

SCOTTISH 2, *adj.* See SCOT 2.

SCOTTISH 3, *adj.* See SCOT 3.

SCRAMBLE (skrăm′ bəl), *v.,* -BLED, -BLING. (Scrambling or mixing up.) The downturned right hand is positioned above the upturned left. The fingers of both are curved. Both hands move in opposite horizontal circles. *Cf.* COMPLICATE, CONFUSE, CONFUSED, CONFUSION, MINGLE 1, MIX, MIXED, MIXED-UP, MIX-UP.

SCRAPE (skrăp), *(voc.)*, *v.*, SCRAPED, SCRAPING, *n.* (The natural motion of using a scraper.) The tips of the right "B" hand move along the upturned left palm, from mid-palm to fingertips. The motion is repeated several times.

SCREW (skrōō), *n., v.* (The movement.) The right index finger makes a clockwise turn in the left palm.

SCRATCH (skrach), *n., v.* (The natural movement.) The signer, with curved index finger, mimes making a quick scratch on the back of the left hand.

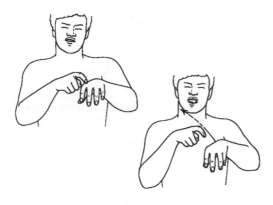

SCRIPTURE (skrip' chər), *n.* (The letter "S"; writing.) The downturned right "S" hand rests on the upturned left palm. Pivoted by the wrist, it moves slightly in a wavy manner, as it goes from the ball of the left palm to the tips of the left fingers.

SCREAM (skrēm), *v.,* SCREAMED, SCREAMING. (Harsh words thrown out.) The right hand, as in CURSE 1, appears to claw words out of the mouth. This time, however, it turns and throws them out, ending in the "5" position. *Cf.* CURSE 2, SHOUT.

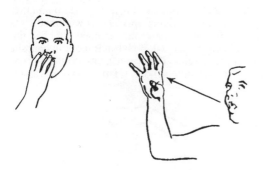

SCULPT (skŭlpt), *v.,* SCULPTED, SCULPTING. (Contours are indicated or outlined.) Both "A" hands, held about a foot apart before the face, with palms facing each other, move down simultaneously in a wavy, undulating motion. *Cf.* FIGURE 2, FORM 1, IMAGE, SCULPTURE, SHAPE, STATUE.

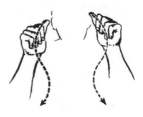

SCULPTOR (skŭlp′ tər), *n.* (An individual who carves.) The thumb of the right "A" hand, placed in the upturned left palm, is twisted up and down several times, as if gouging out material from the left palm. This is followed by the sign for INDIVID-UAL: both open hands, palms facing each other, move down the sides of the body, tracing its outline to the hips.

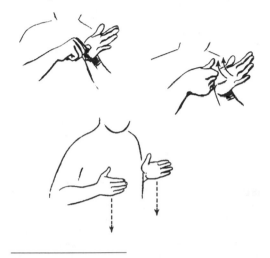

SCULPTURE (skŭlp′ chər), *n., v.,* -TURED, -TURING. See SCULPT.

SEARCH (sûrch), *v.,* SEARCHED, SEARCHING. (Directing the vision from place to place.) The right "C" hand, palm facing left, moves from right to left across the line of vision, in a series of counterclockwise circles. The signer's gaze remains concentrated and his head turns slowly from right to left. *Cf.* CURIOUS 1, EXAMINE, INVESTIGATE, LOOK FOR, PROBE, SEEK.

SEAT (sēt), *n., v.,* SEATED, SEATING. (The act of sitting.) The extended right index and middle fingers are draped across the back of the same two fingers of the downturned left hand. The hands then move straight downward a short distance. *Cf.* BE SEATED, CHAIR, SIT.

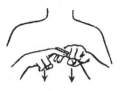

SECOND 1 (sĕk′ ənd), *adj.* (The second finger is indicated.) The tip of the index finger of the right "D" hand is placed on the tip of the middle finger of the left "V" hand. The right hand then executes a short pivotal movement in a clockwise direction. The left "L" hand may be substituted for the left "V" hand, with the right index fingertip placed on the left index fingertip. *Cf.* SECONDARY, SECONDLY.

SECOND 2, *v.,* -ONDED, -ONDING. ("Second"—two fingers.) The right "L" hand, held somewhat above the head, index finger pointing straight up, pivots forward a bit, so that the index finger now points forward. Used in parliamentary procedure. *Cf.* ENDORSE 3.

SECOND 3, *n.* (The ticking off of seconds on the clock.) The index finger of the right "D" hand executes a series of very short movements in a clockwise manner as it rests against the left "S" hand, which is facing right.

SECONDARY (sĕk′ ən dĕr′ ĭ), *adj.* See SECOND 1.

SECONDLY (sĕk' ənd lĭ), *adv.* See SECOND 1.

SECRET (sē' krĭt), *n., adj.* (The sealing of the lips; keeping the words back.) The back of the thumb of the right "A" hand is placed firmly against the closed lips. The thumb, in this position, may move off the lips slightly and return again to the lips. As an optional addition, the thumb may swing down under the downturned cupped left hand, after being placed on the lips as above. *Cf.* PRIVACY, PRIVATE 1.

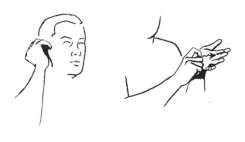

SECRETARY (sĕk' rə tĕr' ĭ), *n.* (Taking a pencil from behind the ear.) An imaginary pencil is taken from the right ear and then is used to go through the motions of writing on the upturned left palm.

SECTION (sĕk' shən), *n.* (Cutting off or designating a part.) The little finger edge of the open right hand moves straight down the middle of the upturned left palm. *Cf.* PART 1, PIECE, PORTION, SHARE 1, SOME.

SEE (sē), *v.,* SAW, SEEN, SEEING. (The eyesight is directed forward.) The right "V" hand, palm facing the body, is placed so that the fingertips are just under the eyes. The hand swings straight out *Cf.* SIGHT.

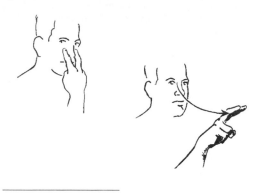

SEEK (sēk), *v.,* SOUGHT, SEEKING. (Directing the vision from place to place.) The right "C" hand, palm facing left, moves from right to left across the line of vision, in a series of counterclockwise circles. The signer's gaze remains concentrated and his head turns slowly from right to left. *Cf.* CURIOUS 1, EXAMINE, INVESTIGATE, LOOK FOR, PROBE, SEARCH.

SEEM (sēm), *v.,* SEEMED, SEEMING. (Something presented before the eyes.) The open right hand, palm flat and facing out, with fingers together and pointing up, is positioned at shoulder level. Pivoting from the wrist, the hand is swung around so that the palm now faces the eyes. Sometimes the eyes glance at the newly presented palm. *Cf.* APPARENT, APPARENTLY, APPEAR 1, LOOK 2.

SEESAW (sē′ sô′), *n.* (The up-and-down movement.) Both downturned "H" hands are held with index and middle fingers touching. They move alternately up and down, always maintaining contact.

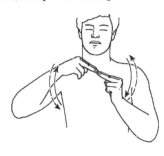

SEETHE (sēth̆), *v.* (A slow boil.) The right hand, palm up, is placed beneath the palm down left hand. The right fingers wriggle under the left palm.

SEIZE (sēz), *v.,* SEIZED, SEIZING. (Grasping something and holding it down.) Both hands, palms down, quickly close into the "S" position, the right on top of the left. *Cf.* CAPTURE, CATCH 2, GRAB, GRASP.

SEIZURE (sē′ zhər), *n.* (The body shakes in a fit.) The right hand, palm up, index and middle fingers curved, is placed in the upturned left palm. The right hand's index and middle fingers open and close slightly as the two fingers tremble. *Cf.* EPILEPSY, FIT.

SELDOM (sĕl′ dəm), *adv.* (The "1" finger is brought up very slowly.) The right index finger, resting in the open left palm, which is facing right, swings up slowly from its position to one in which it is pointing straight up. The movement is repeated slowly, after a pause. *Cf.* OCCASIONAL, OCCASIONALLY, ONCE IN A WHILE 1, SOMETIME(S).

SELECT 1 (sĭ lĕkt′), *v.,* -LECTED, -LECTING. (The natural motion of selecting something from the hand.) The thumb and index fingers of the outstretched right hand grasp an imaginary object on the upturned left palm. The right hand then moves straight up. *Cf.* DISCOVER, DISCOVERY, FIND, PICK 1.

SELECT 2, *v.* (Taking unto oneself.) The right hand, palm out, is extended before the chest, index finger and thumb in an open position, the other fingers separated and pointing up. The hand is drawn in toward the chest, and the index and thumb close at the same time, indicating something taken to oneself. *Cf.* APPOINT, CHOOSE, TAKE.

SELECT 3, *v.* (The natural sign.) The fingertips and thumbtip of the downturned open right hand come together, and the hand moves up a short distance, as if picking something. *Cf.* PICK 2, PICK UP 2.

-SELF 1 (sĕlf), *n.* used with a gender prefix as a reflexive and intensive pronoun; *adj.* (The individual is indicated with the thumb.) The right hand, held in the "A" position, thumb up, moves several times in the direction of the person indicated: *myself, yourself, himself, herself, itself, oneself, ourselves, yourselves, themselves.*

SELF 2, *n.* (The self is carried uppermost.) The right "A" hand, thumb up, is brought up against the chest, from waist to breast. *Cf.* EGOTISM 1.

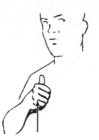

SELF-CENTERED (self' sen' tərd), *adj. phrase.* (SELF and CENTER.) The sign for SELF is made: the right "A" hand, thumb pointing up, is brought against the chest. The sign for CENTER follows: the downturned right fingers describe a small clockwise circle and come to rest in the upturned left palm.

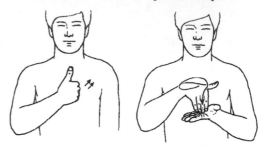

SELFISH 1 (sĕl' fĭsh), *adj.* (Pulling things toward oneself.) Both prone open or "V" hands are held in front of the body with fingers bent. The hands are then drawn quickly and forcefully inward, as if raking things toward oneself. *Cf.* GREEDY 1, STINGY 1, TIGHTWAD 1.

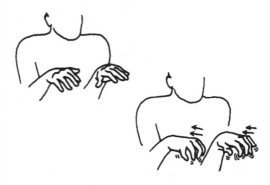

SELFISH 2, *adj.* (Scratching the palm in greed.) The right fingers scratch the upturned left palm several times. A frowning expression is often used. *Cf.* GREEDY 2, STINGY 2, TIGHTWAD 2.

SELFISH 3, *adj.* (Scratching in greed.) The down-turned "3" hands, held side by side, make a scratching motion as they move in toward the body. *Cf.* GREEDY 3, STINGY 3.

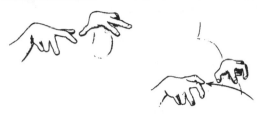

SELL (sĕl), *v.*, SOLD, SELLING. (Transferring ownership of an object.) Both "AND" hands, fingers touching their respective thumbs, are held palms down before the body. The hands are pivoted simultaneously outward and away from the body, once or several times. *Cf.* SALE, VEND.

SELLER (sĕl' ər), *n.* (Transferring ownership.) The sign for SELL is formed. The sign for INDIVIDUAL is then made: both open hands, palms facing each other, move down the sides of the body, tracing its outline to the hips. *Cf.* MERCHANT, SALESMAN, VENDER.

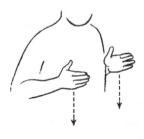

SEMEN (sē' mən), *n.* (The pulsing of the penis during release.) The left index finger, representing the penis, is positioned at the base of the right "E" hand, whose palm faces left. The fingers of the right hand open and close twice, as the two hands, connected,

move forward an inch or so. *Cf.* EJACULATE 1, EJACULATION 1, SPERM.

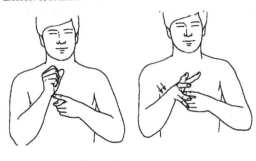

SEMINARY 1 (sĕm' ə nĕr´ ĭ), *(eccles.)*, *n.* (A college dedicated to Christianity.) The sign for JESUS is made: both "5" hands are used. The left middle finger touches the right palm, and then the right middle finger touches the left palm. This is followed by the sign for COLLEGE: the sign for SCHOOL, *q.v.*, is made, but without the clapping of hands. The upper hand swings up in an arc above the lower. The upper hand may form a "C," instead of assuming a clapping position.

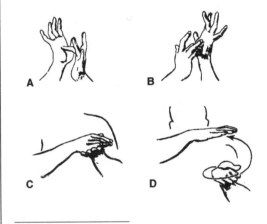

A   B

C   D

SEMINARY 2, *n.* (The letter "S"; a college.) The downturned, right "S" hand rests on the upturned left palm. The right hand moves up toward the right and then over toward the left, describing an arc, as in COLLEGE, *q.v.*

SEND 1 (sĕnd), *v.*, SENT, SENDING. (Sending away from.) The right fingertips tap the back of the down-turned, left "S" hand and then swing forward, away from the hand.

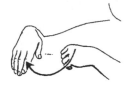

SEND 2, *v.* (Sending something forth.) The right "AND" hand is held palm out. It then opens and moves forcefully outward, in a throwing motion.

SEND AWAY *v. phrase.* (Moving away from.) The fingertips of the right hand move off the top of the left hand.

SENIOR (sēn′ yər), *n., adj.* (College student.) The right index finger touches the thumbtip of the left hand. Also, the open "5" hand, palm down, may rest on the left thumbtip. *Cf.* TOP DOG.

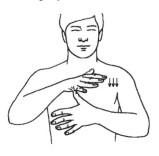

SENSATION (sĕn sā′ shən), *n.* (The welling up of feelings or emotions in the heart.) The right middle finger, touching the heart, moves up an inch or two a number of times. *Cf.* EMOTION 1, FEEL 2, FEELING, MOTIVE 2, SENSE 2.

SENSE 1 (sĕns), *n.* (Patting the head to indicate something of value inside.) The right fingers pat the forehead several times. *Cf.* MENTAL, MIND 1.

SENSE 2, *n., v.*, SENSED, SENSING. See SENSATION.

SENSITIVE (sĕn′ sə tĭv), *adj.* (A nimble touch.) The middle finger of the right hand touches the chest over the heart very briefly and lightly, and is then flicked off. *Cf.* SENSITIVITY.

SENSITIVITY (sĕn′ sə tĭv′ ə tĭ), *n.* See SENSITIVE.

SENTENCE (sĕn' təns), *n., v.,* -TENCED, -TENCING. (A series of letters spelled out on the printed page.) The downturned "F" hands are positioned with thumbs and index fingertips touching. The hands move straight apart to either side in a wavy or straight motion. *Cf.* LANGUAGE 1.

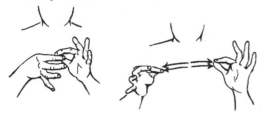

SEPARATE 1 (*v.* sĕp' ə rāt'; *adj., n.* sĕp' ə rĭt), -RATED, -RATING. (The hands are moved apart.) Both hands, in the "A" position, thumbs up, are held together, with knuckles touching. With a deliberate movement they come apart. *Cf.* APART, DIVORCE 1, PART 3.

SEPARATE 2, *v., adj., n.* (Separating to classify.) Both hands, in the right angle position, are placed palms down before the body, knuckles to knuckles. They pull apart or separate, once or a number of times. *Cf.* PART 2.

SEQUEL (sē' kwəl), *n.* (One hand follows the other.) The "A" hands are used, thumbs pointing up. The right is positioned a few inches behind the left. The left hand moves straight forward, while the right follows behind in a series of wavy movements. *Cf.* FOLLOW, FOLLOWING.

SERMON (sûr' mən), *n.* (Placing morsels of wisdom, or food for thought, into the mind.) The right hand, palm out, with thumb and index finger touching, is moved forward and slightly downward a number of times from its initial position near the right temple. *Cf.* PREACH.

SERVANT (sûr' vənt), *n.* (Passing the dishes, one by one.) The upturned "5" hands move alternately toward and away from the chest. *Cf.* SERVE 2, SERVICE, WAITER, WAITRESS.

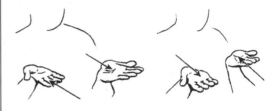

SERVE 1 (sûrv), *v.,* SERVED, SERVING, *n.* (Passing out dishes of food, one by one.) The upturned hands are held before the chest, as if bearing dishes of food. The left moves alternately to the left and back to the right, as if extending the dishes to a diner.

SERVE 2, *v.* See SERVANT.

SERVICE (sûr' vĭs), *n., v.,* -VICED, -VICING. See SERVANT.

SETTLE (set' l), *v.* (Settle down.) Both open hands are held palms down and fingers pointing forward. The hands move straight down a short distance. *Cf.* SIT DOWN.

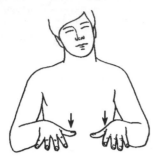

SEVERAL (sĕv' ər əl), *adj.* (The fingers are presented in order, to convey the concept of "several.") The right "A" hand is held palm facing up. One by one the fingers open, beginning with the index finger and ending with the little finger. Some use only the index and middle fingers. *Cf.* FEW.

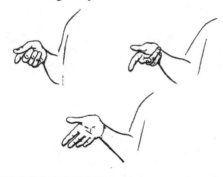

SEWING MACHINE *n.* (The needle moves over the cloth.) The left index finger points straight forward. The right thumb and index, forming a somewhat elongated circle, moves forward repeatedly over the left index, from knuckle to tip, imitating the up–down movement of the needle.

SEX (seks), *n.* (The gender signs, with the letter "X.") The right "X" finger is placed first at the right jawline and then at the right temple.

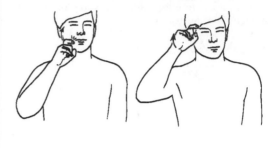

SEXUAL INTERCOURSE *n. phrase.* (The motions of the legs during the sexual act.) The upturned left "V" hand remains motionless, while the downturned right "V" hand comes down repeatedly on the left. *Cf.* COPULATE, FORNICATE.

SHADE (shād), *n.* (The natural sign.) The signer mimes pulling down a window shade.

SHAKESPEARE (shāk' spir), *n.* (Shaking and throwing a spear; a play on signs.) The right fist shakes a bit, and then the right arm mimes throwing a spear.

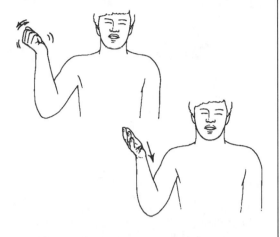

SHALL (shăl, *unstressed* shəl), *v.*, future tense of the verb TO BE. (Something ahead or in the future.) The upright, open right hand, palm facing left, moves straight out and slightly up from a position beside the right temple. *Cf.* FUTURE, IN THE FUTURE, LATER 2, LATER ON, WILL 1, WOULD.

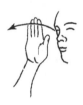

SHAME 1 (shām), *n., v.*, SHAMED, SHAMING. (The color rises in the cheek; an attempt is made to hide the head.) The backs of the fingers of the right hand, held in the right angle position, are placed against the right cheek. The hand moves up along the cheek, pivoting at the wrist, so that the fingers finally point to the rear. *Cf.* ASHAMED, BASHFUL, SHAMEFUL, SHAME ON YOU, SHY 1.

SHAME 2, *n.* Similar to SHAME 1, but both hands are used, at either cheek. *Cf.* SHY 2.

SHAMEFUL (shām′ fəl), *adj.* See SHAME 1.

SHAME ON YOU *phrase.* See SHAME 1.

SHAPE (shāp), *n., v.*, SHAPED, SHAPING. (Contours are indicated or outlined.) Both "A" hands, held about a foot apart before the face, with palms facing each other, move down simultaneously in a wavy, undulating motion. *Cf.* FIGURE 2, FORM 1, IMAGE, SCULPT, SCULPTURE, STATUE.

SHARE 1 (shâr), *n., v.*, SHARED, SHARING. (Cutting off or designating a part.) The little finger edge of the open right hand moves straight down the middle of the upturned left palm. *Cf.* PART 1, PIECE, PORTION, SECTION, SOME.

SHARE 2, *n., v.* (A splitting apart or dividing.) The two hands are crossed, with the right little finger resting on the left index finger. Both hands are dropped down and separated simultaneously, so that the palms face down. *Cf.* DIVIDE, DIVISION.

SHARK (shärk), *n.* (The dorsal fin.) The upturned fingers of the right "B" hand protrude straight up between the left middle and ring fingers. The right fingers move off and away, in a wavy, meandering path.

SHARP (shärp), *adj.* (A sharp-edged hand.) The right hand grasps the little finger edge of the left firmly. As it leaves this position, moving down and out, it assumes the "A" position, palm facing left. *Cf.* ADEPT, EXPERIENCE 1, EXPERT, SKILL, SKILLFUL.

SHE (shē), *pron.* (Pointing at a female.) The FEMALE prefix sign is made: the right "A" hand's thumb moves down along the line of the right jaw, from ear almost to chin. The right index finger then points at an imaginary female. If in context the gender is clear, the prefix sign is usually omitted. *Cf.* HER 1.

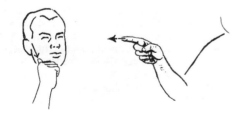

SHELTER (shĕl′ tər), *n.* (A shield.) The "S" hands are held before the chest, the left behind the right, and are pushed slightly away from the body. Then the right hand opens, palm facing out, and moves clockwise as if shielding the left fist. *Cf.* REFUGE, SHIELD 2.

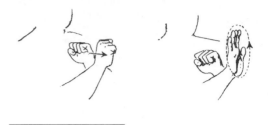

SHIELD 1 (shēld), *n., v.,* SHIELDED, SHIELDING. (Hold down firmly; cover and strengthen.) The "S" hands, downturned, are held side by side in front of the body, the arms almost horizontal, and the left hand in front of the right. Both arms move a short distance forward and slightly downward. *Cf.* DEFEND, DEFENSE, FORTIFY, GUARD, PROTECT, PROTECTION.

SHIELD 2, *n., v.* See SHELTER.

SHINE (shīn), *v.,* SHINED, SHINING, SHONE. (Reflected glistening of light rays.) The left hand, held supinely before the chest, palm down, represents the object from which the rays glisten. The right hand, in the "5" position, touches the back of the left lightly and moves up toward the right, pivoting slightly at the wrist, with fingers wiggling. *Cf.* BRIGHT 2, GLISTEN, SHINING.

SHINE SHOES *v. phrase.* (The act of rubbing.) The right knuckles rub briskly against the outstretched left palm. *Cf.* POLISH, RUB, SANDPAPER.

SHINING (shī′ ning), *adj.* See SHINE.

SHIP (shǐp), *n.* (The ship is transported over the waves; its masts are indicated.) The right "3" hand, palm facing left and resting on the upturned left palm, is moved forward by the left hand, in a series of undulating movements.

SHIRK (shûrk), *v.*, SHIRKED, SHIRKING. (Ducking back and forth, away from something.) Both "A" hands, thumbs pointing straight up, are held some distance before the chest, with the left hand in front of the right. The right hand, swinging back and forth, moves away from the left and toward the chest. *Cf.* AVOID 1, EVADE, EVASION, SHUN.

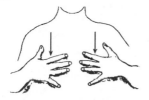

SHIRT (shûrt), *n.* (Draping the clothes on the body.) With fingertips resting on the chest, both hands move down simultaneously. The action is repeated. *Cf.* CLOTHES, CLOTHING, DRESS, FROCK, GARMENT, GOWN, SUIT, WEAR 1.

SHIVER 1 (shĭv′ ər), *v.*, -ERED, -ERING. (The trembling from cold.) Both "S" hands, palms facing, are placed at the sides of the body. In this position the arms and hands shiver. *Cf.* CHILLY, COLD 1, WINTER 1.

SHIVER 2, *v., n.* (Chattering teeth.) Both "V" hands, fingers curved and the right hand held above the left, move very rapidly back and forth, in opposite directions each time, imitating the chattering of teeth. *Cf.* CHILL.

SHOCKED 1 (shŏkt), *v.* (The mind is frozen; the thought is frozen.) The index finger of the right "D" hand, palm facing the body, touches the forehead (modified THINK sign, *q.v.*). Both hands, in the "5" position, palms down, are then suddenly and deliberately dropped down in front of the body. A look of surprise is assumed at this point, and the head jerks back slightly. *Cf.* AT A LOSS, DUMBFOUNDED 1.

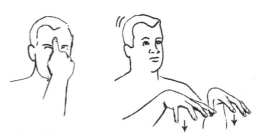

SHOCKED 2, *(colloq.)*, *adj.* (The eyes pop open.) The "S" hands, palms facing each other, are held before the eyes. They suddenly open into the "C" position, with the eyes wide open. *Cf.* OPEN-EYED, SURPRISED.

SHOE(S) 1 (shoo), *n.* Both "S" hands, palms facing down, are brought together sharply twice.

SHOE(S) 2, *n.* (Slipping the foot into the shoe.) The downturned right "B" hand is slipped into the upturned left "C" hand.

SHOOT (shoot), *v.*, SHOT, SHOOTING. (Firing a gun.) The right "L" hand is pointed forward, palm facing left. The right thumb is then moved down, as in the movement of the pistol's hammer. The index or trigger finger may also move.

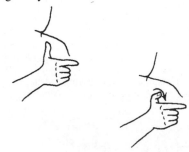

SHOP (shŏp), *n., v.,* SHOPPED, SHOPPING. (Paying out money.) The right hand, palm up and all fingertips touching the thumb, is placed in the upturned left hand. From this position it moves forward and off

the left hand a number of times. The right fingers usually remain against the thumb, but they may be opened very slightly each time the right hand moves forward. *Cf.* SHOPPING.

SHOPPING (shŏp' ĭng), *n.* See SHOP.

SHOPPING CENTER *n.* (SHOP, CENTER.) The sign for SHOPPING is made: the right hand, palm up and all fingertips touching the thumb, is placed in the upturned left hand. The right hand moves forward and off the left hand several times. This is followed by CENTER: the downturned right fingers make a clockwise circle over the upturned open left hand, coming down to stand on the left palm.

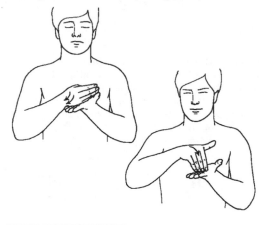

SHORT 1 (shôrt), *adj.* (To make short; to measure off a short space.) The index and middle fingers of the right "H" hand are placed across the top of the index and middle fingers of the left "H" hand, and move a short distance back and forth, along the length of the left index finger. *Cf.* BRIEF 1, SHORTEN.

SHORT 2, *adj.* (A shortness of height is indicated.) The right hand, in right-angle position, pats an imaginary head at approximately chest level. *Cf.* SMALL 2.

SHORTEN (shôr′ tən), *v.*, -ENED, -ENING. See SHORT 1.

SHORTS (shôrtz), *n.* (The length is indicated.) The signer indicates the hem of a pair of shorts on the legs. Indicate the length of the shorts by crossing the thighs.

SHOT (shŏt), *(colloq.), n.* (The natural sign.) The right hand goes through the motions of injecting a substance into the upper left arm. *Cf.* INJECTION, SHOT IN THE ARM.

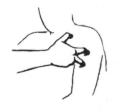 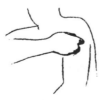

SHOT IN THE ARM *(sl.), n. phrase.* See SHOT.

SHOULD (shŏŏd), *v.* (Being pinned down.) The right hand, in the "X" position, palm down, moves forcefully up and down once or twice. An expression of determination is frequently assumed. *Cf.* HAVE TO, MUST, NECESSARY 1, NECESSITY, NEED 1, OUGHT TO, VITAL 2.

SHOULDER (shōl′ dər), *n.* The right hand taps the shoulder.

SHOUT (shout), *v.,* SHOUTED, SHOUTING. (Harsh words thrown out.) The right hand, as in CURSE 1, appears to claw words out of the mouth. This time, however, it turns and throws them out, ending in the "5" position. *Cf.* CURSE 2, SCREAM.

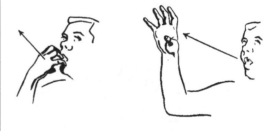

SHOVEL 1 (shŭv′ əl), *n., v.,* -ELED, -ELING. (The natural motion.) Both hands, in the "A" position, right hand facing up and left hand facing down, grasp an imaginary shovel. They go through the natural movements of shoveling earth—first digging in and then tossing the earth aside. *Cf.* DIG.

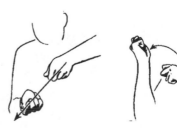

SHOVEL 2, *v.*, -ELED, -ELING. (Turning over the earth.) The upturned right palm, cupped, acts like a scoop for the earth, turning it over to the left. The upturned left palm may act as a foil.

SHOW 1 (shō), *n., v.*, SHOWED, SHOWING. (Directing the attention to something, and bringing it forward.) The right index finger points into the left palm, held facing out before the body. The left palm moves straight out. For the passive form of this verb, *i.e.*, BE SHOWN, the movement is reversed: the left hand, palm facing in, is moved in toward the body, while the right index finger remains pointing into the left palm. *Cf.* DEMONSTRATE, DISPLAY, EVIDENCE, EXAMPLE, EXHIBIT, EXHIBITION, ILLUSTRATE, INDICATE, INFLUENCE 2, PRODUCE 1, REPRESENT, SIGNIFY 1.

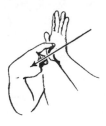

SHOW 2, *n.* (Motion or movement, modified by the letter "A" for "act.") Both "A" hands, palms out, are held at shoulder height and rotate alternately toward the head. *Cf.* ACT 1, ACTOR, ACTRESS, DRAMA, PERFORM 2, PERFORMANCE 2, PLAY 2.

SHOWER (shou′ ər), *n.* (The sprinkling of water on the head.) The right hand sprinkles imaginary water on the head. *Cf.* BAPTISM.

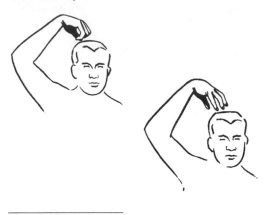

SHOW OFF (shō ôf′), *v.* (Indicating the self, repeatedly.) The thumbs of both "A" hands are alternately thrust into the chest a number of times. *Cf.* BRAG.

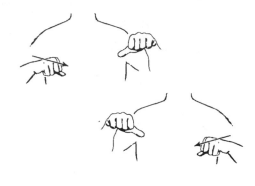

SHRIMP (shrimp), *n.* (The movement in the water.) Both hands, palms out, are held side by side, with the thumbs touching their respective index fingers. The fingers open and close quickly a number of times.

SHRIVEL (shriv′ əl), v. (The natural sign.) The right claw hand, palm down or facing forward, slowly "shrivels" into the "S." The sign is sometimes made with the upright index finger simply waving back and forth in front of the lips.

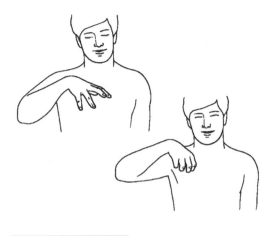

SHUN (shŭn), v., SHUNNED, SHUNNING. (Ducking back and forth, away from something.) Both "A" hands, thumbs pointing straight up, are held some distance before the chest, with the left hand in front of the right. The right hand, swinging back and forth, moves away from the left and toward the chest. Cf. AVOID 1, EVADE, EVASION, SHIRK.

SHUT (shŭt), adj., v., SHUT, SHUTTING. (The act of closing.) Both "B" hands, held palms out before the body, come together with some force. Cf. CLOSE 1.

SHUT UP (shŭt ŭp′), interj. (The natural motion of "shushing.") The index finger of the right "D" hand is brought up forcefully against the lips. An angry expression is assumed.

SHY 1 (shī), adj. (The color rises in the cheek; an attempt is made to hide the head.) The backs of the fingers of the right hand, held in the right angle position, are placed against the right cheek. The hand moves up along the cheek, pivoting at the wrist, so that the fingers finally point to the rear. Cf. ASHAMED, BASHFUL, SHAME 1, SHAMEFUL, SHAME ON YOU.

SHY 2, adj. Similar to SHY 1, but both hands are used, at either cheek. Cf. SHAME 2.

SICILY (sis′ ə lē), n. (Stealing something.) The downturned right "3" or claw-shaped hand, held near the right hip, swivels twice in a clockwise manner, as if picking up something surreptitiously. This sign is highly derogatory, for it implies that all Sicilians are thieves. It should not normally be used. Cf. PALERMO.

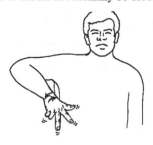

SICK (sĭk), *adj., adv.* (The sick parts of the anatomy are indicated.) The right middle finger rests on the forehead, and its left counterpart is placed against the stomach. The signer assumes an expression of sadness or physical distress. *Cf.* DISEASE, ILL, ILLNESS.

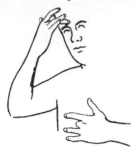

SIGHT (sīt), *n.,* SAW, SEEN, SEEING. (The eyesight is directed forward.) The right "V" hand, palm facing the body, is placed so that the fingertips are just under the eyes. The hand swings straight out. *Cf.* SEE.

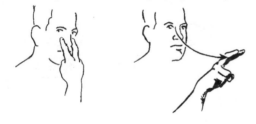

SIGNIFICANCE 1 (sĭg nĭf′ ə kəns), *n.* Both "F" hands, palms facing each other, move apart, up, and together in a smooth elliptical fashion, coming together at the tips of the thumbs and index fingers of both hands. *Cf.* IMPORTANT, SIGNIFICANT, VALUABLE, VALUE, VITAL 1, WORTH, WORTHWHILE, WORTHY.

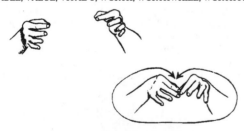

SIGNIFICANCE 2, *n.* (Relative standing of one's thoughts.) A modified sign for THINK is made: the right index finger touches the middle of the forehead. The tips of the right "V" hand, palm down, are then thrust into the upturned left palm (as in STAND, *q.v.*). The right "V" hand is then re-thrust into the upturned left palm, with right palm now facing the body. *Cf.* IMPLY, INTEND, INTENT, INTENTION, MEAN 2, MEANING, MOTIVE 3, PURPOSE 1, SIGNIFY 2, SUBSTANCE 2.

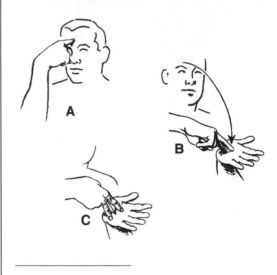

SIGNIFICANT (sĭg nĭf′ ə kənt), *adj.* See SIGNIFICANCE 1.

SIGNIFY 1 (sĭg′ nə fī′), *v.,* -FIED, -FYING. (Directing the attention to something, and bringing it forward.) The right index finger points into the left palm, held facing out before the body. The left palm moves straight out. *Cf.* DEMONSTRATION, DISPLAY, EVIDENCE, EXAMPLE, EXHIBIT, EXHIBITION, ILLUSTRATE, INDICATE, INFLUENCE 2, PRODUCE 1, REPRESENT, SHOW 1.

SIGNIFY 2, *n.* See SIGNIFICANCE 2.

SIGN LANGUAGE (sīn lang′ gwij), *n.* (LANGUAGE 1, *q.v.,* and hand/arm movements.) The "D" hands, palms facing and index fingers pointing back toward the face, describe a series of continuous counter-clockwise circles toward and away from the face, imitating the foot motions in bicycling. This is followed by the sign for LANGUAGE: the downturned "F" hands are positioned with thumbs and index fingertips touching. The hands move straight apart to either side in a wavy motion. The LANGUAGE part is often omitted. *Cf.* LANGUAGE OF SIGNS, SIGNS.

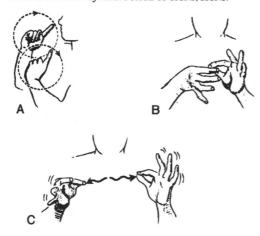

SIGNS (sīnz), *n. pl.* See SIGN LANGUAGE.

SILENCE 1 (sī′ ləns), *interj., n., v.,* -LENCED, -LENCING. (The natural sign.) The index finger is brought up against the pursed lips. *Cf.* BE QUIET 1, QUIET 1, SILENT, STILL 2.

SILENCE 2, *n., interj., v.* (Quiet and peace.) The open hands are crossed before the mouth, the right palm facing left, the left facing right. Then both hands, held palms down, move down from the mouth, curving outward to either side of the body. *Cf.* BE QUIET 2, BE STILL, CALM, QUIET 2.

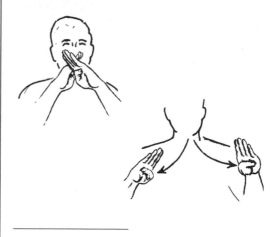

SILENT (sī′ lənt), *adj.* See SILENCE 1.

SILVER 1 (sil′ vər), *n.* (Sparkling from the eyes and shaking the coins.) The right "S" hand is positioned at the right eye. It moves forward, pivoting repeatedly at the wrist, as if shaking imaginary coins.

SILVER 2, *n., adj.* (Sparkling before the eyes.) The fingers of one or both hands wriggle before the eyes.

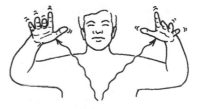

SILLY (sĭl′ ĭ), *adj.* (Thoughts flickering back and forth.) The right "Y" hand, thumb almost touching the forehead, is shaken back and forth across the forehead several times. *Cf.* FOLLY, FOOLISH, NON-SENSE, RIDICULOUS, TRIFLING.

SIMILAR (sĭm′ ĭ lər), *adj.* (Matching fingers are brought together.) The outstretched index fingers are brought together, either once or several times. *Cf.* ALIKE, IDENTICAL, LIKE 2, SAME 1, SUCH.

SIMPLE 1 (sĭm′ pəl), *adj.* (The fingertips are easily moved.) The right fingertips brush repeatedly over their upturned left counterparts, causing them to move. *Cf.* EASY 1.

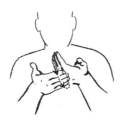

SIMPLE 2, *adj.* (Everything is wiped off the hand, to emphasize an uncluttered or clean condition.) The right hand slowly wipes the upturned left palm, from wrist to fingertips. *Cf.* CLEAN, NICE, PLAIN 2, PURE 1, PURITY.

SIMPLE 3, *adj.* Both hands are held in the "F" position, fingers pointing out and palms facing each other. The right hand comes down past the left, its index finger and thumb smartly striking their left counterparts. The signer often assumes a pursed lips expression.

SIMULTANEOUSLY (sī′ məl tā′ nē əs lē), *adv.* (Time is the same.) The downturned curved right index finger taps the back of the left wrist, and then both hands, in the downturned "Y" position, separate quickly. *Cf.* SAME TIME.

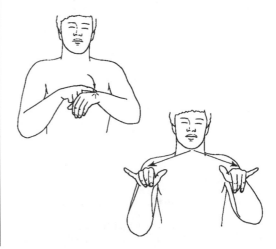

SIN (sĭn), *n., v.,* SINNED, SINNING. (A stabbing pain.) The "D" hands, index fingers pointing to each other, are rotated in elliptical fashion before the chest—simultaneously but in opposite directions. *Cf.* ACHE, HARM 1, HURT 1, INJURE 1, INJURY, PAIN, WOUND.

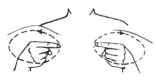

SINCE 1 (sĭns), *adv., prep., conj.* (From a point up and over.) In the "D" position, palms down, both index fingers touch the right shoulder and then are brought up and over, ending in a palm-up position, pointing straight ahead of the body. *Cf.* ALL ALONG, ALL THE TIME, EVER SINCE, SO FAR, THUS FAR.

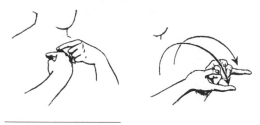

SINCE 2, *conj.* (A thought or knowledge uppermost in the mind.) The fingers of the right hand, or the index finger, are placed on the center of the forehead, and then the hand is brought strongly up above the head, assuming the "A" position, thumb pointing up. *Cf.* BECAUSE, FOR 2.

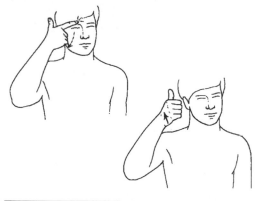

SINCERE 1 (sĭn sîr′), *adj.* (The letter "H," for HONEST; a straight and true path.) The index and middle fingers of the right "H" hand, whose palm faces left,

move straight forward along the upturned left palm. *Cf.* FRANK, HONEST, HONESTY.

SINCERE 2, *adj.* (Coming forth directly from the lips; true.) The index finger of the right "D" hand, palm facing left, is placed against the lips. It moves up an inch or two and then describes a small arc forward and away from the lips. *Cf.* ABSOLUTE, ABSOLUTELY, ACTUAL, ACTUALLY, AUTHENTIC, CERTAIN, CERTAINLY, FIDELITY, FRANKLY, GENUINE, INDEED, POSITIVE 1, POSITIVELY, REAL, REALLY, SURE, SURELY, TRUE, TRULY, TRUTH, VALID, VERILY.

SING (sĭng), *v.,* SANG or SUNG, SUNG, SINGING, *n.* (A rhythmic, wavy movement of the hand, to indicate a melody; the movement of a conductor's hand in directing a musical performance.) The right "5" hand, palm facing left, is waved back and forth next to the left hand, in a series of elongated figure-eights. *Cf.* MUSIC, SONG.

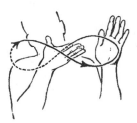

SINK (singk), *n.* (The faucets and the shape.) Both downturned hands mime turning a pair of faucets. The upturned open hands then trace the outline of a sink, from the bottom to the sides.

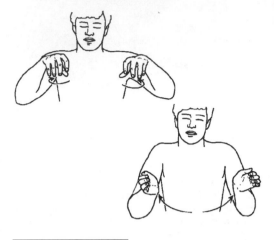

SISSY (sis' ĕ), *n.* (An effeminate gesture.) The right hand lightly taps the back of the limp left hand.

SISTER (sĭs' tər), *n.* (Female root sign: SAME. Meaning a female from the same family.) The FEMALE root sign is made: the thumb of the right "A" hand moves down along the right jawbone, almost to the chin. This is followed by the sign for SAME: the outstretched index fingers are brought together, either once or several times.

SIT (sĭt), *v.*, SAT, SITTING. (The act of sitting.) The extended right index and middle fingers are draped across the back of the same two fingers of the downturned left hand. The hands then move straight downward a short distance. *Cf.* BE SEATED, CHAIR, SEAT.

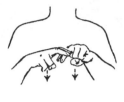

SIT DOWN *v. phrase.* (Act of sitting down.) Both open hands are held palms down and fingers pointing forward before the chest. The hands then move straight down a short distance. *Cf.* SETTLE.

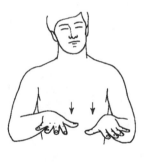

SITUATION (sĭch´ o͞o ā' shən), *n.* (The letter "S"; an encircling environment.) The right "S" hand makes a counterclockwise circle around the upturned left index finger.

SKATEBOARD (skāt' bôrd), *n.* The right index and middle fingers "stand" on the tips of their left counterparts. Both hands, thus connected, move forward in a swaying motion, imitating the rhythms of riding on a skateboard.

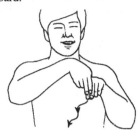

SKELETON (skel' ə tən), *n.* (The crossed bones.) Both "V" hands, fingers bent and palms facing the body, are crossed at the chest. The two "V"s make scratching movements repeatedly as they rest on the biceps.

SKEPTIC 1 (skĕp' tĭk), *n.* (The nose is wrinkled in disbelief.) The right "V" hand faces the nose. The index and middle fingers bend as a cynical expression is assumed. This is followed by the sign for INDIVIDUAL: both open hands, palms facing each other, move down the sides of the body, tracing its outline to the hips. *Cf.* CYNIC, CYNICAL, DISBELIEF 1, DON'T BELIEVE, DOUBT 1, INCREDULITY, SKEPTICAL 1.

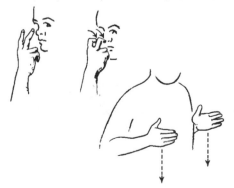

SKEPTIC 2, *n.* (Warding off.) The sign for SKEPTICAL 2 is formed. This is followed by the sign for INDIVIDUAL, as in SKEPTIC 1.

SKEPTICAL 1 (skĕp' tə kəl), *adj.* See SKEPTIC 1.

SKEPTICAL 2, *adj.* (Throwing the fist.) The right "S" hand is held before the right shoulder, elbow bent out to the side. The hand is then thrown forward several times, as if striking at someone. *Cf.* SUSPICION 2.

SKI 1 (skē), *v.* (The ski poles.) The signer, holding an imaginary pair of ski poles, pushes down on them in order to create forward motion.

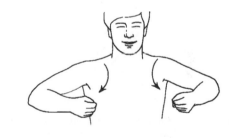

SKI 2, *v.* (Downhill movement.) Both "X" hands, palms up, move downward as if sliding downhill.

SKILL (skĭl), *n.* (A sharp-edged hand.) The right hand grasps the little finger edge of the left firmly. As it leaves this position, moving down and out, it assumes the "A" position, palm facing left. *Cf.* ADEPT, EXPERIENCE 1, EXPERT, SHARP, SKILLFUL.

SKILLFUL (skĭl′ fəl), *adj.* See SKILL.

SKINNY (skĭn′ ĭ), *(sl.), adj.* (A thin, tapering object is described with the little fingers, the thinnest of all.) The tips of the little fingers, touching, one above the other, are drawn apart. The cheeks may also be drawn in for emphasis. *Cf.* BEANPOLE, THIN 2.

SKIP (skip), *v.* (Something is missing.) The extended right index finger strikes against the downturned middle finger of the left hand, which is held palm down and other fingers pointing right or forward.

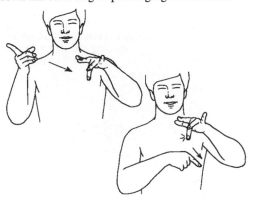

SKY (skī), *n.* (Entering heaven through a break in the clouds.) Both open hands, fingers straight and pointing up, move upward in an arc on either side of the head. Just before they touch above the head, the right hand, palm down, sweeps under the left and moves up, its palm now facing out. *Cf.* HEAVEN.

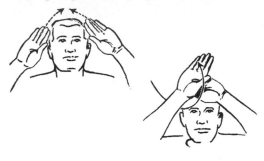

SKYSCRAPERS (skī′ skrā′ pərz), *n. pl.* (The tall buildings are indicated.) Both index fingers move alternately up and down.

SLANG (slang), *n., adj.* (The "S" letters; quotation marks.) Both "S" hands, palms out, are drawn apart an inch or two. The curved "V" hands, palms also out, then draw quotation marks in the air.

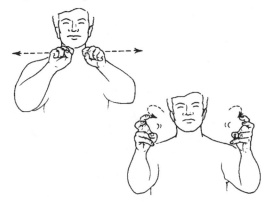

SLAY (slā), *v.*, SLEW, SLAIN, SLAYING. (Thrusting a dagger and twisting it.) The outstretched right index finger is passed under the downturned left hand. As it moves under the left hand, the right wrist twists in a clockwise direction. *Cf.* KILL, MURDER.

SLED (sled), *n.* (The handlebars.) The signer mimes manipulating a sled's handlebars back and forth. The head should be hanging down, as if the body were belly-down on a sled.

SLEEP 1 (slēp), *v.*, SLEPT, SLEEPING, *n.* (The eyes are closed.) The fingers of the right open hand, facing the forehead, are placed on the forehead. The hand moves down and away from the head, with the fingers closing so that they all touch. The eyes meanwhile close, and the head bows slightly, as in sleep. *Cf.* ASLEEP, NAP 1.

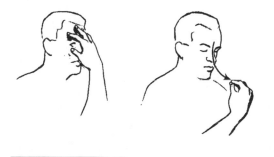

SLEEP 2, *n., v.* (The natural sign.) The signer's head leans to the right and rests in the upturned palm of the open right hand.

SLEEPY (slē′ pĭ), *adj.* (Drooping eyelids.) The right fingers are wiggled in front of the face, and the head is bowed forward.

SLEEVE (slēv), *n.* (Indicating the sleeve.) The thumb and index fingers of either hand move up and down the opposite arm.

SLIDE (slīd), *n.* (Slide being inserted in projector.) The right "H" hand, palm facing the signer and fingertips pointing left, moves into the left palm.

SLIGHT (slīt), *adj.* (Indicating a small mass.) The extended right thumb and index finger are held slightly spread. They are then moved slowly toward each other until they almost touch. *Cf.* PETTY, SMALL 1, TINY.

SLIP AWAY *v. phrase.* (Slipping out and away.) The right index finger is held pointing upward between the index and middle fingers of the prone left hand. From this position the right index finger moves to the right, slipping out of the grasp of the left fingers and away from the left hand. *Cf.* RUN AWAY.

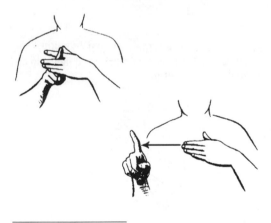

SLIPPER (slĭp′ ər), *n.* The downturned right open hand moves back and forth across the upturned cupped left palm.

SLOW 1 (slō), *adj.* (The movement indicates the slowness.) The right hand is drawn slowly over the back of the downturned left hand, from fingertips to wrist.

SLOW 2, *adv., adj. (loc.)* The right "Y" hand moves slowly down the right cheek.

SMALL 1 (smôl), *adj.* (Indicating a small mass.) The extended right thumb and index finger are held slightly spread. They are then moved slowly toward each other until they almost touch. *Cf.* PETTY, SLIGHT, TINY.

SMALL 2, *adj.* (A shortness of height is indicated.) The right hand, in right-angle position, pats an imaginary head at approximately chest level. *Cf.* SHORT 2.

SMART (smärt), *adj.* (The mind is bright.) The middle finger is placed at the forehead, and then the hand, with an outward flick, turns around so that the palm faces outward. This indicates a brightness flowing from the mind. *Cf.* BRIGHT 3, BRILLIANT 1, CLEVER, INTELLIGENT.

SMASHED IN *v. phrase.* (Collapsing inward.) With fingers interlocked and palms facing the signer, both hands, using the interconnected fingers as hinges, move in toward the chest.

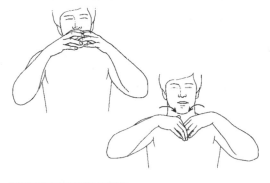

SMELL (směl), *v.*, SMELLED, SMELLING, *n.* (Bringing something up to the nose.) The upturned right hand moves slowly up to and past the nose, and the signer breathes in as the hand sweeps by. *Cf.* FRAGRANT, ODOR, SCENT.

SMILE (smīl), *v.*, SMILED, SMILING, *n.* (Drawing the lips into a smile.) The right index finger is drawn back over the lips, toward the ear. As the finger moves back, the signer breaks into a smile. (Both index fingers may also be used.)

SMOKESTACK (smōk′ stak′), *n.* (The shape.) The open hands, palms facing each other, are held a few inches apart. They move up together a short distance, come together an inch or two, and then continue their upward movement. *Cf.* CHIMNEY.

SNAIL (snāl), *n.* (The shape and function.) The downturned bent right "V" hand is concealed by the downturned cupped left hand. The right "V" fingers protrude from the left as both hands move slowly forward.

SNAKE (snāk), *n.* (The head and fangs gyrating.) The right elbow rests on the palm of the left hand, while the right hand gyrates in imitation of a snake's head, the thumb and first two fingers extended forward to represent fangs.

SNAP (snap), *v.* (Snapping the fingers.) The fingers are snapped.

SNAPS (snapz), *n.* (Fastening snaps on clothes.) The signer mimes closing snaps on the shirt.

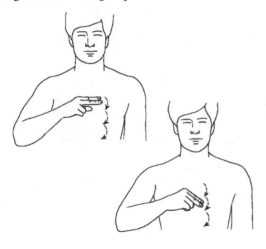

SNATCH UP *(colloq.), v.* (Sleight of hand.) The downturned open hand is positioned at chest height, with the middle finger hanging farther down than the rest of the fingers. With a quick and sudden movement, the hand moves up into the "A" position. For maximum impact, the signer's tongue is visible, sticking out from the pursed lips. As the hand moves up, the tongue is suddenly sucked into the mouth.

SNEEZE (snēz), *v., n.* (Stifling a sneeze.) The index finger is pressed lengthwise under the nose.

SNOB (snob), *n.* (The upturned nose.) The right thumb and index finger, slightly open, are placed at the tip of the nose, and move up, coming together as they do.

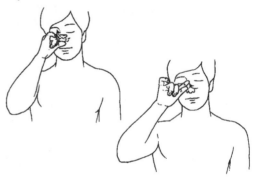

SNOWFLAKE (snō′ flāk′), *n.* (Descending and settling.) The sign for SNOW is made: the fingers wriggle repeatedly as the downturned hands move slowly down. The right thumb and index, forming a circle, then settle gently on the back of the downturned left hand.

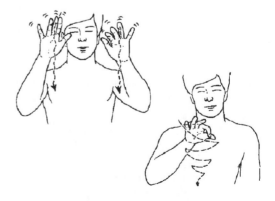

SO (sō), *interj.* (The natural sign, accompanied by a sigh.) With palms facing up, the signer heaves a distinct sigh, causing the shoulders to rise slightly. *Cf.* WELL 3.

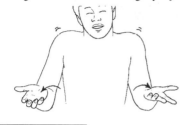

SOAP (sōp), *n., v.,* SOAPED, SOAPING. (Working up a lather in the hand.) The fingertips of the right hand move back and forth on the upturned left palm, in small downturned arcs.

SO-CALLED (sō′ kôld′), *adj.* (The quotation marks are indicated.) The curved index and middle fingers of both hands, held palms out, move slightly to either side of the body, as if drawing quotation marks in the air. *Cf.* CAPTION 1, QUOTATION, QUOTE, SUBJECT, THEME, TITLE, TOPIC.

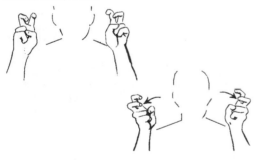

SOCIAL SECURITY *n.* (The "S" letters.) The signer fingerspells the letters "S-S."

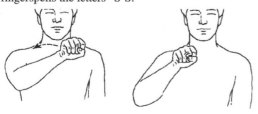

SOCIAL STUDIES *n.* The right hand makes the letter "S" twice, moving slightly to the right after the first time.

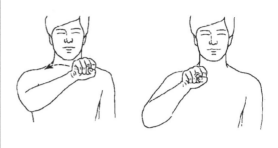

SOCK(S) (sŏk), *n.* (The knitting.) The index fingers, pointing forward, are rubbed back and forth against each other. *Cf.* KNIT, STOCKING(S).

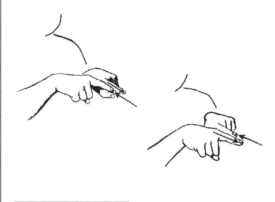

SODA POP *n.* (Corking a bottle.) The left "O" hand is held with thumb edge up, representing a bottle. The thumb and index finger of the right "5" hand represent a cork, and are inserted into the circle formed by the "O" hand. The palm of the open right hand then strikes down on the upturned edge of the "O" hand, as if forcing the cork into the bottle. *Cf.* POP 1, SODA WATER.

SODA WATER *n. phrase.* See SODA POP.

SO FAR *adv. phrase.* (From a point up and over.) In the "D" position, palms down, both index fingers touch the right shoulder and then are brought up and over, ending in a palm-up position, pointing straight ahead of the body. *Cf.* ALL ALONG, ALL THE TIME, EVER SINCE, SINCE 1, THUS FAR.

 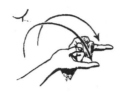

SOFT (sôft, sŏft), *adj.* (Squeezing for softness.) The hands slowly and deliberately squeeze an imaginary object or substance.

SOIL 1 (soil), *n.* (Fingering the soil.) Both hands, held upright before the body, finger imaginary pinches of soil. *Cf.* DIRT, GROUND.

SOIL 2, *v.*, SOILED, SOILING. (A modification of the pig's snout groveling in a trough.) The downturned right hand is placed under the chin. Its fingers, pointing left, wiggle repeatedly. *Cf.* DIRTY, FILTHY.

SOLAR SYSTEM *n.* (The movement of the planets.) The right "S" hand makes a clockwise circle around its left counterpart. Both "S" hands, palms forward, then separate and draw "Z"s in the air. This latter sign means SYSTEM.

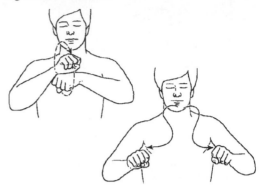

SOLDIER (sōl' jər), *n.* (Bearing arms.) Both "A" hands, palms facing the body, are placed at the left breast, with the right hand above the left, as if holding a rifle against the body. The sign for INDIVIDUAL follows: both open hands, palms facing each other, move down the sides of the body, tracing its outline to the hips. *Cf.* ARMS.

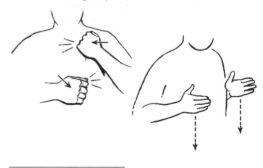

SOLE (sōl), *adj.* (One, wandering around in a circle.) The index finger, pointing straight up, palm facing the body (the number *one*), is rotated before the face in a counterclockwise direction. *Cf.* ALONE, LONE, ONLY.

SO LONG *interj.* (A wave of the hand.) The right open hand waves back and forth several times. *Cf.* GOODBYE, HELLO.

SOME (sŭm; *unstressed* səm), *adj.* (Cutting off or designating a part.) The little finger edge of the open right hand moves straight down the middle of the upturned left palm. *Cf.* PART 1, PIECE, PORTION, SECTION, SHARE 1.

SOMERSAULT (sum' ər sôlt), *n., v.* (The natural sign.) The signer mimes a somersault: the right bent "V" hand, palm facing forward, executes a somersault, twisting into a palm-up position.

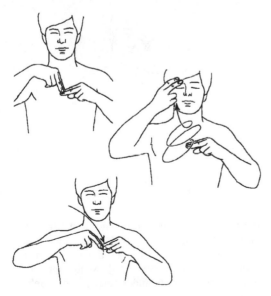

SOMETIME(S) (sŭm' tīmz'), *adv.* (The "1" finger is brought up very slowly.) The right index finger, resting in the open left palm, which is facing right, swings up slowly from its position to one in which it is pointing straight up. The movement is repeated slowly, after a pause. *Cf.* OCCASIONAL, OCCASIONALLY, ONCE IN A WHILE 1, SELDOM.

SON (sŭn), *n.* (Male, baby.) The sign for MALE is made: the thumb and extended fingers of the right hand are brought up to grasp an imaginary cap brim. This is followed by the sign for BABY: the arms are held with one resting on the other, as if cradling a baby.

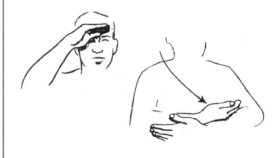

SONG (sông, sŏng), *n.* (A rhythmic, wavy movement of the hand, to indicate a melody; the movement of a conductor's hand in directing a musical performance.) The right "5" hand, palm facing left, is waved back and forth next to the left hand, in a series of elongated figure-eights. *Cf.* MUSIC, SING.

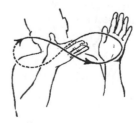

SOPHOMORE (sof' ə môr), *n.* (College student.) The right index finger touches the middle finger of the left hand.

SORROW (sŏr' ō, sôr' ō), *n.* (The heart is circled, to indicate feeling, modified by the letter "S," for SORRY.) The right "S" hand, palm facing the body, is rotated several times over the area of the heart. *Cf.* APOLOGIZE 1, APOLOGY 1, CONTRITION, PENITENT, REGRET, REGRETFUL, REPENT, REPENTANT, RUE, SORROWFUL 2, SORRY.

SORROWFUL 1 (sŏr' ə fəl, sôr'-), *adj.* (The facial features drop.) Both "5" hands, palms facing the eyes and fingers slightly curved, drop simultaneously to a level with the mouth. The head drops slightly as the hands move down, and an expression of sadness isassumed. *Cf.* DEJECTED, DEPRESSED 1, GLOOM, GLOOMY, GRAVE 2, GRIEF 1, MELANCHOLY, MOURNFUL, SAD.

SORROWFUL 2, *adj.* See SORROW.

SORRY (sŏr' ĭ, sôr' ĭ), *adj.* See SORROW.

SORT (sôrt), *v.* (Separating into different groups.) The downturned right-angle hands, knuckles touching, move apart repeatedly as both hands travel from left to right.

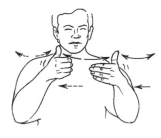

SO-SO (sō' sō'), *phrase.* (Neither this way nor that.) The downturned "5" hand flips over and back several times.

SOUL (sōl), *n.* (Something thin and filmy, *i.e.,* ephemeral.) The hands are held palms facing, with one above the other and index fingers and thumbs touching and almost connected. As the upper hand moves straight up, the index fingers and thumbs of both hands slowly come together, giving the impression of drawing out a thread or other thin substance. *Cf.* GHOST, SPIRIT.

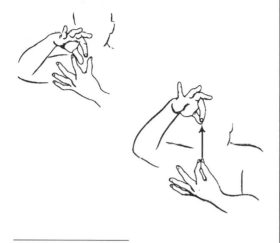

SOUP (sōōp), *n.* (The natural sign.) The upturned open left hand represents the bowl of soup. The index and middle fingers of the right "H" hand form a small scoop to represent the spoon, and move from the left palm to the lips. The movement is usually repeated.

SOUR (sour), *adj.* (Something sour or bitter.) The right index finger is brought sharply up against the lips, while the mouth is puckered up as if tasting something sour. *Cf.* BITTER, DISAPPOINTED, DISAPPOINTMENT.

SPACE (spās), *n.* (The movement upward and outward.) Both "A" hands, palms facing forward and thumbs touching, open to the "5" position as they move upward and outward, with the signer looking up.

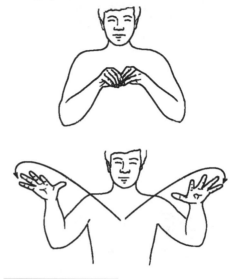

SPAGHETTI (spə gĕt′ ĭ), *n.* (Unraveling a thin string, as indicated by the little fingers.) With palms facing the body, the tips of the extended little fingers touch. As they are drawn slowly apart, they describe very small spirals. *Cf.* STRING, THREAD, TWINE.

SPEAK (spēk), *v.*, SPOKE, SPOKEN, SPEAKING. (Words tumbling from the mouth.) The right index finger, pointing left, describes a continuous small circle in front of the mouth. *Cf.* DISCOURSE, HEARING, MAINTAIN 2, MENTION, REMARK, SAID, SAY, SPEECH 1, STATE 1, TALK 1, TELL, VERBAL.

SPEAKER (spē′ kər), *n.* (The characteristic waving of the speaker's hand as he makes his point.) The right hand is held above the head, palm facing left. The hand, pivoting at the wrist, swings forward and back repeatedly. This is followed by the sign for INDIVIDUAL: both open hands, palms facing each other, move down the sides of the body, tracing its outline to the hips. *Cf.* ORATOR.

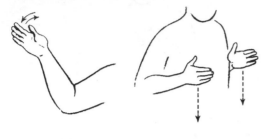

SPECIAL (spĕsh′ əl), *adj.* (Selecting a particular item from among several.) The index finger and thumb of the right hand grasp and pull up the left index finger. *Cf.* EXCEPT, EXCEPTION.

SPECIALIZE (spĕsh′ ə līz′), *v.,* -IZED, -IZING. (A straight, *i.e.,* special, path.) The hands are held in the "B" position, one above the other, with left palm facing right and right palm facing left. The little finger edge of the right hand moves straight forward along the index finger edge of the left. *Cf.* FIELD 1, IN THE FIELD OF, SPECIALTY.

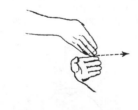

SPECIALTY (spĕsh′ əl tĭ), *n., pl.* -TIES. See SPECIAL-IZE.

SPECIFIC 1 (spĭ sĭf′ ĭk), *adj.* (The fingers come together precisely.) The thumb and index finger of each hand, palms facing, the right above the left, form circles. They are brought together with a deliberate movement, so that the fingers and thumbs now touch. Sometimes the right hand, before coming together with the left, executes a slow clockwise circle above the left. *Cf.* EXACT 1, EXACTLY, EXPLICIT 1, PRECISE.

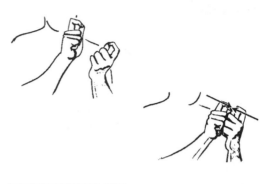

SPECIFIC 2, *adj.* (Pointing.) The signer points to the index finger.

SPECULATE 1 (spĕk′ yə lāt′), *v.,* -LATED, -LATING. (A thought is turned over in the mind.) The index finger makes a small circle on the forehead. *Cf.* CONSIDER 1, MOTIVE 1, RECKON, SPECULATION 1, THINK, THOUGHT 1, THOUGHTFUL.

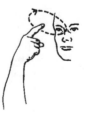

SPECULATE 2, *v.* (Turning thoughts over in the mind.) Both index fingers, pointing to the forehead, describe continuous alternating circles. *Cf.* CONSIDER 2, CONTEMPLATE, PONDER, SPECULATION 2, WEIGH 2, WONDER 1.

SPECULATION 1 (spĕk′ yə lā′ shən), *n.* See SPECULATE 1.

SPECULATION 2, *n.* See SPECULATE 2.

SPEECH 1 (spēch), *n.* (Words tumbling from the mouth.) The right index finger, pointing left, describes a continuous small circle in front of the mouth. *Cf.* DISCOURSE, HEARING, MAINTAIN 2, MENTION, REMARK, SAID, SAY, SPEAK, STATE 1, TALK 1, TELL, VERBAL.

SPEECH 2 *n.* (A gesture of an orator.) The right open hand, palm facing left, is held above and to the right of the head. It pivots, forward and backward, on the wrist several times. *Cf.* LECTURE, ORATE, TALK 2, TESTIMONY 1.

SPEECHLESS (spēch′ lĭs), *(colloq.)*, *adj.* (The mouth drops open.) The fingertips of both "V" hands are held curved and touching before the body, one hand above the other. Then the hands are suddenly drawn apart, and at the same instant the mouth drops open and the eyes open wide. *Cf.* DUMBFOUNDED 2, OPEN-MOUTHED, SURPRISE 2.

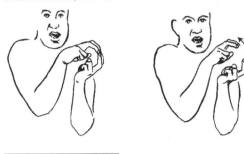

SPEECHREADING *n.* (Reading the lips—the lines of vision, represented by the two fingers, scan the lips.) The right "V" hand, palm facing the body, is placed in front of the face, with slightly curved index and middle fingers directly in front of the lips. The right hand moves in a small counterclockwise circle around the lips. *Cf.* LIPREADING, ORAL, READ LIPS.

SPEED (spēd), *n.*, *v.*, SPED, or SPEEDED, SPEEDING. (A quick movement.) The thumbtip of the upright right hand is flicked quickly off the tip of the curved right index finger, as if shooting marbles. *Cf.* FAST, IMMEDIATELY, QUICK, QUICKNESS, SPEEDY, SWIFT.

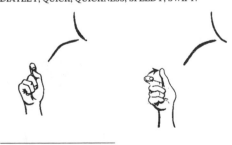

SPEEDY (spē′ dĭ), *adj.* See SPEED.

SPELL (spĕl), *v.*, SPELLED or SPELT, SPELLING. (The movement of the fingers in fingerspelling.) The right hand, palm out, is moved from left to right, with the fingers wriggling up and down. *Cf.* ALPHABET 1, DACTYLOLOGY, FINGERSPELLING, MANUAL ALPHABET, SPELLING.

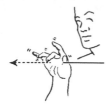

SPELLING (spĕl' ĭng), *n.* See SPELL.

SPEND 1 (spĕnd), *v.*, SPENT, SPENDING. (Repeated giving forth.) The back of the upturned right hand, thumb touching fingertips, is placed in the upturned left palm. The right hand moves off and away from the left once or several times, each time opening into the "5" position, palm up. *Cf.* EXTRAVAGANT, SQUANDER 1, WASTE 1.

SPEND 2, *v.* (Throwing money randomly into the air.) Both hands, closed into fists, palms facing the chest, move alternately up into the air, index fingers flicking out. *Cf.* OVERSPEND, SQUANDER 2.

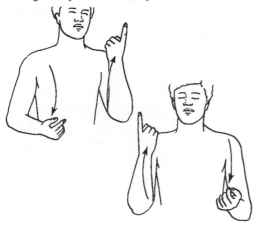

SPERM (spûrm), *n.* (The pulsing of the penis during release.) The left index finger, representing the penis, is positioned at the base of the right "E" hand, whose palm faces left. The fingers of the right hand open and close twice, as the two hands, connected, move forward an inch or so. *Cf.* EJACULATE 1, EJACULATION 1, SEMEN.

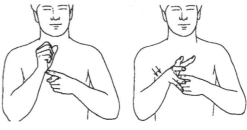

SPILL (spil), *n.*, *v.* (Dropping down and spreading.) Both hands are held in the "AND" position, fingertips touching and palms down. They separate and spread open into the downturned "5" position.

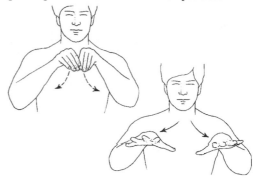

SPIRIT (spĭr' ĭt), *n.* (Something thin and filmy, *i.e.,* ephemeral.) The hands are held palms facing, with one above the other and index fingers and thumbs touching and almost connected. As the upper hand moves straight up, the index fingers and thumbs of both hands slowly come together, giving the impression of drawing out a thread or other thin substance. *Cf.* GHOST, SOUL.

SPLENDID 1 (splěn′ dǐd), *adj.* (The hands gesture toward the heavens.) The "5" hands, palms out and arms raised rather high, are positioned somewhat above the line of vision. The arms move abruptly forward and up once or twice. An expression of pleasure or surprise is usually assumed. *Cf.* EXCELLENT, GRAND 1, GREAT 3, MARVELOUS, SWELL 1, WONDER 2, WONDERFUL 1.

SPLENDID 2, *adj., interj.* (The feelings are titillated.) With the thumb resting on the upper part of the chest, the fingers are wiggled back and forth. *Cf.* ELEGANT, FINE 1, GRAND 2, GREAT 4, SWELL 2, WONDERFUL 2.

SPLINTER (splin′ tər), *n.* (Stuck in the finger.) The right index fingertip sticks an imaginary splinter into the tip of the left index finger.

SPONGE (spunj), *n., v.* (Squeezing and releasing.) The right downturned claw hand mimes squeezing and releasing a sponge.

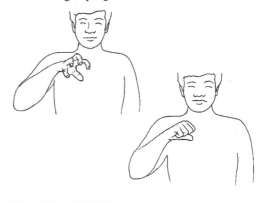

SPOON (spo͞on), *n., v.,* SPOONED, SPOONING. (The shape and action.) The upturned left palm represents a dish or plate. The curved index and middle fingers of the right hand represent the spoon. They are drawn up repeatedly from the left palm to the lips. *Cf.* ICE CREAM 1.

SPOON ON *phrase.* (The natural sign.) The signer, holding an imaginary spoon, tips it over slightly as if pouring off its contents.

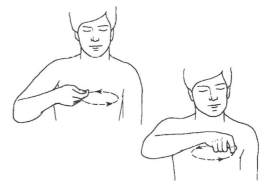

SPORTS (spôrtz), *n.* (A challenge.) Both hands are held in the "A" position, knuckles facing and thumbs standing up. They come together forcefully.

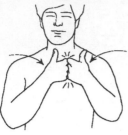

SPREAD (sprĕd), *v.*, SPREAD, SPREADING. (Spreading apart.) Both "AND" hands are held before the body, palms down. They are then directed forward and toward each side, while the fingers open out.

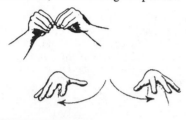

SPRING (sprĭng), *n.* (Flowers or plants emerge from the ground.) The right fingers, pointing up, emerge from the closed left hand, and they spread open as they do. The action may be repeated. *Cf.* BLOOM, DEVELOP 1, GROW, GROWN, MATURE 1, PLANT 1, RAISE 3, REAR 2.

SPRINKLE (sprĭng' kəl), *v.* (The natural sign.) The signer, thumb moving against wriggling fingers, goes through the motions of sprinkling something, like salt, on food.

SQUANDER 1 (skwŏn' dər), *v.*, -DERED, -DERING. (Repeated giving forth.) The back of the upturned right hand, thumb touching fingertips, is placed in the upturned left palm. The right hand moves off and away from the left once or several times, each time opening into the "5" position, palm up. *Cf.* EXTRAVAGANT, SPEND 1, WASTE 1.

SQUANDER 2, *v.* See SPEND 2.

SQUARE (skwâr), *n.*, *v.*, SQUARED, SQUARING, *adj.*, *adv.* (The dimensions are indicated.) The open hands, palms facing and fingers pointing out, are dropped an inch or two simultaneously. They then shift their relative positions so that both palms face the body, with one hand in front of the other. In this new position they again drop an inch or two simultaneously. *Cf.* BOX 1, PACKAGE, ROOM 1, TRUNK.

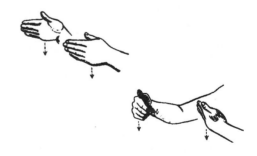

STAGE 1 (stāj), *n.* (The letter "S"; the flat surface.) The right "S" hand is drawn over the back of the downturned left hand, from the wrist to the fingertips.

STAGE 2, *n.* The downturned right "S" hand sweeps forward along the downturned left arm.

STAIR(S) (stâr), *n.* (The natural sign.) The downturned open hands, fingers pointing forward, move in alternate upward "steps" before the body. *Cf.* STEP(S) 1.

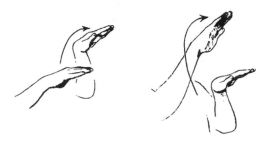

STAMP (stămp), *n.* (Licking the stamp.) The tips of the right index and middle fingers are licked with the tongue, and then the fingers are pressed against the upturned left palm, as if affixing a stamp to an envelope.

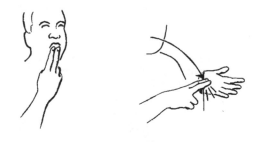

STAND 1 (stănd), *v.*, STOOD, STANDING, *n.* (The feet planted on the ground.) The downturned right "V"

fingers are thrust into the upturned left palm. *Cf.* STANDING.

STAND 2, *v.*, *n.* (Getting onto one's feet.) The upturned index and middle fingers of the right hand, representing the legs, are swung up and over in an arc, coming to rest in the upturned left palm. *Cf.* ARISE 2, GET UP, RAISE 1, RISE 1, STAND UP.

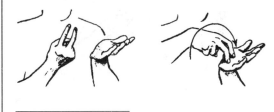

STANDARD (stan' dərd), *adj.*, *n.* (The same all around.) Both downturned "Y" hands execute counterclockwise circles. *Cf.* COMMON.

STANDING (stăn' dĭng), *n.* See STAND 1.

STAND UP *v. phrase.* See STAND 2.

STAPLER (stă′ plər), *n.* (The natural sign.) The signer mimes hitting a stapler with the downturned hand.

START (stärt), *v.*, STARTED, STARTING. (Turning a key to open up a new venture.) The right index finger, resting between the left index and middle fingers, executes a half turn, once or twice. *Cf.* BEGIN, COMMENCE, ORIGIN.

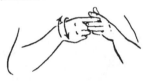

STARVATION (stär vā′ shən), *n.* (The upper alimentary tract is outlined.) The right "C" hand, palm facing the body, is placed with fingertips touching mid-chest. In this position it moves down a bit. *Cf.* APPETITE, CRAVE, DESIRE 2, STARVE, STARVED, WISH 2.

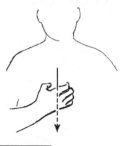

STARVE (stärv), *v.*, STARVED, STARVING. See STARVATION.

STARVED *v.* See STARVATION.

STATE 1 (stāt), *v.*, STATED, STATING. (Words tumbling from the mouth.) The right index finger, pointing left, describes a continuous small circle in front of the mouth. *Cf.* DISCOURSE, HEARING, MAINTAIN 2, MENTION, REMARK, SAID, SAY, SPEAK, SPEECH 1, TALK 1, TELL, VERBAL.

STATE 2, *n.* (The letter "S"; a collection of laws.) The right "S" hand moves down the open left palm, from fingertips to base.

STATEMENT (stāt′ mənt), *n.* The sign for STATE is made. This is followed by the sign for -MENT: the downturned right "M" hand moves down along the left palm, which is facing away from the body.

STATISTICS (stə tis′ tiks), *n.* (The letter "S"; the multiplication symbol.) Both "S" hands repeatedly cross each other as in the "X" symbol for multiplication.

STATUE (stăch' ōō), *n.* (Contours are indicated or outlined.) Both "A" hands, held about a foot apart before the face, with palms facing each other, move down simultaneously in a wavy, undulating motion. *Cf.* FIGURE 2, FORM 1, IMAGE, SCULPT, SCULPTURE, SHAPE.

STAY 1 (stā), *n., v.,* STAYED, STAYING. (Steady, uninterrupted movement.) The "A" hands are held with palms out, thumbs extended and touching, the right behind the left. In this position the hands move forward in a straight, steady line. *Cf.* CONTINUE, ENDURE 2, EVER 1, LAST 3, LASTING, PERMANENT, PERPETUAL, PERSEVERE 3, PERSIST 2, REMAIN, STAY STILL.

STAY 2, *n., v.,* STAYED, STAYING. (Duration of movement from past to present.) The right "Y" hand is held palm down in front of the right shoulder and is then moved slowly down and forward in a smooth curve. *Cf.* STILL 1, YET.

STAY 3, *v.* (Remaining in place.) One "Y" hand, held palm down, drops down a few inches.

STAY STILL *v. phrase.* See STAY 1.

STEAL 1 (stēl), *n., v.,* STOLE, STOLEN, STEALING. (The hand, partly concealed, takes something surreptitiously.) The index and middle fingers of the right hand, somewhat curved, are placed under the left elbow. As they move slowly along the left forearm toward the left wrist, they close a bit. *Cf.* ROB 1, ROBBERY 1, THEFT 1, THIEF 1, THIEVERY.

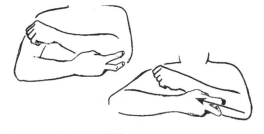

STEAL 2, *(colloq.), v.* (A sly, underhanded movement). The right open hand, palm down, is held under the left elbow. Beginning with the little finger, the hand closes finger by finger into the "A" position, as if wrapping itself around something, and moves to the right. *Cf.* ROB 2, ROBBERY 1, THEFT 2.

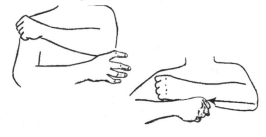

STEAM (stēm), *n.* (Boiling and circling up.) The downturned right "S" hand is held above the wriggling fingertips of the left. The right "S" hand then moves up in a wavy motion. The wavy movement may be substituted for a spiral movement up.

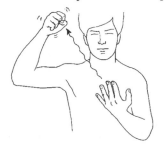

STEP (stĕp), *n.*, *v.*, STEPPED, STEPPING. (The movement of the feet.) The downturned "5" hands move alternately toward and away from the chest. *Cf.* WALK.

STEPBROTHER (stĕp′ bruŧh′ ər), *n.* (Second brother.) The sign for SECOND is made: the right "L" hand, palm facing left and index straight up, moves forward so that the index now faces forward. This is followed by BROTHER: the thumb of the right "L" hand is placed at the right temple. The hand moves down to rest on top of the downturned left hand. The order of the two signs may be reversed.

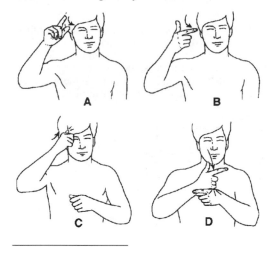

STEPCHILDREN (stĕp′ chil′ drən), *n.* (Second children.) The sign for SECOND is made, as above. This is followed by the downturned right "5" hand, or both "5" hands, miming the patting of children's heads.

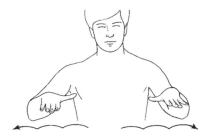

STEPDAUGHTER (stĕp′ dô′ tər), *n.* (Second daughter.) The sign for SECOND is made, as in STEPBROTHER. This is followed by DAUGHTER: the thumb of the right "A" hand moves down the right jawline, and then the upturned right arm is brought down to rest on top of the upturned left arm. The order of the signs may be reversed.

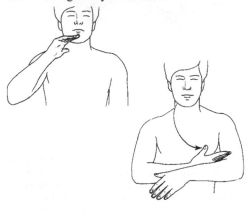

STEPFATHER (stĕp′ fä′ ŧhər), *n.* (Second father.) The sign for SECOND is made as in STEPBROTHER. This is followed by FATHER: the thumb of the right "5" hand is placed on the right temple. The FATHER sign may be made first, followed by SECOND.

STEPMOTHER (stĕp′ muŧh′ ər), *n.* (Second mother.) The sign for SECOND is made as in STEPBROTHER. This is followed by MOTHER: the thumb of the right "5" hand is placed on the right jawline. The MOTHER sign may be made first, followed by SECOND.

STEPS 1 (stĕps), *n.* (The natural sign.) The down-turned open hands, fingers pointing forward, move in alternate upward "steps" before the body. *Cf.* STAIR(S).

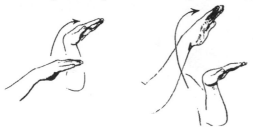

STEPS 2, *n.* (One hand moves forward after the other.) Both downturned "B" hands move forward, one after the other.

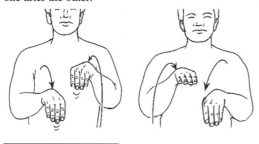

STEPSISTER (stĕp′ sis′ tər), *n.* (Second sister.) The sign for SECOND is made as in STEPBROTHER. This is followed by SISTER: the thumb of the right "L" hand is placed on the right jawline. The hand moves down to rest on top of the downturned left hand. The order of the two signs may be reversed.

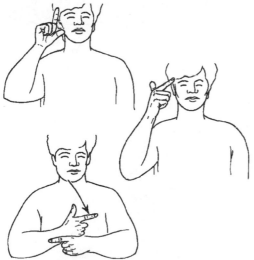

STEPSON (stĕp′ sun′), *n.* (Second son.) The sign for SECOND is made, as in STEPBROTHER. This is followed by SON: the right hand grasps an imaginary cap brim, and then the upturned right arm is brought down to rest on top of the upturned left arm. The order of the signs may be reversed.

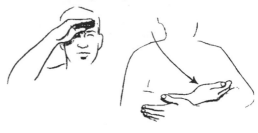

STEREO (ster′ ē ō), *n.* (Sound waves.) One or both fists may be placed against their respective ears. The hand or hands then open and spread out in a wavy or wriggling movement.

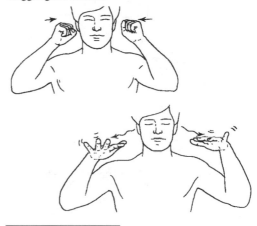

STETHOSCOPE (steth′ ə skōp), *n.* (Miming.) The earpieces are placed in the ears, and then the other end of the instrument touches different spots on the chest.

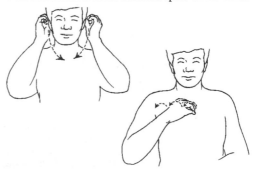

STILL 1 (stĭl), *adv., conj.* (Duration of movement from past to present.) The right "Y" hand is held palm down in front of the right shoulder and is then moved slowly down and forward in a smooth curve. *Cf.* STAY 2, YET.

STILL 2, *adj.* (The natural sign.) The index finger is brought up against the pursed lips. *Cf.* BE QUIET 1, QUIET 1, SILENCE 1, SILENT.

STING (sting), *n., v.* (The natural sign.) The thumb and index of the right "F" hand suddenly come down on the back of the downturned left hand.

STINGY 1 (stĭn' jĭ), *adj.* (Pulling things toward oneself.) Both prone open or "V" hands are held in front of the body with fingers bent. The hands are then drawn quickly and forcefully inward, as if raking

things toward oneself. *Cf.* GREEDY 1, SELFISH 1, TIGHTWAD 1.

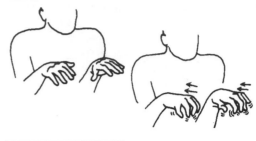

STINGY 2, *adj.* (Scratching the palm in greed.) The right fingers scratch the upturned left palm several times. A frowning expression is often used. *Cf.* GREEDY 2, SELFISH 2, TIGHTWAD 2.

STINGY 3, *adj.* (Scratching in greed.) The downturned "3" hands, held side by side, make a scratching motion as they move in toward the body. *Cf.* GREEDY 3, SELFISH 3.

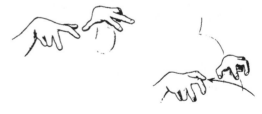

STIR (stûr), *v.* (Miming.) The downturned curved right index finger makes a series of rapid stirring clockwise movements above the "C"-shaped left hand.

STOCKING(S) (stŏk′ ĭng), *n.* (The knitting.) The index fingers, pointing forward, are rubbed back and forth against each other. *Cf.* KNIT, SOCK(S).

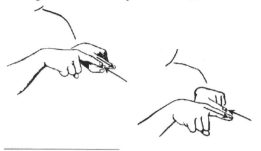

STOMACH (stum′ ək), *n.* (Indicating the stomach.) The signer pats the stomach.

STONE 1 (stōn), *n.* (The hardness is indicated by the striking of the fists.) The back of the right "S" hand is struck several times against the back of the left "S" hand. *Cf.* ROCK 1.

STONE 2, *n.* (A hard, unyielding substance.) The back of the right "S" hand strikes the bottom of the chin twice. *Cf.* ROCK 2.

STOP (stŏp), *v.*, STOPPED, STOPPING, *n.* (A stopping or cutting short.) The little finger edge of the right hand is thrust abruptly into the upturned left palm, indicating a cutting short. *Cf.* HALT.

STORE (stôr), *v.* (Holding back.) The right "V" fingers are tapped once or twice across the back of their left counterparts. Both palms face the chest. *Cf.* RESERVE 3, SAVE 2.

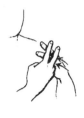

STORM (stôrm), *n.* (The blowing back and forth of the wind.) The "5" hands, palms facing and held up before the body, sway gracefully back and forth, in unison. The cheeks meanwhile are puffed up and the breath is being expelled. The nature of the swaying movement—graceful and slow, fast and violent, etc.—determines the type of wind. The strength of exhalation is also a qualifying device. *Cf.* BLOW 1, BREEZE, WIND.

STORY (stôr′ ĭ), *n.* (The unraveling or stretching out of words or sentences.) Both open hands are held close to each other, with fingers open and palms facing and almost touching. As the hands are drawn apart, the thumb and index finger of each hand come together to form circles. This is repeated several times. *Cf.* DESCRIBE 2, EXPLAIN 2, NARRATE, NARRATIVE, TALE, TELL ABOUT.

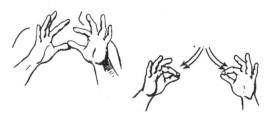

STOUT (stout), *adj.* (The swollen cheeks.) The cheeks are puffed out and the open "C" hands, positioned at either cheek, move away to their respective sides. *Cf.* FAT 1.

STOVE (stōv), *n.* (Cooking and the shape.) The sign for COOK is made: the open right hand rests on the upturned left palm. The right hand flips over and comes to rest with its back on the left palm, as if it has turned over a pancake. The shape of the stove is then indicated: both downturned hands move apart and then, with palms facing each other, downwards.

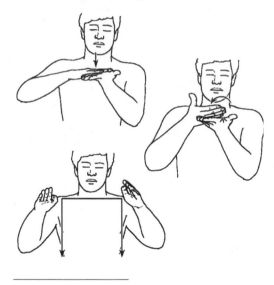

STRAIGHT 1 (strāt), *adj.* (The natural sign.) Both open hands are held with fingers pointing out from the body, the right above the left, the right palm facing left and left palm facing right. The right hand moves its little finger edge along the thumb edge of the left hand, in a straight line outward.

STRAIGHT 2, *adj., sl.* (Heterosexual.) The upright right arm, palm facing left, moves straight forward in an arc. *Cf.* HETEROSEXUAL.

STRANDED (străn' dəd), *adj.* (Impaled on a stick, as a snake's head.) The "V" fingers are thrust into the throat. *Cf.* CAUGHT IN THE ACT 2, STUCK 2, TRAP 1.

STRANGE (strānj), *adj.* (Something which distorts the vision.) The "C" hand describes a small arc in front of the face. *Cf.* CURIOUS 2, GROTESQUE, ODD, PECULIAR, QUEER, WEIRD.

STRAW (strô), *n.* (Miming.) The signer, lips pursed, sips through an imaginary drinking straw, held by one or both hands.

STRAY (strā), *v.*, STRAYED, STRAYING. (The natural motion.) The "G" hands are held side by side and touching, palms down, index fingers pointing forward. Then the right hand moves forward, curving toward the right side as it does. *Cf.* DEVIATE 2, GO OFF THE TRACK.

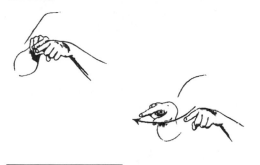

STREET (strēt), *n.* (The path.) Both hands, palms facing and fingers together and extended straight out, move in unison away from the body, in a straight or winding manner. *Cf.* CORRIDOR, HALL, HALLWAY, MANNER 2, METHOD, OPPORTUNITY 3, PATH, ROAD, TRAIL, WAY 1.

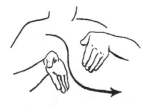

STRENGTH (strĕngkth, strĕngth), *n.* (Strength emanating from the body.) Both "5" hands are placed palms against the chest. They move out and away, forcefully, closing and assuming the "S" position. *Cf.* BRAVE, BRAVERY, COURAGE, COURAGEOUS, FORTITUDE, HALE, HEALTH, HEALTHY, MIGHTY 2, STRONG 2, WELL 2.

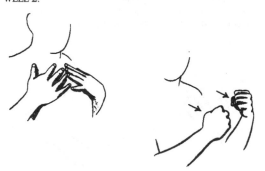

STRESS (strĕs), *n.*, *v.*, STRESSED, STRESSING. (Pressing down to emphasize.) The right thumb is pressed down deliberately against the upturned left palm. Both hands move forward a bit. *Cf.* EMPHASIS, EMPHASIZE, EMPHATIC.

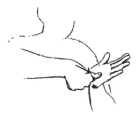

STRETCH (strĕch), *v.*, STRETCHED, STRETCHING. (Pulling apart.) Both "S" hands are pulled apart once or twice slowly, as if stretching something they are holding.

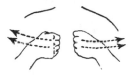

STRICT (strĭkt), *(colloq.)*, *adj.* The extended right index and middle fingers are bent and brought up sharply, so that the edge of the index finger strikes the bridge of the nose.

STRIKE 1 (strīk), *v.*, STRUCK, STRIKING. (The natural sign.) The right "S" hand strikes its knuckles forcefully against the open left palm, which is held facing right. *Cf.* HIT 1, POUND 2, PUNCH 1.

STRIKE 2, *n., v.* (Holding a picket's sign.) Both upright hands grasp the stick of an imaginary display sign. The hands move forward and back repeatedly against the chest. This movement represents the walking back and forth of a striker or picket.

STRIKE THAT *phrase, interj., colloq.* (Sealing the lips to indicate something that should not have been said.) The index finger is brought up sharply against the sealed lips. The head may be shaken slightly. This is known as "repairs" in ASL.

STRING (strĭng), *n., v.* STRUNG, STRINGING. (Unraveling a thin string, as indicated by the little fingers.) With palms facing the body, the tips of the extended little fingers touch. As they are drawn slowly apart, they describe very small spirals. *Cf.* SPAGHETTI, THREAD, TWINE.

STROKE 1 (strōk), *n.* (A blow or accident inside the head.) The right fingertips touch the forehead or the side of the head, and then the right hand forms a fist which strikes the left palm. This sign is used only for a cardiovascular accident.

STROKE 2, *v., n.* (Stroking a person or the head of a pet.) The right hand strokes the back of the left several times. *Cf.* PET, TAME.

STROLLER (strō' lər), *n.* (The back-and-forth movement.) The hands, grasping the handlebar of an imaginary stroller, move forward and back repeatedly.

STRONG 1 (strông, strŏng), *adj.* (Flexing the muscles.) With fists clenched, palms facing down or back, the signer raises both arms and shakes them once, with force. *Cf.* MIGHT 1, MIGHTY 1, POWER 1, POWERFUL 1, STURDY, TOUGH 1.

STRONG 2, *adj.* (Strength emanating from the body.) Both "5" hands are placed palms against the chest. They move out and away, forcefully, closing and assuming the "S" position. *Cf.* BRAVE, BRAVERY, COURAGE, COURAGEOUS, FORTITUDE, HALE, HEALTH, HEALTHY, MIGHTY 2, STRENGTH, WELL 2.

STRUCTURE (struk' chər), *n*. The "S" letters; building something up, by blocks or bricks.) Both downturned "S" hands mime placing bricks one atop the other. The hands meanwhile move up in stages. The walls, finally, are outlined.

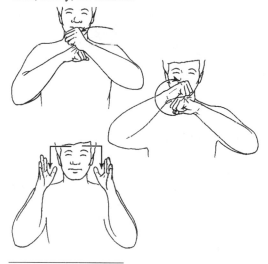

STRUGGLE (strug' əl), *n., v*. (Back and forth movement.) Both index fingers, pointing to each other, move back and forth simultaneously.

STUBBORN (stŭb' ərn), *adj*. (The donkey's broad ear; the animal is traditionally a stubborn one.) The open hand, or the "B" hand, is placed at the side of the head, with palm out and fingers pointing straight up. The hand moves forward and back, pivoting at the wrist, as in the case of a donkey's ears flapping. Both hands may also be used, at either side of the head. *Cf*. DONKEY, MULE, MULISH, OBSTINATE.

STUCK 1 (stŭk), *adj*. (Catching one by the throat.) The right hand makes a natural movement of grabbing the throat. *Cf*. CHOKE.

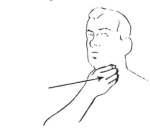

STUCK 2, *adj*. (Impaled on a stick, as a snake's head.) The "V" fingers are thrust into the throat. *Cf*. CAUGHT IN THE ACT 2, STRANDED, TRAP 1.

STUDENT 1 (stū' dənt, stōō'-), *n*. (One who learns.) The sign for LEARN is made: the downturned fingers of the right hand are placed on the upturned left palm. They close, and then the hand rises and the right fingertips are placed on the forehead. This is followed by the sign for INDIVIDUAL: both open hands, palms facing each other, move down the sides of the body, tracing its outline to the hips. *Cf*. PUPIL 1, SCHOLAR.

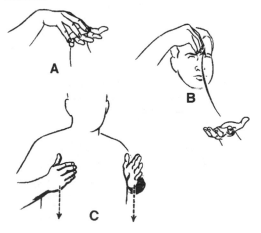

STUDENT 2, *n.* (One who studies.) The sign for STUDY is made. This is followed by the sign for INDIVIDUAL, as in STUDENT 1.

STUFFING (stuf' ing), *n.* The signer goes through the motions of pushing stuffing into the open cavity of a bird.

STUPID 1 (stū' pĭd, stōō'-), *adj.* (Knocking the head to indicate its empty state.) The "S" hand, palm facing the body, knocks against the forehead. *Cf.* DULL 1, DUMB 1, DUNCE.

STUPID 2, *(colloq.), adj.* (The thickness of the skull is indicated, to stress intellectual density.) With the thumb of the right "C" hand grasped by the closed left hand, the right hand is swung away from the body, describing a small arc as it moves. The space between the curved right fingers and the closed left hand indicates the thickness of the skull. *Cf.* DUMB 2, MORON, THICK-SKULLED, UNSKILLED.

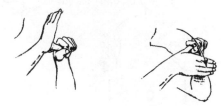

STURDY (stûr' dĭ), *adj.* (Flexing the muscles.) With fists clenched, palms facing down or back, the signer raises both arms and shakes them once, with force. *Cf.* MIGHT 1, MIGHTY 1, POWER 1, POWERFUL 1, STRONG 1, TOUGH 1.

SUBCONSCIOUS (sub kon' shəs), *n., adj.* (The "S" and "C" letters; the mind underneath.) The left hand is held palm facing down. The right "S" hand makes a single counterclockwise circle under the left. It then changes to a "C," and makes another similar circle.

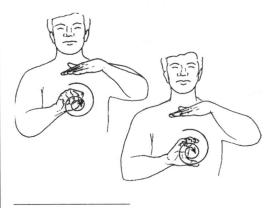

SUBDUE (səb dū', -dōō'), *v.,* -DUED, -DUING. (Forcing the head into a bowed position.) The right "S" hand, placed across the left "S" hand, moves over and down a bit. *Cf.* BEAT 2, CONQUER, DEFEAT, OVERCOME.

SUBJECT (sŭb' jĭkt), *n.* (The quotation marks are indicated.) The curved index and middle fingers of both hands, held palms out, move slightly to either side of the body, as if drawing quotation marks in the air. *Cf.* CAPTION 1, QUOTATION, QUOTE, SO-CALLED, THEME, TITLE, TOPIC.

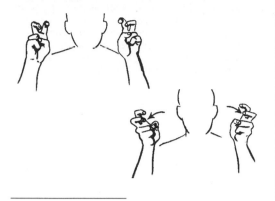

SUBMARINE (sub´ mə rēn´), *n.* (Cruising underwater.) The right "3" hand, palm facing left, moves forward under the shelter of the downturned left hand. The sign may be executed at eye level.

SUBMIT (səb mit´), *v.* (Throwing up the hands in a gesture of surrender.) The hands move palms up in an arc.

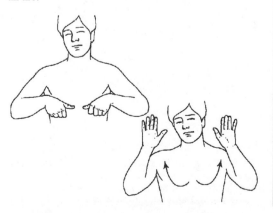

SUBSCRIBE (səb skrīb´), *v.,* -SCRIBED, -SCRIBING. (A regular taking in.) The outstretched open left hand, held palm facing right, moves in toward the body, assuming the "A" position, palm still facing right. This is repeated several times. *Cf.* DIVIDEND 1, INCOME, SUBSCRIPTION.

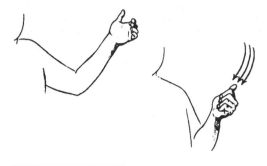

SUBSCRIPTION (səb skrĭp´ shən), *n.* See SUBSCRIBE.

SUBSEQUENT (sub´ sə kwənt), *adj.* (A moving on of the minute hand of the clock.) The right "L" hand, its thumb thrust into the palm of the left and acting as a pivot, moves forward a short distance. *Cf.* AFTER A WHILE, AFTERWARD, LATER 1, SUBSEQUENTLY.

SUBSEQUENTLY (sub´ sə kwənt ly), *adv.* See SUBSEQUENT.

SUBSTANCE 1 (sŭb´ stəns), *n.* (Something shown in the hand.) The outstretched right hand, palm up and held before the chest, is dropped slightly and brought over a bit to the right. *Cf.* OBJECT 1, THING.

SUBSTANCE 2, *n.* (Relative standing of one's thoughts.) A modified sign for THINK is made: the right index finger touches the middle of the forehead. The tips of the right "V" hand, palm down, are then thrust into the upturned left palm (as in STAND, *q.v.*). The right "V" hand is then re-thrust into the upturned left palm, with right palm now facing the body. *Cf.* IMPLY, INTEND, INTENT, INTENTION, MEAN 2, MEANING, MOTIVE 3, PURPOSE 1, SIGNIFICANCE 2, SIGNIFY 2.

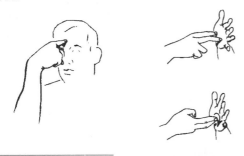

SUBSTANTIAL (səb stăn′ shəl), *adj.* (A full cup.) The left hand, in the "S" position, is held palm facing right. The right "5" hand, palm down, is brushed outward several times over the top of the left, indicating a wiping off of the top of a cup. *Cf.* ABUNDANCE, ABUNDANT, ADEQUATE, AMPLE, ENOUGH, PLENTY, SUFFICIENT.

SUBSTITUTE (sŭb′ stə tūt′), *n., v.,* -TUTED, -TUTING. (Exchanging places.) The right "A" hand, positioned above the left "A" hand, swings down and under the left, coming up a bit in front of it. *Cf.* EXCHANGE, INSTEAD OF 1, REPLACE, TRADE.

SUBTRACT (səb trăkt′), *v.,* -TRACTED, -TRACTING. (Removing.) The right "A" hand, resting in the palm of the left "5" hand, moves slightly up and away, describing a small arc. It is then cast downward, opening into the "5" position, palm down, as if removing something from the left hand and casting it down. *Cf.* ABOLISH, DEDUCT, DELETE 1, ELIMINATE, REMOVE, SUBTRACTION, TAKE AWAY FROM.

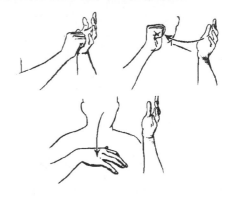

SUBTRACTION (səb trăk′ shən), *n.* See SUBTRACT.

SUBWAY (sub′ wā), *n.* (An underground train.) The sign for TRAIN 1 is made: the downturned right "H" hand slides back and forth on its left counterpart. The right index finger then moves forward under the cupped left hand. The TRAIN 1 sign is often omitted.

SUCCEED (sək sēd′), *v.,* -CEEDED, -CEEDING. (Penetrating the heights.) The "D" hands, palms back, are held at each side of the head, near the temples. With a pivoting motion of the wrists, the hands swing up and around, simultaneously, to a position

above the head, with palms facing out. *Cf.* ACCOM-
PLISH, ACHIEVE, PROSPER, SUCCESS, SUCCESSFUL, TRI-
UMPH 2.

SUCCESS (sək sĕs'), *n*. See SUCCEED.

SUCCESSFUL (sək sĕs' fəl), *adj*. See SUCCEED.

SUCH (sŭch), *adj*. (Matching fingers are brought
together.) The outstretched index fingers are brought
together, either once or several times. *Cf.* ALIKE,
IDENTICAL, LIKE 2, SAME 1, SIMILAR.

SUCKER (sŭk' ər), *(colloq.), n*. (Knocking someone.) The knuckles of the right "S" hand repeatedly
strike the fingertips of the left right-angle hand.

SUDDEN UNDERSTANDING *phrase*. (A sudden
awakening.) Both "S" hands are held in front of the
forehead, the left in front of the right. They suddenly
open into the "C" position, as the hands separate.

The eyes usually open wide at the same time.

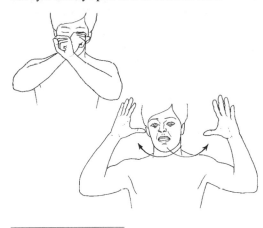

SUFFER 1 (sŭf' ər), *v., -*FERED, -FERING. (A clenching
of the fists; the rise and fall of pain.) Both "S" hands,
tightly clenched, revolve about each other, slowly
and deliberately, while a pained expression is worn.
Cf. ENDURE 1, TOLERATE 2.

SUFFER 2, *v*. (Patience, suffering.) The sign for
PATIENCE is made: the thumb of the right "A"
hand is drawn down across the lips. This is followed
by the sign for SUFFER 1.

SUFFICIENT (sə físh′ ənt), *adj.* (A full cup.) The left hand, in the "S" position, is held palm facing right. The right "5" hand, palm down, is brushed outward several times over the top of the left, indicating a wiping off of the top of a cup. *Cf.* ABUNDANCE, ABUNDANT, ADEQUATE, AMPLE, ENOUGH, PLENTY, SUBSTANTIAL.

SUGAR (shŏŏg′ ər), *n.* (Titillating to the taste.) The fingertips of the right "U" hand, palm facing the body, brush against the chin a number of times beginning at the lips. *Cf.* CANDY 1, CUTE 1, SWEET.

SUGGEST (səg jĕst′), *v.*, -GESTED, -GESTING. (An offering; a presenting.) Both hands, slightly cupped, palms up, are held close to the chest. They move up and out in unison, describing a very slight arc. *Cf.* MOTION, OFFER, OFFERING, PRESENT 1, PROPOSE.

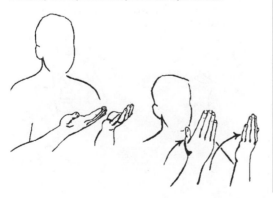

SUIT (sōōt), *n.* (Draping the clothes on the body.) With fingertips resting on the chest, both hands move down simultaneously. The action is repeated. *Cf.* CLOTHES, CLOTHING, DRESS, FROCK, GARMENT, GOWN, SHIRT, WEAR 1.

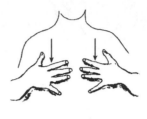

SUITABLE (sōō′ tə bəl), *adj.* The right index finger, held above the left index finger, comes down rather forcefully so that the bottom of the right hand comes to rest on top of the left thumb joint. *Cf.* ACCURATE, CORRECT 1, DECENT, EXACT 2, PROPER, RIGHT 3.

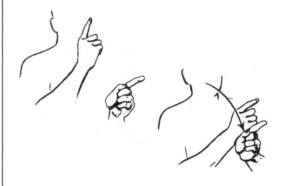

SUITCASE (sōōt′ kās′), *n.* (The natural sign.) The downturned right "S" hand grasps an imaginary piece of luggage and shakes it up and down slightly, as if testing its weight. *Cf.* BAGGAGE, LUGGAGE, VALISE.

SUM (sŭm), *n.*, *v.*, SUMMED, SUMMING. (To bring up all together.) The two open hands, palms and fingers facing each other, with the left hand above the right, are brought together, with all fingers closing simultaneously. This sign is used mainly in the sense of adding up figures or items. *Cf.* ADD 1, ADDITION, AMOUNT 1, SUMMARIZE 2, SUMMARY 2, SUM UP, TOTAL.

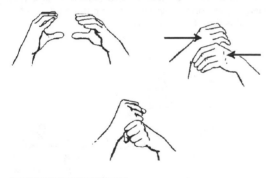

SUMMARIZE 1 (sŭm´ ə rīz´), *v.*, -RIZED, -RIZING. (To squeeze or condense into a small space.) The "C" hands face each other, with the right hand nearer to the body than the left. Both hands draw together and close deliberately, squeezing an imaginary object. *Cf.* ABBREVIATE, BRIEF 2, CONDENSE, MAKE BRIEF, SUMMARY 1.

SUMMARIZE 2, *v.* See SUM.

SUMMARY 1 (sŭm´ ə rĭ), *n.*, *adj.* See SUMMARIZE 1.

SUMMARY 2, *n.* See SUM.

SUMMER (sŭm´ ər), *n.* (Wiping the brow.) The downturned right index finger, slightly curved, is drawn across the forehead from left to right.

SUMMON (sŭm´ ən), *v.*, -MONED, -MONING. (To tap someone for attention.) The right hand is placed upon the back of the left, held palm down. The right hand then moves up and in toward the body, assuming the "A" position. As an optional addition, the right hand may then assume a beckoning movement. *Cf.* CALL 1.

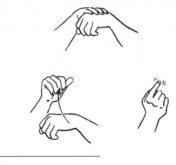

SUM UP *v. phrase.* See SUM.

SUN (sŭn), *n.*, *v.*, SUNNED, SUNNING. (The round shape and the rays.) The right index finger, pointing forward and held above the face, describes a small clockwise circle. The right hand, all fingers touching the thumb, then drops down and forward from its position above the head. As it does so, the fingers open to the "5" position. *Cf.* SUNSHINE.

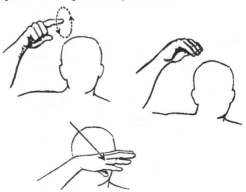

SUNDAE (sŭn' dā), *n.* (The whipped cream is spiraled on.) The right thumb is held pointing down over the left "S" hand, whose palm faces right. The thumb spirals up in a counterclockwise manner.

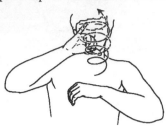

SUNDAY (sŭn' dā), *n.* (A day of quiet, of rest.) The "5" hands, held side by side and palms out before the body, move straight down a short distance. They may also move slightly outward as they move down.

SUNRISE (sŭn' rīz'), *n.* (The natural sign.) The downturned left arm, held horizontally, represents the horizon. The right thumb and index finger form a circle, and this circle is drawn up from a position in front of the downturned left hand.

SUNSET (sŭn' sĕt'), *n.* (The natural sign.) The movement described in SUNRISE is reversed, with the right hand moving down below the downturned left hand.

SUNSHINE (sŭn' shĭn'), *n.* See SUN.

SUPERFICIAL (sōō' pər fish' əl), *adj.* (On the surface.) The right fingertips describe a small circle as they rub against the top of the downturned left hand.

SUPERINTENDENT (sōō' pər ĭn tĕn' dənt, sōō' prĭn-), *n.* The "C" hands, held palms out at either temple, are drawn out and up from the head into the "S" position. *Cf.* PRESIDENT.

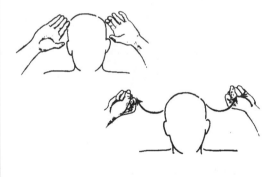

SUPERIOR 1 (sə pĭr' ĭ ər, sōō-), *adj.* (Indicating height.) The right "A" hand, held with thumb pointing upward, moves straight up above the right shoulder. *Cf.* HIGH 2.

SUPERIOR 2, *adj.* (The letter "S"; hovering above others.) The right "S" hand makes a counterclockwise circle as it hovers over the downturned left hand.

SUPERVISE (sōō′ pər vīz′), *v.,* -VISED, -VISING. (The eyes sweep back and forth.) The "V" hands, held crossed, describe a counterclockwise circle before the chest.

SUPPER (sŭp′ ər), *n.* (An evening or night meal.) The sign for NIGHT is made: the left hand, palm down, is positioned at chest height. The downturned right hand, held an inch or so above the left, moves over the left hand in an arc, the sun setting beneath the horizon. This is followed by the sign for EAT: the closed right hand goes through the natural motion of placing food in the mouth. This latter movement is repeated. The NIGHT and EAT signs may be reversed.

SUPPLICATION (sŭp′ lə kā′ shən), *n.* (An act of supplication.) With the right hand clasped over the left, both hands are shaken gently before the body. The eyes often are directed upward. *Cf.* BEG 2, ENTREAT, IMPLORE, PLEA, PLEAD.

SUPPORT 1 (sə pōrt′), *n., v.* -PORTED, -PORTING. (Holding up.) The right "S" hand pushes up the left "S" hand. *Cf.* ENDORSE 1, MAINTENANCE, SUSTAIN, SUSTENANCE, UPHOLD.

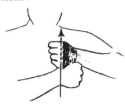

SUPPORT 2, *n., v.* (One hand upholds the other.) Both hands, in the "S" position, are held palms facing the body, the right under the left. The right hand pushes up the left in a gesture of support. *Cf.* ADVOCATE, ENDORSE 2.

SUPPOSE 1 (sə pōz′), *v.,* -POSED -POSING. (Weighing one thing against another.) The upturned open hands move alternately up and down. *Cf.* GUESS 3, MAY 1, MAYBE, MIGHT 2, PERHAPS, POSSIBILITY, POSSIBLY, PROBABLE, PROBABLY.

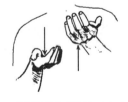

SUPPOSE 2, *v.,* (To have an idea.) The little fingertip of the right "I" hand taps the right temple once or twice.

SUPPRESS FEELINGS *v. phrase.* (Keeping the feelings down.) The curved fingertips of both hands are placed against the chest. The hands slowly move down as the fingers close into the "S" position. One hand only may also be used. *Cf.* CONTROL 2.

SURE (shoor), *adj., adv.* (Coming forth directly from the lips; true.) The index finger of the right "D" hand, palm facing left, is placed against the lips. It moves up an inch or two and then describes a small arc forward and away from the lips. *Cf.* ABSOLUTE, ABSOLUTELY, ACTUAL, ACTUALLY, AUTHENTIC, CERTAIN, CERTAINLY, FIDELITY, FRANKLY, GENUINE, INDEED, POSITIVE 1, POSITIVELY, REAL, REALLY, SINCERE 2, SURELY, TRUE, TRULY, TRUTH, VALID, VERILY.

SURELY (shoor' li), *adv.* See SURE.

SURFING (sûrf' ing), *n.* (The position and motion.) Both hands face down. The right index and middle finger stand on their left counterparts.

SURGERY (sûr' jə ri), *n.* (The action of the scalpel.) The thumb of the right "A" hand is drawn straight down across the upright left palm. *Cf.* OPERATION 1.

SURPRISE 1 (sər prīz'), *v.,* -PRISED, -PRISING, *n.* (The eyes pop open in amazement.) Both hands are held in modified "O" positions with thumb and index fingers of each hand near the eyes. These fingers suddenly flick open, and the eyes simultaneously pop open wide. *Cf.* AMAZE, AMAZEMENT, ASTONISH, ASTONISHED, ASTONISHMENT, ASTOUND.

SURPRISE 2, *(colloq.), adj.* (The mouth drops open.) The fingertips of both "V" hands are held curved and touching before the body, one hand above the other. Then the hands are suddenly drawn apart, and at the same instant the mouth drops open and the eyes open wide. *Cf.* DUMBFOUNDED 2, OPEN-MOUTHED, SPEECHLESS.

SURPRISED *(colloq.), adj.* (The eyes pop open.) The "S" hands, palms facing each other, are held before the eyes. They suddenly open into the "C" position, with the eyes wide open. *Cf.* OPEN-EYED, SHOCKED 2.

SURRENDER (sə rĕn′ dər), *v.*, -DERED, -DERING. (Throwing up the hands in a gesture of surrender.) Both "A" hands are held palms down before the chest and then thrown up in unison, ending in the "5" position. *Cf.* DISCOURAGE, FORFEIT, GIVE UP, RELIN-QUISH, RENOUNCE, RENUNCIATION, YIELD.

SUSPECT (sə spĕkt′), *v.*, -PECTED, -PECTING. (Digging into the mind.) The right index finger scratches at the right temple several times. *Cf.* SUSPICION 1.

SUSPEND (sə spĕnd′), *v.*, -PENDED, -PENDING. (The natural sign.) The curved right index finger "hangs" on the extended left index finger. *Cf.* HANG 1.

SUSPICION 1 (sə spĭsh′ ən). *n.* See SUSPECT.

SUSPICION 2, *n.* (Warding off.) The right "S" hand is held before the right shoulder, elbow bent out to the side. The hand is then thrown forward several times, as if striking at someone. *Cf.* SKEPTICAL 2.

SUSTAIN (sə stān′), *v.*, -TAINED, -TAINING. (Holding up.) The right "S" hand pushes up the left "S" hand. *Cf.* ENDORSE 1, MAINTENANCE, SUPPORT 1, SUSTE-NANCE, UPHOLD.

SUSTENANCE (sŭs′ tə nəns), *n.* See SUSTAIN.

SWEAR 1 (swâr), *v.* SWORE, SWORN, SWEARING. (The arm is raised.) The right index finger is placed at the lips. The right arm is then raised, palm out and elbow resting on the back of the left hand. *Cf.* GUARANTEE, LOYAL, OATH, PLEDGE, PROMISE 1, SWORN, TAKE OATH, VOW.

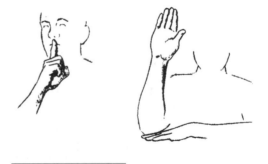

SWEAR 2, *v.* (Harsh words and a threatening hand.) The right hand appears to claw words out of the mouth. It ends in the "S" position, above the head, shaking back and forth in a threatening manner. *Cf.* CURSE 1.

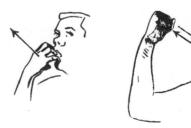

SWEAR 3, *(sl.)*, *v.* (Curlicues, as one finds in cartoon-type swear words.) The right "Y" hand, palm down, pivots at the wrist along the left "G" hand, from the wrist to the tip of the finger. *Cf.* CURSE 3.

SWEAT 1 (swĕt), *n.*, *v.*, SWEAT or SWEATED, SWEATING. (Wiping the brow.) The bent right index finger is drawn across the forehead from left to right and then shaken to the side, as if getting rid of the sweat. *Cf.* PERSPIRATION 1, PERSPIRE 1.

SWEAT 2, *n.*, *v.* (Perspiration dripping from the brow.) The index finger edge of the open right hand wipes across the brow, and the same open hand then continues forcefully downward off the brow, its fingers wiggling, as if shaking off the perspiration gathered. *Cf.* PERSPIRATION 2, PERSPIRE 2.

SWEDEN (swēd' n) *n.* (A "hairy Swede," perhaps borrowed from the image of the early Swedish explorers.) Finger the hair on back of the hand. This is a native sign.

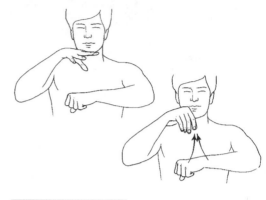

SWEEP 1 (swēp), *v.*, SWEPT, SWEEPING, *n.* (The natural sign.) The hands grasp and manipulate an imaginary broom. *Cf.* BROOM.

SWEEP 2, *v.* (Collecting dust.) The upturned left hand represents the dustpan. The little finger edge of the right hand moves over the left hand repeatedly, sweeping against the fingers from the fingertips to the palm.

SWEET (swēt), *adj.*, *n.* (Titillating to the taste.) The fingertips of the right "U" hand, palm facing the body, brush against the chin a number of times beginning at the lips. *Cf.* CANDY 1, CUTE 1, SUGAR.

SWEETHEART 1 (swĕt' härt´), *(colloq.), n.* (Heads nodding toward each other.) The "A" hands are placed together before the body with thumbs up. The thumbs wiggle up and down. *Cf.* BEAU, LOVER, MAKE LOVE 1.

SWEETHEART 2, *(colloq.), n.* (Locked together.) With little fingers interlocked and palms facing the body, the thumbs of both hands wiggle back and forth.

SWELL 1 (swĕl), *adj.* (The hands gesture toward the heavens.) The "5" hands, palms out and arms raised rather high, are positioned somewhat above the line of vision. The arms move abruptly forward and up once or twice. An expression of pleasure or surprise is usually assumed. *Cf.* EXCELLENT, GRAND 1, GREAT 3, MARVELOUS, SPLENDID 1, WONDER 2, WONDERFUL 1.

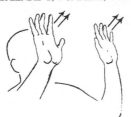

SWELL 2, *adj., interj.* (The feelings are titillated.) With the thumb resting on the upper part of the chest, the fingers are wiggled back and forth. *Cf.* ELEGANT, FINE 1, GRAND 2, GREAT 4, SPLENDID 2, WONDERFUL 2.

SWELL-HEADED *(colloq.), adj.* (The natural sign.) Both downturned "L" hands are positioned with index fingers at the temples. They move away from the head rather slowly, indicating the size or growth of the head. The head is often moved slightly back and forth as the hands move away. An expression of superiority is assumed. *Cf.* BIG-HEADED, BIG SHOT, CONCEITED.

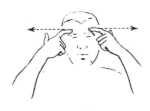

SWIFT (swĭft), *adj.* (A quick movement.) The thumbtip of the upright right hand is flicked quickly off the tip of the curved right index finger, as if shooting marbles. *Cf.* FAST, IMMEDIATELY, QUICK, QUICKNESS, SPEED, SPEEDY.

SWIMSUIT (swim′ soot′), *n.* (Swim clothes.) The motions of swimming (usually the breast stroke) are made, followed by CLOTHES: both downturned "5"hands are posed with thumbs touching the chest. Both hands sweep down the chest repeatedly.

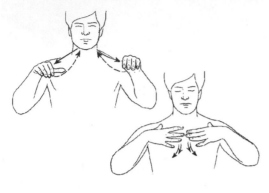

SWORN (sworn), *adj.* (The arm is raised.) The right index finger is placed at the lips. The right arm is then raised, palm out and elbow resting on the back of the left hand. *Cf.* GUARANTEE, LOYAL, OATH, PLEDGE, PROMISE 1, SWEAR 1, TAKE OATH, VOW.

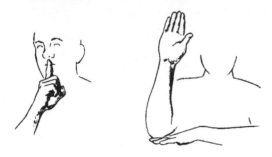

SYMBOL (sim′ bəl), *n.* (The letter "S"; showing something.) The right "S" is placed in the outstretched left palm. Both hands move forward simultaneously.

SYMPATHETIC (sĭm′ pə thĕt′ ĭk), *adj.* (Feeling with.) The tip of the right middle finger, touching the heart, moves up an inch or two on the chest. The sign for WITH is then made: both "A" hands come together, so that the thumbs are side by side. *Cf.* SYMPATHY 1.

SYMPATHY 1 (sĭm′ pə thĭ), *n.* See SYMPATHETIC.

SYMPATHY 2, *n.* (Feelings from the heart, conferred on others.) The middle fingertip of the open right hand touches the chest over the heart. The same open hand then moves in a small, clockwise circle before the right shoulder, with palm facing forward and fingers pointing up. *Cf.* MERCY 2, PITY.

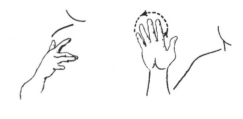

SYPHILIS (sif′ ə lis), *n.* (A fingerspelled loan sign.) The signer fingerspells "V-D," for "venereal disease."

SYRUP (sir′ əp), *n.* (Wiping the mouth and pouring.) The upturned right index sweeps across the mouth, from right to left. The hand then forms the "A" shape, and pivots over so that the thumb represents a left arm.

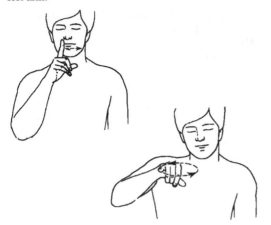

SYSTEM (sis′ təm), *n.* (An arrangement.) Both "S" hands, palms facing out, are positioned side by side. They separate, move down, and separate yet more, tracing a zigzag pattern.

T

TABLE 1 (tā′ bəl), *n.* (The shape and the legs.) The downturned open hands are held together before the chest, fingers pointing forward. From this position the hands separate and move in a straight line to either side, indicating the table top. Then the downturned index fingers are thrust downward simultaneously, moved in toward the body, and again thrust downward. These motions indicate the legs.

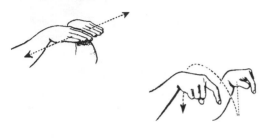

TABLE 2, *v.* (Shelving a motion or proposal.) The right "V" hand is brought down over the upturned left index finger.

TABLECLOTH (tā′ bəl klôth′), *n.* (Laying the cloth on the table.) The closed hands go through the natural motions of flinging the cloth in the air and guiding its descent on the table. This sign may be preceded by the sign for WHITE, *q.v.*

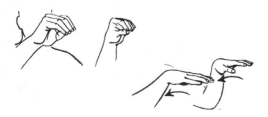

TACKLE (tăk′ əl), *(sports), n.* (The natural motion.) The right open hand closes forcefully over the extended index and middle fingers of the downturned left hand.

TAIL 1 (tāl), *n.* (The shape.) The extended right thumb and index finger come together, and the hand moves away from the body in a downward arc, outlining an imaginary tail.

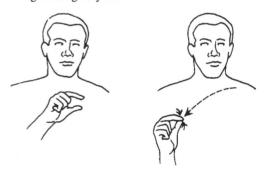

TAIL 2, *n.* (The wagging.) The downturned left arm represents the dog's body. The right "D" hand's base rests against the left fingertips and the right index wags back and forth repeatedly.

TAKE (tāk), *v.* TOOK, TAKEN, TAKING, *n.* (Taking unto oneself.) The right hand, palm out, is extended before the chest, index finger and thumb in an open position, the other fingers separated and pointing up. The hand is drawn in toward the chest, and the index and thumb close at the same time, indicating something taken to oneself. *Cf.* APPOINT, CHOOSE, SELECT 2.

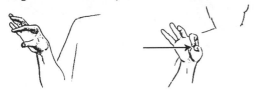

TAKE ADVANTAGE OF *phrase.* (A magician's trick of flipping a coin into the sleeve, and thus cheating someone.) The middle finger of the right downturned hand rests on the upturned left palm. The finger makes a swift backward movement, closing against the right palm. *Cf.* RIP OFF.

TAKE AWAY FROM *v. phrase.* (Removing.) The right "A" hand, resting in the palm of the left "5" hand, moves slightly up and away, describing a small arc. It is then cast downward, opening into the "5" position, palm down, as if removing something from the left hand and casting it down. *Cf.* ABOLISH, DEDUCT, DELETE, ELIMINATE, REMOVE, SUBTRACT, SUBTRACTION.

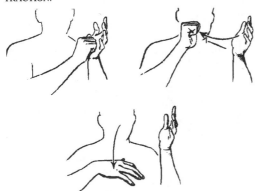

TAKE CARE OF 1, *v. phrase.* (The "K" for *keep* in the sense of *keeping carefully*.) Both "K" hands are crossed, the right atop the left. The right hand moves up and down a very short distance, several times, each time coming to rest on top of the left. *Cf.* BE CAREFUL, CAREFUL 3.

TAKE CARE OF 2, *v. phrase.* (Slow, careful movement.) The "K" hands are crossed, the right above the left, little finger edges down. In this position the hands are moved up and down a short distance. *Cf.* CARE 2, CAREFUL 2, KEEP, MAINTAIN 1, MIND 3, PRESERVE, RESERVE 2.

TAKE CARE OF 3, *v. phrase.* (Slow, careful movement.) The "K" hands are crossed, the right above the left, little finger edges down. In this position they describe a small clockwise circle in front of the chest. *Cf.* CARE 1, CARE FOR, CAREFUL 1.

TAKE OATH (ōth), *v. phrase.* (The arm is raised.) The right index finger is placed at the lips. The right arm is then raised, palm out and elbow resting on the back of the left hand. *Cf.* GUARANTEE, LOYAL, OATH, PLEDGE, PROMISE 1, SWEAR 1, SWORN, VOW.

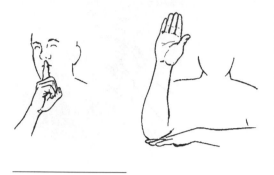

TAKE TURNS *phrase.* (First one then the other.) The thumb of the right "L" hand is pointed to the chest. The hand swings around so that the thumb now points out.

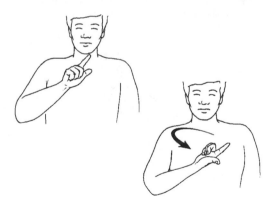

TAKE UP *v. phrase.* (Responsibility.) Both hands, held palms down in the "5" position, are at chest level. With a grasping upward movement, both close into "S" positions before the face. *Cf.* ASSUME, PICK UP 1.

TALE (tāl), *n.* (The unraveling or stretching out of words or sentences.) Both open hands are held close to each other, with fingers open and palms facing and almost touching. As the hands are drawn apart, the thumb and index finger of each hand come together to form circles. This is repeated several times. *Cf.* DESCRIBE 2, EXPLAIN 2, NARRATE, NARRATIVE, STORY.

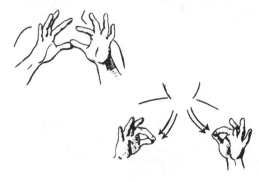

TALK 1 (tôk), *v.,* TALKED, TALKING. (Words tumbling from the mouth.) The right index finger, pointing left, describes a continuous small circle in front of the mouth. *Cf.* DISCOURSE, HEARING, MAINTAIN 2, MENTION, REMARK, SAID, SAY, SPEAK, SPEECH 1, STATE 1, TELL, VERBAL.

TALK 2, *n., v.* (A gesture of an orator.) The right open hand, palm facing left, is held above and to the right of the head. It pivots on the wrist, forward and backward, several times. *Cf.* LECTURE, ORATE, SPEECH 2, TESTIMONY 1.

TALK 3, *n., v.* (Movement forward from, and back to, the mouth.) The tips of both index fingers, held pointing up, move alternately forward from, and back to, the lips. *Cf.* CONVERSATION 1, CONVERSE.

TALL 1 (tôl), *adj.* (The height is indicated.) The index finger of the right "D" hand moves straight up against the palm of the left "5" hand. *Cf.* HEIGHT 1.

TALL 2, *adj.* (The height is indicated.) The right right-angle hand, palm facing the left, is held at the height the signer wishes to indicate. *Cf.* BIG 2, HEIGHT 2, HIGH 3.

TALL 3, *(loc.), adj.* (The stooped position.) The curved index finger of the right "D" hand, held up before the body, moves forward, away from the body, in a series of small bobbing motions. The head may be stooped and may also bob slightly in cadence with the hand.

TAME (tām), *adj., v.,* TAMED, TAMING. (Stroking the head of a pet.) The right hand strokes the back of the left several times. *Cf.* PET, STROKE 2.

TAPE RECORDER *n.* (The movement of the spools.) Both hands are held downturned, with middle fingers hanging down. Both hands move in unison, in a clockwise direction.

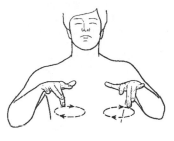

TARDY (tär' dǐ), *adj.* (Hanging back.) The "5" hand and forearm, hanging loosely and straight down from the elbow, move back and forth under the armpit. *Cf.* LATE, NOT DONE, NOT YET.

TASK (tăsk), *n.* (Striking an anvil.) Both "S" hands are held palms down. The right hand strikes against the back of the left a number of times. *Cf.* JOB, LABOR, OCCUPATION, TOIL, TRAVAIL, VOCATION, WORK.

TATTLE 1 (tăt′ əl), v., -TLED, -TLING. (Words moving outward from the mouth.) The right hand is held with index and middle fingertips touching the thumbtip, and with its thumb edge at the mouth. The hand then moves outward from the mouth, with its extended thumb and first two fingers alternately opening and closing. Cf. TATTLETALE 1, TELLTALE 1.

TATTLE 2, v. (Words shooting out from the mouth.) The right "S" hand is held palm out before the mouth, with the knuckle of the index finger touching the lips. From this position the hand moves forward, away from the mouth. At the same time the index finger straightens and points forward. Cf. TATTLE-TALE 2, TELLTALE 2.

TATTLETALE 1 (tăt′ əl tāl′), n. See TATTLE 1.

TATTLETALE 2, n. See TATTLE 2.

TAX 1 (tăks), n., v., TAXED, TAXING. (Nicking into one.) The knuckle of the right "X" finger is nicked against the palm of the left hand, held in the "5" position, palm facing right. Cf. CHARGE, COST, EXPENSE, FEE, FINE 2, PENALTY, PRICE 2, TAXATION 1, TOLL.

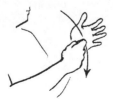

TAX 2, n., v. (Making a nick, as in "nicking the pocketbook.") The tip of the right index finger, moving downward in an arc, makes a nick in the open left palm, which is facing right. Cf. TAXA-TION 2.

TAXATION 1 (tăks ā′ shən), n. See TAX 1.

TAXATION 2, n. See TAX 2.

TEA 1 (tē), n. (Dipping the teabag.) The right index finger and thumb raise and lower an imaginary teabag into a "cup" formed by the left "C" or "O" hand, held thumb side up.

TEA 2, n. (Stirring the teabag.) The hand positions in TEA 1 are assumed, but the right hand executes a circular, stirring motion instead.

TEACH (tēch), *v.*, TAUGHT, TEACHING. (Giving forth from the mind.) The fingertips of each hand are placed on the temples. They then swing out and open into the "5" position. *Cf.* EDUCATE, INDOCTRINATE, INDOCTRINATION, INSTRUCT, INSTRUCTION.

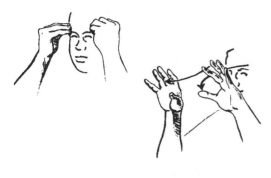

TEACHER (tē' chər), *n.* The sign for TEACH is made. This is followed by the sign for INDIVID-UAL: both open hands, palms facing each other, move down the sides of the body, tracing its outline to the hips. *Cf.* INSTRUCTOR.

TEAR 1 (târ), *n., v.*, TORE, TORN, TEARING. (The natural motion.) Both "A" hands, held palms down before the body, grasp an imaginary object; then they move forcefully apart, as if tearing the object.

TEAR 2 (tĭr), *n.* (Tears streaming down cheeks.) Both index fingers, in the "D" position, move down the cheeks, either once or several times. Sometimes one finger only is used. *Cf.* BAWL 1, CRY, TEARDROP, WEEP.

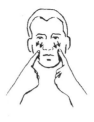

TEARDROP (tĭr' drŏp´), *n.* See TEAR 2.

TEASE 1 (tēz), *n., v.*, TEASED, TEASING. (Striking sparks off one.) The knuckles of the right "A" hand move sharply forward along the thumb edge of the left "A" hand. *Cf.* TORMENT.

TEASE 2, *n., v.* The movements in TEASE 1 are duplicated, except that the "X" hands are used.

TEASE 3, *n., v.* The movements in TEASE 1 are duplicated, except that the "G" hands are used. *Cf.* CRUEL 2.

TECHNICAL (tek′ ni kəl), *adj.* (Forming a T-shape with both hands.) The left open hand faces the chest. The middle finger of the right "5" hand, palm facing the signer, is placed at the little finger edge of the left.

TECHNICAL REHEARSAL (tek′ ni kəl ri hûr′ səl), *n.* (Tightening a screw in the head.) The right index and middle fingers, held straight together, turn repeatedly in a clockwise manner on the right temple. This sign is reserved for stagecraft; it refers to taking care of the technical details of a stage production.

TEDDY BEAR (ted′ ē bâr), *n.* (The sign for BEAR; hugging.) Both crossed hands make a series of scratching movements against the shoulders. The signer then mimes a bear hug.

TEDIOUS (tē′ dǐ əs, tē′ jəs), *adj.* (The nose is pressed, as if to a grindstone wheel.) The right index finger touches the tip of the nose, as a bored expression is assumed. The right hand is sometimes pivoted

back and forth slightly, as the fingertip remains against the nose. *Cf.* BORING 1, MONOTONOUS.

TEEN (tēn), *n.* (The letter "T"; female and male.) The right "T" hand is placed first at the jaw and then at the temple.

TEETH (tēth), *n. pl.* (The natural sign.) The extended right index finger passes over the exposed teeth.

TEL AVIV (tel′ ä vĕv′), *n.* The right thumb and index finger, held at the right eye, open and close. A local sign.

TELEPHONE (tĕl′ ə fōn′), *n., v.,* -PHONED, -PHONING. (The natural sign.) The right "Y" hand is placed at the right side of the head with the thumb touching the ear and the little finger touching the lips. This is the more modern telephone receiver. *Cf.* PHONE.

TELESCOPE (tel′ ə skōp), *n.* (Miming.) The signer mimes opening a telescope and peering through the eyepiece.

TELETYPE (tel′ ə tīp), *n., v.* (Holding a phone and typing.) The right "Y" hand is placed at the side of the head, little finger touching the mouth and thumb touching the ear. The signer then mimes using a typewriter.

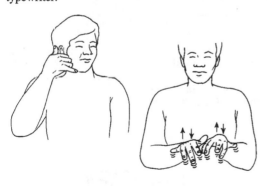

TELL (tĕl), *v.,* TOLD, TELLING. (Words tumbling from the mouth.) The right index finger, pointing left, describes a continuous small circle in front of the mouth. *Cf.* DISCOURSE, HEARING, MAINTAIN 2, MENTION, REMARK, SAID, SAY, SPEAK, SPEECH 1, STATE 1, TALK 1, VERBAL.

TELL ABOUT *v. phrase.* (The unraveling or stretching out of words or sentences.) Both open hands are held close to each other, with fingers open and palms facing and almost touching. As the hands are drawn apart, the thumb and index finger of each hand come together to form circles. This is repeated several times. *Cf.* DESCRIBE 2, EXPLAIN 2, NARRATE, NARRATIVE, STORY, TALE.

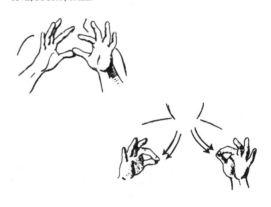

TELL ME *phrase.* (The natural sign.) The tip of the index finger of the right "D" hand, palm facing the body, is first placed at the lips and then moves down to touch the chest.

TELLTALE 1 (tĕl′ tāl′), *n.* (Words moving outward from the mouth.) The right hand is held with index and middle fingertips touching the thumbtip, and with its thumb edge at the mouth. The hand then moves outward from the mouth, with its extended thumb and first two fingers alternately opening and closing. *Cf.* TATTLE 1, TATTLETALE 1.

TELLTALE 2, *n.* (Words shooting out from the mouth.) The right "S" hand is held palm out before the mouth, with the knuckle of the index finger touching the lips. From this position the hand moves forward, away from the mouth. At the same time the index finger straightens and points forward. *Cf.* TATTLE 2, TATTLETALE 2.

TEMPERATE (tĕm′ pər ĭt), *adj.* (In between.) The little finger edge of the right "5" hand is placed between the thumb and index finger of the left "C" hand, whose palm faces the body. The right hand moves back and forth.

TEMPERATURE 1 (tĕm′ pər ə chər, -prə chər), *n.* (The rise and fall of the mercury in the thermometer.) The index finger of the right "D" hand, pointing left, moves slowly up and down the index finger of

the left "D" hand, which is held pointing up. *Cf.* FEVER, THERMOMETER.

TEMPERATURE 2, *n.* (A unit of temperature.) The tip of the index finger of the right "D" hand travels up and down the upturned left index finger. *Cf.* DEGREE 1.

TEMPLE (tĕm′ pəl), *n.* (The letter "T"; an establishment, *i.e.*, something placed upon a foundation.) The base of the right "T" hand comes down against the back of the downturned left "S" hand. The action is repeated.

TEMPT (tĕmpt), *v.*, TEMPTED, TEMPTING. (Tapping one surreptitiously at a concealed place.) With the left arm held palm down before the chest, the curved right index finger taps the left elbow a number of times. *Cf.* TEMPTATION.

TEMPTATION (tĕmp tā′ shən), *n.* See TEMPT.

TEND (tĕnd), *v.*, TENDED, TENDING. (The feelings of the heart move toward a specific object.) The tip of the right middle finger touches the heart. The open right hand, palm facing the body, then moves away from the heart toward the palm of the open left hand. *Cf.* DISPOSE, DISPOSED TO, INCLINATION, INCLINE, INCLINED, TENDENCY.

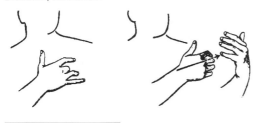

TENDENCY (tĕn′ dən sĭ), *n.* See TEND.

TENNIS (ten′ is), *n.* (Holding the racket.) The signer goes through the motions of manipulating a tennis racket. *Cf.* RACKET.

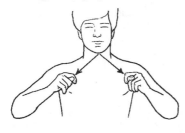

TEPEE (tĕ′ pē), *n.* (The letter "T"; the shape.) Both "T" hands, joined together, come apart as they move down, describing the sloping roof of a tent or tepee.

TERRIBLE (tĕr′ ə bəl), *adj.* (Throwing out the hands.) Both hands, their fingertips touching their respective thumbs, are held, palms facing each other, near the temples. They are thrown out before the face, assuming "5" positions, palms still facing. *Cf.* AWFUL, DREADFUL, TRAGEDY 1, TRAGIC.

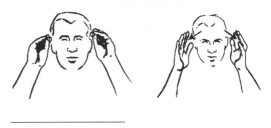

TERRITORY (ter′ ə tôr′ ē), *n.* (The letter "T"; an area.) The "T" hands are held together before the body, palms out. They separate and move back in a circle toward the chest, coming together again an inch or so from the chest.

TERROR 1 (tĕr′ ər), *n.* (The heart is suddenly covered with fear.) Both hands, fingers together, are placed side by side, palms facing the chest. They quickly open and come together over the heart, one on top of the other. *Cf.* AFRAID, FEAR 1, FRIGHT, FRIGHTEN, SCARE(D).

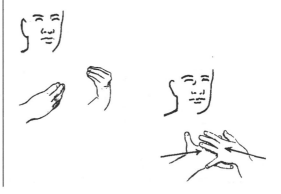

TERROR 2, *n.* (The hands attempt to ward off something which causes fear.) The "5" hands, right behind left, move downward before the body, in a wavy motion. *Cf.* DREAD, FEAR 2, TIMID.

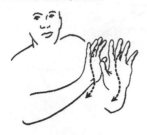

TEST (tĕst), *n., v.,* TESTED, TESTING. (A series of questions, spread out on a page.) Both "D" hands, palms down, simultaneously execute a single circle, the right hand moving in a clockwise direction and the left in a counterclockwise direction. Upon completion of the circle, both hands open into the "5" position and move straight down a short distance. (The hands actually draw question marks in the air.) *Cf.* EXAMINATION 1, QUIZ 1.

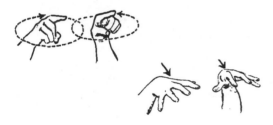

TESTES (tes' tēz), *n.* (Holding the testes.) Both upturned cupped hands move up and down a short distance near the lower abdomen. *Cf.* TESTICLES.

TESTICLES (tes' ti kəlz), *n.* See TESTES.

TESTIMONY 1 (tĕs' tə mō' nĭ), *n.* (A gesture of an orator.) The right open hand, palm facing left, is held above and to the right of the head. It pivots on the wrist, forward and backward, several times. *Cf.* LECTURE, ORATE, SPEECH 2, TALK 2.

TESTIMONY 2, *n.* (The letter "T"; to show or indicate.) The right "T" hand is placed against the outfacing left palm. Both hands move forward in unison.

THANKS (thăngks), *n. pl., interj.* See THANK YOU.

THANK YOU *phrase.* (Words extended politely from the mouth.) The fingertips of the right "5" hand are placed at the mouth. The hand moves away from the mouth to a palm-up position before the body. The signer meanwhile usually nods smilingly. *Cf.* THANKS, YOU'RE WELCOME 1.

THAT (t͟hat, *unstressed* t͟hət), *pron.* (Something specific.) The downturned right "Y" hand is placed on the upturned left palm. *Cf.* THIS.

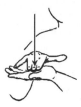

THAT ONE *(colloq.), phrase.* The downturned "Y" hand drops down abruptly, ending with a finger pointing at the one referred to. A knowing expression is assumed, or sometimes an exaggerated grimace, as if announcing a surprising fact.

THEFT 1 (thĕft), *n.* (The hand, partly concealed, takes something surreptitiously.) The index and middle fingers of the right hand, somewhat curved, are placed under the left elbow. As they move slowly along the left forearm toward the left wrist, they close a bit. *Cf.* ROB 1, ROBBERY 1, STEAL 1, THIEF 1, THIEVERY.

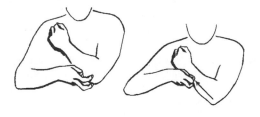

THEFT 2, *(colloq.), n.* (A sly, underhanded movement.) The right open hand, palm down, is held under the left elbow. Beginning with the little finger, the hand closes finger by finger into the "A" position, as if wrapping itself around something, and

moves to the right. *Cf.* ROB 2, ROBBERY 1, STEAL 2.

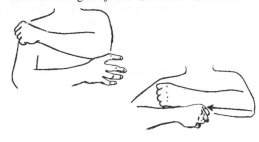

THEFT 3, *n.* (A mustachioed thief.) The fingertips of both "H" hands, palms facing the body, are placed above the lips and are drawn slowly apart, describing a mustache. Sometimes one hand only is used. *Cf.* BANDIT, BURGLAR, BURGLARY, CROOK, ROB 3, ROBBER, ROBBERY 1, THIEF 2.

THEIR(S) (t͟hâr, *unstressed* t͟hər), *pron.* (Belonging to; pushed toward.) The open right hand, palm facing out and fingers together and pointing up, moves out a short distance from the body. This is repeated several times, with the hand moving an inch or two toward the right each time. The hand may also be swept in a short left-to-right arc in this position.

THEM (t͟hĕm, *unstressed* t͟həm), *pron.* (The natural sign.) The right index finger points in turn to a number of imaginary persons or objects. *Cf.* THEY.

THEME (thēm), *n.* (The quotation marks are indicated.) The curved index and middle fingers of both hands, held palms out, move slightly to either side of the body, as if drawing quotation marks in the air. *Cf.* CAPTION 1, QUOTATION, QUOTE, SO-CALLED, SUBJECT, TITLE, TOPIC.

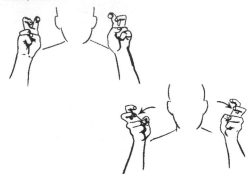

THEMSELVES (ŧħəm sĕlvz′), *pron. pl.* (The thumb indicates an individual, *i.e.,* a *self;* several are indicated.) The right hand, in the "A" position with thumb pointing up, makes a series of short forward movements as it sweeps either from right to left, or from left to right.

THEN 1 (ŧħĕn), *adv.* (Going from one specific point in time to another.) The left "L" hand is held palm facing right and thumb pointing left. The right index finger, positioned behind the left thumb, moves in an arc over the left thumb and comes to rest on the tip of the left index finger.

THEN 2, *adv.* (Same basic rationale as for THEN 1, but modified to incorporate the concept of nearness, *i.e.,* NEXT. The sign, then, is "one point [in time] to the next.") The left hand is held as in THEN 1. The extended right index finger rests on the ball of the thumb. The right hand then opens and arcs over,

coming to rest on the back of the left hand, whose index finger has now closed.

THEORY 1 (thē′ ə rĭ, thĭr′ ĭ), *n.* (A thought coming forward from the mind, modified by the letter "I" for "idea.") With the "I" position on the right hand, palm facing the body, touch the little finger to the forehead, and then move the hand up and away in a circular, clockwise motion. The hand may also be moved up and away without this circular motion. *Cf.* CONCEIVE, IMAGINATION 1, IMAGINE, THOUGHT 2.

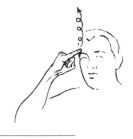

THEORY 2 (The letter "T"; turning over a thought in the mind.) The right "T" hand makes a small counterclockwise circle against the forehead.

THERAPY (ther′ ə pē), *n.* (The letter "T"; helping.) The right "T" hand is placed palm down or palm left on the left palm. The left palm pushes up the right a short distance.

THERE 1 (t͡hâr), *adv.* (The natural sign.) The right index finger points to an imaginary object, usually at or slightly above eye level, *i.e.,* "yonder."

THERE 2, *adv.* (Something brought to the attention.) The right hand is brought forward, simultaneously opening into the palm-up position.

THEREABOUTS (t͡hâr′ ə boutz), *adv.* (In the general area.) The downturned open "5" hand moves in a counterclockwise direction in front of the body. *Cf.* ABOUT 3.

THEREFORE 1 (t͡hâr′ fōr′), *adv.* (In proportion.) Both "D" or "P" hands, palms facing down, are held before the body. They describe a short arc from right to left and, while unnecessary, they may return to their original position. *Cf.* PROPORTION, THUS.

THEREFORE 2, *adv.* (The mathematical symbol.) The index finger describes three dots in the air, in pyramidal arrangement. This is used in the mathematical context.

THERMOMETER (thər mŏm′ ə tər), *n.* (The rise and fall of the mercury in the thermometer.) The index finger of the right "D" hand, pointing left, moves slowly up and down the index finger of the left "D" hand, which is held pointing up. *Cf.* FEVER, TEMPERATURE.

THERMOS (thûr′ məs), *n.* (Closing a bottle.) The sign for BOTTLE is made: the right "C" hand is held little finger edge against the upturned left palm. The right hand moves straight up, describing the shape of a bottle. The right hand then mimes tightening a bottle cap on the left hand, which now holds the imaginary bottle.

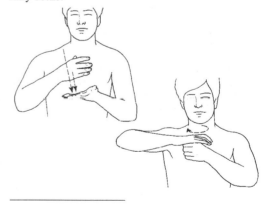

THEY (t͡hā), *pron.* (The natural sign.) The right index finger points in turn to a number of imaginary persons or objects. *Cf.* THEM.

THICK-SKULLED *(colloq.), adj.* (The thickness of the skull is indicated, to stress intellectual density.) With the thumb of the right "C" hand grasped by the closed left hand, the right hand is swung away from the body, describing a small arc as it moves. The space between the curved right fingers and the closed left hand indicates the thickness of the skull. *Cf.* DUMB 2, MORON, STUPID 2, UNSKILLED.

THIEF 1 (thēf), *n.* (The hand, partly concealed, takes something surreptitiously.) The index and middle fingers of the right hand, somewhat curved, are placed under the left elbow. As they move slowly along the left forearm toward the left wrist, they close a bit. This is followed by INDIVIDUAL, as in THIEF 2. *Cf.* ROB 1, ROBBERY 1, STEAL 1, THEFT 1, THIEVERY.

THIEF 2, *n.* (A mustachioed thief.) The fingertips of both "H" hands, palms facing the body, are placed above the lips and are drawn slowly apart, describing a mustache. Sometimes one hand only is used. This is followed by the sign for INDIVIDUAL: both open hands, palms facing each other, move down the sides of the body, tracing its outline to the hips. *Cf.* BANDIT, BURGLAR, BURGLARY, CROOK, ROB 3, ROBBER, ROBBERY 1, THEFT 3.

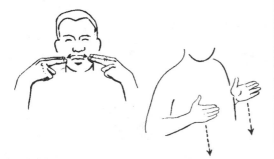

THIEVERY (thē′ və rĭ), *n.* See THIEF 1.

THIN 1 (thĭn), *adj.* (The drawn face.) The thumb and index finger run down the cheeks, which are drawn in.

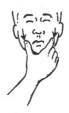

THIN 2, *(sl.), adj.* (A thin, tapering object is described with the little fingers, the thinnest of all.) The tips of the little fingers, touching, one above the other, are drawn apart. The cheeks may also be drawn in for emphasis. *Cf.* BEANPOLE, SKINNY.

THING (thĭng), *n.* (Something shown in the hand.) The outstretched right hand, palm up and held before the chest, is dropped slightly and brought over a bit to the right. *Cf.* OBJECT 1, SUBSTANCE 1.

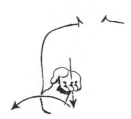

THINK (thĭngk), v., THOUGHT, THINKING. (A thought is turned over in the mind.) The index finger makes a small circle on the forehead. Cf. CONSIDER 1, MOTIVE 1, RECKON, SPECULATE 1, SPECULATION 1, THOUGHT 1, THOUGHTFUL.

THIRST (thûrst), n. (The parched throat.) The index finger moves down the throat a short distance. Cf. THIRSTY.

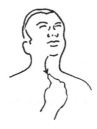

THIRSTY (thûrs′ tĭ), adj. See THIRST.

THIRTY (thûr′ tĭ), adj. (Three and zero.) The right "3" hand moves slightly to the right, closing into a modified "0" position.

THIS (thĭs), pron., adj. (Something specific.) The downturned right "Y" hand is placed on the upturned left palm. Cf. THAT.

THIS MONTH phrase. (Now, month.) The sign for NOW is made: the upturned right-angle hands drop down rather sharply. The "Y" hands may also be used. This is followed by the sign for MONTH: the extended right index finger moves down along the upturned, extended left index finger. The two signs are sometimes given in reverse order.

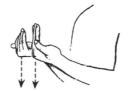 

THORN (thôrn), n. (The shape.) The right index and thumb rest on the upturned left index and trace the pointed shape of a thorn.

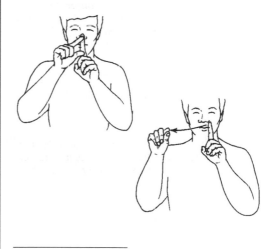

THOUGHT 1 (thôt), n. (A thought is turned over in the mind.) The index finger makes a small circle on the forehead. Cf. CONSIDER 1, MOTIVE 1, RECKON, SPECULATE 1, SPECULATION 1, THINK, THOUGHTFUL.

THOUGHT 2, *n.* (A thought coming forward from the mind, modified by the letter "I" for "idea.") With the "I" position on the right hand, palm facing the body, touch the little finger to the forehead, and then move the hand up and away in a circular, clockwise motion. The hand may also be moved up and away without this circular motion *Cf.* CONCEIVE, IMAGINATION 1, IMAGINE, THEORY 1.

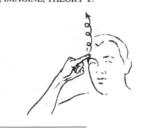

THOUGHTFUL (thôt' fəl), *adj.* See THOUGHT 1.

THREAD (thrĕd), *n.* (Unraveling a thin string, as indicated by the little fingers.) With palms facing the body, the tips of the extended little fingers touch. As they are drawn slowly apart, they describe very small spirals. *Cf.* SPAGHETTI, STRING, TWINE.

THREE OF US *phrase.* (Three all around.) The right "3" hand, palm facing the body, moves in a half circle from right shoulder to left shoulder.

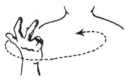

THRILL 1 (thrĭl), *n., v.,* THRILLED, THRILLING. (The heart beats violently.) Both middle fingers move up alternately to strike the heart sharply. *Cf.* EXCITE, EXCITEMENT, EXCITING.

THRILL 2, *(colloq.), n., v.* (The feelings well up and come out.) The open hands are placed near the chest, with middle fingers resting on the chest. Both hands move up and out simultaneously. A happy expression is assumed. *Cf.* WHAT'S NEW? 1, WHAT'S UP?

THROUGH (thrōō), *adv., prep., adj.* (The natural movement.) The open right hand is pushed between either the middle and index or the middle and third fingers of the open left hand.

THROW (thrō), *v.,* THREW, THROWN, THROWING. (The natural movement.) The right "S" hand is thrown forward and up a bit, as it opens into the "5" position.

THUMB (thum), *n.* (Indicating the thumb.) The right index and thumb grasp and sometimes shake the outstretched left thumbtip.

THUNDER (thŭn' dər), *n.* (A shaking which disturbs the ear.) After placing the index finger on the ear, both hands assume the "S" position, palms down. They move alternately back and forth, forcefully. *Cf.* NOISE, NOISY.

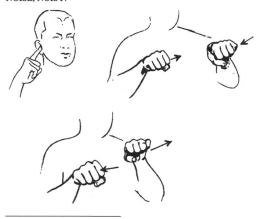

THUS (thŭs), *adv.* (In proportion.) Both "D" or "P" hands, palms facing down, are held before the body. They describe a short arc from right to left and, while unnecessary, they may return to their original position. *Cf.* PROPORTION, THEREFORE 1.

THUS FAR *adv. phrase.* (From a point up and over.) In the "D" position, palms down, both index fingers touch the right shoulder and then are brought up and over, ending in a palm-up position, pointing straight ahead of the body. *Cf.* ALL ALONG, ALL THE TIME, EVER SINCE, SINCE 1, SO FAR.

TICKET 1 (tĭk' ĭt), *n.* (The natural sign.) The sides of the ticket are outlined with the thumb and index finger of each hand. *Cf.* CARD.

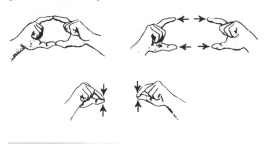

TICKET 2, *n.* (A baggage check or ticket.) The sign for TICKET 1 is made. Then the middle knuckles of the second and third fingers of the right hand squeeze the outer edge of the left palm, as a conductor's ticket punch.

TIE 1 (tī), *v.,* TIED, TYING. (The act of tying.) Both hands, in the "A" position, go through the natural hand-over-hand motions of tying and drawing out a knot. *Cf.* BIND, KNOT.

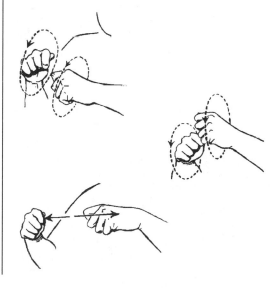

TIE 2, *n.* (The natural motion.) The "H" hands go through the natural hand-over-hand motions of tying a knot in a necktie at the throat. The right "H" hand then moves down the front of the chest to indicate the fall of the tie. *Cf.* NECKTIE.

TIGER (tī′ gər), *n.* (The stripes on the face.) The claw hands trace the cat's stripes on the face.

TIGHT (tīt), *adj.* (The squeezing movement.) The fingers of one hand squeeze the other.

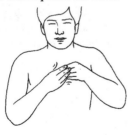

TIGHTFISTED (tīt′ fis′ tid), *adj.* (Holding onto money tightly.) The signer makes a tight fist, shaking it slightly. *Cf.* PENNY-PINCHING.

TIGHTROPE (tīt′ rōp′), *n.* (The natural activity.) The signer, arms outstretched, mimes walking a tightrope.

TIGHTS (tīts), *n.* (The natural activity of donning tights.) The signer mimes struggling into a pair of tights, pulling down the top over the chest, and showing the effort on the face. *Cf.* LEOTARDS.

TIGHTWAD 1 (tīt′ wŏd′), *n.* (Pulling things toward oneself.) Both prone open or "V" hands are held in front of the body with fingers bent. The hands are then drawn quickly and forcefully inward, as if raking things toward oneself. *Cf.* GREEDY 1, SELFISH 1, STINGY 1.

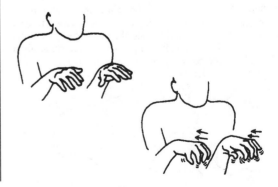

TIGHTWAD 2, *n.* (Scratching the palm in greed.) The right fingers scratch the upturned left palm several times. A frowning expression is often used. *Cf.* GREEDY 2, SELFISH 2, STINGY 2.

TILL (tĭl), *prep.* (From one point to the next.) The extended right index finger moves forward slowly and comes to rest on the tip of the extended, upturned left index finger. *Cf.* TO 1, TOWARD 1, UNTIL, UNTO, UP TO, UP TO NOW.

TIME 1 (tīm), *n.* (Time by the clock, indicated by the ticking of the clock or watch.) The curved right index finger taps the back of the left wrist several times. *Cf.* WATCH 3.

TIME 2, *n.* (Time in the abstract, indicated by the rotating of the "T" hand on the face of a clock.) The right "T" hand is placed palm to palm in the open left hand. It describes a clockwise circle and comes to rest again in the left palm.

TIME 3, *(sports)*, *n.* (The gesture employed in sports.) The fingertips of the right hand, pointing up, are thrust into the open left hand, whose palm is facing down. A "T" is thus formed. This movement may be repeated. *Cf.* TIME OUT.

TIME OUT *(sports)*, *phrase.* See TIME 3.

TIMID (tĭm' ĭd), *adj.* (The hands attempt to ward off something which causes fear.) The "5" hands, right behind left, move downward before the body, in a wavy motion. *Cf.* DREAD, FEAR 2, TERROR 2.

TINY (tī' ni), *adj.* (Indicating a small mass.) The extended right thumb and index finger are held slightly spread. They are then moved slowly toward each other until they almost touch. *Cf.* PETTY, SLIGHT, SMALL 1.

TIP 1 (tĭp), *n., v.,* TIPPED, TIPPING. (A tapering or sharp point is indicated.) The index finger and thumb of the left hand grasp the tip of the index finger of the right "D" hand. The left hand then moves away a short distance, and its index finger and thumb come together.

TIP 2, *n., v.* (Putting a coin in someone's hand.) The right hand places an imaginary coin in the upturned left palm.

TIP 3, *n., v.* (Fingering a coin or a bill.) The upturned right hand holds an imaginary coin or bill. As it moves forward, the thumb rubs against the fingertips, from middle finger to index, assuming the "A" position.

TIPTOE (tĭp′ tō′), *n., v.* (The feet touch lightly.) With both index fingers pointing down, the signer very lightly, slowly, and deliberately moves forward first one and then the other index finger. The shoulders

are a little stooped, and with each successive forward movement of the index fingers, the signer moves forward very slightly.

TIRE (tīr), *v.,* TIRED, TIRING. (The hands collapse in exhaustion.) Both "C" hands are placed either on the lower chest or at the waist. The palms face the body. They fall away into a palms-up position. At the same time, the shoulders suddenly sag in a very pronounced fashion. An expression of weariness may be used for emphasis. *Cf.* TIRED.

TIRED (tīrd), *adj.* See TIRE.

TIRES (tīrz), *n.* (The shape.) Both index fingers, held on either side of the chest, outline the round shape of a pair of tires or wheels.

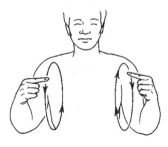

TITLE (tī′ təl), *n.* (The quotation marks are indicated.) The curved index and middle fingers of both hands, held palms out, move slightly to either side of the body, as if drawing quotation marks in the air. *Cf.* CAPTION 1, QUOTATION, QUOTE, SO-CALLED, SUBJECT, THEME, TOPIC.

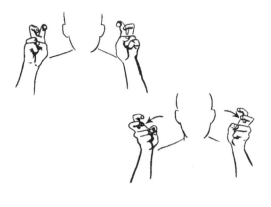

TO 1 (tōō), *prep.* (From one point to the next.) The extended right index finger moves forward slowly and comes to rest on the tip of the extended, upturned left index finger. This sign should never be used for an infinitive; it is simply omitted in that case. *Cf.* TILL, TOWARD 1, UNTIL, UNTO, UP TO, UP TO NOW.

TO 2, *prep.* (The thoughts are directed outward, toward a specific goal or purpose.) The right index finger, resting on the right temple, leaves its position and moves straight out in front of the face. *Cf.* FOR 1.

TOAST (tōst), *n., v.,* TOASTED, TOASTING. (The fork is thrust into each side of the toast, to turn it around.) With the left hand held upright, the tips of the right "V" fingers are thrust into the open left palm and then into the back of the same hand.

TOASTER (tōs′ tər), *n.* (Popping the bread into a box.) The downturned right fingers are thrust into the left hand. The sides of the toaster are then indicated.

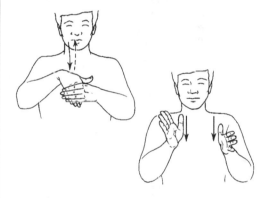

TODAY 1 (tə dā′), *n.* (Now, day.) The sign for NOW is made: the upturned right-angle hands drop down rather sharply. The "Y" hands may also be used. This is followed by the sign for DAY: the left arm, held horizontally, palm down, represents the horizon. The right elbow rests on the back of the left hand, with the right arm in a perpendicular position. The right "D" hand, palm facing left, moves in an arc to the left until it is just above the left elbow. The two signs may be reversed.

TODAY 2, *prep.* (Right before one, *i.e.,* now.) The right-angle or "Y" hands, palms up, drop down twice.

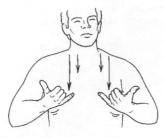

TOE(S) (tō), *n.* (Touching them in turn.) The downturned left "5" hand is held at chest height. The right thumb and index finger (or the right "T" hand) moves from the left thumb to the little finger, indicating the toes, one by one.

TOGETHER (tŏŏ gĕŧħ′ ər), *adv.* (To go along with.) Both "A" hands, knuckles together and thumbs up, are moved in a counterclockwise ellipse in front of the chest.

TOIL (toil), *n., v.,* TOILED, TOILING. (Striking an anvil.) Both "S" hands are held palms down. The right hand strikes against the back of the left a number of times. *Cf.* JOB, LABOR, OCCUPATION, TASK, TRAVAIL, VOCATION, WORK.

TOILET (toi′ lĭt), *n.* (The letter "T.") The right "T" hand is shaken slightly.

TOKYO (tō′ kē ō), *n.* (The skyscrapers.) Both "L" hands, palms facing out, move alternately up and down.

TOLERATE 1 (tŏl′ ə rāt′), *v.,* -ATED, -ATING. (A permissive upswinging of the hands, as if giving in.) Both hands, palms facing and fingers pointing away from the body, are held at chest level, almost a foot apart. With an upward movement, using their wrists as pivots, the hands sweep up until the fingers point almost straight up. *Cf.* ALLOW, GRANT 1, LET, LET'S, LET US, MAY 3, PERMISSION 1, PERMIT 1.

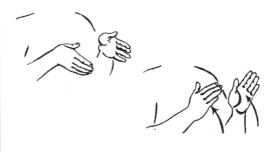

TOLERATE 2, *v.* (A clenching of the fists; the rise and fall of pain.) Both "S" hands, tightly clenched, revolve about each other, slowly and deliberately, while a pained expression is worn. *Cf.* ENDURE 1, SUFFER 1.

TOLL (tōl), *n.* (Nicking into one.) The knuckle of the right "X" finger is nicked against the palm of the left hand, held in the "5" position, palm facing right. *Cf.* CHARGE, COST, EXPENSE, FEE, FINE 2, PENALTY, PRICE 2, TAX 1, TAXATION 1.

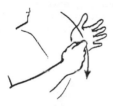

TOMATO (tə mā′ tō), *n.* (The slicing is indicated.) The sign for RED is made: the tip of the right index finger moves down across the lips. The open right hand, palm facing left, is then brought down against the thumb side of the downturned left "S" hand in a slicing movement. This latter movement is repeated a number of times. The slicing may also be done with the index finger.

TOMORROW (tə môr′ ō, -mŏr′ ō), *n., adv.* (A single step ahead, *i.e.,* into the future.) The thumb of the

right "A" hand, placed on the right cheek, moves straight out from the face, describing an arc.

TONIGHT (tə nīt′), *n.* (Now, night.) The sign for NOW is made: the upturned right-angle hands drop down rather sharply. The "Y" hands may also be used. This is followed by the sign for NIGHT: the left hand, palm down, is positioned at chest height. The downturned right hand, held an inch or so above the left, moves over the left hand in an arc, as the sun setting beneath the horizon. The two signs may be reversed.

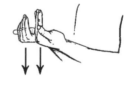 

TONSILS (ton′ səlz), *n.* (Pointing to the tonsils.) The signer points to both sides of the throat.

TOO (tōō), *adv.* (A likeness; a sameness.) Both index fingers, held together at one side of the body near waist level, point forward. As they travel to the other side of the body they separate an inch or two and come together again. *Cf.* ACCORDING (TO), ALSO, AS, SAME AS.

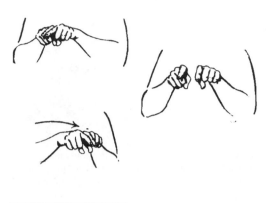

TOOTHPASTE (tōōth′ pāst′), *n.* (Squeezing the tube.) The signer mimes squeezing toothpaste onto the outstretched left index finger.

TOP (top), *n.* (Winding up a top and spinning it.) The signer mimes winding up a toy top and spinning it.

TOP DOG (top′ dôg) *n.* *(sl.)* (The senior year at school.) The downturned open right palm rests on the tip of the left thumb. *Cf.* SENIOR.

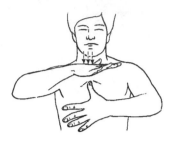

TOPIC (tŏp′ ĭk), *n.* (The quotation marks are indicated.) The curved index and middle fingers of both hands, held palms out, move slightly to either side of the body, as if drawing quotation marks in the air. *Cf.* CAPTION 1, QUOTATION, QUOTE, SO-CALLED, SUBJECT, THEME, TITLE.

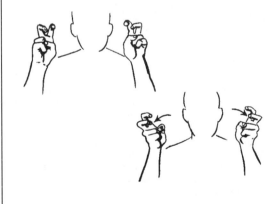

TORMENT (*n.* tôr′ mĕnt; *v.* tôr mĕnt′), -MENTED, -MENTING. (Striking sparks off one.) The knuckles of the right "A" hand move sharply forward along the thumb edge of the left "A" hand. *Cf.* TEASE 1.

TOSS AND TURN *colloq. phrase.* (The body moves around in bed.) The upturned curved index and middle fingers of the right hand, swiveled from the right wrist, move back and forth in the upturned open left palm.

TOTAL (tŏ′ təl), *adj., n., v.,* -TALED, -TALING. (To bring up all together.) The two open hands, palms and fingers facing each other, with the left hand above the right, are brought together, with all fingers closing simultaneously. This sign is used mainly in the sense of adding up figures or items. *Cf.* ADD 1, ADDITION, AMOUNT 1, SUM, SUMMARIZE 2, SUMMARY 2, SUM UP.

TOUCH (tŭch), *n., v.,* TOUCHED, TOUCHING. (The natural movement of touching.) The tip of the middle finger of the downturned right "5" hand touches the back of the left hand a number of times. *Cf.* CONTACT 1, FEEL 1.

TOUCHED (tŭcht), *adj.* (A piercing of the heart.) The tip of the middle finger of the right "5" hand is thrust against the heart. The head, at the same time,

moves abruptly back a very slight distance. *Cf.* FEEL TOUCHED, TOUCHING.

TOUCHING (tŏŭch′ ĭng), *adj.* See TOUCHED.

TOUGH 1 (tŭf), *adj.* (Flexing the muscles.) With fists clenched, palms facing back, the signer raises both arms and shakes them once, with force. *Cf.* MIGHT 1, MIGHTY 1, POWER 1, POWERFUL 1, STRONG 1, STURDY.

TOUGH 2, *(sl.), adj.* (Striking the chest to indicate toughness, *i.e.,* a "tough guy.") The little finger edge of the upturned right "S" hand strikes the chest repeatedly.

TOURIST (tŏŏr′ ĭst), *n.* (One who wanders around.) Using the downturned curved "V" fingers, the signer describes a series of small counterclockwise circles as the fingers move in random fashion from right to left. This is followed by the sign for INDIVIDUAL.

TOURNAMENT (tûr' nə mənt), *n.* (First one team leads, then the other.) The curved index fingers and thumbs of both hands, palms facing, move up and down alternately.

TOW (tō), *n., v.,* TOWED, TOWING. (Hooking on to something and pulling.) With index fingers interlocked, the right hand pulls the left hand from left to right. *Cf.* HITCH, HOOK, PULL 2.

TOWARD 1 (tōrd, tə wôrd'), *prep.* (From one point to the next.) The extended right index finger moves forward slowly and comes to rest on the tip of the extended, upturned left index finger. *Cf.* TILL, TO 1, UNTIL, UNTO, UP TO, UP TO NOW.

TOWARD 2, *prep.* (Coming close to.) Both hands are held in the right angle position, fingers facing each other, with the right hand held between the left hand and the chest. The right hand slowly moves toward the left. *Cf.* APPROACH, NEAR 2.

TOWEL 1 (tou' əl), *n.* (The natural sign.) The signer goes through the motions of wiping his face with a towel. *Cf.* WASH 2.

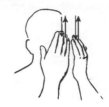

TOWEL 2, *n.* (Drying off the back.) The signer mimes using a large towel to dry off the back.

TOWN (toun), *n.* (A collection of rooftops.) The fingertips of both hands are joined, the hands and arms forming a pyramid. The fingertips separate and rejoin a number of times. Both arms may move a bit from left to right each time the fingertips separate and rejoin. *Cf.* CITY, COMMUNITY.

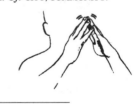

TOY (toi), *n.* (The "T"s; playing.) Both downturned "T" hands swivel alternately from their wrists. The swiveling movement is derived from the sign to PLAY.

TRADE (trād), *n., v.,* TRADED, TRADING. (Exchanging places.) The right "A" hand, positioned above the left "Λ" hand, swings down and under the left, coming up a bit in front of it. *Cf.* EXCHANGE, INSTEAD OF 1, REPLACE, SUBSTITUTE.

TRAGEDY 1 (trăj' ə dĭ), *n.* (Throwing out the hands.) Both hands, their fingertips touching their respective thumbs, are held, palms facing each other, near the temples. They are thrown out before the face, assuming "5" positions, palms still facing. *Cf.* AWFUL, DREADFUL, TERRIBLE, TRAGIC.

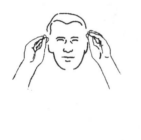

TRAGEDY 2 (The "T" letters; tears running down the cheeks.) Both "T" hands move down the side of the face. A look of sadness is assumed.

TRAGIC (trăj' ĭk), *adj.* See TRAGEDY 1.

TRAIL (trāl), *n.* (The winding movement.) Both hands, palms facing and fingers together and extended straight out, move in unison away from the body, in a winding manner. *Cf.* CORRIDOR, HALL, HALLWAY, MANNER 2, METHOD, OPPORTUNITY 3, PATH, ROAD, STREET, WAY 1.

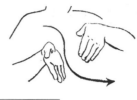

TRAILER (trā' lər), *n.* (The rig swings back and forth.) Both downturned hands are positioned with the left fingertips against the heel of the right hand, the cab. Both hands sway slightly back and forth as they move forward.

TRAIN 1 (trān), *n.* (Running along the tracks.) The "V" hands are held palms down. The right "V" moves back and forth over the left "V." *Cf.* RAILROAD 1, TRANSPORTATION 2.

TRAIN 2, *v.,* TRAINED, TRAINING. (Polishing or sharpening up.) The knuckles of the downturned right "A" hand are rubbed briskly back and forth over the side of the hand and index finger of the left "D" hand. *Cf.* PRACTICE 1.

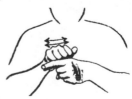

TRANSFER (trans′ fər), *n., v.* (Shift position or travel.) The downturned curved right "V" fingers move forward in a horizontal arc.

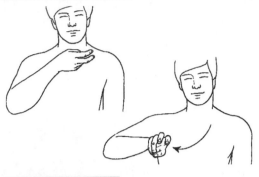

TRANSIENT (trăn′ shənt), *adj.* A variation of TRAVEL 1 and TRAVEL 2, but using the downturned curved "V" fingers. *Cf.* JOURNEY 3, TRAVEL 3, TRIP 3.

TRANSMISSION (trans mish′ ən), *n.* (The internal working of an automobile transmission.) Both claw hands are held up, palms facing each other. They rotate repeatedly from the wrists, in opposite directions.

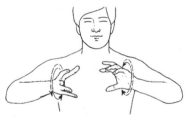

TRANSPORTATION 1 (trăns′ pər tā′ shən), *n.* (The natural sign.) The right "A" hand, palm facing left and thumb held straight up, moves back and forth repeatedly from left to right.

TRANSPORTATION 2, *n.* (Running along the tracks.) The "V" hands are held palms down. The right "V" moves back and forth over the left "V." *Cf.* RAILROAD 1, TRAIN 1.

TRAP 1 (trăp), *n., v.,* TRAPPED, TRAPPING. (Impaled on a stick, as a snake's head.) The "V" fingers are thrust into the throat. *Cf.* CAUGHT IN THE ACT 2, STRANDED, STUCK 2.

TRAP 2, *n.* (The jaws of the trap snap together.) Both "X" hands, palms out, are held a few inches apart. They suddenly snap together.

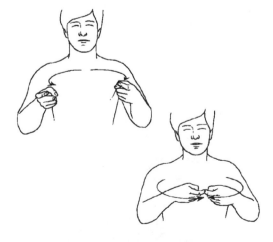

TRAPEZE ARTIST (trə pēz' är' tist), *n.* (The natural movements.) The outstretched left index finger represents the bar of the trapeze. The right index and middle fingers stand on the left index finger and, maintaining contact, swing back and forth.

TRAVAIL (trăv' āl), *n.* (Striking an anvil.) Both "S" hands are held palms down. The right hand strikes against the back of the left a number of times. *Cf.* JOB, LABOR, OCCUPATION, TASK, TOIL, VOCATION, WORK.

TRAVEL 1 (trăv' əl), *n., v.,* -ELED, -ELING. (Moving around from place to place.) Both "D" hands are held palms facing, the index fingers pointing to each other. In this position the hands describe a series of small counterclockwise circles as they move in random fashion from right to left. *Cf.* JOURNEY 1, TRIP 1.

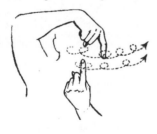

TRAVEL 2, *n., v.* A variation of TRAVEL 1, but using only the right hand. *Cf.* JOURNEY 2, TRIP 2.

TRAVEL 3, *n., v.* A variation of TRAVEL 1 and TRAVEL 2, but using the downturned curved "V" fingers. *Cf.* JOURNEY 3, TRANSIENT, TRIP 3.

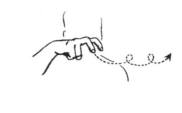

TREE (trē), *n.* (The shape.) The elbow of the upright right arm rests on the palm of the upturned left hand. This is the trunk. The right "5" fingers wiggle to imitate the movement of the branches and leaves.

TRESPASS (trĕs' pəs), *n., v.,* -PASSED, -PASSING. (An encroachment; parrying a knife thrust.) The left "A" hand is held palm toward the body, knuckles facing right. The extended thumb of the right "A" hand is brought sharply over the back of the left. *Cf.* DANGER, DANGEROUS, INJURE 2, PERIL, VIOLATE.

TRIFLING (trī′ fling), *adj.* (Thoughts flickering back and forth.) The right "Y" hand, thumb almost touching the forehead, is shaken back and forth across the forehead several times. *Cf.* FOLLY, FOOLISH, NONSENSE, RIDICULOUS, SILLY.

TRIP 1 (trĭp), *n.* (Moving around from place to place.) Both "D" hands are held palms facing, the index fingers pointing to each other. In this position the hands describe a series of small counterclockwise circles as they move in random fashion from right to left. *Cf.* JOURNEY 1, TRAVEL 1.

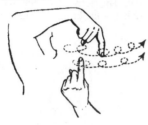

TRIP 2, *n.* A variation of TRIP 1, but using only the right hand. *Cf.* JOURNEY 2, TRAVEL 2.

TRIP 3, *n.* A variation of TRIP 1 and TRIP 2, but using the downturned curved "V" fingers. *Cf.* JOURNEY 3, TRANSIENT, TRAVEL 3.

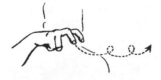

TRIUMPH 1 (trī′ əmf), *n., v.,* -UMPHED, -UMPHING. (Waving a flag.) The right "A" hand goes through

the natural movement of waving a flag in circular fashion. Preceding this, the right hand may go through the motion of grabbing the flagstaff out of the left hand. *Cf.* EXULTATION, VICTORY 2, WIN 2.

TRIUMPH 2, *n.* (Penetrating the heights.) The "D" hands, palms back, are held at each side of the head, near the temples. With a pivoting motion of the wrists, the hands swing up and around, simultaneously, to a position above the head, with palms facing out. *Cf.* ACCOMPLISH, ACHIEVE, PROSPER, SUCCEED, SUCCESS, SUCCESSFUL.

TROLLEY CAR (trŏl′ ĭ), *n.* (Running along the overhead cable.) The extended index finger of the downturned left "D" hand represents the overhead cable. The knuckles of the curved right index and middle fingers, grasping the left index finger, move along its length, from base to tip.

TROUBLE (trŭb′ əl), *n., v.,* -BLED, -BLING. (A clouding over; a troubling.) Both "B" hands, palms facing each other, are rotated alternately before the forehead. *Cf.* CONCERN, FRET, PROBLEM 1, WORRIED, WORRY 1.

TRUE (trōō), *adj.* (Coming forth directly from the lips; true.) The index finger of the right "D" hand, palm facing left, is placed against the lips. It moves up an inch or two and then describes a small arc forward and away from the lips. *Cf.* ABSOLUTE, ABSOLUTELY, ACTUAL, ACTUALLY, AUTHENTIC, CERTAIN, CERTAINLY, FIDELITY, FRANKLY, GENUINE, INDEED, POSITIVE 1, POSITIVELY, REAL, REALLY, SINCERE 2, SURE, SURELY, TRULY, TRUTH, VALID, VERILY.

TRULY (trōō′ lĭ), *adv.* See TRUE.

TRUNK (trŭngk), *n.* (The dimensions are indicated.) The open hands, palms facing and fingers pointing out, are dropped an inch or two simultaneously. They then shift their relative positions so that both palms face the body, with one hand in front of the other. In this new position they again drop an inch or two simultaneously. *Cf.* BOX 1, PACKAGE, ROOM 1, SQUARE.

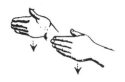

TRUST (trŭst), *n., v.,* TRUSTED, TRUSTING. (Planting a flagpole, *i.e.,* planting one's trust.) The "S" hands grasp and plant an imaginary flagpole in the ground. This sign may be preceded by the extended index finger placed against the forehead. *Cf.* CONFIDENCE.

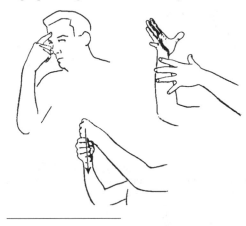

TRUSTEE (trus tē′), *n.* (The "T"; the Roman toga.) The right "T" hand moves from the left shoulder to the right shoulder.

TRUTH (trōōth), *n.* See TRUE.

TRY 1 (trī), *n., v.,* TRIED, TRYING. (Trying to push through.) The "A" hands, palms facing before the body, are swung around and a bit down, so that the palms now face out. The movement indicates an attempt to push through a barrier. *Cf.* ATTEMPT 1, EFFORT 1, ENDEAVOR, PERSEVERE 1, PERSIST 1.

TRY 2, *v., n.* (Trying to push through, using the "T" hands, for "try.") This is the same sign as TRY 1, except that the "T" hands are employed. *Cf.* ATTEMPT 2, EFFORT 2, PERSEVERE 2.

TTY/TDD 1, *n., v.* (Phone and type.) The "Y" hand is held at the side of the face, indicating the phone's receiver. The signer then executes typing motions.

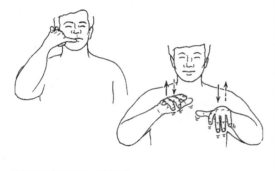

TTY/TDD 2, *n., v.* (A fingerspelled loan sign.) The signer fingerspells either "T-T-Y" or "T-D-D."

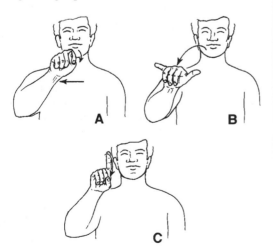

TUBA (tōō′ bə), *n.* (The shape and function.) One hand grasps the mouthpiece and holds it at the pursed lips, while the other hand, in the "5" position, facing out, traces the outline of the instrument and its sweep over the head.

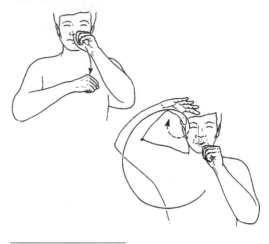

TURKEY (tûr′ kĭ), *n.* (The wattle shakes.) The "G" hand, palm down, is shaken before the nose or under the chin.

TUTOR (tōō′ tər), *n., v.* (The letter "T"; taking knowledge from the mind and giving it to someone.) Both "T" hands, palms facing, are placed at the temples. They move forward and back again several times. Used as a noun, this sign is followed by the sign for INDIVIDUAL.

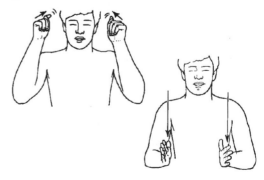

TWICE (twīs), *adv.* (Two fingers are brought up.) The right "V" fingers rest in the open left palm, and are then swung in an arc to an upright position.

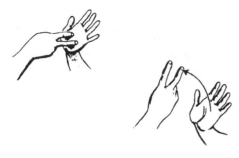

TWINE (twīn), *n., v.,* TWINED, TWINING. (Unraveling a thin string, as indicated by the little fingers.) With palms facing the body, the tips of the extended little fingers touch. As they are drawn slowly apart, they describe very small spirals. *Cf.* SPAGHETTI, STRING, THREAD.

TWINS 1 (twinz), *n.* The right "T" hand moves from the left corner of the mouth to the right corner.

TWINS 2, *n.* The thumb edge of the right "T" hand is placed on the left corner of the mouth. It moves away

and over to the right corner of the mouth.

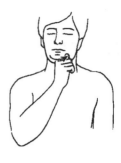

TWO MORE *(colloq.), phrase.* (Two fingers beckon.) The right hand is held palm up, with the index and middle fingers making very small and rapid beckoning movements.

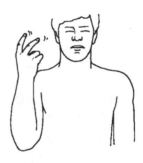

TWO WEEKS *n. phrase.* ("2"; week.) The base of the right "2" hand is drawn across the upturned left palm, from its base to its fingertips. See WEEK.

U

UGLINESS 1 (ŭg′ lĭ nəs), *n.* (The facial features are distorted.) The "X" hands are moved alternately up and down in front of the face, whose features are distorted with a pronounced frown. *Cf.* GRIMACE, HOMELY 1, UGLY 1.

UGLINESS 2, *n.* The "X" hands, palms down, move back and forth in a horizontal direction in front of the face whose features are distorted with a pronounced frown. *Cf.* HOMELY 2, UGLY 2.

UGLINESS 3, *n.* This is a variant of UGLINESS 1. The "X" hands, crossed in front of the face, alternately move apart and recross. The facial features are distorted with a pronounced frown. *Cf.* UGLY 3.

 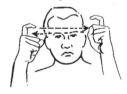

UGLY 1 (ŭg′ lĭ), *adj.* See UGLINESS 1.

UGLY 2, *adj.* See UGLINESS 2.

UGLY 3, *adj.* See UGLINESS 3.

ULTIMATE (ŭl′ tə mĭt), *adj.* (The little, *i.e.,* LAST, fingers are indicated.) With the hands in the "I" position, the tip of the right little finger strikes the tip of its left counterpart. The right index finger may be used instead of the right little finger. *Cf.* END 1, EVENTUALLY, FINAL 1, FINALLY 1, LAST 1, LASTLY, ULTIMATELY.

ULTIMATELY *adv.* See ULTIMATE.

UMBRELLA (ŭm brĕl′ ə), *n.* (The natural sign.) The signer goes through the motions of opening an umbrella.

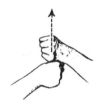

UMPIRE (ŭm′ pĭr), *n.* (Judge, individual.) The sign for JUDGE is formed: the two "F" hands, palms facing each other, move alternately up and down. This is followed by the sigh for INDIVIDUAL: both open hands, palms facing each other, move down the sides of the body, tracing its outline to the hips. *Cf.* JUDGE 2, REFEREE.

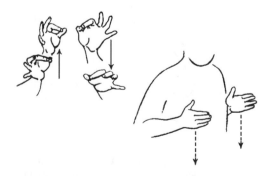

UN- *prefix.* (Crossing the hands—a negative gesture.) The downturned open hands are crossed at the wrists. They are drawn apart rather quickly. *Cf.* NOT.

UNABLE (ŭn ā′ bəl), *adj.* (One finger encounters an unyielding quality in striking another.) The right index finger strikes the left and continues moving down. The left index finger remains in place. *Cf.* CANNOT 1, CAN'T.

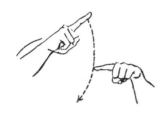

UNCERTAIN (ŭn sûr′ tən), *adj.* (On a fence.) The index and middle fingers of the right hand, palm down, straddle the index finger edge of the left "B" hand, which is held palm facing right. In this position the right hand rocks deliberately back and forth, from left to right. *Cf.* INDECISION, UNSURE, WAVER 1.

UNCLE (ŭng′ kəl), *n.* (The letter "U"; the "male" or upper portion of the head.) The right "U" hand is held near the right temple and is shaken slightly.

UNCLEAR (un′ klir′), *adj.* (One hand obscures the other.) The "5" hands are held up palm against palm in front of the body. The right hand moves in a slow, continuous clockwise circle over the left palm, as the signer tries to see between the fingers. *Cf.* BLURRY, VAGUE.

UNCONSCIOUS (un kon′ shəs), *adj.* (The "U" and "C" letters; under the conscious level.) The signer makes a "U" and then a "C" with the right hand, which is held under the downturned left and moving in a small counterclockwise circle.

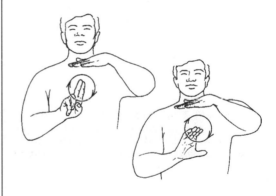

UNDER 1 (ŭn′ dər), *prep.* (Underneath something.) The right hand, in the "A" position, thumb pointing straight up, moves down under the left hand, held outstretched, fingers together, palm down. *Cf.* BELOW 2, UNDERNEATH.

UNDER 2, *prep.* (The area below.) The right "A" hand, thumb pointing up, moves in a counterclockwise fashion under the downturned left hand. *Cf.* BELOW 3.

UNDERNEATH (ŭn´ dər nĕth´, -nĕth), *prep.* See UNDER 1.

UNDERSTAND 1 (ŭn´ dər stănd´), *v.,* -STOOD, -STANDING. (An awakening of the mind.) The right "S" hand is placed on the forehead, palm facing the body. The index finger suddenly flicks up into the "D" position.

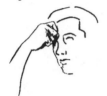 

UNDERSTAND 2, *v.* (See rationale for UNDERSTAND 1.) The curved index finger of the right hand, palm facing the body, is placed with the fingernail resting on the middle of the forehead. It suddenly flicks up into the "D" position. *Cf.* UNDERSTANDING, UNDERSTOOD.

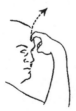

UNDERSTANDING (ŭn´ dər stăn´ dǐng), *n.* See UNDERSTAND 2.

UNDERSTOOD (ŭn´ dər stŏŏd´), *v., adj.* See UNDERSTAND 2.

UNDERSTUDY (un´ dər stud´ ē), *n.* (One who is behind another, *i.e.,* backup.) The upturned right thumb is held behind the upturned left thumb. The sign for INDIVIDUAL 1 then follows.

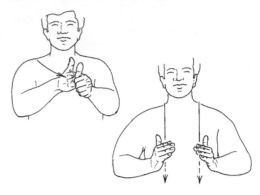

UNDERWEAR (un´ dər wâr´), *n.* (Pointing to the underclothes.) The right index finger, pointing down, is held on the upper chest, near the opening of the collar. It moves down repeatedly an inch or two, returning each time to its original place.

UNEMPLOYMENT INSURANCE (un em ploi´ ment in shŏŏr´ əns), *n.* (A fingerspelled loan sign.) The letters "U-I" are fingerspelled.

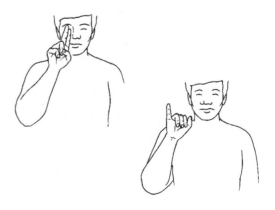

UNFAIR 1 (ŭn fâr'), *adj.* (NOT, EQUAL.) The sign for the prefix UN- is made: the downturned open hands are crossed at the wrists. They are drawn apart rather quickly. This is followed by the sign for EQUAL: the downturned "B" hands, held at chest height, are brought together repeatedly, so that the index finger edges come into contact.

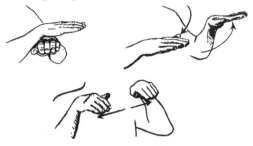

UNFAIR 2, *adj.* (Nicking into one.) The "AND" hands are held one above the other, palms toward the body, the right fingers pointing left, the left fingers pointing right. The upper hand then moves forcefully downward, striking its fingertips across those of the lower hand as it passes by. The "F" hands may also be used. *Cf.* UNJUST, UNJUSTIFIED.

UNFAITHFUL (un fāth' fəl), *adj. sl.* (Activity carried on out of view.) The downturned left hand, fingers pointed forward, is held at chest level. The slightly curved right hand, palm facing left, travels across the left fingertips, continuing on to the little finger side of the left hand. The sign is usually made twice. Typical expressions accompanying this sign would be one of guilt, or eyes narrowed or pursed lips.

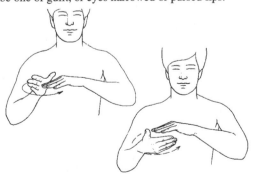

UNFORGIVABLE (un' fər giv' ə bəl), *adj.* (NOT, FORGIVE.) The sign for the prefix UN-, as in UNFAIR 1, is made. This is followed by the sign for FORGIVE: the right hand, palm flat, facing down, is brushed over the left hand, held palm flat and facing up. This action may be repeated twice.

UNIFORM (yōō' nə fôrm), *adj.* (Parallel movement.) Both downturned "Y" hands, held a few inches apart, move simultaneously from left to right or toward and away from each other. *Cf.* SAME 3, UNIFORMLY.

UNIFORMLY *adv.* See UNIFORM.

UNION (yōōn' yən), *n.* (The "U" fingers, making a circle to indicate unity.) Both "U" hands, touching, with palms out, move in a circle until they touch again, with palms now facing in.

UNITE (yōō nīt′), *v.,* UNITED, UNITING. (Joining together.) Both hands, held in the modified "5" position, palms out, move toward each other. The thumbs and index fingers of both hands then connect. *Cf.* AFFILIATE, ANNEX, ATTACH, BELONG, CONNECT, ENLIST, ENROLL, JOIN, PARTICIPATE.

UNIVERSAL (yōō′ nə vûr′ səl), *adj.* (Encompassing; a gathering together.) Both hands are held in the right angle position, palms facing the body, and the right hand in front of the left. The right hand makes a sweeping outward movement around the left, and comes to rest with the back of the right hand resting in the left palm. *Cf.* ALL, ENTIRE, WHOLE.

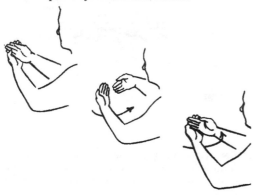

UNIVERSE (yōō′ nə vûrs), *n.* (The letter "U"; the planet.) The right "U" hand, palm out, makes a clockwise circle around the left "S" hand, representing a planet.

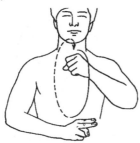

UNIVERSITY (yōō′ nə vûr′ sə tē), *n.* (The letter "U"; a higher school.) The base of the right "U" hand rests in the upturned left palm. It swings to the left a bit and up a few inches, describing an arc. See also COLLEGE, SCHOOL.

UNJUST (ŭn jŭst′), *adj.* (Nicking into one.) The "AND" hands are held one above the other, palms toward the body, the right fingers pointing left, the left fingers pointing right. The upper hand then moves forcefully downward, striking its fingertips across those of the lower hand as it passes by. The "F" hands may also be used. *Cf.* UNFAIR 2, UNJUSTIFIED.

UNJUSTIFIED (ŭn jŭs′ tĭ fīd), *adj.* See UNJUST.

UNLIKE (ŭn līk′), *adj.* (Separated; different.) The "D" hands, palms down, are crossed at the index fingers or are held side by side. They separate once or a number of times. *Cf.* ASSORTED, DIFFERENCE, DIFFERENT, DIVERSE 1, DIVERSITY 1, VARIED.

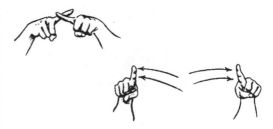

UNNECESSARY (un nes′ ə ser′ ə), *adj.* (Nothing there, in the area of necessity.) The sign for NECESSARY: the downturned curved index finger is thrust down and then the hand opens with a flourish to the palm-up position.

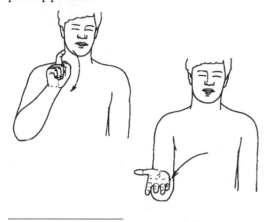

UNSKILLED (ŭn skĭld′), *(colloq.)*, *adj.* (The thickness of the skull is indicated, to stress intellectual density.) With the thumb of the right "C" hand grasped by the closed left hand, the right hand is swung away from the body, describing a small arc as it moves. The space between the curved right fingers and the closed left hand indicates the thickness of the skull. *Cf.* DUMB 2, MORON, STUPID 2, THICK-SKULLED.

UNSURE (ŭn shŏŏr′), *adj.* (On a fence; uncertain.) The downturned right "V" hand straddles the index finger edge of the left "B" hand, whose palm faces right. The right hand sways slightly, from left to right. *Cf.* INDECISION, UNCERTAIN, WAVER 1.

UNTIL (ŭn tĭl′), *prep.* (From one point to the next.) The extended right index finger moves forward slowly and comes to rest on the tip of the extended, upturned left index finger. *Cf.* TILL, TO 1, TOWARD 1, UNTO, UP TO, UP TO NOW.

UNTO (ŭn′ tōō), *prep.* See UNTIL.

UPHOLD (ŭp hōld′), *v.*, -HELD, -HOLDING. (Holding up.) The right "S" hand pushes up the left "S" hand. *Cf.* ENDORSE 1, MAINTENANCE, SUPPORT 1, SUSTAIN, SUSTENANCE.

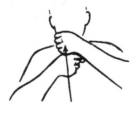

UPSET (up set′), *adj.*, *v.* (The stomach is turned upside down.) The downturned open right hand is positioned horizontally across the stomach. It flips over so that it is now palm up.

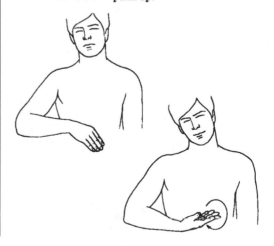

UP TO *prep. phrase.* (From one point to the next.) The extended right index finger moves forward slowly and comes to rest on the tip of the extended, upturned left index finger. *Cf.* TILL, TO 1, TOWARD 1, UNTIL, UNTO, UP TO NOW.

UP TO NOW *adv. phrase.* See UP TO.

UP TO YOU *phrase.* (Think by yourself.) The sign for THINK is made: the right index finger touches the center of the forehead. The SELF sign follows: the upturned right thumb moves straight forward from the signer toward the person addressed. *Cf.* DO AS ONE WISHES.

URGE 1 (ûrj), *v.,* URGED, URGING, *n.* (Pushing forward.) Both "5" hands are held, palms out, the right fingers facing right and the left fingers left. The hands move straight forward in a series of short movements. *Cf.* ENCOURAGE, MOTIVATE, MOTIVATION.

URGE 2, *v.* (Shaking someone, to implant one's will into another.) Both "A" hands, palms facing, are held before the chest, the left slightly in front of the right. In this position the hands move back and forth a short distance. *Cf.* COAX, PERSUADE, PERSUASION, PROD.

URINATE 1 (yŏŏr′ ə năt), *v.* The right index finger, held pointing forward at the groin area, shakes up and down. Used for the male only.

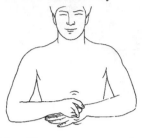

URINATE 2, *v.* (The letter "P," for "pee.") The middle finger of the right "P" hand brushes off the tip of the nose. *Cf.* PENIS 2, URINATION.

URINATION (yŏŏr′ ə nā shən), *n.* See URINATE 2.

US (ŭs), *pron.* (The letter "U"; an encompassing gesture.) The right "U" hand, palm facing the body, swings from right shoulder to left shoulder.

USE (*n.* ūs; *v.* ūz), USED, USING. (The letter "U.") The right "U" hand describes a small clockwise circle. *Cf.* CONSUME 2, USED, USEFUL, UTILIZE, WEAR 2.

USED (yōōzd), *v.* See USE.

USEFUL (yōōs′ fəl), *adj.* See USE.

USE UP (yōōz up), *v. phrase.* (Pull something off the hand.) The right "C" hand, palm facing left, is placed on the upturned left hand. The right hand, moving right, quickly leaves the left, while closing into a fist.

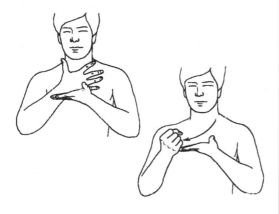

USHER (ŭsh′ ər), *v.,* -ERED, -ERING. (Opening or leading the way toward something.) The open right hand, held up before the body, sweeps down in an arc and over toward the left side of the chest, ending in the palm-up position. Reversing the movement gives the passive form of the verb, except that the hand does not arc upward but rather simply moves outward in a small arc from the body. *Cf.* INVITE, WELCOME.

US TWO *phrase.* (Two people interacting.) The right "V" hand, palm up and fingers pointing left, is swung in and out to and from the chest. *Cf.* BOTH OF US, WE TWO.

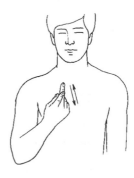

UTILIZE (ū′ tə līz′), *v.,* -LIZED, -LIZING. See USE.

UZI (ew zē), *n.* (A machine gun held in one hand.) The signer, holding an imaginary small machine gun in one hand, takes aim and the arm and body shake repeatedly from the weapon's recoil.

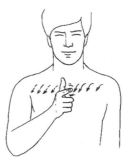

V

VACANCY (vā′ kən sǐ), *n.* (Devoid of everything on the surface.) The middle finger of the downturned right "5" hand sweeps over the back of the downturned left hand, from wrist to knuckles, and continues beyond a bit. *Cf.* BARE, EMPTY, NAKED, NUDE, OMISSION, VACANT, VOID.

VACANT (vā′ kənt), *adj.* See VACANCY.

VACATION (vā kā′ shən), *n.* (A position of idleness.) With thumbs tucked in the armpits, the remaining fingers of both hands wiggle. *Cf.* HOLIDAY, IDLE, LEISURE, RETIRE.

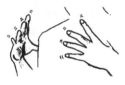

VACUUM CLEANER (vak′ yōōm), *n.* (Sucking up the dirt.) The extended right fingers are positioned above the upturned left palm. The right fingers move back and forth across the palm, while the fingers open and close very rapidly.

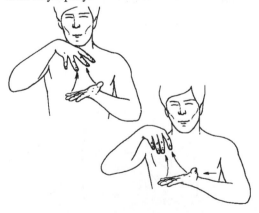

VAGINA (və jī′ nə), *n.* (The shape of the vagina's opening.) The right index and thumb, touching the left index and thumb, are held pointing forward.

VAGUE (vāg), *adj.* (One hand obscures the other.) The "5" hands are held up, palm against palm in front of the body. The right hand moves in a slow, continuous clockwise circle over the left palm, as the signer tries to see between the fingers. *Cf.* BLURRY, UNCLEAR.

VAIN (vān), *adj.* (All eyes upon oneself.) The "V" hands, held on either side of the face with palms facing the body, swing back and forth simultaneously, pivoting at the wrists. *Cf.* VAINLY, VANITY.

VAINLY (vān′ lǐ), *adv.* See VAIN.

VALID (văl′ ĭd), *adj.* (Coming forth directly from the lips; true.) The index finger of the right "D" hand, palm facing left, is placed against the lips. It moves up an inch or two and then describes a small arc forward and away from the lips. *Cf.* ABSOLUTE, ABSOLUTELY, ACTUAL, ACTUALLY, AUTHENTIC, CERTAIN, CERTAINLY, FIDELITY, FRANKLY, GENUINE, INDEED, POSITIVE 1, POSITIVELY, REAL, REALLY, SINCERE 2, SURE, SURELY, TRUE, TRULY, TRUTH, VERILY.

VALISE (və lēs′), *n.* (The natural sign.) The downturned right "S" hand grasps an imaginary piece of luggage and shakes it up and down slightly, as if testing its weight. *Cf.* BAGGAGE, LUGGAGE, SUITCASE.

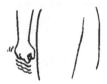

VALUABLE (văl′ yōō ə bəl, văl′ yə bəl), *adj.* Both "F" hands, palms facing each other, move apart, up, and together in a smooth elliptical fashion, coming together at the tips of the thumbs and index fingers of both hands. *Cf.* IMPORTANT, SIGNIFICANCE 1, SIGNIFICANT, VALUE, VITAL 1, WORTH, WORTHWHILE, WORTHY.

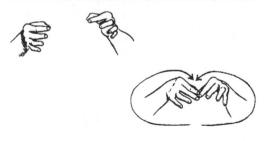

VALUE (văl′ ū), *n.* See VALUABLE.

VAMPIRE (vam′ pīr), *n.* (Biting the neck.) The right curved thumb, index, and middle fingers make a "bite" at the right side of the neck.

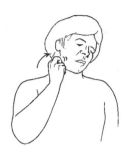

VANILLA (və nil′ ə), *adj.* (The letter "V.") The outstretched right "V" is shaken slightly.

VANISH (văn′ ĭsh), *v.*, -ISHED, -ISHING. (A disappearance.) The right open hand, palm facing the body, is held by the left hand and is drawn down and out, ending in a position with fingers drawn together. The left hand, meanwhile, may close into a position with fingers also drawn together. *Cf.* ABSENCE, ABSENT, DISAPPEAR, GONE 1.

VANITY (văn′ ə tǐ), *n.* (All eyes upon oneself.) The "V" hands, held on either side of the face with palms facing the body, swing back and forth simultaneously, pivoting at the wrists. *Cf.* VAIN, VAINLY.

VARIED (vâr′ ĭd), *adj.* (Separated many times; different.) The "D" hands, palms down, are crossed at the index fingers or are held side by side. They separate and return to their initial position a number of times. *Cf.* ASSORTED, DIFFERENCE, DIFFERENT, DIVERSE 1, DIVERSITY 1, UNLIKE.

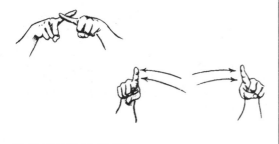

VARIOUS (vâr′ ĭ əs), *adj.* (The fingertips indicate many things.) Both hands, in the "D" position, palms out and index fingertips touching, are drawn apart. As they move apart, the index fingers wiggle up and down. *Cf.* DIVERSE 2, DIVERSITY 2, VARY.

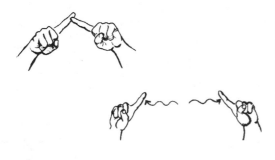

VARY (vâr′ ĭ), *v.,* VARIED, VARYING. See VARIOUS.

VCR *n.* (A fingerspelled loan sign.) The signer fingerspells "V-C-R."

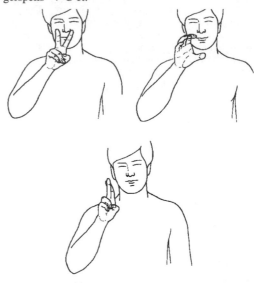

VEND (vĕnd), *v.,* VENDED, VENDING. (Transferring ownership of an object.) Both "AND" hands, fingers touching their respective thumbs, are held palms down before the body. The hands are pivoted simultaneously outward and away from the body, once or several times. *Cf.* SALE, SELL.

VENDER (vĕn′ dər), *n.* (Transferring ownership.) The sign for VEND is formed. The sign for INDIVIDUAL is then made: both open hands, palms facing each other, move down the sides of the body, tracing its outline to the hips. *Cf.* MERCHANT, SALESMAN, SELLER.

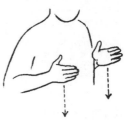

VENETIAN BLINDS *n.* (The slats.) Both hands, palms down at chest level, are positioned with the right above the left, left fingers pointing right and right fingers pointing left. They both move down, while each wrist swivels back and forth, imitating the opening and closing of the blinds.

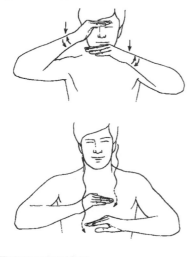

VERB (vûrb), *n.* (The letter "V.") The right "V" hand, palm facing the body and fingers pointing left, moves across the mouth from left to right.

VERBAL (vûr′ bəl), *adj.* (Words tumbling from the mouth.) The right index finger, pointing left, describes a continuous small circle in front of the mouth. *Cf.* DISCOURSE, HEARING, MAINTAIN 2, MENTION, REMARK, SAID, SAY, SPEAK, SPEECH 1, STATE 1, TALK 1, TELL.

VERDICT (vûr′ dĭkt), *n.* (The mind stops wavering, and the pros and cons are resolved.) The right index finger touches the forehead, the sign for THINK, *q.v.* Both "F" hands, palms facing each other and fingers pointing straight out, then drop down simultaneously. The sign for JUDGE, *q.v.,* explains the rationale behind the movement of the two hands here. *Cf.* DECIDE, DECISION, DETERMINE, MAKE UP ONE'S MIND, MIND 5, RESOLVE.

VERILY (věr′ ə lĭ), *adv.* (Coming forth directly from the lips; true.) The index finger of the right "D" hand, palm facing left, is placed against the lips. It moves up an inch or two and then describes a small arc forward and away from the lips. *Cf.* ABSOLUTE, ABSOLUTELY, ACTUAL, ACTUALLY, AUTHENTIC, CERTAIN, CERTAINLY, FIDELITY, FRANKLY, GENUINE, INDEED, POSITIVE 1, POSITIVELY, REAL, REALLY, SINCERE 2, SURE, SURELY, TRUE, TRULY, TRUTH, VALID.

VERSUS (vûr′ səs), *prep.* (Two individuals pitted against each other.) The hands are held in the "A" position, thumbs pointing straight up, palms facing the body. They come together forcefully, moving down a bit as they do, and the knuckles of one hand strike those of the other. *Cf.* CHALLENGE, GAME, OPPORTUNITY 2.

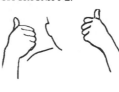

VERTICAL (vûr′ ti kəl), *adj.* (The upright or vertical position.) The outstretched right hand, palm facing left, moves straight up and down. Alternately, the "V" hand moves straight up, either independently or from an initial position on the upturned left palm.

VERY (vĕr′ ĭ), *adv.* (The "V" hands, with the sign for MUCH.) The fingertips of the "V" hands are placed together, and then moved apart.

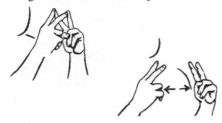

VETERINARIAN (vet′ ər ə när′ ē ən), *n.* (A finger-spelled loan sign.) The signer spells out "V-E-T" with the fingers.

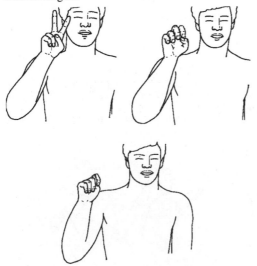

VICINITY (vĭ sin′ ə tĭ), *n.* (One hand is near the other.) The left hand, cupped, fingers together, is held before the chest, palm facing the body. The right hand, also cupped, fingers together, moves a very short distance back and forth, as it is held in front of the left. *Cf.* CLOSE (TO) 2, NEAR 1, NEIGHBOR, NEIGHBORHOOD.

VICTORY 1 (vĭk′ tə rĭ), *n.* (Waving of flags.) Both upright hands, grasping imaginary flags, wave them in small circles. *Cf.* CELEBRATE, CELEBRATION, CHEER, REJOICE, WIN 1.

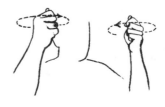

VICTORY 2, *n.* (Waving a flag.) The right "A" hand goes through the natural movement of waving a flag in circular fashion. Preceding this, the right hand may go through the motion of grabbing the flagstaff out of the left hand. *Cf.* EXULTATION, TRIUMPH 1, WIN 2.

VIDEOTAPE (vid′ ē ō tãp), *n., v.* (The turning of the tape.) The left hand is held open, palm facing right. The right "V" hand makes a circle around the left palm, ending in the letter "T," and resting on the palm.

VIE 1 (vī), *v.*, VIED, VYING. (Two opponents come together.) Both hands are closed, with thumbs pointing straight up and palms facing the body. From their initial position about a foot apart, the hands are brought together sharply, so that the knuckles strike. The hands, as they are drawn together, also move down a bit, so that they describe a "V." *Cf.* COMPETE 1, COMPETITION 1, RACE 1, RIVAL 2, RIVALRY 1.

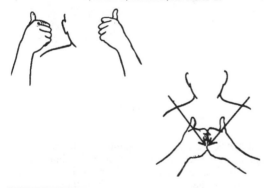

VIE 2, *v.* (Opposing objects.) The "A" hands are held side by side before the chest, palms facing each other and thumbs pointing forward. In this position the hands move alternately back and forth, toward and away from the body. *Cf.* COMPETE 2, COMPETITION 2, RACE 2, RIVAL 3, RIVALRY 2.

VIE 3, *v.* (The changing fortunes of competitors.) The "A" hands are held facing each other, thumbs pointing up in front of the body. Both hands are moved alternately backward and forward past each other several times. *Cf.* RACE 3, RIVAL 4, RIVALRY 3.

VIEW (vū), *n., v.*, VIEWED, VIEWING. (Look around.) The sign for LOOK is made: the right "V" hand, palm facing the body, is placed so that the fingertips are just under the eyes. Then both "V" hands are held with palms down and fingers pointing forward in front of the body. In this position the hands move simultaneously from side to side several times. *Cf.* VISION 1.

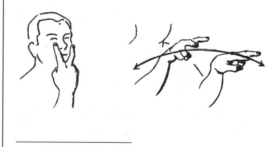

VIOLATE (vī′ ə lāt′), *v.*, -LATED, -LATING. (An encroachment; parrying a knife thrust.) The left "A" hand is held palm toward the body, knuckles facing right. The extended thumb of the right "A" hand is brought sharply over the back of the left. *Cf.* DANGER, DANGEROUS, INJURE 2, PERIL, TRESPASS.

VIRGIN 1 (vûr' jin), *n.* The fingers of the right "V" hand are placed at the right corner of the mouth.

VIRGIN 2, *n., adj.* (One who has never had intercourse.) The sign for NEVER: the outstretched hand moves down in an "S" curve. This is followed by INTERCOURSE: both "V" hands are held palms facing, with the right above the left. The right hand comes down on the left repeatedly.

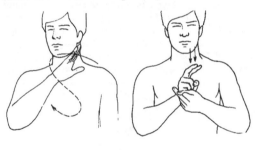

VIRGIN 3, *sl. n., adj.* (CHERRY, an extended slang term for hymen.) The sign for CHERRY is made: the fingertips of the right hand grasp the end of the left little finger and twist back and forth as if loosening a cherry from a branch. *Cf.* BERRY, CHERRY.

VISION 1 (vĭzh' ən), *n.* (Look around.) The sign for LOOK is made: the right "V" hand, palm facing the body, is placed so that the fingertips are just under the eyes. Then both "V" hands are held with palms down and fingers pointing forward in front of the body. In this position the hands move simultaneously from side to side several times. *Cf.* VIEW.

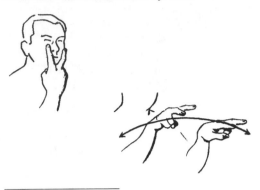

VISION 2, *n.* (The vision is directed forward, into the distance.) The right "V" fingertips are placed under the eyes, with palm facing the body. The hand is then swung around and forward, moving under the down-turned prone left hand and continuing forward and upward. *Cf.* FORECAST, FORESEE, FORETELL, PERCEIVE 2, PREDICT, PROPHECY, PROPHESY, PROPHET.

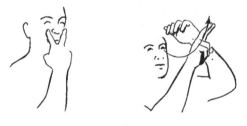

VISION 3, *n.* (A sudden opening of the mind.) The sign for DREAM is made: the tip of the right index is placed on the forehead. Then both "S" hands are held in front of the forehead, the left in front of the right. They open into the "C" position, as the hands separate. The sign for DREAM may be omitted.

VISIT (vĭz′ĭt), *n., v.,* -ITED, -ITING. (The letter "V"; random movement, *i.e.,* moving around as in visiting.) The "V" hands, palms facing, move alternately in clockwise circles out from the chest.

VISUAL AID (vizh′ ōō əl ād′), *n.* (To see and to help.) The index and middle fingers of the right hand, palm facing the body, move away from the eyes. The left upturned open hand then pushes up the right fist.

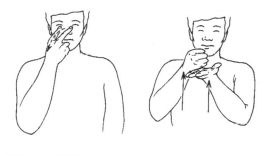

VITAL 1 (vī′ təl), *adj.* Both "F" hands, palms facing each other, move apart, up, and together in a smooth elliptical fashion, coming together at the tips of the thumbs and index fingers of both hands. *Cf.* IMPORTANT, SIGNIFICANCE 1, SIGNIFICANT, VALUABLE, VALUE, WORTH, WORTHWHILE, WORTHY.

VITAL 2, *adj.* (Being pinned down.) The right hand, in the "X" position, palm down, moves forcefully up and down once or twice. An expression of determination is frequently assumed. *Cf.* HAVE TO, MUST,

NECESSARY 1, NECESSITY, NEED 1, OUGHT TO, SHOULD.

VOCATION (vō kā′ shən), *n.* (Striking an anvil.) Both "S" hands are held palms down. The right hand strikes against the back of the left a number of times. *Cf.* JOB, LABOR, OCCUPATION, TASK, TOIL, TRAVAIL, WORK.

VOID (void), *adj., n.* (Devoid of everything on the surface.) The middle finger of the downturned right "5" hand sweeps over the back of the downturned left "A" or "S" hand, from wrist to knuckles, and continues beyond a bit. *Cf.* BARE, EMPTY, NAKED, NUDE, OMISSION, VACANCY, VACANT.

VOLCANO (vol kā′ nō), *n.* (The shape and the eruption.) Both "V" hands move up, coming together to form a peak. The hands are then closed and opened explosively, describing the eruption.

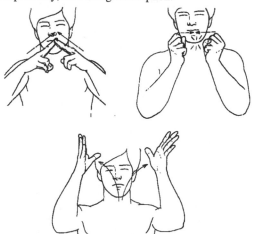

VOLUME (vol′ yoom), *n.* (The "V" letters; an area is indicated.) Both upturned "V" hands, palms facing out, move forward, executing a circle, so that they now face the signer.

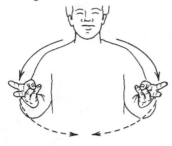

VOLUNTEER (vŏl′ ən tir′), *n., v.,* -TEERED, -TEERING. (Bringing oneself forward.) The right index finger and thumb grasp the clothing near the right shoulder (often the lapel of a suit or the collar of a dress) and tug it up and down gently several times. Sometimes one tug only is used. *Cf.* CANDIDATE.

VOTE 1 (vōt), *n., v.,* VOTED, VOTING. (Placing a ballot in a box.) The right hand, holding an imaginary ballot between the thumb and index finger, places it into an imaginary box formed by the left "O" hand, palm facing right. *Cf.* ELECT, ELECTION.

VOTE 2, *n., v.* (Placing the ballot in the box.) The thumb and index finger drop an imaginary ballot into a slot.

VOW (vou), *v.,* VOWED, VOWING. (The arm is raised.) The right index finger is placed at the lips. The right arm is then raised, palm out and elbow resting on the back of the left hand. *Cf.* GUARANTEE, LOYAL, OATH, PLEDGE, PROMISE 1, SWEAR 1, SWORN, TAKE OATH.

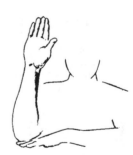

W

WAFFLE (wŏf′ əl), *n.* (The grid pattern.) Both hands face each other, fingertips forward and interlocked, right above left. The right hand moves down and back up a number of times, representing the cover of the waffle grill.

WAGE(S) (wāj), *n.* (Gathering in.) The right "5" hand, its little finger edge touching the upturned left palm, is drawn in an arc toward the body, closing into the "S" position as it sweeps over the base of the left hand. *Cf.* ACCUMULATE, COLLECT, EARN, SALARY 1.

WAGON (wăg′ ən), *n.* (Miming.) The signer pulls an imaginary wagon with both hands.

WAIT (wāt), *n.*, *v.*, WAITED, WAITING. (The fingers wiggle with impatience.) The upturned "5" hands are positioned with the right behind the left. The fingers of both hands wiggle.

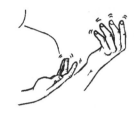

WAITER (wā′ tər), *n.* (Passing the dishes, one by one.) The upturned "5" hands move alternately toward and away from the chest. *Cf.* SERVANT, SERVE 2, SERVICE, WAITRESS.

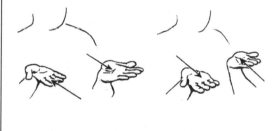

WAITRESS (wā′ trĭs), *n.* See WAITER.

WAIVE (wāv), *v.* (A wiped off and clean slate.) The right hand wipes off the left palm several times.

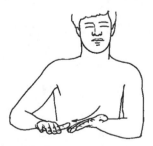

WAKE UP (wāk), *v. phrase.* (Opening the eyes.) Both hands are closed, with thumb and index finger of each hand held together, extended, and placed at the corners of the closed eyes. Slowly they separate, and the eyes open. *Cf.* AWAKE, AWAKEN.

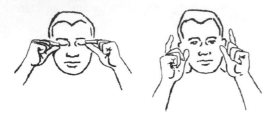

WALK (wôk), *n., v.,* WALKED, WALKING. (The movement of the feet.) The downturned "5" hands move alternately toward and away from the chest. *Cf.* STEP.

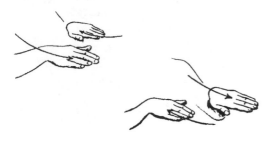

WALKIE-TALKIE (wô′ kē tô′ kē), *n.* (The shape at the ear.) The "Y" hand is held thumb against mouth, and then it moves up so that the thumb is against the ear. The movement is repeated.

WALK TO *v. phrase.* (The fingers do the walking.) The downturned index and middle fingers of either hand execute forward walking movement.

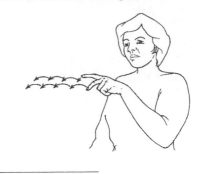

WALLET 1, (wol′ it), *n.* (Folding the wallet.) The two hands held with fingertips touching are brought together palm to palm and move flat against each other as if closing a wallet. This is a generic sign.

WALLET 2, *n.* (Placing the bills in.) The little finger edge of the open right hand, palm facing the body, is slipped into the space created by the thumb and other fingers of the left hand. The signer then mimes placing the wallet into a back pocket. *Cf.* BILLFOLD 1.

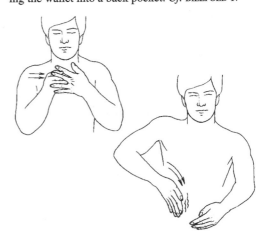

WANDER (wŏn' dər), v., -DERED, -DERING. (Random movement.) The right "D" hand, palm facing left, moves to and fro from right to left. Cf. ROAM.

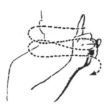

WANT (wŏnt, wônt), v., WANTED, WANTING. (Grasping something and pulling it in.) The upturned "5" hands, held side by side before the chest, close slightly into a grasping position as they move in toward the body. Cf. DESIRE 1, LONG 2, NEED 2, WILL 2, WISH 1.

WAR (wôr), n., v., WARRED, WARRING. (The contending armies.) The "4," "W," or "5" hands face each other, and move simultaneously from side to side, representing the successive advance and retreat of contending armed forces.

WARM (wôrm), adj., v., WARMED, WARMING. (The warmth of the breath is indicated.) The upturned cupped right hand is placed at the slightly open mouth. It moves up and away from the mouth, opening into the upturned "5" position, with fingers somewhat curved.

WARN (wôrn), v., WARNED, WARNING. (Tapping one to draw attention to danger.) The right hand taps the back of the left several times. Cf. ADMONISH, CAUTION, FOREWARN.

WAS (wŏz, wŭz; *unstressed* wəz), v. (Something past, behind.) The upraised right hand, in the "5" position with palm facing the body, is held just above the right shoulder and is thrown back over it. Cf. AGO, FORMERLY, ONCE UPON A TIME, PAST, PREVIOUS, PREVIOUSLY, WERE.

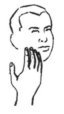 

WASH 1 (wŏsh, wôsh), n., v., WASHED, WASHING. (Rubbing the clothes.) The knuckles of the "A" hands rub against one another, in circles.

WASH 2, v. (The natural sign.) The signer goes through the motions of wiping his face with a towel. Cf. TOWEL 1.

WASH 3, *v.* (The natural sign.) The closed hands move up and down against the chest as if scrubbing it. *Cf.* BATH, BATHE.

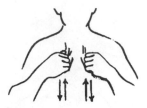

WASH DISHES *v. phrase.* (The natural sign.) The downturned right "5" hand describes a clockwise circle as it moves over the upturned left "5" hand. *Cf.* DISHWASHING.

WASHING MACHINE *n.* (The clothes are tumbled around.) The cupped, open hands, palms facing and one above the other, execute opposing circular movements.

WASTE 1 (wāst), *n., v.,* WASTED, WASTING. (Repeated giving forth.) The back of the upturned right hand, thumb touching fingertips, is placed in the upturned left palm. The right hand moves off and away from the left once or several times, each time opening into the "5" position, palm up. *Cf.* EXTRAVAGANT, SPEND 1, SQUANDER 1.

WASTE 2, *n., v.,* (The "W" is indicated.) The same movement as in WASTE 1 is used, except that the right hand assumes the "W" position and keeps it.

WATCH 1 (wŏch), *v.,* WATCHED, WATCHING. (Careful, constant vision.) The downturned, left "V" hand sweeps back and forth from side to side beneath the downturned, right "V" hand, which remains stationary and pointing forward.

WATCH 2, *n., v.* (The eyesight is directed forward.) The right "V" hand, palm facing the body, is placed so that the fingertips are just under the eyes. The hand swings around and out, so that the fingertips are now pointing forward. *Cf.* LOOK 1, PERCEIVE 1, PERCEPTION, SEE, SIGHT.

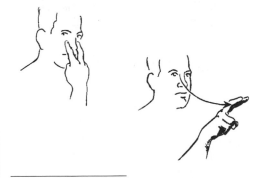

WATCH 3, *n.* (Time by the clock, indicated by the ticking of the clock or watch.) The curved right index finger taps the back of the left wrist several times. *Cf.* TIME 1.

WATCH 4, *n.* (The shape of the wristwatch.) The thumb and index finger of the right hand, forming a circle, are placed on the back of the left wrist. *Cf.* WRISTWATCH.

WATER (wô′ tər, wŏt′ ər), *n.* (The letter "W" at the mouth, as in drinking water.) The right "W" hand, palm facing left, touches the lips a number of times.

WAVER 1 (wā′ vər), *v.,* -VERED, -VERING. (On a fence; uncertain.) The downturned right "V" hand straddles the index finger edge of the left "B" hand, whose palm faces right. The right hand sways slightly back and forth, from left to right. *Cf.* INDECISION, UNCERTAIN, UNSURE.

WAVER 2, *v.* (The wavering.) The downturned "S" hands swing alternately up and down. *Cf.* DISBELIEF 2, DOUBT 2, DOUBTFUL.

WAVER 3 *v.* (On a fence; uncertain.) The downturned right "V" palm faces right. The right hand sways slightly, from left to right.

WAY 1 (wā), *n.* (The winding movement.) Both hands, palms facing and fingers together and extended straight out, move in unison away from the body, in a winding manner. *Cf.* CORRIDOR, HALL, HALLWAY, MANNER 2, METHOD, OPPORTUNITY 3, PATH, ROAD, STREET, TRAIL.

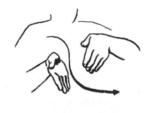

WAY 2, *n.* (The letter "W.") The sign for WAY 1 is made, but with the "W" hands.

WE 1 (wē; *unstressed* wĭ), *pron.* (An encompassing movement.) The right index finger points down as it swings over from the right shoulder to the left shoulder.

WE 2, *pron.* (The letter "W.") The right "W" hand, fingers pointing up, goes through the same motion as in WE 1.

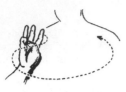

WEAK (wĕk), *adj.* (The knees buckle.) The right "V" hand is placed with fingertips resting in the upturned left palm. The knuckles of the "V" fingers buckle a bit. This motion may be repeated. *Cf.* FAINT, FEEBLE, FRAIL, WEAKNESS.

WEAKNESS (wĕk′ nĭs), *n.* See WEAK.

WEALTH (wĕlth), *n.* (A pile of money.) The sign for MONEY is made: the back of the upturned right hand, whose thumb and fingertips are all touching, is placed in the upturned left palm. The right hand then moves straight up, as it opens into the "5" position, palm facing down and fingers somewhat curved. *Cf.* RICH, WEALTHY.

WEALTHY (wĕl′ thĭ), *adj.* See WEALTH.

WEAR 1 (wâr), *n. v.,* WORE, WORN, WEARING. (Draping the clothes on the body.) With fingertips resting on the chest, both hands move down simul-

taneously. The action is repeated. *Cf.* CLOTHES, CLOTHING, DRESS, FROCK, GARMENT, GOWN, SHIRT, SUIT.

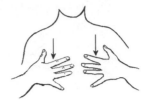

WEAR 2, *v.* (To use; the letter "U.") The right "U" hand describes a small clockwise circle. *Cf.* CONSUME 2, USE, USED, USEFUL, UTILIZE.

WEATHER (wĕth′ ər), *n.* (The letter "W.") The right "W" hand, palm out, moves straight down before the body, trembling slightly as it does.

WEDDING (wĕd′ ĭng), *n.* (A joining of hands.) The downturned "B" hands are joined together with a flourish.

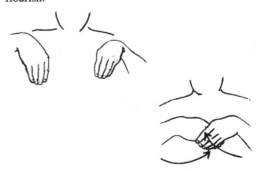

WEEK (wĕk), *n.* The upright, right "D" hand is placed palm-to-palm against the left "5" hand, whose palm faces right. The right "D" hand moves along the left palm from base to fingertips.

WEEP (wēp), *v.,* WEPT, WEEPING. (Tears streaming down the cheeks.) Both index fingers, in the "D" position, move down the cheeks, either once or several times. Sometimes one finger only is used. *Cf.* BAWL 1, CRY, TEAR 2, TEARDROP.

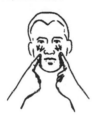

WEIGH 1 (wā), *v.,* WEIGHED, WEIGHING. (The balancing of the scale is described.) The fingers of the right "H" hand are centered on the left index finger and rocked back and forth. *Cf.* POUND 1, SCALE 1, WEIGHT.

WEIGH 2, *v.* (Turning thoughts over in the mind.) Both index fingers, pointing to the forehead, describe continuous alternating circles. *Cf.* CONSIDER 2, CONTEMPLATE, PONDER, SPECULATE 2, SPECULATION 2, WONDER 1.

WEIGHT (wāt), *n.* See WEIGH 1.

WEIGHTY (wā′ tĭ), *adj.* (The hands drop under a weight.) The upturned "5" hands, held before the chest, suddenly drop a short distance. *Cf.* HEAVY.

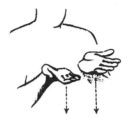

WEIRD (wĭrd), *adj.* (Something which distorts the vision.) The "C" hand describes a small arc in front of the face. *Cf.* CURIOUS 2, GROTESQUE, ODD, PECULIAR, QUEER, STRANGE.

WELCOME (wĕl′ kəm), *n., v.,* -COMED, -COMING. (Opening or leading the way toward something.) The open right hand, held up before the body, sweeps down in an arc and over toward the left side of the chest, ending in the palm-up position. Reversing the movement gives the passive form of the verb, except that the hand does not arc upward but rather simply moves outward in a small arc from the body. *Cf.* INVITE, USHER.

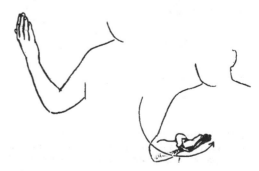

WELL 1 (wĕl), *adv.* (Tasting something, approving it, and offering it forward.) The fingertips of the right "5" hand are placed at the lips. The right hand then moves out and into a palm-up position on the upturned left palm. *Cf.* GOOD 1.

WELL 2, *adj.* (Strength emanating from the body.) Both "5" hands are placed palms against the chest. They move out and away, forcefully, closing and assuming the "S" position. *Cf.* BRAVE, BRAVERY, COURAGE, COURAGEOUS, FORTITUDE, HALE, HEALTH, HEALTHY, MIGHTY 2, STRENGTH, STRONG 2.

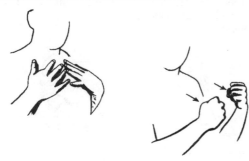

WELL 3, *interj.* (The natural sign, accompanied by a sigh.) With palms facing up, the signer heaves a distinct sigh, causing the shoulders to rise slightly. *Cf.* SO.

WE'LL SEE *phrase.* (Modified from the sign for SEE.) The index finger of the right "V" hand, palm facing left, is placed at the corner of the right eye. The hand makes several very small back and forth movements. This is often accompanied by a very slight nodding.

WERE (wûr, *unstressed* wər), *v.* (Something past, behind.) The upraised right hand, in the "5" position with palm facing the body, is held just above the right shoulder and is thrown back over it. *Cf.* AGO, FORMERLY, ONCE UPON A TIME, PAST, PREVIOUS, PREVIOUSLY, WAS.

WET (wĕt), *adj., n., v.,* WET or WETTED, WETTING. (The wetness.) The right fingertips touch the lips, and then the fingers of both hands open and close against the thumbs a number of times. *Cf.* DAMP, MOIST.

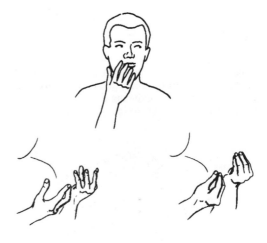

WE TWO *phrase.* (Two people interacting.) The right "V" hand, palm up and fingers pointing left, is swung in and out to and from the chest. *Cf.* BOTH OF US, US TWO.

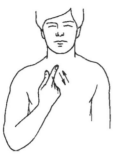

WHALE 1 (hwāl), *n.* (The blowhole.) The right hand, in the AND position, fingers pointing up, is placed on top of the head. It moves up off the head and opens into the "5" position, representing the whale blowing out through the blowhole.

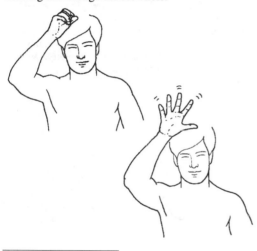

WHALE 2, *n.* (The letter "W"; the movement.) The right "W" hand makes a series of undulating dive movements in front of the downturned left arm, which represents the surface of the water.

W-H-A-T? *(colloq.), interj.* (A fingerspelled loan sign.) The letters "W-H-A-T" are spelled out rather slowly, but with force and deliberation, while the signer assumes a look of incredulity. This is the equivalent of a shouted interjection.

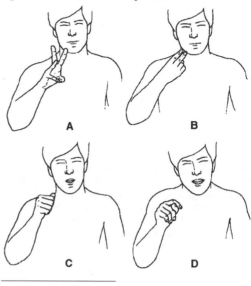

WHAT 1 (hwŏt, hwŭt; *unstressed* hwət), *pron., adj., adv., interj., conj.* (The finger passes over several specifics to bring out the concept of "which one?") The right index finger passes over the fingers of the upturned left "5" hand, from index to little finger.

WHAT 2, *pron., adj., adv., interj., conj.* (Throwing out the hands as a gesture of inquiry.) Both upturned open hands move slightly back and forth in front of the chest. The signer assumes a look of wonderment, emphasized by slightly upturned shoulders, raised eyebrows, or furrowed brow.

WHAT FOR? *(colloq.), phrase.* (For—For—For?) The sign for FOR is made repeatedly: the right index finger, resting on the right temple, leaves its position and moves straight out in front of the face. The sign is usually accompanied by an expression of inquiry, or annoyance.

WHAT IS THE PRICE? (Amount of money is indicated.) The sign for MONEY is made: the upturned right hand, grasping some imaginary bills, is brought down into the upturned left palm a number of times. The right hand then moves straight up, opening into the "5" position, palm up. *Cf.* HOW MUCH MONEY?, PRICE 1.

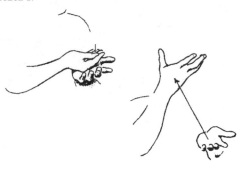

WHAT'S NEW? 1 (The feelings well up and come out.) The open hands are placed near the chest, with middle fingers resting on the chest. Both hands move up and out simultaneously. A happy expression is assumed. *Cf.* THRILL 2, WHAT'S UP?

WHAT'S NEW? 2, *phrase.* (What are your feelings?) Both middle fingers quickly sweep up and out from the chest. The eyebrows are raised in inquiry. *Cf.* HOW ARE YOU?

WHAT'S UP? See WHAT'S NEW? 1

WHAT TO DO? *(colloq.), phrase.* (Do—Do—Do?) This is a modified fingerspelled loan sign. The signer makes palm-up "D"s with both hands. These quickly assume the "O" position, with the palms remaining up. This is repeated several times, quickly, with an expression of despair or inquiry.

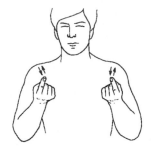

WHEELBARROW (hwēl′ bar′ ō), *n.* (Holding the handles and moving forward.) Grasping an imaginary pair of handles and lifting with effort, the signer moves slightly forward. *Cf.* PUSHCART.

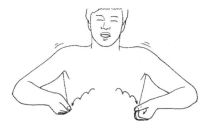

WHEELCHAIR (hwēl′ châr), *n*. (The wheels.) The signer makes simultaneous large forward circles at the sides of the body.

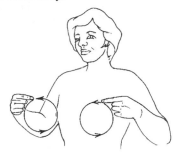

WHEN (hwĕn), *adv., conj., n.* (Fixing a point in time.) The left "D" hand is held upright, palm facing the body. The right index finger describes a clockwise circle around the left, coming to rest on the left index fingertip.

WHERE 1 (hwâr), *adv.* (Alternate directions are indicated.) The right "D" hand, with palm out and index finger straight or slightly curved, moves a short distance back and forth, from left to right.

WHERE 2, *adv.* The open "5" hands, palms up and fingers slightly curved, move back and forth in front of the body, the right hand to the right and the left hand to the left. *Cf.* HERE.

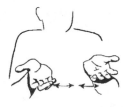

WHEREVER (hwâr ĕv′ ər), *conj.* Both hands, in the "5" position, are held before the chest, fingertips facing each other. With an alternate back-and-forth movement, the fingertips are made to strike each other. *Cf.* ANYHOW, ANYWAY, DESPITE, DOESN'T MATTER, HOWEVER 2, INDIFFERENCE, INDIFFERENT, IN SPITE OF, MAKE NO DIFFERENCE, NEVERTHELESS, NO MATTER.

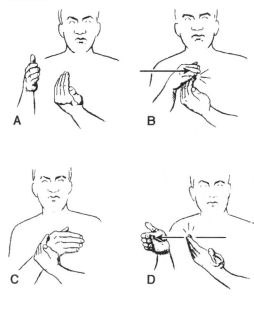

A   B

C   D

WHETHER (hwĕth′ ər), *conj.* (Considering one thing against another.) The "A" hands, palms facing and thumbs pointing straight up, move alternately up and down before the chest. *Cf.* EITHER 3, OR, WHICH.

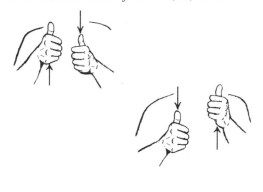

WHICH (hwĭch), *pron. (esp. interrog. pron.), adj.* See WHETHER.

WHILE (hwīl), *conj. only.* (Parallel time.) Both "D" hands, palms down, move forward in unison, away from the body. They may move straight forward or may follow a slight upward arc. *Cf.* DURING, MEANTIME.

WHILE AGO, A 1, *phrase.* (The slight movement represents a slight amount of time.) With the closed right hand held with knuckles against the right cheek, the thumbtip flicks off the tip of the curved index finger a number of times. The eyes squint a bit and the lips are drawn out in a slight smile. The hand remains against the cheek during the flicking movement. Sometimes, instead of the flicking movement, the tip of the curved index finger scratches slightly up and down against the cheek. In this case, the palm faces back toward the shoulder. The same expression is used as in the flicking movement. *Cf.* RECENT, RECENTLY.

WHILE AGO, A 2, *phrase.* (Time moved backward a bit.) The right "D" hand, palm facing the body, is placed in the palm of the left hand, which is facing right. The right hand swings back a bit toward the body, with the index finger describing an arc. *Cf.* FEW SECONDS AGO, JUST A MOMENT AGO.

WHIP (hwĭp), *n., v.,* WHIPPED, WHIPPING. (The natural sign.) The left hand is held in a fist before the face, as if grasping something or someone. The right hand, at the same time, is held as if grasping a stick or whip; it strikes repeatedly at the imaginary object or person dangling from the left hand. *Cf.* BEAT 1.

WHISKEY (hwĭs′ kĭ), *n.* (The size of the jigger is indicated.) The right hand, with index and little fingers extended and the remaining fingers held against the palm by the thumb, strikes the back of the downturned "S" hand several times. *Cf.* ALCOHOL, LIQUOR 1.

WHISPER 1 (hwĭs′ pər), *n., v.* (Two people talk back and forth.) The right index and middle fingers rest on the lips. They individually go back and forth repeatedly striking the lips.

WHISPER 2, *n., v.* (Covering the mouth.) Cupping the hand over the mouth, the signer leans to one side, as if imparting private information to someone.

WHISTLE (hwis' əl), *n., v.* (Using the fingers to whistle.) The index and middle fingers, or the index and little fingers, are placed in the mouth and the signer mimes whistling.

WHO (hōō), *pron.* (The pursed lips are indicated.) The right index finger traces a small counterclockwise circle in front of the lips, which are pursed in the enunciation of the word. *Cf.* WHOM.

WHOLE (hōl), *adj., n.* (Encompassing; a gathering together.) Both hands are held in the right angle position, palms facing the body, and the right hand in front of the left. The right hand makes a sweeping outward movement around the left, and comes to rest with the back of the right hand resting in the left

palm. *Cf.* ALL, ENTIRE, UNIVERSAL.

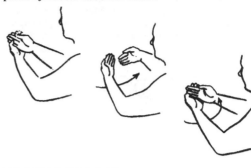

WHOLE (THE) *n.* (An inclusion, in the sense of a total number.) The left hand is held in the "C" position, fingers pointing right. The right hand, in the "5" position, fingers facing out from the body, palm down, is held above the left. With a horizontal swing to the right, the right hand describes an arc, as the fingers close and are thrust into the left "C" hand, which closes over it. *Cf.* INCLUDE, INCLUSIVE.

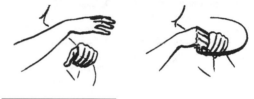

WHOM (hōōm), *pron.* See WHO.

WHOOPEE! (hwōō' pē), *interj.* (Jumping up and down.) The downturned right index and middle fingers "jump" up and down repeatedly from the upturned left palm. The signer assumes an expression of unbridled glee.

WHORE (hōr), *n.* (The blood rushes up the cheek in shame—several times for emphasis.) The curved back of the right hand, placed against the right cheek, moves up and off the cheek several times. *Cf.* PROSTITUTE.

WHOSE (hōōz), *pron.* (Who; outstretched open hand signifies possession, as if pressing an item against the chest of the person spoken to.) The sign for WHO is made: the right index finger traces a small counterclockwise circle in front of the lips, which are pursed in the enunciation of the word. Then the right "5" hand, palm facing out, moves straight out toward the person spoken to or about.

WHY (hwī), *adv., n., interj.* (Reason—coming from the mind—modified by the letter "Y," the phonetic equivalent of WHY.) The fingertips of the right hand, palm facing the body, are placed against the forehead. The right hand then moves down and away from the forehead, assuming the "Y" position, palm still facing the body. Expression is an important indicator of the context in which this sign is used. Thus, as an interjection, a severe expression is assumed; while as an adverb or a noun, the expression is blank or inquisitive.

WIDE (wīd), *adj.* (The width is indicated.) The open hands, fingers pointing out and palms facing each other, separate from their initial position an inch or two apart. *Cf.* BROAD, WIDTH.

WIDTH (wĭdth), *n.* See WIDE.

WIFE (wīf), *n.* (A female whose hand is clasped in marriage.) The FEMALE root sign is made: the thumb of the right "A" hand moves down along the right jawbone, almost to the chin. The hands are then clasped together, right above left.

WIGWAM (wig' wom), *n.* (The letter "W"; the sloping top.) Both "W" hands form the top. They move down, in the shape of a pyramid.

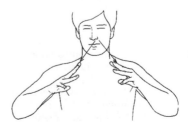

WILD (wīld), *adj.* (The "W"s; the mind is in a state of disarray.) Both "W" hands, palms facing, describe alternate clockwise circles at the temples. This sign should be accompanied by an appropriate look of agitation, or a threatening look.

WILL 1 (wĭl), *v.* (Something ahead or in the future.) The upright, open right hand, palm facing left, moves straight out and slightly up from a position beside the right temple. *Cf.* FUTURE, IN THE FUTURE, LATER 2, LATER ON, SHALL, WOULD.

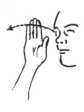

WILL 2, *n.* (Grasping something and pulling it in.) The upturned "5" hands, held side by side before the chest, close slightly into a grasping position as they move in toward the body. *Cf.* DESIRE 1, LONG 2, NEED 2, WANT, WISH 1.

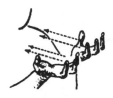

WILLING 1 (wĭl' ĭng), *adj.* (A taking of something unto oneself.) Both open hands, palms down, are held in front of the chest. They move in unison toward the chest, where they come to rest, all fingers closed. *Cf.* ACCEPT.

WILLING 2, *adj.* (A pleasurable feeling on the heart.) The open right hand is circled on the chest, over the heart. *Cf.* APPRECIATE, ENJOY, ENJOYMENT, GRATIFY 1, LIKE 3, PLEASE, PLEASURE.

WIN 1 (wĭn), *v.,* WON, WINNING, *n.* (Waving of flags.) Both upright hands, grasping imaginary flags, wave them in small circles. *Cf.* CELEBRATE, CELEBRATION, CHEER, REJOICE, VICTORY 1.

WIN 2, *v., n.* (Waving a flag.) The right "A" hand goes through the natural movement of waving a flag in circular fashion. Preceding this, the right hand may go through the motion of grabbing the flagstaff out of the left hand. *Cf.* EXULTATION, TRIUMPH 1, VICTORY 2.

WIND (wĭnd), *n.* (The blowing back and forth of the wind.) The "5" hands, palms facing and held up before the body, sway gracefully back and forth, in unison. The cheeks meanwhile are puffed up and the breath is being expelled. The nature of the swaying movement—graceful and slow, fast and violent, etc.—determines the type of wind. The strength of exhalation is also a qualifying device. *Cf.* BLOW 1, BREEZE, STORM.

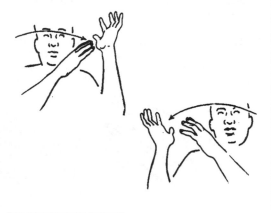

WINDSURFING (wind′ sûrf′ ing), *n.* (The natural movement.) The signer, standing on an imaginary windsurfer and grasping the boom, executes a series of swaying maneuvers, as if guiding a surfboard.

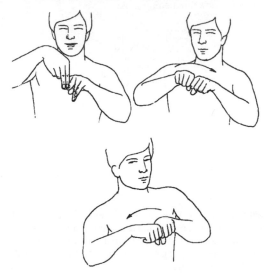

WIND (wīnd), *v.* (Turning the wind-up key.) The signer mimes turning a wind-up key on the left palm.

WINE (wīn), *n.* (The "W" hand indicates a flushed cheek.) The right "W" hand, palm facing the face, rotates at the right cheek, in either a clockwise or a counterclockwise direction.

WINDOW (wĭn′ dō), *n.* (The opening of the window.) With both palms facing the body, the little finger edge of the right hand rests atop the index finger edge of the left hand. The right hand then moves straight up and down. *Cf.* OPEN THE WINDOW.

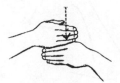

WING (wing), *n.* (The flapping.) The right elbow moves in repeatedly against the right ribs.

WINTER 1 (wĭn′ tər), *n.* (The trembling from cold.) Both "S" hands, palms facing, are placed at the sides of the body. In this position the arms and hands shiver. *Cf.* CHILLY, COLD 1, SHIVER 1.

WINTER 2, *n.* (The letter "W.") The upright "W" hands, palms facing or forward, are brought together forcefully before the body one or two times.

WIPE (wīp), *v.* (Wiping with a cloth or towel.) The flattened right hand makes a series of clockwise wiping movements against the open left palm.

WISDOM (wĭz′ dəm), *n.* (Measuring the depth of the mind.) The downturned "X" finger moves up and down a short distance as it rests on mid-forehead. *Cf.* WISE.

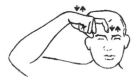

WISE (wīz), *adj.* See WISDOM.

WISH 1 (wĭsh), *v.*, WISHED, WISHING. (Grasping something and pulling it in.) The upturned "5" hands, held side by side before the chest, close slightly into a grasping position as they move in toward the body. *Cf.* DESIRE 1, LONG 2, NEED 2, WANT, WILL 2.

WISH 2, *v.*, *n.* (The upper alimentary tract is outlined.) The right "C" hand, palm facing the body, is placed with fingertips touching mid-chest. In this position it moves down a bit. *Cf.* APPETITE, CRAVE, DESIRE 2, STARVATION, STARVE, STARVED.

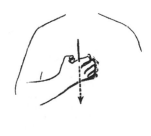

WITH (wĭth), *prep.* (The two hands are together, *i.e.*, WITH each other.) Both "A" hands, knuckles together and thumbs up, are moved forward in unison, away from the chest. They may also remain stationary.

WITHDRAW 1 (wĭŧħ drô', wĭŧħ-), *v.*, -DREW, -DRAWN, -DRAWING. (Pulling away.) The downturned open hands are held in a line, with fingers pointing to the left, the right hand behind the left. Both hands move in unison toward the right. As they do so, they assume the "A" position. *Cf.* DEPART, LEAVE 1.

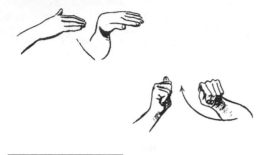

WITHDRAW 2, *v.* (Removing.) The right "A" hand, resting in the palm of the left "5" hand, moves slightly up and away, describing a small arc. It is then cast downward, opening into the "5" position, palm down, as if removing something from the left hand and casting it down. *Cf.* ABOLISH, DEDUCT, DELETE, ELIMINATE, REMOVE, SUBTRACT, SUBTRACTION, TAKE AWAY FROM.

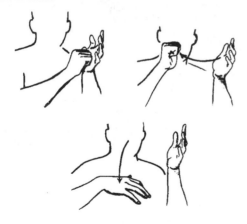

WITHDRAW 3, *v.* (Pulling out.) The index and middle fingers of the right "H" hand are grasped by the left hand. The right hand pulls out of the left. *Cf.* QUIT, RESIGN.

WITHIN (wĭŧħ ĭn', wĭŧħ-), *adv., prep.* (The natural sign.) The fingers of the right hand are thrust into the left. *Cf.* IN, INSIDE, INTO.

WITHOUT (wĭŧħ out', wĭŧħ-), *prep., adv.* (The hands fall away from the WITH position.) The sign for WITH is formed. The hands then drop down, open, and part, ending in the palms-down position.

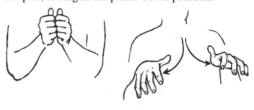

WITNESS (wĭt' nĭs), *v.*, -NESSED, -NESSING. (The vision is directed forward.) The tips of the right "V" fingers point to the eyes. The right hand is then swung around and forward a bit. *Cf.* GAZE, LOOK AT, OBSERVE.

WOMAN (wo͝om' ən), *n.* (A big female.) The FEMALE prefix sign is made: the thumb of the right "A" hand moves down along the line of the right jaw, from ear almost to chin. This outlines the string used to tie ladies' bonnets in olden days. This is a root sign to modify many others. The downturned right hand then moves up to a point above the head, to indicate the relative height.

WONDER 1 (wŭn' dər), v., -DERED, -DERING. (Turning thoughts over in the mind.) Both index fingers, pointing to the forehead, describe continuous alternating circles. Cf. CONSIDER 2, CONTEMPLATE, PONDER, SPECULATE 2, SPECULATION 2, WEIGH 2.

WONDER 2, n. (The hands gesture toward the heavens.) The "5" hands, palms out and arms raised rather high, are positioned somewhat above the line of vision. The arms move abruptly forward and up once or twice. An expression of pleasure or surprise is usually assumed. Cf. EXCELLENT, GRAND 1, GREAT 3, MARVELOUS, SPLENDID 1, SWELL 1, WONDERFUL 1.

WONDERFUL 1 (wŭn' dər fəl), adj. See WONDER 2.

WONDERFUL 2, adj., interj. (The feelings are titillated.) With the thumb resting on the upper part of the chest, the fingers are wiggled back and forth. Cf. ELEGANT, FINE 1, GRAND 2, GREAT 4, SPLENDID 2, SWELL 2.

WON'T (wŏnt, wŭnt), v. Contraction of *will not*. (Holding back.) The right "A" hand, palm facing left, moves up sharply to a position above the right shoulder. Cf. REFUSE.

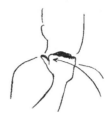

WOOD (wŏŏd), n. (The sawing of wood.) The little finger edge of the open right hand moves back and forth in a sawing motion over the back of the downturned left hand. Cf. SAW 1.

WOODCUTTER (wŏŏd' kut' ər), n. (Chopping down a tree.) The left upraised fist or open hand represents the tree. The upturned right hand (the axe) strikes the left elbow repeatedly. The sign for INDIVIDUAL 1 then follows.

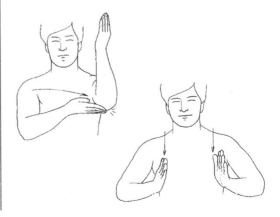

WORD (wûrd), *n.* (A small part of a sentence, *i.e.*, a word.) The tips of the right index finger and thumb, about an inch apart, are placed on the side of the outstretched left index finger, which represents the length of a sentence.

WORD PROCESSING *n.* (A fingerspelled loan sign.) The signer fingerspells "W-P."

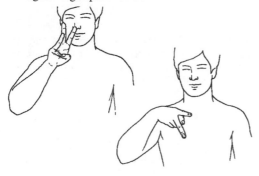

WORK (wûrk), *n., v.*, WORKED, WORKING. (Striking an anvil.) Both "S" hands are held palms down. The right hand strikes against the back of the left a number of times. *Cf.* JOB, LABOR, OCCUPATION, TASK, TOIL, TRAVAIL, VOCATION.

WORLD (wûrld), *n.* (The letter "W" in orbit.) The right "W" hand makes a complete circle around the left "W" hand and comes to rest on the thumb edge of the left "W" hand. The left hand frequently assumes the "S" position instead of the "W," to represent the stationary sun. *Cf.* GLOBE 2.

WORRIED (wûr' ĕd), *v.* (A clouding over; a troubling.) Both "B" hands, palms facing each other, are rotated alternately before the forehead. *Cf.* CONCERN, FRET, PROBLEM 1, TROUBLE, WORRY 1.

WORRY 1 (wûr' ē), *v.*, -RIED, -RYING. See WORRIED.

WORRY 2, *v., n.* (Drumming at the forehead, to represent many worries making inroads on the thinking process.) The right fingertips drum against the forehead. The signer frowns somewhat, or looks very concerned.

WORSE 1 (wûrs), *adj.* The "V" hands, palms facing the body, cross quickly. The comparative degree suffix sign -ER is often used after this sign: the upright thumb of the right "A" hand is brought sharply up to a level opposite the right ear. *Cf.* WORST 1.

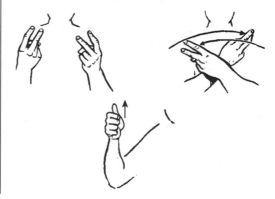

WORSE 2, *adj.* The same movements as in WORSE 1 are used, except that the "W" hands are employed. The comparative degree suffix sign may likewise follow. *Cf.* WORST 2.

WORSHIP (wûr′ ship), *v.* (Bowing to show respect or deference.) The right "W" hand comes down on its left counterpart as the signer's head remains bowed.

WORST 1 (wûrst), *adj.* The sign for WORSE 1 is made. This is followed by the superlative degree suffix -EST: the upright thumb of the right "A" hand is brought sharply up to a level a bit above the right side of the head. *Cf.* WORSE 1.

WORST 2, *adj.* The sign for WORSE 2 is repeated, followed by the superlative degree suffix sign, as in WORST 1. *Cf.* WORSE 2.

WORTH (wûrth), *adj., n.* Both "F" hands, palms facing each other, move apart, up, and together in a smooth elliptical fashion, coming together at the tips of the thumbs and index fingers of both hands. *Cf.* IMPORTANT, SIGNIFICANCE 1, SIGNIFICANT, VALUABLE, VALUE, VITAL 1, WORTHWHILE, WORTHY.

WORTHLESS (wûrth′ lĭs), *adj.* (The hands are thrown out from the sign for WORTH.) The "F" hands, palms down and held side by side or touching, close into the "S" or "E" position, palms still down. They are then thrown out and apart, opening into the "5" position, palms still down.

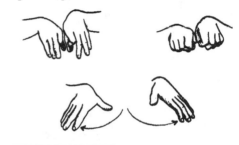

WORTHWHILE (wûrth′ hwīl′), *adj.* See WORTH.

WORTHY (wûr′ t̸hĭ), *adj.* See WORTH.

WOULD (wŏŏd, *unstressed* wəd), *v.* (Something ahead or in the future.) The upright, open right hand, palm facing left, moves straight out and slightly up from a position beside the right temple. *Cf.* FUTURE, IN THE FUTURE, LATER 2, LATER ON, SHALL, WILL 1.

WOUND (wo͞ond), *n.* (A stabbing pain.) The "D" hands, index fingers pointing to each other, are rotated in elliptical fashion before the chest—simultaneously but in opposite directions. *Cf.* ACHE, HARM 1, HURT 1, INJURE 1, INJURY, PAIN, SIN.

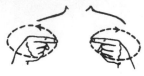

WOW! (wou), *interj.* The limp right hand is shaken up and down repeatedly, while the signer assumes a look of open-mouthed surprise.

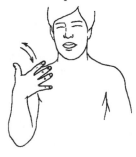

WRAP (rap), *v.*, *n.* (Wrapping up a package.) Both downturned hands, fingers pointing to each other, make a series of alternate clockwise circles, as if spreading wrapping paper around an object.

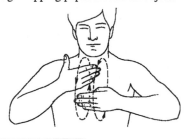

WRISTWATCH *n.* (The shape of the wristwatch.) The thumb and index finger of the right hand, forming a circle, are placed on the back of the left wrist. *Cf.* WATCH 4.

WRITE (rīt), *v.*, WROTE, WRITTEN, WRITING. (The natural movement.) The right index finger and thumb, grasping an imaginary pen, write across the open left palm.

WRONG 1 (rông, rŏng), *adj.*, *n.* (Rationale obscure; the thumb and little finger are said to represent, respectively, right and wrong, with the head poised between the two.) The right "Y" hand, palm facing the body, is brought up to the chin. *Cf.* ERROR, MISTAKE.

WRONG 2, *adj.*, *n.* (Going astray.) The open right hand, palm facing left, is placed with its little finger edge resting on the upturned left palm. The right hand curves rather sharply to the left as it moves across the palm. *Cf.* DEVIATE 1.

X

XEROX (zĭr′ ŏks), *n.* (The letter "X"; the movement of the light as it moves under the item to be copied.) The "X" finger moves back and forth rather rapidly under the downturned hand.

XMAS *n.* See CHRISTMAS

YARD (yärd), *n*. (The letter "Y"; arm's length.) The downturned right "Y" hand is placed on the shoulder of the downturned left arm. The right hand moves down the arm to the left fingertips.

YARN (yärn), *n*. The letter "Y"; unraveling.) The right "Y" hand is placed against the left little finger. The right hand moves away from the left in a series of small circular clockwise movements.

YEAR (yĭr), *n*. (A circumference around the sun.) The right "S" hand, palm facing left, represents the earth. It is positioned atop the left "S" hand, whose palm faces right, and represents the sun. The right "S" hand describes a clockwise circle around the left, coming to rest in its original position.

YEARLY (yĭr' lĭ, yûr'-), *adj., adv., n*. (Several years brought forward.) This sign is actually a modification of the sign for YEAR, *q.v.* The ball of the right "S" hand, moving straight out from the body, palm facing left, glances over the thumb side of the left "S" hand, which is held palm facing right. As this contact is made, the right index finger is flung straight out, and the right hand, in this new position, continues forward. This is repeated several times, to indicate several years. *Cf.* ANNUAL, EVERY YEAR.

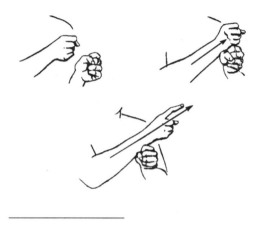

YEAR-ROUND (yĭr' round'), *adj*. (Making a revolution around the sun.) The right index finger, resting on the left index, goes forward around the left once, coming back to where it began.

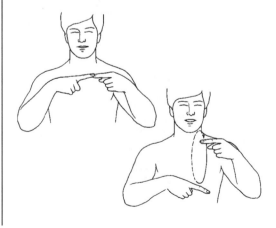

YEARS (yĭrs), *n. pl.* The sign for YEAR is made twice.

YEARS OLD *phrase (regional).* (Showing relative height of a person.) The downturned "B" hand is placed against the stomach and moves off and up, coming to rest at chest level. This sign indicates the growth marks some parents make on the wall, to chronicle the growth of children.

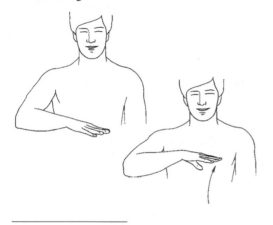

YES (yĕs), *(colloq.), adv., n.* (The nodding.) The right "S" hand, imitating the head, "nods" up and down.

YESTERDAY (yĕs′ tər dĭ, -dā′), *adv., n.* (A short distance into the past.) The thumbtip of the right "A" or "Y" hand, palm facing left, rests on the right cheek. It then moves back a short distance.

YET (yĕt), *adv., conj.* (Duration of movement from past to present.) The right "Y" hand is held palm down in front of the right shoulder and is then moved slowly down and forward in a smooth curve. *Cf.* STAY 2, STILL 1.

YIELD (yēld), *v.,* YIELDED, YIELDING. (Throwing up the hands in a gesture of surrender.) Both "A" hands are held palms down before the chest and then thrown up in unison, ending in the "5" position. *Cf.* DISCOURAGE, FORFEIT, GIVE UP, RELINQUISH, RENOUNCE, RENUNCIATION, SURRENDER.

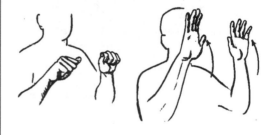

YOM KIPPUR (yom kip′ ər), *n.* (The letter "Y"; beating the breast in penitence.) The right "Y" hand strikes the left breast several times.

YOU 1 (ū), *pron. sing.* (The natural sign.) The signer points to the person he is addressing.

YOU 2, *pron. pl.* (The natural sign.) The signer points to several persons before him, or swings his index finger in an arc from left to right.

YOUNG (yŭng), *adj.* (The spirits bubbling up.) The fingertips of both open hands, placed on either side of the chest just below the shoulders, move up and off the chest, in unison, to a point just above the shoulders. This is repeated several times. *Cf.* YOUTH, YOUTHFUL.

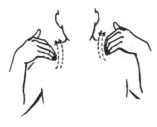

YOUR (yo͞or), *pron., adj.* (The outstretched open hand indicates possession, as if pressing an item against the chest of the person spoken to.) The right "5" hand, palm facing out, moves straight out toward the person spoken to. *Cf.* YOURS.

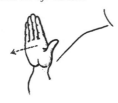

YOU'RE WELCOME 1, *phrase.* (Words extended politely from the mouth.) The fingertips of the right "5" hand are placed at the mouth. The hand moves away from the mouth to a palm-up position before the body. The signer meanwhile usually nods smilingly. *Cf.* THANKS, THANK YOU.

YOU'RE WELCOME 2, *phrase.* (A straightening out.) The right hand, fingers together and palm facing left, is placed in the upturned left palm, whose fingers point away from the body. The right hand slides straight out along the left palm, over the left fingers, and stops with its heel resting on the left fingertips. *Cf.* ALL RIGHT, O.K. 1, PRIVILEGE, RIGHT 1, RIGHTEOUS.

YOURS (yo͞orz, yôrz), *pron.* See YOUR.

YOURSELF (yo͞or sĕlf'), *pron.* The signer moves his upright thumb in the direction of the person spoken to. *Cf.* -SELF 1.

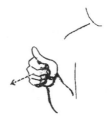

YOURSELVES (yo͞or sĕlvz'), *pron. pl.* The signer moves his upright thumb toward several people before him, in a series of small forward movements from left to right.

YOUTH (ūth), *n.* See YOUNG.

YOUTHFUL (ūth' fəl), *adj.* See YOUNG.

YO-YO (yō′ yō′), *n.* (Manipulating the toy.) The downturned "Y" hand moves up and down repeatedly, in rhythmic progression.

 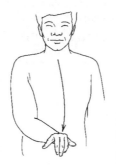

Z

ZEAL (zēl), *n*. (Rubbing the hands together in zeal or ambition.) The open hands are rubbed vigorously back and forth against each other. *Cf.* AMBITIOUS, ANXIOUS, DILIGENCE, DILIGENT, EAGER, EAGERNESS, ENTHUSIASM, ENTHUSIASTIC, INDUSTRIOUS, METHODIST, ZEALOUS.

ZEALOUS (zĕl′ əs), *adj*. See ZEAL.

ZERO 1 (zĭr′ ō), *(colloq.)*, *n*. (An emphatic movement of the "O," *i.e.*, ZERO, hand.) The little finger edge of the right "O" hand is brought sharply into the upturned left palm.

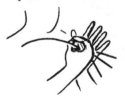

ZERO 2, *n*. (The natural sign.) The right "O" hand, palm facing left, is held in front of the face. It then moves an inch or two toward the right.

ZIPPER (zip′ ər), *n*. (The movement of the zipper.) The signer mimes opening and closing a zipper on the chest or the side of the body.

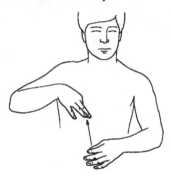